THE LAST KNIGHT

DOMINE·DANOBIS·PACEM·IN·DIEB9   NOSS   62

Edited by
Pierre Terjanian

THE LAST KNIGHT

The Art, Armor, and Ambition of
MAXIMILIAN I

THE METROPOLITAN MUSEUM OF ART, NEW YORK

DISTRIBUTED BY YALE UNIVERSITY PRESS, NEW HAVEN AND LONDON

This catalogue is published in conjunction with *The Last Knight: The Art, Armor, and Ambition of Maximilian I*, on view at The Metropolitan Museum of Art, New York, from October 7, 2019, through January 5, 2020.

The exhibition is made possible by Jo Carole and Ronald S. Lauder.

Additional support is provided by Alice Cary Brown and W.L. Lyons Brown, the Sherman Fairchild Foundation, the Gail and Parker Gilbert Fund, Kathleen and Laird Landmann, and Marica and Jan Vilcek.

The publication is made possible by the Grancsay Fund, The Carl Otto von Kienbusch Memorial Fund, and The Andrew W. Mellon Foundation.

Published by The Metropolitan Museum of Art, New York
Mark Polizzotti, Publisher and Editor in Chief
Gwen Roginsky, Associate Publisher and General Manager
Peter Antony, Chief Production Manager
Michael Sittenfeld, Senior Managing Editor

Edited by Anne Blood Mann
Designed by Rita Jules, Miko McGinty Inc.
Production by Christopher Zichello
Bibliographic editing by Jayne Kuchna
Image acquisitions and permissions by Shannon Cannizzaro
Translations from German by Elisabeth Lauffer and Adam B. Brandow
Map by Adrian Kitzinger

Photographs of works in The Met collection are by Bruce J. Schwarz, Imaging Department, The Metropolitan Museum of Art, unless otherwise noted.

Photographs of armor from European collections are by Bruce M. White, 2019, unless otherwise noted.

Additional photography credits appear on page 340.

Typeset in SangBleu Kingdom, Founders Grotesk, and Lyon by
    Tina Henderson
Printed on 150gsm Perigord
Printed and bound by Trifolio S.r.l., Verona, Italy

Cover illustrations: front, Ceremonial Armor of Charles V (detail of cat. 82); back, *Emperor Maximilian I on Horseback* (detail of cat. 107)
Page 2: *Tournament Tapestry of Frederick the Wise* (detail of cat. 70); page 7: Field Armor of Maximilian I (detail of cat. 17): page 16: Portions of an Armour for the Joust of Peace of Maximilian I (detail of cat. 26); pages 38, 62–63, 64, 88, 130, 188, 218, and 260: *Arch of Honor* (details of cat. 165); page 52: *The Golden Knight (Life Is a Struggle)* (detail of fig. 21)

The Metropolitan Museum of Art
1000 Fifth Avenue
New York, New York 10028
metmuseum.org

Distributed by
Yale University Press, New Haven and London
yalebooks.com/art
yalebooks.co.uk

Cataloguing-in-Publication Data is available from the Library of Congress.
ISBN 978-1-58839-674-7

Note to the Reader
For the sake of clarity, individuals other than Maximilian I are assigned the highest title they attained during their lifetime. The dimensions are given in the following sequence: height precedes width precedes depth. When necessary, the abbreviations H. (height), L. (length), W. (width), D. (depth), and Diam. (diameter) are given for clarity.

CONTENTS

DIRECTOR'S FOREWORD

In the Renaissance, just as now, the capacity to mobilize people and resources to achieve goals was an essential characteristic of a leader. No one was as keenly aware of this as Maximilian I. He tirelessly promoted an image of himself as an exemplary individual, a role model who upheld values and causes worth fighting (and paying) for, and a leader who should be served, praised, and remembered for generations.

Maximilian is a familiar figure in the collective imagination of Europeans because of the works of art that he commissioned and the myths and legends that his life inspired. But he is relatively unknown in the United States and many other parts of the world. The five hundredth anniversary of his death provides a unique opportunity to shed light on this master communicator and to consider his extraordinary artistic legacy as well as the abiding power of objects, especially armor, to forge alliances and convey ambition.

This exhibition and book bring a remarkable range of artworks into conversation with one another thanks to generous loans from institutional and private collections in Europe, the Middle East, and the United States, together with pieces from The Met's own permanent holdings. The exhibition would not have been conceivable without the critical participation of our Austrian counterparts. We are especially grateful to the Kunsthistorisches Museum of Vienna, Director General Sabine Haag, and Director of Schloss Ambras Veronika Sandbichler; the Albertina Museum of Vienna and Director Klaus Albrecht Schröder; the Tiroler Landesmuseum Ferdinandeum in Innsbruck and Director Wolfgang Meighörner; the Landeshauptstadt Innsbruck and Mayor Georg Willi; the Landesmuseum für Kärnten in Klagenfurt, former Director, now Head of the Art and Culture Section of the State of Carinthia,

Igor Pucker, and present Director Christian Wieser; the Haus-, Hof- und Staatsarchiv in Vienna and Director Thomas Just; and the Tiroler Landesarchiv in Innsbruck and Director Ronald Bacher for their marvelous loans, which include works of art and precious documents that have never been seen abroad before.

For the opportunity to include other outstanding objects, which have rarely if ever been exhibited outside their homelands, we also wish to acknowledge the invaluable contributions of museums and archives in Belgium, the Czech Republic, France, Italy, Spain, the United Arab Emirates, the United Kingdom, and the United States. Among these generous lenders, we especially recognize the Musée des Beaux-Arts de Valenciennes and Director Vincent Hadot; the Musée de la Chasse et de la Nature, Paris, and Director Claude d'Anthenaise; the Musée de l'Armée, Paris, and Director and Général de Brigade Alexandre d'Andoque de Sériège; the Royal Armouries, Leeds, and Director General and Master Edward Impey; the Morgan Library and Museum, New York, and Director Colin B. Bailey; the National Gallery of Art, Washington, D.C., and Director Kaywin Feldman; the Philadelphia Museum of Art and Director Timothy Rub; the Victoria and Albert Museum, London, and Director Tristram Hunt; and the Patrimonio Nacional, Madrid, and Director of the Colecciones Reales José Luis Díez García. Our deepest gratitude goes to all other lenders, including two private collectors who wish to be anonymous, and Drs. Kenneth and Vivian Lam, for entrusting us with treasures from their collections.

Mounting this exhibition would be impossible without the expertise and assistance of the Museum's many departments, working in unison. I wish to thank our accomplished staff for bringing this undertaking to fruition. The exhibition and book were conceived and organized by Pierre Terjanian, Arthur Ochs Sulzberger Curator in Charge of the Department of Arms and Armor, who has worked prodigiously to ensure the excellence of *The Last Knight*. We are most grateful to the other distinguished experts who contributed to this publication.

I wish to express both my personal and our institutional gratitude to Jo Carole and Ronald S. Lauder for their outstanding support of the exhibition. Their commitment to scholarship and to the study of arms and armor has been an inspiration. We are also indebted to Alice Cary Brown and W.L. Lyons Brown, the Sherman Fairchild Foundation, the Gail and Parker Gilbert Fund, Kathleen and Laird Landmann, and Marica and Jan Vilcek for their generous contributions to this project. Finally, we are grateful to Stephen V. Grancsay, Carl Otto von Kienbusch, and The Andrew W. Mellon Foundation, whose vital endowments for publications have made this beautiful catalogue possible.

Max Hollein
Director
The Metropolitan Museum of Art

ACKNOWLEDGMENTS

The idea for this project was sparked in 2014 by a conversation with Stefan Krause, then curator in the Kunsthistorisches Museum's Imperial Armoury, about the merits of an exhibition on the occasion of the five hundredth anniversary of Maximilian I's death in 2019. I quickly realized that a close examination of the ruler's passion for armor and the trappings of chivalry would provide an incomparable opportunity to consider the relevance and influence of these objects on the grand stage of European Renaissance politics. Previous exhibitions had established that armor played an important part in the representation of power, but none had focused on its broader role in the ambition of a single ruler. It is my hope that *The Last Knight* will illuminate the true function of armor in a larger, more complex context than the combats or ceremonies for which they were designed.

I am indebted to Thomas P. Campbell, former Director of The Metropolitan Museum of Art, for the invitation to begin work on this project, and to Jennifer Russell, then Associate Director for Exhibitions, and the Exhibition Advisory Group for their invaluable feedback during its inception. For their encouragement, support, and guidance, my deepest thanks go to Max Hollein, Director, as well as Quincy Houghton, Deputy Director for Exhibitions, and Gillian Fruh, Manager for Exhibitions. Max's commitment to promoting alternative readings of objects through dissimilar, even conflicting perspectives increased the show's ambition.

The exhibition would have been impossible without the ongoing interest and support of the Department of Arms and Armor's devoted friends. A large debt of gratitude is owed to Jo Carole and Ronald S. Lauder for their leadership gift. I would like to thank Alice Cary Brown and W.L. Lyons Brown, the Sherman Fairchild Foundation, the Gail and Parker Gilbert Fund, Kathleen and Laird Landmann, and Marica and Jan Vilcek for additional funding. I also acknowledge the important support of the Grancsay Fund, The Carl Otto von Kienbusch Memorial Fund, and The Andrew W. Mellon Foundation in making possible this beautiful catalogue.

The institutions that lent works to the exhibition have been very generous, as have the three private collectors, including Drs. Kenneth and Vivian Lam. I am especially indebted to Sabine Haag, Director General, and Stefan Krause, Director of the Imperial Armoury, Kunsthistorisches Museum, Vienna; Veronika Sandbichler, Director of Schloss Ambras, Innsbruck, Austria; Klaus Albrecht Schröder, Director, and Christof Metzger, Chief Curator, Albertina Museum, Vienna; and Peter Scholz, Curator in Charge of the Ältere Kunstgeschichtliche Sammlungen, Tiroler Landesmuseum Ferdinandeum, Innsbruck, for their enthusiastic and staunch support of our project. For their loans to the exhibition, I am also grateful to Christof Metzger, Julia Zaunbauer, Kristina Liedtke, Karine Bovagnet, and Sonja Eiböck, Albertina Museum, Vienna; Mireille Jean, Alexis Donetzkoff, and Lucile Froissart, Archives Départementales du Nord, Lille; Laurence Perry and Franck Burckel, Archives de la Ville et de l'Eurométropole, Strasbourg; Isabella Fiorentini, L'Archivio Storico Civico e Biblioteca Trivulziana, Milan; José Luis Díez García and Álvaro Soler del Campo, Colecciones Reales and Real Armería, Madrid; Salvador Salort-Pons and Yao-Fen You, Detroit Institute of Arts; Brian Henderson and Ed Gyllenhaal, Glencairn Museum, Bryn Athyn, Pennsylvania; Thomas Just and Kathrin Kininger, Haus-, Hof- und Staatsarchiv, Vienna; Stephan Weppelmann, Guido Messling, and Francesca del Torre, Gemäldegalerie, Kunsthistorisches Museum, Vienna; Matthias Pfaffenbichler, Stefan Krause, Petra Fuchs, and Jorge Sepúlveda Herreros, Imperial Armoury, Kunsthistorisches Museum, Vienna; Fritz Fischer and Franz Kirchweger, Kunstkammer and Schatzkammer, Kunsthistorisches Museum, Vienna; Timothy Potts and Elizabeth Morrison, J. Paul Getty Museum, Los Angeles; Sara Lammens and Benoît Labarre, Koninklijke Bibliotheek van België, Brussels;

Michel Draguet and Philippe Goris, Koninklijke Musea voor Kunst en Geschiedenis, Brussels; Igor Pucker, Christian Wieser, Alexandra Krug, and Robert Wlattnig, Landesmuseum für Kärnten, Klagenfurt; Manuel Rabaté and Souraya Noujaim, Louvre Abu Dhabi; Colin B. Bailey, John Marciari, Frank Trujillo, Roger S. Wieck, and Sophie Worley, Morgan Library and Museum, New York; Alexandre d'Andoque de Sériège, Olivier Renaudeau, and Chantal Vigouroux, Musée de l'Armée, Paris; Vincent Hadot, Musée des Beaux-Arts de Valenciennes, France; Claude d'Anthenaise and Karen Chastagnol, Musée de la Chasse et de la Nature, Paris; Hélène Lobir, Musée de l'Hospice Comtesse, Lille; Jean-Luc Martinez, Sébastien Allard, Sophie Caron, Hélène Grollemund, and Cécile Scaillérez, Musée du Louvre, Paris; Matthew Teitelbaum, Benjamin Weiss, and Annette Manick, Museum of Fine Arts, Boston; Earl A. Powell III, Kaywin Feldman, Jonathan Bober, Mollie Berger, David Brown, Michelle Facini, Kimberly Schenck, National Gallery of Art, Washington, D.C.; Bruno Girveau and Laetitia Barragué-Zouita, Palais des Beaux-Arts, Lille; Timothy Rub, Dirk H. Breiding, Jack Hinton, and Sally Malenka, Philadelphia Museum of Art; Edward Impey, Suzanne J. Dalewicz-Kitto, Keith Dowen, Georgia Grant, Rebecca Hayton, Ellie Rowley-Conwy, Lauren Piper, Giles Storey, Karen Watts, and Martin Wills, Royal Armouries, Leeds; Veronika Sandbichler and Thomas Kuster, Schloss Ambras Innsbruck; Ronald Bacher and Nadja Krajicek, Tiroler Landesarchiv, Innsbruck; Wolfgang Meighörner, Lourdes-Maria Canizares-Flores, Katharina Niedermüller, and Peter Scholz, Tiroler Landesmuseen, Innsbruck and Hall; Helena Koenigsmarková and Radim Vondráček, Uměleckoprůmyslové Museum, Prague; Lynne Farrington and Abigail C. Lang, University of Pennsylvania Libraries, Philadelphia; Tristram Hunt and Terry Bloxham, Victoria and Albert Museum, London; Natasja Peeters and Elke Otten, War Heritage Institute, Brussels; Amy Meyers and Sarah Welcome, Yale Center for British Art, New Haven, Conn.; and Bürgermeister Georg Willi, Landeshauptstadt Innsbruck.

For the loan of objects in their care, I am also thankful to my Met colleagues Nadine M. Orenstein, Drue Heinz Curator in Charge, and Freyda Spira, Drawings and Prints; Keith Christiansen, John Pope-Hennessy Chairman, Andrea Bayer (now Deputy Director for Collections and Administration), and Maryan Ainsworth, European Paintings; Sarah Ellen Lawrence, Iris and B. Gerald Cantor Curator in Charge, Elizabeth Cleland, Wolfram Koeppe, Marina Kellen French Curator, and Denny Stone, European Sculpture and Decorative Arts; Dita Amory and Alison Manges Nogueira, the Robert Lehman Collection; and C. Griffith Mann, Michel David-Weill Curator in Charge, Medieval Art and the Cloisters.

For their assistance with our application for US Governmental Indemnity, I express my gratitude to Christie's and David Williams, Antique Arms and Armor Department, Bonhams. A prime motivation for this exhibition was to shed new light on Maximilian's armors and patronage by uncovering previously unknown information in public European archives. I wish to thank the staff of the Staatsarchiv Augsburg, Germany; the Algemeen Rijksarchief, Brussels; the Tiroler Landesarchiv, Innsbruck; the Archives Départementales du Nord, Lille; the Staatsarchiv Nürnberg, Germany; the Archives de la Ville et Eurométropole, Strasbourg; and the Haus-, Hof- und Staatsarchiv, Vienna, for the opportunity to research their records.

The preparation of the exhibition and accompanying catalogue entailed the assistance of many other colleagues and independent scholars. For their time and advice I wish to especially thank Lloyd de Beer, British Museum, London; Michael Vigl and Julia Amman, Abteilung für Konservierung und Restaurierung, Bundesdenkmalamt, Vienna; Wilfried Magnet, Klagenfurt, Austria; Marija Milchin, Institut für Konservierung und Restaurierung, Universität für angewandte Kunst, Vienna; Jonathan Graindorge Lamour, Moulins-le-Carbonnel, France; Pierre Curie and Hélène Couot Echiffre, Musée Jacquemart-André, Paris; Karin Schmid-Pittl, Amt der Tiroler Landesregierung, Abteilung Kultur, Tiroler Kunstkataster, Innsbruck; Diane Bodart, Department of Art History and Archaeology, Columbia University; and Marina Viallon, Paris.

At The Metropolitan Museum of Art, many departments enthusiastically supported and contributed to the exhibition and publication. For their invaluable help with outside loans, I am grateful to Meryl Cohen and Mary McNamara, Registrar's Office; Martha Deese, Exhibitions Office; and Amy Lamberti and Nicole Sussmane, Counsel's Office. For their expert guidance and support, I thank Lisa Pilosi, Sherman Fairchild Conservator in Charge, Drew Anderson, Linda Borsch, Frederick Sager, Jack Soultanian, Jr., and Marlene April Yandrisevits, Objects Conservation; Michael Gallagher, Sherman Fairchild Chairman, and Michael Alan Miller, Paintings Conservation; Marjorie Shelley, Sherman Fairchild Conservator in Charge, Rachel Mustalish, and Yana van Dyke, Paper Conservation; Janina Poskrobko, Cristina B. Carr, and Olha Yarema-Wynar, Textile Conservation; and Marco Leona, David H. Koch Scientist in Charge, and Federico Carò, Scientific Research Department. For their respective contributions, I am also grateful to Taylor Miller and Matthew Lytle, Buildings; Emile Molin, Anna Rieger, Brian Butterfield, Christopher DiPietro, Patrick Herron, Ria Roberts, and Alejandro Stein, Design; Clyde B. Jones III and Daphne Butler Birdsey, Development; Sofie Andersen, Evander Batson, Melissa Bell, Lynn Burke, Paul Caro, Skyla Choi, Nina Diamond, Kate Farrell, William Fenstermaker, Sumi Hansen, Benjamin Korman, Bryan Martin, Bora Shehu, Digital; Jennifer Bantz, Publications and Editorial; Kenneth Weine, Ann M. Bailis, Meryl Cates, and Claire Lanier, External Affairs; Marianna Siciliano, Emily Blumenthal, Marie Clapot, Erin Flannery, Rebecca McGinnis, Darcy-Tell Morales, Julie Marie Seibert, and Leslie Tait, Education; Sharon Cott, Counsel's Office; Kenneth Soehner, Arthur K. Watson Chief Librarian, Deborah Vincelli, Robyn Fleming, and Gwen Mayhew, Thomas J. Watson Library.

For their scholarly contributions to the catalogue, I am indebted to Andrea Bayer, Adam B. Brandow, Chassica Kirchhoff, Alison Manges Nogueira, and above all Freyda Spira at The Metropolitan Museum of Art and to Lisa Demets, Stefan Krause, Guido Messling, Elizabeth Morrison, Matthias Pfaffenbichler, Veronika Sandbichler, Delia Scheffer, Peter Scholz, Roland Sila, Larry Silver, Robert Wlattnig, Barbara Wolf, and Christina Zenz.

For their dedication and attention to detail in creating such a beautiful and informative publication, I wish to thank the *Last Knight* team—Anne Blood Mann, Shannon Cannizzaro, Jayne Kuchna, and Christopher Zichello—as well as Mark Polizzotti, Peter Antony, Elizabeth De Mase, Michael Sittenfeld, Publications and Editorial. For the splendid photography specially commissioned for this book, I wish to thank Barbara J. Bridgers and Bruce J. Schwarz, Imaging, as well as Bruce M. White and Christina Ewald, who traveled to Europe to shoot armor, weapons, and other loans to the exhibition.

Neither this exhibition nor the publication would have been possible without the tireless efforts, expertise, and encouragement from all of my dear colleagues in the Department of Arms and Armor: Sean P. Belair, Stephen J. Bluto, Adam B. Brandow, John Byck, Catherine Chesney, Edward A. Hunter, Jennafer Julien, Donald J. La Rocca, Stuart W. Pyhrr, Markus Sesko, and George Sferra. I am especially indebted to Edward Hunter for the coordination of all conservation-related needs of the exhibition, and to him and Sean Belair for the assessment, treatment, and mounting of many objects for photography and display. For his attentiveness, dedication, advice, and scholarly contributions, I also wish to express my gratitude to Adam B. Brandow, who as Research Associate played a pivotal role in the making of this project. I also would like to acknowledge the help we received from Chassica Kirchhoff, Andrew W. Mellon Curatorial Research Fellow in our department, and from Maud Leclair, then an intern in our department and now Research Assistant, Department of Asian Art.

Lastly, I am ever grateful to my parents and grandparents for fostering my early interest in history, art, and culture and to my family, Sonya, Violette, and Rémy, for their understanding, love, and encouragement during the long hours of study and travel that were required to bring this project to fruition.

Pierre Terjanian
Arthur Ochs Sulzberger Curator in Charge
Department of Arms and Armor

LENDERS TO THE EXHIBITION

Albertina Museum, Vienna
Archives de la Ville et de l'Eurométropole, Strasbourg, France
Archives Départementales du Nord, Lille, France
Archivio Storico Civico e Biblioteca Trivulziana, Milan
Detroit Institute of Arts
Glencairn Museum, Bryn Athyn, Pennsylvania
Haus-, Hof- und Staatsarchiv, Vienna
J. Paul Getty Museum, Los Angeles
Koninklijke Bibliotheek van België, Brussels
Koninklijke Musea voor Kunst en Geschiedenis, Brussels
Kunsthistorisches Museum, Vienna
Drs. Kenneth and Vivian Lam
Landeshauptstadt Innsbruck, Austria
Landesmuseum für Kärnten, Klagenfurt, Austria
Louvre Abu Dhabi
The Metropolitan Museum of Art, New York
Morgan Library and Museum, New York
Musée de l'Armée, Paris
Musée de la Chasse et de la Nature, Paris
Musée de l'Hospice Comtesse, Lille, France
Musée des Beaux-Arts de Valenciennes, France
Musée du Louvre, Paris
Museum of Fine Arts, Boston
National Gallery of Art, Washington, D.C.
Palais des Beaux-Arts, Lille, France
Patrimonio Nacional, Madrid, Real Armería
Philadelphia Museum of Art
Private collections
Royal Armouries, Leeds
Tiroler Landesarchiv, Innsbruck, Austria
Tiroler Landesmuseum Ferdinandeum, Innsbruck, Austria
Uměleckoprůmyslové Museum, Prague
University of Pennsylvania Libraries, Philadelphia
Victoria and Albert Museum, London
Yale Center for British Art, New Haven, Connecticut

CONTRIBUTORS TO THE CATALOGUE

Andrea Bayer (AB)
Deputy Director for Collections and Administration,
The Metropolitan Museum of Art, New York

Adam B. Brandow (ABB)
Research Associate, Department of Arms and Armor,
The Metropolitan Museum of Art, New York

Lisa Demets (LD)
Doctoral Fellow, Research Foundation Flanders (FWO),
Henri Pirenne Institute for Medieval Studies,
Department of History, Ghent University, Belgium

Chassica Kirchhoff (CK)
Andrew W. Mellon Curatorial Research Fellow, Department
of Arms and Armor, The Metropolitan Museum of Art,
New York

Stefan Krause (SK)
Director, Imperial Armoury,
Kunsthistorisches Museum, Vienna

Guido Messling (GM)
Curator of German Painting, Gemäldegalerie,
Kunsthistorisches Museum, Vienna

Elizabeth Morrison (EM)
Senior Curator of Manuscripts, J. Paul Getty Museum,
Los Angeles

Alison Manges Nogueira (AMN)
Associate Curator, Robert Lehman Collection,
The Metropolitan Museum of Art, New York

Matthias Pfaffenbichler (MP)
Former Director, Imperial Armoury, Kunsthistorisches
Museum, Vienna

Veronika Sandbichler (VS)
Director, Schloss Ambras Innsbruck,
Kunsthistorisches Museum, Vienna

Delia Scheffer (DS)
Associate Curator, Ältere Kunstgeschichtliche
Sammlungen, Tiroler Landesmuseum Ferdinandeum,
Innsbruck, Austria

Peter Scholz (PS)
Curator in Charge, Ältere Kunstgeschichtliche
Sammlungen, Tiroler Landesmuseum Ferdinandeum,
Innsbruck, Austria

Roland Sila (RS)
Library Curator, Tiroler Landesmuseum Ferdinandeum,
Innsbruck, Austria

Larry Silver (LS)
James and Nan Wagner Farquhar Professor Emeritus of
History of Art, University of Pennsylvania, Philadelphia

Freyda Spira (FS)
Associate Curator, Department of Drawings and Prints,
The Metropolitan Museum of Art, New York

Pierre Terjanian (PT)
Arthur Ochs Sulzberger Curator in Charge, Department
of Arms and Armor, The Metropolitan Museum of Art,
New York

Robert Wlattnig (RW)
Head of the Abteilung für Kunstgeschichte,
Landesmuseum für Kärnten, Klagenfurt, Austria

Barbara Wolf (BW)
Associate Curator, Ältere Kunstgeschichtliche
Sammlungen, Tiroler Landesmuseum Ferdinandeum,
Innsbruck, Austria

Christina Zenz (CZ)
Associate Curator, Ältere Kunstgeschichtliche
Sammlungen, Tiroler Landesmuseum Ferdinandeum,
Innsbruck, Austria

THE HOLY ROMAN EMPIRE
ca. 1519

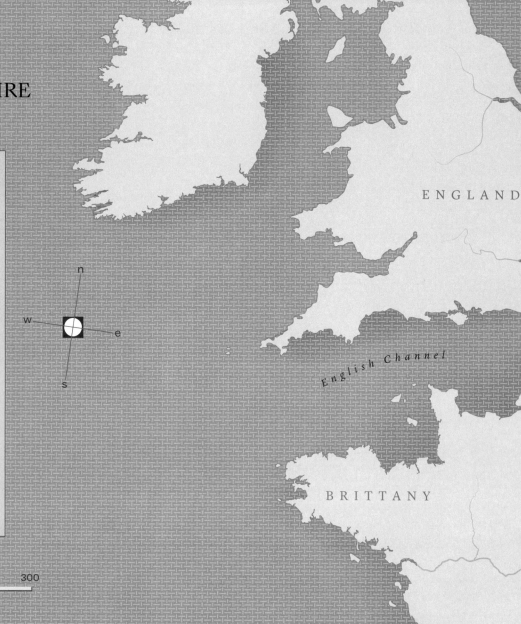

KEY

〰〰〰 Bounds of the Holy Roman Empire

HABSBURG TERRITORIES, FROM:

⬜ Burgundian lands

⬜ Austrian hereditary lands

CENTERS OF MAXIMILIAN'S
ARMOR MANUFACTURE

▪ Brussels —For his personal use

▪ Lille —For his officials, troops,
and arsenals

Key Sieges or Battles

✳ *Guinegate*

Other cities

▪ Paris

miles

0	100	200	300

0	100	200	300	400

kilometers

ENGLAND

English Channel

BRITTANY

ATLANTIC OCEAN

Bay of Biscay

SPAIN

NORTH SEA

Oder

Elbe

Ems

Ruhr

SAXONY

Gueldern

Bruges

Flanders Antwerp

Ghent Mechelen

Brabant Brussels

Lille Cologne

Guinegate

Meuse

Rhine

Mosel

BOHEMIA

Vltava

Luxembourg Worms

Nuremberg

Wenzenbach *Danube*

Lower
Austria

is Nancy

SWABIA BAVARIA Upper

Strasbourg Ulm Augsburg Linz Vienna

Inn Austria

Wiener Neustadt

FRANCE Further Austria *Lech* Styria HUNGARY

Kufstein

Saône Mühlau Graz

Mur

Dornach Innsbruck

Arbois SWISS Tyrol Carinthia *Drava*

Franche-Comté CONFEDERATION Ljubljana

Sava

Trento Carniola

Rhône Brescia Venice

Milan *Adige*

Po

Ferrara

OTTOMAN
EMPIRE

MEDITERRANEAN SEA Florence

ADRIATIC SEA

Rome

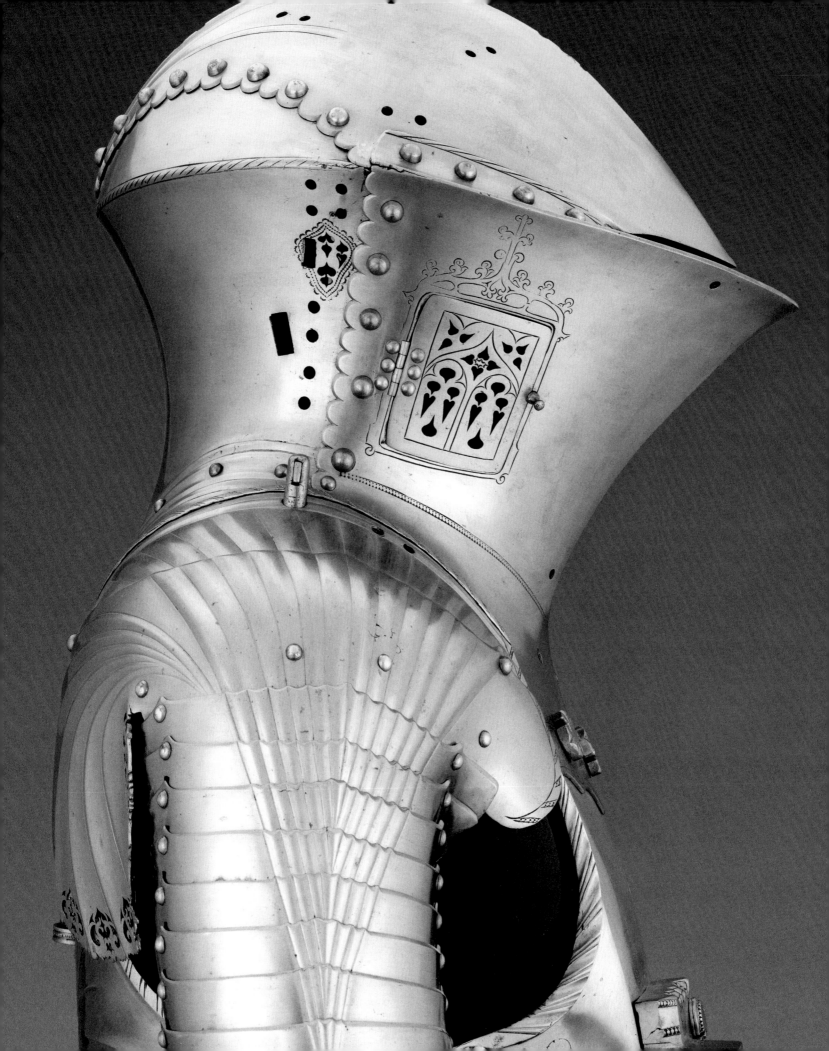

THE CURRENCY OF POWER
The Central Place of Armor in the Ambitions and Life of Maximilian I

Pierre Terjanian

"What could be more precious to a king than an armor that will safeguard his body in combat?" When Emperor Maximilian I (1459–1519) instructed his secretary to feature this question in the *Weisskunig*, an ambitious pseudo-autobiographical work he intended to have printed and widely distributed, he did not merely mean to rhetorically emphasize the practical value of armor as bodily protection, a point that readers would have readily agreed with; instead, he wished to call attention to his personal contribution to—and expertise in—the art of making armor.[1] Yet, why would an emperor have wanted to meddle with armor design? And, even more importantly, why would he have viewed his involvement as something worthy of recording in a book meant to extol his virtues as a ruler, preserve the legacy of his reign, and set an example for others to follow? These questions illuminate the chief reasons Maximilian's life provides the perfect lens through which to recapture and better understand the significance of the armorer's art in late medieval and Renaissance European politics. Maximilian and most of his contemporaries prized armor deeply, and not simply for its functional use in battle or the tournament. The claim that it surpasses a king's other material possessions because of its defensive qualities, like so many other assertions put forth in the *Weisskunig*, should not be taken literally. Maximilian knew better, and his actions prove it. The true significance of armor extends to the part it played in his efforts to construct his identity, enhance his own legitimacy as a ruler and that of his descendants, shape the memory of his deeds, and, at all times, consolidate his political authority and spheres of influence. Armor, in so many ways, was the currency of power.

If Maximilian was not fundamentally different from his peers in the appreciation he showed for armor, his sincere and lifelong commitment to forge and actively manage the impression others would form of him and his actions is unrivaled. He did not wish to be misunderstood, and he did not wish to be overlooked or forgotten either. While the literary and artistic projects that the emperor patronized to deliberately pursue these goals may be viewed as propaganda, his letters, reports, account books, and other archival documents provide opportunities to review the works that he authored or commissioned, and the part he actually took in them, in a different, more objective light, illuminating some of his specific motives, and certainly his methods, which Maximilian never expected the world to see. This rich documentation is especially invaluable for exposing the role armor played in the realization of Maximilian's ambitions.

SEMINAL YEARS

As duke consort of Burgundy, King of the Romans, and Holy Roman Emperor, Archduke Maximilian of Austria spent a great deal of his energy and resources on shaping opinion on his merits and accomplishments. The idea that a ruler in a nondemocratic political system should preoccupy himself or herself with such things as the judgment of others may surprise the modern observer. Indeed, if authority is defined as the power to give orders and requires compliance, then authority figures such as kings and queens and emperors and empresses probably should not need the approval of others. By seeking it, was Maximilian exhibiting weakness and perhaps even signaling insecurity? The emperor's behavior, including his extraordinary artistic patronage, reflects something else, namely, an acute awareness that communication has the power to build trust, inspire loyalty, and attract support. Atypical as it may have been, Maximilian's determination to present himself, and what he wished to represent—the House of Habsburg, the Holy Roman Empire—in a purposeful and impactful manner is one of the most remarkable dimensions of the man and his legacy.[2] The origins of his lifelong engagement with image management, in

which chivalry and armor played such an important part, are to be found in the early years of his rule as duke consort in the Burgundian Low Countries, where he underwent his difficult apprenticeship as a ruler (fig. 1).

Born and raised in the German-speaking lands, Maximilian was abruptly thrown into a world with which he had had no direct contact when, at the age of eighteen, he married Mary of Burgundy (1457–1482) and went to the Low Countries to rule jointly with her over the extensive territories that she had inherited from her father. As the only child of Charles the Bold (1433–1477), duke of Burgundy, Mary was the sole heiress to his dominions. After her father's death in battle near Nancy in 1477, she consented to marry Maximilian, in keeping with her father's wishes and in the hope that her spouse would be able to defend her inheritance from powerful neighbors such as the king of France, who sought to reclaim some of her lands, and from her own subjects, who wished to undermine her authority and recover some of the autonomy and privileges her father had succeeded in wresting away.

Maximilian was not ideally suited for the task of succeeding Charles the Bold and ruling over the Low Countries. He spoke neither French nor Flemish, the languages of his subjects.[3] Although he bore the prestigious title of archduke of Austria, he had no lands of his own, and he had never been given an opportunity to administer any under the control of his father, Emperor Frederick III (1415–1493). He thus had neither an independent source of income nor prior experience in governance. To make matters worse, as his father had been fighting wars, Maximilian could not count on meaningful financial support from his family. In fact, Mary had to send him money so that he could undertake the long journey that would take him from Lower Austria to her in the Low Countries, and equip himself and his retinue in keeping with his distinguished standing as the emperor's son and her consort. Mary had feared a poor showing would have compromised her husband's ability to inspire confidence among their subjects.

Although Maximilian made a positive impression at first, he faced numerous obstacles in the Burgundian Low Countries. From 1477, the date of his arrival,

FIG. 1 *Great Seal of Maximilian I and Mary of Burgundy as Counts of Flanders*, from Olivier de Wree, *Les seaux des comtes de Flandre et inscriptions des chartres par eux publiées, avec un esclaircissement historique* (fol. 40). South Netherlandish (Bruges), 1641. Engraving. Archives Nationales, Paris, Département du Moyen Âge et de l'Ancien Régime, Centre de sigillographie et d'héraldique

through 1489, when he departed to visit his great-uncle Archduke Sigismund (1427–1496) in Innsbruck, Maximilian was confronted with ceaseless military, financial, and political challenges. His merit and aptitude as a ruler were put to the test by the invasion of his lands by the French, the defection of key vassals, the unexpected death of his wife, the open rebellion of his subjects, the resulting subjugation of his children, his own imprisonment, the devastation of his lands, and the general disruption of the income sources required to fund his actions. They were years of intense struggle, during which his right to govern and his ability to uphold his authority and conserve his dominions were continually contested.

The widespread questioning and even rejection of his authority in the Low Countries forced Maximilian to ponder the kernel issue of his legitimacy as a ruler and consider ways he could hold on to and actually strengthen his position. It is during this turbulent but seminal period that he became preoccupied with shaping opinion and actively managing his image to validate his political status and build support for his cause. The ideas that he developed during these years would inform his decisions and actions for the rest of his life.

As he was not a native prince (ruler) of the realms, but a foreigner who derived his power solely from his marriage with a princess of the blood, Maximilian could not expect to enhance the legitimacy of his rule over the Burgundian Low Countries by emphasizing who he was; instead, he had to promote what he stood for. Because his audience included noblemen whose loyalty and support were critical for maintaining his authority, Maximilian could rely on the ideals of chivalry, which they all shared, to strengthen their mutual bonds and set an example that would inspire confidence in his leadership. It is in this context that he acquired his reputation as an exemplary knight, whose spirit and deeds embodied the virtues that they all respected—among them courage, fidelity, and perseverance.

On the battlefield Maximilian was prompt to lead by example. At Guinegate in 1479, when he defeated an invading French army, he fought much of the battle on foot, facing capture or death, alongside his men and in the first ranks. He called attention to his honorable conduct by taking great chances to rescue one of the lords in his service, who was imperiled. In numerous other encounters, he never hesitated to expose himself, engage in close combat, incur serious wounds, and all too often run the risk of being taken by his enemies.[4] By partaking in battles, he offered a stark contrast to many of his peers, such as Louis XI of France (1423–1483), who would not personally lead the forces that he sent against Maximilian. This point was made even more eloquently by Maximilian's participation in the duel-like preludes to battles, contests in which a knight from one camp traditionally challenged anyone from the other to defeat him, after which the armies would effectively clash. On at least two occasions, one during his military campaign in the duchy of Luxembourg, and the other during his campaign in the duchy of Guelders, Maximilian reportedly challenged French knights to run against him. Although there was no formal difference from the jousts held in the context of tournaments, the intent in these encounters on the battlefield was not merely to win but to inflict maximum harm. In each case, Maximilian killed his opponent with the thrust of his lance. These politically charged displays of bravado, watched by the opposing armies, validated his heroic image. By embracing duel-like combat in which his rank conferred no particular advantage, and by publicly accepting the possibility of losing his life, Maximilian did not act before his men so much as a prince or commander but as a fearless peer and a formidable role model, a first among equals.[5]

Maximilian's performance on the battlefield was matched by his prowess in the tournament, and it is in this arena that he acquired the greatest fame. From its early medieval origins as a brutal reenactment of warfare, the tournament had by the fifteenth century evolved into distinct, codified mock (i.e., friendly) combats, which could be either held privately for recreation or practice, or staged before a broad audience as part of festivities. The free tourney was a mass combat in which two groups of knights, armed in field armor supplemented with reinforcing elements, charged toward each other with lances, then continued the fight with swords. The joust normally opposed only two horsemen who charged toward each other with lances, aiming to break the shaft of their own lance (an indication that they had delivered the proper blow), unhorse their opponent, or both. While jousting was initially fought in field armor, over time the contest evolved into two distinct forms. The first, the joust of war, was fought with lances with sharpened heads, and the contestants wore field or specialized tournament armor that mimicked the features of field armor. The second, the joust of peace, was fought with lances fitted with multi-pronged heads, and the contestants wore specialized tournament armor that bore little resemblance to field armor. In the German-speaking lands, the jousts of war and peace were traditionally fought at large, meaning in an open space, and without anything to separate the contestants. In France, Italy, and the Low Countries, the joust of peace was normally fought with a tilt, a barrier of cloth or wood, that stood between the contestants. The multiple forms of joust and the presence or absence of a tilt introduced enough variety for the contests to be quite challenging, as each required practice and the mastery of distinct skills. Alongside other forms of equestrian combat (such as the tourney fought with swords or specialized clubs, which was a group combat not preceded by a joust), another popular tournament contest was the foot combat. Taking place in field or specialized tournament armor in an enclosed space known as the lists, it originated from the judicial duel and could be fought with a wide range of weapons, including axes, daggers, maces, pollaxes, and swords. Although it no longer was concluded by the killing of one's opponent, the foot combat remained a brutal, vicious, and most perilous contest, for which specialized armor and a knowledge of wrestling were indispensable.[6]

Maximilian distinguished himself in all of those mock combats. A few months before the battle of Guinegate, for example, he jousted over three days in Bruges and broke sixteen lances, an accomplishment for which he was awarded the tournament's first prize.[7] The accounts of his treasurers show that Maximilian, who had seldom if ever jousted in public before he became duke consort of Burgundy, was touring his realms and taking part in and even organizing jousts in many of the places that he visited.[8] Although jousting armors were specifically designed to provide maximum protection, the contests were rough—in some the contestants rode on saddles that facilitated their fall from their horses—and accidents were common and occasionally fatal. By taking part in these contests, Maximilian was continually running the risk of getting injured.[9] Undeterred by the inherent dangers and quite possibly stimulated by the prospect of surmounting them, Maximilian actively sought to measure himself against those who

had demonstrated the greatest proficiency in the tournament. At times he used all the authority he wielded to ensure that worthy opponents would be able to come to him, petitioning their masters to give them permission to leave their service for the occasion. This certainly was the case in 1498, when he sought to joust against Gaspare Sanseverino d'Aragona (ca. 1455–1519), alias Fracasso, one of the most famous Italian jousters of the time, and corresponded with the duke of Milan to persuade him to grant Fracasso a leave of absence without which the latter could not come to Innsbruck (see cat. 38).

While there were times when he had no wish to fight certain individuals, the etiquette of the period dictated that it would have been shameful to turn down the challenge of a qualified opponent. Maximilian was thus forced to face Claude de Vaudrey (ca. 1445–ca. 1518), a Burgundian knight who had openly challenged him. Although much older than Maximilian, Vaudrey was a formidable opponent, perhaps one of the bravest knights of his era, and an expert in martial arts who had acquired an illustrious reputation in both battle and the tournament. The contest took place in Worms in 1495 before a distinguished audience, including various princes of the empire, foreign ambassadors, and Bianca Maria Sforza (1472–1510), Maximilian's second wife. It ended in Maximilian's victory and public exchanges of gifts between the two men, which advertised their gallantry and the chivalric standards of behavior that united them (see cat. 37). Both the acceptance of the contest and his irreproachable conduct during the event made an impression on the audience. Six years later Olivier de La Marche (1425–1502), a prominent Burgundian courtier who had served Charles the Bold, cited them in his memoirs as proofs of Maximilian's chivalrous character.[10]

Additionally, Maximilian devised variants of the established forms of mock combats, creating more perilous and unpredictable contests. By 1478, only a year after he had arrived in the Low Countries, he wrote to a confidant that he had conceived new knightly games.[11] These may have included the idea for the mixed joust, in which one contestant was armed for the joust of war and the other for the joust of peace, or variants of the joust of war in which the contestants left areas of their bodies dangerously exposed, or carried shields of unprecedented form, or shields covered with plates that would dramatically disperse in the air once struck by an opponent's lance, or shields mounted on the armor in such a way that they would be propelled into the air upon impact. While the contestants may have enjoyed the unique complications that these innovations introduced, spectators are likely to have found them just as rewarding, as they challenged conventions and increased the visual drama of the contests. In the seventeenth century, panegyrists of the House of Habsburg counted these inventions among Maximilian's most outstanding achievements, pointing out that ever since the time of

King Arthur and the knights of the round table, there had been no other court than his own for all princes, counts, lords, and nobles to seek glory in chivalry, and no better school in knightly education (fig. 2).[12]

In his exemplary demonstrations of knightly virtues, Maximilian showed not only courage but also great panache. Under his predecessors, the Burgundian court had eclipsed most others in Europe in sophistication and flamboyance. No matter how precarious his financial position periodically was, Maximilian understood the importance of upholding the grandeur of his forebearers, no doubt because extravagance was viewed as the material measure of one's wealth and correlated to one's ability to afford costly wars. In short, since opulence was readily equated with might, maintaining the former was key to inspiring confidence and attracting support.

Maximilian was resplendent in battle and the tournament. His treasurers' accounts record the acquisition of a crimson satin robe lined with green taffeta silk for him to wear over his field armor and his use of a leather bard covered in blue cloth of gold to protect his horse at the battle of Guinegate in 1479.[13] He also owned a number of caparisons made of velvet or cloth of gold. Even his smallest accessories were luxurious: the laces used to secure the elements of a bard together were made of silk and sometimes fitted with points of solid silver.[14] In the countless tournaments in which he participated in the Low Countries, he wore sumptuous textiles over his armors, and plumes enriched with goldsmiths' work over his helmets.[15] Despite the fact that these trappings would likely be ruined during the contest, Maximilian regularly spent more on his ornaments than on his equipment and horse. In 1479, for example, the Bruges goldsmith Martin Boucher (recorded 1472–1479) made for him several plume holders, including one that was set with a large flower of diamonds, rubies, and pearls, for which the gold alone cost the sum of 138 florins, currency of Flanders.[16] In anticipation of each tournament, expensive cloth was acquired and turned over to tailors to make doublets for armor, caparisons for horses, and coverings for the jousting shields and lances.[17] The splendor of the

FIG. 2 *King Arthur*. Cast by Peter Vischer the Elder (1455–1529). German (Nuremberg), 1513. Bronze. Hofkirche, Innsbruck

archduke at these knightly games was magnified by that of his entourage. On occasion Maximilian outfitted the key courtiers who were his jousting companions, and their servants and horses.[18] The objects awarded to the winners of the tournaments that he organized were commensurate with the exuberance of the attire worn on these occasions. The diamonds, rubies, and hyacinth gemstone that were the prizes for the joust he staged in Ghent in September 1478, as well as the gold fleur-de-lis inset with a ruby and the miniature jousting helm of gold that he acquired for another tournament held the same year, are symptomatic of the care with which he sought to perpetuate the opulent ways of his predecessors.[19]

Although near continuous warfare in the Low Countries made it difficult to organize lavish tournaments there until 1493, when peace returned, Maximilian found opportunities to stage—and shine in—jousts elsewhere, particularly in the German-speaking lands and above all in Innsbruck, where he established his chief residence upon becoming archduke of Tyrol in 1490. The reports of foreign ambassadors indicate that at times Maximilian's jousts monopolized everyone's attention, so much so that no other business could be discussed. The contests themselves often lasted many days and were said to be magnificent.[20] A sense of their grandeur can be gleaned from one of Maximilian's pseudo-autobiographical projects, in which Freydal, his alter ego, meets numerous opponents in jousts and the foot combat. A series of surviving drawings provides a good indication of the accoutrements in which Maximilian appeared in the contests he wished to commemorate: the hero always sports a different crest or accessory on his helmet, and fancy textiles over his armor (cats. 39–52). Although Freydal was a fictional character, he was grounded in historical fact, and each combat and each opponent referred to specific events in Maximilian's life (fig. 3).

If battles and tournaments provided arenas in which to acquire esteem and fame, as such they had inherent limitations. To make his prowess known to a broader audience and to ensure it would be remembered, Maximilian resolved to document his deeds, or, rather,

FIG. 3 *Joust of War between Wolfgang von Polheim and Freydal.* South German, 1512–15. Gouache with gold and silver highlights over pen, pencil, and leadpoint on paper, 15 1/16 x 10 9/16 in. (38.2 x 26.8 cm). Kunsthistorisches Museum, Vienna, Kunstkammer (5073, fol. 212)

portray them in literary and artistic productions that reflected and amplified his actions.[21] While *Theuerdank* is perhaps the most fictional among them, the *Weisskunig* and *Freydal* are closely inspired by actual historical, political, and military events. In the mind of the emperor, these fictional works had to be imbued with veracity and thus fact-checking was an integral part of their development. Needless to say, Maximilian's direct involvement and editorial ambitions were among the reasons only a deluxe version of *Freydal*, meant for his personal enjoyment, was produced. The printed version that he had also envisioned was still in an early stage of development by the time he died and was never completed.

The bulk of the projects commemorating his knightly deeds seem to have been initiated after he relocated to Innsbruck and gained the greatest momentum during the last decade of his life; yet, Maximilian's interest in projects of this nature is documented at a

much earlier date in the Low Countries (fig. 4). In 1479 he paid a large sum to a poet at the University of Leuven for having written an account of his victory at Guinegate the same year.[22] Although it is not clear whether it had been proposed to or commissioned by him, Maximilian's desire to commemorate his martial accomplishments is evident in the purchase of the work. Notably, he also gave one of his personal armors to the church of Notre Dame of Halle, then a major pilgrimage site in the Low Countries. While the votive gift may have been motivated by a pious vow, and was thus a sincere manifestation of Maximilian's gratitude for divine protection, the donation of the armor to a place of worship that had been consistently patronized by his predecessors, its installation in a prominent location, and its display on a lifesize statue of Maximilian himself kneeling in prayer all point to the fact that the donation also ensured the representation of the armed prince in a sacred place, where his image would be seen and admired by many. As the earliest mention of the armor dates to 1512 and the armor already needed to be polished and repaired, it is likely that the donation was made some time earlier (see cats. 151, 152).

Maximilian wanted his martial accomplishments to resonate beyond the battlefields and the market squares in which tournaments commonly occurred, and for that reason he generally appeared before his subjects adorned in the shining trappings of a warrior prince. After his victory at Guinegate he rode into Ghent in triumph, wearing full armor, parading with his one-year-old son seated on his lap. He made other spectacular entries in armor into Burgundian towns during this period of intense fighting and continued to do so in more peaceful times when visiting imperial cities in the German-speaking lands, particularly on the occasions of Imperial Diets (meetings of the Imperial Estates, assemblies that represented the constituents of the Holy Roman Empire).[23] Significantly, Maximilian is often depicted in armor in portraits that he commissioned, especially in stained-glass panels, paintings, and sculpture. Armor expressed knightly virtues, authority, and majesty, and it became a fixture of the official iconography. Over time, as Maximilian became

King of the Romans (1486) and Holy Roman Emperor (1508), armor was complemented by the corresponding attributes of his new titles, including mantle, scepter, and, of course, crown in official portraiture (see cats. 113, 161).

If armor was indispensable for Maximilian's knightly activities, it was equally if not more so for the construction of his image as a martial hero. Like any other self-respecting ruler from the period, he owned several armors: some for war and numerous others for the tournament, as each form of mock combat required a distinct type. As a young man, Maximilian did not initially have the time or the resources to commission or purchase all the different specialized armors, and he had to rent equipment from armorers in order to participate in jousts.[24] Eventually, he was able to assemble an armory that befitted his rank, inclinations, and reputation. Upon his death in 1519, his personal armors and those that he would lend to his guests were kept in specialized depots, or armories, which were located in Innsbruck and Augsburg, where professionals oversaw their care and maintenance.[25] Maximilian's holdings were so extensive that he purchased a private residence in Augsburg for the sole purpose of housing his armors and weapons, even though the magistrate of the city was opposed to the idea, not least because Maximilian refused to pay the customary property taxes.

Like clothing or jewelry, armor adorns the individual who wears it, and in doing so also shapes their image. As ordinary soldiers and even knights could hardly afford one, a quality armor immediately signaled a person's higher standing or association with people who had the power and means to provide it. For Maximilian, it was essential that the armors he used live up to the image he was fashioning of himself. To bolster his appearance as the rightful continuator of Charles the Bold, he owned magnificent armors, often either covered in costly textiles or decorated with precious materials, which were perhaps solely intended for ceremonial use. In 1479 a merchant supplied black satin to line one of his war hats, a helmet that was covered in black velvet.[26] The same year the Brussels goldsmith Jaspar de Bacquere (first recorded 1479, died

ca. 1487) received a payment for having embellished one of his armors with gilded silver. The work included the creation of a border of silver to be applied to the archduke's leg defenses, and the repair of branches and paillettes of silver that adorned one of his war hats.[27]

For the battlefield and the tournament, however, Maximilian needed highly functional and dependable armor, the intrinsic qualities of which would surpass, as his own deeds did, those of his entourage as well as the rulers who were his peers. At the battle of Guinegate, during which the French were able to loot Maximilian's camp and baggage, there were entirely gilded pieces among the spare armors that the Brussels armorer Franck Scroo (recorded 1479–1496) had kept in a carriage for Maximilian's use.[28] In 1479 Scroo was also paid for an armor made for Maximilian that must have been either very fine or richly decorated as it cost three times more than a typical made-to-measure field armor.[29] The archduke was deeply interested in and pleased with the quality of his personal armors. In a letter written in 1478 he enthusiastically reported having had several armors made for him, including a "French" (i.e., probably Walloon) example, all of which were superior to any others seen within living memory.[30] Maximilian was a great patron of armorers in the Low Countries. Although he gave work to other Netherlandish masters, he seems to have been particularly pleased with the abilities of Scroo, so much so that a decade later the latter was still making armors for Maximilian's personal use and for presentation as gifts.[31]

By appearing to his entourage and subjects magnificently clad in locally made armor styled in the fashion of his dominions, Maximilian could emphatically stress his role as the continuator and defender of the Burgundian state. Nevertheless, he did not deny himself the pleasure of wearing armor made elsewhere.[32] If anything, the possession of a variety of armors was likely to inspire the admiration of others, as it suggested a high degree of sophistication.[33] Any self-respecting fifteenth-century European ruler, for example, would have typically owned armor made in Milan, then one of the most prestigious armor-making centers in Europe. Charles the Bold had owned several and even installed

FIG. 5 *Maximilian on Horseback*, from an *Album of Armor Drawings*. South German (Augsburg), ca. 1550. Lead point, ink, watercolor, and metallic pigments on paper; bound in vellum, 12⅜ x 9½ in. (31.4 x 24 cm). Uměleckoprůmyslové Museum, Prague (GK 11.572-B, fol. n29r)

Milanese armorers in the Burgundian lands. His rival Louis XI had sought and accomplished the same in France.[34] During his time in the Low Countries, Maximilian occasionally commissioned armor for his personal use from the German-speaking lands, especially from Augsburg, which complemented the ones that he had received as gifts from the same territories.[35]

In this regard, the works that the Augsburg armorer Lorenz Helmschmid (first recorded 1467, died 1516) made for Maximilian and personally delivered to his court in the Low Countries in 1480 signal the archduke's intent to dazzle those around him. Their description in the accounts of Maximilian's treasurers, their astounding cost, and the qualities of their surviving elements indicate that in conception, execution, and style, the armors and the horse bard were superlative (cats. 16, 17). The bard, in particular, included articulated defenses for the horse's belly and legs, unprecedented feats of design made possible by the genius of the German armorer and ambition of his patron. Significantly, these works were paraded on solemn occasions: Maximilian rode into the city of Luxembourg on September 29, 1480, wearing one of Helmschmid's field armors, while his troops were repelling a French invasion (fig. 5). Acting as his representative, the official in charge of Maximilian's armory had similarly entered Namur six days earlier, riding on a horse clad in Helmschmid's bard. Contemporaries were awed by these armors. They were depicted in paintings commemorating the events at which they were observed, which is most unusual for the time, and a Venetian envoy who saw Maximilian in Strasbourg twelve years later recorded in minute detail the bard that protected the ruler's horse.[36]

By presenting himself in innovative and superbly crafted armor, Maximilian was no longer providing the measure of his greatness in terms of sheer expenditure. Deliberately seeking to amaze his audience with technological wonders, a year earlier he had acquired a war saddle equipped with spring-loaded steel brackets to hold the shaft of a banner and free the rider's hand, a novel invention and the first of several examples made for the Burgundian court over the ensuing

FIG. 6 Unicorn Sword of Charles the Bold. Netherlandish, before 1477. Steel, narwhal tooth, gold, silver, enamel, ruby, and pearls. Sword: L. 34⅛ in. (86.7 cm). Kunsthistorisches Museum, Vienna, Weltliche Schatzkammer (WS XIV 3)

decades (cat. 124). Similarly, in 1480 Helmschmid delivered a mechanism designed to carry a shield, which may have been intended for a new variant of the joust of war that required the use of a mechanical breastplate (see cats. 31–33). As this joust appears to have been practiced only at Maximilian's court, it seems likely that the archduke was responsible for its development or, at the very least, its promotion. For the rest of his life, Maximilian would encourage armorers to push the limits of their art (see cats. 34, 36, 88, 128).

While Maximilian counted on new armor to impress his audience, the dire state of his finances forced him to discreetly part with prized possessions, the very kind that he could have only benefited from in his efforts to legitimize his place at the helm of the Burgundian state. To fund the defense of his realms and to put down rebellions, he pawned the so-called unicorn sword, one of Charles the Bold's most valuable possessions (fig. 6). It took more than a century for the Habsburgs to reacquire the famed sword.[37] Similarly, Maximilian pawned extraordinary defenses for arms and legs, armor elements that he had either inherited from Charles the Bold or commissioned for himself. Enriched with jewels, including rubies and pearls, they were never recovered.[38] As Philip the Good (1396–1467) and Charles the Bold had also owned and worn armor similarly covered with gems, by pawning these objects Maximilian was effectively relinquishing their power to associate him with his predecessors.[39] His ordinary subjects were unaware of these transactions, which were conducted in secrecy with merchants in Bruges. To the casual eye, and certainly in public ceremonies, Maximilian succeeded in posing as the formidable, staunch continuator of a line of ambitious Burgundian dukes.

FIG. 7 Circle of the Master of the London Wavrin. *Maximilian I*, from the *Statutes of the Order of the Golden Fleece*. South Netherlandish (Bruges), ca. 1481–86. Gouache with gold and silver highlights over pen on paper. British Library, London (Harley 6199, fol. 73v)

FROM KNIGHT TO KNIGHT-MAKER

Upon becoming duke consort of Burgundy in 1477, Maximilian quickly realized the importance of upholding the customs and traditions of his distinguished predecessors as a way to legitimize his own power. It is for that reason that Maximilian consented, at the request of the few remaining loyal members, to join the Order of the Golden Fleece and become its sovereign in 1478 (fig. 7).[40] Founded by Philip the Good in 1430, the order, once one of Europe's most prestigious and exclusive chivalric institutions, had suddenly turned into a moribund body as most of its members had either died in action during Charles's military campaigns or defected to France after the latter's death. By joining it Maximilian signaled his intention to follow the example of his predecessors, and by becoming its head he demonstrated his resolution to exercise their privileges. The unfavorable circumstances under which he did so left no doubt about his commitment to uphold one of their most famous creations.

Maximilian, however, had to be knighted in order to join the Order of the Golden Fleece. Although he initially wanted his own father, Emperor Frederick III, to perform the honor, the prospect of having to wait for him to come to the Low Countries pushed Maximilian to accept the offer of being knighted by one of the order's senior members, Adolf of Cleves (1425–1492), lord of Ravenstein. On April 30, 1478, he was made a knight and shortly thereafter was received as a member and the sovereign of the order in a solemn ceremony held in Bruges.[41] In a single day Maximilian had thus been awarded the coveted knightly status and propelled to the head of one of Europe's most exalted chivalric orders.

As soon as he was knighted, Maximilian began to confer knighthoods upon others. He did so on the battlefield, as well as on solemn occasions such as Imperial Diets, his coronation as King of the Romans, and his proclamation as Holy Roman Emperor. Olivier de La Marche marveled at the fact that, unlike the Burgundians, the Germans seemed to have desired this honor to be bestowed as frequently as possible. Maximilian thus occasionally knighted the same individuals multiple times.[42] By awarding the coveted distinction, he reminded the men—most of them nobles—who fought by his side of the kindred ethos that united and distinguished them from everyone else. Maximilian sometimes further honored the recipients with gifts of armor.[43]

After joining the exclusive Order of the Golden Fleece, Maximilian proudly wore its collar with the distinctive pendant of a sheep's fleece. The order's prestigious symbols henceforth surrounded his coat of arms, while the flints and fire steels, which were its badges, and the cross of Saint Andrew, an evocation of its patron saint, graced his personal effects, including his weapons, and, uniquely, his personal armors. On September 29, 1480, Maximilian rode into the city of Luxembourg on a horse protected by an imposing bard of steel that was adorned with the order's badges and collar on the peytral and crupper (see fig. 5).[44] Similarly, the hilt and blade of a battle sword, probably made for him during the same period, are decorated with the order's badges (cat. 97). Although following the death of his first wife, Mary of Burgundy, Maximilian had to share the sovereignty of the order with his descendants—first his son, Philip I (1478–1506), and then his eldest grandson, Charles V (1500–1558)—he continued to sport its insignia. A jousting armor made for him in Innsbruck, which has the cross of Saint Andrew prominently engraved on the breastplate, and a sallet made for him in Augsburg, which has fire steels fretted on the brow plate, are telling examples of his attachment to the order as well as early milestones in the development of the custom for members of the House of Habsburg to celebrate their close association with the chivalric order in the decoration of their personal armors (see cat. 110).

As its leader, Maximilian did everything he could to revive the order, expand its ranks, and restore its former splendor, and in these endeavors he was quite successful. He expelled the members who had defected to France. In their stead he admitted his devotees, loyal Burgundians at first, and soon also trusted German servitors and companions such as Bertram von Liechtenstein (1478); Martin von Polheim (1481); Albrecht, duke of Saxony (1491); Christoph, margrave

of Baden (1491); Wolfgang von Polheim (1501); and Eitelfriedrich, count of Zollern (1501). In the meantime, Maximilian secured a place of honor for his own lineage, beginning with the admission of his son, Philip I (1481), followed by his father, Frederick III (1491). The subsequent admission of his grandsons, Charles V (1501) and Ferdinand I (1515), ensured that the association between the noble institution and the House of Habsburg would endure. In parallel, Maximilian relied on the institution to co-opt and consolidate ties by inviting foreign rulers, including Henry VII of England (1491); Henry VIII of England while he was prince of Wales (1505); Francis I of France (1515); Manuel of Portugal (1515); and Louis II of Hungary (1515), to join its ranks. The chivalric order was an instrument of his diplomacy.

Following his election and coronation as King of the Romans in 1486, which made him the presumptive heir to the Holy Roman Empire, Maximilian became increasingly involved in the empire's affairs. Upon the death of his father in 1493, he inherited the remaining Habsburg hereditary lands as well as the patronage of the Order of Saint George, which his father had established in 1469 (fig. 8). With these came the responsibility of safeguarding the empire and, in particular, the Habsburg hereditary lands threatened by the expansion of the Ottoman Empire. Unlike the Order of the Golden Fleece, the Order of Saint George was modeled on medieval militant chivalric orders that required their members to lead a communal and austere life, praying to God and fighting infidels in his name. Established for the purpose of bolstering the defense of the empire and expelling the Ottomans from Europe, the order never commanded substantial resources and had too few members. From a military point of view, it had little significance. Yet, for Maximilian, who had to share the sovereignty of the Order of the Golden Fleece with his descendants, and who in 1497 would fail to persuade Philip I to consent to the creation of two distinct branches of the order, a Burgundian and an Austrian one, the Order of Saint George opened up possibilities for greater and perhaps more fruitful engagement.[45] The idea of launching a new Crusade had been

FIG. 8 *Investiture of the First Grand Master of the Order of Saint George, Johann Siebenhirter, by Pope Paul II and Emperor Frederick III on January 1, 1469, in the Lateran Basilica in Rome*, detail showing Emperor Frederick III holding the order's mantle and Pope Paul II blessing Siebenhirter. Austrian, ca. 1490. Tempera on panel. Landesmuseum für Kärten, Klagenfurt, Austria (K 86)

Bold (who had contemplated launching a Crusade), and as the head of the empire and the Habsburg hereditary lands, Maximilian had both the moral obligation and the practical incentives to finally transform the order into the powerful instrument its founder had intended it to be.[46]

Since he lacked the material resources to increase the order's wealth, Maximilian primarily relied on his own influence and prestige to revitalize the order and build support for its cause. Only a month after his father's death, he decreed the creation of the Fraternity of Saint George, which anyone—irrespective of gender, birth, or wealth—was exhorted to join, to provide physical and material assistance to the order of the same name. As this call to arms was not successful, Maximilian established the Society of Saint George in 1503. It was at this time that he envisioned the creation of a lavishly illustrated prayer book for the order. He commissioned portraits of himself in armor, wearing the order's cross on his breastplate or its insignia on a mantle, in the presence of the saint, as his mirror image, or as the saint himself (see cats. 102, 103, 105–7).[47] He naturally owned armor that similarly relayed his fervor for the order's cause (fig. 9). Although his attention was periodically redirected to military conflicts and to the correlated issue of funding his campaigns, Maximilian was sincerely committed to the Order of Saint George and the organizations he had founded to strengthen it. He became a member of the fraternity upon its creation and succeeded in persuading Pope Alexander VI (r. 1492–1503) and his cardinals to nominally join it as well. He also considered becoming the order's grand master, but he could not do so as long as the incumbent, who died in 1508, was alive and he himself remained a married man. Following the death of his second wife, Bianca Maria Sforza, however, Maximilian joined the order.[48] Despite his best intentions and efforts, the order neither gained influence nor contributed in any notable way to the defense of the Habsburg hereditary lands against the Ottomans. Its ongoing military insignificance and inactivity, which led to its eventual dissolution in 1598, are among Maximilian's most spectacular failures.

promoted by successive popes and secular rulers who had been given the mandate to carry it out. The foundation of the Order of Saint George had been sanctified in Rome and its first grand master, a trusted servitor of Frederick III, solemnly inducted there by Pope Paul II (r. 1464–1471) in the emperor's presence. As Frederick's son, as a Christian prince, as the heir of Charles the

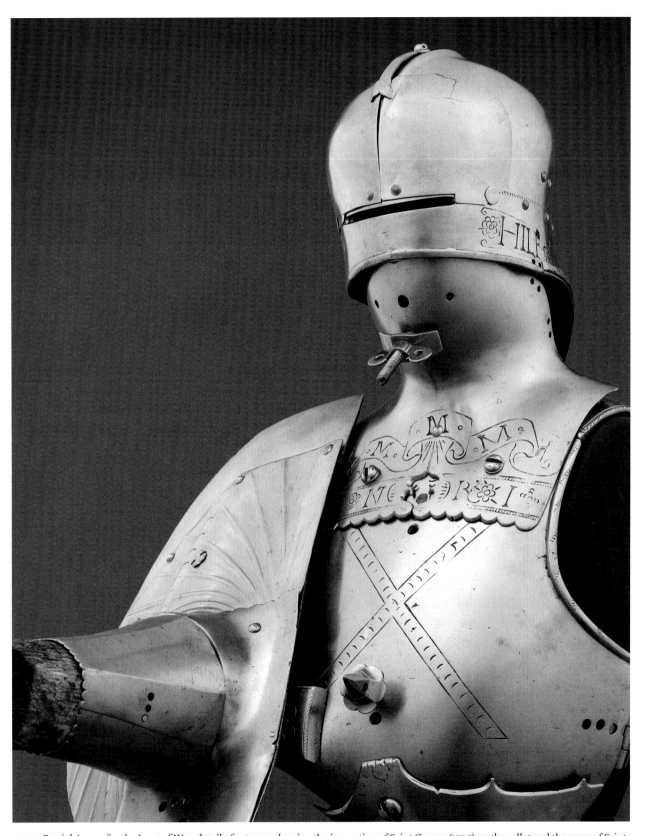

FIG. 9 Partial Armor for the Joust of War, detail of cat. 110, showing the invocation of Saint George (HILF) on the sallet and the cross of Saint Andrew on the breastplate

THE PERFECT GIFT

Although it was customary in medieval times for a knight who entered the service of a lord to acquire for himself the military equipment that he would need, the expense was not inconsiderable and a decision from a lord to provide a fine armor, or the monetary means to purchase one, was thus both welcome and viewed as a mark of interest and favor. Charles the Bold was well aware of armor's power to strengthen such bonds. In 1468, to celebrate his wedding with Margaret of York (1446–1503), he acquired and liberally distributed more than a hundred fine armors to his entourage and guests. In the years that followed, he periodically honored one man or another with comparable gifts.[49]

Maximilian also knew the value of armor and what made a good one particularly desirable. Because many other men shared his appreciation for well-made, dependable, beautiful works, he saw in gifts of armor opportunities to establish or affirm connections, show his appreciation or friendship, and elicit loyalty or gratitude. While several hundred recipients, most of whom were members of his military household and guard, remain anonymous, the available documentation, despite being uneven and incomplete, yields the names of well over a hundred individuals to whom Maximilian presented gifts of armor during his lifetime. This group includes craftsmen, administrative officials, squires, lesser and great noblemen, princes, kings, and relatives.

At the beginning of his rule in the Low Countries, Maximilian's situation seems to have initially been too precarious for him to consistently give his gifts much thought. The available record of his activity shows the acquisition of armors for many members of his household, from armorers and merchants in Brussels and Bruges, and gifts of cash to various individuals for the purpose of buying their military equipment. The varying costs and quantities of the armors awarded reveal that the gifts were allocated on a case-by-case basis, though one's respective position at court appears to have generally commanded a predetermined measure of liberality, with the most influential courtiers typically receiving more expensive armors. Recorded exceptions

to this scale, however, make it clear enough that Maximilian presented special gifts to those who might provide the greatest service.[50]

During this early period, the primary motive for Maximilian's gifts seems to have been limited to equipping individuals for war. In some cases, the records explicitly link the gifts to the services that recipients are providing or are about to provide in military campaigns.[51] Maximilian also compensated some men who had lost their armors (or horses) in his service, although it is not entirely clear whether he was under the obligation to do so by virtue of a medieval practice, known as *droit de restor*, according to which an overlord was bound to replace the horses and equipment his vassals had lost in his service, or whether it was a favor that he freely granted to chosen individuals.[52] Whatever his reasons were, it seems clear that at this time the archduke had no direct communications with the armorers who made the works, and that he had no hand in their design or production.

By 1488, two years after he had become King of the Romans, Maximilian's gift giving had become more sophisticated.[53] Records show that his trusted Brussels armorer, Franck Scroo, was paid for custom-made armors that Maximilian later presented to worthy recipients. By distributing armors wrought by the master from whom he commissioned many of his own pieces, the king was no longer merely providing military equipment that was valuable and useful; he was now also presenting a token of favor, an object that intimated to others the existence of a privileged connection. The knight Vincent von Swanenburch (recorded 1478–1519) was certainly honored in this way. Although he had neither a high social standing nor an appointment at the Burgundian court, his recent military conduct in Utrecht in 1488 had caught Maximilian's attention and prompted his inclusion along with a knight from Zeeland among the handful of individuals who were presented with armors specially commissioned from Scroo, including Philip I, Wolfgang von Polheim (1458–1512), Maximilian's longtime companion and trusted adviser, and Jan van Houthem (ca. 1440–1504), chancellor of Brabant. The gift was a tangible marker of

FIG. 10 Epitaph of the Armorer Jörg Helmschmid and His Daughter Anna. Austrian, dated 1502. Sandstone. Hofkirche, Vienna

Maximilian's appreciation, one that implicitly placed Swanenburch in the sphere of much more eminent and influential men.[54]

The beginning of Maximilian's personal rule over Tyrol in 1490, the establishment of his chief residence in Innsbruck, and his inheritance of all other Habsburg hereditary lands upon his father's death three years later provided him with easier access to accomplished German armorers and greater financial resources to pay for their services. Significantly, Maximilian promptly appointed Lorenz Helmschmid of Augsburg, the master from whom he had acquired extraordinary armors in 1480, as his court armorer for life, a status

that guaranteed Maximilian preferential treatment and the right to summon Helmschmid to his court.[55] Within a few years he also took Lorenz's brother, Jörg (first recorded 1488, died 1502), another gifted armorer, into his service, and installed him in Vienna (fig. 10),[56] and later Hans Laubermann (recorded 1490–1521), then the wealthiest armorer in Innsbruck.[57] Finally, he recruited leading Milanese armorers to create and operate an armorer's workshop in Arbois in the Franche-Comté (see cat. 125).

Maximilian had dramatically greater access to high-quality armor in Innsbruck than he had had in the Low Countries. Under the patronage of Archduke Sigismund, his great-uncle and predecessor, armorers active in nearby Mühlau had been given the opportunity to specialize in the manufacture of very fine armor, producing works that Sigismund had presented to peers across Europe, as far as France, Hungary, Portugal, Scotland, and Silesia.[58] Maximilian benefited from their experience and exceptional knowledge of metallurgy, which made their creations singularly effective against projectiles and edged weapons. In his new position Maximilian could commission gift armors that were coveted not just for their aesthetic merits but also for their superior defensive qualities. In addition, he began to train handpicked armorers that he took in his service. Among them was Conrad Seusenhofer (first recorded 1500, died 1517), who in 1504 entered into an agreement to work exclusively for Maximilian for six years in return for set wages and prime working conditions. In 1509 Seusenhofer was made the head of a fully subsidized court workshop that became the chief source of Maximilian's gift armors until the latter's death.[59] Unlike independent armorers who had multiple clients, and who generally had too few helpers to take on many commissions at once and complete them promptly, the Innsbruck court workshop was always available and theoretically sized to meet Maximilian's demands. In practice, and despite the growth of its premises and staff, it continually struggled to meet the ever-expanding volume of his requests. Nevertheless, it became one of Maximilian's greatest assets in all of his pursuits: it produced functional armors for the

FIG. 11 Lorenz Helmschmid (first recorded 1467, died 1516). Combination Sallet and Bevor, view of cat. 128

sovereign's personal guard and household as well as luxury armors for his relatives and select individuals.[60]

The image of Maximilian visiting an armorer's workshop in the *Weisskunig* is no exaggeration (cats. 114, 115). His correspondence suggests that he often gave Seusenhofer his instructions in person and frequently commented on designs, specifying desired types and styles, and even expressing preference for the fixtures used to assemble the elements.[61] In 1515, for example, he instructed Seusenhofer to make helmets in a new form.[62] A year later, in relation to an armor intended for an eleven-year-old prince, he reminded the armorer of the need to use a system of bolts to ensure that the armor would be able to fit the boy's growing body for three years (see cat. 141). In return, Seusenhofer often confirmed the styles of the armors he had completed. In 1504 he wrote that he had made an armor with a breastplate in the Italian fashion for a cardinal and a cuirass with long tassets intended for a certain Dyllemee, which was fluted to resemble the pleats of Netherlandish clothing.[63]

Maximilian was proud of the unique features found on the armors made under his supervision in the court workshop. As part of the instructions he gave to Seusenhofer to make a field armor for an Italian nobleman, he insisted that the armorer should also let the recipient know about the particular technical features and peculiarities that distinguished the objects made in the imperial court workshop.[64] In his communications, he made it clear when extra care was to be paid to certain work, notably stressing the quality required for a field armor for an ambassador of the king of Aragon in 1513.[65] Maximilian took such pride in the Innsbruck court workshop that he wanted its premises to look as engaging as possible. In 1506 he requested that the building's upper floor be turned into a hall in which armors and cuirasses could be hung alongside a tapestry.[66]

Maximilian's need for gift armors was so great, however, that additional Innsbruck armorers were entrusted with their manufacture. In some instances, it was clear that the commissions were primarily motivated by Seusenhofer's workload.[67] When such armors were ordered in Augsburg or Vienna, other factors, such as the physical proximity of the armorers to the intended recipients, were likely taken into consideration.[68]

Following the death of his father, which effectively placed him at the head of the empire even though he had yet to be crowned emperor, Maximilian became so involved in the affairs of the Holy Roman Empire that his gifts of armor increasingly took on a tactical and strategic nature. He honored men whose goodwill or support he needed, including ambassadors of the Ottoman sultan and of the kings of Aragon, England, and Naples; French and Italian cardinals; the marquises of Mantua; and the pope's brother.[69] The protracted war against the Republic of Venice, during which interests and alliances regularly shifted, fueled many of these commissions as Maximilian attempted to secure the collaboration of dependable partners. He also used gift armors to build lasting alliances, ordering grand armors for presentation to Frederick IV (1452–1504), king of Naples, in 1499, when Louis XII of France (1462–1515) was invading his lands;[70] Henry VIII (1491–1547), king of England, in 1511, when the latter was about to join the Holy League that the pope was forming against the king of France;[71] and Louis II of Hungary (1506–1526), in 1514, for the celebration of Louis's prospective marriage with his granddaughter Mary of Austria (1505–1558).[72] Similarly, a mail shirt and cap covered in cloth of gold, trimmed with velvet, and adorned with seven sapphires and two garnets was specially made in 1510 to be given to a figure described as "the Great Wallachian," presumably Mircea III Dracul (d. 1534), who had just become prince of Wallachia, and whose anti-Ottoman views made him a prospective ally.[73]

For these strategic undertakings Maximilian would spare no expense even though he chronically lacked funds and could not always make the payments necessary to ensure the smooth completion of the required gifts. An armor of Charles V, which was produced by Seusenhofer's workshop and designed along the same lines as one made for presentation to Henry VIII, may give a fair idea of the sophistication and opulence of the gifts that were deployed by Maximilian to strengthen ties with his peers (cat. 82). As the donor,

Maximilian also hoped to project an ideal image of himself as a munificent knightly ruler. The words that he dictated to his secretary, and which are reproduced in the *Weisskunig*, leave no doubt that for Maximilian the armor he distributed mirrored his own greatness: "And in his aforementioned armory the said White King had armors made with this induced hardness, which was secret to all others, and [he had them] presented to many kings, princes, and mighty lords, whereby the White King had outdone the generosity of all other kings."[74]

Maximilian was equally extravagant with the gifts he ordered for his family. He had high hopes for his descendants, especially his son, Philip I. In 1488, finally freed after having been held prisoner in Bruges for three months, he had Franck Scroo make a partly gilded armor that included three different helmets for Philip, who was then still in the custody of a council appointed by the Flemish rebels.[75] The armor provided a powerful visual assertion of the connection between the young boy and his imperious father, as once clad in it, his son would mirror his father's image. Undoubtedly moved by a similar understanding, Philip wrote Archduke Sigismund of Tyrol a few months later, after Maximilian's guardianship had been restored, to request the favor of having an armor made for him in Innsbruck, so that he would be able to stand by his father's side to fight their enemies.[76] As it is doubtful that Maximilian would have allowed his ten-year-old son to take part in a battle, the requested armor, which is preserved in the Kunsthistorisches Museum, Vienna, was first and

foremost a symbol of the alignment of father and son and of the Houses of Austria and Burgundy, which they represented, in the defense of their shared heritage.[77]

Following Philip I's death, Maximilian became the guardian of his grandson Charles V. Soon after, he commissioned from Hans Rabeiler (first recorded 1501, died 1519) an armor shaped and decorated with puffs and slashes in the manner of the fashionable male clothing of the time. For reasons unknown, Rabeiler was unable to complete the work, and the armor was retained in its rough, unfinished state (cat. 81). Either dissatisfied with Rabeiler's services or convinced that the armor would no longer fit Charles, Maximilian ordered another one for his grandson, this time from Conrad Seusenhofer. Completed in 1514, the resulting armor is a masterpiece: it has a steel skirt and is adorned throughout with etched ornament and strips of gilded silver fretted with the badges of the Order of the Golden Fleece, which were applied over a ground of dark velvet. This extravagant armor, which would fit the fourteen-year-old Charles only for a few years, signaled the teenager's great prospects as he was about to begin his personal rule as duke of Burgundy and claim the crowns of Castile and Aragon (cat. 82).

EPILOGUE

Under Maximilian the art of the armorer blossomed like never before (fig. 11). In various parts of Europe, masters were tasked with creating objects that were the measure of his ambitions. While some made only ordinary armor for his troops, others were invited to achieve unprecedented refinement and novelty. Maximilian was an exacting patron but also a supportive one. He was interested in armor design and metallurgy. He wanted to outshine his peers by presenting them with works that they could not obtain by themselves. The armor that Maximilian commissioned from Kolman Helmschmid (1471–1532) in 1516, which was completed by the time of the emperor's death in 1519, was a superlative work made of solid silver and adorned with gilding and gems (fig. 12). Maximilian may have hoped that the extravagant piece would help erase from his memory the humiliation of having had to part with bejeweled armor elements for the sake of raising funds and ensuring his political survival at the very beginning of his rule. Sadly, his mounting debts prevented him from ever taking possession of the masterpiece. Charles V acquired the armor, gave it away, and within a few decades it was destroyed. Nevertheless, Maximilian left an extraordinary artistic and political legacy. Writing at the end of his life, when he had nothing to expect from flattery, the prominent Burgundian courtier Olivier de La Marche thought the emperor deserved the nickname of "heart of steel" (*coeur d'acier*) on the grounds that "steel is a more noble thing than gold, silver, lead, or iron, for it is of steel, as the noblest of metals, that are made the armors and harnesses with which the preeminent people in the world adorn themselves and protect their bodies against war and else."[78] Maximilian, who was then alive and well, would never hear the compliment, which was first published in 1562. And yet, through his pursuits and actions, he proved himself deserving of it.

FIG. 12 Lucas Cranach the Elder (1472–1553) and workshop. *Saint Maurice*, detail of cat. 160, showing the saint wearing the now-lost silver armor

Er zoch darnach in niderlanndt
Zu hilff dem Künig von Engellandt
Pald sampten sy ein heere gros
Dy Frantzosen soltchs verdros
Ir maniger der nider lag
Terrauan ward gschlaifft Tornay sich gab

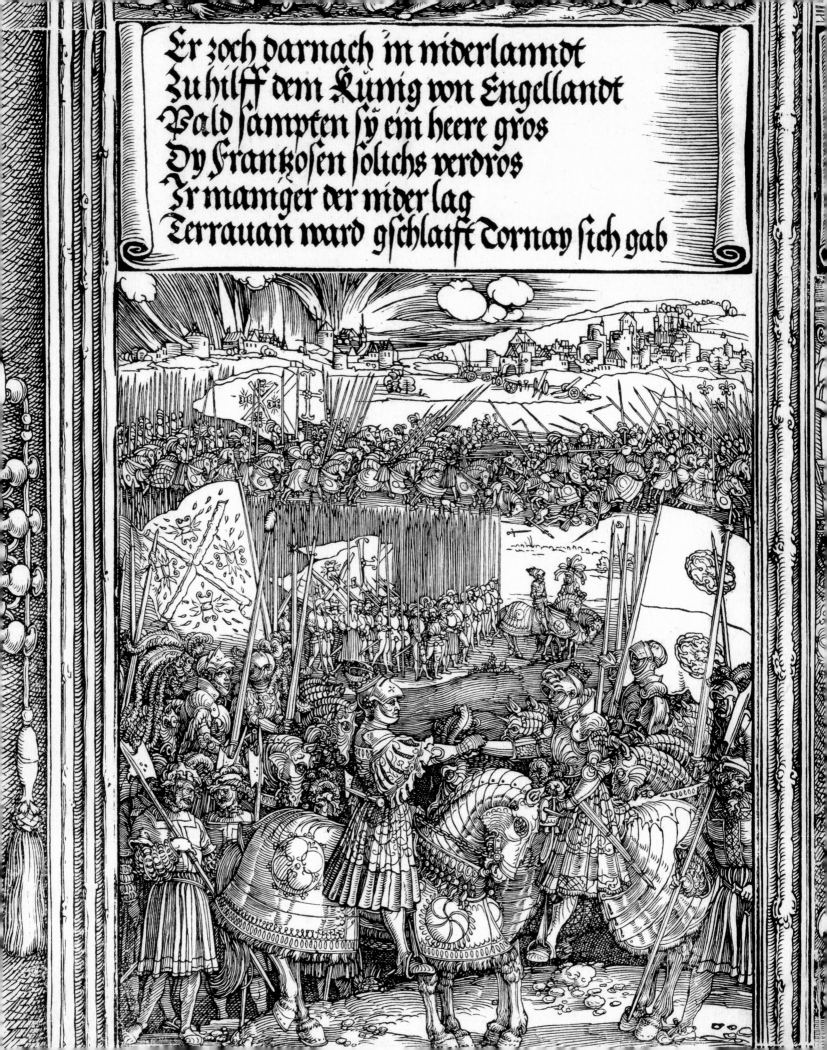

POLITICAL STRUGGLE AND DYNASTIC TRIUMPH

Maximilian I and the Rise of the House of Habsburg

Adam B. Brandow and Matthias Pfaffenbichler

As Holy Roman Emperor, Maximilian I (1459–1519) wielded nominal imperial authority over hundreds of fragmented political entities, stretching from the North Sea to the Mediterranean. Since Charlemagne had been crowned Holy Roman Emperor in 800, the empire's sheer scale and diversity had hindered efforts to centralize its administration and rule under a single figure. The constitutional regulations set out in the Golden Bull of 1356 had established the process by which the monarch was chosen by a college of seven secular and ecclesiastical prince electors, whose collective power ultimately overshadowed that of the emperor. By the time Maximilian's father, Frederick III (1415–1493), became Holy Roman Emperor, the imperial crown had lost much of its prestige and agency, leaving Frederick with little political influence beyond the largely titular prerogatives of the office itself. Realizing that the only means of bolstering his authority was to secure his own strong territorial base, Frederick devoted much of his fifty-three-year reign to reuniting the Habsburgs' ancient hereditary lands that spread across the eastern Alps and Upper Danube region. Although these distinct political entities were loosely held together under the aegis of the empire, the sovereignty of them had been divided in preceding generations among competing dynastic lines. Frederick's consolidation of the geographic nucleus of Habsburg power and his skill for arranging politically strategic marriages for his children, particularly Maximilian, paved the way for his decedents' dynastic ascent and provided a model for them to follow.

FIG. 13 *Banner of Saint George*. Netherlandish, before 1474. Silk, 46¹⁄₁₆ in. x 11 ft. 3¹³⁄₁₆ in. (117 x 345 cm). Museum Altes Zeughaus, Solothurn, Switzerland (MAZ 1145)

It was into this climate that Maximilian was born on March 22, 1459, at Wiener Neustadt Castle in Lower Austria, approximately twenty-eight miles (forty-five kilometers) south of Vienna, the only surviving son of Frederick III and Eleanor of Portugal (1434–1467).[1] As a child he received a typical princely education meant to prepare him for life at court and on the battlefield, including instruction in languages, music, dancing, woodworking, hunting, and the handling of weapons for tournaments and war. This training would guide his future patronage of the arts and inspire his efforts to craft an idealized self-image. Maximilian's awareness of his father's diplomatic struggles and the bitter conflict with his uncle Archduke Albrecht VI of Austria (1418–1463) over the inheritance of the Habsburg hereditary lands established his political worldview and calibrated his imperial and dynastic objectives.

The events of Maximilian's life can be divided roughly into two distinct periods, which hinge around the year 1490. After his marriage to Mary of Burgundy (1457–1482), Maximilian directed his attention toward the west, where he was preoccupied with ongoing political and territorial disputes in the Low Countries, as well as warfare on the French border. Through the 1490s Maximilian's focus shifted toward the east and

south, where he placed greater emphasis on expanding the Habsburg hereditary lands. After becoming Holy Roman Emperor, he sought to reestablish imperial power in Italy, which resulted in the devastating wars against the French and the Venetians.

THE LOW COUNTRIES

Maximilian's marriage to Mary of Burgundy was the most significant event of his youth, and it propelled the archduke into the arena of European politics. As early as 1463 Pope Pius II (r. 1458–1464) had encouraged a marriage between Maximilian and Mary, heiress to the Burgundian lands, in the hope that this union might foster support for the Holy See's proposed Crusade against the Ottoman Turks. Frederick III approved of this prospect, but he rejected the petition by Charles the Bold (1433–1477), Mary's father, to elevate his status from duke to king in exchange for Mary's hand. In September 1473 the emperor and fourteen-year-old Maximilian met Charles the Bold at Trier to negotiate the marriage. It was at this lavish event that Maximilian first witnessed the material splendor of the Burgundian court, the luxury and sophistication of which was unrivaled in Europe. For Maximilian, whose background was relatively modest despite his status as the

FIG. 14 *Maximilian I and Mary of Burgundy*, detail from the *Counts of Flanders*, panel X. South Netherlandish, 1401–1500. Oil on panel. Grootseminarie, Bruges, Belgium

emperor's only son, the experience was a revelation. It was also the only time that he and his future father-in-law would meet (fig. 13).

Undeterred by the summit's unsuccessful resolution, the two parties continued diplomatic negotiations, and Maximilian and Mary were betrothed in 1476. Charles the Bold's sudden death in January 1477 on the battlefield near Nancy, the site of the final clash in his devastating war against the Old Swiss Confederacy and its allies, left Burgundy nearly bankrupt and politically vulnerable. Motivated by a French claim to the duchy of Burgundy under Salic Law, which prohibited women

and descendants in the female line from dynastic succession, King Louis XI (1423–1483) took the opportunity to annex Burgundian territory, seizing the territories of Burgundy, Picardy, and Artois. With her inheritance in peril and facing pressure from Louis to marry his son, the dauphin Charles VIII (1470–1498), Mary sought to secure a swift alliance with Maximilian, and they were married by proxy in Bruges on April 21.[2] Maximilian and his entourage entered Ghent on August 18, and as the court was still in mourning for Charles the Bold, a private wedding ceremony was held in the court chapel (fig. 14).

Maximilian's youth and martial energy, as well as the prestige he brought as son of the Holy Roman Emperor, compensated for his inability to refill the depleted Burgundian coffers with funds needed to defend Mary's dominions against the French. After gaining monetary support from the Netherlandish Estates (assemblies that represented the provinces of the Burgundian Low Countries), Maximilian was able to resist further French incursions into his wife's territories and defeat the French at the battle of Guinegate in August 1479.

In addition to the foreign threat from France, Maximilian and Mary faced internal rebellion from the citizens of Flemish towns who demanded the restoration of ancient privileges and political autonomy that had been lost as a result of Charles the Bold's efforts to centralize the administration of his territories and consolidate his sovereignty. Mary agreed to the estates' demands in return for financial support to fund Maximilian's war against France, thus undoing her father's political legacy. While the birth of Maximilian and Mary's son, Philip I (1478–1506), secured the Burgundian succession, the arrival of their daughter, Margaret (1480–1530), two years later presented the possibility for an advantageous marriage alliance. Louis XI proposed that the young archduchess become engaged to the dauphin Charles VIII, recommending the division of the Burgundian territories as her dowry, a suggestion that Maximilian rejected.

Mary of Burgundy's tragic death following a riding accident in March 1482 led to a crisis in the Burgundian succession. Maximilian was already despised throughout Brabant and Flanders, especially by the burghers of Ghent and Bruges who viewed him as a foreigner and resented his interference in their affairs and the continued taxation to fund his war against France. The guardianship of Maximilian and Mary's children was key to maintaining the balance of power between the ruler and the bodies representing his subjects. The Netherlandish Estates vehemently opposed Maximilian's demand to act as regent for four-year-old Philip, who had inherited the duchy on his mother's death. Instead, they demanded the right to raise the young prince and his sister, which Maximilian

refused as securing his children's guardianship was vital to legitimizing his authority.[3]

Louis XI took advantage of the conflict and aggressively stoked rebellion among the Flemish people in the hope of further undermining Maximilian's position and winning territorial gains. His clandestine talks with the burghers of Ghent resulted in the treaty of Arras on December 23, 1482, according to which two-year-old Margaret was to become engaged to the dauphin Charles VIII in 1483. Maximilian was forced to let his daughter be raised in Paris as the future queen of France and to relinquish territories including Artois and the Franche-Comté as her dowry. Philip remained under the guardianship of the council appointed by the Netherlandish Estates. Maximilian, who had not been consulted in the negotiations, viewed this treaty as a grave personal defeat.[4]

The political situation shifted after Louis XI's death in August 1483. The following summer Maximilian dissolved the council in whose care Philip had been placed, sparking open Flemish rebellion led by the cities of Ghent, Bruges, and Ieper. Adding to Maximilian's troubles was a renewed declaration of war by the young French king Charles VIII, who sought to capitalize on Maximilian's domestic distractions. Maximilian was able to take the Flemish city of Oudenarde that winter, and subsequent victories against Ghent and Bruges forced his rebellious subjects into a peace agreement. Maximilian declared amnesty for all but the rebel leaders, who were executed or banished. Philip was returned to his father in July 1485 and placed under the care of Mary's stepmother, Margaret of York.

Following his triumphs in the Low Countries Maximilian directed his attention to securing his election as King of the Romans, a title that would indicate his status as heir apparent to the imperial throne. According to imperial custom, the monarch was chosen by the archbishops of Mainz, Cologne, and Trier, the count palatine of the Rhine, the duke of Saxony, the margrave of Brandenburg, and the king of Bohemia, who collectively acted as the nominal successors to the Roman Senate. Despite Frederick III's opposition to his son's elevation, seemingly concerned by Maximilian's encroachment on his authority, Maximilian was elected in Frankfurt am Main on February 16, 1486, and crowned in Aachen on April 9. He returned to the Low Countries in August.[5]

For decades Frederick III and the Hungarian king Matthias Corvinus (1443–1490) had fought for control over the southeastern region of the Habsburg hereditary lands, which led to outright warfare between 1477 and 1488. Although Maximilian had planned to come to his father's aid after Hungarians seized the duchy of Lower Austria and occupied Vienna in 1485, the unrest in the Low Countries prevented him from doing so. Maximilian's renewed demand for more financial support angered the Flemish people, and he entered Bruges at the beginning of 1488, intending to use the city as a base from which to lead a campaign against a rebellion in Ghent. On February 1, armed guild members of Bruges took Maximilian prisoner in the name of the city council. Only Maximilian's royal status and the House of Habsburg's prestige saved his life, while one of his most trusted companions was executed by the mob. The news that the King of the Romans had been imprisoned sparked outrage throughout the empire, and Frederick quickly raised an army to free his son. Yet before the seventy-two-year-old emperor and his army arrived in the Low Countries, Maximilian had succeeded in negotiating his own release and agreed to sign a treaty, whereby he relinquished his title of count of Flanders. However, neither Frederick nor Maximilian intended to adhere to the terms of the treaty, as they were incompatible with the notion of imperial power and the emperor's supreme authority.

After twelve years of fighting rebellious subjects and defending his northwestern territories against the French, Maximilian handed military command of the Low Countries to his cousin Duke Albrecht of Saxony (1443–1500) and abandoned the region to support his father's efforts in the empire's southeast.

HUNGARY

The long conflict between Frederick III and Matthias Corvinus, in which the Hungarians had achieved significant territorial gains in the Habsburg hereditary lands, ended abruptly in April 1490 when Corvinus died in Vienna without a legitimate heir. Recognizing the power vacuum as an opportunity to aid his father in reclaiming the family's lost possessions on the other side of the empire, Maximilian led an army eastward that summer.[6] Meanwhile in Lower Austria, the citizens of Wiener Neustadt, Tulln, Baden, St. Pölten, and Vienna rose up against the occupying Hungarian garrisons. On August 19 Maximilian, with an army of four thousand men, retook Vienna, and by the beginning of October had succeeded in driving all Hungarian forces out of the Habsburg hereditary lands in Austria.[7] Maximilian crossed into Hungary at the end of October and on November 17 took the royal city of Stuhlweissenburg (Székesfehérvár). His continued march to the Hungarian capital, Buda, was hindered by cold weather, and the troops, whom Maximilian was unable to pay, refused to lay siege to the city. Maximilian's only option was to negotiate with the Hungarians, and after months of diplomacy, they signed the peace of Pressburg (Bratislava), acknowledging the legitimacy of the Bohemian king Ladislaus Jagiellon (1456–1516), now Ladislaus II of Bohemia and Hungary, on November 7, 1491. Ladislaus II, in turn, renounced his claim to Lower Austria and recognized the Habsburgs' fundamental right to succession in Hungary in the event that he were to die without a legitimate male heir.[8]

In 1505 the growing tensions between the Hungarian magnates and Ladislaus II led to a brief war between the Hungarian Estates and the king. Maximilian sided with Ladislaus II, and the Austrian advance toward Eisenburg (Vasvár) and Ödenburg (Sopron) promptly forced the Hungarian magnates to the negotiating table. In the treaty of Vienna, signed on July 19, 1506, Maximilian gained 200,000 florins and the confirmation of the validity of his claim to the Hungarian throne, according to the previous terms set by the peace of Pressburg. This treaty led to talks between Ladislaus II and Maximilian about a strategic marriage between Princess Anne of Bohemia and Hungary (1503–1547) and one of Maximilian's grandsons, though at this time it was unclear whether Charles V (1500–1558) or Ferdinand I (1503–1564) would be chosen as the bridegroom. They also agreed that Ladislaus II's son Louis II

(1506–1526) would marry Mary of Austria (1505–1558), one of Maximilian's granddaughters. This contract, signed in autumn 1507, set the stage for the "double marriage" that would take place at the Congress of Vienna in 1515.

BRITTANY, THE LOW COUNTRIES, AND TYROL

The rivalry between Maximilian and Charles VIII came to a head in September 1488 following the death of Duke Francis II of Brittany (1433–1488), who had spent his rule fighting to preserve his duchy's autonomy from the French. Situated on a peninsula jutting into the Atlantic Ocean off the northwest coast of France, the sovereign duchy of Brittany was of economic and military significance due to its strategic coastal position between England and the Low Countries. Seeking to prevent the French from annexing the duchy, Maximilian married Anne of Brittany (1477–1514)—who had inherited the Breton throne from her father, Francis II—by proxy in December 1490. Unfortunately, Maximilian's absence due to his Hungarian campaigns left the Breton peninsula undefended, and with no Habsburg aid in sight Anne was forced to renounce her marriage to Maximilian and marry Charles VIII at the end of 1491.

Charles VIII's duplicitous conduct was doubly insulting to Maximilian, for in addition to stealing his wife, the king had retracted his long-standing engagement to Margaret of Austria, who had been isolated from her family since being taken to live at the French court at the age of three. To aggravate the situation, Charles showed no willingness to hand back Margaret's substantial territorial dowry, and even refused to release the archduchess herself as a means of ensuring Maximilian's continued diplomatic cooperation. Maximilian responded by forming an alliance with England and Spain against France, though this effort failed when Charles bribed these allies into neutrality. Ultimately, the rejection of Maximilian's further attempts to gain imperial support for a war against France at the 1492 Imperial Diet (a meeting of the Imperial Estates, the deliberative assemblies that represented the constituents of the empire), together

with Charles's weakened position due to his ongoing involvement in Italian politics, led both parties to settle the conflict in May 1493 with the treaty of Senlis. Margaret was finally returned to her father, hostilities over the Habsburgs' control of the Burgundian Low Countries ceased, and Artois, Flanders, and the Franche-Comté reverted to Maximilian.

For sixteen years, since the death of Charles the Bold, Maximilian had struggled to fund his military efforts to hold on to the Burgundian inheritance. Unable to rely on financial support from the Imperial Estates or to draw sufficient tax income from the Habsburg hereditary lands in Austria, Maximilian sought another means to shore up his fiscal resources with the acquisition of Tyrol. A wealthy alpine county of the Holy Roman Empire, Tyrol owed its prosperity to its silver and salt mines, and it had been controlled by another branch of the Habsburg family since 1363. By the mid-1480s, the extravagant lifestyle of Maximilian's great-uncle Archduke Sigismund of Tyrol (1427–1496) had left him deeply in debt to Duke Albrecht IV of Bavaria (1447–1508). As partial payment against a loan of 216,000 florins, Sigismund offered Albrecht the margraviate of Burgau in 1486, and in 1487 proposed the sale of Further Austria, which included Habsburg possessions in parts of present-day Tyrol and Bavaria.[9]

To prevent Sigismund from squandering more of Tyrol's resources on his debts and on the disastrous War of Rovereto against the Republic of Venice, Frederick III intervened and appealed to the nobles of Tyrol, who in August 1487 summoned a diet. In addition to demanding the dismissal of Sigismund's councilors and the cancellation of the sale of Further Austria, the Tyrolian Estates imposed rigorous austerity measures that severely limited the operating budget of the archducal household. Sigismund failed to adhere to the demands, and in March 1490 he abdicated in favor of Maximilian, who was formally recognized as the new ruler of Tyrol (fig. 15). Maximilian was in residence in Innsbruck when he learned of his father's death in Linz on August 19, 1493, which left him as the sole ruler of the Habsburg hereditary lands.

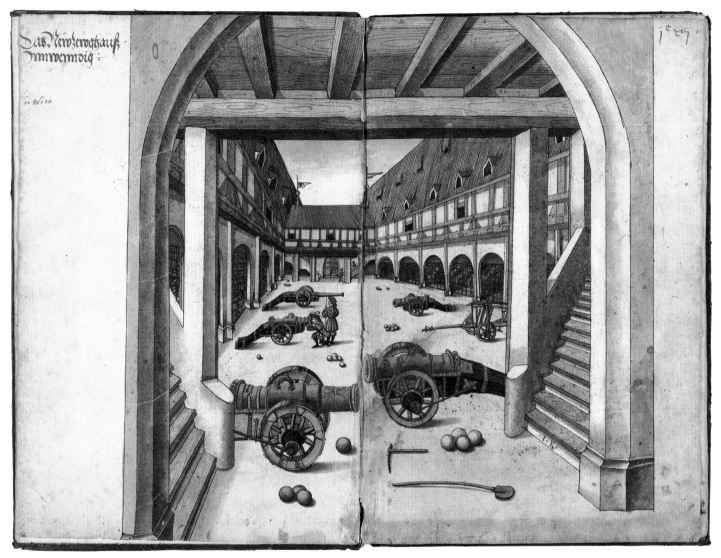

FIG. 15 Jörg Kölderer (ca. 1456/70–1540). *Interior Courtyard of Maximilian's Armory*, from the *Inventory of Maximilian I's Armaments in Tyrol* (cat. 153)

ITALY, THE GÖRZ INHERITANCE, AND THE WAR OF THE SUCCESSION OF BAVARIA-LANDSHUT

After Maximilian's bitter dispute with Charles VIII over the marriage with Anne of Brittany, the conflict with France shifted from the Low Countries to Italy. Frederick III had been the first Habsburg emperor to be crowned by the pope in Rome, and Maximilian dreamt of restoring the emperor's authority over the ancient imperial peninsula. In order to strengthen his family ties in Italy and motivated by the prospect of pocketing the considerable dowry offered by Ludovico Sforza (1452–1508), regent of Milan, Maximilian married Ludovico's niece Bianca Maria Sforza (1472–1510) by proxy in November 1493, though they did not meet until 1494. In return for a payment and an assurance of military support against France, Ludovico was invested by Maximilian as duke of Milan.

Although Maximilian had intended to spend the money from the dowry on a Crusade against the Ottoman Turks, he was forced to reconsider his priorities when Charles VIII led a French army into Italy in 1494. The following year, Maximilian entered a coalition with Agostino Barbarigo (1419–1501) of the Republic of Venice, Ludovico of Milan, and Ferdinand II of Aragon (1452–1516), who had joined together ostensibly to protect the Church's sovereignty in the Papal States, but who, in reality, were determined to expel the French from Italy. This coalition, known as the Holy League, enabled Maximilian's pursuit of a double marriage between his children Philip and Margaret with Joanna of Castile (1479–1555; fig. 16) and John of Asturias (1478–1497), the children of King Ferdinand II of Aragon and Queen Isabella I of Castile (1451–1504). The marriage contracts that were ratified on January 3, 1496, cemented the dynastic unions that, in the coming generations, would spread Habsburg rule across Europe and throughout the New World.

Despite Maximilian's acquisition of Tyrol, the county's estates refused to take on additional debt to pay for his military campaigns in Italy, and Maximilian's foreign policy objectives were again curtailed by a lack of funds. Nevertheless, the defeat of the French forces by members of the Holy League in 1495 at the battle of Fornovo forced Charles VIII to withdraw from Italy. Although he tried to restore his army and resume the campaign, Charles was unable to rebound from the large debts he had incurred in Italy. After the French king's death a few years later in 1498, the Holy League was disbanded.

Concurrent with his activities in Italy, Maximilian worked toward resolving the long-standing conflict between the Habsburgs and the powerful counts of Görz, who for centuries had controlled territories that separated Tyrol and Carinthia, Habsburg hereditary lands in Austria. Because the Görz dynasty was in the hands of the elderly and childless Count Leonhard (1440–1500), Maximilian saw an opportunity to finally unite the divided hereditary lands. Although he faced competition for the territories from the Republic of Venice, which bordered Görz on the south, Maximilian was able to negotiate an agreement with Leonhard in 1497, whereby the Görz lands would pass to the Habsburgs. Following the count's death in 1500,

FIG. 16 *Joanna of Castile*, right panel from the *Zierikzee Triptych*. South Netherlandish, 1495–1506. Oil on canvas, 49³⁄₁₆ x 18⅞ in. (125 x 48 cm). Koninklijke Musea voor Schone Kunsten van België, Brussels (2406)

Maximilian acted immediately to secure his inheritance, sending troops to occupy the town of Gorizia to cut off any Venetian attempts to claim the region. The Venetians were enraged by Maximilian's success, and the Görz conflict added to the brewing tensions between Venice and the Holy Roman Empire, which would lead to the great war between the two powers that lasted from 1508 to 1516.

Following his election in 1503, Pope Julius II (r. 1503–1513) planned to break the Venetian hegemony in northern Italy that since the fourteenth century had challenged papal authority and threatened the Papal States. Julius II wanted to seize Venetian territories and divide them among the Holy See, King Louis XII of France (1462–1515), and Maximilian. To gain the support of Maximilian, who was now King of the Romans, the pope promised him the honor of being crowned emperor in Rome. Enticed by the prospect of limiting Venetian power and the promised coronation ceremony, Maximilian signed the treaty of Blois with Louis XII in September 1504, relinquishing Milan to the French, agreeing to a marriage between his grandson Charles V and the king's daughter Claude (1499–1524), and concluding an offensive pact against the Venetians.

Unfortunately, Maximilian's perpetual diplomatic conflicts with the Imperial Estates and his involvement, starting in 1504, in the War of the Succession of Bavaria-Landshut prevented the treaty of Blois from being put into practice. After the death of the imperial chancellor Berthold von Henneberg (1442–1504), who had led the Imperial Estates' efforts to contain Maximilian's influence in the empire, Maximilian was able to regain his authority over the assembly.[10] This authority became apparent in the ensuing conflict between the duchies of Bavaria-Munich and Bavaria-Landshut over who would inherit were one house to become extinct, as the 1329 treaty of Pavia had established the inheritance of the surviving house despite imperial law designating the emperor as heir. Violence erupted in 1503 when Duke George of Bavaria-Landshut (1455–1503) died without a male heir but left the duchy to his daughter Elisabeth (1478–1504). Maximilian sided with Duke Albrecht IV of Bavaria in contesting

FIG. 17 *Kufstein: Siege by Imperial Troops in October 1504*, from *Ehrenspiegel des Hauses Österreich*. 16th century. Watercolor. Bildarchiv der Österreichische Nationalbibliothek, Vienna (Cod. 8614)

the inheritance, and they fought against Elisabeth's husband, Ruprecht (1481–1504), count palatine of the Rhine, who had supported Berthold von Henneberg's imperial reforms. The War of the Succession of Bavaria-Landshut showed Maximilian at the height of his diplomatic and imperial military power. In addition to taking possession of the territories of Rattenberg, Kufstein, and Kitzbühel, Maximilian personally led his troops to victory over Bohemian opponents at the battle of Wenzenbach (fig. 17).[11] In the peace treaty signed at Cologne on July 30, 1505, Albrecht IV won a large portion of Lower Bavaria, while Maximilian gained additional territories, further consolidating the Habsburg power base in central Europe.[12]

FIG. 18 Albrecht Altdorfer (ca. 1480–1538) and workshop. *The Great Venetian War*, detail from the *Triumphal Procession of Maximilian I* (see cat. 162). Albertina Museum, Vienna (25224)

WAR WITH THE REPUBLIC OF VENICE

Maximilian's intention to travel with a military escort to Rome for his imperial coronation infuriated the Venetians, who were still bitter over their failure to win Görz. The republic's demand that he pass through their territory unarmed was immediately rejected by Maximilian. Despite sending troops to the area around Trento, Maximilian found that his army was too weak to force its way through enemy territory. Unable to reach Rome, Maximilian accepted the title Holy Roman Emperor elect from Pope Julius II on February 4, 1508.

With continued encouragement from the pope to attack the Venetians, Maximilian claimed the failed coronation journey as justification to wage war and moved his army across the border toward Vicenza (fig. 18). The numerous border skirmishes with Venice that followed were disastrous for Maximilian. His troops suffered a serious defeat at Cadore in the northern Veneto, after which the victorious Venetian troops crossed the Isonzo River and lay siege to Görz and Trieste. Görz was forced to surrender on April 26, 1508, and the Venetians quickly occupied the city of Trieste, the castles of Duino, Reifenberg, Santangelo, and Wippach, and the peninsula of Istria. When the Venetian advance threatened the Habsburg hereditary duchy of Carniola (in present-day Slovenia), Maximilian saw the need to negotiate a truce in order to retain control of the region.[13]

After Maximilian's disastrous invasion, Pope Julius II turned to Louis XII of France, who he knew was motivated to resume his cousin Charles VIII's Italian campaigns. When the Venetians filled the vacant bishopric of Vicenza without papal consent, Julius II called for a unified coalition against the republic. In response, on December 10, 1508, the Holy See, Louis XII, Maximilian, and Ferdinand II of Aragon formed the League of Cambrai, with the objective of conquering and dividing all Venetian territories in the

north (fig. 19). The war opened decisively with the French occupying Verona and imperial troops seizing Vicenza and Padua. In their distress, the Venetians sent envoys to Maximilian offering peace, including the return of all territories that they had conquered in 1508 and interest payments for imperial territories in northern Italy. Maximilian's rejection of this offer was a grave political error.

The Venetians, with their nearly inexhaustible wealth, raised enough troops to retake Padua in July 1509. Maximilian arrived in August to lay siege to the city, but ran out of food by September, and unable to pay his mercenaries, he was forced to retreat to Tyrol. His attempts to recapture Friuli and Treviso in the summer campaigns of 1510 and 1511 were equally unsuccessful. In order to protect Tyrol from enemy incursion, Maximilian instituted a decree known as the Tyrolian *Landlibell* in June 1511, which required the conscription of Tyrolians in the event of military

emergencies. It lay the responsibility of provisioning troops on the territorial rulers rather than the emperor and forbade the participation of these troops in campaigns outside Tyrol without permission from the Tyrolian Estates.

In addition to military setbacks, rifts occurred among the allies in the League of Cambrai. A synod, called by Louis XII, of French bishops at Tours in September 1510 threatened to dethrone the pope, and in response Julius II excommunicated the king of France. Louis XII courted Maximilian to remain by his side, and the emperor confirmed his alliance with France at the Congress of Blois that November. As Pope Julius II lay gravely ill in September 1511, Maximilian imagined the possibility of uniting Christendom's highest temporal and spiritual offices and assuming the papal throne himself. But the dream faded when Julius II recovered. Having turned against France, the pope formed a new Holy League with Spain and the

FIG. 19 *Pope Julius II in Armor Exhorting Emperor Maximilian, King Louis XII of France, and King Ferdinand of Aragon to War on Venice*, from *Hoc in volumine haec continentur. Vlr. De Hvtten Eq. Ad Caesarem Maximil. vt bellum in Venetos coeptum prosequatur.* German (Augsburg), 1519. Universitätsbibliothek Heidelberg, Germany

Republic of Venice in 1511, the nominal purpose of which was to protect the Papal States, but, in reality, it sought to drive the French out of Italy. Maximilian's tendency to shift alliances for personal and political gain led him to be swayed by Julius II's offer to restore imperial dominion in Italy, and so the emperor agreed to join the new Holy League. But disputes over the division of territories recovered from the French stirred up old feelings, and Maximilian's hatred of Venice resurfaced when he refused to make any land concessions to his republican ally. This angered the Venetians, who once again turned their backs on Maximilian and the pope and united with France.

In April 1513, Maximilian refocused his military efforts north after he forged an alliance with King Henry VIII of England (1491–1547), who sought to take advantage of the opportunity to win territory in northern France (fig. 20). Henry VIII landed in Calais in June with a large army and besieged the city of

Thérouanne with Maximilian's support. On August 16, Henry VIII and Maximilian's united Anglo-Imperial army defeated the French at the Battle of the Spurs, and shortly afterward captured the towns of Thérouanne and Tournai. This was Maximilian's last personal victory on the battlefield, not far from where he had celebrated his first triumph against the French decades before. Despite these victories and encouragement from Maximilian, Henry VIII was anxious about provisioning his troops through the coming winter and returned to England without accomplishing his objective of territorial gain.

Imperial troops led by Georg von Frundsberg (1473–1528) won a military victory over the Venetians at the battle of La Motta near Vincenza in October, though this failed to end the costly war for Maximilian. His attempts at secret peace negotiations with France and Spain backfired when Henry VIII, who felt betrayed by Maximilian for not being included in the talks, switched sides and allied with Louis XII of France. The new pope, Leo X (r. 1513–1521) had less interest than his predecessor in military affairs and dissolved the Holy League after his election.

Following the recapture of Milan by the young French king Francis I (1494–1547) in 1515, Maximilian set out on a new Italian campaign with an army of German and Swiss mercenaries. Yet his attempts to take the city by siege or to force the French into open combat failed, and as was so often the case, Maximilian had to abandon the campaign for lack of funds.

The treaty of Noyon in 1516 between Francis I and Maximilian's grandson Charles V, who had inherited the Spanish crown after the death of Ferdinand II of Aragon, ended the fighting between France and Spain, and Maximilian no longer had the resources to continue the Italian campaign on his own. In the end, the eight-year war over the control of northern Italy left Maximilian politically isolated and with oppressive debts. Forced to negotiate with the Republic of Venice, the emperor won only a few square miles around Rovereto, Riva, Ala, and Cortina d'Ampezzo as compensation for the territories that had fallen to the Venetians.[14]

At the Augsburg Diet of 1518, Maximilian was able to convince the prince electors of Mainz, Cologne, Pfalz, Brandenburg, and Bohemia to sign a secret deal guaranteeing their votes for the election of his grandson Charles V as King of the Romans. Yet, while he had ensured Habsburg imperial succession, by this time Maximilian was disastrously in debt: he owed the exorbitant sum of five million florins, more than twenty times his annual income from the hereditary lands, and as a result the emperor's own political career was at an end.[15] Maximilian was already sick when he traveled from Augsburg to Wels, where he spent his final days and died on January 12, 1519. In spite of Maximilian's ultimate personal bureaucratic weakness, his diplomatic and dynastic ambitions had transformed the House of Habsburg into a global political force that would last into the twentieth century. Outgrowing the inherited patchwork of central European territories, the dominions of his grandsons, Charles V and Ferdinand I, would reach across Europe and the New World, manifesting Frederick III's cryptic device A.E.I.O.U.: *Alles Erdreich ist Österreich untertan*, or "All the earth is subject to Austria."

FIG. 20 *The Meeting of Henry VIII and Emperor Maximilian I, circa 1513.* Netherlandish, 16th century. Oil on panel, 39 x 81 in. (99.1 x 205.7 cm). Royal Collection Trust, United Kingdom (RCIN 405800)

THE MAKING OF THE "LAST KNIGHT"

Maximilian I's Commemorative Projects and Their Impact

Stefan Krause

"As I read the last lines of your book one regret alone arose in my mind and that one was that the Frenchmen did not succeed in defeating Max. I should have liked it well had Dame Fortune smiled on them for one short hour, but she seemed to have preferred Max." The New York banker Amory Sibley Carhart (1851–1912) wrote these lines in an 1890 letter to John O. Sargent (1811–1891), who had sent Carhart his translation of *The Last Knight: A Romance-Garland* by the Austrian poet Anastasius Grün (1806–1876).[1]

Originally composed in German as *Der letzte Ritter: Romanzen-Kranz*, Grün's dramatic cycle of poems was first published in Munich in 1830 and would go on to appear in nine editions until 1906.[2] The English author Charles Boner (1815–1870) had tried his hand at rendering the work into English in the 1840s,[3] but Sargent was the first to succeed at the undertaking. Grün's work and Sargent's translation, published in New York in 1871, exemplify the glorified image of Emperor Maximilian I (1459–1519) that emerged in the nineteenth century and still resonates today.[4] The book also cemented Maximilian's sobriquet, the "Last Knight," in common usage. However, the roots of what this modern term stands for extend much farther back, and far more broadly, in history. They can be traced to paintings by Romantic artists, such as Anton Petter (1781–1858) and Moritz von Schwind (1804–1871); to a tomb "rediscovered" and opened under much attention by the imperial court in 1770; to a late Renaissance saga about a miracle in the mountains of Tyrol and a 1679 play by the Spanish dramatist Pedro Calderón de la Barca (1600–1681); and finally to the emperor himself. Maximilian was a master of self-promotion.[5] In the final two decades before his death in 1519, he expended tremendous effort in preparing his own image for posterity. He ordered heroic autobiographical epics written, the finest genealogical tree created for his family, and designs for a triumphal procession and arch drawn up. He also commissioned one of the greatest monuments of the European Renaissance, his tomb. Although many of these works ultimately went unfinished, for lack of either funding or time, they all hinge on motifs that later informed the hugely popular image of the Last Knight. They depict Maximilian as a noble warrior (fig. 21), fearless hunter, and loving husband—in short, as the *ideal* knight. The one image Maximilian did not apply to himself, however, was that of the *last* knight.

Maximilian did not think that historians would view him as one of the last in a succession or consider his reign as the end of an epoch; this trope first emerged in retrospect centuries later. The noble past and gallant present that the emperor constructed for himself and his family were intended to provide the foundations for a glorious future. The distant objective of these efforts was to rebuild the Roman Empire under Christian, Habsburg rule. As he aged, Maximilian increasingly came to view his progeny, rather than himself, as those who would consummate this political vision. He projected this role first onto his son, Philip I (1478–1506), then, after Philip's early death, onto his grandsons, Charles V (1500–1558) and Ferdinand I (1503–1564). Charles, the heir apparent, was to "complete and lead [the project] to its favorable conclusion," a charge included in the eulogy for his grandfather, delivered on January 16, 1519, in the parish church at Wels, the city of Maximilian's death.[6]

The Last Knight sobriquet actually arose from early nineteenth-century Romantic literature, which produced a number of melancholy "lasts," including Thomas Moore's "Last Rose of Summer" (1805) and James Fenimore Cooper's *Last of the Mohicans* (1826). The Austrian historian Joseph von Hormayr (1781/82–1848) first used the term in reference to Maximilian in 1810.[7] It was immediately adopted by other authors and historians,[8] Grün among them, and quickly came

FIG. 21 Gustav Klimt (1862–1918). *The Golden Knight (Life Is a Struggle)*, 1903. Oil, tempera, and gold leaf on canvas, 39⅜ x 39⅜ in. (100 x 100 cm). Aichi Prefectural Museum of Art, Nagoya (FO199000002000)

to occupy a permanent place in the lexicon, even beyond Germany.

The idea of the Last Knight epitomizes the Romantics' tendency to idealize traditional courtly culture; their latter-day yearning for an ostensibly superior, glorified past culminated in this chivalric image.[9] These ideals were particularly pronounced in the German-speaking world during the early nineteenth century, a time bookended by Napoleonic supremacy and the political reprisals of the Age of Metternich. Emperor Maximilian I—at once mighty and just, noble and genial—embodied these much-desired ideals. Echoes of the loaded concepts underlying the Last Knight, albeit without direct reference to Maximilian, can be found even in modern-day, mostly pop cultural, iterations of the expression, as in the film titles *Star Wars: The Last Jedi* and *Transformers: The Last Knight*.[10]

A series of monumental publications forms the backbone of the commemorative works commissioned by Maximilian. Three verse epics—the *Weisskunig* (cats. 114–17), *Freydal* (cats. 39–55), and *Theuerdank* (cats. 108, 109)—adopt the allegorical model of medieval heroic literature and portray the emperor's life in elaborate symbolic language. The *Weisskunig* describes the ruler's childhood and youth as well as his military campaigns; *Freydal* depicts the tournaments in which the eponymous protagonist participates as he searches for a wife; and *Theuerdank* centers around the dangers the titular hero faces on his journey to marry Princess Ehrenreich (or "Rich in Honor," Maximilian's first wife, Mary of Burgundy, 1457–1482).[11]

The *Genealogy* (cat. 166) and the so-called *Book of Habsburg Family Saints* (*Sipp-, Mag- und Schwägerschaft*) illustrate the emperor's largely fictitious ancestral line.[12] Maximilian traced his ancestry back—by way of the Franconian and Merovingian royal houses—to Hector, prince of Troy. Such a comprehensive ancestral line was essential to the emperor's political vision: it positioned him as Europe's noblest ruler, whose legitimacy could derive from his incomparable origins alone. It also conveyed dynastically argued, and thus seemingly incontrovertible, claims to nearly all European dominions. Genealogy therefore functioned in both the past and the future for Maximilian.

Uniting the most important figures and events from the emperor's life, the monumental series of woodcut prints known as the *Triumphal Procession of Maximilian I* and the *Arch of Honor* (cat. 165) can be considered summations of the works commemorating him. The *Triumphal Procession,* also painted in miniature by Albrecht Altdorfer (ca. 1480–1538, cat. 162), includes representatives from every stratum of German aristocracy as well as delegations from the *Landsknecht,* the emperor's critical mercenary force. There are images of the emperor's ancestors and military battles; even "people of Calicut" march along in the parade (the Indian city of Kolkata had become a synonym for all exotic riches after Vasco da Gama had reached it by ocean route in 1498). The *Arch of Honor,* on the other hand, combines representations of Virtues and the emperor's military victories with emblems of his lineage and myriad symbolic details to yield an exceptionally rich, layered image. Its antecedents lie in antiquity and in the decorative motifs used in so-called *Joyeuse Entrées*, festive entries into cities, common in France and Burgundy.[13]

The crowning achievement of Maximilian's self-memorialization is his tomb. Greatly diminished in scope and seven decades behind schedule, the project was ultimately completed in 1589 in the Court Church (Hofkirche), Innsbruck, which had been constructed for the purpose. Twenty-eight larger-than-life ancestral figures (from his son, Philip, to Theoderic the Great, king of the Ostrogoths) flank a monumental sarcophagus, itself adorned with twenty-four marble reliefs depicting militarily and politically noteworthy moments from the emperor's life. The tomb was never occupied, however, as Maximilian's will stipulated he be interred under the high altar in the Castle Chapel in his home city of Wiener Neustadt, located south of Vienna.[14]

A characteristic common to many of the projects commemorating the emperor is their enormous size. The painted miniatures of the *Triumphal Procession,* of which only about a half remains, stretched over 328 feet (over 100 meters) in length. At more than 11 feet (3.54 meters) high, the *Arch of Honor* is more reminiscent of a wall tapestry than a woodblock print. *Theuerdank* inspired 118 illustrations, the *Weisskunig* featured 251, and *Freydal*'s 255 surviving miniatures cover a total area of 145 square feet (13.5 square meters). Perhaps most notably, the emperor's tomb was originally intended to include forty larger-than-life ancestral statues as well as a further thirty-four busts of Roman emperors and one hundred statues of saints. Assembling a monument of this scope would have necessitated a space designed for that purpose alone; indeed, a sepulchral church with an attached monastery of Saint George was slated for construction in the mountains high above the Upper Austrian pilgrimage site of Sankt Wolfgang—a plan as grandiose as it was unrealistic.

In order to see this staggering range of commissions to completion, Maximilian divided the work among many artists. In fact, South German art around 1510 was thoroughly dominated by projects commemorating the emperor. Even artists from the Low Countries, such as Cornelis Liefrinck (d. ca. 1545), a block cutter from Antwerp, were summoned to provide support in Augsburg.[15] Designs for the printed *Triumphal Procession* were created by Hans Burgkmair, Altdorfer, Hans Springinklee, Leonhard Beck, Dürer, Schäufelein, and Wolf Huber.[16] More than thirty, mostly anonymous artists of varied skill were involved in creating the miniatures for *Freydal*; at least one of these came from the Low Countries, while others appear closely tied to Altdorfer's workshop.[17]

Peculiar to the commemorative works produced in honor of Maximilian is the personal involvement of the emperor himself: Maximilian not only ordered the projects, he was also their driving force. As such, he was involved in every step of the creative process. In consultation with his collaborators, who included Marx Treitzsaurwein (ca. 1450–1527), Melchior Pfinzing (1481–1535), and Johannes Stabius (1450–1522), the emperor wrote outlines, revised drafts, and dictated texts. He signed off on illustrations personally, shifted them between works, and discarded them altogether if he deemed them unsatisfactory.[18] Maximilian discussed the very smallest details with his collaborators. In the specifications for a sketch in *Freydal*, for instance, he ordered that the heraldic crest of one of the riders be changed from a pelican head to a whole pelican, which is how it appears in the final design.[19] The emperor's perfectionism also contributed to the numerous delays and changes in plan that ultimately prevented the completion of most of the projects.

The body of works memorializing Maximilian is also characterized by its broad spectrum of content and concepts. In addition to medieval German heroic literature, influences include ancient sources and Burgundian representational forms. Maximilian incorporated ultramodern media such as woodblock printing, while maintaining an appreciation for traditional book illumination. These two techniques are even combined occasionally in the same work: *Theuerdank,* accomplished by means of printing, has the appearance of an illuminated manuscript.

Maximilian's concept of commemoration extended far beyond his own glorification for posterity.[20]

For him, commemoration also meant the detailed documentation of the present, from a pictorial inventory of an arsenal (see cat. 153) to descriptions of the hunting grounds and records of the Tyrolian castles.[21] The emperor's memorial books mention plans for further volumes on armor production, architecture, falconry, and the kitchens, cellars, and barns of the court; also planned was a book on the pleasure gardens and seven *ruem* (honor) gardens.[22] The emperor noted in one of his memorial books that any archival material of interest was generally to be stored in cases designed for this purpose.[23] In his will, drafted on December 30, 1518, two weeks before his death, Maximilian ordered that his "books, chronicles and like material are to be faithfully preserved and looked after until my dear son [Charles V] expresses his will and further intentions."[24]

The emperor's broader concept of memory also applied to safeguarding historical artifacts, including restoring older works of art, collecting ancient objects, and studying archival sources. Maximilian was not bound by the modern historical conventions that distinguish between antiquity and the Middle Ages, the sacred and the secular. His historical curiosity was as readily piqued by a newly discovered Roman relief depicting Neptune as it was by an inscription from 1415 at the Kufstein Fortress. The rediscovery of the Holy Tunic (*Tunica Domini*)—the garment supposedly worn by Christ at the time of the Crucifixion, housed in the cathedral of Trier—carried the same archaeological weight for him as the quest to find the bones of Siegfried, the hero of the *Nibelungenlied*.[25]

Maximilian felt it was imperative to preserve significant source material, both old and new. He complained in the *Weisskunig* that "people paid too little attention to memory."[26] For this reason, he "ordered that all histories be diligently compiled in a chronicle."[27] Furthermore, as Philipp Melanchthon (1497–1560) noted in his *Cronica Carionis* (1569), Maximilian "had also recorded [his own actions] so diligently that later scholars would want to describe them."[28]

Maximilian died on January 12, 1519, at three o'clock in the morning at Wels Castle. He was fifty-nine years, nine months, and twenty-five days old.[29] Two forms of commemoration work ensued after his death. For one, his descendants continued work on the unfinished projects Maximilian had left behind. They completed the tomb and issued first and new editions of the publications.[30] In addition, the efforts the emperor had made toward his own commemoration started to take effect, and his second life, as one of the greatest symbolic figures in German-Austrian historical consciousness, started to take shape.

In the very year of Maximilian's death, two portraits were created that are among the most famous depictions of the emperor, yet they could not be more different. Dürer's painting is an idealized state portrait (fig. 22), minimal in appurtenances but furnished with an inscription that meets every last requirement for a monarch's panegyric: Maximilian was, the text states, the Very Most Powerful and Inviolable Emperor.[31] Juxtaposed to this is the postmortem portrait, now in Graz, painted around the same time, an unsettlingly realistic depiction of the emperor's emaciated corpse, following weeks of decline.[32] This picture, as visual evidence of Maximilian's exemplary death, may be thought to represent the final facet of the emperor's posthumous propaganda.[33]

Likenesses of Maximilian were of key importance for the iconography of images designed to legitimize the rule of the Habsburg dynasty during the Renaissance and Baroque eras. The emperor's heirs, the later emperors Charles V and Ferdinand I, were repeatedly portrayed in the 1520s and 1530s alongside their deceased grandfather so as to highlight their familial ties and, therefore, the legitimacy of their rule.[34] A depiction of Maximilian's marriage to Mary of Burgundy, painted by Jacob Jordaens (1593–1678), adorned one of the triumphal arches constructed in honor of Cardinal-Infante Ferdinand II's (1609–1641) arrival in Antwerp in April 1635 (fig. 23). The image of Maximilian and Mary underscored the rightfulness of the Habsburg claim to power in the Low Countries, which the imperial nuptials had established in 1477 (fig. 24).[35]

From the sixteenth into the nineteenth century, a popular saga—that of Maximilian on the Martinswand— not only provided religious justification for Habsburg

FIG. 22 Albrecht Dürer (1471–1528). *Portrait of Emperor Maximilian I*, 1519. Oil on panel, 29⅛ x 24¼ in. (74 x 61.5 cm). Kunsthistorisches Museum, Vienna, Gemäldegalerie (825)

sovereignty but also was fundamental to the court's Catholic self-image. According to legend, the young archduke Maximilian was hunting chamois on the face of the Martinswand, a steep rock wall to the northwest of Innsbruck, when he found himself stuck, unable to move either forward or back. For three days, he prayed for rescue, until a messenger of God, disguised as a youth in peasant's clothing, appeared and showed him the route to safety.[36] Parts of this tale were in circulation during Maximilian's life, but it was first presented in full in *Hercules Prodicius*, written by the Dutch historian Stephanus Vinandus Pighius (1520–1604) and published in Antwerp in 1587.[37]

The Martinswand saga became a cornerstone of Pietas Austriaca, the concept of Habsburg Catholic piety propagated in the late Renaissance and Baroque

FIG. 23 Jacob Jordaens (1593–1678). *The Wedding of Mary of Burgundy with Maximilian of Austria*, 1634–35. Oil on canvas, 128 x 141¾ in. (325 x 360 cm). Musée des Beaux-Arts et d'Archéologie, Troyes, on loan from the ville de Sainte-Savine

FIG. 24 *Maximilian and Mary of Burgundy in Ghent in 1477*, 17th century(?), after Netherlandish model. Gray and gray-brown ink, skin tones scumbled in red, 9¹⁵⁄₁₆ x 6¹⁵⁄₁₆ in. (25.3 x 17.6 cm). Albertina Museum, Vienna (24425)

eras. It can be found in late sixteenth-century objets d'art (fig. 25),[38] early seventeenth-century Netherlandish paintings,[39] and eighteenth-century church frescoes, such as those in Ljubljana Cathedral (Giulio Quaglio the Younger, consecrated 1707) and the Assumption of Mary (Mariä Himmelfahrt) parish church in Scheppach, Bavaria (Franz Martin Kuen, 1769).[40] Calderón de la Barca drew upon the Martinswand saga in his 1679 ecclesiastical play *Austria's Second Glory* (*El segundo blasón del Austria*). The same year, the actor Augustín Manuel de Castilla (d. 1695) was released from debtors' prison in Segovia for the express purpose of portraying the young Maximilian in Calderón's play on stage in Madrid.[41] Romantic artists elevated the emperor's deliverance from the Martinswand to an allegory of personal and private trust in God; in 1860 the Austrian painter Moritz von Schwind (1804–1871) produced the depiction of the saga best known today (fig. 26).[42]

FIG. 25 *The Martinswand near Innsbruck, a So-Called Coral Mountain*, detail, latter half 16th century. Painted plaster and coral, H. 21¼ in. (54 cm). Schloss Ambras Innsbruck (AM PA 999)

FIG. 26 Moritz von Schwind (1804–1871). *Maximilian on the Martinswand*, ca. 1860. Oil on panel, 23⅝ x 16⁹⁄₁₆ in. (60 x 42 cm). Österreichische Galerie Belvedere, Vienna (2125)

FIG. 27 Hans Burgkmair (1473–1531). *The Joy and Skill He Showed in His Instructions for Paintings . . . ,* from the *Weisskunig,* 1514–16. Woodcut, 8¹¹⁄₁₆ x 7⅞ in. (22 x 20 cm). Albertina Museum, Vienna (DG2012/129/21)

In the late eighteenth century, a shift occurred in the popular perception of Maximilian.[43] The emperor had always been central to the story of the Habsburg dynasty; he had laid the foundations for its ascension to world power and had served as a model of Catholic piety. Now, however, he was increasingly viewed as an emblem of the entire era centered around 1500, which was considered a turning point in German history. In 1769 the German writer Johann Gottfried Herder (1744–1803) noted that Maximilian's reign provided the "basis for all new European constitutions," while the foreword of the 1775 first edition of the *Weisskunig* claimed that he had begun to "raise the level of the Austrian throne."[44] Maximilian had in effect transformed from a dynastic figure to a national symbol.

In the midst of this change, an occurrence in 1770 caused a considerable stir, as the emperor's casket was disturbed during renovations at Castle Wiener Neustadt's chapel. After Empress Maria Theresa (1717–1780) granted permission for it to be opened, Maximilian's corpse was revealed, clothed in "a white

damask robe and cloak of red flowered silk," as described in an article in the *Wienerisches Diarium* from April 11, 1770.[45] For the emperor's reburial, a trilevel structure encasing the bier, known as a *castrum doloris,* was erected. A patrician cadet corps installed outside the chapel discharged three salvos, and—to the "sound of all of the bells in the chapel, and in the city"—the casket containing the emperor's mortal remains was reinterred in a Baroque sarcophagus under the newly renovated high altar of the chapel.[46] Nearly two hundred years later, on August 6, 1946, Maximilian's sarcophagus was recovered, unscathed, from the wreckage of the chapel, which had been destroyed at the end of World War II. Four years later, on October 20, 1950, the emperor was ceremoniously laid to rest for the third time in the renovated church.[47]

In the nineteenth century, under the influence of Romanticism and later of historicism, the image of Emperor Maximilian developed in many new directions.[48] Maximilian was seen as both a genial ruler and a chivalric ideal;[49] the depiction of an armor-clad knight by Gustav Klimt (1862–1918; see fig. 21) from 1903, for example, referred to prints by Burgkmair and Dürer as well as to the emperor's two late Gothic armors (see cats. 16, 17), which were on display in the imperial collections in Vienna at the time.[50] Artists such as Josef Mathias von Trenkwald (1824–1897) and Petter portrayed Maximilian's union with Mary of Burgundy as the epitome of a romantic marriage for love.[51] The double wedding in Vienna that Maximilian arranged with the Bohemian-Hungarian House of Jagiellon in 1515 was celebrated as the establishment of the Austro-Hungarian "Danube Monarchy" and in 1898 immortalized by the Czech artist Václav Brožik (1851–1901) in his monumental *You, Happy Austria, Marry (Tu felix Austria nube),* measuring fourteen by twenty-four feet.[52]

Not least, the emperor's relationship with Dürer represented an ideal of art patronage in late medieval Germany (fig. 27). In 1886 the Nuremberg-based artist Karl Jäger (1833–1887) painted the marvelous scene of the emperor sitting for his portrait in Dürer's workshop.[53] August Siegert (1820–1883), a member of the Düsseldorf School of painting, revisited an anecdote

FIG. 28 August Siegert (1820–1883). *Emperor Maximilian Holds the Ladder for Albrecht Dürer*, 1849. Oil on canvas, 29¹⁵⁄₁₆ x 22⅞ in. (76 x 58 cm). Museen der Stadt Nürnberg, on loan from the Albrecht-Dürer-Haus-Stiftung, Nuremberg (Gm 3029)

that can be traced back to the Flemish artist and writer Karel van Mander (1548–1606): in a special demonstration of honor, and to the great surprise of his attending noblemen, Maximilian braced Dürer's ladder as the artist worked on a mural (fig. 28).[54]

The nineteenth century stylized the stories and myths surrounding Maximilian as key moments in the German-Austrian self-image. At the heart of these pictures, however, is the commemorative work the emperor had undertaken centuries earlier. In the

Weisskunig, Maximilian muses that "he who during his life provides no remembrance for himself has no remembrance after his death and the same person is forgotten with the tolling of the bell." Therefore, he continues, "the money that I spend on remembrance is not lost."[55] For Maximilian, commemorative work was an investment with unmatched returns; for us the modern manifestation of this investment has proved to be the Last Knight.

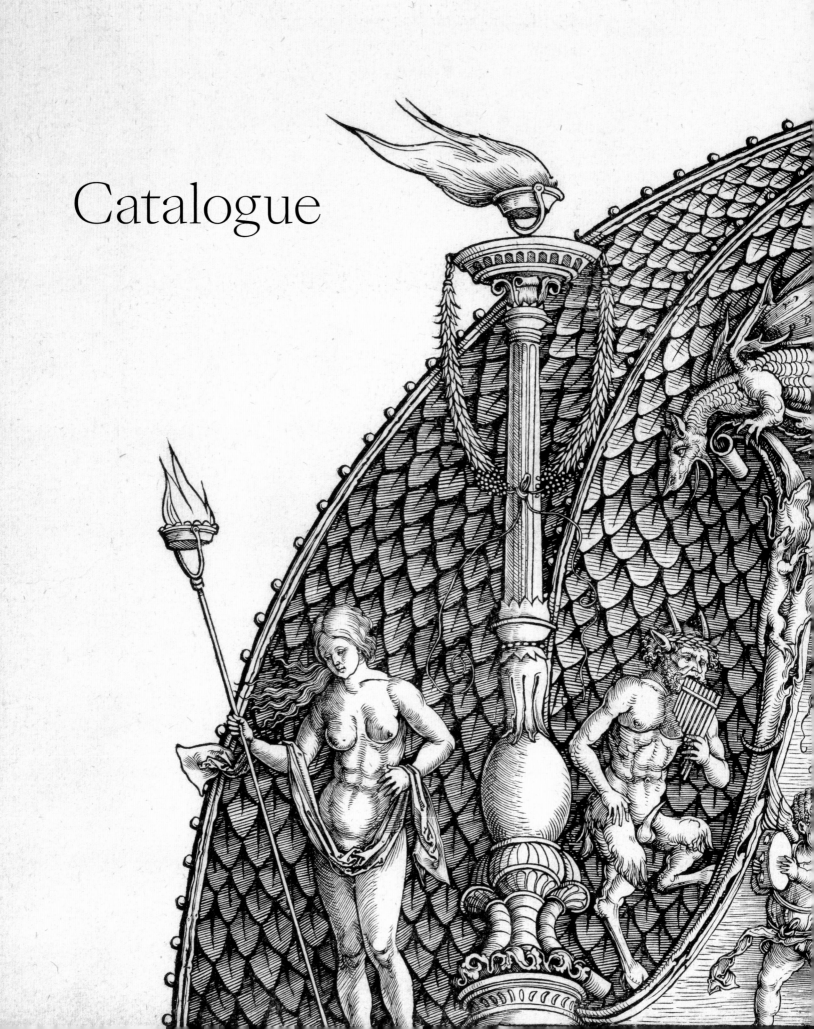

Catalogue

Burgundian Inheritance

The Valois dukes of Burgundy built one of the wealthiest and most powerful European states over the fourteenth and fifteenth centuries. When Duke Charles the Bold died in 1477 without a male heir, the Burgundian state was thrown into an existential crisis. By marrying Mary of Burgundy, Charles's only daughter, Maximilian I became his successor at the age of eighteen. Born and raised in the German-speaking lands, Maximilian moved to the Burgundian Low Countries to join his wife and defend her territories from the king of France, who immediately invaded her lands, and from her own subjects, who saw an opportunity to undermine the authority that the dukes had so successfully built at their expense. With no prior experience in governance and no independent resources, Maximilian struggled to be accepted as a ruler, especially after his wife, from whom he derived his ducal title and authority, died unexpectedly. These years of external and internal political, military, and financial challenges prompted Maximilian to develop ways of legitimizing his rule, a mission that would inform his actions for the rest of his life. He sought to affirm his position by promoting what he stood for: he constructed a persona as an intrepid knight whose principles and deeds made him the deserving continuator of his august predecessors. On the battlefield and in the tournament, he exhibited uncommon bravery and skill, showcasing chivalric virtues that commanded respect and inspired loyalty.

Armor was critical in Maximilian's cultivation of his image as a martial hero. He became a major patron of armorers in the Low Countries, from whom he ordered stylish equipment that likened him to his Valois predecessors. He also made powerful statements by acquiring works from one of the greatest masters in Germany that are likely to have surpassed in sophistication anything that had ever been seen in the Low Countries. Although his financial resources were limited, Maximilian succeeded in upholding the grandeur that had made the Burgundian court one of the most admired in Europe.

Cat. 1

Charles the Bold, Duke of Burgundy
Netherlandish, ca. 1500
Oil on oak panel
Framed: 21½ x 16⅞ in. (54.7 x 43 cm)
Palais des Beaux-Arts, Lille, France, deposited at the Musée de l'Hospice Comtesse, Lille, France (P 1173)

This painting belongs to a suite of nine portraits on similarly sized oak panels that feature the successive rulers of the Burgundian Low Countries from Philip the Bold to Maximilian I. Except for Maximilian's portrait, which was produced a few decades later and is probably posthumous, the suite was painted at the turn of the sixteenth century and by the same hand. This portrait depicts Charles the Bold, the last duke of Burgundy from the House of Valois. Eight months after he lost his life in battle in January 1477, Mary, his daughter and only heir, married Maximilian in accordance with her father's wishes, ushering in an extended period of Habsburg rule in the Low Countries, which would last until the very end of the eighteenth century.

The portrait has often been claimed to have been copied from a much finer picture, now in the Gemäldegalerie, Staatliche Museen, Berlin, which was painted in Rogier van der Weyden's workshop before Charles became duke of Burgundy (as his father was still alive).[1] However, notable differences in composition, such as the position of the hands, and in the expression and physiognomy of the sitter support the view that another model was used for this panel. The cropping of the arms, the distinctive position of the only visible hand, and the slashes in the doublet (which seem to be a misinterpretation of vertical folds on the model) relate closely to those same elements in a similar bust portrait of Charles in reverse by the Bruges illuminator Simon Bening in the statute book of the Order of the Golden Fleece, now in the collection of the Österreichische Nationalbibliothek, Vienna.[2] As the miniature is thought to have been painted about 1518–19, it seems likely that the two works were copied after a common model, or variants thereof, rather than each other.

Conceived as part of a suite honoring the memory of successive rulers of the Burgundian Low Countries, Charles's portrait belongs to a long tradition of representing the sovereign in civilian dress. Although the tradition is continued in the later painting of Maximilian, it was precisely under the Habsburgs that male sovereigns were more frequently portrayed in armor.

Probably made when Maximilian's portrait was added to the group, the later sixteenth-century frame bears inscriptions that identify the sitter as a duke of Burgundy and spell out his motto "I have dared it" (*jelay em Prins* [*sic*]); in addition, his coat of arms is painted at the bottom. The actual picture, by contrast, only signals the sitter's distinguished standing through his expensive velvet attire and, most importantly, the collar of the Order of the Golden Fleece, of which Charles was made a member when he was just four months old, and of which he became the sovereign in 1467.[3]   PT

REFERENCES: Châtelet and Goetghebeur 2006, pp. 185–86, 188–90, 222–26, no. 240, ill. no. 1; Till-Holger Borchert in *Charles the Bold* 2009, p. 175, no. 3, ill.

1. Staatliche Museen, Berlin, Gemäldegalerie (545); see Stephan Kemperdick in *Master of Flémalle* 2009, pp. 371–73, no. 42, ill.
2. Österreichische Nationalbibliothek, Vienna, Cod. 2606, fol. 70v.
3. Châtelet and Goetghebeur 2006, p. 225.

Prayer Book of Charles the Bold

Lieven van Lathem (ca. 1430–1493) and workshop, and Vienna Master of Mary of Burgundy (active ca. 1470–ca. 1480) and workshop
Scribe: Nicolas Spierinc (active ca. 1455–1499)
South Netherlandish and French, 1469 and ca. 1471
Tempera, gold, silver, and ink on parchment; bound between wood boards covered with purple velvet
Leaf: 4⅞ x 3⅝ in. (12.4 x 9.2 cm)
J. Paul Getty Museum, Los Angeles (MS 37, fol. 6r)

Charles the Bold, an important patron of the arts, inspired the collecting habits of his court, commissioning paintings, metalwork, and especially illuminated manuscripts. In addition to numerous secular books, he owned at least four personal devotional manuscripts.[1] This prayer book is unusual for incorporating three portraits of the patron himself, all in association with Saint George. This connection with the classic military saint was particularly appropriate to Charles, given the duke's territorial ambitions and perceived position as a warrior of God.[2] One of the manuscript's presentation portraits on folio 6 was modeled after the famed gold reliquary of George presenting Charles (who holds a finger relic of a saint) commissioned by the duke himself from Gerard Loyet.[3] In the illumination, Charles wears a blue surcoat over his armor and retains his sword by his side with his helmet lying next to the prie-dieu (prayer bench). Saint George, identified by the dragon at his feet, stands behind Charles and presents him to the Virgin and Child on the facing page. In the first portrait, a full-page illumination on folio 1 verso depicting a similar composition of Saint George presenting the duke (this time to Saint Veronica), Charles wears a long robe of lavish cloth of gold and his fur hat rests on the floor nearby. Together, these images convey the two most important aspects of his role as duke of Burgundy: he is represented first as a nobleman of high rank, with his wealth prominently indicated, and second as a warrior, emphasized by his armor and weaponry. In all the portraits, the illuminator Lieven van Lathem has shown Charles and George sharing the same facial features, linking patron and patron saint even closer together in intent and purpose.[4]   EM

REFERENCES: Van der Velden 2000, p. 124, fig. 74; Thomas Kren in Kren and McKendrick 2003, pp. 128–31, no. 16, ill. nos. 16a–d; *Gebetbuch Karls des Kühnen* 2007; De Schryver 2008; Kren in *Charles the Bold* 2009, p. 254, no. 67, ill., and pls. 43, 44, 47a; Morrison 2015, pp. 103–5, figs. 15, 16

1. Kren 2003, p. 121.
2. On Charles's devotion to Saint George, see Van der Velden 2000, pp. 122–51.
3. Saint Paul's Cathedral, Liège; ibid., p. 124.
4. De Schryver 2008, pp. 17–26.

Excellen
tissima
et glori
osissima
Atq̃ z
sanctis
sima virgo semper ma
ria mater domini nos
tri ihu xp̃i. Domina
mea regina z domina
totius creature. Qui
milium dextigius ntal
tium despiras. Nullum

Charles the Bold at the Battlefield of Nancy,
from the *Excellent Chronicle of Flanders, 1420–77*
(*Excellente Cronike van Vlaenderen, 1420–77*)

Continuation written by Anthonis de Roovere (ca. 1430–1482)

Scribe: Hendrik Bollekin (ca. 1460–ca. 1498)

South Netherlandish (Bruges), ca. 1484

Watercolor, ink, and lead point on paper

11 x 8¼ in. (28 x 21 cm)

Morgan Library and Museum, New York (MS M.435, fol. 352r)

This richly illustrated manuscript belongs to one of the most important fifteenth-century Middle Dutch chronicle traditions, known as the *Excellent Chronicle of Flanders* (*Excellente Cronike van Vlaenderen*). Based on the Latin *Flandria Generosa C*, a clerical chronicle probably written in the Eeckhout Abbey in Bruges, the *Excellent Chronicle* was expanded and rewritten over the course of the fifteenth and early sixteenth centuries, mainly in urban milieus, resulting in notable differences between copies.[1] This manuscript belongs to a distinct group of seven copies, referred to as the Bruges manuscripts, which focus on Flemish history from a Bruges perspective and include a continuation written by the rhetorician Anthonis de Roovere (see also cat. 94).[2] In addition to composing a rich poem collection, De Roovere was involved in the organization of many public events in Bruges, such as processions, joyous entries, and weddings.

While most *Excellent Chronicle* manuscripts start with the mythical origin of the county of Flanders, this example only narrates the history of the Burgundian dukes, starting with the early reign of Philip the Good in 1420 and ending with the death of Charles the Bold in 1477.[3] The choice to conclude with Charles and to omit the reign of his successor, Mary of Burgundy, is notable. Probably at the request of his patron, the scribe updated De Roovere's text with details on public and religious life in late medieval Bruges. The scribe also added several paragraphs on the papal dynasty, which he derived from the *Little Bundle of Time* (*Fasciculus Temporum*), printed by Jan Veldener in Utrecht in 1480. Many of these elements suggest that the manuscript had a clerical owner, and, on the final pages, a miniature of the owner, dressed in clerical garments, appears kneeling toward a depiction of Christ on the opposite folio. The coat of arms and the motto—"to hold dear" (*om te ghelievene*)—help identify the owner as Lieven de Jonckheere (ca. 1457–1507), secular canon at Saint Donatian Church, Bruges. De Jonckheere was also one of the ambassadors at the peace negotiations in Tours in 1489, organized by

King Charles VIII of France. Another important member of the peace envoy was Golden Fleece knight Louis of Gruuthuse, who, along with De Jonckheere, supported the Flemish cause during the uprising against Maximilian I from 1482 to 1492.[4]

The present manuscript contains seven full-page color miniatures and many marginal drawings, including a small sketch of the important Bruges Holy Blood relic. In the concluding miniature, Charles the Bold is depicted armored, ready for action, wearing his collar of the Order of the Golden Fleece, most probably at the fatal battlefield near Nancy. He raises his sword with his right hand (another one hangs at his waist), as he sits astride his armored horse, holding the reins with his left hand. In the background is a campground of tents, behind which cannons are aimed at a city surrounded by water. The image of the duke is similar to a smaller miniature in an *Excellent Chronicle* manuscript preserved in the Bibliothèque Municipale, Douai.[5] Several miniatures in the Bruges manuscripts were based on existing depictions of the Burgundian dukes and duchesses that were paraded during urban festivities or ceremonies. It is very likely that this image of Charles was based on an existing panel.

On the folio preceding Charles's miniature, the scribe ends his text with rumors of the duke's supposed return after the battle of Nancy. Nevertheless, he adds: "I have waited for Duke Charles's return for seven years, seven months, seven weeks, seven days, seven hours and seven minutes. I write now: Duke Charles will not return." Apart from the melancholy tone and the religious symbolism, the scribe has also cleverly communicated the writing date: 1484. Beneath this closing line, the scribe has left a small signature, which was used by Hendrik Bollekin, a cloth merchant. Although it is not clear if Bollekin was a rhetorician himself, he had close ties with rhetoricians in Bruges and other *Excellent Chronicle* scribes, such as Jan de Lenesse.[6] Moreover, he knew the manuscript's owner, Lieven de Jonckheere, through a religious confraternity, Our Lady of the Snow, which had a particularly strong connection with the Bruges Chambers of Rhetoric and the Burgundian dukes.[7]   LD

REFERENCES: Brown 1999; Oosterman 2002; Haemers 2014; Demets 2016; Demets and Dumolyn 2016

1. Demets 2016.
2. Oosterman 2002.
3. The manuscript is missing one or two quires at the beginning.
4. Haemers 2014. On the close relation between the *Excellent Chronicle* manuscripts and the Flemish revolt, see Demets and Dumolyn 2016.
5. Bibliothèque Municipale, Douai, MS 1110, fol. 248r.
6. Jan de Lenesse was one of the scribes of MS 437 in the Openbare Bibliotheek Brugge.
7. Brown 1999.

Cats. 4, 5

Unit of Nineteen Soldiers on Foot and *Ten Knights on Horseback*, from *War and Camp Scenes from the Burgundian Wars*

Master W with the Key (also known as Master WA; active ca. 1465–ca. 1490)

Netherlandish, ca. 1467–ca. 1477

Engravings

Albertina Museum (DG1928/402): 3⅜ x 5¾ in. (8.7 x 14.8 cm); Albertina Museum (DG1928/400): 5⅜ x 7 in. (13.6 x 17.8 cm)

Albertina Museum, Vienna (DG1928/402; DG1928/400)

Although very little is known definitely about the innovative printmaker Master W with the Key, he is believed to have been active in the southern Netherlands and perhaps was based at certain moments in his career in the city of Bruges.[1] These prints, two of a series of nine variously sized engravings depicting Burgundian soldiers, are likely part of Charles the Bold's ongoing efforts to create visual and textual propaganda in the years following the death of his father, Philip the Good, in 1467.[2] Master W with the Key also produced another print that served the propagandistic mission of Charles's court. Known as the *Achievement of Charles the Bold*, it displays in heraldic terms the full armorial bearing to which Charles was entitled.[3]

The complete series includes tent scenes along with regimented detachments of cavalrymen, foot soldiers, and archers. Although the detachments are precisely ordered,

interest and spontaneity are added to the prints by showing the horses untamed as they move, sway, and stomp in formation and by varying the arms and armor worn and held by the military men, especially their adorned helmets. As with the Master's other engravings, the precise dating of this series is unclear, but given the years of the artist's activity and his connection to Charles, it can be safely assigned to the period of his rule from 1467 to 1477. In the most sizable engraving of the series, known as the *Large Tent*, the detachments are clearly marked as part of the Burgundian armies, using the Burgundian coat of arms, emblems of the Golden Fleece, and the cross of Saint Andrew.[4] Some scholars have suggested that the series commemorated the battles and encampments of Philip the Good, but it may also be related to Charles the Bold's famous military ordinances, which he penned and

enacted between 1468 and 1473 (see cat. 7).[5] These sweeping measures codified nearly every aspect of the duke's military. While the particular troop groupings illustrated do not correspond with any of those explicitly detailed in the ordinances, nonetheless the images' specificity and variety in terms of the organization and numbers of troops align them with the directives laid out by Charles. FS

REFERENCES: W. Boerner 1927, pp. 62–65; Byck 2015, pp. 28–30

1. For more on Master W with the Key, see W. Boerner 1927; Byck 2015.
2. Hollstein 1949–2010, vol. 12 (1955), pp. 218–19, nos. 25–33.
3. Ibid., p. 225, no. 48.
4. Ibid., p. 218, no. 25.
5. Marti 2009a, pp. 322–23, fig. 129a–d. On the series relation to Philip the Good, see M. P. McDonald 2005, p. 217. For the ordinances, see Michael 1983, pp. 10–16; for more on Charles's military, see Vaughan 2002, pp. 197–229.

Cat. 6

Seal Box (Skippet) with the Arms of Charles the Bold

South Netherlandish, ca. 1473–77
Gilded copper
Diam. 4¹⁵⁄₁₆ in. (12.5 cm)
Philadelphia Museum of Art, Purchased with funds from the bequest of Elizabeth Gilkison Purves in memory of G. Colesberry Purves from the Edmond Foulc Collection, 1930 (1930-1-40)

This circular seal box, or skippet, was intended to receive and protect a wax seal impression attached to an official document. Similar in form and function to the seal box of Massimiliano Sforza (cat. 63), it emphasizes seals' singular importance as legally binding marks of individual authority and suggests the care with which they were fashioned and safeguarded.

In contrast to earlier examples typically made of leather, wood, or bone, this gilt-metal box reflects the opulence of functional objects in use at the Burgundian court shortly before Maximilian I's marriage to Mary of Burgundy in 1477. That the box dates to the reign of Charles the Bold, Mary's father, can be inferred from its elaborate surface decoration, which includes his coat of arms and motto "I have dared it"

(*Je lay emprins* [*sic*]), as well as the collar and other symbols of the Burgundian Order of the Golden Fleece, of which he was sovereign. The sixteen coats of arms adorning the box's edge, which identify Charles's various dominions, establish that the box cannot have been made earlier than 1473, as they include the duchy of Guelders, which he acquired that year. Since the duke was killed at the battle of Nancy in January 1477, the box appears to have been made within the last four years of his rule.[1] The designs of Charles's seals evolved throughout his reign to reflect the acquisition of new territories and titles, with what was known as the secret seal used for personal correspondence and a larger equestrian seal reserved for state business. The date, dimensions, and decoration of this seal box correspond precisely to the state seal used by Charles the Bold in the final years of his life.[2]

The Philadelphia Museum of Art acquired this seal box in 1930 along with other works from the collection of Edmond Foulc.[3] It also belonged to notable collector Didier Petit, and it is included in the 1843 sale catalogue of his collection.[4]   ABB

REFERENCE: Leman 1927, p. 33, no. 40, pl. XXVIII

1. See Roberts 2004, pp. 136–37.
2. Wree 1639.
3. Leman 1927, p. 33, no. 40, pl. XXVIII.
4. *Catalogue de la collection formée par M. Didier Petit* 1843, p. 62, no. 627.

Cat. 7

Maximilian I's Personal Copy of Charles the Bold's Military Ordinances

Netherlandish, 1473

Illumination on vellum

12 x 8⅞ in. (30.5 x 22.5 cm)

Haus-, Hof- und Staatsarchiv, Vienna (Hs. Böhm, Suppl. 1332, Sign Weiss 1096)

This luxury copy of the regulations for the organization and administration of a permanent Burgundian army was presented as a gift by Charles the Bold to Maximilian I. It is possible that Charles gave the manuscript to Maximilian at their first and only meeting, in Trier in 1473. The summit between Maximilian's father, Emperor Frederick III, and Charles the Bold—which the fourteen-year-old archduke attended—was motivated by Charles's ambition to turn his disparate dominions into a powerful, unified kingdom and to be solemnly crowned as king of Burgundy by the emperor. Conversely, Frederick wished to secure the marriage of Mary, the duke's daughter and only heiress, with Maximilian. The meeting was, in many ways, a failure. Charles outshone

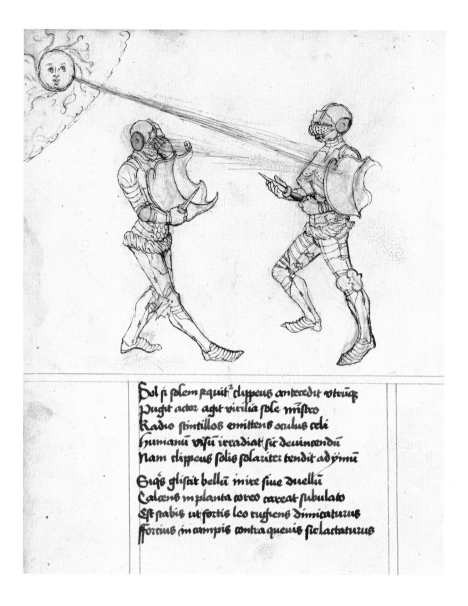

Frederick with displays of magnificence, and Frederick abruptly left after having announced, then rescheduled, the coronation ceremony. Although Charles would never become king, Maximilian did marry his daughter four years later.[1]

Probably inspired by the standing army King Charles VII of France had established twenty-six years earlier, Charles the Bold issued regulations in 1471, 1472, and 1473 to create and structure a comparable force of his own. As there was no standing army in medieval Europe other than the one in France, Charles's regulations were novel for their time and potentially of great military value. The splendor of Charles's court made a lasting impression on the young Maximilian, whose careful study of this manuscript is evident from the notes he added in the margins.   PT

REFERENCES: *Maximilian I.* 1959, p. 10, no. 28, pl. 7; *Maximilian I.* 1969, "Katalog," p. 18, no. 43; Susan Marti in *Charles the Bold* 2009, p. 221, no. 48, ill.

1. On this meeting, see Marti 2009b.

Cat. 8

Strong in War (*Bellifortis*)
Written by Conrad Kyeser (1366–1405)
South German, ca. 1455
Pen and ink and watercolor
Open: 12⁹⁄₁₆ x 20⁷⁄₁₆ in. (32 x 52 cm)
Tiroler Landesmuseum Ferdinandeum, Innsbruck, Austria, Bibliothek (FB 32009)

Conrad Kyeser, a physician from Eichstätt, completed the original *Strong in War* (*Bellifortis*) manuscript on parchment in 1405, making it the first illustrated European treatise on warfare. This seminal late medieval work was composed for a courtly audience as a compendium of military technology, knowledge that the author had acquired as a soldier in the Bavarian service. This magnificent copy includes vivid images of weapons, such as crossbows, rockets, and chariots, as well as technical drawings of mills, conveyors, and other mechanisms.

The book was produced during a period defined by the rise of firearms, which had a lasting impact on military technology. Although the manuscript was composed well before Maximilian I's reign, its impressive illustrations convey realistically the nature of battle and the armaments knights used at the time. There are, however, notable gaps in information, as Kyeser seems to have been more concerned with rhyme scheme in his written passages than with correct technical descriptions, and he may very well have lacked certain expertise. Surviving copies indicate that by 1460 Kyeser's work had been duplicated more than twenty times, demonstrating its strong reception and significance.[1]

Watermark analysis performed on the copy now in Innsbruck has dated it to about 1455 and suggests it was produced in southern Germany.[2] Its structure and chapter arrangement mirror the original exactly, although there are many omissions in the text as well as postscripts added later by a different hand.   RS

REFERENCES: Leng 2002, pp. 106–49; Leng 2009, pp. 220–22, no. 39.4.6; Cermann 2013; Thomas Kuster in *Ritter!* 2013, pp. 92–93, no. 1.9

1. See Cermann 2013.
2. Leng 2009, pp. 220–22. According to Rainer Leng, the watermark is a tower; see Piccard 1970, sect. II, pp. 28, 89, no. 332; see also Piccard-Online, no. 100470, http://www.piccard-online.de.

Cat. 9

Medal of Maximilian I and Mary of Burgundy

Giovanni Filangieri Candida (ca. 1445/50–ca. 1498/9?)
Netherlandish, probably 1477–80
Cast bronze
Diam. 1⅞ in. (4.88 cm)
The Metropolitan Museum of Art, New York,
Gift of Ogden Mills, 1925 (25.142.37)

The second of two portrait medals attributed to amateur medalist Giovanni Filangieri Candida that depict Maximilian I and Mary of Burgundy, this example probably dates to the early years of their marriage. Although the work is unsigned and undated, the attribution is based on stylistic similarities to the signed medal of Mary's father, Charles the Bold, and Maximilian that Candida produced in 1476 or 1477 to commemorate the couple's engagement. While he may have received some training as a medalist in Rome, Candida practiced the art only as it contributed to his career as a diplomat. Known to have produced a mere six medals while at the Burgundian court, Candida served as private secretary to Charles the Bold and continued to work for Maximilian

after the duke's death in 1477, until falling out of favor and moving to France in 1480.[1]

Maximilian's marriage to one of Europe's wealthiest heiresses was a spectacular triumph for the Habsburgs following years of diplomatic and military conflicts with the duke of Burgundy. A meeting between Emperor Frederick III and Charles the Bold in 1473 to negotiate the union was abruptly abandoned when they failed to reach an agreement over terms including Charles's desire to elevate his own position from duke to king. This first and only encounter with his future father-in-law had a lasting impact on the fourteen-year-old Maximilian, who later sought to emulate the ceremony, splendor, and authority of the Burgundian court during his own reign. Despite Maximilian's political and military inexperience, the marriage offered Mary's dominions greater security against threats from France. Her decision to honor her late father's wish and marry Maximilian suggests her keen understanding of international diplomacy and the importance of the union as a means of securing her future inheritance.   ABB

REFERENCE: Mark Wilchusky in *Currency of Fame* 1994, p. 123, no. 37, ill. p. 140

1. See Mark Wilchusky in *Currency of Fame* 1994, pp. 123–26, nos. 37, 38, ill., and ill. p. 140; Waldman 1994; Daniel Schmutz in *Charles the Bold* 2009, pp. 226–29, no. 53, ill., and ill. pp. 224, 225; Schmutz 2009; Heinz Winter in *Kaiser Maximilian I.* 2014, pp. 210–18, nos. III.1–III.21, ill.; Winter 2014.

Panels of Maximilian I as Archduke of Austria and Mary of Burgundy, from the Chapel of the Holy Blood, Bruges

South Netherlandish, probably ca. 1483 and later
Clear and colored glass with painted details and silver stain
Each panel: 72¹⁄₁₆ x 30¹⁵⁄₁₆ in. (183 x 78.5 cm)
Victoria and Albert Museum, London (C.438-1918; C.439-1918)

These stained-glass panels originally belonged to a series of windows from the chapel of the Holy Blood in Bruges, which featured full-figure representations and armorial bearings of the dukes of Burgundy and their consorts. The chapel, which was connected to the medieval residence of the counts of Flanders and named for the holy relic of Christ's blood that it housed, was rebuilt in the Gothic style and completed sometime after 1482.[1] Accounts in the archive of the Noble Brotherhood of the Holy Blood include payments for glazing in 1483 and 1496. Although the records do not identify the subjects of the windows, it is likely that the panels depicting Maximilian I and Mary of Burgundy date from the earlier commission. What is clear, however, is that the work was funded by the thirty-one members of the Noble Brotherhood, who were among the city's most prominent citizens. Although the windows were removed by revolutionary officials at the end of the eighteenth century and subsequently sold in England, where they were extensively restored, their original appearance is recorded in a set of sixteenth-century drawings in the archive of the Noble Brotherhood (fig. 29).[2] This remarkable evidence is critical in efforts to interpret and contextualize the present works.

Mary's untimely death in 1482 sparked a succession crisis in the Burgundian state, and Maximilian faced numerous challenges to his claim to rule on behalf of their four-year-old son, Philip I, who was his mother's rightful heir. By consenting to a marriage between his daughter, Margaret, and the dauphin of France, Maximilian neutralized the foreign threat at the cost of a part of his Burgundian inheritance, which he was forced to cede as a dowry. Despite maintaining control over the wealthy and fiercely autonomous county of Flanders, Maximilian endured periodic and often violent revolts by his Flemish subjects, notably the citizens of Bruges, who deeply resented his rule, viewing him as a foreigner and a usurper. It is in this tense political climate that the chapel of the Holy Blood windows were conceived.

Standing alongside his wife's ancestors in a monumental genealogy, Maximilian's appearance as Austrian archduke emphasizes his status as an outsider and conceals signs of his

FIG. 29 *Drawing of the Window Depicting Maximilian I and Mary of Burgundy, from the Chapel of the Holy Blood, Bruges.* South Netherlandish, 16th century(?). Ink and watercolor on parchment, 26 x 10 in. (66 x 25.5 cm). Museum van het Heilig-Bloed, Bruges

Burgundian claim. He is immediately identifiable by his arch-ducal cap and armorial surcoat, on which the arms of Austria (dexter) impale those of Burgundy (sinister), a heraldic expression of his marital and political union with Mary. Yet the mantle draped over his left shoulder obscures all but the smallest portion of the Burgundian arms. Although Maximilian's position to Mary's left may have been dictated by the placement of the windows relative to the altar or other practical considerations, it may also reflect the greater status of his wife as Charles the Bold's rightful heir. This visual trope is repeated in another series of panels depicting the counts of Flanders, commissioned for the Bruges Seminary (see fig. 14).[3] ABB

REFERENCES: cat. 10: Vallance 1911, pp. 189–92, pl. I; *Grosvenor Thomas Collection* 1913, vol. 1, pp. 7–8, pl. I; Rackham 1940; Polleross 2012, pp. 103–4, fig. 3; cat. 11: Vallance 1911, pp. 189–92, pl. II; *Grosvenor Thomas Collection* 1913, vol. 1, p. 6, pl. II; Rackham 1940; Polleross 2012, pp. 103–4

1. Gailliard 1846, p. 99.
2. See Yvette Vanden Bemden in *Magie du verre* 1986, p. 51, no. 10, ill.; Vanden Bemden 2000, p. 39, ill. p. 95, fig. 31, and pp. 133, 145, 147, n. 19, ill. p. 137, fig. 56; Williamson 2003, pp. 144–45, nos. 57–61, ill. pp. 77–80; Marsh 2009.
3. See Roberts 2004, pp. 139–40.

Cat. 12

Crowned Female Figure with an Angel

Netherlandish, ca. 1500
Stone with polychromy
H. 31½ in. (80 cm), W. 18 in. (45.8 cm), D. 10 in. (25.3 cm)
Glencairn Museum, Bryn Athyn, Pennsylvania (09.SP.152)

Collector Raymond Pitcairn acquired this enigmatic sculpture, which appears in payment records as "Donatrice," from the estate of the Belgian art dealer Georges Demotte in 1935. The work's approximate date and geographic origin may be inferred from the unidentified figure's distinctly Netherlandish appearance and costume, as well as from the escutcheon with Charles the Bold's coat of arms carved on the base. Whether the heraldry refers to the work's donor or subject is unknown, although the sculpture must represent either a prominent young woman at the Burgundian court or a religious figure.

The young woman's age and delicate physiognomy suggest that the most obvious secular candidate is Mary of Burgundy. Yet the figure does not conform to typical posthumous representations of the duchess, who almost always appears with a head covering and elaborate jewelry.[1] Likewise Mary's arms were most commonly not depicted on their own but rather impaled with those of her husband, according to heraldic custom.[2] The figure's flowing hair and *demi-ceint* girdle seem to indicate that she is unmarried, thus limiting the contexts in

which this work could represent Mary of Burgundy to the period before her marriage to Maximilian in 1477.[3] While no known sculptural representations of Maximilian and Mary's marriage survive, the visual and armorial similarities between this work and an illustration of Mary as a bride from a copy of the *Excellent Chronicle of Flanders* are evident (fig. 30).

The more likely possibility is that this sculpture represents a virgin saint or the Virgin Mary, perhaps given her orientation and gesture at the scene of the annunciation. Saints such as Margaret of Antioch or Barbara were frequently depicted with characteristics comparable to those of the present figure, for example with a crown and uncovered hair, a *demi-ceint* girdle, and a red dress with a blue mantle.[4] The figure's missing limbs and the lack of any evidence of a saintly attribute can only lead to speculation on her identity. While it would be unconventional for an angel—here identified by his bare feet and the now-empty slots that once held wings—to accompany such a saint,

FIG. 30 *Marriage of Maximilian I and Mary of Burgundy*, from the *Excellent Chronicle of Flanders* (*Excellente Cronike van Vlaenderen*). South Netherlandish (Bruges), ca. 1485–1515. Paper, 10¼ x 7⅝ in. (26 x 19.3 cm). Openbare Bibliotheek, Bruges (MS 437, fol. 384r)

an angelic attendant would not be unusual in the presence of
the Virgin. A remarkable comparison appears in the Grimani
Breviary, in which Mary and the Christ Child lead a procession
of saints with angelic supporters holding her mantle.   ABB

REFERENCE: Donna L. Sadler in Holladay and Ward 2016, pp. 345–46,
no. 233, ill.

1. Roberts 2008.
2. See Wree 1639, p. 101.
3. See Lightbown 1992, pp. 306–41; Decker 2018.
4. A late fifteenth-century alabaster sculpture of Saint Margaret of Antioch,
patron and namesake of Mary of Burgundy's stepmother Margaret of York,
in the collection of the Metropolitan Museum (2000.641) makes a compelling
comparison, as does a sculpture of Saint Barbara also at the Glencairn
Museum (12.SP.23).

Helm for the Joust of Peace

South Netherlandish (Brussels), ca. 1490–1500
Steel
H. 17 in. (43.1 cm), Wt. 21 lb. 8 oz. (9,750 g)
Koninklijke Musea voor Kunst en Geschiedenis,
Brussels, deposited at the Koninklijke Museum van het Leger en de
Krijgsgeschiedenis, Brussels (10057,01)

Aside from a near-complete example in the Kunsthistorisches Museum, Vienna, none of the many jousting armors that were made in the Low Countries for Maximilian I, Philip I, Charles V, and Ferdinand I have survived.[1] They are only known from inventories, payment records, and related archival documents; from their representation in later paintings; and from a few, now widely scattered elements of which this helm is a particularly fine example.

The helm consists of three plates firmly riveted together. Although it is much stouter than contemporary German specimens, the helm is not nearly as massive as its Italian counterparts. It is especially distinctive for the curvature of the top and rear plates, which follow the contours of the skull and the nape of the neck; for the presence of a keel-shaped medial comb on the same plates; for the ornamental scalloped cut of the front plate's side edges and of the top plate's rear edge; and for the method for attaching the helm to the breast, with a massive hinge in the center and a hole for a large screw at each side. The outline of the hinge-half, which is shaped with fleurons, like a crown, is especially uncommon. In form, construction, and decoration, the helm compares closely to one in the Royal Collection, Windsor, which was modified for funerary use and bears marks that may be securely attributed to a Brussels armorer, Anthonis van Ghindertaelen.[2]

On the present helm, the maker's marks on the upper right side of the rear plate, an open coronet struck once at the top, and an orb and cross struck twice beneath it, do not match the mark attributed to Van Ghindertaelen, in which an orb and cross are surmounted by an open coronet, shown in strict profile, all struck as a whole with a single punch (see cat. 15). Significantly, Van Ghindertaelen's helm in Windsor is struck thrice with his mark, instead of with a combination of different marks. Accordingly, the helm under discussion was probably made by another Netherlandish armorer, perhaps Lancelot van Ghindertaelen, who may have used marks similar to those of Anthonis, his son.

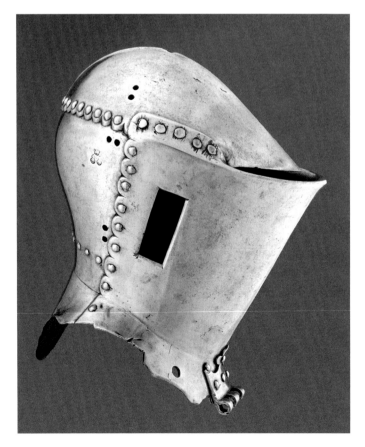

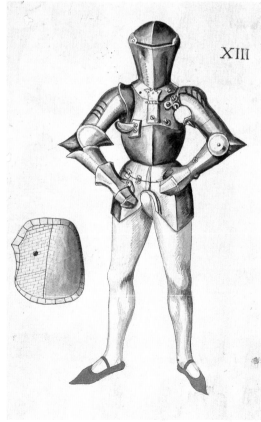

FIG. 31 Armor for the Joust of Peace from the pictorial inventory of Charles V's armory. German, ca. 1544. Watercolor and ink on paper. Patrimonio Nacional, Madrid, Real Armería (N18A, fol. 25r)

A comparable helm is illustrated in a pictorial inventory of Charles V's armory, which was compiled sometime before Charles abdicated and took most of his armors with him to Spain in 1556 (fig. 31). The helm may have belonged to one of the thirteen similar jousting armors that Charles owned and seemingly left in Brussels, representations of which appear in seventeenth-century allegorical pictures by Netherlandish painters who had access to the armory in the ducal palace on the Coudenberg, such as *Allegory of Touch* (1617–18) by Jan Brueghel the Elder and Peter Paul Rubens.[3] Those armors must have included examples originally made for Philip I, Charles's father, as following Philip's death and an intervention by Maximilian, thirteen such armors had effectively been deposited into Charles's armory in Brussels in 1510.

In the Musée d'Armes Anciennes, d'Armures, d'Objets d'Art et de Numismatique of Brussels by 1835, the present helm became part of the collections of the Koninklijke Musea voor Kunst en Geschiedenis in 1889.   PT

REFERENCES: Terjanian 2006, pp. 153–54, 157, no. 3, p. 159, no. 72; Norman and Eaves 2016, pp. 232–33, under no. 17

1. See Thomas and Gamber 1976, pp. 149–50, no. S. II, fig. 91.
2. See Norman and Eaves 2016, pp. 230–33, no. 17, ill.
3. Museo del Prado, Madrid (1398); see Ariane van Suchtelen in Woollett and Van Suchtelen 2006, pp. 90–99, no. 8, and fig. 56.

Cats. 14, 15

Right Gauntlet and Left Arm Defense for the Joust of Peace

Anthonis van Ghindertaelen (first recorded 1491, died 1520)
South Netherlandish (Brussels), ca. 1500
Steel
Gauntlet: L. 12¾ in. (32.4 cm), Wt. 2 lb. 1.6 oz. (951 g);
arm defense: L. 29½ in. (74.9 cm), Wt. 9 lb. 15.6 oz. (4,524 g)
Collection of Drs. Kenneth and Vivian Lam

This right gauntlet and left arm defense belonged to an armor designed for the joust of peace, a contest that in the Low Countries was generally undertaken with a tilt, a barrier of cloth or wood that separated the jousters from each other. As the target for the lance was a small shield fastened in front of the left shoulder, the lower left arm and hand that the shield failed to cover were vulnerable; thus the defenses guarding them were made in one to provide a rigid surface. Contrary to

conventional German examples, Netherlandish specimens are constructed with two articulated plates over all the fingers other than the thumb, which helped the rider to hold the reins and guide the horse's course. The right gauntlet has a series of faceted ridges that extend from the back of the hand over to the cuff, en suite with the lower cannon for the left arm.

The quality of design and execution found on these pieces speaks to the abilities of the armorers working for Maximilian I and his descendants in the Burgundian Low Countries. The upper cannon of the left arm defense is struck with the maker's mark of an orb and cross surmounted by an open coronet, which belonged to Anthonis van Ghindertaelen, a Brussels armorer who worked for Maximilian, Philip I, and Charles V (see cats. 76, 77). These elements are believed to be the remnants of one of their jousting armors and are likely to originate from the armory of the ducal palace in Brussels. An idea of the general appearance of the type of armor to which they belonged is provided by an illustration in a pictorial inventory of Charles's armory, which suggests that he owned thirteen such armors (see fig. 31).[1]

These elements were in the collection of Count Hector Economos in Paris until 1924, when the collection was purchased en bloc by William Randolph Hearst in New York. The left vambrace and its reinforcing pieces were subsequently purchased at auction from Galerie Fischer, Lucerne, in 1953 by Luigi Marzoli of Brescia.[2] Later bought privately by Enrico Minervino of Milan, the vambrace was sold by him through Geoffrey Jenkinson to R. T. Gwynn of Epsom, United Kingdom, before 1990. Also bought by Minervino, the reinforcing pieces were sold separately to Gottlob-Herbert Bidermann of Stuttgart before 1980; they were eventually acquired by Gwynn and reunited with the vambrace before 1990. The gauntlet was purchased independently by Gwynn at auction from Galerie Fischer, Lucerne, in 1961.[3] The ensemble was purchased by the present owners at the sale of the Gwynn Collection at Christie's London in 2001.[4]   PT

REFERENCES: cat. 14: Christie's 2001, pp. 72–74, no. 68, ill.; Gwynn 2016, pp. 228–29, no. 35, ill.; cat. 15: Christie's 2001, pp. 72–74, no. 68, ill.; Gwynn 2016, pp. 222–26, no. 34, ill.

1. Patrimonio Nacional, Madrid, Real Armería, N18A, fol. 25r.
2. Galerie Fischer 1953, p. 77, no. 1409, pl. 21.
3. Galerie Fischer 1961, p. 15, no. 124, ill. p. 18.
4. Christie's 2001, pp. 72–74, no. 68, ill.

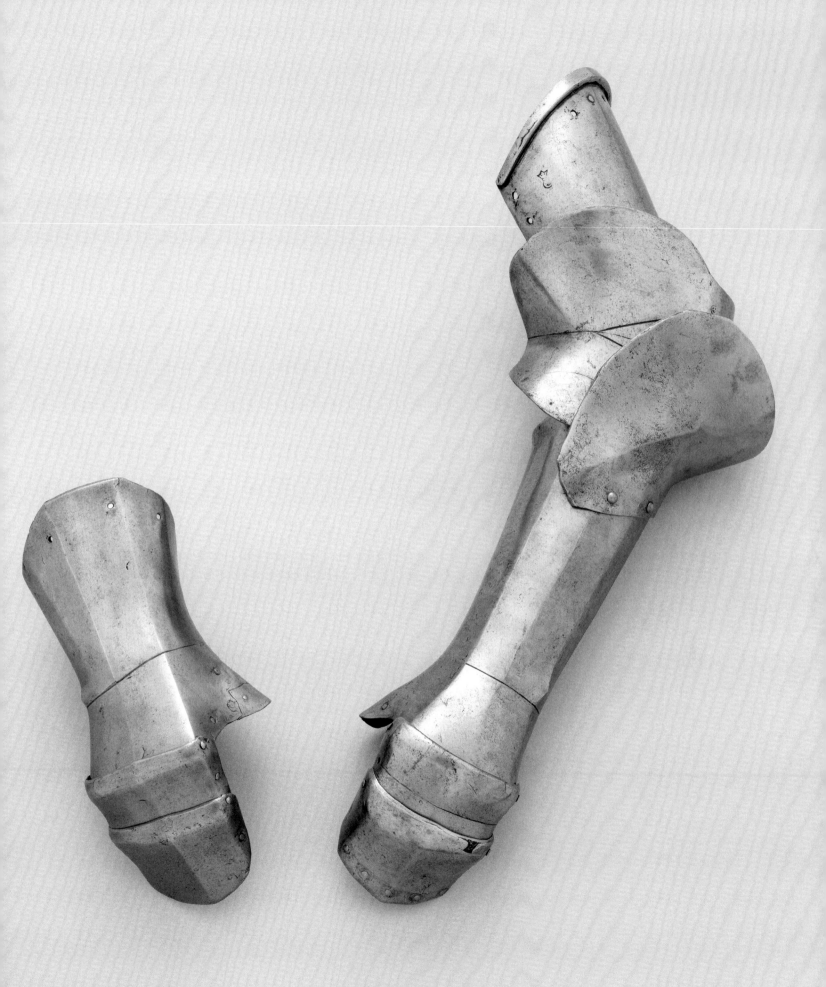

Field Armor of Maximilian I

Lorenz Helmschmid (first recorded 1467, died 1516)
South German (Augsburg), 1480
Steel, copper alloy, and leather
As mounted: H. 70⅝ in. (179.5 cm), W. 29⅞ in. (76 cm),
D. 27 in. (68.5 cm)
Sallet: Private collection, New York; all other elements of the armor:
Kunsthistorisches Museum, Vienna, Imperial Armoury (A 60)

A masterpiece by the hand of the Augsburg armorer Lorenz Helmschmid, this field armor is one of the most sophisticated German examples ever made in the late Gothic style, only rivaled by a few other works by Lorenz and his brother Jörg. Created for Maximilian I just over two years after he became duke of Burgundy and had moved to the Low Countries, the armor is tailored to his measure, elaborately worked with flutes and pierced designs, and constructed with copper-alloy components and decorative bands that offer a rich visual contrast to the cool tonality of the steel plates. In its present, exhibited state, it consists of twenty elements: a sallet, a bevor, a breastplate with a lance rest and a short fauld, a backplate with a culet, asymmetrical pauldrons, upper cannons, couters, lower cannons, gauntlets, cuisses, greaves, and sabatons. Originally, the pauldrons would have each been supplemented with a reinforcing piece at the front.

The armor is unusually well documented. It appears to be depicted in a sixteenth-century copy of a lost fifteenth-century painting, which shows Maximilian in armor as he enters the city of Luxembourg on horseback on September 29, 1480, and in a more detailed sixteenth-century illustration in an album of armor drawings (see fig. 5).[1] A series of payments recorded in the account books of Maximilian's chief treasurer in the Low Countries indicates that the armor was brought along with many others—all expressly described as being for Maximilian's personal use and body—over to the Low Countries by Lorenz no later than February 1480.

The armors that Maximilian acquired from the Augsburg master on that occasion constitute the single largest ensemble of luxury armors known to have been purchased in the fifteenth and sixteenth centuries. The payment records specifically list five complete field armors; two armors for the joust of war; an armor without a helmet; two "incomplete" armors; a field helmet and a war hat, both in the German fashion; two pairs of pauldrons; four pairs of besagews; three pairs of gauntlets; a pair of tassets or jousting sockets; three steel targes; several lance rests as well as a mechanical device "for carrying the shield"; a horse bard constructed with plates over the belly and articulated defenses for the legs; four half-bards of steel; and three war saddles. There were other items in the delivery that were evidently not made by Lorenz himself, as they are of a different nature. These include three mail shirts, four German swords and additional edged weapons, horse bits, rein guards, stirrups, and spurs, as well as rivets and armorer's tools. The whole cargo weighed 2,500 pounds of Flanders (about 2,399 pounds in modern weights, or about 1,088 kilograms) and cost Maximilian—with shipping, tolls, and couriering expenses—2,043 florins, 21 sols, 2 pence of the Rhine, or 2,656 livres, 19 sols, 2 pence of Flanders, which was a huge sum.[2]

Although the payment records do not provide a lengthy description of each piece, they make it clear that at least two complete armors, one targe, two pairs of besagews, and a pair of gauntlets were "garnished with latten [an alloy of copper and zinc] in the fashion of Germany." Two additional complete armors and a single helmet must also have been quite sumptuous, as the former cost Maximilian 110 florins apiece, and the latter 50. By way of comparison, Maximilian commonly awarded a squire the equivalent of 33 florins to purchase an armor made to his measure;[3] thus, two of the armors in this order were three times more expensive than a standard armor made to order, and the horse bard with articulated legs, for which Maximilian paid 800 florins, was the equivalent of twenty-four such armors.

The order included armors for war and peace, which Maximilian would have used in very different situations. The present field armor, in which he is portrayed when entering Luxembourg, emphasized his role as the supreme commander of the forces that opposed the king of France's attempts to take possession of Artois and other territories. In view of its exceptional workmanship and unmistakable German style, there can be little doubt that it would have eclipsed any armor that had been seen in the town within living memory.

The elements of the armor other than the sallet were kept in the imperial armory of Vienna until 1889, when they

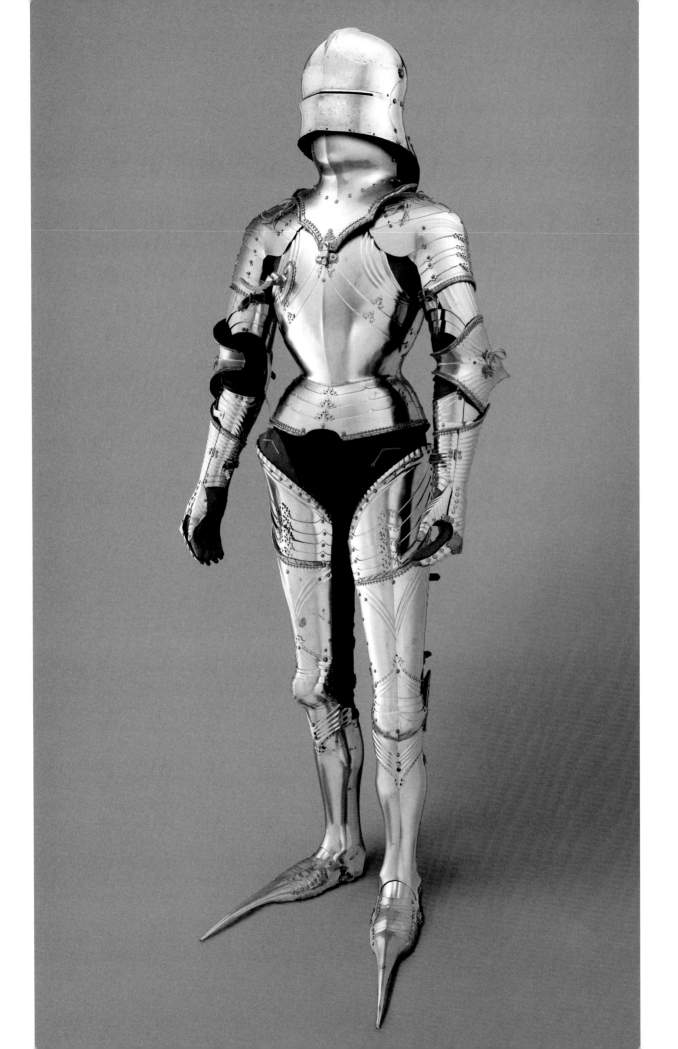

became part of the Kunsthistorisches Museum's Arms Collection (Waffensammlung).[4] The sallet was in the collection of Count August Breuner-Enckevoirt at Grafenegg Castle in Austria by 1894 and was inherited through his eldest daughter by Victor II, duke of Ratibor. Bought for William Randolph Hearst at a sale held by Galerie Fischer in 1934, the sallet was then kept in Saint Donat's Castle, Wales.[5] Later acquired by Hearst's restorer, Raymond Bartel, it was sold in 1952 at Sotheby's, London, where it was purchased by R. T. Gwynn of Epsom, United Kingdom;[6] it was privately acquired from his estate in 2001.   PT

REFERENCES: cat. 16: Galerie Fischer 1934, p. 8, no. 67, pl. 14 (erroneously shown as part of no. 88); Beard 1939b, pp. 130–31, ill. no. v; Sotheby's 1952, p. 4, no. 13, frontispiece; *Charles-Quint et son temps* 1955, p. 169, no. 430, fig. 126; *Art of the Armourer* 1963, p. 16, no. 28, ill.; Pyhrr 2011, pp. 74–75, fig. 13; *Ronald S. Lauder Collection* 2011, p. 524, no. 62, and p. 194, pl. 62; Gwynn 2016, pp. 132–43, no. 14, ill., figs. 12–14; cat. 17: Leitner 1866–70, pp. 1–2, pl. I; *Maximilian I.* 1959, pp. 156–57, no. 486, pl. 69; Thomas and Gamber 1976, pp. 106–7, no. A 60, fig. 40

1. On these two representations and a third, later one in Wolfenbüttel, see Buttin 1929; Anzelewsky 1963, pp. 77–81, figs. 1, 3, 4.
2. Archives Départementales du Nord, Lille, B 2124, fols. 295v–296r.
3. See, for example, Archives Départementales du Nord, Lille, B 2121, fol. 407r.
4. The Imperial Armoury department was known as the Waffensammlung until 1989.
5. Galerie Fischer 1934, p. 8, no. 67, pl. 14 (erroneously shown as part of no. 88). The sale was held at Zunfthaus zur Meise, Zurich.
6. Sotheby's 1952, p. 4, no. 13, frontispiece.

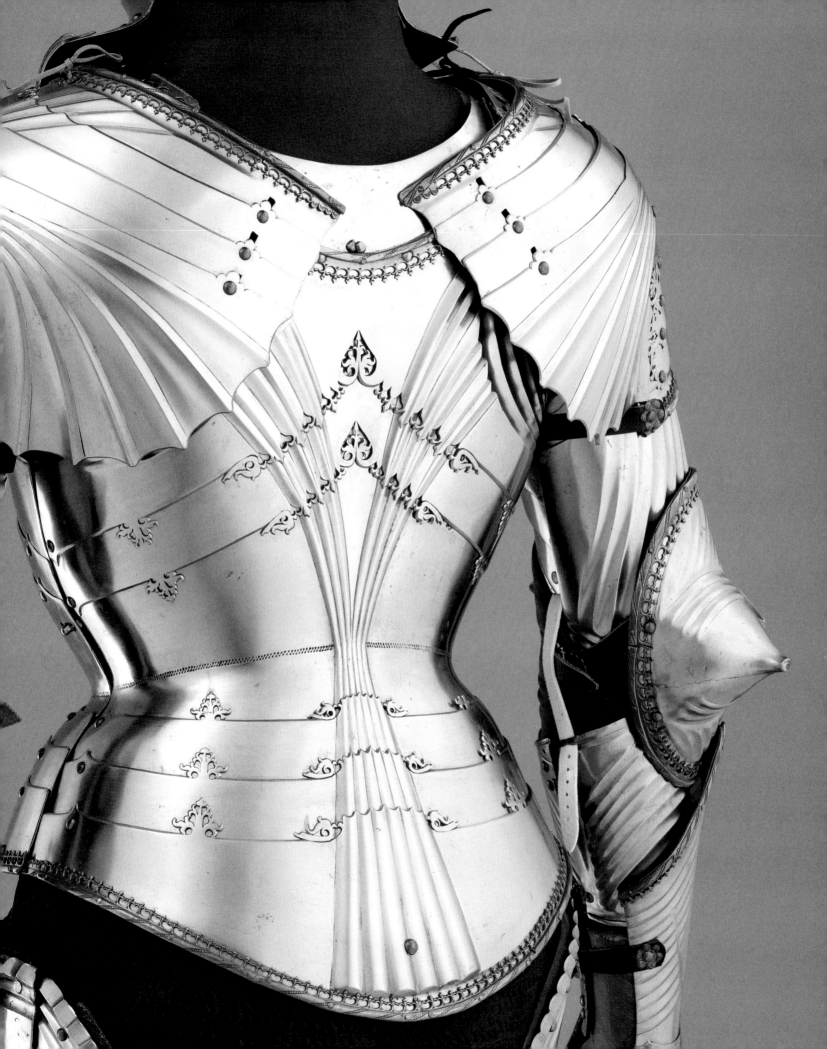

Martial Hero

From its origins as a brutal reenactment of warfare, the tournament gradually developed into a variety of mock combats in which the contestants could measure and display their valor and proficiency in the use of different arms. Often performed in front of an audience, and belonging to the customary celebrations of major events, these combats aided Maximilian I in his campaign to be recognized as one of the greatest knights that ever lived.  He organized and personally participated in countless tournaments, and extraordinary armors were especially made for him to shine and prevail on those momentous occasions. He invented and promoted unusual variants of the joust, which became common fixtures at his court and contributed to his renown. He even appears to have encouraged, if not actually imagined, the creation of technologically advanced mechanical devices that greatly contributed to the theatrical spectacle of the contests.

Maximilian also collected armors to commemorate his historic encounters with the most illustrious tour-neyers of the age: some were trophies he won by defeating them and others were gifts he received as tokens of his opponents' regard for his position and reputation. Together with the armors that he ordered for his own use, these mementos reinforced Maximilian's claims to fame. He commissioned chronicles of his knightly exploits, with the ambition of making his heroic deeds known to a broad audience by turning them into prints, then a relatively new medium. These accounts were so important to him that he personally oversaw their development, dictating and editing the narratives and reviewing the planned illustrations for accuracy.

In Innsbruck, where Maximilian established his chief residence after having succeeded his great-uncle Sigismund as archduke of Tyrol in 1490, he commissioned a spectacular loggia covered in golden tiles from which he could watch tournaments on the town square below. The loggia's polychrome stone reliefs suitably illustrated the range of his realms with an impressive row of coats of arms and asserted his position as a sovereign.

Cat. 18

King Maximilian as Hercules Germanicus (recto)

German, ca. 1493 or 1500

Woodcut

11³⁄₁₆ x 7 in. (28.4 x 17.8 cm)

Albertina Museum, Vienna (DG1948/224)

This double-sided woodcut was commissioned by Johannes Tolhopf, a professor of canon law at the University of Regensburg and a friend of the humanist Conrad Celtis. Also known by the Latinized name Janus Tolophus, Tolhopf referred to himself as the "Hercules Priest," an appellation that appears in the inscription on the reverse of the work, which shows his coat of arms. In 1493 Tolhopf exchanged letters with Celtis concerning his plan to write a volume about the mythic hero Hercules, who is sometimes claimed as a progenitor of the ancient Germans. The book was never completed, and all that is left is this tribute to Maximilian I. The woodcut identifies Maximilian as King of the Romans, a title he used from 1486 until 1508, when he assumed that of Holy Roman Emperor elect. During this period, as Maximilian was accruing power, several German humanists, including Celtis, Sebastian Brant, and Joseph Grünpeck, were developing the association between the young ruler and Hercules.[1]

In the upper register of the print, Maximilian stands on a patch of ground with his arms and legs outstretched; he is clothed in the pelt of Hercules's Nemean lion, with the face of the animal near his own. Maximilian wears Hercules's crown of poplar leaves, his nudity emphasizing his mythic power, and he holds a full arsenal of weapons, including a three-knotted club (*clavia trinodis*) and a bow whose arrow is looped with a snake labeled as *hidra* (hydra), another beast the hero overcame during his Twelve Labors. Between his legs lies an escutcheon with charges commemorating his achievements. The text praises Maximilian not only as the restorer of order and as an almost Christ-like savior of the world but also as a promoter of knowledge and virtue.

On the lower half of the print, in a landscape setting, Maximilian sits astride his horse in full armor with the crown of the King of the Romans on his head, while surrounded by troops from the far-flung regions of the empire, all labeled by means of their banners: Bohemians, Milanese, Swiss, and Burgundians, among others. Riding above the fray as the world leader, Maximilian appears above a large crowned

shield encircled by the collar of the Order of the Golden Fleece and enclosing his heraldic arms—the King of the Romans' single-headed eagle bearing on its breast an escutcheon with the arms of Austria.   FS

REFERENCES: Erwin Pokorny in *Hispania—Austria* 1992, pp. 349–50, no. 162, ill.; Thomas Schauerte in *Emperor Maximilian I* 2012, p. 186, no. 31, ill.

1. For more on the humanists' celebration of Maximilian as Hercules, see W. C. McDonald 1976; see also Wood 2005, p. 1133.

Eighteen Reliefs from the Golden Roof (Goldenes Dachl)

Design attributed to Jörg Kölderer (ca. 1465/70–1540)
Carving by Nikolaus Türing (died 1517) and Gregor Türing
(ca. 1475–1543)
Austrian (Innsbruck), ca. 1496/97–1500
Mittenwald sandstone with remnants of pigment
Dimensions variable, largest relief: H. 32¼ in. (82 cm), W. 29¹⁵⁄₁₆ in.
(76 cm), D. 7⅞ in. (20 cm)
Landeshauptstadt Innsbruck, Austria, deposited at the Tiroler
Landesmuseum Ferdinandeum, Innsbruck, Austria, Ältere
Kunstgeschichtliche Sammlungen (P 974–991)

In celebration of his marriage with Bianca Maria Sforza,
Maximilian I commissioned the court builder Nikolaus Türing
to add a loggia to the front of the three-story Neuer Hof (the new
ducal residence commissioned by Duke Frederick IV of Austria,
which Archduke Sigismund expanded after 1459), then still a
simple structure on a city square in Innsbruck. Known as the
Golden Roof (Goldenes Dachl), for its more than 2,500 fire-
gilded copper shingles, this work is singular in European art

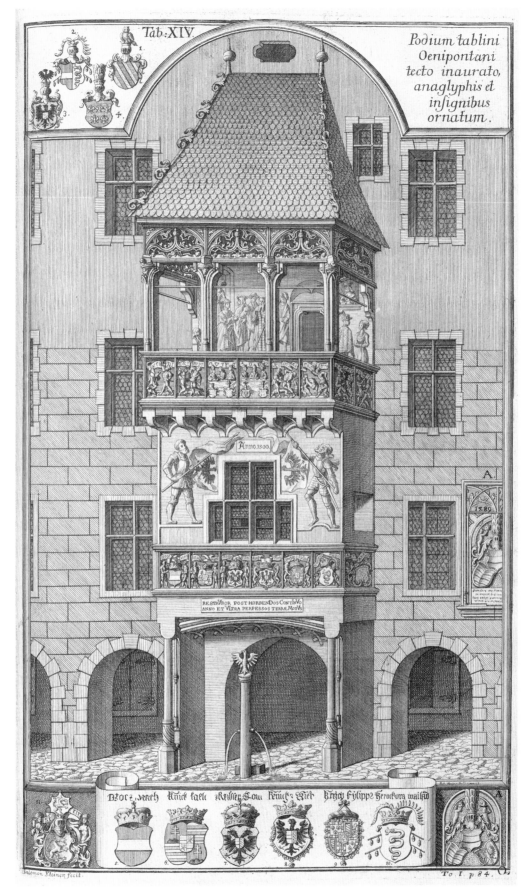

FIG. 32 Salomon Kleiner (1700–1761). *Golden Roof* (*Goldenes Dachl*), from *Monumenta Aug. Domus Austriacae*. 1750. Engraving, 17¹/₁₆ x 10¹/₁₆ in. (43.4 x 25.6 cm). Beinecke Rare Book and Manuscript Library, Yale University, New Haven, Connecticut

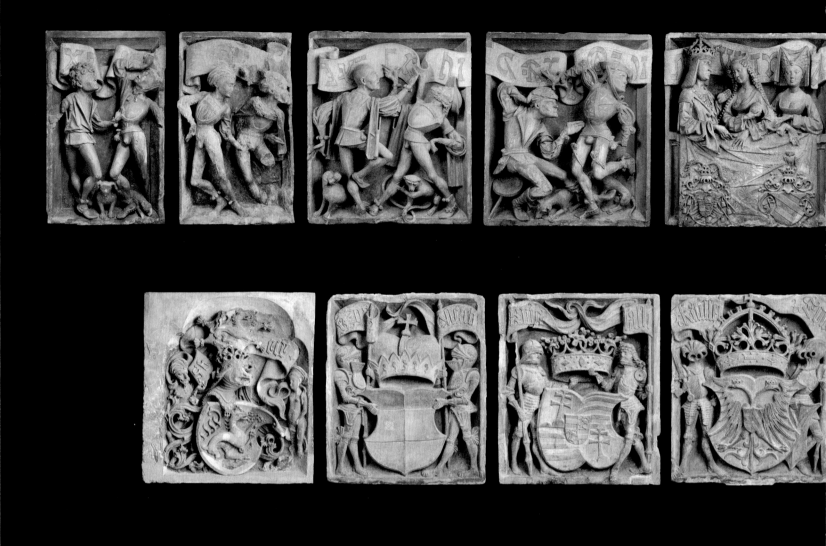

(fig. 32).[1] As an artistic synthesis of architecture, sculpture, and painting, it not only communicates the Habsburg dynasty's claim to dominion, but it also reflects courtly festival customs and displays of splendor. The loggia, constructed of Kramsach marble and set upon two pillars, was produced between 1497 and 1500. During this period, or perhaps earlier, Türing also created the reliefs carved in Mittenwald sandstone that adorn the loggia, possibly following designs by the court painter Jörg Kölderer. Originally, the reliefs were less colorful; following the Italian example, they were painted white with a few gold sections, giving them an elegant, marble-like appearance.

A large window, a painting of two immense standard-bearers waving the banners of the Roman kingdom and county of Tyrol, and an eight-part frieze of coats of arms hierarchically arranged and furnished with explanatory inscriptions dominate the second-story balustrade. The two most significant scenes in this frieze are positioned at the center of the six reliefs facing the square. On the left, knights brandish the heraldic arms of the Holy Roman Empire with the double-headed eagle and imperial crown, accompanied by the inscription KAISSERTOM (Empire, P 977). On the right, griffins hold aloft the crown and arms of the Roman kingdom, accompanied by the inscription KINGRICH (Kingdom, P 978). The inclusion of the Austrian-Burgundian inescutcheon and the collar of the Order of the Golden Fleece on both reliefs indicates that they depict Maximilian's personal coats of arms.

These two central reliefs are flanked by heraldic arms of the next-most important Habsburg territories. On the left, two knights in armor hold the arms of Hungary with the inscription K*ING LASLE, for King Ladislaus II (P 976). On

the right, two lions present the arms of Burgundy with the collar of the Order of the Golden Fleece and an inscription honoring the founder of the order, Duke Philip the Good, HERZOG FYLIPP (P 979). On the far left, two knights carry the arms of the duchy of Austria, with the inscription H*ZOG* OSTRICH (Duke of Austria, P 975). On the far right, the relief communicates the Habsburgs' dynastic connection to the Sforza family: doubled rods hung with water buckets (an allusion to a devastating fire in the city's history) frame the heraldic serpent of the duchy of Milan, and the inscription reads HERZOG VON MAILA*T (Duke of Milan, P 980). On the left side of the loggia is a relief featuring the arms of the duchy of Styria with the inscription STEIR (P 974), and on the right side is a relief displaying the arms of Tyrol with the inscription TIROL (P 981).

As a group, the reliefs on the second-story balustrade symbolize the chief Habsburg territories and the reach of Maximilian's monarchical influence, under which he now counted the duchy of Milan. Since Maximilian did not ascend to Holy Roman Emperor until 1508, it seems likely either that the imperial relief was installed later, replacing another, or that it reflected his claim to the future imperial title (P 977). Originally, the arms and/or shield bearers and the backgrounds were probably painted white to draw attention to the colorful shields and golden letters.

The reliefs in the ten-part frieze on the third-story balustrade produce a far more remarkable iconographic effect than those below. Maximilian appears in both of the central reliefs. In the left relief, he is in half profile, wearing his crown and the collar of the Order of the Golden Fleece (P 991). He faces his two wives: Bianca Maria Sforza, who holds an apple that was presumably gilded at one time, and Mary of Burgundy, who gazes straight ahead, toward the viewer. The arms of the allied Sforza family and duchy of Burgundy embellish the fabric hanging from the balustrade. It is unusual that Bianca Maria is placed in the middle of the composition and not Maximilian. This placement reveals that the relief is dedicated to his wives, who are crucial to the survival of the dynasty. In the relief to the right, Maximilian is represented as a ruler, centered and facing forward, displaying emblems of his power, such as a scepter and scroll (P 990). His arms are positioned to the left beneath him, only without the standard double-headed eagle; instead, a single eagle occupies the shield, with a second placed above the crown. To Maximilian's left is a jester, wearing the typical jester's cap with donkey ears. To Maximilian's right is a high-ranking male figure, whose identity can no longer be determined because his heraldic arms have chipped off. Although there is no narrative link between the two central reliefs, the jester establishes a connection between them—an axis of communication, even—as he levels his gaze directly at Maximilian in the left-hand relief. The senior courtier also turns to face Maximilian in the neighboring frame.

The remaining eight reliefs depict sixteen paired dancers in expressive positions and grotesque poses, performing a *moresca* (P 982–89). This exhibition dance, which featured acrobatic step and jump sequences, derived from Moorish culture and enjoyed tremendous popularity at courts during the fifteenth and sixteenth centuries because of its "exotic" or, rather, "Saracenic" character. Accordingly, the pairs of figures—accompanied by animals, some foreign—wear fashionable costumes with slashed sleeves and headdresses that are at once contemporary and orientalizing. The semblance of the "exotic" complements the unreadable text composed of pseudo Greek, Hebrew, and Latin characters on the banner that runs through the background of all the reliefs, examples of which exist from fifteenth-century Burgundy.

As an element of courtly masquerade, the *moresca* was a form of entertainment in which noblemen sometimes participated too. For example, one of Maximilian's confidants, Michael von Wolkenstein, is included in the Innsbruck *moresca*, identifiable by the heraldic arms on his back (P 989). Maximilian himself often partook in these dances. Moreover, the *moresca* had the character of a burlesque courtship dance, directed toward a lady in a manner echoing courtly love. The dancer with the most daring contortions was awarded a golden apple, suggested here by the apple held by Bianca Maria, who is ready to give the prize (P 991).

Although the Golden Roof was produced on the occasion of Maximilian's marriage to Bianca Maria, it was not meant as a record of specific historic celebrations. Instead, the staging and communication of power in the imagery presented make recourse to such festivities in general and to other representations of sovereignty, such as tournaments, that may have played out in the square below. The depiction of Maximilian and his wives behind a balustrade on one of the reliefs alludes to the royals' actual appearance on the loggia, and in this way, it reflects the possible uses for this architectural space for the delivery of homages or proclamations.

It was no happy accident that the Golden Roof was constructed in a significant urban location, at the convergence of some of the most important roads in Habsburg territory. The liminal zone the loggia occupied between court and city allowed Maximilian to come into contact with the public, without leaving the safety of the Neuer Hof. The portraits on the reliefs, in combination with the courtly frescoes behind them, performed a representative function—through them, the royal couple was permanently present, even when they were not. The reliefs were therefore not intended merely to communicate the Habsburg claim to power or to commemorate wedding festivities. Their primary purpose was to stabilize Maximilian's sovereignty during his frequent absences. PS

REFERENCES: M. Koller 2001, p. 173, ill.; Morscher and Grossmann 2004; Ulrich Söding in Naredi-Rainer and Madersbacher 2007, p. 256, no. 166, ill., and ill. p. 424; Eva Michel in *Emperor Maximilian I* 2012, p. 144, no. 9, ill.; Franke and Welzel 2013, pp. 15–51, fig. 3, colorpls. 2–4

1. Hye 1997; Morscher and Grossmann 2004.

Cat. 20

Foot Combat Armor of Maximilian I

Francesco da Merate (active 1480–1496)
Burgundian (Arbois), before 1508
Steel, copper alloy, leather, and gold pigments
As mounted: H. 70⅞ in. (180 cm), W. 27½ in. (70 cm),
D. 25⅝ in. (65 cm)
Kunsthistorisches Museum, Vienna, Imperial Armoury (B 71)

This armor is designed for the foot combat, a contest in which two heavily armored men fought inside an enclosure with pollaxes, swords, or daggers (fig. 33). Originating from the judicial duel, in which the killing of the claimant or defendant was thought to show God's will and would have concluded a legal dispute, the foot combat had evolved by the mid-fifteenth century, if not earlier, into a friendly though brutal competition

that allowed its participants to showcase their prowess in front of an audience.

In the joust, the horse, the saddle, and the tilt that sometimes separated the contestants effectively protected certain areas of the body. In the foot combat, however, one's entire body was vulnerable. As a result, the armors that were specially developed for it generally seek to leave nothing exposed. Virtually all examples encase the thighs, which on horseback would have been protected by the animal's ribs. On some the buttocks and groin are also fully encased in steel; while, on others, these same parts are protected by a tonlet, a deep steel skirt that widens downward to facilitate leg movement (see cat. 37).

Made for his personal use and originally blued or russeted (the gold pigments on its surface were brushed on sometime before 1555), this is Maximilian I's only near-complete foot combat armor to survive. Missing only the gauntlets, it consists of eleven elements: a helm that can be firmly attached to the breastplate and backplate by hook and eye, and by strap and buckle, respectively; a breastplate made in one with a deep fauld of seven lames; a backplate secured to the breastplate by hinges at the left and by strap and buckle at the right, and made in one with a similarly deep culet, which, together with the breastplate's fauld, makes the tonlet; wide, symmetrical pauldrons; vambraces constructed with wide couter wings to guard the inside of the elbows; cuisses with comparable poleyn wings to defend the knees, made in one with greaves pierced at the bottom to suspend borders of mail (now lost); and a pair of sabatons that fully enclose the heels.

Besides the tonlet, several features make this sturdy and carefully thought-through armor particularly apt for the hazards of the strenuous foot combat. The helm is suitably ample to accommodate the padding that would have minimized the impact of blows and perhaps also to allow the wearer's head to freely rotate inside. Its face defense has an unusually large number of apertures to provide greater peripheral vision and facilitate ventilation; these apertures are narrow to prevent the point of a weapon from harming the person inside. The helm has a spring-loaded catch on the right side and a hook and eye on the left side to keep the face defense locked to the bevor and prevent it from accidentally opening. The vambraces have lower cannons with turned upper edges to direct the point of a weapon away from the elbows, and the cuisses fully enclose the thighs. As mobility was key in the foot combat, the upper cannons of the vambraces are constructed with flush turning joints, and the sabatons are independent of the greaves so that the feet could rotate freely, in contrast to the standard design of armor used on horseback.

Along with a much-corroded breastplate with tassets, its reinforcing breastplate, and an armet, now all in Zurich,[1] this foot combat armor is one of the few works known to have been made in the workshop Maximilian established under the supervision of the two brothers and Milanese armorers Gabriele and Francesco da Merate at Arbois in the county of Burgundy in 1495 (see cat. 125). The breastplate bears the workshop's mark of the letters ARBOIS as well as the mark of a closed coronet, which is thought to represent the crown Maximilian would have been entitled to as King of the Romans. As this crown would have been replaced by a different one upon his assumption of the title of Holy Roman Emperor elect in 1508, the armor is likely to have been made prior to that date.[2]

The construction of the breastplate and backplate each in two parts (to make forward and backward bending easier), the choice of a helm, and the reliance on a tonlet to cover the groin all represent time-tested solutions that draw from a medieval tradition. Although some foot combat armors continued to be built with helms and tonlets through the third quarter of the sixteenth century, the design of Maximilian's armor looks conservative when compared to that of the armors for Louis II of Hungary and Giuliano de' Medici (see cats. 86, 119), which are believed to have been made at the emperor's orders in or around 1515. In this regard, the traditional features of Maximilian's armor might betray the relative age of Francesco da Merate, who directed the Arbois workshop (Gabriele remained in Milan), by the time it was made. Already a prominent master in 1480, when he was working for the duke of Ferrara, Francesco presumably began his career one or two decades earlier.[3] By 1500 his experience was considerable enough that he may have had limited inclination to depart from trusted designs with which, by then, he was very well acquainted.

Maximilian's armor is first recorded and identified as having belonged to him in an inventory of the archducal armory of Innsbruck in 1555. In Ambras Castle by 1596, it was removed to Vienna in 1806, and became part of the Kunsthistorisches Museum's Arms Collection (Waffensammlung) in 1889.[4]   PT

FIG. 33 Master of the Getty Lalaing (active ca. 1530). *Jacques de Lalaing Fighting the Esquire Jean Pitois at the Passage of Arms of the Fountain of Tears.* Netherlandish, ca. 1530. Tempera colors, gold leaf, gold paint, and ink, 14⁵⁄₁₆ x 10⁵⁄₁₆ in. (36.4 x 26.2 cm). J. Paul Getty Museum, Los Angeles (MS 114 [2016.7], fol. 129v)

REFERENCES: *Maximilian I.* 1959, pp. 189–90, no. 540, pl. 79; Thomas and Gamber 1976, pp. 194–95, no. B 71, fig. 89; Boccia, Rossi, and Morin 1980, pp. 94–95, and ill. nos. 83, 84

1. See Boccia 1982, p. 288, no. 96, and figs. 168, 169, 205a, b.
2. Thomas and Gamber 1976, p. 195, no. B 71; Boccia 1982, p. 292, nos. 147, 148.
3. Ortwin Gamber in Thomas 1958/1977, p. 1003.
4. Thomas and Gamber 1976, p. 195, no. B 71; see also *Maximilian I.* 1959, p. 189, no. 540. The Imperial Armoury department was known as the Waffensammlung until 1989.

Cats. 21–23

Lance Heads for the Joust of War

German, ca. 1475–1540

Steel

Metropolitan Museum (14.25.439): L. 8½ in. (21.6 cm), Diam. 2⅝ in. (6.7 cm), Wt. 1 lb. 10.6 oz. (754.1 g); Metropolitan Museum (42.50.39): L. 12 in. (30.5 cm), Diam. 2⅝ in. (6.7 cm), Wt. 2 lb. 9.8 oz. (1,185 g); Metropolitan Museum (42.50.38): L. 9⁵⁄₁₆ in. (23.7 cm), Diam. 2¾ in. (7 cm), Wt. 3 lb. 3 oz. (1,446 g)

The Metropolitan Museum of Art, New York, Gift of William H. Riggs, 1913 (14.25.439); Gift of Stephen V. Grancsay, 1942 (42.50.39, .38)

In the joust of war, contestants were required to wear armor that resembled field armor, though often of outdated style, and, most importantly, to use lances fitted with heads projecting forward into a single point, as one would in battle. The customary designation of this contest as a "joust with lances with sharpened heads" (*joute à fers émoulus*) at the Burgundian court of Maximilian I is symptomatic of the importance of lance heads in defining the nature of such mock combats.[1]

Although they projected into a single point, the lance heads for the joust of war were rarely long or symmetrical like those designed for field use. Instead, they were rather stout, and the point was often slightly off-center, presumably to minimize its ability to penetrate metal and encourage it to glide on impact.

Exemplifying the varied proportions and forms such heads could have, these three examples, now in the Metropolitan Museum, originate from two different collections. One was owned by William Henry Riggs in Paris and was donated by him in 1913 (cat. 21). The other two were purchased by Clarence H. Mackay of Roslyn, Long Island, New York, at the auction house Orell Füssli-Hof, Zurich, in 1928. They were subsequently acquired by Stephen V. Grancsay and donated by him to the Metropolitan Museum in 1942.[2] PT

REFERENCE: Orell Füssli-Hof 1928, p. 12, nos. 65, 66, pl. III

1. See, for example, Archives Départementales du Nord, Lille, B 2124, fol. 295v. For earlier references at the Burgundian court, see Buchon 1838, pp. 70, 172.
2. Orell Füssli-Hof 1928, p. 12, nos. 65, 66, pl. III.

Cat. 24

Armor for the Joust of War of Maximilian I

South German, ca. 1494

Steel, copper alloy, wood, and leather

As mounted (approx.): H. 52¾ in. (134 cm), W. 29 in. (73.5 cm), D. 31⅛ in. (79 cm), Wt. 112 lb. 14 oz. (51,260 g)

Royal Armouries, Leeds, acquired with support from the Art Fund and The Pilgrims Trust (II 167)

Central to the joust of war was the idea that the contest should seem to take place in the context of a battle rather than in a tournament. Although it was probably conducted in field armor at first, safety concerns and perhaps also the rules of engagement led to the development of specialized armor over the course of the fifteenth century. Designed to evoke the appearance of field armor, the examples made in the German-speaking lands naturally sported sallets, the kind of helmets most knights then wore in battle. German armors for the joust of peace, by contrast, included distinctive helms that no longer bore any resemblance to helmets for the field (see cats. 26, 59), as was the case in most other parts of Europe (see cat. 13).

This armor is one of several that Maximilian I is known to have commissioned and kept both for his personal use and for his guests. It includes a sallet with two detachable brow plates, a bevor, a breastplate fitted with a rest and a queue at the right side for the jousting lance, a backplate composed of a plate that covers the middle of the buttocks and the tailbone, a waist

plate with a deep fauld of six lames and tassets each of ten lames, and a plate worn beneath the fauld and fitted with strap and buckle to be secured to the lowermost plate of the backplate. The armor is complemented by a large shield, or targe, of leather-covered wood, which can be secured sturdily to the armor's bevor and breastplate by bolt and nut and by a bolt with pointed head, respectively; a vamplate for the lance, constructed on an inner plate and three outer plates attached to it by screws; a pair of jousting sockets to cover the thigh and knee, which would have been suspended from the saddle; and, finally, a blind shaffron with a poll plate at the top and a rondel on the brow.

The workmanship of the pieces is consistently high. The jousting targe and vamplate are designed to cover the entire front part of the torso, the throat and chin, and the jouster's arms, which in the German joust of war were always left unarmored. The waist plate is made of thicker metal than the rest of the elements to prevent the sharp point of the opponent's lance from causing injury. The thigh defenses do not merely protect the rider; they also safeguard the horse. The sallet, which has a series of holes along the lower edge for riveting an applied decorative border in place, is among the shapeliest surviving examples of its kind and is likely to have been made by either Lorenz or Jörg Helmschmid.

This armor was in the collection of the Kunsthistorisches Museum, Vienna, until about 1935, when it was offered at auction by Galerie Fischer.[1] Acquired for William Randolph Hearst at the sale, it was kept at Saint Donat's Castle, Wales, until 1952, when it was purchased along with other objects by the Royal Armouries with the help of a grant from the National Art Collections Fund, the Pilgrim Trust, and a special Exchequer Grant.   PT

REFERENCES: Boeheim 1889, p. 162, no. 1007; Galerie Fischer 1935, p. 6, nos. 38–41, pls. 8–11; Beard 1939a, p. 8, and p. 9, ill. no. XI; Norman and Wilson 1982, pp. 34–35, no. 1, pl. 1; Pyhrr 2014, p. 93, fig. 25

1. Galerie Fischer 1935, p. 6, nos. 38–41, pls. 8–11. The sale was held at Zunfthaus zur Meise, Zurich.

Cat. 25

Lance Head for the Joust of Peace

Northern European, perhaps Netherlandish, ca. 1520–50
Steel
L. 7¾ in. (19.7 cm), Diam. 2⅝ in. (6.7 cm), Wt. 3 lb. (1,360.8 g)
The Metropolitan Museum of Art, New York, Gift of Stephen V. Grancsay, 1942 (42.50.40)

The joust of peace required specialized armor and lances that bore little resemblance to the equipment used in battle. This lance head is an example of the type intended solely for the contest. Unlike a lance head for the joust of war, it does not project forward into a single point. Instead it develops into four blunt prongs, reducing the risk of its head accidentally penetrating the opponent's armor by distributing the impact of the lance onto multiple points.[1] Most heads appear to have been made with three or four prongs. On account of their distinctive profile, which resembles the outline of a crown, they were generally called coronels. This example is notable for the high quality of the workmanship and the presence of a mark, now partly defaced, of the letter R

in a shield surmounted by an open coronet, which may be tentatively attributed on the basis of its typology to a Flemish armorer or cutler.

Clarence H. Mackay of Roslyn, Long Island, New York, purchased this lance head from the auction house Orell Füssli-Hof, Zurich, in 1928.[2] It was subsequently acquired by Stephen V. Grancsay and donated by him to the Metropolitan Museum in 1942.   PT

REFERENCES: Orell Füssli-Hof 1928, p. 12, no. 64, pl. III; Fallows 2010, p. 116, fig. 57

1. On coronels, see Fallows 2010, pp. 114–16; Matthias Pfaffenbichler in *Kaiser Maximilian I.* 2014, p. 152, nos. II.21, II.22, ill.; Breiding 2017, pp. 26–27.
2. Orell Füssli-Hof 1928, p. 12, no. 64, pl. III.

Portions of an Armor for the Joust of Peace of Maximilian I

Jörg Helmschmid the Younger (first recorded 1488, died 1502)
South German (Augsburg), ca. 1494
Steel, copper alloy, and leather
As mounted: H. 76⅜ in. (194 cm), W. 28¾ in. (73 cm),
D. 27⁹⁄₁₆ in. (70 cm)
Kunsthistorisches Museum, Vienna, Imperial Armoury (S XI)

Of the many tournament armors that Maximilian I owned, this example for the joust of peace is one of the finest and the only one to be so elaborately decorated. It presently consists of a

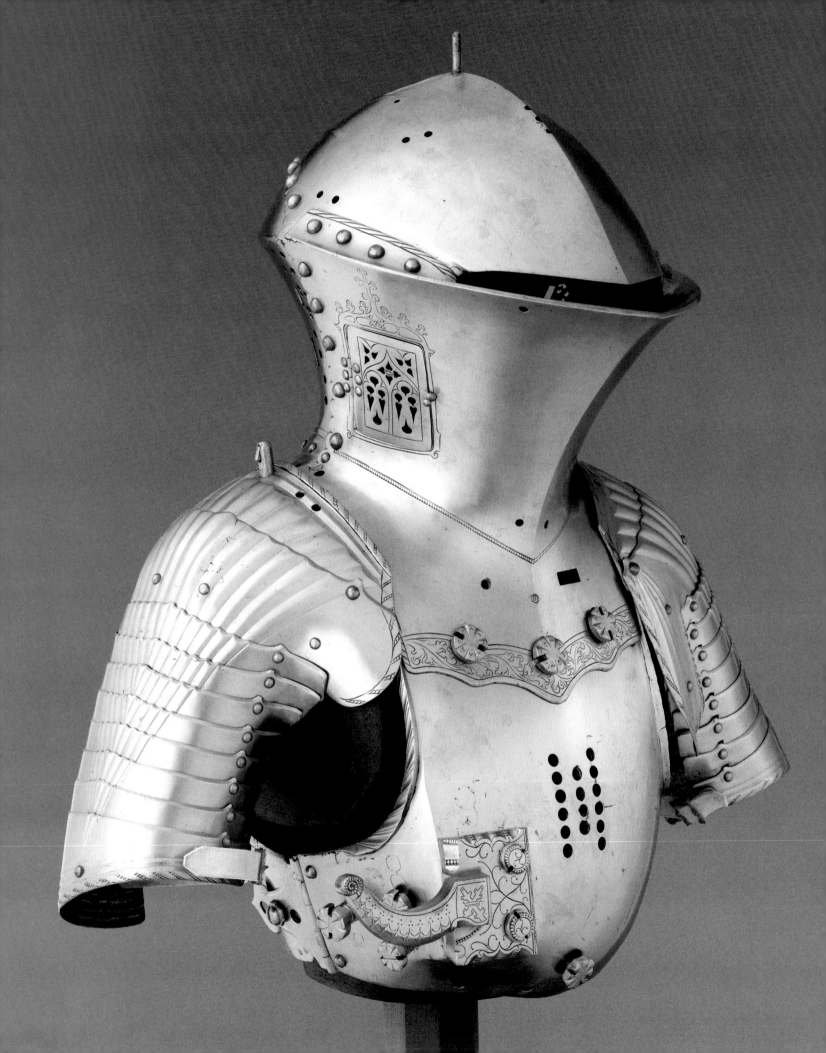

helm, a breastplate, a backplate, a lance rest, and asymmetrical pauldrons; in its original state, the armor would have also included besagews, asymmetrical arm defenses,[1] a queue for stabilizing the jousting lance, a waist plate fitted with a fauld and short tassets, and a plate that would have been worn beneath the fauld and secured by strap and buckle to a plate that extended down the buttocks to protect the tailbone. The helm is firmly secured to the upper part of the breastplate by three screws and to the lower part of the backplate by a hinged turnbuckle. A standard device on armors of this type, the turnbuckle was more than a clever way of ensuring a tight fit; it also made it possible to slightly tilt the helm backward and align its sight with the eyes of the person inside. The three vertical rows of holes in the center, along with the many plugged holes immediately above the area where the lance rest is currently attached and on the right side, behind the rest, where the lost queue would have been attached, prove the armor was modified during its working life, as new holes were added and old ones were filled. Such changes were typical for armors of this type that saw active use at Maximilian's court.

The armor's rich decoration was achieved through a combination of different techniques. The pauldrons, backplate, and rear base of the helm are embossed with bundles of flutes and gadroons. The pauldrons are additionally punched and engraved along their upper and lower edges to mimic the hammered-and-filed twists of the breastplate's integral gussets, and fretted at the rear with delicate foliate scrollwork in the late Gothic fashion. The helm's face plate similarly has fretted and engraved late Gothic ornament over and around the trapdoor on its right side (which may be temporarily opened to provide ventilation), and engraved scrolling acanthus leaves (probably added later) along its lower edge, which in character and execution seem to match the raguly cross of Saint Andrew engraved on the outer face of the lance rest. The scalloped trim on the rear edges of the helm's brow and face plates, as well as on the rear edges of the backplate's two side plates, completes the decorative scheme.

The maker's mark of a helm for the joust of peace facing dexter, which is struck on each of the steel shoulder straps hinged to the breastplate, belongs to Jörg Helmschmid the Younger, who with his brother Lorenz fulfilled commissions for Maximilian in Augsburg before becoming his court armorer in 1496 and relocating to Vienna in 1497. This armor is likely to be among those Maximilian ordered from the two brothers in 1494, the year many tournaments were held in celebration of his marriage with Bianca Maria Sforza (see

cat. 59).[2] It became part of the Kunsthistorisches Museum's Arms Collection (Waffensammlung) in 1889.[3] PT

REFERENCES: Thomas 1956/1977, p. 1140, and p. 1139, fig. 40, p. 1141, fig. 41, p. 1144, fig. 43c; Thomas and Gamber 1976, p. 144, no. S. XI; Matthias Pfaffenbichler in *Kaiser Maximilian I*. 2014, pp. 148–49, no. II.17, ill.

1. On the left arm defense of this armor, now lost, see Thomas 1956/1977, p. 1140, and p. 1139, fig. 40.
2. On Jörg Helmschmid the Younger's activity in Augsburg and Vienna, see Reitzenstein 1951, pp. 183–84; Thomas 1956/1977.
3. The Imperial Armoury department was known as the Waffensammlung until 1989.

Cat. 27

Padded Coif for the Joust of Peace

Austrian (Innsbruck), 1484
Linen, tow, hemp, leather, and iron
H. 15¾ in. (40 cm), W. 9⅞ in. (25 cm), D. 9⅞ in. (25 cm)
Kunsthistorisches Museum, Vienna, Imperial Armoury (B 47)

Although perhaps less hazardous than the joust of war because its participants wore massive helms and used lances fitted with coronels (see cat. 25), the joust of peace was a perilous mock combat, not least because one of its aims was to unhorse

one's opponent and the saddles used in this contest purposely had no back in order to facilitate one's fall. To make matters worse, the formidable blows delivered with the lances were enough to occasionally bring both the opponent and his horse down to the ground.

This padded coif would have been worn beneath the helm. It is fitted with numerous laces, the ends of which could be pulled through grommets in the helm and tied together on its exterior, as is shown in great detail in a watercolor by Albrecht Dürer, to ensure that it would be correctly positioned inside.[1] In addition, it has two leather straps, one round the forehead and one round the chin, the ends of which could be pulled through openings at either side of the helm and tightly buckled round its back, to immobilize the wearer's head and to keep the coif against the rear of the helm, as far away as possible from the side likely to receive a blow.

Originally belonging to Maximilian I's great-uncle Archduke Sigismund of Tyrol, who abdicated in his favor in 1490, it is one of six padded coifs in the collection of the Kunsthistorisches Museum, and of the kind that would have been worn beneath several armors in this volume (see cats. 26, 59). The coif was in Sigismund's armory, of which Maximilian took possession either when Sigismund abdicated or after he died in 1496. It was removed to Vienna in 1806 and entered the Kunsthistorisches Museum's Arms Collection (Waffensammlung) in 1889.[2] PT

REFERENCES: Thomas and Gamber 1976, pp. 152–53, no. B 47, fig. 72; Matthias Pfaffenbichler in *Kaiser Maximilian I.* 2014, p. 146, no. II.14, ill. p. 147; Pfaffenbichler in *Feste feiern* 2016, p. 200, no. 69.3, ill. p. 201

1. Musée du Louvre, Paris, Département des Arts Graphiques (R.F. 5640); see Mathias F. Müller in *Albrecht Dürer* 2003, p. 198, no. 38, and ill. pp. 197, 199.
2. The Imperial Armoury department was known as the Waffensammlung until 1989.

Cat. 28

Blind Shaffron

Attributed to Lorenz Helmschmid (first recorded 1467, died 1516)
South German, ca. 1485–90
Steel, copper alloy, and leather
H. 21⅞ in. (55.5 cm), W. 11⅝ in. (29.5 cm)
Kunsthistorisches Museum, Vienna, Imperial Armoury (B 19a)

This shaffron was designed to blind a horse when jousting at large—that is, without a tilt, a barrier that separated the contestants as they charged at each other with their lances— as was the custom in the German-speaking lands for both the jousts of peace and war. By ensuring that the horse would

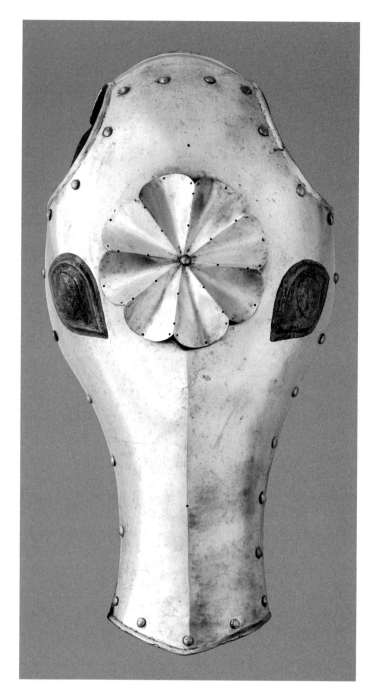

not deviate from its course out of fear of colliding with the oncoming opponent, a blind shaffron gave the rider greater control and the ability to focus on his target. Because it was so effective, however, it greatly increased the danger of the contest. Head-on collisions regularly took place, occasionally killing the animals and their riders.[1] Although Maximilian I knew of the Italian tradition of jousting across a tilt, and was intrigued enough to have regularly jousted in this foreign manner himself, it took a long time for the safer tilting tradition to take root in the German lands and supplant the native forms of engagement.[2] Although the latter were more hazardous, they were closer to the experience of war and as such daunting and exciting. They also importantly provided greater opportunities for contestants to showcase their horsemanship since the careful direction of the horses was critical. The courts of middle and northern German rulers became the final bastions for the genre, which eventually died out in the eighteenth century.

Forged from a single plate and fitted with a poll plate at the top and with a reinforcing rondel on the brow, this shaffron was designed to closely fit a horse's head, and it is embossed and blued to suggest the presence of eyes. The blued coloration was achieved by heating the steel plate up to about three hundred degrees Celsius, before rapidly cooling the hot metal by plunging it into oil. The bright surface was obtained by selectively grinding away the unwanted bluing, which was no more than a superficial oxidation of the metal.   PT

REFERENCE: Thomas and Gamber 1976, pp. 156–57, no. B 19a

1. Anglo 2000, p. 227.
2. For a report on a joust in the Italian fashion, in which Maximilian ran against an envoy from Naples, see *Regesta Imperii* 1993, p. 304, no. 5966 (document dated March 11, 1498, Innsbruck).

Cat. 29

Rowel Spur for the Left Foot

South German, ca. 1500
Iron and copper alloy
L. 9⅝ in. (24.4 cm), W. 2¾ in. (7 cm), Diam. of rowel: 1¾ in. (4.5 cm), Wt. 9½ oz. (269.3 g)
The Metropolitan Museum of Art, New York, Gift of William H. Riggs, 1913 (14.25.1701b)

Overlaid with a copper alloy, this spur is made of iron and constructed with a long shank at the extremity of which a rowel is attached. Because the prevailing riding style in fifteenth-century Germany and most parts of Europe required horsemen to keep their legs forward, riders had to wear spurs with long shanks in order to reach their steeds' flanks to give them instructions. Gilded spurs belonged to the trappings of knighthood and were often ritually placed around the heels of aspirants during the knighting ceremony. It is not known whether the copper-alloy overlay on this example was originally gilded.

This spur once formed a pair with an example now preserved in the Kunsthistorisches Museum, Vienna; both are struck with the maker's mark—a shield enclosing the letter R—of an unidentified South German spur maker.[1]

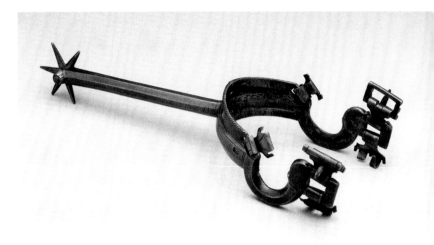

The existence of a mate in Vienna strongly suggests that the pair was originally made for use either at the court of Archduke Sigismund of Tyrol or at that of his great-nephew and successor, Maximilian I. William Henry Riggs of Paris acquired the Metropolitan Museum's spur from the collection of Prince Peter Soltykoff and later donated it to the Museum in 1913.   PT

REFERENCE: Grancsay 1955, n.p., no. 92, ill.

1. See Thomas and Gamber 1976, p. 210, no. A 131.

Cat. 30

Sallet for the Joust of War

Matthes Deutsch (active 1480–ca. 1515)
German (Landshut), ca. 1490
Steel
H. 9½ in. (24 cm), W. 8¼ in. (21 cm), D. 15⅜ in. (39 cm)
Musée de l'Armée, Paris (G 1)

Maximilian I was proud of the range of mock combats that were typically staged at his court, and he frequently took part in them. According to his autobiographical works, however, he also personally devised some of these knightly games. It is likely that he invented the variants of the joust of war in which the contestants were equipped with mechanical breastplates and shields (see cats. 31–33). In such jousts, the opponent's shield was the target for the sharp point of one's lance. Upon impact the mechanism freed the shield and propelled it into the air, much to the spectators' delight.

This exceptional sallet has a roller riveted along the front edge, a feature that strongly suggests that it was designed for one of the jousts of war for which mechanical breastplates and shields were required. Aside from two other specimens now in

London and New York,[1] it is the only example of its kind known to survive. The roller presumably ensured that the shield would not catch the helmet's lower edge and hit the wearer's face when the shield was struck and suddenly sprung upward. Over time, this safety feature seems to have been more commonly affixed to the bevor, the piece worn along with the sallet to protect the chin and throat, for this is how it appears in the woodcuts of Maximilian's *Triumphal Procession* (see cat. 162).[2] Because it was firmly bolted to the breastplate, the bevor was likely found to be a much more dependable place to attach the roller that guided the shield's ejection.

This sallet is forged in one piece; the lower part is flanged and pierced at each side with a pair of holes, the lower one now plugged. Stylized animal ears, horns, or other ephemeral adornments may have been fastened to these holes, just as the helmets are adorned in contemporary representations of the joust of war, including in *Freydal*, another of Maximilian's pseudo-autobiographical works (see cat. 50).[3]

The inspection mark and the maker's mark struck on each side of its tail indicate that the sallet was wrought in the Bavarian town of Landshut by Matthes Deutsch, a sought-after master who was one of the preferred makers of jousting armor in his day. An armor for the joust of war by his hand and now in the Kunsthistorisches Museum, Vienna, is believed to have been a gift that Maximilian received from Duke John of Saxony, one of Deutsch's chief patrons.[4]

This sallet was purchased by the Musée de l'Artillerie, Paris, at the sale of the collection of Dr. A. Hebray in 1838 and incorporated into the Musée de l'Armée upon its foundation in 1905.[5]   PT

REFERENCES: Penguilly L'Haridon 1862, p. 165, no. G. 1; Robert 1889–93, vol. 2 (1890), p. 43, no. G. 1; Reitzenstein 1963, p. 95, n. 14; *Landshuter Plattnerkunst* 1975, p. 23, no. 2, ill. no. 5

1. On the London example, see Mann 1962, vol. 1, p. 99, no. A80, pl. 56; Norman 1986, p. 43, no. A80. On the New York example, see Pyhrr 1989, pp. 102–11, figs. 32–35.
2. See Appelbaum 1964, p. 8, pls. 54, 55.
3. For examples of such attachments, see *Ritterturnier* 2014, p. 20, fig. 12, p. 100, fig. 97, pp. 220–21, fig. 224, and p. 167, no. 21b, ill.
4. Kunsthistorisches Museum, Vienna (R. IV). For the armor, see Thomas and Gamber 1976, pp. 163–64, no. R. IV. On Deutsch's oeuvre, see Reitzenstein 1963; Terjanian 2011, pp. 35–36.
5. Bonnefons de Lavialle 1838, no. 39, ill.

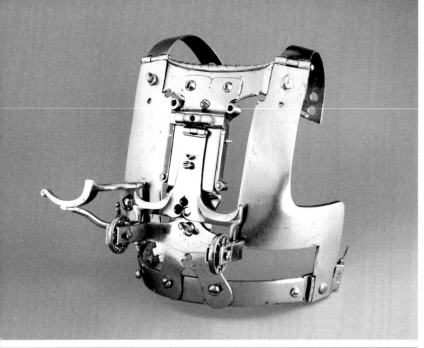

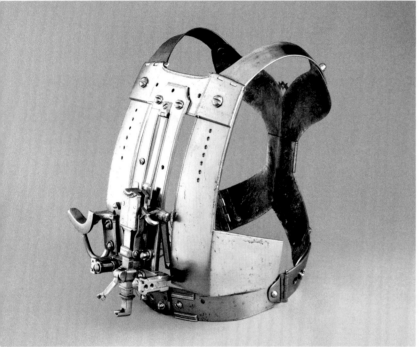

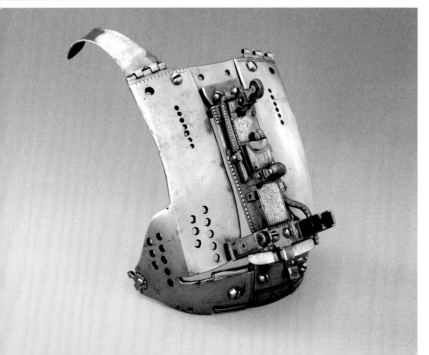

Cats. 31–33

Mechanical Breastplates for Variants of the Joust of War

South German, ca. 1480–1500

Steel and copper alloy

Kunsthistorisches Museum (B 21): H. 19^{11}⁄₁₆ in. (50 cm), W. 18½ in. (47 cm), D. 9½ in. (24 cm); Kunsthistorisches Museum (B 25): H. 14⁹⁄₁₆ in. (37 cm), W. 14⁹⁄₁₆ in. (37 cm), D. 19^{11}⁄₁₆ in. (50 cm); Musée de l'Armée (G 528): H. 13⅜ in. (34 cm), W. 12¼ in. (31 cm), D. 8⅝ in. (22 cm)

Kunsthistorisches Museum, Vienna, Imperial Armoury (B 21; B 25); Musée de l'Armée, Paris (G. 528)

Mechanical marvels for their time, these three unusual breastplates were designed to be worn by jousters and are the only examples of their kind known to survive. Each one has a spring-loaded mechanism that would have released an ejectable targe above the jouster's head the moment the targe was hit by the opponent's lance. The three breastplates were all made in the German-speaking lands, but not in the same way or in the same workshop, as there are notable variations in their execution, decoration, and mechanisms.

Although the breastplates are now all missing parts, a comparative study of their mechanisms establishes that they shared the same general working principles. They all have a central mechanical block that is, or was originally, fitted with a spring-loaded arm at each side. The lowest end of each arm was secured to the block, allowing the arm to pivot laterally and away from the block. The two arms were brought close together over the top of the block to firmly grab a piece on the back of the targe. The action of bringing them to that position placed springs inside the block under tension and activated an internal locking mechanism that prevented the springs from operating. The locking mechanism was released by depressing one or several levers that were kept by springs in close contact with movable rollers mounted on a forked structure at the bottom of the chest. When the targe was struck, the springs that held the rollers forward of the breastplate were overpowered, causing the rollers to slide backward and depress the levers that controlled the locking mechanism for the arms. The arms would then abruptly pivot sideways and release the targe from their catch. The presence of a small rest, either on the structure supporting the rollers or on the piece that prolongates the structure downward, suggests that the targe was loosely secured to the breastplate by another device on its backside. As there are no springs to propel it upward, it is likely that the targe would have been fitted with its own ejecting mechanism.

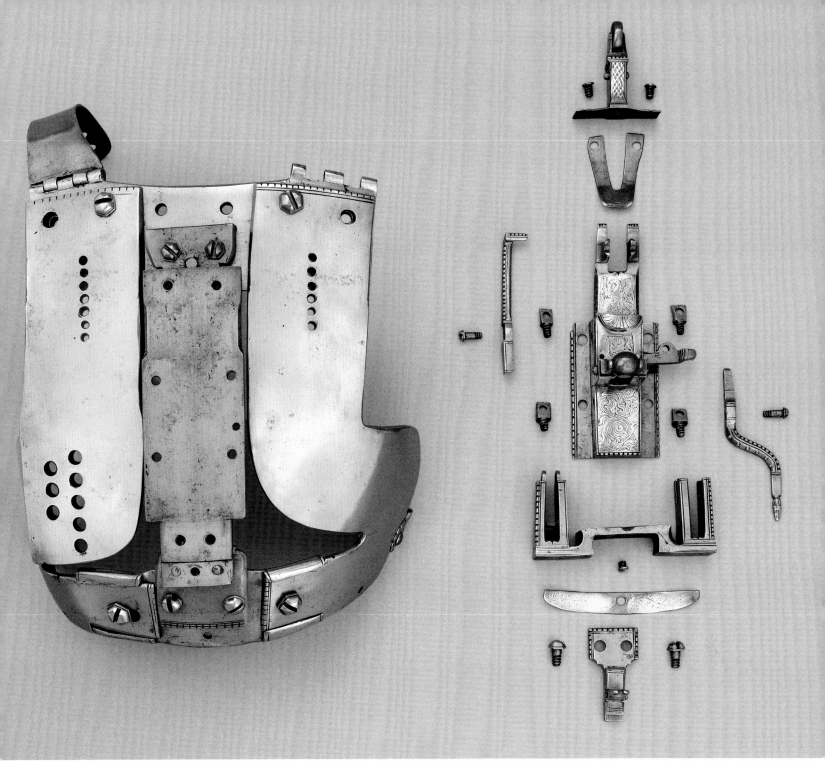

CAT. 33

Of these three breastplates, the one that retains two large rollers at the bottom is likely the earliest as it stylistically recalls late Gothic works by Innsbruck armorers and its mechanism, though robust, is less sophisticated (cat. 31).[1] The other two breastplates seem somewhat later. Closely related to each other in construction, they offer multiple settings for adjusting the force required to trigger their mechanisms and are also more carefully wrought and decorated. The example in the Musée de l'Armée is the more opulent of the two, as it has

copper-alloy pieces engraved with scrolling foliage, a mother pelican feeding her young with her blood to prevent starvation (a Christian symbol of redemption), and an escutcheon enclosing the figure of a lion rampant facing dexter. Once erroneously thought to represent the lion of the Palatinate, from which it differs in not having a crown, the heraldic beast might allude to the duchy of Brabant or the county of Flanders.[2] The first breastplate was possibly intended for a form of the joust of war known in German as the *Wulstrennen*, as it has no provisions for attaching a bevor or other type of face guard, and it does not completely cover the chest unlike the breastplates used in other variants of the joust of war. The other two were perhaps intended for the *Bundrennen*, a contest in which a large steel bracket fitted with a roller rose from each side of the breastplate to guard the jouster's face; the vertical series of holes beneath each shoulder would have provided suitable means of attachment for such brackets.[3]

The two breastplates now in Vienna unquestionably belonged to Maximilian I, who took great pride in staging, and personally participating in, an extravagant range of tournaments at his court. Although most of the works on paper celebrating the variety of mock combats that he favored date to the final decade of his life, the ideas for them came much earlier. Already in 1478, Maximilian informed his father's chief chamberlain that he had conceived many rare knightly games.[4] The truth of these claims is strongly suggested by the inclusion of a mechanical device to carry a shield among the pieces that the Augsburg armorer Lorenz Helmschmid delivered to Maximilian in 1480, and by the presence of a full-time locksmith among the personnel in charge of maintaining his armory (see cats. 16, 17).[5]

The breastplates now in Vienna may possibly be the two examples for the *Bundrennen* that were in the archducal armory of Innsbruck in 1555.[6] They entered the Kunsthistorisches Museum's Arms Collection (Waffensammlung) in 1889.[7] The example in Paris was in the collection of the Musée de l'Artillerie by 1862.[8] Its earlier history is not known. PT

REFERENCES: cat. 31: Thomas and Gamber 1976, pp. 172–73, no. B 21, fig. 82; cat. 32: Thomas and Gamber 1976, p. 173, no. B 25, fig. 83; Gamber and Beaufort-Spontin 1978, pp. 17–18, fig. 1; cat. 33: Penguilly L'Haridon 1862, p. 231, no. G. 164, ill.; Reverseau 1982, p. 70, and p. 71, ill. no. 8; Reverseau 1990, p. 84, no. 65, ill.

1. For examples of Innsbruck armor of plain steel and comparable simplicity, see Thomas and Gamber 1954, pls. 8, 9, 16, 17, 22.
2. Lorey 1941, p. 114, no. 1488.
3. On the *Wulstrennen* and the general appearance of the brackets used in the *Bundrennen*, see Appelbaum 1964, p. 8, pls. 56, 50, respectively.
4. Maximilian I to Sigmund Prüschenk, June 24, 1478, in Kraus 1875, p. 35.
5. On the device in question, see Archives Départementales du Nord, Lille, B 2124, fol. 295v; on the locksmith Hans Kyeringen, alias Hans Slosser, "maker of the locks" in Maximilian's armory, see Archives Départementales du Nord, Lille, B 2127, fols. 191r, 196r, 221r, 234v.
6. Schönherr 1890, p. CLVIII, no. 7164.
7. The Imperial Armoury department was known as the Waffensammlung until 1989.
8. See Penguilly L'Haridon 1862, p. 231, no. G. 164, ill. The Musée de l'Artillerie, Paris, merged with the Musée Historique de l'Armée in 1905 to form the Musée de l'Armée.

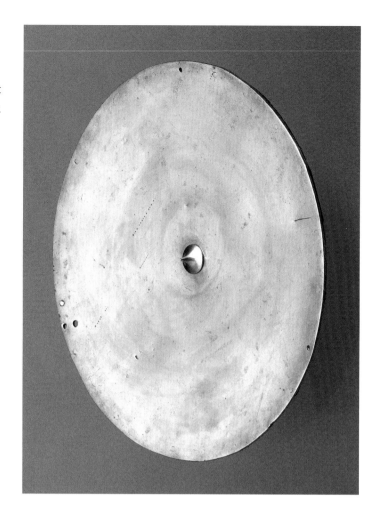

Cat. 34

Rondel for the Joust of War

South German, ca. 1490–1510
Steel
Diam. 16⅛ in. (41 cm)
Musée de l'Armée, Paris (G. 529)

This rondel, a large disk of steel, was intended for one of the unusual forms of the joust of war favored by Maximilian I. As a target for the opponent's lance, it may have been affixed by a contraption to the breastplate and overlaid with smaller plates, which would scatter dramatically upon impact as if the rondel had shattered from the force of the blow. The visual effect made possible by this conceit can be appreciated thanks to the Augsburg artist Hans Burgkmair, who represented it in a print that features jousters equipped for this specific contest (known in German as the *Scheibenrennen*) and belongs to a suite of 137 woodcuts generally known as the *Triumph of Maximilian* (fig. 34).

Alternatively, the rondel may have been a reinforcing piece for the steel targe worn in the Italian joust of war (*Welschrennen* in German), a contest for which specialized tournament armor mimicking the appearance of Italian field armor was required (see cats. 35, 36). Jousters armed with shields and rondels for this type of mock combat can be seen in another print by Burgkmair for the *Triumph of Maximilian* (fig. 35). The vacant holes along the edge of the rondel were meant for rivets that would have secured a lining on the opposite side of the piece, as is made clear by a comparable rondel in the Musée de l'Armée's collection, which retains its original leather lining.[1] The present rondel was in the collection of the Musée de l'Artillerie, Paris, by 1890.[2]   PT

REFERENCE: Robert 1889–93, vol. 2 (1890), p. 126, no. G. 529

1. This and the comparable rondel are grouped under the same inventory number.
2. The Musée de l'Artillerie, Paris, merged with the Musée Historique de l'Armée in 1905 to form the Musée de l'Armée.

FIG. 34 Hans Burgkmair (1473–1531). *Joust of War with Disks*, detail from the *Triumph of Maximilian*, 1796 (first edition 1526). Woodcut. Albertina Museum, Vienna (DG1931/35/52)

FIG. 35 Hans Burgkmair (1473–1531). *Italian Joust of War*, detail from the *Triumph of Maximilian*, 1796 (first edition 1526). Woodcut. Albertina Museum, Vienna (DG1931/35/49)

Helm for the Italian Joust of War

Attributed to Lorenz Helmschmid (first recorded 1467, died 1516)
South German, ca. 1490
Steel and leather
H. 12⅝ in. (32 cm), W. 9⁷⁄₁₆ in. (24 cm), D. 13⅜ in. (34 cm),
Wt. 11 lb. 5.31 oz. (5,140 g)
Royal Armouries, Leeds, acquired with support from the Art Fund and The Pilgrims Trust (IV.502)

The only helm of its kind to survive, this piece was designed for a rare variant of the joust of war, one that the Germans generally called the *Welschrennen* (*Welsch* translates as Gallic) in reference to the Romance languages of the places in which it was most popular, such as Italy. Whereas the Italian joust of war normally took place in the open field, the Italian joust of peace typically required a tilt, a barrier of cloth or wood that separated the contestants. The German-made armors for the *Welschrennen* were intended to be used in the Italian fashion and designed to resemble Italian field armor. For that reason, they were modeled after—though constructed differently from—Italian prototypes and featured helms reminiscent of the Italian men-at-arms' helmet of choice, the armet.

An armet is traditionally worn with a buffe, a reinforcing element that provides additional protection for the lower half of the face and that bridges the vulnerable gap between the helmet and breastplate that would have otherwise been exposed. Unlike an armet, this helm has no cheekpieces hinged to the bowl; instead, it has two plates to guard the face that are pivoted on the same points as the brow defense, in the manner of a close helmet. Although the upper edges of the deep plates that extend below the neckline at the front and back visually suggest that the wearer could have freely rotated his head, the plates are riveted to the bowl and lowermost face guard, making it impossible for those pieces to move independently of them. In addition, the same plates are pierced at the bottom with circular holes so that the helm could be firmly screwed to the cuirass and become capable of withstanding the impact of an incoming lance fitted with a sharp-pointed head.

The excellent workmanship that went into making this helm is evident in the careful modeling and close fit of the plates. Although plain, it includes decorative refinements such as simple but effective fretting near the lower edge of the front neck plate. The helm has been conclusively shown to be part of an ensemble of pieces made by the Augsburg armorer Lorenz Helmschmid for Maximilian I. The majority of these items are

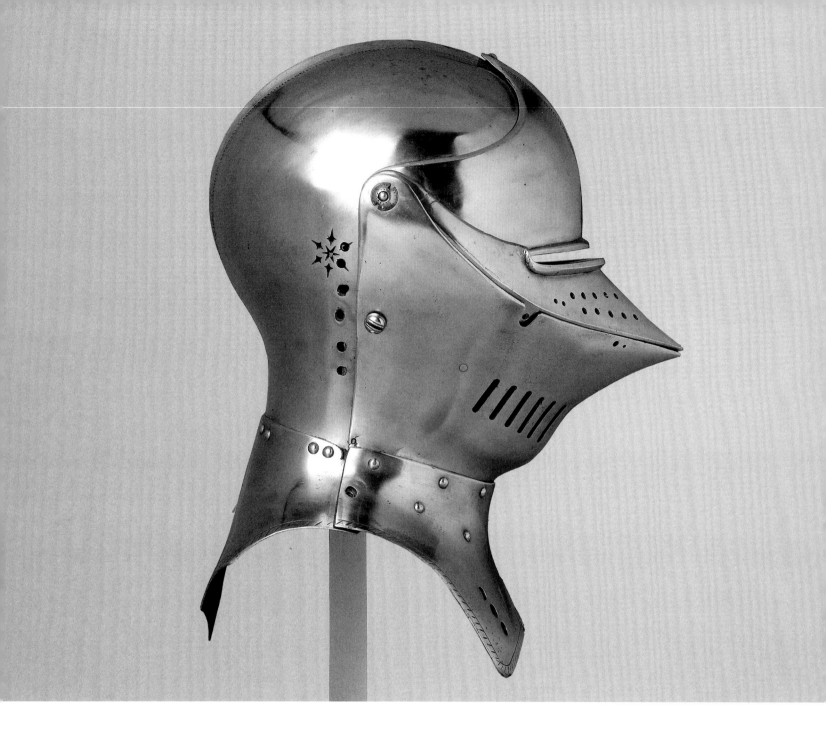

now in Vienna, though it is probable that a similarly formed and decorated armet with buffe, reinforcing pate, and nape defenses in the armory of the counts of Trapp at Churburg Castle in South Tyrol originally belonged to the same group.[1]

The present helm was in the Arms Collection (Waffensammlung) of the Kunsthistorisches Museum, Vienna,[2] until about 1936, when it was offered at auction and purchased at the sale for William Randolph Hearst.[3] Kept in Saint Donat's Castle, Wales, it was one of fifty-two objects that the Royal Armouries purchased in 1952 from the National Magazine Company, one of Hearst's enterprises, with the help of the

Pilgrim Trust, National Art Collections Fund, and a special Exchequer Grant. PT

REFERENCES: Gamber 1959a, pp. 6, 10–11, and p. 8, fig. 8, p. 9, fig. 10; Scalini 1996, p. 98, and p. 105, ill. no. III.15; Pyhrr 2014, p. 93, and p. 94, fig. 27

1. On the related armet, see Thomas and Gamber 1954, pp. 61–62, no. 44, pl. 24 (erroneously attributed to the armorer Hans Müllner); Gamber 1959a, pp. 6, 14 (fol. 64v), and p. 9, fig. 14; Scalini 1996, p. 98, ill. pp. 230, 284, no. CH S66.
2. The Imperial Armoury department was known as the Waffensammlung until 1989.
3. Formerly Kunsthistorisches Museum, Vienna (B 24). See Sotheby's 1936, p. 20, no. 133, ill.; Pyhrr 2014, p. 93, and p. 94, fig. 27.

Cat. 36

Left Arm Defense for the Italian Joust of War

Attributed to Lorenz Helmschmid (first recorded 1467, died 1516)
or Jörg Helmschmid the Younger (first recorded 1488, died 1502)
South German (Augsburg), ca. 1490
Steel
L. 24⅝ in. (62.6 cm), W. 8½ in. (21.5 cm), D. 5⅛ in. (13 cm)
Kunsthistorisches Museum, Vienna, Imperial Armoury (B 169)

This defense for the left arm would have been worn in the
Welschrennen, the Italian variant of the joust of war as it was
practiced in the German-speaking lands. It consists of an
upper cannon formed from a single plate on the outer side
and a vertical row of nine overlapping lames on the interior.
A couter projects to a point over the outside of the elbow, with
two articulating lames above and another two below, the lowermost of which has a scalloped lower edge. A lower cannon,
shaped from a single plate to enclose the entire forearm, continues over the back of the hand and is extended by one plate
over the thumb and two wider plates over the remaining fingers.
Two vacant holes on the lower cannon, one in the forearm and
the other in the back of the hand, would have been used to
secure a protective rondel over each.

Like the helm for the same contest discussed in catalogue
entry 35, this arm defense exhibits the highest quality of
workmanship and is a masterpiece of deception. The lower
cannon is embossed with a chevron-like rib to simulate the
peaked cuff of a gauntlet. Five flutes flank this rib to under-
score its shape and contribute to the illusion that a separate
gauntlet is present, while comparable flutes replicate the
artifice over the back of the hand and thumb. The series of
punched lines that extend across the plates guarding the
fingers until they meet strategically placed rivets serve no
purpose other than to falsely signal the existence of articulated plates.

The artifice and skill required to give elements specially
constructed for the joust the appearance of conventional
items for the field are likely to have appealed to such a great
connoisseur as Maximilian I, for whom this piece was made,
not least because they contributed to making the contests that
he organized both unique and memorable. Additional examples of this rare type of arm defense are preserved in the
Kunsthistorisches Museum of Vienna, the Real Armería of
Madrid, and the Metropolitan Museum.[1] This arm defense
entered the Kunsthistorisches Museum's Arms Collection
(Waffensammlung) in 1889.[2]   PT

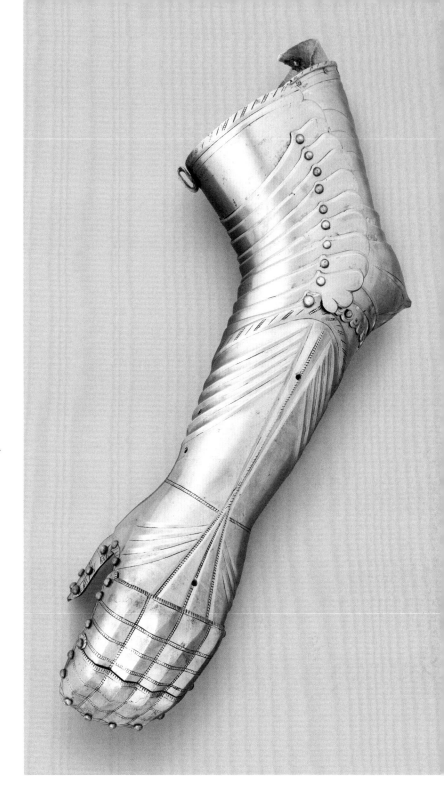

REFERENCE: Thomas and Gamber 1976, p. 154, no. B 169

1. On these elements, see Gamber 1959a, p. 6, and p. 9, fig. 16; *Arte y
caballería en España* 2007, pp. 100–101, 490, no. 6, ill. The Metropolitan
Museum's example (25.135.99b) is unpublished.
2. The Imperial Armoury department was known as the Waffensammlung
until 1989.

Foot Combat Armor of Claude de Vaudrey

Italian (Milan), ca. 1485
Steel, copper alloy, and leather
H. 70½ in. (179 cm), W. 35⅜ in. (90 cm), D. 24 in. (61 cm)
Kunsthistorisches Museum, Vienna, Imperial Armoury (B 33)

This armor belonged to the Burgundian nobleman Claude de Vaudrey and was worn by him in a historic contest that he fought against Maximilian I in the German city of Worms, probably on September 3, 1495, in which Vaudrey was ultimately defeated. Maximilian kept the armor as a trophy and material evidence of his superior prowess. His victory in this momentous encounter is also celebrated in his pseudo-autobiographical work *Freydal*, which includes a scene of the combat (see cats. 39, 48).

Vaudrey was one of the most illustrious knights in late fifteenth-century Europe. Renowned for his bravery in both the tournament and battle, he called attention to his martial abilities at the festivities held to celebrate the marriage of Charles the Bold and Margaret of York in 1468, as well as in other mock combats thereafter, many of which he personally organized. As a loyal servant of the dukes of Burgundy, he staunchly defended their dominions from French attacks following Charles's death, frequently putting his life at risk in combat.[1] His conduct earned him the admiration of his enemies, among them Charles VIII of France, who after seeing him fight in a tournament held in Paris willingly restituted lands that he had seized from Vaudrey in wartime. Another eyewitness at the Paris tournament, the German knight Conrad Grüneberg, makes a special mention of Vaudrey in the celebrated armorial that he compiled.[2]

Maximilian had a chance to behold the singular vigor and skills of the larger-than-life Burgundian hero at a tournament held in Antwerp in 1494. The opportunity to fight him materialized when Vaudrey, reportedly moved by a vision that he should compete against the "premier king in the world" in an arena, begged Maximilian to accept his challenge a few months before the ruler was to attend an imperial summit, or diet, in Worms in 1495. Although the existing accounts of the encounter that ultimately took place there do not quite agree on the scope of the contest, which apparently began with a joust, it is clear enough that it was concluded on foot and with swords, inside an enclosure. The end of the fight triggered a larger combat, also fought with swords, by two groups of armored men massed around the enclosure for the spectators' enjoyment. Onlookers included Maximilian's wife Bianca Maria Sforza, as well as many more women of rank, various German and Burgundian noblemen, and envoys from Spain, Venice, and other foreign powers. Maximilian and Vaudrey impressed their distinguished audience with demonstrations of chivalrous politeness. As a token of appreciation of his opponent's bravery, Maximilian awarded to Vaudrey a golden chain and ring, the prizes to which, as the victor, he was entitled. Vaudrey, in turn, refused the prizes and presented them to Maximilian's wife instead.[3]

The armor consists of sixteen elements: a large helm; a breastplate and backplate secured together by hinges at the left and snapping pegs at the right; a deep tonlet of eight lames at the front and back, originally hinged at the left side and closed with snapping pegs at the right; deep symmetrical pauldrons of six lames each; vambraces; gauntlets (the left one is associated); cuisses that fully enclose the thighs; greaves; and sabatons that entirely encase the feet.

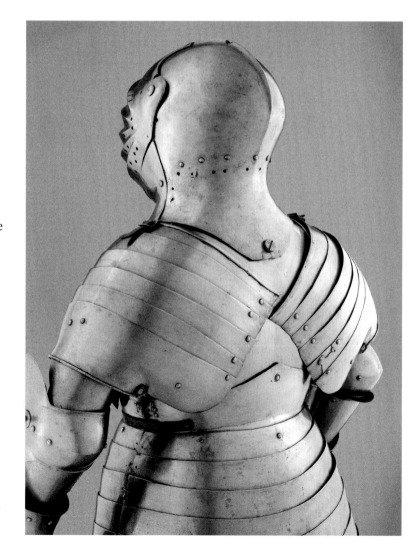

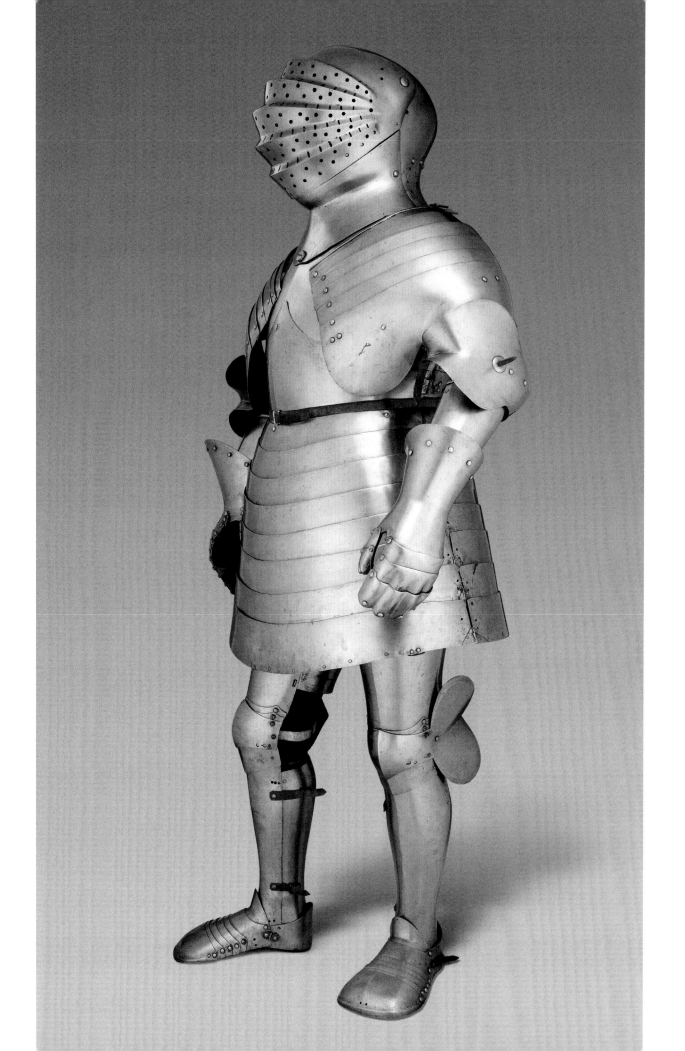

The armor is struck with the mark of the letters MER at the top of each vambrace, and with the mark of the letters DMY around the split legs of a cross on the helm and right gauntlet. These are the marks of Milanese armorers. The first one could conceivably refer to members of either the Merate or Meravaglia family, while the second can be attributed to the armorer Damiano Missaglia, who is documented in Milan from 1472 to 1514.[4] The conjunction of these marks raises the possibility that the present armor was not made as a unit, but customized by Vaudrey from elements he acquired from diverse sources. A noted armor connoisseur, Vaudrey is said to have continually sought to perfect armor design. He owned an extensive personal armory that apparently made a big impression on those able to see it.[5]

The armor was in the archducal armory in Innsbruck in 1555, when it was described as the victor's prize earned by Maximilian in a foot combat against Vaudrey. In Ambras Castle by 1596, it was removed to Vienna in 1806 and became part of the Kunsthistorisches Museum's Arms Collection (Waffensammlung) in 1889.[6]   PT

REFERENCES: Boccia and Coelho 1967, pp. 222–23, 230–31, pl. 153; Thomas and Gamber 1976, pp. 183–84, no. B 33, fig. 88

1. Molinet 1827–28, vol. 2 (1828), pp. 44–55.
2. Bischoff 2003, pp. 168–70.
3. Angermeier 1981, vol. 1, pt. 2, p. 1117, vol. 2, pp. 1680–82, 1708–10, 1803, 1811–12.
4. On these marks, see Boccia 1982, p. 292, nos. 145, 146.
5. Anglo 2000, p. 214; Bischoff 2003, p. 168.
6. Schönherr 1890, p. CLIX, no. 7164; Luchner 1958, p. 21. The Imperial Armoury department was known as the Waffensammlung until 1989.

Cat. 38

Armor for the Italian Joust of Peace of Gaspare Sanseverino d'Aragona, alias Fracasso

Missaglia workshop
Italian (Milan), ca. 1490
Steel, gold, and copper alloy
As mounted: H. 72⅞ in. (185 cm, including mount),
W. 26¾ in. (68 cm), D. 26¾ in. (68 cm)
Kunsthistorisches Museum, Vienna, Imperial Armoury (S I)

This massive Italian jousting armor, one of only three known examples of its kind, was specially made in Milan for Gaspare Sanseverino d'Aragona. Also known as Fracasso, a nickname he earned for his impetuosity and physical strength, Gaspare was a mercenary captain and diplomat famous in Italy for his skills in the tournament.

Maximilian I was intrigued by Fracasso's reputation as an expert jouster in the Italian fashion, which was not commonly practiced in the German-speaking lands, and formally invited him to the Innsbruck court in January 1498, requesting that he arrive with the appropriate armor and horses.[1] As in the German joust of peace, the opponents in the joust in the Italian fashion wore specialized armor and used lances with heads terminating in multiple prongs, or coronels, instead of single sharp points. Unlike the German tradition, in which the jousters' horses ran toward each other at large, or in an open setting, opponents in the Italian joust were separated by a barrier, often cloth but more commonly a solid wood fence called the tilt. Because the tilt prevented the horses from accidentally colliding, the riders were able to run as close to the tilt as possible and maximize the impact of their lances.[2] The contest was thus quite dangerous.

Less than a month after he received the invitation, Fracasso arrived with a retinue of thirty-three horsemen in Innsbruck, where he was received with great honor and immediately invited to watch a tournament.[3] In a private meeting the next day, Maximilian told Fracasso of his ambition to personally joust against him in the Italian fashion.[4] Visibly curious about the contest, Maximilian was ready to put his abilities to the test against one of its most illustrious and successful practitioners in all of Italy. According to a papal legate who was present, the jousts in the German and Italian fashions being staged in Innsbruck were the sole focus of everyone's attention.[5] Fracasso was a formidable opponent. Authorized to compete with one of Maximilian's masters of arms and jousting instructors, he wounded the man when his lance found its way into the latter's helm.[6]

Although Fracasso was scheduled to joust against Maximilian a few weeks later, the much-awaited contest was canceled after the latter sustained a leg injury in another tournament; Fracasso jousted against an envoy from Naples instead.[7] As Fracasso was a high-ranking official at the duke of Milan's court, Maximilian had no choice but to grant him permission to return to his master since the prospect of running against him had faded.[8] He wrote the duke to thank him for having allowed such a remarkable man to participate in his tournaments and presented Fracasso with gifts that included a horse and goldsmiths' works.[9] In return, the celebrated Italian jouster presented Maximilian with an armor and four horses, which were estimated together at 400 ducats.[10] Although Maximilian appears to have purchased one of Fracasso's armors for the remarkable sum of 73 florins of the Rhine in 1502, the object seems to have been a field armor.

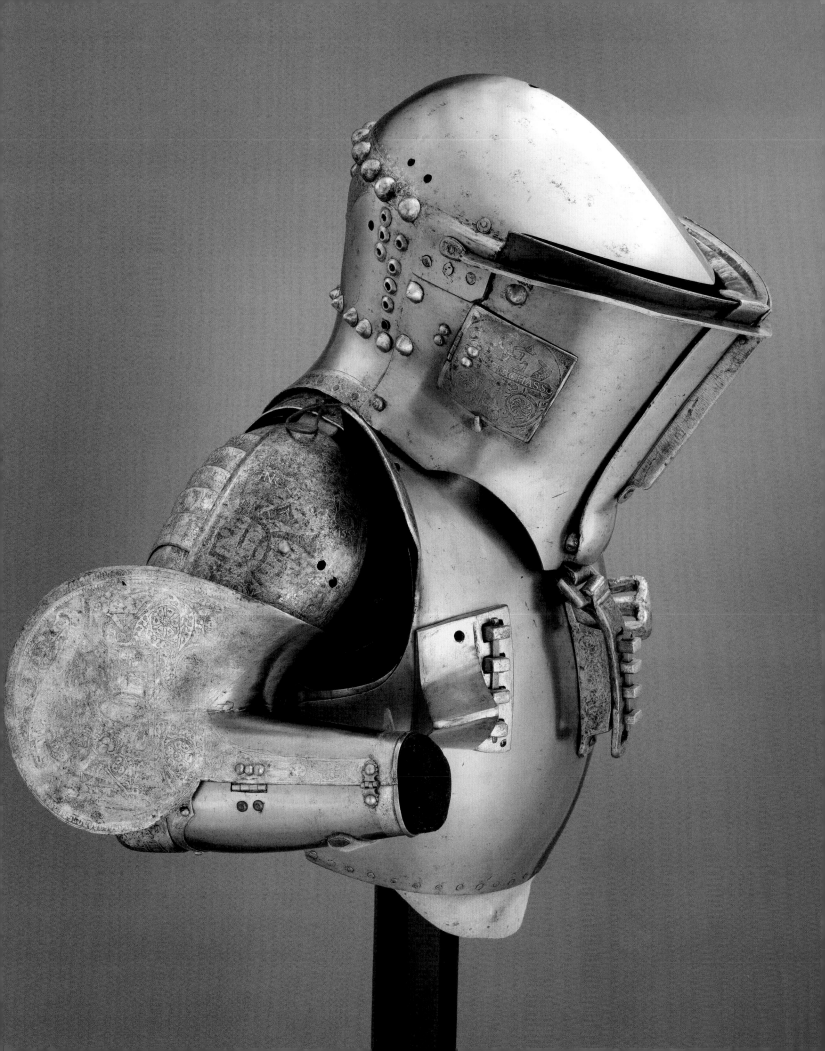

Accordingly, the jousting armor under consideration is likely to be the one that Fracasso had brought with him to Innsbruck and presented to Maximilian upon his departure.[11]

Although it is now missing several elements (such as the left pauldron and arm, a pair of besagews, a waist plate with a left tasset, and a tilting targe), Fracasso's armor is outstanding for its completeness, workmanship, and opulence. Comprising a helm, a breastplate and backplate secured by steel straps at the shoulders, a reinforcing breastplate with a protective flange at the right shoulder, a right pauldron with a reinforcing plate, and a right arm defense, it is the finest surviving example of its kind. The massive helm—almost twice the size of a German helm for the joust of peace and fitted with a wide reinforce at the left side of the face plate—is etched and gilded on the right side with an emblem of three interlocking Gs (for Fracasso's first name), each letter fitted with a diamond as if it were a ring, and with a banderole that encloses the words SIGNOR FRACHASSO. Other parts of the armor are etched and gilded with the same motifs as well as with foliage, trophies of arms, putti, unicorns, and other mythological figures, all set against a hatched ground.

The armor is struck on the right side of the face plate and on the right arm defense with the maker's mark of the letters MY surmounted by an open coronet. The same mark is repeated twice, albeit in etched and gilded form, on the back of the nape plate. Used by successive members of the Missaglia, a family of illustrious Milanese armorers, it identifies Fracasso's armor as one of their works. In the absence of records conclusively linking the mark to a specific individual, the identity of the master who created this exceptional object cannot be determined.

Likely to be Fracasso's gift to Maximilian, the armor remained in Tyrol. In the collection of Ambras Castle by 1595, it was removed to Vienna in 1806 and became part of the Kunsthistorisches Museum's Arms Collection (Waffensammlung) in 1889.[12] PT

REFERENCES: Gamber 1958, pp. 83–85, fig. 65; Boccia and Coelho 1967, pp. 221, 228–29, pl. 145; Thomas and Gamber 1976, pp. 184–85, no. S. I (B 2), fig. 86

1. *Regesta Imperii* 1993, p. 268, no. 5745 (document dated January 17, 1498, Innsbruck).
2. Anglo 2000, pp. 227–38.
3. *Regesta Imperii* 1993, p. 290, no. 5881 (document dated February 16, 1498, Hall near Innsbruck).
4. Ibid., p. 291, no. 5884 (document dated February 17, 1498, Innsbruck).
5. Ibid., pp. 299–300, no. 5934 (document dated March 3, 1498, Hall near Innsbruck).
6. Ibid., pp. 295–96, no. 5910 (document dated February 24, 1498, Innsbruck).
7. Ibid., pp. 298–99, no. 5930 (document dated March 2, 1498, Innsbruck), pp. 299–300, no. 5934 (document dated March 3, 1498, Hall near Innsbruck), p. 304, no. 5966 (document dated March 11, 1498, Innsbruck).
8. Ibid., p. 298, no. 5926 (document dated March 1, 1498, Innsbruck), p. 308, no. 5999 (document dated March 18, 1498, Innsbruck).
9. Ibid., p. 308, no. 5994 (document dated March 17, 1498, Innsbruck), p. 308, no. 5997 (document dated March 17, 1498, [Innsbruck]).
10. Sanuto 1496–1533/1879–1903, vol. 1 (1879), cols. 921–22 (diary entry of March 1498).
11. *Regesta Imperii* 2002, p. 117, no. 16477 (document dated May 17, 1502, Augsburg).
12. The Imperial Armoury department was known as the Waffensammlung until 1989.

CAT. 39 *Foot Combat between Claude de Vaudrey and Freydal* (fol. 39)

Cats. 39–43

The *Freydal* Miniatures in Vienna

South German, 1512–15
Gouache with gold and silver highlights over pen, pencil,
and leadpoint on paper
Each sheet: 15¹⁄₁₆ x 10⁹⁄₁₆ in. (38.2 x 26.8 cm)
Kunsthistorisches Museum, Vienna, Kunstkammer (5073)

The *Freydal* illuminated manuscript housed at the Kunsthistorisches Museum, Vienna, is the largest tournament book of the late Middle Ages and the most important surviving record of Maximilian I's incomplete memorial project of the same name.[1] In preparing his own commemoration for posterity, Maximilian commissioned *Freydal* alongside such printed works as the *Triumphal Procession* (see cat. 162), the *Arch of Honor* (cat. 165), *Theuerdank* (cats. 108, 109), and the *Weisskunig* (cats. 114–17), as well as his monumental tomb in the Court Church (Hofkirche), Innsbruck.

Freydal is most closely related to the emperor's other autobiographically inspired, poetic volumes, the *Weisskunig* and *Theuerdank*, in which parts of Maximilian's life are encrypted in literary form. Both *Theuerdank* and *Freydal* are based on the events leading up to Maximilian's marriage to Mary of Burgundy, which took place in Ghent in 1477. *Freydal* portrays the titular hero's performance in tournaments during his search for a wife, whereas *Theuerdank* documents the subsequent dangers the eponymous hero of this tale faces on the journey to marry his betrothed.

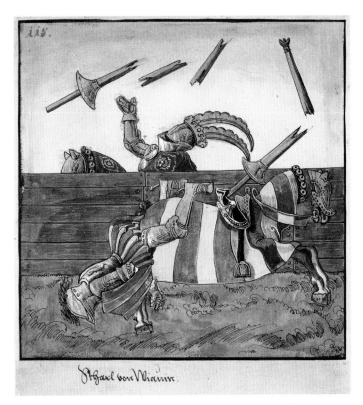

CAT. 40 *Italian Joust of Peace between "Scharl von Wiauin" and Freydal* (fol. 118)

CAT. 41 *Joust of War between Freydal and Anton von Yvan* (fol. 101)

In *Freydal*, the young hero must enter a series of tournaments to prove himself worthy to ask for the hand of a princess. The tale opens with three noble maidens enjoining the hero to compete in these tournaments to demonstrate his love. Freydal accepts the challenge and participates in competitions hosted by the finest courts in the realm. He engages in sixty-four tournaments, each featuring two types of joust and one combat on foot, and each followed by a masquerade ball. At the end of the tournament series, one of the three maidens—a powerful queen—confesses her love to the hero in a letter, whereupon Freydal strikes out to find her. The book ends at this point, but the story continues in *Theuerdank*.[2]

Both *Freydal* and *Theuerdank* were intended to appear in print. *Theuerdank* was completed in 1517, with copies printed on paper and vellum. At that time, and even by the emperor's death in 1519, *Freydal* was nowhere near complete. The text remained in draft form, and a mere five of the 256 total scenes were trial printed. Fortunately, however, all of the scenes had been outlined in miniature for the emperor's review and approval, and they are now preserved in the Viennese manuscript (only 255 scenes remain as one of the miniatures has been missing since at least about 1600). In nearly all of these images, the participants—the tournament opponents and the mummery dancers—are identified by name; archival evidence places most of these individuals within the emperor's

entourage, such as Claude de Vaudrey in folio 39 (cat. 39) and Anton von Yvan in folio 101 (cat. 41).

Across the 127 miniatures in *Freydal* that depict horseback jousts, no fewer than eleven varieties of this chivalrous sport are depicted, making the volume a vital pictorial source on late medieval tournaments (see cats. 40–42).[3] The joust known as the Italian joust of peace (*Welsches Gestech*) was carried out over a wood plank, or tilt, that separated the riders. The tilt allowed jousters to ride more closely past each other and to strike frontally, which was more forceful and thus caused their lances to splinter in spectacular fashion. In the *Scharfrennen* (joust of war with "flying" shields), opponents rode toward each other with pointed spears. The objective was to dislodge the shield hooked loosely on the opponent's chest and throw him from his horse. In the *Anzogenrennen* (joust of war with fixed shields), the shield was screwed tightly to the armor so that it could not be knocked off; instead, the aim was to unseat one's opponent from his horse, aided by the increased impact of the lance. In the *Bundrennen* (joust of war with "flying" shields and without bevors), competitors wore special breastplates equipped with a complicated spring mechanism that held their shields loaded in place; if a contestant managed to strike his opponent's shield in the right spot, the mechanism released and shot the shield high into the air (see cats. 32, 33). Riders in this joust wore a guard of iron brackets and rollers

CAT. 42 *Free Tourney between Freydal and Charles de Croÿ* (fol. 109)

CAT. 43 *Masquerade* (fol. 207)

designed to guide the shield upward. In the *Feldrennen* (or *Kampfrennen*, joust of war in reinforced field armor), riders attempted to reconstruct wartime skirmishes under tournament conditions; their equipment therefore approximated that used on the battlefield, and both rider and horse were fully armored. A rare variant of horseback jousting was the *Krönlrennen* (mixed form of joust of war and joust of peace), in which one rider wore the armor typical of a joust of peace and brandished the pointed lance used in a joust of war, while the other dressed for a joust of war and wielded the pronged lance used in a joust of peace.

The Viennese manuscript also provides the most extensive visual record of mummery, the costumed dance of the late medieval court. Mummery was the earliest type of courtly masquerade and served as the precursor to ballet, which would emerge as the preferred dance form of the nobility over the course of the seventeenth century. Mummery can be traced back to the early Middle Ages in France, but it first reached its pinnacle in Germany under Maximilian, who had encountered it in Burgundy in the 1470s and 1480s. An established component of early modern tournaments, mummery was the evening's entertainment after the day's contests. The somewhat (and only somewhat) more relaxed manners on display in the evening allowed for levels of communication that were otherwise unavailable in the highly regimented

life of the court. The costumes worn at late medieval masquerades typically reflected national identities, professions, or social classes, such as Burgundian or Ottoman styles or the attire of hunters, merchants, or miners. Coats of hair were fashioned for mummeries featuring so-called "wild men," dances with giants used superstructures constructed of wood and papier-mâché, and numbers starring heroes of antiquity sometimes even included dancers wearing costumes that made them appear to be naked. One of the most surprising forms of mummery can be found in folio 207 (cat. 43), in which the men dancing don women's dresses. Cross-dressing is no modern invention. Although the names of participants in this mummery have not survived, records show that a similar costume ball was held in honor of Frederick the Wise, prince elector of Saxony, and John, prince elector of Saxony, who visited Innsbruck in March 1498. SK

REFERENCES: Leitner 1880–82; Krause 2019a; Krause 2019b

1. See Leitner 1880–82; Krause 2019a; Krause 2019b.
2. Drawn from draft text for "Ritter Freydalb," Österreichische Nationalbibliothek, Vienna, Cod. 2831*, fol. 83v.
3. For a discussion on English terminology for these very specific German forms of the joust, see Capwell 2019. Importantly, there is a notable difference between the joust of war of the High Middle Ages and the German *Rennen* depicted in *Freydal*. Initially a warlike contest, by the fifteenth century the joust of war had predominantly become a sport-like mock combat.

Cats. 44–52

The *Freydal* Sketches in Washington, D.C.

South German, ca. 1512–15

Pen in brown and black ink with watercolor over black chalk and leadpoint on laid paper

Each sheet: 13 x 10⅜ in. (33 x 26.3 cm)

National Gallery of Art, Washington, D.C., Rosenwald Collection

The genesis of *Freydal* has proven difficult to reconstruct in detail, given the paltry body of source material on the tournament book. Now, fortunately, many previously unknown planning sketches have been rediscovered, including several rough drawings in Rome[1] and an extensive collection of colored illustrations at the National Gallery of Art in Washington, D.C. Studied alongside the Viennese manuscript, these sketches provide a new perspective on the artistic evolution of the tournament book as well as Maximilian I's commemorative works as a whole.

The sketches are first recorded in the collection of Prussian Grand Master of Ceremonies Frédéric de Pourtalès in the first half of the nineteenth century.[2] In 1929 and 1930, the drawings were acquired by Lessing J. Rosenwald of Jenkintown, Pennsylvania, and later they found their way to Washington.[3] The Washington collection has 203 colored sketches, including 120 devoted to jousting events on horseback, fifty-five to foot combat, and twenty-eight to mummeries. An additional page from this set is today housed in the British Museum, London, while another was last recorded at auction at Sotheby's in 1923.[4]

In 1502 Maximilian appears to have begun plans to document his masquerades in a book, ordering court tailor Martin Trummer to "have drawn in a book all those costumes as yet seen in mummeries organized by his majesty."[5] Although the work on *Freydal* is not verifiably documented until 1512, the first planning sketches may have been created in the intervening years. In a letter from October 14, 1512, addressed to his counselor and close confidant Sigmund von Dietrichstein, Maximilian writes that "*Freydal* is half conceived, the largest part of which we have made in Cologne," and that "the figures [i.e., printing blocks] belonging to *Freydal*, of which there are two and one half hundred, have not yet been carved."[6]

Maximilian took up residence in Cologne from mid-June to mid-October 1512; he appears to have used this time to develop a number of his commemorative projects, because the same letter contains discussions of his work on *Theuerdank* (cats. 108, 109), the *Genealogy* (cat. 166), the *Triumphal Chariot* (cat. 164), and the *Weisskunig* (cats. 114–17). According

CAT. 44 *Masquerade* (1943.3.4393)

CAT. 45 *Mixed Joust of War and Joust of Peace between Felix von Werdenberg and Freydal* (1943.3.4418)

CAT. 46 *Joust of War between Christoph Lamberger and Freydal* (1943.3.4461)

CAT. 47 *Joust of War between Freydal and Christoph Schenk von Limpurg* (1943.3.4491)

CAT. 48 *Foot Combat between Claude de Vaudrey or Ramyng and Freydal* (1943.3.4530)

CAT. 49 *Italian Joust of Peace between Freydal and Friedrich von Horn* (1943.3.4505)

CAT. 50 *Joust of War between Freydal and Sigmund von Welsberg* (1943.3.4476)

to the letter, the final number of illustrations (approximately 250) in *Freydal* had been decided by 1512. There is no surviving documentation to elucidate which part of the book Maximilian is discussing when he writes that *Freydal* "is half conceived," but this was more likely in reference to preparatory designs—such as those in Washington—than to the Viennese miniatures.

The *Freydal* sketches in Washington also shed light on the editorial work behind the emperor's commemorative project. They are an earlier version of the illustrations intended for *Freydal*, and they were revised for the Viennese miniatures according to the emperor's wishes. Recent infrared reflectograms taken of folio 207 (cat. 43) of the Viennese manuscript reveal that the artist initially copied the double-arched window used in one of the Washington sketches (cat. 44), before overlaying the image with a balcony, from which a queen watches the dance.[7] Beneath the scene of the *Krönlrennen* (mixed form of joust of war and joust of peace; cat. 45), Maximilian had his editor add the correction, "the encounter should be reversed" (*das treffen sol verkert werden*), and the image was crossed out several times. The emperor's desired revision is seen in folio

86 of the Viennese manuscript, in which the image of the noblewoman on the horse trapper to the right has been moved to the one on the left.

Furthermore, several errors in the depiction of various jousting contests in the Washington sketches were later amended in the respective Viennese miniatures. For instance, all of the sketches that depict *Geschifttartschen-Rennen* (joust of war with "flying" and "exploding" shields) events mistakenly portray the riders' shields covered with fabric (cat. 50); the Viennese miniatures accurately show them without cloth covering. The *Geschifttartschen-Rennen* is one of the most spectacular variations of jousting on horseback, in which riders loaded their shields into a complex spring mechanism mounted on their breastplate. Should one rider's lance make perfect impact with the trigger on his opponent's torso, the mechanism would release the shield and launch it high into the air. Triangular metal plates—which had been loosely affixed to the shield—then rained down, like a fireworks display of iron; this would be impossible, of course, had the shields been covered in fabric, as suggested by the Washington sketches. The corrections made in the Viennese miniatures to errors of this sort imply an

CAT. 51 *Mixed Joust of War and Joust of Peace between Wolfgang von Polheim and Freydal* (1943.3.4428)

CAT. 52 *Italian Joust of Peace between Jacob de Heere and Freydal* (1943.3.4503)

editorial review of the sketches that could only have been conducted by the emperor himself, because no one else involved knew more about the often highly specific characteristics of individual tournament events.

A significant feature found on many of the Washington sketches is small slips of paper inscribed with brief descriptions for the artists to follow. Maximilian's collaborators, or editors, who oversaw his projects during his frequent travels, composed these notes, and the assigned artists later pasted them onto the respective sketches as proof that they had composed the scene as directed. Eighty-three of these notes survive, while many more have been lost, as suggested by spots the adhesive left on the pages.

The note pasted to one sketch reads: "Freydal has competed in an *Anzogenrennen* in a damask blanket, white on one side and green-red-yellow on the other, a scarlet jousting surcoat with long slashed Spanish sleeves, on the sallet a beautiful ostrich feather with glittering gold flake and jewelry, such as a diadem" (cat. 46). The trapper on the horse to the right is marked with color codes: "gl" for *gelb*, or yellow; "r" for *rot*, or red; and a leaf to represent green. The artist has not added pigment to the rider's surcoat, but in folio 54 of the Viennese miniature, it appears in red, as requested in the note.   SK

REFERENCES: Leitner 1880–82; Krause 2019a; Krause 2019b

1. Biblioteca Apostolica Vaticana, Vat. Lat. 8570.
2. A bookplate for the Pourtalès library, dating to about 1820/30, is affixed to the modern binding of the Washington *Freydal,* which was added in the 1920s. For the provenance, see Krause 2019c, sect. C, "Die *Freydal*-Skizzen in Washington, D.C., National Gallery of Art."
3. Sometime after Pourtalès's death, the sketches were divided into two groups: mummeries and jousts. The mummery sketches entered the collection of Richard von Passavant-Gontard in Frankfurt, before they were sold at auction in 1929 (C. G. Boerner 1929, p. 52, no. 469, ill.; see also *Sammlung von Passavant-Gontard* 1929, p. 32, no. 469) to J. Leonard Sessler, Charles Sessler Rare Books, Philadelphia. Sessler sold the group to Lessing J. Rosenwald that same year. The joust sketches were acquired during World War I from an unnamed art dealer in Paris by E. P. Goldschmidt, who sold this group to J. Leonard Sessler, Charles Sessler Rare Books, Philadelphia, in 1930. Rosenwald purchased this group from Sessler that same year. See Dodgson 1926; Dodgson 1928; see also the provenance information in Krause 2019c, sect. C, "Die *Freydal*-Skizzen in Washington, D.C., National Gallery of Art."
4. British Museum, London (1926,0713.9); Sotheby's 1923, no. 59, ill.
5. Quoted from the "Erstes Gedenkbuch Kaiser Maximilians I.," 1502, Österreichisches Staatsarchiv, Vienna, Haus-, Hof- und Staatsarchiv, HS B 376, fol. 147r.
6. Copy of a letter from Maximilian I to Sigmund von Dietrichstein, Niederwesel, October 14, 1512, Österreichische Nationalbibliothek, Vienna, Cod. 7425, fols. 3r–4r.
7. Schenck 2019; see also the technical discussion in Krause 2019c, sect. C, "Die *Freydal*-Skizzen in Washington, D.C., National Gallery of Art" (1943.3.4393).

CAT. 53 *Italian Joust of Peace between Jacob de Heere and Freydal,* National Gallery of Art, Washington, D.C., Rosenwald Collection (1943.3.3682)

The *Freydal* Woodblock Prints

Albrecht Dürer (1471–1528)

South German, ca. 1517–18

Woodcut

Each sheet (trimmed to image): 8¹³/₁₆ x 9⁹/₁₆ in. (22.4 x 24.3 cm)

Like the *Weisskunig* (cats. 114–17) and *Theuerdank* (cats. 108, 109), *Freydal* was intended to appear in print. The preliminary sketches in Washington, D.C., and the miniatures in Vienna were intermediate steps leading up to the print edition, which never made it past the initial stages of planning how to convert the illustrations into woodblock prints; only five are known to have been produced in about 1517–18.[1] In the Viennese manuscript, which was the emperor's review copy, the five images that were later printed are each marked with a small x on the upper edge of the page. The selection of scenes for trial printing thus appears to have been carried out according to the Viennese manuscript, or this selection was simply noted in the manuscript for the emperor's reference.

CAT. 54 *Masquerade*, National Gallery of Art, Washington, D.C., Rosenwald Collection (1943.3.3683)

CAT. 55 *Joust of War between Freydal and Anton von Yvan*, The Metropolitan Museum of Art, New York, Rogers Fund, 1921 (21.9.4)

Records indicate that work on the print version of *Freydal* had begun by 1516. Conrad Peutinger, the Augsburg city secretary and humanist who served as an editor for many of the emperor's commemorative projects, informed Maximilian in a letter dated June 9, 1516, that three images from *Freydal* would be engraved by the Augsburg book printer and publisher Hans Schönsperger the Elder. However, Peutinger continues, Schönsperger is unsure how large the images should be rendered, and Peutinger thus requests that the emperor make a decision with regard to their size.[2]

In this same letter, Peutinger expresses uncertainty about the allocation of these images, writing that he had received "six figures" from the emperor's secretary, of which—per the emperor's instructions—two belonged in the *Weisskunig* and two in *Theuerdank*. Peutinger also asks for further clarification, noting that in an earlier letter, dated February 28, 1516, Maximilian had informed him that, of these illustrations, three were intended for *Freydal*, one for *Theuerdank*, and two for the *Weisskunig*.[3] These miscommunications provide insight into the practical problems artists and editors encountered as they worked on the emperor's commemorative projects. In the years around 1515, work was underway on a whole range of richly illustrated publications that Maximilian had commissioned; more than six hundred images were planned for the three autobiographical volumes alone. Misunderstandings such as those Peutinger highlights in his 1516 letter were thus unavoidable. They were one of the reasons for the constant delays and for the fact that, by the emperor's death in 1519, many of his commemorative works remained incomplete.

Albrecht Dürer is credited almost unanimously today for converting the five miniatures into woodcuts. Dürer appears to have been instructed to closely follow the templates, which could explain why his authorship has been questioned.[4] In spite of these specific instructions, Dürer asserted creative license to improve some compositional details. In the print of the Italian joust of war (cat. 53), he deviated from both the preliminary sketch (cat. 52) and the miniature on folio 82, and moved the riders closer to each other, thereby concentrating the scene. The fallen rider, his horse, and his lance no longer hover strangely in the foreground, as in the sketch; having been thrown to the ground, they now lie there with their full weight.

The five print proofs were likely produced in a very limited run. The court historian Johannes Stabius, who, like Peutinger, was involved in editorial work on *Freydal*, did not even know about them. About 1519–20, when Stabius presented to Charles V an overview of Maximilian's commemorative projects, he reported that not a single printing block for *Freydal* had been fashioned.[5]

The same missive from Stabius to Charles contains two further important details on the evolution of *Freydal*. First, Stabius states that a copy of the work could be found with the provost of Saint Sebald Church in Nuremberg, Melchior Pfinzing. The letter also reveals that, shortly before his death, Maximilian had reached an agreement with the Nuremberg woodblock-cutter Hieronymus Andreae regarding the manufacture of printing blocks for the images in *Freydal*, for which he was contracted to receive one thousand florins. Andreae presumably produced the first five blocks used for the *Freydal* proofs, as he later circulated copies of the images.[6] The *Freydal* printing blocks may also have remained in Nuremberg, because Hans Glaser, another woodblock cutter and book printer in the city, signed a later copy of the scene of the *Anzogenrennen*.[7] One of the *Freydal* printing blocks, depicting the masquerade (see cat. 54), has survived and is now in the Kupferstichkabinett of the Staatliche Museen, Berlin.[8] SK

REFERENCES: Leitner 1880–82; Krause 2019a; Krause 2019b

1. See Mende 2004; Matthias Mende in Schoch, Mende, and Scherbaum 2001–4, vol. 3 (2004), pp. 154–64, nos. 272.1–272.5, ill.
2. Stadtarchiv, Augsburg, Literaliensammlung Personenselekte Peutinger, June 9, 1516; see König 1923, pp. 268–71, no. 168.
3. The letter from Maximilian, dated February 28, 1516, is mentioned only in Peutinger's own letter, and nothing else is known about this now-lost piece of communication.
4. See Tietze and Tietze-Conrat 1928–38, vol. 2, pt. 1 (1937), pp. 162–63, no. W 97, ill. p. 316.
5. Formerly Staatsarchiv (today Niedersächsisches Landesarchiv), Hannover, Cod. Ms Y 17, vol. 1, fol. 299 (lost to war, 1943), quoted in Steinherz 1906, p. 154.
6. A copy of the mummery print, housed in Hamburg, bears the signature "Jeronimus Formschneyder," attributable to Andreae; Hamburger Kunsthalle, Kupferstichkabinett (10988); Meder 1932, pp. 203, 204, no. 250.
7. The signature on this copy of the print reads: "[H]anns Glaser Brieffmaler zu Nürmberg am Panersberg"; Germanisches Nationalmuseum, Nuremberg (H 367); Meder 1932, p. 203, no. 246.
8. Staatliche Museen, Berlin, Kupferstichkabinett (D 428); Schoch, Mende, and Scherbaum 2001–4, vol. 3 (2004), p. 162, fig. 1.

Head of a Lineage

After the death of Mary of Burgundy in 1482, Maximilian I fought his subjects to secure the guardianship of Philip I, their son, and serve as regent of the Burgundian Low Countries. Many years later, following Philip's unexpected death in 1506, Maximilian became the guardian of his eldest grandson, Charles V, while Charles's brother Ferdinand I was effectively placed in the care of his maternal grandfather, Ferdinand II of Aragon. Maximilian personally looked after the well-being of his heirs and acted to help them expand their authority and dominions. The marriages that he arranged for his descendants created the conditions for the further rise of the House of Habsburg and the considerable increase of its influence in the political affairs of Europe, with Philip becoming king of Castile, Charles V king of all Spain and the ruler of parts of Italy and the New World, and Ferdinand I king of Bohemia and Hungary.

Maximilian commissioned lavish armors for his son and grandsons to promote their standing and uphold their political and dynastic claims. Unfortunately, the execution of such grand plans was frequently hampered by Maximilian's chronic shortages of funds. A remarkable costume armor that he commissioned in Innsbruck for presentation to Charles, which remains unfinished, probably was the victim of his ongoing struggle with his own treasurers to pay his armorers in a timely fashion. A group of drawings by Albrecht Dürer raises the possibility that Maximilian took advantage of his relations to the famed Nuremberg artist to plan a richly decorated armor intended for Charles just before he was to become king of all Spain.

Maximilian also procured armor for members of his extended family. Following his second marriage in 1493 to Ludovico Sforza's niece, Bianca Maria, Maximilian took Ludovico's son, Ercole, who had been renamed Massimiliano in his honor, under his protection after Milan fell to the French in 1499. Maximilian had fine armor made for him in Innsbruck and in Brussels after the young prince took up residence in the Burgundian Low Countries. The prospective marriage of Maximilian's granddaughter Mary of Austria and one of his grandsons with the children of Ladislaus II of Bohemia and Hungary prompted Maximilian to give important horse bards to Ladislaus's brother Sigismund of Poland and to order splendid armor in Innsbruck for presentation to the bridegroom Louis II, whom he adopted. Armor thus played a key role in the all-important matrimonial arrangements through which Maximilian secured peace, alliances, and influence.

Cat. 56

Maximilian I
Giovanni Ambrogio de Predis (ca. 1455–after 1508)
Italian (Milan), 1502
Oil on oak or walnut panel
17⁵⁄₁₆ x 11¹⁵⁄₁₆ in. (44 x 30.3 cm)
Kunsthistorisches Museum, Vienna, Gemäldegalerie (4431)

In this austere painting from 1502, Maximilian I wears a black hat and a black-collared gown, with the chain of the Burgundian Order of the Golden Fleece around his neck. The majuscule inscription positioned at chest height, which identifies him as "Roman king" (Maximilian was not anointed Holy Roman Emperor until 1508), is the sole indication of his monarchical status.

The portrait is the only known work signed and dated by Giovanni Ambrogio de Predis, who is otherwise noted for his occasional collaboration with Leonardo da Vinci in Milan (from 1483) and his engagement, also in Milan, as an artist in the court of Ludovico Sforza, from about 1479 until the duke's ouster in 1499. This painting could be seen as resulting from that position, since it was executed after 1493, the year of Maximilian's betrothal to his second wife, Bianca Maria Sforza, Ludovico's niece. The artist's portrait of the young bride, which today hangs in Washington, D.C., was painted shortly before the wedding (cat. 58). In its composition—the subject set in profile against a black background—Bianca Maria's portrait resembles that of her consort, painted approximately ten years later.

Given the vegetal pattern in Maximilian's garb, which echoes that on his bride's attire, and the rather archaic style, Karl Schütz has recently proposed that the present painting may represent the artist's own second version of a previous portrait of Maximilian.[1] It is possible that Predis was in Innsbruck when he first painted the monarch's distinctive profile, which is especially pronounced against the deep black background. This possibility would gain considerable support if the wood used for the picture could be shown to be oak, while the similar-looking walnut is encountered on a few pictures by Leonardo and his circle.[2] Documentation for the time Predis spent in Innsbruck, where he was occupied with a host of further commissions from Maximilian, exists only for the period directly following the wedding, when he accompanied Bianca Maria there as a member of her court.

This painting has often been linked to a black chalk portrait drawing of Maximilian, today in Berlin, that was subsequently dated 1504 (or 1507) in ink and furnished with Albrecht Dürer's monogram. Widely considered a Venetian work, the drawing has also tentatively been ascribed to Predis.[3]   GM

REFERENCES: Primisser 1819, p. 94, no. 66; Shell 1998, pp. 128, 130, and p. 129, ill. no. 6; Elena Ginanneschi in *Cinquecento lombardo* 2000, p. 106, no. III.16, ill.; Margot Rauch in *Werke für die Ewigkeit* 2002, p. 28, no. 2, ill. p. 29; Andrea Bayer in *Renaissance Portrait* 2011, pp. 263–67, no. 106, ill.; Karl Schütz in *Emperor Maximilian I* 2012, pp. 146–47, no. 11, ill.

1. Karl Schütz in *Emperor Maximilian I* 2012, p. 146.
2. Based on visual assessment; the wood has not yet undergone scientific analysis.
3. Staatliche Museen, Berlin, Kupferstichkabinett (KdZ 10). For the attribution, see Andrea Bayer in *Renaissance Portrait* 2011, pp. 263–67, no. 107, ill.

Cat. 57

Ludovico Sforza

Circle of Benedetto Briosco

Italian, ca. 1500

Marble

Diam. 21⅝ in. (55 cm)

Private collection

Carved in high relief, accentuating the volume and texture of Ludovico Sforza's thick hair, fleshy neck, and magnificent chain collar, this marble portrait of the Milanese duke belongs to a tradition of *all'antica* tondo effigies of the ruling dynasty that adorned the ducal residences, private palaces, and churches of Milan and its environs.[1] These portraits frequently formed an extensive genealogical series that asserted the authority of the ruling duke as the rightful heir to an illustrious and long-standing dynasty composed of his Sforza predecessors, their forerunners the Visconti, and sometimes even legendary ancestors from antiquity.[2]

About 1497 Ludovico commissioned an elaborate series of tondo portraits of the Sforza and Visconti from the Lombard sculptor Benedetto Briosco to adorn the transept portals in the Certosa di Pavia.[3] In format and physiognomy, the present work is closely related to Ludovico's relief portrait in the Certosa, as well as to numismatic and medallic effigies of the duke. Equally significant is an element that distinguishes the tondo under discussion, namely, Ludovico's open-link chain collar, a prominent attribute worn by the duke in the celebrated *Pala Sforzesca*, but otherwise very rarely seen.[4] Painted in 1494, this altarpiece commemorated Ludovico's long-awaited investiture, bestowed by Maximilian in exchange for a substantial payment and the promise of his niece, Bianca Maria Sforza, in marriage.

Maximilian's granting of the ducal title, sought after by the Visconti and Sforza since 1395, legitimized the tenuous rule of Ludovico, who usurped power from his nephew in 1480 and faced escalating French claims upon Milan in the 1490s. This tondo portrait of Ludovico, adorned with a chain that may symbolize his investiture, was probably commissioned within this political context, perhaps by Ludovico (before his imprisonment in 1500) or by one of his supporters.[5]   AMN

REFERENCES: Sismann 2006, pp. 19–20, ill.; *Galerie Sismann* 2012, pp. 20–23, no. 8, ill.

1. Sismann 2006, pp. 19–20, ill.; *Galerie Sismann* 2012, pp. 20–23, no. 8, ill.; Albertario 2015; Luca Tosi in *Arte lombarda* 2015, pp. 38–39, nos. 2–4, ill. pp. 36, 37.
2. The most extensive example is Ludovico's patronage of seventy-five frescoed roundels bearing portraits of the Sforza, ancient heroes, and ducal emblems above the arcade surrounding the Piazza Ducale of Vigevano; see Zaffignani 1991.
3. The Certosa di Pavia, a Carthusian monastery near Milan, was a significant site of Visconti/Sforza patronage and portraiture. Ludovico's portrait appears above the portal leading to the old sacristy; *Certosa di Pavia* 2006, p. 190, ill. pp. 208, 210. The closest copy is the marble medallion in the Musée Jacquemart André, Paris (R.F. 615).
4. Ludovico is most often portrayed wearing armor. For the *Pala Sforzesca*, see Pietro C. Marani in *Pinacoteca di Brera* 1988, pp. 325–30, no. 145, ill.
5. Families loyal to the Sforza dukes commissioned series of ducal portraits for their private palaces, including the sculpted tondi attributed to a Lombard sculptor and to Briosco that adorned the Palazzo Fontana Silvestri and the Palazzo Pellizzoni in Milan; see Tosi in *Arte lombarda* 2015, pp. 38–39, nos. 1–4, ill. pp. 34, 36, 37.

Cat. 58

Bianca Maria Sforza

Giovanni Ambrogio de Predis (ca. 1455–after 1508)

Italian (Milan), probably 1493

Oil on wood panel

20 1/16 x 12 13/16 in. (51 x 32.5 cm)

National Gallery of Art, Washington, D.C.,

Widener Collection (1942.9.53)

This painting is at the heart of an important Renaissance betrothal story. In September 1492 a Milanese courtier reported that "*uno Todesco*" (a German) had come to the city to get a glimpse of Bianca Maria Sforza, daughter of Duke Galeazzo Maria Sforza and niece of the current ruler, Ludovico Sforza, Il Moro, as a possible bride for Maximilian I. The visitor was able to observe her in church, and he took a charcoal drawing of her by Giovanni Ambrogio de Predis back with him. Returning to Milan sometime later, he asked for information about her dowry (enormous) and for another portrait, now in color. The parties agreed upon the arrangement, and in late November 1493, Bianca Maria and Maximilian were married by proxy in an elaborate ceremony in Milan Cathedral, with the bride delivered to the church in a great carriage drawn by four white horses. She then crossed a rough Lake Como and made her way to Innsbruck, where bride and bridegroom finally met some months later.[1]

Predis depicted Bianca Maria at the time of her betrothal, as signaled by the carnation that she wears tucked into her belt. He shows her in strict profile, with emphasis on her carefully described dress and ornament, all of which reflect recent fashion in Milan, much of it inflected by Spanish tastes. Her jewels are particularly sumptuous, including pearls threaded through her headdress (known as a *coazzone*) and down her plait, and as part of her necklace, which includes an elaborate hanging pendant. Some of the ornaments act as Sforza emblems, such as the brush-shaped jewel in her hair, known as a *spazzola*, which includes the motto MERITO ET TEMPORE (With merit and time).[2] Thus, this young woman is presented in her role as Sforza bride, the instrument of dynastic negotiations with positive outcomes for Ludovico, whose status in Milan was legitimized, and for Maximilian, who got an influx of resources. The artist also captured Bianca Maria's own girlish appearance more sensitively in a silverpoint drawing of her profile that delicately describes the overhang of her upper lip and fleshy chin.[3] It may date to the time of her betrothal, or from her first months in Innsbruck, a happy moment before her husband's arrival, when we know Predis made drawings of

her court women.[4] The artist continued to work for the court, painting Maximilian's portrait in 1502 (cat. 56).

Bernhard Strigel's portrait of Bianca Maria (cat. 60) shows her more than a decade later, in completely different, albeit equally elaborate, attire, and now a matron. It is interesting that the severity of the strict profile has there yielded to a pose that mitigates the implied distance between sitter and viewer. In each case, we know with historical hindsight that the wealth and station demonstrated in these paintings did not lead her to a contented family life. AB

REFERENCES: Welch 1995, p. 243, and p. 244, fig. 135; Venturelli 1996, pp. 50–53, fig. 1; David Alan Brown in Boskovits and Brown 2003, pp. 596–601, ill.; Fahy 2008, pp. 21–22, fig. 11

1. David Alan Brown in Boskovits and Brown 2003, p. 599. Ludovico's wife, Beatrice d'Este, described the ceremony in a letter to her sister Isabella. Welch 1995, p. 249, and Fahy 2008, pp. 21–22, offer an alternative interpretation to that given by Brown concerning the German visitor's original client. It is most likely he was always working on Maximilian's behalf.
2. For an analysis of the costumes and gems, see Venturelli 1996.
3. Hamburger Kunsthalle, Kupferstichkabinett (21478).
4. Andrea Bayer in *Renaissance Portrait* 2011, pp. 262–63, no. 105, ill.

Cat. 59

Armor for the Joust of Peace of Maximilian I

Lorenz Helmschmid (first recorded 1467, died 1516)

South German (Augsburg), ca. 1494

Steel and leather

As mounted: H. 26 3/8 in. (58 cm), W. 17 15/16 in. (45.5 cm), D. 19 1/8 in. (48.5 cm), Wt. 43 lb. 15 oz. (19,935 g)

Philadelphia Museum of Art, Purchased with Museum funds, 1930 (1930.63.1a–t)

Made by Lorenz Helmschmid at his request, this armor is one of several that Maximilian I used himself when jousting or lent to his guests participating in the sumptuous tournaments and more casual contests staged regularly at his court. Designed for the joust of peace, a mock combat fought with lances fitted with heads projecting into several prongs, or coronels, it is one of the finest examples Maximilian is known to have owned. Notably, its elements were carefully marked with a distinctive symbol to ensure that they would be reunited after being disassembled for repair or cleaning. Because comparable armors lack markings of this sort, this example must have enjoyed a special status, and was perhaps reserved for Maximilian's use only.

The mark, a segment that splits into two parts at one end and intersects with two crossed segments at the splitting point, is engraved on the front right side of the helm, near the lower edge; on the middle of the breastplate and backplate,

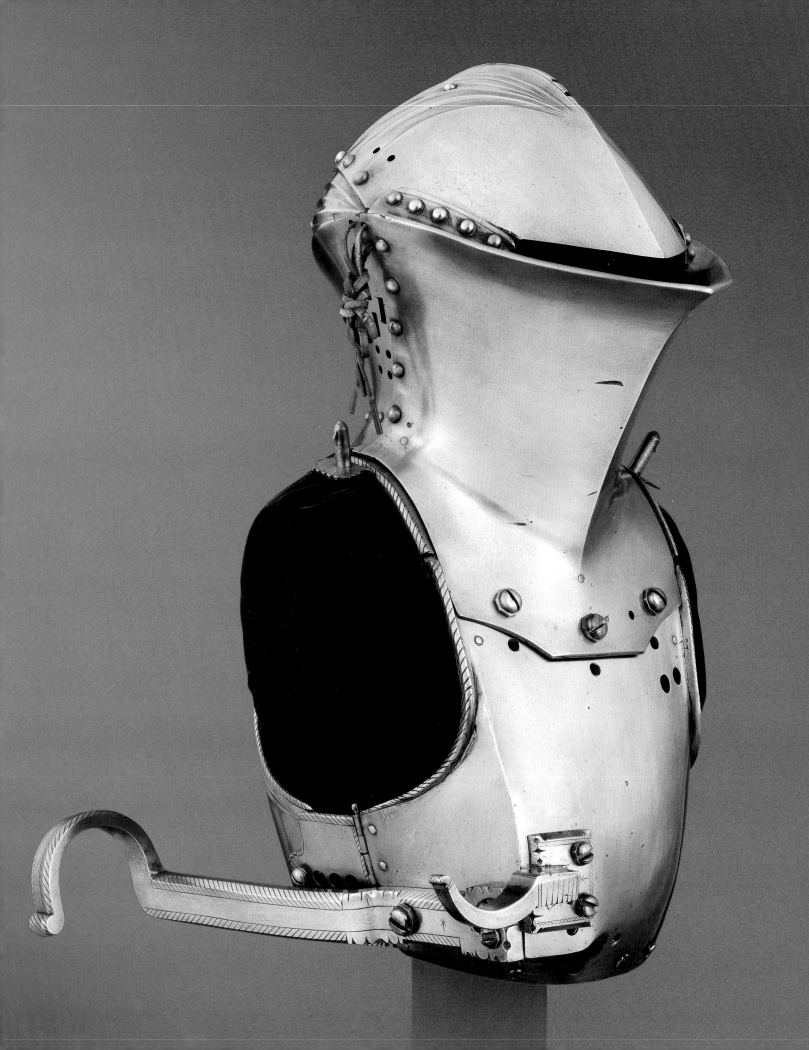

near their upper edges; on the middle of the base of the lance rest; and on the right side of the queue, toward the front. These pieces were already assembled together, along with elements that did not originally belong to the same armor and specially made modern replacements, when it entered the Kunsthistorisches Museum in the late nineteenth century.

The original pauldrons and left arm defense of this armor, each of which bears the same engraved mark, are preserved in the Kunsthistorisches Museum's Imperial Armoury.[1] Because they had already been mistakenly remounted with another armor of the same type, they were not included with the present armor when the Kunsthistorisches Museum deaccessioned it in 1928 and the Philadelphia Museum of Art purchased it in 1930. The relationship between the dispersed elements appears to have remained unnoticed until now.

In its present state, the armor in Philadelphia consists of a helm, a breastplate and a backplate secured together by steel straps at the shoulders and by hinged hasps beneath the gussets, and a lance rest and queue fastened by large screws to the breastplate. Originally, the armor would have had additional elements, including symmetrical pauldrons, left and right arm defenses, besagews, a waist plate with tassets, and a culet.

Beyond the exceptional quality of its execution, the armor is remarkable for its refined design, which extends to subtleties such as the placement of shock-absorbing strips of leather in the areas where the plates of the helm overlap and are riveted together. These strips would have prevented a blow on one of the plates from causing the others to vibrate in the manner of a bell, and thus would have spared the jouster a serious and well-known inconvenience.[2] The deep gouges in the helm's face plate were left by opponents' lances.

The armor is traditionally believed to have been commissioned by Maximilian for the tournaments held following his marriage with Bianca Maria Sforza in 1494. The elements now in Philadelphia were in the Kunsthistorisches Museum from 1889 until 1928,[3] when they were deaccessioned, in exchange for other objects, to the German dealer Hans Schedelmann; they were purchased by the Philadelphia Museum of Art through Thomas T. Hoopes in 1930. The elements remaining in the Kunsthistorisches Museum became part of its Arms Collection (Waffensammlung) in 1889.[4]   PT

REFERENCES: Taylor 1931, pp. 25, 27, ill. facing p. 2; Grancsay 1956; Thomas 1956/1977, p. 1133

1. These elements are part of armor S XIV; Thomas and Gamber 1976, pp. 145–46, figs. 69, 71.
2. On the issue of helm resonance, or clangor, see Anglo 2000, p. 214.
3. Formerly Kunsthistorisches Museum, Vienna (B 63).
4. The Imperial Armoury department was known as the Waffensammlung until 1989.

Cat. 60

Bianca Maria Sforza
Bernhard Strigel (1460–1528)
South German (Memmingen), 1505–10
Oil on wood panel
29 7/16 x 17 15/16 in. (74.7 x 45.5 cm)
Tiroler Landesmuseum Ferdinandeum, Innsbruck, Austria, Ältere Kunstgeschichtliche Sammlungen (Gem 100)

Well into the modern era, marriages between members of royal families were not the expression of loving relationships; instead, they served to forge alliances and thus bore political and dynastic implications. Maximilian I's second marriage, to

Bianca Maria Sforza, exemplifies this custom. In 1490, following the death in 1482 of his first wife, Mary of Burgundy, Maximilian married Anne of Brittany by proxy. The marriage was never consummated, however, and Charles VIII of France could therefore intervene to take Anne as his wife. Despite Maximilian's protestations to the pope, he was ultimately forced to acquiesce.

This is how Bianca Maria, daughter of the fifth duke of Milan, Galeazzo Maria Sforza, came onto the scene. Born in 1472, she grew up under the guardianship of her uncle Ludovico, who ruled Milan in place of her brother, the ailing Gian Galeazzo. In June 1493 a prenuptial agreement was arranged between Maximilian and Bianca Maria, and the standard yet still opulent marriage by proxy followed in Milan Cathedral. Although the bride arrived in Innsbruck that December, she and Maximilian did not meet or consummate the union until March 1494.

This arrangement benefited both parties. The Sforza family ennobled their recently secured sovereignty, and Maximilian enfeoffed them with the duchy of Milan and county of Pavia (Maximilian's father, Frederick III, had long withheld these territories from the Sforza, who did not occupy an equivalent social stratum). For Maximilian, who routinely struggled with finances, the staggering dowry of 400,000 florins was a godsend, supplemented as it was by additional trappings and jewels valued at 40,000 gold ducats. Furthermore, he had now established another ally in Italy.

Bianca Maria's clothing in this half-figure portrait satisfies sartorial expectations for a queen and one of the wealthiest brides in Europe.[1] Beneath her décolleté, her gown features an elaborately embroidered bodice with two distinct decorative panels. The upper has two peacocks facing each other in a meadow on either side of a vase containing sinuous floral vines. The lower depicts scenes of courtly amusement: men and women fowling and strolling alongside a pool. About 1500 embroidery of this sort was the most notable and costly form of ornamentation for clothing.[2] Surviving records show, for instance, that in 1507 Bianca Maria's silk embroiderer received 50 florins for gold thread from Venice.

Backed by a brocade baldachin cloth of honor, allowing a view to the left of a landscape probably meant to be the Inn Valley, Bianca Maria displays a stately appearance that is emphasized by her gold mesh bonnet, golden link chain collars, elegant gloves, precious rings, and capacious, richly draped sleeves. In a virtuosic detail, part of her left sleeve rests on the parapet before her. The motif of a foreground balustrade, which had emerged primarily in fifteenth-century northern Italian portraiture, accentuated both the viewer's distance from the subject and the boundaries of the image. However, the sleeve on the parapet here crosses this line and the distance it denotes. This oscillation between shielding and overstepping the aesthetic barrier offers a reflection on the imagery and media of the portrait. With this device, Strigel distinguishes himself among those painters who embraced the northern Italian influence.

Bianca Maria's exquisite necklace, decorated in pearls and featuring the conspicuous Christian monogram IHS, may allude to her increasing gravitation toward religion. Her piety provided her with some stability during her unhappy, childless marriage to Maximilian, who lost interest in his wife and did not see her for months at a time. The striking appearance of Bianca Maria's eyes in many of her portraits has led scholars to speculate that she may have suffered from Graves' disease, and was therefore infertile.[3] She died at the age of thirty-eight on December 31, 1510, and was buried—without Maximilian's attendance—at Stams Abbey in Tyrol.   PS

REFERENCES: *Maximilian I.* 1969, "Katalog," pp. 23–24, no. 72; Gert Ammann in *Hispania—Austria* 1992, pp. 262–63, no. 78, ill.; Weiss 2010, p. 224, and p. 163, fig. 143; Frieling 2013, pp. 96–97, no. 11, ill.

1. A similar version of the portrait is in the collection of the Dumbarton Oaks Research Library and Collection, Washington, D.C. (HC.P.1930.04.(O)).
2. Frieling 2013, p. 90.
3. Weiss 2010, pp. 174–75.

Cat. 61

Massimiliano Sforza, from *A Treatise on Latin Grammar by Aelius Donatus* (*La Grammatica del Donato*)

Giovanni Ambrogio de Predis (ca. 1455–after 1508)
Italian, ca. 1496–99
Tempera on parchment
$10^{13}/_{16}$ x $6^{15}/_{16}$ in. (27.4 x 17.7 cm)
Archivio Storico Civico e Biblioteca Trivulziana, Milan
(Cod. 2167, fol. 1v)

This stately portrait of the Milanese prince Massimiliano Sforza, portrayed around the age of five, conveys his authority as a born ruler, armed for his future role as duke of Milan. Despite the child's delicate physiognomy, his precocious grandeur is suggested by the imposing scale of his body relative to the picture plane, and above all, by his expansive, armor-clad torso, which fills the lower half of the composition and is central to his identity as a ruler. Painted on parchment, this full-page portrait forms the frontispiece of a grammar book commissioned for Massimiliano by his father, the Milanese duke Ludovico Sforza.[1]

Massimiliano's portrait and that of his father on the manuscript's final folio (fol. 54r) are the most monumental illuminated portraits of the Renaissance.[2] Painted by Giovanni Ambrogio de Predis, one of the leading portraitists in late fifteenth-century Milan, these portraits closely approximate panel painting in scale, composition, and format. Predis, who collaborated with Leonardo da Vinci in 1483 on the *Virgin of the Rocks* (National Gallery, London), was a painter, illuminator, and coin designer at the Sforza court during the 1490s,

while also working in the service of Maximilian at Innsbruck. Predis represents a significant artistic and political bridge between the Sforza dynasty and Maximilian. In 1492–93 Maximilian commissioned Predis to paint the portrait of his potential bride, Ludovico's niece, Bianca Maria Sforza (cat. 58). In addition to arranging this marriage, Ludovico covertly paid Maximilian an enormous sum in order to secure the long-sought-after privilege of the ducal title of Milan. Predis accompanied Bianca Maria to Innsbruck in 1493, serving as her artist, working at the mint in 1494, and designing tapestries for Maximilian in 1498. Predis returned to the Innsbruck court permanently in 1502, joining the other Sforza exiles residing there, including Bianca Maria, Massimiliano, and his brother Francesco, following the French conquest of Milan in 1499. In 1502 Predis painted the celebrated panel portrait of Maximilian, his only signed work (cat. 56).

This manuscript, containing a Latin grammatical text by the fourth-century author Aelius Donatus, was one of two richly illuminated educational codices made for Massimiliano (the second is the *Liber Iesus*, cat. 62) that contain an elaborate series of miniatures illustrating the prince in the act of preparing for his impending duties.[3] With depictions of Massimiliano appearing at a courtly banquet, in a triumphal procession, and as a diligent student, these images constitute a pictorial "mirror for princes," a literary genre in which young princes were instructed in the proper skills and decorum of the ideal ruler.

While in the *Liber Iesus* Massimiliano encounters the model of rulership in his godfather Maximilian, in the present manuscript he looks to his father, though indirectly. Massimiliano, facing right on the manuscript's opening folio, is paired with a full-page, bust-length portrait of Ludovico in armor, who appears on the final folio, facing left. Massimiliano and Ludovico engage in a dialogue, with the intervening folios bearing the instructions for the prince to master to reach his paternal model.

The two pioneering portraits by Predis vividly illustrate a larger phenomenon at the Milanese court, namely that educational manuscripts for the Sforza children contain the most prominent and significant examples of illuminated portraiture, produced by preeminent court painters and illuminators. The quality of these portraits, as well as the numerous propagandistic images of Massimiliano mastering the skills of rulership, suggests that the manuscripts were intended for an audience beyond the prince and his tutor. There was a tradition of staging public recitations of rhetorical exercises at the Sforza court, and these educational manuscripts may well have played a role in such displays.

When commissioning these luxurious manuscripts for his son, Ludovico was undoubtedly inspired by his own childhood schoolbook and those of his siblings.[4] He and Predis, however, were also probably familiar with the three educational manuscripts, containing grammar lessons and prayers, commissioned between 1465 and 1468 by Frederick III to instruct the young Maximilian, who is depicted in prayer and reading with his teacher in several miniatures.[5]   AMN

REFERENCES: Giovanni M. Piazza in *Codice di Leonardo da Vinci* 2006, pp. 57–60, no. 3, ill.; Pier Luigi Mulas in *Arte lombarda* 2015, p. 379, no. v.46; Nogueira 2015, pp. 200, 218, n. 53, pp. 220–21, and p. 201, fig. 4; Alexander 2016, pp. 12, 14, fig. 1; Mulas 2016, pp. 72–73, 87, fol. 1v; Pontone 2016, p. 98

1. Giovanni M. Piazza in *Codice di Leonardo da Vinci* 2006, pp. 57–60, no. 3, ill.; Pier Luigi Mulas in *Arte lombarda* 2015, p. 379, no. v.46, ill. p. 353; Alexander 2016; Mulas 2016; Pontone 2016.
2. For the portrait of Ludovico Sforza in this manuscript, see Alexander 2016, pp. 14, 24; Mulas 2016, pp. 72–73, 89, fol. 54r, fig. 34. There are two precedents for full-page, bust-length illuminated portraits: that of the Venetian general Jacopo Marcello ("Life and Passion of Saint Maurice," Bibliothèque de l'Arsenal, Paris, MS 940, fol. 38v) from 1453, and, more importantly, that of Ludovico's father Francesco Sforza, in the schoolbook for his children Ippolita and Galeazzo Maria from about 1460 ("Grammatica di Baldo Martorelli," Archivio Storico Civico e Biblioteca Trivulziana, Milan, Cod. 786).
3. Alexander 2016; for a broader discussion of Sforza schoolbooks, see Nogueira 2015.
4. Nogueira 2015.
5. These manuscripts include a reading book in German and Latin, a Latin grammar, and the "Doctrinale Puerorum" by Alexander de Villa Dei (Österreichische Nationalbibliothek, Vienna, Cod. 2289, Cod. 2368, Cod. 2617), with illuminations attributed to the Master of the Maximilian Schoolbooks; Alexander 2016, pp. 14–15.

Cat. 62

Massimiliano Sforza Welcomes Maximilian During His Visit to Italy in 1496, from the *Liber Iesus*

Attributed to Boccaccio Boccaccino (before 1466–1525)
Italian, 1496–97
Tempera on parchment
7¾ x 5⅜ in. (19.8 x 13.8 cm)
Archivio Storico Civico e Biblioteca Trivulziana, Milan
(Cod. 2163, fol. 6r)

For his son and heir Massimiliano, the Milanese duke Ludovico Sforza commissioned two luxuriously illuminated educational manuscripts, which are distinguished for their numerous portraits of the young prince fulfilling the courtly, civic, military, and diplomatic duties of a good ruler. These images served both as propaganda for the Sforza dynasty and as instructions for the future duke, evoking the literary tradition known as mirrors for princes, which outlines their requisite skills and conduct. In the present manuscript, consisting of grammatical texts and prayers, Massimiliano's edification culminates in the image of his encounter with the supreme model of rulership, his godfather Maximilian I, who was closely tied to the Sforza family. In 1493, Ludovico secretly paid Maximilian for the long-coveted privilege of the ducal title of Milan, arranged for Maximilian to marry his niece Bianca Maria Sforza, and agreed to rename Ercole, his infant son, Massimiliano in Maximilian's honor.

In this miniature of exceptional quality and political resonance, Maximilian and his young namesake shake hands in the company of attendants before a panoramic vista of northern Italy. The image (and perhaps the manuscript as a whole) commemorates their historic meeting in 1496, when the emperor convened with Ludovico to discuss a defensive alliance against the French, either on July 26 near Bormio or on September 1 near Lake Como.[1] Massimiliano's preparations for this occasion are reflected in the text on the facing page, which includes German phrases for the prince to learn, as well as a dialogue with the emperor, who professes his affection for both Massimiliano and his father.

The illumination's stylistic resemblance to panel painting, its attribution to one of the leading painters in and around Milan, and the quality of the manuscript as a whole indicate the significance of the commission. Furthermore, the involvement of multiple illuminators in its production suggests that the manuscript was to be completed quickly, perhaps for a specific occasion.[2] Undoubtedly destined for an audience beyond Massimiliano and his tutor (portrayed at the far right), the manuscript could have been displayed to Ludovico's esteemed guests when his son performed public recitations of his learning, as was the tradition for children at the Sforza court.

An image celebrating the emperor as a model, ally, and protector of Massimiliano and the dynasty would have also served as significant political propaganda in the mid- to late 1490s. Faced with the impending threat of further French advancement into Italy, in 1495, an alliance, known as the Holy League, was formed by Pope Alexander VI, which included Ludovico and Maximilian. Milan was acutely vulnerable due to the long-standing claims to the duchy by the French dukes of Orléans, which culminated in King Louis XII of France's conquest of the city in 1499. Following Ludovico's imprisonment in 1500, the seven-year-old Massimiliano was brought to Innsbruck and put under the protection of Maximilian, who helped to prepare the prince as a ruler, commissioning armor for him. While Maximilian appeared to support Massimiliano's successful claim of Milan in 1512, in fact, he had hoped his grandson Charles V would assume the ducal title. AMN

REFERENCES: Giovanni M. Piazza in *Codice di Leonardo da Vinci* 2006, pp. 55–56, no. 2, ill.; Pier Luigi Mulas in *Arte lombarda* 2015, p. 379, no. v.45, ill. p. 353; Alexander 2016, p. 24; Mulas 2016, pp. 73, 81, 86, fol. 6r, figs. 37, 39, 41; Pontone 2016, p. 99

1. Alexander 2016, p. 23; Mulas 2016, pp. 81, 85–86.
2. Giovanni M. Piazza in *Codice di Leonardo da Vinci* 2006, pp. 55–56, no. 2, ill.; Pier Luigi Mulas in *Arte lombarda* 2015, p. 379, no. v.45, ill. p. 353.

Cat. 63

Seal Box (Skippet) with the Arms of Massimiliano Sforza

Italian (Lombardy), ca. 1512–15
Copper alloy and gold
H. 13/16 in. (2 cm), W. 3 1/16 in. (7.8 cm), D. 3 5/16 in. (8.5 cm)
Tiroler Landesmuseum Ferdinandeum, Innsbruck, Austria, Ältere Kunstgeschichtliche Sammlungen (G0 17)

Seals have been used to authenticate or secure documents since antiquity. Starting in the fifteenth century, fragile wax seals were frequently stored in metal boxes for protection. These boxes were often gilded and occasionally embellished with the owner's crest and initials.[1]

This seal box, now empty, is made of fire-gilded copper alloy. A dove flying over a banner is depicted on the half-rounded underside, three interlocked diamond rings adorn the inside of the lid, and the Sforza coat of arms appears on the outside. The latter features the single-headed imperial eagle quartered with the Sforza serpent, which holds a person in its mouth. It is surmounted by a crown, and flanked on each side by three burning rods, hung with water buckets. The initials MA are engraved over the rods to the left, and SF over those to the right.

Until now it had been assumed that this box belonged to Bianca Maria Sforza because the Sforza coat of arms on the lid recalls the ones that appear as her coat of arms in Innsbruck on the balustrade of the Golden Roof (Goldenes Dachl; cat. 19) and on the Tower of Coats of Arms (Wappenturm), designed in 1499.[2] There are several reasons, however, why this attribution of ownership is quite unlikely. In no other known sources is Bianca Maria's name shortened to only the initials MA, leaving out Bianca, which was usually shortened to BL (BLanca).[3] This coat of arms was also not exclusive to Bianca Maria; in fact, it was used by a number of members of the Sforza family before, during, and after her lifetime. Most importantly, two very similar seal boxes that still contain their original seals have come to light in Milan. The two Milan boxes and the one in Innsbruck have a shared style and design, suggesting that they were created at the same Lombard workshop during the same period. The first Milan seal box, now at Castello Sforzesco, is almost identical to the Innsbruck one, but it does not have the initials MA and SF on the lid, although the wax seal inside does contain the full name and title for Massimiliano Sforza, Bianca Maria's younger cousin.[4] The initials MA and SF are inscribed on the second Milan seal box,

now at the Archivio di Stato, along with the letters DV and MLI (DVx MedioLanI, for the duke of Milan), which appear underneath the burning rods. This box is still fixed to the document it was sealing, a book of statutes of the union of herb and spice traders in Como. It was sealed by Duke Massimiliano Sforza as a symbol of his assent as the ruler of Lombardy, where Como is located.[5]

Massimiliano was duke of Milan from 1512 to 1515, after the Sforza territory had been claimed back from the French, who had occupied it since 1499. In 1515 the French recaptured Milan and took Massimiliano prisoner. He was compensated financially and had to live in exile in France for the remainder of his days.[6] The three boxes were very likely created during his three-year rule.   DS

REFERENCES: Hye 1969, especially p. 63; *Maximilian I.* 1969, "Katalog," p. 27, no. 91; Gert Ammann in Tiroler Landesmuseum Ferdinandeum 1979, p. 39; Claudia Helm in *Kaiser, Reich, Reformen* 1995, p. 237, no. D 4, ill.; Weiss 2010, p. 213, fig. 176

1. Kittel 1970, especially p. 172.
2. This interpretation was proposed by Franz-Heinz Hye; see Hye 1969, especially p. 63. His interpretation was successively accepted by all authors who mentioned the Innsbruck seal box. Regarding the Wappenturm, see also Hye 2004, p. 85.
3. The initials can be found in two illuminated books made for Bianca Maria Sforza at the Österreichische Nationalbibliothek, Vienna, Cod. 2369 and Cod. Ser. n. 2621; see Unterkircher 1983.
4. Zastrow 1993, pp. 129–30, no. 80, ill.
5. See Statuti del Paratico e dell'Università degli Aromatari e degli Speziari della città di Como, 1514, Fondo Cimeli, cart. 5, doc. 6, Archivio di Stato, Milan.
6. Angermeier 1982, especially pp. 177–86.

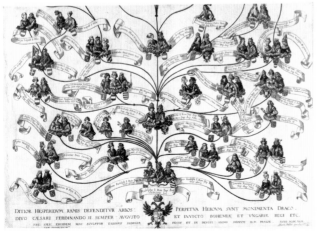

Cat. 64

Family Tree of the House of Habsburg
Aegidius Sadeler II (ca. 1570–1629) and
Marcus Christoph Sadeler (1614–after 1650)
South Netherlandish, 1629
4 engravings
Each sheet: 21 x 26½ in. (53.3 x 67.3 cm)
The Metropolitan Museum of Art, New York,
Harris Brisbane Dick Fund, 1953 (53.601.10[84-88])

This multiplate engraving was executed by Aegidius
Sadeler II, the most gifted member of an Antwerp family of
printmakers, print publishers, and art dealers. The German
artist and art historian Joachim von Sandrart, writing in the
1670s, praised his friend and mentor as "a phoenix among
engravers."[1] Aegidius was equally celebrated in his own lifetime; he worked as engraver to three successive Habsburg
emperors, creating portraits, landscapes, religious images,
and propaganda for the court. This family tree of the House of
Habsburg was commissioned at a key moment for Emperor
Ferdinand II (1578–1637). After eleven years of war with the
Protestants, Ferdinand had just secured an important victory
with the establishment of the Edict of Restitution in 1629.[2]
This edict sought to restore religious and territorial agree-
ments reached in the 1555 Peace of Augsburg, which had
halted the secularization of Catholic Church lands. The militant political and religious climate of Ferdinand's court called
for artistic programs that propagandized the Habsburgs' commitment to Catholicism and their joint causes. Although
Ferdinand's victory was short-lived, it did provide a moment
of great celebration and empowerment for the embattled
ruler during the Thirty Years' War.

The engraved ensemble is composed of four sheets and
a title page. In both the title and the lengthy inscription at the
base of the tree, Ferdinand II is lauded as always victorious
and as an august and divine Caesar, using the same ancient
Latin words employed for Maximilian I in the woodcut portrait
by Hans Weiditz the Younger after Albrecht Dürer (cat. 154).
Ferdinand, like the dragon in the Hesperides, guards the
golden apples produced in that legendary garden at the western edge of the world. Here, his ancestors and descendants
are the golden apples of the tree. The progenitor of the
Habsburg line is Emperor Rudolf I, from whom all branches
of the family sprout. Each member is shown as a half-length
figure attached by fronds to the central stem with text to identify him or her. The successive emperors occupy the trunk of
the tree with their wives and children; the childrens' spouses

Caroli Emanuel Philippi II
Hispaniarum & c. Regis filiæ
Maritus

Maria Philippi II. Hispa-
norum. & c. Regis. Vxor

Maria
Maximiliani Vxor

Elisabetha sive Isabella
Philippi II. Hisp. Reg Vxor

Maria Philippi II Hi-
spanorum & c. Regis
prima Regi Vxor

Aug. felix Ferdinandi
Rom. Imp. Aug. primoge

Albertus Annæ Ferdinandi
Rom. Imp. Aug. Filiæ Mari

Catharina Ferdinandi I. Rom
Imp. Aug. Filia quinta

Guglielmus alijs Franciscus I. ca
Ferdinandi I Rom. Imp.
Aug. Filiæ prior Maritus

Sigismundus Augustus Polonica
Rex, alter Catharinæ Maritus

Philippus II. Caroli V. Rom. Imp.
Aug. Filius Hispaniarum & C.
Rex potentissimus.

Anna Maximiliani II Romani
Aug. filia p. Philippi II Hispa-
niæ. & c. Regis Vxor num

Elisabetha Ferdinandi I. Rom.
Aug filia. filia prima

Sigismundus
Augustus Elisabethæ
Ferdin I & c. filiæ Marit

Anna Ferdinandi I. Rom.
Imp. Aug. Filia altera

Guglielmus Dux Claus. Ma
Ferdinandi I Rom. Imp.
Aug. Filiæ 3ª

Magdalena
di I. Rom
Filia

Philippi I. Archiducis Austriæ
Filia 3ª

Ludovicus Hungariæ et
Boemiæ Rex, Mariæ Phi-
lippi I. Arch. Aust. filiæ Marit

Elisabetha Anna Ferdinandi I
Rom. Imp. Aug. Vxor

Maria Ferdinandi I. Rom.
Imp. Aug. Filia 3.a

Barbara Ferdina
Rom. Imp. Aug. fi

Isabella Caroli V.
Rom. Imp. Aug. Vxor

Carolus hæc nomine primus in incluta
Austriæ domo sed V. Rom. Imp. Aug. Philippi I. Archid Austriæ et c. Filius.

Ferdinandus I. hoc nomine & e. iu
Austriæ domo et Rom. Imp. Aug.
Philippi I. Archid. Aust & c. Filius Prim

Isabella Philippi I. Arch. Aust.
& c. Filia altera

Iæ Rex et c.
I. Arch. Au

Christianus Isabella Philippi
Arch. Aust. & c. filiæ Maritus

Iohanna Philippi I. Archiducis Aust.
Vxor.

Philippus I. Maximiliani I. Rom. Imp. Aug.
Filius.

Margareta Maxi
Aug. Arch. Aust.

Franciscus Maximiliani I. Rom.
Imp. Aug. et c. Filius

Maximilianus I. huius nominis in Archid
Aust. domo Augusta et Imperio Rom. Imp. Au
1486.

Ioannes Margaretæ Maximiliani I.
et c. Filiæ prior Maritus

Maria Maximiliani I. Rom.
Imp. Aug. Vxor prima

Blanca Maria Maximiliani I.
Rom. Imp. Aug. Vxor altera

Christophorus Friderici IV.
Rom. Imp. Aug. Filius

Ioannes II. Friderici IV.
Rom. Imp. Aug. Filius

Albertus Kunigundis Archidu-
cissæ Austriæ Maritus

Ernestus II. Ernesti Feren
Arch. Aust. Filius

Rudolphus V. Ernesti Feren
Archid. Austria Filius

Albertus VI. Ernesti Fe
Archid. Austriæ Filius M

Leopoldus V. Alberti Ferr.
Archid. Aust. Filius

Eleonora Friderici IV. Rom.
Imp. Aug. Vxor

Fridericus VI. in familia Ar.
ducum huius nominis IV. aut
Rom. Imp. Aug. Filius 1415

Machtildis Alberti VI. Archid.
Austriæ Vxor

Catharina Ernesti Fer
in Arch. Aust. Filia

Casimirus Poloniæ Rex et c.
Elisabetha, Alberti V. Rom.
Aug. filiæ Maritus

Anna Alberti V. Rom.
Imp. Aug. Filia

Wilhelmus Annæ Alberti
Rom. Imp. Aug. filiæ Mari

Alexandra Ernesti
Arch. Aust. Filia

Rom. Imp. Aug. A
arch. Aust. Filius
437.

Anna Ernesti Fer
Arch. Aust. Filia

Leopoldi III. Archid.

Georgius alijs Wolfgan
us Friderici V. Ar
Filius

and their offspring radiate out from the center. At the top of the tree, the artist left space for future generations to be added. In this impression, signed by Aegidius's cousin Marcus, which was likely printed between 1650 and 1700, the final members of the brood include Maria Margarita of Austria (1651–1673) and Emperor Leopold I (1640–1705). An impression of this rare print in London has even later additions to the family and can be dated to approximately 1750.[3] The continuation of this family tree not only speaks to the Sadeler family's popularity at court but also to the focus on recording and celebrating Habsburg genealogy from the time of Maximilian until well into the eighteenth century.   FS

REFERENCE: Hollstein 1949–2010, vol. 21 (1980), p. 78, nos. 371–76

1. See the biography of Aegidius Sadeler in Sandrart 1675, pt. 2, pp. 355–57 (quotation on p. 357). This quotation is cited by Dorothy Limouze in Limouze 1989, p. 3.
2. For more on the Edict of Restitution, see Foster 2014.
3. British Museum, London (1874,0214.73.1-4).

Cat. 65

Procession of the Counts and Countess of Holland on Horseback: Mary of Burgundy, Maximilian I, Philip I, and Charles V

Jacob Cornelisz. van Oostsanen (ca. 1470–1533)
Printed by Doen Pietersz. (ca. 1480–after 1536)
Netherlandish (Amsterdam), 1518
Woodcut
15¹⁄₁₆ x 10¹¹⁄₁₆ in. (38.2 x 27.1 cm)
The Metropolitan Museum of Art, New York, The Elisha Whittelsey Collection, The Elisha Whittelsey Fund, 1949 (49.95.25)

In 1517 the Amsterdam printer Doen Pietersz. published a series of woodcuts by Jacob Cornelisz. van Oostsanen that shows the major historical rulers of the Dutch provinces mounted on horseback. The present example is one section of a procession that likely consisted of eighteen blocks, printed on fourteen sheets of paper to be joined together to form a frieze. The same visual strategy was employed in the painted and woodcut versions of the *Triumphal Procession*, which Albrecht Altdorfer, Hans Burgkmair, and Albrecht Dürer, among others, worked on between 1507 and 1518 (see cat. 162). The woodcut version of the *Triumphal Procession*, meant to disseminate Maximilian's *Gedächtnis*, or memorial, presents scenes relating to court life, including hunts,

tournaments, territories, marriages, wars, family trees, soldiers, and captives. By contrast, Cornelisz.'s woodcuts emphasize Charles V's Dutch ancestry by depicting counts and countesses of the provinces from the Houses of Habsburg, Burgundy, Wittelsbach, and Avesnes, all the way back to the House of Gerolfingen, which ruled from the ninth to the twelfth century. Maximilian's printed *Triumphal Procession* remained unfinished at his death, but one of its scenes shows his marriage in 1477 to Mary of Burgundy, which sealed the ties between the Habsburgs and the duchy of Burgundy.[1]

This sheet, the last in Cornelisz.'s series, arranges the figures in the order in which they ruled over Holland. Mary of Burgundy ruled first, from 1477 to 1482, then Maximilian, initially from 1482 to 1494 and again from 1506 to 1515 after the death of their son, Philip I, known as Philip the Handsome, who ruled from 1494 to 1506. Maximilian's grandson Charles V ruled the territory from 1515 to 1555. Below the figures are lengthy Latin texts about the rulers, while their coats of arms float above. This sheet belongs to the Latin edition of the series, which was printed simultaneously with one in French. By 1518 Mary and Philip were long dead, but Maximilian and Charles were still vibrant and powerful; they are accompanied here by their mottoes: HALT MAES (Dutch for Maintain Moderation) for the former, and PLUS OVTRE (Latin for Even Further) for Charles, who through his Spanish territories already had transatlantic realms.

At the time this woodcut was made, the *Triumphal Procession* undoubtedly had great patriotic appeal for the Low Countries, which in 1516 were celebrating Charles's succession to the Spanish throne after the death of King Ferdinand II of Aragon. Also created during this period of celebration was Cornelius Aurelius's *Chronicle of Holland, Zeeland, and Friesland* (Leuven: Jan Seversz, 1517), which similarly presented the history of the Dutch nation along with portraits of former rulers.[2] Although the *Chronicle* probably influenced Cornelisz.'s woodcuts, it seems equally significant that his adoption of the procession form and his emphasis on genealogy and symbols of power derive from Maximilian's printed projects, including not only the *Triumphal Procession* but also the *Arch of Honor* (cat. 165).   FS

REFERENCES: Jacobowitz and Stepanek 1983, pp. 272–73, no. 112, ill.; Ilona van Tuinen in Vogelaar et al. 2011, p. 316, no. 110.3

1. For connections between the two series, see Silver 2005.
2. Tilmans 1988; Marieke van Delft in Vogelaar et al. 2011, pp. 353–54, no. 153.

HALT MAES PLVS OVTR

De Maria Caroli filia.

Maria Caroli (de q̄ mō loquuti sumus) filiā vnicā formā excellentē vginē cū nobilissimi pricipes/Frederic̞ ipator et Lodouicus Gallorū rex certati hic Carolo ille Maximiliano filio vxorē peterēt. Cōuocati sunt Iouaniū patrie primores q̄ auditis q̄ postulabāt reuerūt ex patris Caroli volūtate Maximiliano Frederici ipatoris filio Mariā dādā ī matrimoniū q̄ adeo iīquo aīo tulisse Gallus dicitur vt statim oib; q̄b; perat Maria/bello idicto Atrebatū hostiliter adortus/admissi sq; p cōditiones pacis in vrbē celis primorib; direptisq; eor bonis/etiā sine discrimie iusserit occidi oēs q̄ Marie faueret/Vastauit inde quicq̄ agri opido circuiacet/In Hānonijs Auēnas vi captas icēdit missis Parrhisiosijs q̄b; ducibus icole restituerāt q̄ postea nō nisi ingēti pecunia sese redemerunt/eodē tēpore cū Gallus et mari p̄meret ab Hollādis auspicio ducat; Amstelredamoriū potissimū p̄spere pugnatū captanaui a Ianuensibus emissa/ciuis magnitudine nostri homines admirabantur.

De Maximiliano Austrio Imp. S. Au.

Maximilian̞ Caroli ducis filiai matrimoniū Gaudaui recepta/factusq; Hollādie Comes ditionis sue pricipes oēs/litteris et nūtijs hortatus est vt ad bellū Gallo q̄ vsq; ī eam diē Marie pūicias magnis cladibus affecerat/inferendū arma secū induerēt/ad quā expeditionē vnō pauci nobiles viri opimiōe celeri? aduenissent ī Morinēsem agrū egressus cū Gallis acie cōflixit/fuit ea pugna Gallox ducib; iselix/Hecū ab eo adhuc romite gesta/q̄ postea gesserit et nunc Imperat ad cōmune vtilitate bella gerit meditatur; neq; hui̞ eī situt ī scribere neq; si eēt oia scriberē Noluteni hoies nīi nisi restrictissime aliq̄d lris mādari de ijs q̄ viuunt/ īo vīnā Tironiā etate viuat M. S. A. de cui̞ vnī̞ fato oēs nīe pendent fortune.

De Philippho M. filio

Philipphus p etatē admistrationi maturus vlt̄o cedēte Maximiliano patre gubernacula Hollādie suscepit. Arame moriā hic p̄uceps magno pediti̞ ī eq̄tū globo igressus Gheldriā vt eā terrā oli a maiorib; su subactā repeteret/atq; adeo veluti intusq̄ posse scorib; occupatā iure post liminio assererēt oia terroreq̄ pleuit pleraq; opida p cuilsa metu ad p̄mū stati potētissimi ducis aduētū sese dedidere In his p̄icipijs videbaē breui vniuersaq̄ Gheldriā dominu̞ nisi repēte mutat (vt fieri solet) reb̞ in Hispaniā p̄fect̞ fuisset vt Castellano regno inauguraret̞ fuit ea Philippo maxime pacata magnificaq̄ p̄sectio vt altera illa nobis plane non tristis solū/veruētiā luctuosa/nā tūc in Hispanijs decessit adhuc iuuenis/et amplissimis imperijs destinatus.

Ad Carolū catholicum Philipphi filiū illustrissimū Hispaniarū regem.

Perduxim̞ iuuante deo cathalogū Hollādie comitū ad celsitudinē tuā illustrissime Carole de quo iā p̄dē tui ciues oēs nihil expectat mediocre/oib̞ certissima spes est te aliq̄ magnū illū Philippū pietate/Carolū q̄ ob rerū gestarū magnitudinē bellator a q̄busdā dicit̞/et quē tu noie referes/bellica virtute/auū Maximilianū clemētia/patrem comitate facilitateq̄ superaturum. In hanc autē amplissimā spem tui amātissimos/tuiq̄ obsequijs impēsissime deditos ciues adduxit/cum nature tue bonitas/tū exacta sub incorruptissimis magistris pueritia tua ex quiā iam egressus maioribus indole aperte representas

Cū gr̄a ⁊ priuilegio Car. Catho. Hisl. Reg.

Cats. 66–68

Heraldic Panels with the Arms of Maximilian I, Philip I, and Charles V

South Netherlandish, ca. 1505/6
Pot-metal glass, white glass, vitreous paint, and silver stain
Each panel: 34 x 21 in. (86.4 x 53.3 cm)
The Metropolitan Museum of Art, New York, The Cloisters
Collection, 1937 (37.147.1–.3)

These stained-glass panels feature the armorial achievements of Maximilian I, Philip I, and Charles V at the turn of the sixteenth century. Viewed together, they chronicle the Habsburgs' rapidly expanding spheres of political authority and reflect Maximilian's successes in arranging advantageous marriages for his descendants. The specific circumstances for the creation of the windows are unknown. Yet their approximate date may be inferred from significant events in the lives of the individuals whose identities are revealed through the heraldry that conveys lineage, alliance, and sovereignty in a concise visual form.[1]

Maximilian's shield of arms bears the single-headed eagle of the King of the Romans, a title he held from 1486 that reflected his status as heir apparent to the imperial throne. These arms frequently represent Maximilian during this period and appear, for example, above the arms of Hungary, Austria, Burgundy, and Tyrol in the 1502 woodcut from the *Revelations of Saint Bridget of Sweden*, attributed to the circle of Dürer (cat. 95), as well as in one of the armorial reliefs from the Golden Roof (Goldenes Dachl; cat. 19).

The armorial bearings of Philip and Charles document the family's remarkable advancement in only three generations from provincial archdukes to rulers of the Burgundian Low Countries and claimants of the Spanish crown, including its possessions in Italy and the New World. The differences between Charles's and Philip's arms, although visually subtle, carry significant heraldic implications. While the shield presently in Philip's panel includes the castle and rampant lion of Castile and León, the shield in Charles's panel additionally features the arms of Aragon, Sicily, and Granada, kingdoms of which he became the ruler. The present configuration of these panels, however, reflects a curatorial decision in 1937 to switch the shields of Philip and Charles before the windows were installed in the Cloisters, as the state in which they were acquired was thought to be incorrect (fig. 36). Thus, the shield now in Charles's window was originally in Philip's and vice versa. This action, taken in retrospect on unconvincing

FIG. 36 The windows with the coats of arms in the original arrangement

scholarly grounds, imposes false chronological assumptions on the images and obscures more than it clarifies. The issue is complicated by the fact that Charles did eventually adopt the arms presently installed in his window (as seen, for example, in cat. 65), but only after he inherited the kingdom of Aragon in 1516 and not at the time the windows were created.

Queen Isabella I of Castile's death in 1504 sparked a bitter personal standoff between her husband, Ferdinand II of Aragon, and their son-in-law Philip over Habsburg claims to the Spanish inheritance. As their only surviving child, Joanna of Castile, Philip's wife, was to inherit the kingdoms of Castile and Aragon through her parents' marriage. Ferdinand's unsuccessful attempt to remarry and produce a rival heir that might have prevented the Spanish crown from falling into foreign hands left him no choice but to allow Philip to become

king consort of Castile in 1506, thus paving the way for six-year-old Charles to become king of all of Spain. The presence of the united Spanish arms in Philip's window, as they appeared before 1937, can be read as a provocative statement of Maximilian's dynastic ambitions over the Habsburgs' right to inherit Spain.

Extensive visual and documentary evidence corroborates the accuracy of the panels' original configurations. All of the arms on Philip's seals from this period include Castile, León, Aragon, Sicily, and Granada, as does the heraldic decoration of his surcoat and Joanna's mantle in the double portrait on the *Zierikzee Triptych* (see fig. 16).[2] Charles's arms as prince of Castile, which did not include quarterings for Aragon or Granada until after his maternal grandfather's death, appear on his seal of 1507 and on a contemporaneous

diptych featuring the portraits of Philip and Joanna's six children, formerly in the collection of the Museo de Santa Cruz, Toledo.[3]   ABB

REFERENCES: Rorimer 1938, p. 14, fig. 11; Helbig 1939; Steinberg 1939, pp. 218–22, pls. A, B, D; "Stained-Glass Windows" 1971–72, n.p.; Jane Hayward in Caviness et al. 1985, pp. 136–37, nos. A–C, ill.

1. In addition to the three Habsburg panels, the series includes two windows featuring the arms of Count Henry III of Nassau-Dillenburg (1483–1538), who served Charles as chamberlain, and Roland le Fèvre (d. 1517), who served Maximilian as chamberlain and Philip as treasurer-general. The date of Henry of Nassau's entry into the Order of the Golden Fleece on November 17, 1505, and Philip's death on September 25, 1506, provide the start and end dates for the series. See Helbig 1939; Steinberg 1939; Jane Hayward in Caviness et al. 1985, pp. 136–37, nos. A–E, ill.
2. Wree 1639, pp. 137–40.
3. Ibid., p. 142; Menéndez Pidal de Navascués 1982, p. 213; Zalama 2006, ill. p. 33.

Cat. 69

Margaret of Austria

Jean Hey (called the Master of Moulins, active ca. 1480–1500)

Netherlandish, ca. 1490/1

Oil on oak panel

12⅞ x 9 in. (32.7 x 23 cm)

The Metropolitan Museum of Art, New York, Robert Lehman Collection, 1975 (1975.1.130)

This regal portrait of the ten-year-old Margaret of Austria, daughter of Maximilian I and Mary of Burgundy, vividly evokes her early role as a political instrument in the dynastic and territorial conflicts between the Habsburgs and the French crown. Under the treaty of Arras of 1482, Maximilian was forced to concede to the French king Louis XI by giving Margaret's hand in marriage to the dauphin Charles VIII, thereby relinquishing significant Burgundian territories in her dowry. Following their betrothal in 1483, the three-year-old Margaret was sent to the French court in preparation for her role as queen of France. However, in 1491, in a double assault against Maximilian, Charles renounced Margaret in favor of Anne of Brittany, whom Maximilian had married by proxy the prior year.

In late 1490 or early 1491, shortly before Charles dissolved his engagement to Margaret, the present portrait was painted when the young couple visited the Bourbon court in Moulins in central France.[1] The Netherlandish-born artist Jean Hey served as painter to the thriving Bourbon court and produced portraits of several members of the dynasty. Conceived within this artistic and political milieu, Margaret's portrait could have been commissioned by Charles's sister Anne de Beaujeu, who served as regent during his youth and was responsible for the education of his intended bride.

Hey's virtuosity in rendering the luxurious material quality of Margaret's garments and jewels—the textures of velvet and fur and the iridescent pearls—enhances the splendor of her courtly attire. The "little queen," as she was known, is bedecked in symbols evoking her affiliation with the Bourbon dynasty and the French crown. Her ermine-trimmed red velvet gown is embellished at the collar with the initials C and M, signifying her union with Charles, while the shells along the edge of her headdress are Bourbon emblems. Margaret's elaborate jeweled pendant celebrates her royal status in its fleur-de-lis form—a symbol also associated with the Virgin Mary—while the pelican mounted on top, a traditional reference to Christ's sacrifice and resurrection, emphasizes her piety.[2] Such accoutrements were listed in the 1493 inventory of her possessions and may have been nuptial gifts from Charles.[3] Holding a pearl rosary, a self-referential symbol of her piety given that *margarita* means pearl in Latin, the young queen recites her prayers as she gazes to the right, possibly toward what was originally the object of her devotion: an image of Christ's Passion that may have adorned the now-lost right-hand wing of a diptych.[4]

The Lehman panel is among several images of the young Margaret that illustrate her role, and that of portraiture, in matrimonial politics, including one painted at age three, around the time of her betrothal to Charles, and another at age fifteen, in anticipation of Maximilian's arrangement of her marriage into the Spanish dynasty in 1496.[5] In 1495 Margaret's portrait was also included in the tournament tapestry of Frederick the Wise, prince elector of Saxony (cat. 70). As regent of the Burgundian Low Countries beginning in 1507, Margaret became a notable ruler and patron in her own right, assembling a significant collection of dynastic portraits at her court in Mechelen.   AMN

REFERENCES: Maryan W. Ainsworth in *From Van Eyck to Bruegel* 1998, pp. 181–83, no. 35, ill.; Charles Sterling and Ainsworth in Sterling et al. 1998, pp. 11–18, no. 3, ill.; Borchert 2002, p. 251, no. 73, ill.

1. Charles Sterling and Maryan W. Ainsworth in Sterling et al. 1998, p. 12; see also Martha Wolff in *Kings, Queens, and Courtiers* 2011, p. 126.
2. Sterling and Ainsworth in Sterling et al. 1998, p. 15. For a discussion of the themes of sacrifice and resurrection, see Ainsworth in *From Van Eyck to Bruegel* 1998, p. 181, no. 35.
3. Eichberger 2002, pp. 29–32.
4. The pun on *margarita* is referenced in Borchert 2002, p. 251, no. 73.
5. The 1483 portrait by the Master of the Legend of Mary Magdalen (Musée National du Château de Versailles, MV 4026) and the double portrait of Margaret and Philip the Fair painted in 1493–95 by Pieter van Coninxloo (National Gallery, London, NG 2613.2).

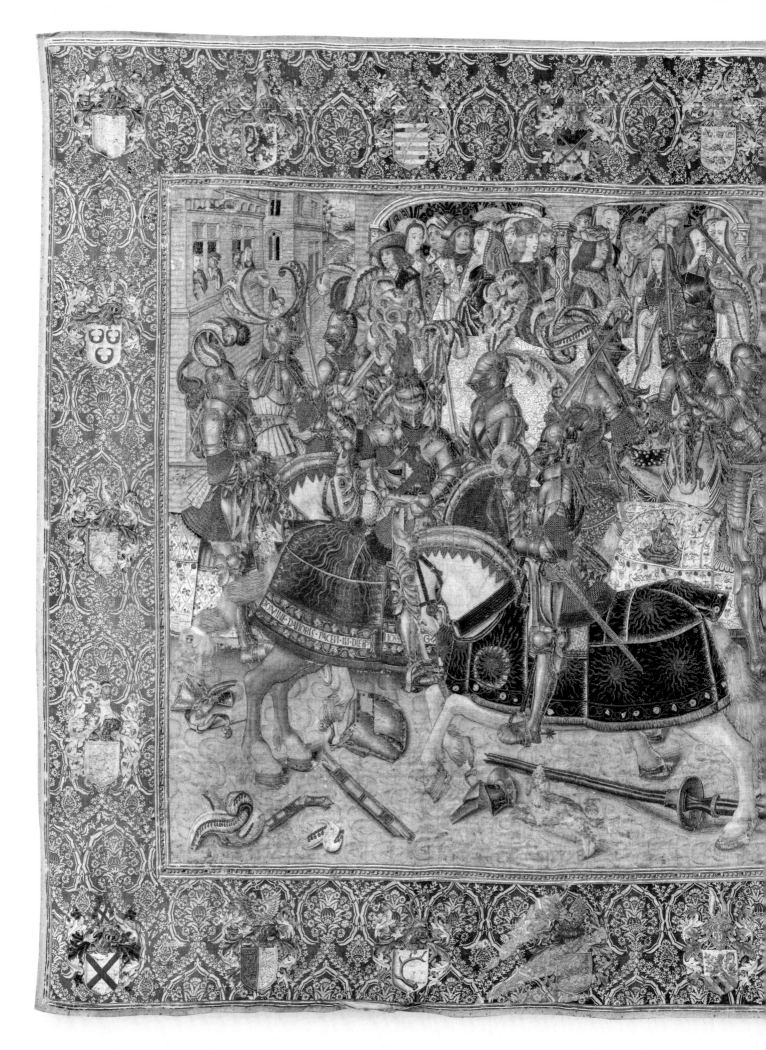

Tournament Tapestry of Frederick the Wise
South Netherlandish (probably Brussels), ca. 1490
Silk, silver, and gold threads
16 ft 3¹¹⁄₁₆ in. x 18 ft 11¹⁵⁄₁₆ in. (497 x 579 cm)
Musée des Beaux-Arts de Valenciennes, France (O.A.87.19)

This grand panel occupies a special place among the tapestries woven in the Low Countries not only for its quality and luxury, but also for its portrayal of a distinctive form of tournament, known as the free tourney, and for the notable spectators watching it from a central loggia. Popular in the Burgundian Low Countries, the free tourney was a mock combat structured to evoke the successive phases of a battle fought by mounted knights. The participants were divided into two groups who first charged toward each other with lances and then engaged in a group fight with swords. The tapestry depicts the second phase of the free tourney: the ground is strewn with the reinforcing elements and broken lances that the participants used during its first phase, and the fury of their sword fight is made clear by the chopped plumes of their helmets, which the horses trample. The members of one group wear the cross of Saint Andrew (a Burgundian badge) made of costly textiles over their breastplates, while the others keep their breastplates bare.

Irrespective of team, some knights sport sizable crests over their helmets—almost certainly heraldic crests that complement their coats of arms, which would have helped spectators identify them and follow their respective deeds. The crest of the knight riding on a horse covered with a red caparison is a case in point, as it features a seated lion, akin to the heraldic crest of the Reimerswaele family of Zeeland, whose coat of arms is prominently displayed on the escutcheon of his horse's shaffron. The crests of other participants—a salamander(?); a griffin's claw; a six-pointed star; and a sword with its point up, standing on a ball—would have been recognized by contemporary observers but their owners currently elude us.

There are several reasons to believe that the tapestry represents actual people and events: the unparalleled care with which the armor, weaponry, and textile accoutrements for the contestants and their horses are represented; the verisimilitude and variety of the knights' armors and equipment; and the presence of crests on helmets, a coat of arms on a shaffron, and ciphers and mottos on horse caparisons. The coats of arms in the tapestry's integral border, which represent territories in the dominion of Frederick the Wise, prince elector of Saxony, indicate that the work was commissioned either by him or for presentation to him. Among them, the arms of

Biberstein (third to the right, at the bottom left corner) and Sagan (second above the bottom right) importantly identify a territory of which Frederick took possession in 1490 and another that he and his brother ceded to Duke George of Saxony in 1508, respectively. The presence of these coats of arms suggests that the cartoon after which the tapestry was woven was executed sometime between these two dates.

Because Philip I is recognizable among the spectators in the loggia,[1] and because Frederick the Wise was in the Low Countries in 1494 for Philip's legal emancipation from his guardian, Maximilian, it has often been suggested that the tapestry commemorates a tournament held in celebration of Philip's coming of age in Antwerp, on October 19 and 20, which Frederick is known to have attended.[2] This interpretation, however, should be reconsidered. Notably, Philip, who wears the collar of the Order of the Golden Fleece, does not occupy a particularly prominent place in the loggia: he stands with his back turned to the woman holding a pink (a conventional symbol of love and fidelity),[3] almost pressed against the central column. In fact, the spectators surrounding him hardly pay any attention to him. If the depicted tournament was held in his honor, it seems doubtful that he would have been relegated to such an insignificant position.

The couple so prominently featured on the right side of the loggia raises an additional problem. The two figures are Charles VIII of France, wearing the collar of the royal French order of Saint Michael, and Margaret, Philip's sister.[4] Yet, Philip, Charles, and Margaret never were together in the same place at the same time; further, Charles did not attend the inauguration of Philip's personal rule or the tournaments held in his honor. Even more significantly, by the time Philip was solemnly emancipated, Charles had become an odious figure in pro-Habsburg circles. Although he was betrothed to Margaret in 1483, Charles chose to renege on his engagement in order to marry Anne, duchess of Brittany, in 1491, and sent Margaret back to the Burgundian Low Countries in 1493. Adding insult to injury, Anne had recently been married by proxy with Maximilian. By marrying her, Charles both ravished Maximilian's wife and dismissed Maximilian's daughter. As it is unlikely that Frederick, then one of Maximilian's strongest supporters, would have wanted to include such an unpopular figure as Charles in a sumptuous tapestry, it seems probable that the piece was commissioned while Charles VIII and Margaret were still betrothed, that is before December 6, 1491, when Charles married Anne, several years before Philip was emancipated and the Antwerp tournament took place.

The presence of Charles and Margaret in the loggia, and the careful placement of her left hand over the right one to show the engagement ring on her finger, can only reference their betrothal, and the implicit hope that their union might restore peace between Louis XI, Charles's father, and Maximilian. In support of this idea, the inscription adorning

one of the caparisons, DOMINE DANOBIS PACEN IN DIEB NOSS, which corresponds to the Latin words for the Christian hymn or psalm "O Lord, give us peace in our days," would have been a fitting one for a tourney celebrating a peace or a truce.[5] In view of these historical and iconographic considerations, it is conceivable that the tapestry might celebrate the treaty of Arras (December 23, 1482), whereby Maximilian made peace with Louis XI and Margaret was engaged to Charles VIII; the treaty of Frankfurt (July 22, 1489), whereby Maximilian, on behalf of Philip, and Charles VIII agreed on a truce (as hostilities had resumed between them after the 1482 treaty); or the treaty of Montil-les-Tours (October 31, 1489), whereby the same individuals agreed on a peace that included the Flemish cities that had rebelled against Maximilian. While the woman holding a pink and many other distinctive figures in the loggia have not been conclusively identified, and the ultimate meaning of this magnificent work remains open to question, the tournament tapestry is an unequivocal reminder of the significance of matrimonial arrangements in the political affairs of the time, and of the particular importance mock combats played in their celebration, the memory of which it was meant to preserve from oblivion.   PT

REFERENCES: Hénault 1910, pp. 145–56, ill. facing p. 148, figs. 2, 4 (details); Kretschmar 1909–11, pp. 166–71, ill. facing p. 168; Geneviève Souchal in *Chefs-d'oeuvre de la tapisserie* 1973, pp. 72–75, no. 17, ill.; Cetto 1977; Ramade 1995, pp. 241–44, ill.; Delmarcel 1999, p. 52, ill. p. 50

1. The figure is closely related to a number of painted portraits, including examples in the Koninklijke Musea voor Schone Kunsten van België, Brussels (6355), Musée du Louvre, Paris (2085), and Upton House, National Trust, collection of the viscount of Bearsted, near Banbury, Warwickshire (160); see Micheline Comblen-Sonkes in Lorentz and Comblen-Sonkes 2001, pt. 1, pp. 228–38, no. 200, pt. 2, pls. CLXXIV–CLXXIX, a, on the Paris portrait, and pt. 1, pp. 233–35, on related examples.

2. Kretschmar 1909–11, p. 166; Geneviève Souchal in *Chefs-d'oeuvre de la tapisserie* 1973, p. 73; Ramade 1995; Delmarcel 1999, p. 52.

3. On the imagery of women holding pinks in Netherlandish portraits from the period, and its meanings, see Anne Dubois and Géraldine Patigny in Dubois et al. 2009, p. 181.

4. The figure of Charles VIII is closely related to a portrait in the Institute of Fine Arts, New York University, the existence of which was kindly brought to the author's attention by Vincent Hadot. It may have been based on that portrait or a lost variant thereof; see Dupont 1936, pp. 186–89, ill. The figure of Margaret is closely related to a portrait attributed to the Master of the Legend of Mary Magdalene in the Musée du Louvre, Paris (R.F. 2259), a variant attributed to Pieter van Coninxloo thought to have been presented to Henry VII of England in 1505, in the Royal Collection at Hampton Court Palace (RCIN 403428), and yet another variant in a private collection. The similarities extend to the position of her hands and the jewel pendant worn around her neck. The brocade of her dress relates more closely to a portrait in the National Gallery, London (NG2613.2), and a comparable picture in the Kunsthistorisches Museum, Vienna, Gemäldegalerie (4447). On these portraits, see Comblen-Sonkes in Lorentz and Comblen-Sonkes 2001, pt. 1, pp. 216–27, no. 199, especially pp. 222–24, pt. 2, pls. CLXVIII–CLXXIII, CLXXIX, b; Gisela Sachse in *Kaiser Maximilian I.* 2002, p. 250, no. 323, ill. p. 181.

5. The proper Latin inscription reads "Domine da nobis pacem in diebus nostris." The suggestion that this inscription participates in the celebration of a truce or peace is already put forth by Souchal in *Chefs-d'oeuvre de la tapisserie* 1973, p. 73.

Toy Figures Armed for the Joust of War

Austrian (probably Mühlau), ca. 1505

Bronze

Each toy: H. 4⁵⁄₁₆ in. (11 cm), W. 2½ in. (6.5 cm), D. 4¾ in. (12 cm)

Kunsthistorisches Museum, Vienna, Kunstkammer (81; 92)

Late medieval and early modern toys are rare; those produced for elite children were often specially commissioned from artisans and workshops otherwise engaged in the manufacture of wares for adults.[1] These toy jousting figures may have been cast at Maximilian's bronze foundry at Mühlau near Innsbruck by highly skilled craftsmen who specialized in firearms.[2] Maximilian established the foundry in 1503 to secure independent access to cast-bronze weapons, recruiting craftsmen from the free imperial city of Nuremberg, which previously had maintained strict control over the craft.[3]

Each of these toys has a horse mounted onto a base plate with functioning spoked wheels and a rider riveted to a saddle allowing it to tilt backward when struck by an opponent's lance. Such a game is depicted in Hans Burgkmair's well-known woodcut from the chapter recounting the education of the young prince in Maximilian's pseudo-autobiographical romance the *Weisskunig* (cat. 116). Despite the book's sensational literary style and frequent exaggerated claims, the passage emphasizes the importance of tournaments as models of combat in the education of noble boys. These toys are thought to have been commissioned for Maximilian's grandsons, Charles V and Ferdinand I, to whom the *Weisskunig* was dedicated. Maximilian also ordered two jousting toys for his adopted son Louis II, the future king of Hungary, Bohemia, and Croatia, from armorer Kolman Helmschmid in 1516, demonstrating his continued personal interest in the education of his descendants.[4]   ABB

REFERENCES: Gröber 1928, pp. 13–15, ill. no. 29; Weihrauch 1963, pp. 17–20, fig. 3; Blair 1966, pp. 43–47, fig. 1; Thomas and Gamber 1976, p. 171, nos. P 81, P 92, fig. 84; Stefan Krause in *Kaiser Maximilian I.* 2014, p. 140, no. II.1, ill.

1. Gröber 1928, pp. 10–21.
2. See Palme 2000.
3. Ibid., pp. 142–43.
4. Gröber 1928, p. 14.

Cat. 73

Toy Figure Armed for the Joust of Peace

Austrian (probably Mühlau), ca. 1510

Bronze

H. 2⅞ in. (7.3 cm), W. 1⁷⁄₁₆ in. (3.7 cm), D. ¹⁵⁄₁₆ in. (2.4 cm)

Tiroler Landesmuseum Ferdinandeum, Innsbruck, Austria, Ältere Kunstgeschichtliche Sammlungen (B 186)

Very few knight figurines from before 1600 survive, and only eight cast-bronze toys from the early sixteenth century are known to exist worldwide.[1] This figurine—unearthed in 1875 during construction on Welsergasse in Innsbruck and gifted to the Ferdinandeum the following year—can be identified as a jouster, although both horse and lance have been lost. The helmet, shaped like a ship's bow, is of a type commonly used in jousting, as is the shield secured to the torso and the surviving piece of plate armor that protects the figure's thigh (the second piece is missing). In jousting, two opponents charge at one another, each trying to unhorse his rival with a lance. The figurine's right hand is positioned to wield a lance, which might have been a removable element inserted in the hole.

The toy jouster, which may have been made for Maximilian I's grandsons—Charles V and Ferdinand I—was probably manufactured, like two other figurines now housed in Vienna (see cats. 71, 72), in a bronze foundry active for Maximilian in Mühlau, just outside Innsbruck. Mounted on wheeled bronze horses and originally outfitted with string, the Vienna figurines could be pulled toward each other with gusto and reflect a different form of jousting, known in German as *Anzogenrennen*. Nevertheless, the three toys illustrate the enduring importance of the chivalric system around 1500, into which the sons of European rulers were initiated. Just as a young Maximilian is depicted playing with toy knights in the *Weisskunig* (cat. 116), his progeny would also use these figurines to learn the various tournament forms and structures as children, before their own training for tourneying began in adolescence.   PS

REFERENCES: Gert Ammann in *Ruhm und Sinnlichkeit* 1996, pp. 94–95, no. 14, ill.; Monika Frenzel in *Maximilian I.* 2005, p. 43, II.15; Martin Baumeister in *Mythos Burg* 2010, p. 152, no. 4.21, ill.; Stefan Krause in *Kaiser Maximilian I.* 2014, p. 140, under no. II.1

1. On the group, see Blair 1966.

Cat. 74

Philip I

Attributed to the Master of the Portraits of Princes
(active ca. 1470–ca. 1492)

South Netherlandish, ca. 1490

Oil on panel

10⅝ x 6⅞ in. (27 x 17. 5 cm)

Musée du Louvre, Paris, deposited at the Musée de la Chasse
et de la Nature, Paris (RF 1969–18)

As he descended through his mother from the Valois dukes
of Burgundy, and was born in Bruges, the three-year-old
Philip I was viewed by many of his prospective subjects as
Mary of Burgundy's only rightful successor when she died
suddenly in an accident in 1482. Maximilian I, his father,
may have borne the title of duke of Burgundy, but that was
only his privilege as her consort; a foreigner, he was widely
unpopular in the Burgundian Low Countries, especially in
the Flemish towns of Bruges, Ghent, and Ieper, which
resented his manners, his constant need for subsidies to
fight the king of France, and his disregard for the privileges
that guaranteed their autonomy and curtailed his authority.
A long struggle over the legal guardianship of Philip thus
began, with many disputing Maximilian's claim to be the
regent of the Low Countries for his son, leading to revolt and
open war, peaking with Maximilian's imprisonment in Bruges
in 1488, only to end with the submission of his opponents.

As a prince who was too young to rule personally, Philip
was the object of considerable attention and strife. In this portrait, his exceptional standing is apparent in the regal quality
of his attire—a doublet of gold brocade, a coat of silk velvet
lined with ermine, and a bejeweled hat—and the collar of the
Order of the Golden Fleece round his neck. The hooded hawk
on his left hand refers to the noble pursuit of falconry, of which
his mother and certainly Maximilian were very fond.[1]
It is unclear whether the picture simply conforms to an established genre, as some important figures at the Burgundian
court were similarly represented, or whether it might allude to
an important aspect of princely education since Philip's son
Charles V was similarly portrayed at the age of seven.[2]

Philip is depicted wearing the same clothes in the *Marriage
at Cana*, the left panel of an altarpiece in the collection of the
National Gallery of Victoria, Melbourne. The present portrait
seems to date from about the same period and has been
attributed on stylistic grounds to the Master of the Portraits of
Princes, an anonymous painter thought to have been active
in Brussels.[3]   PT

REFERENCES: Friedländer 1975, pp. 14–15, pl. 22, no. 31; Périer-D'Ieteren
1990, pp. 4–11, 16, figs. 4, 8b; Bücken 2013, p. 225, and p. 226, ill. no. III.156

1. Brigitte Mersich in *Herrlich Wild* 2004, pp. 29–31, no. 1.7, ill.; Sandbichler
2004, p. 135.
2. See, for example, the portrait of Engelbrecht II of Nassau; Matthias Ubl
in *Héritage de Rogier van der Weyden* 2013, pp. 228–29, no. 43, ill. For
Charles's portrait, see Katharina Seidl in *Herrlich Wild* 2004, pp. 143–44,
no. 5.6, ill.
3. For a discussion of the two pictures and their attribution to the Master of
the Portraits of Princes, see Périer-D'Ieteren 1990; Périer-D'Ieteren 2013,
pp. 72–73, and p. 74, ill. nos. 48, 49.

Cat. 75

Cuirass of an Armor of Philip I

Master of the Crowned H (active ca. 1480–1500)

South Netherlandish, ca. 1485

Steel, leather, copper alloy, and gold

H. 14⅛ in. (36 cm), W. 9⅞ in. (25 cm), D. 8¼ in. (21 cm)

Kunsthistorisches Museum, Vienna, Imperial Armoury (A 109a)

In late medieval and Renaissance Europe it was customary
for noble families' eldest sons to train from a young age in the
areas that befitted their higher rank—among them horsemanship and the various martial arts including the tournament.
The armors that were made to their measure were not only
required for practical purposes; they were also worn to signal
the boys' distinguished standing and calling. Emblematic of
their privileges, their armors typically mirrored those of adults
in construction, form, and decoration.

During the five years they were married, Maximilian I and
Mary of Burgundy had two sons and one daughter. After their
youngest son died in infancy, Philip I became their sole male
heir and he was groomed accordingly. Maximilian commissioned armors for him to wear when training in knightly pursuits and appearing before his future subjects in the guise of a
promising successor and a burgeoning leader. This cuirass was
made to serve both practical and symbolic purposes, when
Philip was perhaps six to eight years old. It is all that is known
to remain of what must have originally been a full armor,
which in its complete state would have also included a helmet,
as well as defenses for the neck, shoulders, arms, hands, legs,
and feet. The presence of a gilded rest on the right side of
the chest, to steady the lance that could be couched under
the armpit and to absorb the shock when the lance struck the
desired target, indicates that the armor was designed for
cavalry use.

In addition to being the earliest surviving example of a
boy's armor, the cuirass is unprecedented for the fact that its

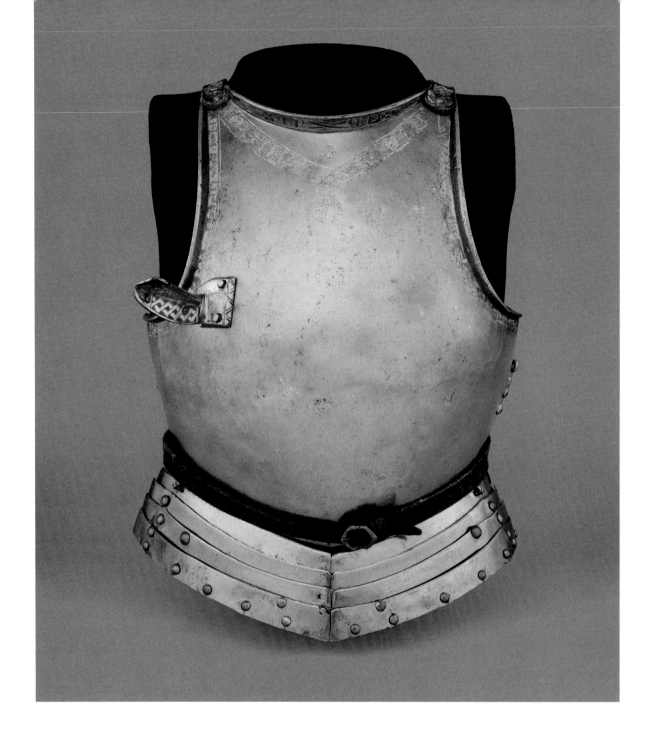

etched and gilded ornamentation includes the collar of the Order of the Golden Fleece round the neck. As the presumptive heir to his mother's dominions, Philip was made a member of this prestigious chivalric order at the age of two, whereas all other members had to be adult men. The collar on the boy's armor signaled his preeminence, and it would have reminded onlookers of his bright future, as the eventual sovereign of the order and their prospective ruler. Subsequent armors created for the personal use of members of the House of Habsburg were often decorated with the order's collar. One of the latest known examples is an armor garniture for the field and tournament, which was made by Franz Groszschedel in Landshut in 1571 for Maximilian II of Austria and is now preserved in Vienna.[1]

The workmanship and decoration of Philip's cuirass show the care with which Maximilian—whose right to be his son's guardian (following the death of his wife) was periodically contested and even became a cause for war with his Burgundian subjects—sought to strengthen the future of his line and the position of his son in particular.[2] In form and construction, the cuirass is resolutely modern: its breastplate and backplate are each formed from a single main plate, in contrast to the prevailing fifteenth-century practice of joining two or more plates together in the center to create the pieces to

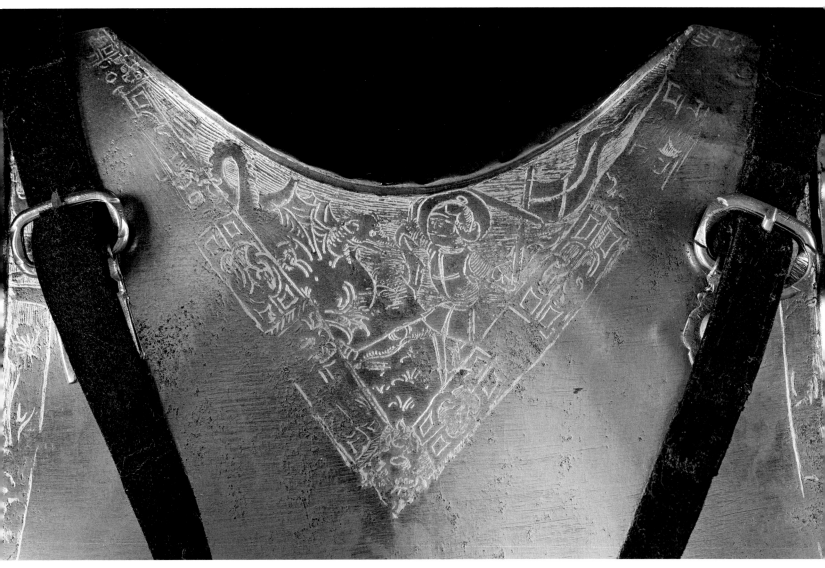

DETAIL OF BACKPLATE

guard the upper and lower parts of the torso. Comparable single-piece breastplates are recorded in the Low Countries from the 1480s, for example on the figure of Saint George in a panel from a diptych by Hans Memling in Munich.[3] The cuirass also has a detachable fauld and culet, each of which consists of four lames and is secured at the top by turning pins that engage into keyhole slots at the sides. The turned edges along the cuirass's neck and gussets are decorated with etched and gilded ornament consisting of the cross of Saint Andrew, Philip's monogram of two confronted letters P, and flower heads. On the right gusset is the biblical quotation "But Jesus, passing through the midst of them, went His way"

(IHEZUS AVTEM TRANCIAM PER MEDIVM ILLORVM IBAT; Luke 4: 30), and on the left, the supplication "Mary, full of Grace, O Mother of God, remember me" (MARIA MATER GRA O MATER DEI MEM).

The mark of the letter H surmounted by an open coronet, which is struck beneath the neck on the breastplate, belonged to an armorer working in the Low Countries for the Habsburg court. The same mark occurs on a number of other pieces, most importantly on elements of a jousting armor made for Philip when he was in his teens, which is now in Vienna.[4] As the registers of accounts of Maximilian's treasurers for expenses of this nature are virtually all lost, his identity remains uncertain. He was not Hugues Brugman, to whom the mark has been tentatively attributed, as Brugman was a cutler, and as such made swords, lance heads, and the like. A better candidate is Franck Scroo, one of Maximilian's preferred armorers in Brussels, who in 1488 was paid the sum of 62 livres 8 sols, currency of Flanders, for a full armor he had made for Philip when the boy was nine years old.[5]

The cuirass is first recorded in Ambras Castle in 1596,[6] where it remained until 1806, when it was removed for safekeeping to Vienna. It was kept in the Lower Belvedere Palace until 1891, when it entered the collections of the Kunsthistorisches Museum. It may be the remnants of a boy's armor Charles V sent to Maximilian in 1517.[7]   PT

REFERENCE: Thomas and Gamber 1976, pp. 127–28, no. A 109a, fig. 49

1. Kunsthistorisches Museum, Vienna (A 474); see Beaufort-Spontin and Pfaffenbichler 2005, pp. 174–75, no. 61, ill.
2. Haemers 2014.
3. Scalini 1996, p. 106, ill. no. III.18.
4. See Thomas and Gamber 1976, pp. 149–50, no. S. II. On this master and his known works, see Blair 1998, pp. 291–94.
5. On Brugman, see Thomas and Gamber 1976, pp. 127–28, no. A 109a, pp. 149–50, no. S. II; Blair 1998, p. 294. On Scroo's delivery, see Algemeen Rijksarchief, Brussels, CC 1924, fol. 130v.
6. Auer 1984, p. XXXIV, no. 46.
7. Archives Départementales du Nord, Lille, B 2267, fol. 321r.

Cat. 76

Armor of Philip I

Anthonis van Ghindertaelen (first recorded 1491, died 1520)
South Netherlandish (Brussels), 1500
Steel, gold, leather, and copper alloy
As mounted: H. 67¾ in. (172 cm), W. 25¼ in. (64 cm),
D. 19¹¹⁄₁₆ in. (50 cm)
Patrimonio Nacional, Madrid, Real Armería (A 11)

Although no longer entirely homogeneous, and also missing some elements, this work is the most complete and luxurious surviving example of a Netherlandish field armor from the turn of the sixteenth century. Notably, it was made for Philip I and reverently kept by all of his descendants. Wrought by Anthonis van Ghindertaelen, one of Philip's favorite armorers, its original elements presently include a helmet in the shape of a hat, a bevor, a breastplate, pauldrons made in one with the vambraces, besagews, and gauntlets, as well as the culet lames of a backplate, which are all etched and gilded with the same designs. The mark of an orb and cross surmounted by an open coronet, which is struck on the breastplate, the couters, and the backplate, can be securely attributed to Van Ghindertaelen

on the basis of a rare document by his hand, which he signed with a sketch of the same mark.[1] Although by the same master, the current backplate must once have belonged to another armor as its decoration does not match that of the other pieces. When still complete, the armor would have presumably also had a matching backplate, tassets, cuisses, greaves, and poleyns, and quite possibly exchange pieces such as an armet. The unique hat-like helmet was probably not intended for cavalry use with a lance, in contrast to the breastplate, which has three staples on the right side to attach a rest over which the lance could be couched when engaging in combat. This disparity suggests there may have been a second helmet. Moreover, while the bevor would have covered the front of the neck, the symmetrical, hat-like helmet does not protect the nape of the neck, which supports the hypothesis that another kind of helmet, such as a war hat or sallet, must have also originally existed.

The original elements are all etched and gilded with multiple patterns, including scrolling foliage and narrow bands enclosing half flower heads separated from one another by a zigzag line. Set against a hatched or crosshatched ground, the ornamentation also includes numerous religious invocations in Latin and Flemish on all pieces, and the representation of the chain collar and pendant of the Order of the Golden Fleece on the breastplate. Although rather crudely executed, the etching would have looked magnificent when completely covered in gold. The shortcomings of the execution raise the possibility that the pieces were etched not by a painter or an artist specializing in the graphic arts, but perhaps by the armorer himself or an assistant in his workshop.

Van Ghindertaelen was held in high regard. The account books of Philip's chief treasurer in the Burgundian Low Countries from 1499 record commissions for the armorer to manufacture field harnesses that Philip presented as gifts to Duke John II of Cleves, King Ferdinand II of Aragon, and the latter's illegitimate son, Alfonso of Aragon, the archbishop of Saragossa. After Philip's death he was patronized by Charles V and made important armors on the occasion of the latter's coronation as King of the Romans in 1520.[2]

The present armor must have held a special place in Philip's armory, for among the many pieces that Van Ghindertaelen had made for his father, it is the one that Charles ultimately took with him to Spain after his abdication. It is illustrated in a pictorial inventory of Charles's armory and also recognizable in the earliest surviving inventory of Philip II's armory in Madrid.[3] It is Philip II who, by declaring the royal Spanish armory an inalienable property of the crown, created the

conditions for this and other Habsburg heirlooms to remain protected and cared for through the centuries.[4]   PT

REFERENCES: Valencia de Don Juan 1898, pp. 8–10, no. A. 11, figs. 11, 12, pl. I; José A. Godoy in *Resplendence of the Spanish Monarchy* 1991, pp. 114–17, no. 17, ill.; Godoy in *Tapices y armaduras del Renacimiento* 1992, pp. 124–27, ill.; Godoy in *Paz y la guerra* 1994, pp. 296–97, no. 227, ill.

1. The publication of this important document is in preparation by the present author.
2. On Van Ghindertaelen's accomplishments, see Terjanian 2006, pp. 153–54.
3. Patrimonio Nacional, Madrid, Real Armería, N18A, fol. 21r.
4. José A. Godoy in *Tapices y armaduras del Renacimiento* 1992, pp. 101–3, 124–27.

Cat. 77

Shaffron of Philip I

Anthonis van Ghindertaelen (first recorded 1491, died 1520)
South Netherlandish (Brussels), ca. 1505
Steel, copper alloy, and gold
H. 27 9/16 in. (70 cm), W. 9 7/8 in. (25 cm), D. 4 5/16 in. (11 cm)
Patrimonio Nacional, Madrid, Real Armería (A. 15)

Charles V formally abdicated as duke of Burgundy and king of Spain in favor of his son Philip II in October 1556, and eight months later also abdicated as Holy Roman Emperor in favor of his younger brother Ferdinand I. Before sailing to Spain, where he chose to spend the rest of his life, he ensured that the major part of his armory in Brussels, among which were heirlooms from his father, Philip I, including this shaffron, would follow him. The shaffron probably entered Charles's armory when he was only ten, thanks to the energetic intervention of his grandfather Maximilian I, who would not allow such significant objects to go astray (see cat. 76).[1]

Forged from a single plate, this shaffron has a hinged poll plate at the top and a large faceted rondel over the brow. Shaped to fit a horse's head, it is embossed with a ridge down the nose, and flanged over the ears, eyes, and mouth. The flanged sections have cusped edges and are bordered by flutes except at the eyes. The poll plate has similar flutes at each side of its medial ridge. Engraved on its lower part with knobby staves tied together to evoke the cross of Saint Andrew and with fire steels, flints, and flames, the shaffron sports the badges of the Order of the Golden Fleece, of which Philip was made a member when he was only two years old, and of which he became the sovereign upon his mother's death the following year. The badges were likely gilded in their original state.

The mark of an orb and cross surmounted by an open coronet, which is struck immediately below the base of the ears,

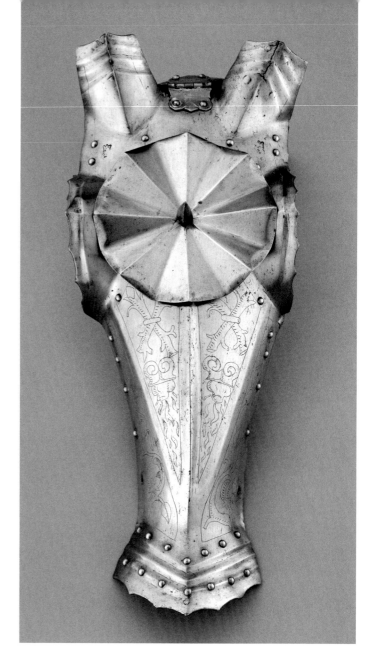

identifies this shaffron as a work by Anthonis van Ghindertaelen, one of Philip I's favorite armorers.[2] Likely to be one of four examples illustrated in a pictorial inventory of Charles's armory, which was compiled sometime after 1544, the shaffron was among the items that Philip II acquired from his father's armory and incorporated into his own in Madrid in 1565.[3]   PT

REFERENCES: Valencia de Don Juan 1898, p. 11, no. A. 15; Blair 1965, p. 27, pl. XVI, c (erroneously as no. A. 11); José A. Godoy in *Tapices y armaduras del Renacimiento* 1992, pp. 128–29, ill.; Godoy in *Paz y la guerra* 1994, p. 297, no. 228, ill.

1. On the removal of objects from Charles's armory in Brussels to Spain, see Soler del Campo 1998. On the objects that originally belonged to Philip I that entered Charles's armory in 1510, see Terjanian 2006.
2. On this armorer, see Terjanian 2006, pp. 153–54.
3. The pictorial inventory is in the collections of the Patrimonio Nacional, Madrid, Real Armería, N18A, N18B.

Sallet of Philip I

Probably Netherlandish, ca. 1500
Steel and gold
H. 15⅜ in. (39 cm), W. 8¼ in. (21 cm), D. 13 in. (33 cm)
Patrimonio Nacional, Madrid, Real Armería (D. 14)

As was typical of his time, Maximilian I relied on marriages to cement alliances and secure political advantages for himself and his kin. The betrothal of his son, Philip I, to Joanna of Castile and their subsequent marriage in 1496 proved to be one of his greatest coups. Philip became king of Castile in 1506 once his wife succeeded her mother, Isabella, as queen. In turn, their eldest son, Charles V, became king of all Spain in 1516 once the crown of Aragon, which had remained with

Joanna's father, Ferdinand II of Aragon, became available after his death. Charles inaugurated a long line of Habsburg kings of Spain, which lasted until 1700.

Made for Philip, this sallet is unique for the steel pomegranate that surmounts it. Possibly a replacement for a similarly formed finial, which in 1793 was thought to be of silver, it unequivocally refers to the kingdom of Granada, which Joanna's parents had successfully recaptured in 1492.[1] As Granada was the last kingdom under Moorish control in Spain, its fall effectively completed the reconquest of the Iberian Peninsula, and this major event was celebrated all over Christendom. By sporting a pomegranate on his helmet, as he did in his own heraldic arms, Philip—who systematically used the title of king of Granada in his correspondence from the time he became king consort of Castile—associated himself with the accomplishments of his parents-in-law and claimed for himself some of the prestige that came with the Castilian crown Maximilian had secured for him.

The sallet was probably made after Philip's marriage with Joanna, perhaps in anticipation of his second trip to Spain (1504–6), where he was to be crowned king. It is recognizable in a pictorial inventory of Charles V's armory, in which it appears among old Flemish arms and armor that Charles had brought to Spain following his abdication.[2] It is perhaps the same piece as the sallet with a gilded visor and bevor that had been brought back from Spain following Philip's unexpected death, and incorporated, thanks to Maximilian's intervention, into Charles's armory in 1510.[3]

In its original state the sallet was extensively ornamented: the back of its crown and the bottom edge of its nape defense were enriched with gilded appliqués. The sallet's provenance and decoration, including the longitudinal flutes on its bowl, which converge toward the apex, and the stepped profile of

the lower part of its visor, suggest it was likely made in the Burgundian Low Countries. Specimens with similarly fluted bowls are frequently represented in Netherlandish art, for example in a tapestry panel from the Story of Alexander, which is now in Genoa.[4] The mark struck on the rear left side of the sallet's bowl, which consists of the stacked upper edges of three open coronets, is not known to occur on any other piece. The armorer who used it remains unidentified.[5]   PT

REFERENCES: Valencia de Don Juan 1898, pp. 143–44, no. D. 14, figs. 83, 84; José A. Godoy in *Resplendence of the Spanish Monarchy* 1991, pp. 108–9, no. 15, ill.; Godoy in *Tapices y armaduras del Renacimiento* 1992, pp. 118–19, ill.; Soler del Campo 2009, pp. 72–73, no. 13, ill.

1. Abadia 1793, pp. 47–48, cited by José A. Godoy in *Resplendence of the Spanish Monarchy* 1991, p. 108, n. 1.
2. Patrimonio Nacional, Madrid, Real Armería, N18A, fol. 20v; see also Godoy in *Resplendence of the Spanish Monarchy* 1991, p. 108, ill.
3. Terjanian 2006, p. 158, no. 23.
4. Campbell 2007, p. 46, fig. 3.2.
5. The mark is illustrated in Valencia de Don Juan 1898, p. 143, fig. 84.

Cat. 79

Sallet of Philip I

Negroli workshop (active ca. 1475–ca. 1575)
Italian (Milan), ca. 1496–1500
Steel, silver, and gold
H. 9⅞ in. (25 cm), W. 8¼ in. (21 cm), D. 16 in. (40.7 cm),
Wt. 3 lb. 15 oz. (1,800 g)
Patrimonio Nacional, Madrid, Real Armería (D. 13)

Philip I died unexpectedly in 1506 while traveling in Castile, leaving some of his officials with the practical problem of what to do with his personal objects. In the case of the numerous armors and weapons that he had brought with him from the Low Countries, and perhaps also had acquired during his time in Spain, the matter proved particularly complicated. After many tribulations, the armory that the sovereign had with him in Spain ended up in multiple places, among them the port cities of Bilbao and Santander. For years, items from his armory were kept in rented spaces, but without proper supervision; thus, by the beginning of 1510, when they were finally brought back to the Low Countries, most were corroded and in need of professional cleaning and repair. On March 8, 1510, Maximilian I and Charles V formally took possession of them, releasing the court official in whose care they had remained of his responsibility and compensating him for the various costs he had personally incurred in the process of rescuing and recovering the objects. The items were then incorporated into the Brussels armory of the ten-year-old Charles.[1]

Among the weapons and armor thought to have originally belonged to Philip that subsequently came to his son Charles, this sallet is one of the most opulent and distinctive. It is certainly among the most cosmopolitan, as it brings together very different stylistic traditions. Constructed and formed in the German fashion, it has a bowl that develops into a long tail at the rear, and a visor that pivots on its sides. Silvered, gilded, and punched with a dense pattern of foliate scrolls and

interlacing strapwork, and with Islamic-inspired knots, the helmet is further adorned with applied bands riveted along the main lower edges and the lower edge of the brow. Uncommon on European armor, its decoration is derived from Islamic ornament and of a kind that was especially prized in parts of Italy and the Iberian Peninsula. The mark struck on the rear right side of the bowl—a pair of two crossed keys surmounted by an open coronet, with the bits of the keys turned toward each other—identifies the helmet as a work by a member of the Negroli family of Milanese armorers.[2]

A pictorial inventory of Charles's armory suggests that the sallet was originally gilded overall, surmounted by an elaborate gilded or gold mount with a finial, and fitted with a band of gilded or gold beads round the base of its tail. The similarly decorated and complementary bevor is lost.[3] In view of its place of manufacture and unusual decoration, the helmet is likely to have been presented to, or purchased by, Philip I during one of his two sojourns in Spain. It was among the items that Philip II of Spain acquired from Charles's armory and incorporated into his own in Madrid in 1565.   PT

REFERENCES: Valencia de Don Juan 1898, pp. 142–43, no. D. 13, pl. XX; José A. Godoy in *Paz y la guerra* 1994, pp. 299–300, no. 232, ill.; Pyhrr and Godoy 1998, p. 6, and p. 5, figs. 5, 6

1. On Philip I's armory, see Terjanian 2006.
2. For a related helmet struck with the same mark similarly decorated, also originating from Charles's armory, see Soler del Campo 2009, pp. 70–71, no. 12, ill.
3. Patrimonio Nacional, Madrid, Real Armería, N18A, fol. 21r.

Cat. 80

Charles V in Armor and Holding a Sword

South German, ca. 1515
Oil on pine panel
23½ x 16⅝ in. (59.8 x 42.2 cm)
Kunsthistorisches Museum, Vienna, Gemäldegalerie (5618)

In this portrait, Charles V, depicted between the ages of twelve and fifteen, is shown wearing the collar of the Order of the Golden Fleece over a fine field armor, holding an unsheathed sword with his left hand, and clasping the grip of a dagger with his right. Set against a green background, crowned by a red hat, and framed by pale long hair, the boy's youthful face is striking as is his armored body, which stands out against the luxurious red cloth hung immediately behind him. The picture is not so much a portrait of an individual as an iconic representation of the authority that he wields.

The collar of the prestigious Burgundian chivalric order, of which Charles was made a member at the age of eleven months and of which he became the sovereign five years later, signals his preeminence, as ordinary members of the order were admitted only after having reached adulthood. His armor, a fine example of the latest German fashion, confirms his privileged birth. As the eldest son of a territorial ruler, Charles began to wear armor at the age of five.[1] Although the monotonous distribution of the flutes on the breastplate, which are incorrectly depicted running parallel above the hips, is a clear indication that the armor was not painted from life, the more careful representation of details, such as the hinged articulation of the lance rest and the gilded cusped lines with stylized trefoils bordering the main edges, suggests a degree of verisimilitude.

The sword visually confirms Charles's authority to rule; he holds it with great ease in a position known in heraldry as erect. The weapon is presented unsheathed with its point upward, in a manner often seen in medieval depictions of emperors and kings and in public ceremonies, such as the parading of swords of state before rulers on solemn occasions.[2] An effective device for conveying the authority secular and even ecclesiastical rulers claimed to derive from God,[3] the sword was a potent symbol in official representations of Maximilian I (cats. 10, 161, and 166) and his immediate descendants,[4] and one that has precedents in medieval portraiture and in representations of Burgundian rulers (cat. 3).[5] As powerful signs of divine rulership, swords were also exchanged as diplomatic gifts by secular and ecclesiastical authorities (cat. 93). The purely symbolic function of the sword in this portrait is readily apparent in the imbalance between the long grip, which could have accommodated two hands, and the blade, which the artist had to shorten so that it would fit within the available space. Driven by practical considerations, this imbalance is inconsequential and would not have affected the substance of the message the weapon imparted.

The picture was probably commissioned in anticipation of Charles's legal emancipation from Maximilian I and Margaret of Austria, his guardians, which was proclaimed in Brussels on January 5, 1515, and opened the era of his personal rule over the Burgundian Low Countries.[6] As the portrait was in Ambras Castle before 1806, when it was removed to Vienna, it seems likely that it was a Habsburg family heirloom.   PT

REFERENCES: Sacken 1855, vol. 2, p. 59, no. 73; Heinz and Schütz 1976, pp. 62–63, no. 21, fig. 37; Karl Schütz in *Kaiser Karl V.* 2000, p. 131, no. 36, ill. p. 132; Margot Rauch in *Werke für die Ewigkeit* 2002, p. 72, no. 28, ill. p. 73

1. On an armor made for his body by the Brussels armorer Jehan Wat in 1505, see Archives Départementales du Nord, Lille, B 2191, fol. 361v.
2. On the representation and symbolic function of swords in later portraits of Charles V, see Woods-Marsden 2013.
3. On the metaphorical use of swords in a famous fourteenth-century power struggle, see Curley 1927, pp. 200–202, 214. On swords as symbols in the Middle Ages and the Renaissance, see *A bon droyt* 2007; Scalini 2007; *Epée* 2011, especially the essay by Michel Huynh (Huynh 2011).
4. For a portrait of Philip I, see Domínguez Casas 2006, p. 92, ill.
5. For a portrait of Charles the Bold possibly copied from a fifteenth-century original, see *Epée* 2011, p. 131, no. 94, and p. 58, fig. 62.
6. Margaret was Maximilian's representative as Charles's guardian.

Cat. 81

Unfinished Field Armor of Charles V

Hans Rabeiler (first recorded 1501, died 1519)
Austrian (Innsbruck), ca. 1511–12
Steel and leather
As mounted: H. 58⅛ in. (147.5 cm), W. 24⁷⁄₁₆ in. (62 cm)
Kunsthistorisches Museum, Vienna, Imperial Armoury (A 186)

Because armor played such an important role in the representation of a young prince's status and authority, Maximilian I made sure that his male descendants—his son, Philip I, and subsequently his grandsons, Charles V and Ferdinand I—were all outfitted in examples befitting their station until they came of age and were able to order armor for themselves. If Maximilian's personal interest in the subject was his original motivation for providing armor for his grandchildren, it became his responsibility after Philip died unexpectedly at the age of twenty-eight, leaving his sons, Charles and Ferdinand, then aged six and three, fatherless. Since Ferdinand was born in Spain and had remained there, his maternal grandfather, Ferdinand II of Aragon, was quick to take him under his protection. Since Charles, by contrast, was born in Ghent and had grown up in the Low Countries, Maximilian became his legal guardian and protector, with the help of his daughter, Margaret, who was his proxy in those lands. Together Maximilian and Margaret ensured that Charles would lack nothing, periodically commissioning armor for his personal use as his body grew and his range of activities expanded. The account registers of their chief treasurer in the Low Countries record the delivery of various armors for use on horseback and foot, all made in Brussels to Charles's measure when he was about seven, eleven, and thirteen to fourteen years old.[1]

Unlike the Brussels works, of which no elements are known to survive, this armor was made for Charles in the German-speaking lands and in a distinctly German style. Commissioned from the Innsbruck armorer Hans Rabeiler when Charles was eleven, it was never completed. It is entirely possible that Rabeiler stopped working on it because he was not paid in a timely fashion, a chronic problem that plagued Maximilian's reign and often stood in the way of his ambitious projects (see cats. 120, 121). The officials to whom Maximilian sent his instructions in Innsbruck when he was not personally in residence in the town routinely ignored many of them on the grounds that there was not enough money at their disposal for the requested works to be undertaken. They quibbled over costs with the armorers and reluctantly paid them, often occasioning delays and halts in the manufacturing process. It is thus possible that Charles had outgrown the armor, the only one approved by officials of three that the emperor had ordered, by the time it was ready to be decorated and assembled. Another slightly more plausible explanation for the armor to have remained unfinished was Maximilian's impatience, for only eight months after he had ordered it, the emperor instructed Conrad Seusenhofer, his court armorer in Innsbruck, to make another armor for Charles (cat. 82).[2]

Unpolished and left rough from the hammer, the armor has no visor, which was perhaps never produced. Comprising an armet, a gorget, a breastplate with a fauld and short tassets of three lames each, a backplate with a culet of three lames, asymmetrical pauldrons, vambraces, gauntlets, cuisses, and greaves made in one with the sabatons, it was meant to be a field armor as the right pauldron is notched at the front to allow a lance to be couched under the armpit and the decoration of the breastplate leaves a blank space at the right side for affixing the base of a lance rest. The absence of holes for screwing the lance rest in place suggests that the latter was never made or at least not finished. The armor is a fine example of a style, much favored in the German-speaking lands, that emulated contemporary male fashion, in particular the puffed and slashed dress of German and Swiss mercenaries. The metal is embossed with gadrooned ribs and the gadroons in turn have oblique indentations that simulate the look of slashed fabric. In its finished state, the modeling of the metal would have probably been underscored and refined with etched ornamentation of the type found on most surviving armors in the same style.[3] In order to further mimic the appearance of clothing, the armor was not constructed and tailored in the usual manner. For example, the pauldrons have no provisions for attaching haute-pieces, upright plates that would have redirected the points of weapons away from the neck and that were a normal fixture of field armors from the period (see the armors in cat. 70). Similarly, the tassets

are uncharacteristically curved at their outer sides, gradually rising toward the culet and meeting its lower edge to create the semblance of the pleated skirts commonly worn by men at the time.

Rabeiler was one of several independent masters in Innsbruck from whom Maximilian periodically commissioned fine armors. In 1509 Rabeiler and the armorer Michael Witz the Elder received the substantial sum of 128 florins toward the full payment of the armor they had jointly produced at Maximilian's request for Francesco II Gonzaga, marquis of Mantua. In 1511 Rabeiler was paid 60 florins for an armor he had made for Girolamo della Torre, a nobleman from Verona who had fulfilled diplomatic missions for Maximilian in Italy.[4] He was thus in excellent standing with Maximilian when he was asked to undertake Charles's armor. The absence of subsequent commissions from the emperor raises the possibility that Rabeiler fell from favor.[5]

Although left unfinished, the armor was not discarded and appears to have remained in Innsbruck. At Ambras Castle by 1596,[6] it was removed to Vienna in 1806 and became part of the Kunsthistorisches Museum's Arms Collection (Waffensammlung) in 1889.[7]   PT

REFERENCES: Thomas and Gamber 1954, p. 64, no. 53, pl. 40; Thomas and Gamber 1976, pp. 215–16, no. A 186, fig. 111

1. Archives Départementales du Nord, Lille, B 2207, fol. 319v, B 2218, fols. 317r, 320r, B 2251, fol. 380v.
2. On these commissions, see Schönherr 1884, p. LIV, nos. 1032, 1034, p. LVII, no. 1063.
3. On armor in this style, see Krause 2016, especially pp. 31–62.
4. Schönherr 1884, p. XLV, no. 952, p. LII, no. 1024, p. LIV, no. 1029. On a mission of Della Torre in Genoa, see Montagnini 1769, vol. 2, pp. 101–8.
5. On armors privately commissioned from him by the marquis of Mantua and his son, which Maximilian decided to pay for in 1518, see Schönherr 1884, p. LXXXVII, no. 1337.
6. Auer 1984, p. XXI, no. 34.
7. The Imperial Armoury department was known as the Waffensammlung until 1989.

Cat. 82

Ceremonial Armor of Charles V

Conrad Seusenhofer (first recorded 1500, died 1517)
Austrian (Innsbruck) and South German (Augsburg), ca. 1512–14
Steel, silver, gold, copper alloy, textile, and leather
As mounted: H. 58⅝ in. (149 cm), W. 27½ in. (70 cm),
D. 21⅝ in. (55 cm)
Kunsthistorisches Museum, Vienna, Imperial Armoury (A 109)

In 1512 Maximilian I commissioned this armor from his Innsbruck court armorer Conrad Seusenhofer as a gift for his eldest grandson, Charles V. It was designed after an armor Conrad had made two years earlier, which Maximilian had presented as a gift to one of his trusted councilors and military commanders. Charles's armor was completed and delivered in 1514, along with a comparable but larger armor intended as a gift for King Henry VIII of England. Aside from an altered helmet likely to have belonged to Henry's suit, the armor for Charles is the sole known survivor of these gifts.[1]

Like the example Maximilian commissioned from the Innsbruck armorer Hans Rabeiler, which was also intended for Charles but never completed (cat. 81), the armor made by Conrad simulates the appearance of contemporary fashionable male dress. The style specifically referenced clothing worn by nobles that resembled—and possibly originated from—the extravagant attire of German and Swiss mercenary soldiers. Unlike Rabeiler's work, however, Conrad's armor possesses broad short sleeves and a pleated skirt. Suitable for use on horseback, the armor has a square opening on the right side of the breastplate that was fitted with a concealed rest for couching a lance. In addition, the skirt was constructed with two detachable panels, one at the front and the other at the back, which could be removed to allow the wearer to ride a horse. Unfortunately, the armor is now incomplete, as this modularity resulted in the separation and loss of the panels. Only one armor, which was made during the same period but in a different workshop for Margrave Albrecht of Brandenburg-Andbach, was spared a similar fate and can provide a sense of the original visual effect the skirt might have had when still complete.[2]

Charles's armor comprises a helmet fitted with a visor (not an original part of it); a gorget; a breastplate and backplate; a skirt formed of two halves hinged at the rear and secured by hook and eye at the front; fully articulated, symmetrical pauldrons in the form of sleeves; vambraces with series of articulated lames protecting the inner joint of the upper arm and forearm; mitten gauntlets; cuisses; and greaves made in one with the sabatons. Remarkable in terms of construction, the armor has articulated pauldrons that guard the armpits and overlap the breastplate, lames that protect the inside of the elbows on the vambraces, and no prominent turned upper edge on the breastplate. Commonly found on foot combat armor (see cats. 20, 37, 86, and 119), these features also occur, for lack of a better term, on "costume armors," such as Charles's suit. Other examples include the previously mentioned armor of Margrave Albrecht and another, made in Augsburg, for Wilhelm von Roggendorf, which is also in the Kunsthistorisches Museum.[3]

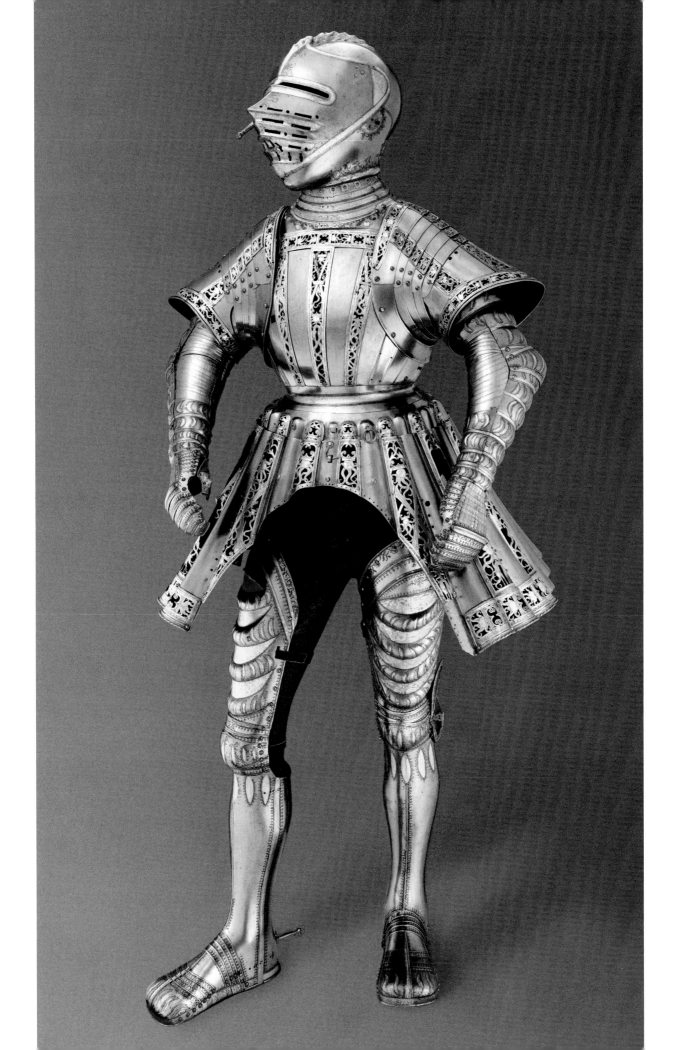

Charles's armor was sent to be decorated by craftsmen in Augsburg, whose skills were apparently superior to those in Innsbruck at the time. There, an unknown goldsmith cast, chased, and gilded the fretted silver bands applied over strips of violet velvet (now modern replacements for the decayed originals) down the breastplate, backplate, pauldrons, and skirt, as well as along the edges of the same elements and along the wings of the poleyns guarding the knees. These bands prominently feature the cross of Saint Andrew and the flaming fire steels and flints of the Order of the Golden Fleece, of which Charles was the sovereign. Halfway down the medial band of the breastplate is a representation of the fleece itself, in reference to the pendant of the prestigious order, which also adorns a cuirass made for Charles's father (cat. 75). The etched ornament on the remainder of the armor was presumably executed by another unidentified Augsburg artist, as it differs notably in conception and execution from the etched ornament on other armors made in Innsbruck during the same period (see cat. 145).

Evidently a showpiece meant to bolster Charles's standing and to promote the vision Maximilian had for his future, the armor proved both expensive, with its extensive use of silver and gold, and complicated to execute. Overburdened by the labor involved, Conrad Seusenhofer had to hire additional staff to enable his workshop to keep up with Maximilian's commissions and pressing demands to see his orders completed and delivered. As was typical, Charles's armor generated tensions among Maximilian, his representatives, and the various craftsmen involved over costs, payments, and deadlines, since the emperor's chronic shortages of funds stood in the way of a smooth workflow.[4]

It became part of the Kunsthistorisches Museum's Arms Collection (Waffensammlung) in 1889.[5]   PT

REFERENCES: Thomas 1949/1977, pp. 545–57, figs. 3–5, 14; Thomas and Gamber 1954, pp. 66–67, no. 62, pls. 41–43; Blair 1965, pp. 17–19, pls. VII, a, IX, a, b; Thomas and Gamber 1976, pp. 216–17, no. A 109, fig. 110

1. On these armors, see Thomas 1949/1977, p. 545; Blair 1965, pp. 8–20.
2. See Thomas and Gamber 1976, pp. 218–19, no. A 78, fig. 118.
3. On Roggendorf's armor and fragments of a comparable armor in The Metropolitan Museum of Art and the Musée de l'Armée, Paris, see Krause 2016.
4. Blair 1965, pp. 10–13.
5. The Imperial Armoury department was known as the Waffensammlung until 1989.

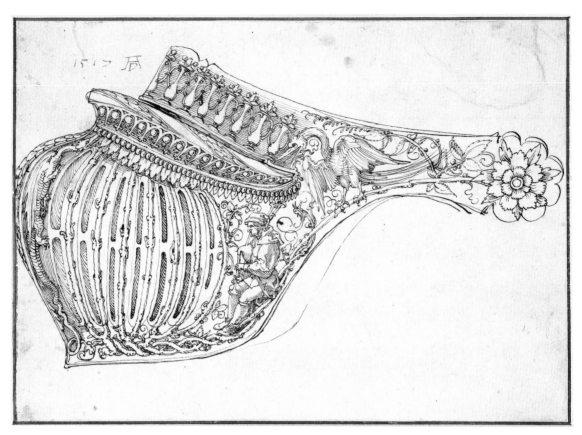

CAT. 83

Cats. 83–85

Designs for the Ornamentation of an Armor
Albrecht Dürer (1471–1528)
South German (Nuremberg), dated 1517
Pen in brown ink on paper
Albertina Museum (3151): 7⅝ x 10⅞ in. (19.4 x 27.5 cm);
Albertina Museum (3152): 7⅝ x 10⅞ in. (19.3 x 27.6 cm); and
Morgan: 8⅝ x 11⁵⁄₁₆ in. (22 x 28.7 cm)
Albertina Museum, Vienna (3151; 3152); Morgan Library and
Museum, New York (I, 256)

These three drawings, together with two additional drawings
preserved in Berlin, are the only works known to remain of a
group of designs by the hand of the Nuremberg artist Albrecht
Dürer for the etched ornamentation of a luxurious armor. Each
sheet documents the decoration of a single plate, thus only a
portion of a given armor element, which suggests that the drawings belong to what must have been a much larger ensemble. The
Albertina Museum's sheets provide models for the decoration
of the left side of the visor of a cavalry helmet (fig. 37) and for
the outer side of a haute-piece, a plate that would have been
affixed to the left pauldron protecting the wearer's neck. The
specific piece for which the Morgan's drawing was intended is
less clear. However, due to its scale and the distribution of

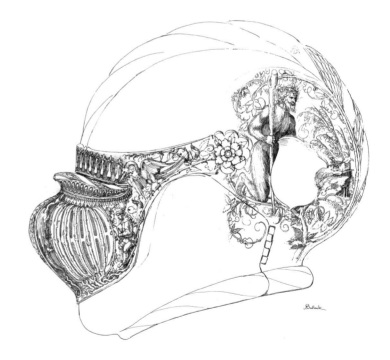

FIG. 37 Tentative reconstruction of the helmet for which two designs by Albrecht
Dürer were intended. Composed by Randolph Bullock. The Metropolitan Museum
of Art, New York, Archives of the Department of Arms and Armor

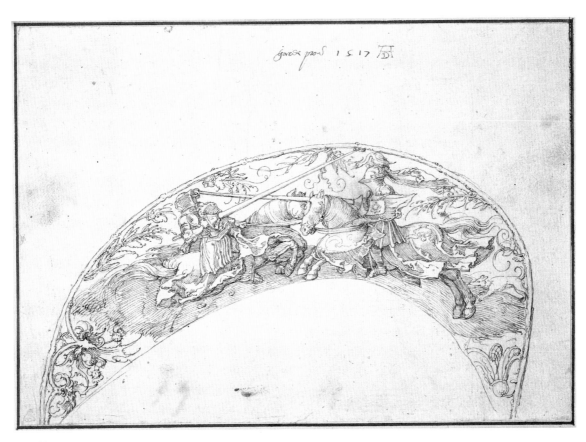

CAT. 84

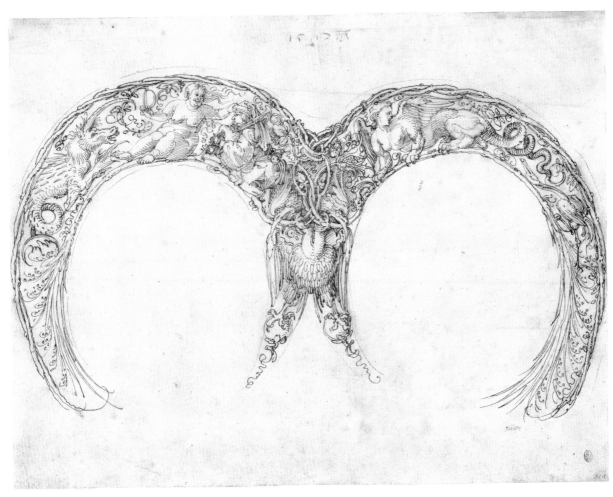

CAT. 85

the ornament, it is possible that it depicts the adornment for the exterior side of a war saddle's cantle. The two remaining drawings, both in the collection of the Kupferstichkabinett of the Staatliche Museen, Berlin, include designs for the ornamentation of additional unidentified plates. A sixth drawing, destroyed in 1871 but known through publications, provided a model for the left side of the bowl of a cavalry helmet.[1]

Only a highly influential patron such as Maximilian I could have engaged an artist as famous as Dürer, who is otherwise not known to have created designs for armor decoration, to produce this unusual group of drawings. It was long believed that the drawings, which all bear the date 1517, were intended for the ornamentation of an extravagant solid silver armor commissioned that same year by the emperor for his personal use.[2] The claim is strengthened by the emperor's documented patronage of the artist, his lifelong interest in commissioning magnificent armors, and his membership in the Aragonese chivalric Order of the Stole, the collar of which features prominently in one of the Albertina's drawings (cat. 83). While Maximilian clearly preferred the emblems of the Burgundian Order of the Golden Fleece once he became a member and its sovereign in 1478, his continued attachment to the Order of the Stole, into which he was received as a youth, is demonstrated by prominent references to its symbols around the pillars of his *Arch of Honor* (see cat. 165).

While there is no cause to question the identification of Maximilian as Dürer's patron, the traditional association of the drawings with Maximilian's silver armor should be reconsidered and probably even dismissed. From a practical standpoint, the execution of Dürer's intricate and lively designs would have been possible only by etching or gilding and bluing. These were the sole techniques for the surface ornamentation of armor in use at the time in the German-speaking lands. Yet, during this period silver was never etched, and silver, unlike ferrous metals, cannot be fire-blued.[3] Another problem is that the date 1517, which is the basis for the argument connecting the drawings to the silver armor, appears to have been added in all cases by another hand, and thus may not be original or correct.[4] Finally, the critical iconographic evidence for the silver armor, which was completed but destroyed soon thereafter, strongly suggests that it was not etched or decorated with intricate designs such as those created by Dürer (see cat. 160). When taken together, these considerations cast serious doubt on the time-honored view that the drawings relate to Maximilian's grand silver armor. It is more likely that they were created in the context of another important, yet unknown, imperial commission.

The representation of the collar of the Order of the Stole raises the previously unconsidered possibility that the drawings may have been commissioned by Maximilian in relation to his grandson Charles V's claim to, and eventual inheritance of, the Aragonese throne. Following the death of his maternal grandfather, Ferdinand II of Aragon, Charles—already king of Castile—was able at last to inherit Aragon and thus become king of all Spain. The reference to the chivalric order of which he thereby became the sovereign, and to which Maximilian was attached, could have been a suitable reference to his Aragonese inheritance and standing, especially after Ferdinand II of Aragon had considered making Ferdinand I, Charles's younger brother, the sovereign of all Spanish knightly orders, and even his successor to the throne of Aragon instead.[5] In the absence of known designs for the gorget and breastplate, it is impossible to tell whether the collar of the Order of the Golden Fleece, of which Charles also was sovereign, would have been given, as one would expect, the place of honor on the armor.   PT

REFERENCES: cats. 83, 84: Ephrussi 1882, pp. 210–12; Boeheim 1891, pp. 177–79; Post 1939, pp. 253–58, figs. 1, 2; Williams 1941, pp. 73–82, figs. 1, 3; Mathias F. Müller in *Albrecht Dürer* 2003, pp. 446–47, nos. 152, 153, ill.; Christof Metzger in *Emperor Maximilian I* 2012, pp. 340–41, nos. 104, 105, ill.; cat. 85: Post 1939, pp. 253–58, fig. 5; Williams 1941, pp. 73–82, fig. 4; Müller in *Albrecht Dürer* 2003, p. 446, under nos. 152, 153; Metzger in *Emperor Maximilian I* 2012, pp. 340–41, under nos. 104, 105

1. On the drawings in Berlin, see Post 1939, p. 255, figs. 3, 4; Anzelewsky and Mielke 1984, pp. 88–90, nos. 87, 88, ill. On the destroyed drawing, see Williams 1941, pp. 81–82, and p. 79, fig. 7, p. 80, fig. 9.
2. Boeheim 1891, pp. 178–79; Post 1939; Williams 1941; Christof Metzger in *Emperor Maximilian I* 2012, pp. 340–41, nos. 104, 105, ill.
3. On this decorative technique, see Krause 2011–12, p. 57.
4. Metzger in *Emperor Maximilian I* 2012, pp. 340–41, nos. 104, 105, ill.
5. Raurell 2003, pp. 53–54; Rudolf 2003, pp. 42–45.

Cat. 86

Portions of a Foot Combat Armor of Louis II of Hungary

Attributed to Conrad Seusenhofer (first recorded 1500, died 1517)
Austrian (Innsbruck), ca. 1515
Steel and leather
As mounted: H. 55⅞ in. (142 cm), W. 25⁹⁄₁₆ in. (65 cm),
D. 10⅝ in. (27 cm)
Kunsthistorisches Museum, Vienna, Schloss Ambras Innsbruck (E 1)

In 1515, at the First Congress of Vienna, Maximilian I met with King Ladislaus II of Bohemia and Hungary to conclude a double marriage of their descendants. A major political summit in which Ladislaus's brother King Sigismund of Poland also took part, the congress resulted in the marriage of Ladislaus's daughter Anne to one of Maximilian's grandsons (precisely which one was to be determined later; Maximilian married her as their proxy), and the marriage of Ladislaus's son Louis II to Maximilian's granddaughter Mary. Although all parties could anticipate great benefits—above all, peace and mutual aid—from this union, the congress proved to be a particularly great diplomatic success for Maximilian. Within eleven years, Louis was killed in action at the battle of Mohács, and the emperor's grandson Ferdinand I was offered the crowns of both Bohemia and Hungary. The first Habsburg to rule over these lands, Ferdinand inaugurated a long period of Habsburg rule that would last through World War I.

In order to secure the coveted double marriage, however, Maximilian took the extraordinary steps of adopting the nine-year-old Louis as his son, appointing him as vicar general (imperial administrator) of the Holy Roman Empire, and declaring him an heir to the empire during the summit. As a result, Louis became a protégé of the emperor and was to be considered a member of his family.[1] This foot combat armor, of which the core elements remain, was presumably made for Louis in the wake of the congress—unless it was meant to be among the emperor's gifts at the event, but had not been completed in time (see cats. 88, 89).

Already in the armory of Ambras Castle by 1583, when it belonged to Archduke Ferdinand II of Tyrol, the piece is likely to have been among several armors made for boys that were in the Innsbruck armory in 1555. It was expressly recorded in 1583 as being Louis's armor and as also comprising a helmet, gorget, pauldrons, vambraces, and gauntlets, all now lost.[2] In its present state, the armor guards the body from the torso to the feet. It is unique in being constructed of two halves, one for the front and the other for the back, that are joined at the sides. The front half has a breastplate with movable gussets, made in one with the waist plate, five fauld lames, the codpiece, and the front halves of the cuisses and greaves, as well as with the poleyns and sabatons. The back half is comparable except for the large plate over the buttocks and numerous lames over the inside of the knees. Ingeniously designed, the armor is remarkable for the extensive articulation of the abdomen, loins, thighs, knees, and feet, and for its overall form, which is so carefully modeled after the anatomy of the body as to become sculptural.

Presumably intended as a gift, the armor was perhaps never delivered to Louis, possibly because by the time it was completed it would obviously no longer fit his growing body. Despite the loss of some elements, its great refinement of form places the piece among the finest foot combat armors that have survived.   PT

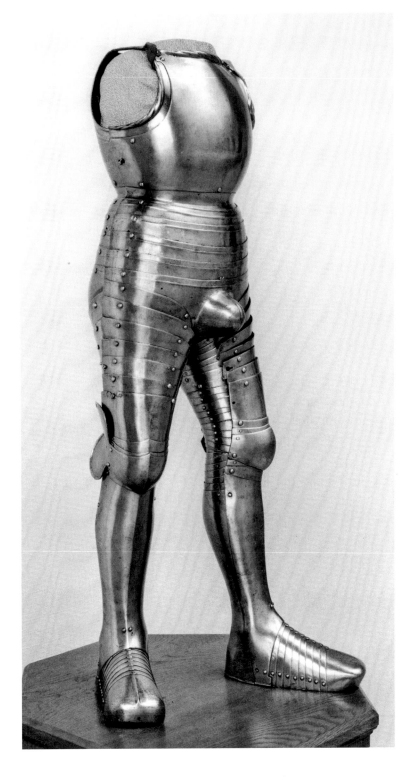

REFERENCES: Thomas 1949/1977, pp. 573, 574, and p. 568, figs. 26, 27; Thomas and Gamber 1954, p. 69, no. 74; Thomas 1971, pp. 58–60, figs. 46, 47; Gamber 1981, p. 37; Alfred Auer and Ortwin Gamber in Gamber and Auer 1981, pp. 64–65, no. E 1; Auer in Auer et al. 2008, pp. 28–29, no. 3, ill.

1. For a fictive family portrait in which Louis II is prominently featured, see Karl Schütz in *Emperor Maximilian I* 2012, pp. 152–53, no. 13, ill.
2. Thomas 1971, p. 59. For the 1555 inventory, see Schönherr 1890, pp. CLVII–CLXI, no. 7164.

Cat. 87

Presentation Coin of Maximilian I

Ulrich Ursentaler (first recorded 1508, died 1561/62)
Coin: South Netherlandish (Antwerp), minted 1517;
die: Austrian (Hall), cut and dated 1509
Silver
Diam. 2⅛ in. (5.4 cm)
The Metropolitan Museum of Art, New York,
Gift of George D. Pratt, 1926 (26.261.14)

Called a double florin (*Doppelguldiner* in German) because it was equal in value to two gold coins, this heavy silver coin was not intended as currency but as a token of the existing or supposed relationship between Maximilian I, the donor, to the person fortunate enough to receive it as a gift. As such, it manifested the existence of a bond between the two, the strength of which was verified by the limited numbers of such coins actually made with the help of the dies Maximilian commissioned from Ulrich Ursentaler, die-cutter at the Mint of Hall in Tyrol. Indirectly, the possession of the coin also marked one's membership in the exclusive circle of individuals deemed worthy of the honor, and thus it provided a measure of one's standing in relation to others.

Commissioned in 1508 in celebration of Maximilian's coronation as Holy Roman Emperor, the double florin still retained much of its appeal years later. In 1517, while the emperor was in the Low Countries, he requested the Mint of Hall to send him three dies, which he needed to issue new presentation coins. The present example was struck in Antwerp with one of those dies.

Maximilian's double florin is remarkable for the imagery on the obverse, which shows him in full armor riding a horse armored to the hooves. Bards constructed with defenses for the legs were most unconventional and, insofar as evidence for their manufacture has come to light, all were made by the Augsburg armorer Lorenz Helmschmid and his son Kolman. The earliest recorded example of such a bard, now lost, was delivered by Lorenz to Maximilian in 1480. Its appearance is preserved in a drawing and a painting, both sixteenth-century copies of earlier sources (see fig. 5).[1] A second bard, also made by Lorenz, was offered by the armorer in 1511 to Francesco II Gonzaga, marquis of Mantua, who declined the opportunity to acquire it. This bard was perhaps the same one that Kolman submitted to Federico II Gonzaga, Francesco's successor, in 1520, although it is unlikely that the piece would have been kept so long and still been considered fashionable enough for such an important patron. Federico's bard, placed in the custody of one of his men, was said to arm a horse like a man, and it was not to be shown to any professional armorer for fear that its design would be copied and replicated. These precautions, and the fact that Federico was intrigued and had inquired about it, make it clear that the type remained far from common.[2]

While the horse armor shown on Maximilian's double florin might, of course, have been imaginary, its verisimilitude, down to the placement of the lames for the articulation of its leg defenses, suggests the opposite. Since Lorenz was Maximilian's court armorer and continually fulfilling commissions in his service, the emperor would have had no trouble adding another exceptional bard to the one he already owned. That he still thought highly of these singular bards, and actually relied on them to help conclude important affairs, is made clear by his gift of one to King Sigismund of Poland in 1515, to cement a critical agreement (cat. 88). PT

REFERENCE: Dirk H. Breiding in Pyhrr, La Rocca, and Breiding 2005, pp. 31–32, no. 3, ill.

1. See Anzelewsky 1963, pp. 77–82, figs. 1, 4; Terjanian 2011–12, pp. 307–9, figs. 5, 6, pp. 342–43, image 30.
2. On these bards, see Bertolotti 1889, pp. 130–32; Buttin 1929, pp. 9–32, 38–49, 52–55, 58–60, 66–67, pls. II, III, XI, XIV, XV.

Cat. 88

Defense for the Leg of a Horse

Attributed to Lorenz Helmschmid (first recorded 1467, died 1516)

South German (Augsburg), ca. 1515

Steel, copper alloy, and leather

H. 10¾ in. (27.3 cm)

Koninklijke Musea voor Kunst en Geschiedenis, Brussels, deposited at the Koninklijke Museum van het Leger en de Krijgsgeschiedenis, Brussels (10212)

This unique defense for the thigh of a horse is all that seems to remain of a horse armor, or bard, that in its original state would have included fully articulated defenses for the limbs, just as armor for men typically did. Constructed of five main plates riveted to one another, the lowermost one shaped to fully wrap around the limb, and extended with six comparable plates in the areas that require greater articulation, the piece is analogous in form and function to the pauldrons formed like short sleeves that armors mimicking the male dress of the period often featured. However, certain elements clearly indicate that this example was intended for a different purpose: its large scale; the twin holes along the bottom edge of its lowermost plate, meant to secure a lining strip on the interior and minimize friction with an underlapping piece, which on

pauldrons is always on the top edge of the uppermost lame and thus at the opposite end; and the direction of its plates, which underlap one another downward, unlike those on the comparable pauldrons.

Like the pauldrons, however, this piece was connected to another at the top and made wide enough at the bottom to overlap yet another. The twin holes on the bottom suggest that the piece it overlapped was likely to move and cause friction. For this reason, it seems clear enough that the defense was designed to function as a sleeve-like cover for the upper part of a piece of armor equivalent to a man's vambrace, but in this case designed for the leg of a horse. Like the comparable

pauldrons of armors mimicking the features of contemporary male dress, it was unconnected to the defenses for the limb so that the latter could freely rotate within and achieve maximum mobility. The slight asymmetry of the entire piece, which is longer on one side than the other, and of its lowermost main plate, the top edge of which gently curves in the direction of the articulating plates on one side and abruptly drops on the other, suggests that it was intended for use on a right leg, possibly the front one in view of its proportions.

Sophisticated and distinctive, the etched ornamentation of this remarkable piece leaves no doubt that it was decorated in Augsburg about 1515. The trefoil designs adorning the edges of the inner articulating plates, for example, display the exact same pattern as decoration found on a ceremonial armor made for Charles V, which was forged in Innsbruck but probably etched in Augsburg in 1513 or 1514 (see cat. 82). More importantly, the foliage, leafy masks, cornucopia, and additional motifs etched along the main borders and between the sets of flutes are comparable in conception and execution with those adorning a field armor and matching horse bard now in the Historisches Museum, Bern. Wrought by Lorenz Helmschmid, whose mark is struck on the man's armor, the ensemble was made no later than 1516, the year of the armorer's death.[1] A comparison of the execution of this piece with those of the Bern ensemble and further works of Augsburg manufacture strongly suggests that the object under consideration was not merely decorated in Augsburg, but it was probably wrought there as well.[2]

In view of its probable date of manufacture and its stylistic analogies to contemporary Augsburg armor, this element of a rare type of bard is likely to reflect the character and sophistication of an example that Lorenz Helmschmid sought to sell to Francesco II Gonzaga, marquis of Mantua, in 1511.[3] Since no armorers other than Lorenz and his son Kolman are known to have created such bards, and since both successively became Maximilian I's court armorers, the present piece may also give an idea of another bard that the emperor must have acquired from them either for himself or as a gift he may have presented to King Sigismund of Poland at the First Congress of Vienna in 1515. At that political summit, Maximilian arranged a double marriage between his granddaughter Mary and one of his grandsons, on the one hand, and Louis II and Anne, the only children of Sigismund's brother Ladislaus, king of Bohemia and Hungary, on the other. In this way, Maximilian not only secured peace with powerful neighbors, but he also created the conditions for the Habsburgs' future rule over Bohemia and Hungary, a prospect that became a reality when his grandson Ferdinand I was offered the crowns of both kingdoms in 1526.

Although the emperor did not refrain from presenting more conventional objects, such as goldsmiths' works, jewelry, horses, and birds of prey, he appears to have favored gifts of weapons and armor whenever he wanted to impress the prospective recipients (invariably men) and their entourages. A technologically marvelous bard armoring a horse down to the hooves, one of two that Maximilian presented to Sigismund at the congress, caused a sensation that chroniclers duly noted (see cat. 89). The young Louis, who was only nine years old, received a more conventional bard as well as an armor for himself, which was observed to be decorated with gold and most ingeniously fabricated.[4]

In the Musée d'Armes Anciennes, d'Armures, d'Objets d'Art et de Numismatique of Brussels by 1835, this horse leg defense became part of the collections of the Koninklijke Musea voor Kunst en Geschiedenis of Brussels in 1889.   PT

REFERENCES: Dillon 1902, pp. 14, 18, 19; Buttin 1929, pp. 66–67, pls. XIV, XV; Metzger 2009, p. 527, no. WZ 6; Krause 2011–12, p. 63, n. 66

1. For a comparison of the present piece and the etched ornamentation of Charles's armor, see Blair 1965, pl. IX, b. On the field armor and bard in Bern, see Wegeli 1920–48, vol. 1 (1920), pp. 55–60, no. 81, figs. 32–36, pls. X, XII; on their etched ornamentation, see Krause 2011–12, pp. 61–63, nn. 65, 67.
2. Similar features include the execution of the turns of the main edges as well as the form, grouping, and placement of the sunken bands and decorative flutes—details that show the armorer's hand, not that of the etcher. See, for example, Thomas 1938/1977, especially p. 1150, fig. 2, p. 1152, fig. 4, p. 1153, fig. 6.
3. Bertolotti 1889, pp. 130–31.
4. On these gifts, see Bartolini 1515, p. 96; Cuspinian 1515, p. 26; Newe Zeitung 1515, p. 12; Villinger 1515, p. 27; Boeheim 1899, p. 302.

Cat. 89

Where and How His Imperial Majesty and the Kings of Hungary, Poland, and Bohemia Got Together and Rode into Vienna (*Wo und wie Ro. Kay. Maiestat und die Kunig von Hungern, Poln, un[d] Peham zusamen kumen und zu Wienn eingeritten sendt*)
Compiled by Johannes Spiessheimer (known as Cuspinian, 1473–1529)
Published by Johannes Singriener (1480–1545)
Austrian (Vienna), 1515
Bound volume
H. 6⅞ in. (17.5 cm), W. 4¹⁵⁄₁₆ in. (12.6 cm), D. ⁷⁄₁₆ in. (1 cm)
University of Pennsylvania Libraries, Philadelphia, Kislak Center for Special Collections, Rare Books and Manuscripts (GC5 C9624 515w)

The first Congress of Vienna was a political summit that took place in 1515, and it proved to be one of Maximilian I's greatest diplomatic achievements. The congress also was one of the most widely published events of its time. Compiled by Johannes Spiessheimer (the Viennese humanist who wrote under the Latinized pseudonym Cuspinian), this account was published in two languages: Latin for educated Christian circles across Europe and German for a broader audience within the Holy Roman Empire.[1]

The author was not merely a key eyewitness; as Maximilian's ambassador, Cuspinian had actually been instrumental in arranging the double marriage of the emperor's grandchildren with the son and daughter of King Ladislaus II of Bohemia and Hungary, which was the chief motive for the summit. These unions were meant to complete

Maximilian's reconciliation with Ladislaus, with whom he had previously been at war, and to consolidate ties with Ladislaus's younger brother, King Sigismund of Poland.

As one of the most detailed accounts of the event, Cuspinian's publication provides a wealth of information about the ceremonies and festivities surrounding the double marriage, including the gifts that were exchanged over several days. The attention paid to the armored horses on which the participants, their distinguished guests, and everyone's retinue rode into the city in the days preceding the congress is symptomatic of the prestige one derived from the ownership of such costly equipment. The account makes special mention of a gift of an armor and a horse bard from Maximilian to Ladislaus's son, Louis II of Hungary, and of another gift of two horse bards to Sigismund (see cat. 86). Significantly, the account specifies that Louis's armor was ingeniously built and that one of the bards presented to Sigismund included complete leg defenses—a marvel of design (see cats. 87, 88).

Sigismund was apparently so moved by the sight of the extraordinary bard that he is reported to have spontaneously pledged his lifelong support to Maximilian. Maximilian had carefully planned these lavish gifts and borrowed considerable sums of money from the banker Jacob Fugger to ensure that the summit would be a complete success. His gifts were meant to seal this historic alliance that would allow the three rulers to better resist Ottoman expansion. In reality, the Congress of Vienna laid the foundation for Maximilian's youngest grandson, Ferdinand I, to ascend to the thrones of Bohemia and Hungary after Louis was defeated and killed in combat against the Ottomans in 1526.   PT

1. Liske 1866.

Cat. 90
Anne of Hungary
Hans Maler (ca. 1475/80–ca. 1526/29)
Austrian (Schwaz), 1521
Oil on wood panel
11⁵⁄₁₆ x 7¹⁵⁄₁₆ in. (28.7 x 20.2 cm)
Tiroler Landesmuseum Ferdinandeum, Innsbruck, Austria, Ältere Kunstgeschichtliche Sammlungen (Gem 1919)

One of Maximilian I's most successful marital projects was the dynastic alliance with Bohemia and Hungary, which brought his house significant gains in territory. In the early sixteenth century, these lands were ruled by King Ladislaus II of Bohemia and Hungary, who had a son and daughter. Following an agreement sealed in 1507, nine-year-old Louis II of Hungary was engaged to Mary, Maximilian's granddaughter, at the Congress of Vienna in the summer of 1515. On the same occasion, the emperor promised one of his grandsons, either Charles V or Ferdinand I, by proxy to twelve-year-old Anne of Bohemia and Hungary. Although the Hungarian nobility hoped that Charles, the heir to the Habsburg crown, would marry Anne, they also accepted his younger brother as the bridegroom after Ferdinand received hereditary lands in a division of the Habsburg estate. Ferdinand and Anne married in 1521 in Linz. After Louis's early death in 1526, his lands were ceded to Austria.[1]

The Tyrolian artist Hans Maler, who created this portrait of seventeen-year-old Anne in the year of her marriage, had previously painted several portraits of the princess during her residence in Innsbruck. She is identified as a queen in the inscription here, although this does not reflect her actual rank at the time, but rather her ambitions.[2] Anne wears a red dress

detailed in gold and a black partlet draped with a gold chain. Her gold cap is topped with a black beret decorated with a golden pendant bearing the initials AW. The painting is one of many similar, small-format portraits of the princess; about 1521, these were often created in combination with a corresponding image of her husband, Ferdinand.   DS

REFERENCES: Mackowitz 1955, p. 79; Krause 2008, pp. 42, 114, 151–52, no. 13, ill. p. 212; Anna Moraht-Fromm in *Dürer, Cranach, Holbein* 2011, pp. 318–19, no. 205, ill.; Krause 2012, p. 80, fig. 15; Moraht-Fromm 2016, pp. 10, 85, 172, no. 32, ill., and p. 11, fig. 2b, p. 84, fig. 87b

1. See Heilingsetzer 2003.
2. Krause 2008, pp. 40–41.

Cat. 91

Meeting of Charles V and Ferdinand I before the City of Worms

Hans Daucher (1486–1538)
South German (Augsburg), dated 1527
Honestone relief with pigments and gold
6¹³⁄₁₆ x 8⅝ in. (17.3 x 21.9 cm)
Morgan Library and Museum, New York,
Purchased by Pierpont Morgan, 1916 (AZ051)

As Ferdinand I was born and raised in Spain, he grew up apart from his elder brother Charles V and did not see him until the latter went to Spain to be solemnly recognized as king of Castile and Aragon in 1517. The two brothers first met near Valladolid on November 12 of that year, only to part again on April 20, 1518, when Charles left for Aragon and Ferdinand went in the opposite direction to sail to the Low Countries, which he reached on June 16.[1]

This relief by Hans Daucher was likely made to commemorate the brothers' second meeting at the Imperial Diet of Worms. The representation of the brothers greeting each other on horseback would be an apt image for their encounter outside the city, out of which Charles had ridden with many German princes to personally greet Ferdinand on April 2, 1520. The significance of the event lies less in the summit of Worms than in the arrangements Charles made to split up the territories he had inherited, whereby Ferdinand received all of the Habsburg hereditary lands, including the duchies of Carinthia, Carniola, Upper and Lower Austria, and Styria.[2] The destinies of the two brothers is announced by ornamentation of their horses' bards: the double-headed eagle on Charles's signals his status as future emperor, a title that he assumed six months later at his coronation as King of the Romans in Aachen, while the two-tailed crowned rampant lion on Ferdinand's foretells his accession to the throne of Bohemia in 1526. Incidentally, this last heraldic reference to the kingdom of Bohemia confirms the authenticity of the date engraved at the top, which had been questioned.[3] In this light, the relief may be read as a retrospective celebration of the great destinies of Maximilian's two grandsons, and by implication the success the former attained by carefully arranging marriages for his progeniture.   PT

REFERENCES: Pierpont Morgan Library 1993, p. 47, no. 11, ill.; Eser 1996, pp. 166–71, no. 16, fig. 33

1. Rudolf 2003, p. 45.
2. Heilingsetzer 2003, pp. 69–70.
3. Pierpont Morgan Library 1993, p. 47, no. 11.

Grand Master of Knights

The values and fellowship promoted by exclusive chivalric institutions provided unique leverage for Maximilian I to enhance his image as a virtuous knight and mobilize political support. He joined and became sovereign of the Burgundian Order of the Golden Fleece in 1478, and in 1493 he also became the chief protec-

tor and advocate of the Austrian Order of Saint George, which was closer in character and purpose to austere early medieval orders such as the Teutonic knights. He commissioned and proudly wore armor that bolstered his association with these exclusive groups and the ideals that they stood for.

The Order of the Golden Fleece, which had been one of the most prestigious institutions in Europe, was almost defunct by the time Maximilian became its head. Most of its members had been killed in recent battles or had defected to the enemy. Nevertheless, Maximilian was successful in restoring its repute and replenishing its ranks. He also exploited its prestige for diplomatic aims, using offers of coveted membership to co-opt key figures in the Low Countries, reward trusted German companions and servitors, and strengthen

his ties to other European rulers. By securing the admission of his father and his descendants into the order, he was able to associate the House of Habsburg firmly with Burgundy.

Established in 1469 to launch a Crusade to expel the Ottoman Turks from Europe, the Order of Saint George was in an even worse state than the Order of the Golden Fleece when Frederick III, its founder, died in 1493. As much of the territory he inherited upon his father's death was under Ottoman attack, and as promoting a Crusade would both affirm his identity as a well-rounded knight and help his relations with the Holy See, Maximilian saw the Order of Saint George as a worthy institution, despite its low membership and meager resources. Through artistic commissions and the armor that he wore, Maximilian openly cultivated his association with the order and its patron saint. Despite his personal efforts and the multiple organizations that he established to attract support for it, the order ultimately failed to live up to his dreams and remained politically and militarily insignificant.

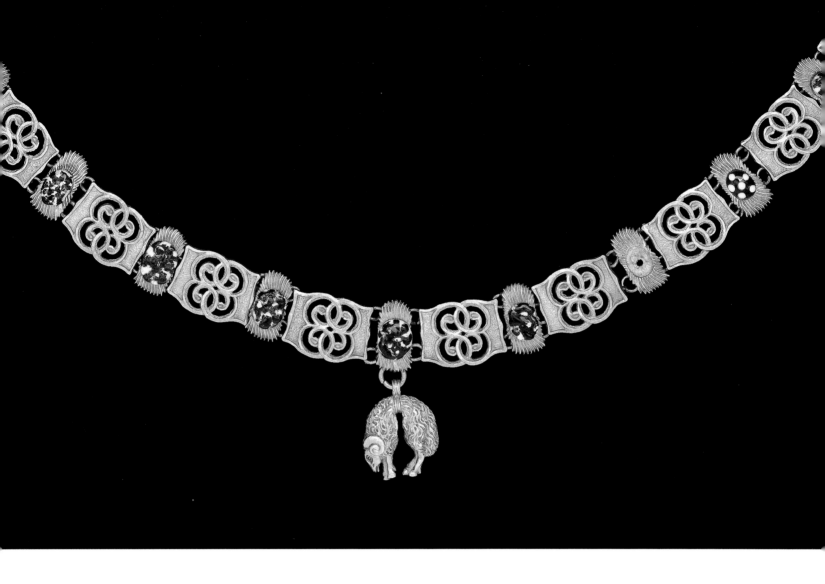

Cat. 92

Collar of the Order of the Golden Fleece

Netherlandish, 16th century

Enameled gold

L. 46½ in. (118 cm)

Louvre Abu Dhabi (LAD 2010-014)

This exceptionally rare collar of the Order of the Golden Fleece is one of only three examples known to survive from the fifteenth and sixteenth centuries. Founded in 1430 by Philip the Good, the Order of the Golden Fleece was the preeminent symbol of the Burgundian dynasty and among the most important European knightly societies. The order's name was inspired by two distinct legends: the biblical story of Gideon collecting the dew of heaven in a fleece (Judges 6: 37–40), and the ancient Greek myth of Jason and the Argonauts capturing the golden fleece from the distant shores of the Black Sea. The combination of religious and secular references was significant, as the biblical association emphasized the order's devotion to Christian ideals and the allusion to

antiquity reflected a novel view of heroism and a foreshadowing of Renaissance humanism.

Members, who were drawn from the nobility of the realm, pledged to live according to chivalric and Christian ideals and swore allegiance to the sovereign head of the order, who by inheritance was the duke of Burgundy. While the order had no explicit political function, it served to forge an intimate bond between the duke and the princes and noblemen within and outside of his dominions, and ultimately strengthened his position as a ruler. Members espoused the tenets of unity and fraternity, and the hierarchy of knights depended not on social status but rather on date of entry into the order.

The future of the order was cast into jeopardy when Charles the Bold died in 1477 without a male heir. However, it survived as a result of his daughter Mary's marriage to Maximilian I, who had himself installed as the order's sovereign head in April 1478. Maximilian's move signaled his claim—and that of his descendants—to the inheritance of the Valois dukes of Burgundy, and he embraced the order's ritual and visual tradition with enthusiasm, frequently employing

the order's symbols and badges. The right to the order's sovereignty passed to their son, Philip I, after Mary's premature death in 1482, and to his son Charles V in 1506. Following his election as emperor in 1516, Charles chose to abandon all other chivalric orders and promote the Golden Fleece, thus making it one of the most prestigious in Christendom.

According to the order's statutes each member was required to wear his collar daily, and his family was obliged to return it following the knight's death. For this reason, the only other known early collar is now in the Weltliche Schatzkammer in Vienna;[1] a slightly later herald's collar, which still belongs to the Austrian order, is on permanent loan to the same collection.[2] By law, neither of these examples is permitted to leave Austria. The present collar descended in the De Croÿ (Croÿ-Roeulx) family, which rose to prominence under the dukes of Burgundy and counted several members as knights of the order. According to family tradition, the collar belonged to Adrien de Croÿ (ca. 1500–1553), a close childhood friend of Charles V and governor of Lille, Douai, and Orchies, as well as the counties of Flanders and Artois, who was made a knight of the order in 1519.   ABB

REFERENCES: Lucie Ninane in *Flanders in the Fifteenth Century* 1960, pp. 292–94, no. 130, ill.; Henri Pauwels in *Toison d'Or* 1962, p. 178, no. 120, ill.; Gruben 1997, pp. 43–48, ill.; Van der Velden 2000, pp. 43–44, and p. 45, figs. 19, 20

1. Kunsthistorisches Museum, Vienna, Weltliche Schatzkammer (WS XVI 263).
2. Kunsthistorisches Museum, Vienna, Weltliche Schatzkammer (Dep. Prot. 4).

Cat. 93

Papal Presentation Sword

Italian, ca. 1510 and later
Steel, brass, wood, velvet, and enamel
Overall length: 37⅜ in. (95 cm); blade: 29⅛ in. (74 cm)
Kunsthistorisches Museum, Vienna, Imperial Armoury (A 453)

Late medieval and Renaissance popes and secular sovereigns frequently exchanged lavish gifts to promote diplomatic and dynastic objectives (see cat. 86). Yet the belief that the Church's authority was superior to that of temporal rulers, as Pope Boniface VIII argued in the bull *Unam Sanctam* (1302), meant that receiving a papal gift carried additional spiritual significance with an unmistakable message of hierarchy.[1] Perhaps the most important of these traditional papal gifts were known as blessed swords, which originated in the fourteenth century as rewards for noblemen celebrating Christmas Matins at the papal court. By Maximilian I's time, the gift had become a strategic and highly ritualized political tool, dispatched once a year to honor a Catholic ruler (and occasionally a municipality) with the expectation of support for the Holy See's aims and its claim to heavenly authority.[2] Although there is no comprehensive record of the recipients of blessed swords, Philip I is known to have received one from Julius II in 1503, and his father Maximilian one from Alexander VI in 1493 and another from Leo X in 1517.[3]

The present weapon was undoubtedly a gift to a senior member of the House of Habsburg from Pope Julius II, as revealed through the decoration of the blade with oak branches from the pontiff's family arms and escutcheons bearing papal tiaras crowning double-headed eagles. The precise identity of the recipient remains open to question.[4] The most recent hypothesis that Maximilian received this sword in 1509, together with another for Charles,[5] to celebrate their entry into the knighthood of Saint Peter is problematic as the short-lived pontifical College of Saint Peter (*Collegium Sancti Petri*) was not established until 1521, three years after Maximilian's death.[6] Moreover, the emperor was an unlikely recipient of such a gift given his long-standing conflict with Julius II over control of the Italian peninsula and, after 1511, Maximilian's desire to unite the temporal and spiritual offices and become pope himself. An additional mystery surrounds the matching hilts on this sword and the slightly older sword purportedly for Charles, both of which appear to have been added in the later sixteenth century at the orders of an unknown descendant.[7] These alterations suggest that both weapons were deemed valuable enough to warrant these upgrades after their owners' lifetimes, and as such highlight the importance of objects associated with individuals in the construction of legacies.   ABB

REFERENCES: Boeheim 1898, p. 8, pl. XVII, 2; Modern 1901, pp. 162–66, and p. 157, fig. 5, p. 158, fig. 6, p. 159, fig. 7; *Maximilian I.* 1959, p. 181, no. 528, pl. 81; *Maximilian I.* 1969, "Katalog," pp. 60–61, no. 237, fig. 10; Thomas and Gamber 1976, pp. 192–93, no. A 453, fig. 93b (sword at right); Beaufort-Spontin and Pfaffenbichler 2005, p. 122, no. 37, ill.

1. See Curley 1927.
2. See Cornides 1967.
3. Maximilian gave the 1517 sword to Albrecht of Brandenburg on the occasion of his investiture as cardinal, and it is illustrated at the beginning of the 1520 *Hallesches Heiltumsbuch*; see Ainsworth, Hindriks, and Terjanian 2015, p. 29, and p. 30, fig. 36.
4. See Sacken 1859; Boeheim 1890; Boeheim 1898; Modern 1901.
5. Kunsthistorisches Museum, Vienna (A 454).
6. See Leo X 1521; Cardinale 1985, p. 21.
7. Modern 1901, p. 162.

Cat. 94

Maximilian of Austria's Inauguration as Knight of the Golden Fleece, from the *Excellent Chronicle of Flanders, 1071–1482* (*Excellente Cronike van Vlaenderen, 1071–1482*)
Continuation written by Anthonis de Roovere (ca. 1430–1482)
South Netherlandish (Bruges), ca. 1485
Paper
8 11/16 x 6 5/16 in. (22 x 16 cm)
Koninklijke Bibliotheek van België, Brussels (MS 13073-74, fol. 335v)

This manuscript belongs to the late medieval Middle Dutch chronicle tradition known as the *Excellent Chronicle of Flanders* (*Excellente Cronike van Vlaenderen*), which consists of various manuscripts that narrate Flemish history from the legendary origin of the county up to the period of the Burgundian dukes.[1] Only a distinct group of seven manuscripts includes a continuation of the chronicle—from the rule of Philip the Good until

the death of the last Burgundian duchess, Mary of Burgundy, in 1482—written by the Bruges master-mason Anthonis de Roovere, one of the most productive fifteenth-century rhetoricians in the county of Flanders.[2] Rhetoricians (*rederijkers*) were organized in literary confraternities, or guilds, known as Chambers of Rhetoric. In the Low Countries and northern France, these guilds were especially involved in the organization of public events. Unsurprisingly, in his section of the *Excellent Chronicle*, De Roovere focuses on the urban festivities in Bruges, such as the celebrations on the occasion of the wedding of Charles the Bold and Margaret of York in 1468, a narrative that was also incorporated in a separate manuscript.[3]

Among the oldest examples with a full version of De Roovere's text, the present manuscript is also one of two surviving copies (the second copy is in the public library in Bruges)[4] that contain an extensive version of the chronicle with additional information on Bruges urban life, in particular on the political situation and faction war during the Bruges Revolt of 1436–38 against Philip the Good. It is unclear whether these additions were made by De Roovere or an enthusiastic scribe. Little is known about the context in which the present manuscript was created as the names of the scribes and owners are unknown. It was written by three unidentified scribes; the scribe who wrote the last part of the chronicle, from folio 274 recto to folio 401 verso, also recorded the first section of another *Excellent Chronicle* manuscript with a shorter version of the text.[5] The present manuscript is currently missing the first quire narrating the origin myth of the county of Flanders.

The colophon states that the manuscript was finished around Christmas Eve in 1485, shortly after De Roovere completed his text in 1482. The year 1485 was quite turbulent in the history of Bruges. For more than three years the city had rebelled against Maximilian I, the county's new regent, but in 1485 the Habsburg ruler managed to reclaim control of Flanders, albeit for a short period of time, as in 1488 he was imprisoned by rebels in Bruges. The *Excellent Chronicle* manuscripts, with their strong urban perspective on Flemish history, were very popular in Bruges during this revolt.[6]

This manuscript and the nearly identical copy in the public library in Bruges are particularly well known for their rich illustrations. The present manuscript contains five full-page miniatures, as well as many coats of arms and decorated initials. Although other *Excellent Chronicle* manuscripts also include portraits of the different counts of Flanders, this

manuscript and the copy preserved in the public library are the only two that contain full-page illustrations related to the reign of Mary of Burgundy, most of which represent important public political events (see fig. 30). In style, these miniatures greatly resemble the illustrations in the manuscript discussed in catalogue entry 3.

The miniature illustrated here portrays the inauguration of the nineteen-year-old Maximilian as a knight of the Order of the Golden Fleece in Saint Salvator's Church, Bruges, in 1478. The young ruler kneels as he is knighted by a member of the order and receives his collar. The inauguration and festivities in Bruges are described in detail in the text;[7] De Roovere even wrote a poem on the occasion.[8] Founded by Philip the Good in 1430, the Order of the Golden Fleece was the most important Burgundian noble organization.[9] By establishing his own order of knights, Philip increased the status of his dynasty and tied the nobility of both the northern and the southern Burgundian territories to it. At the end of the fifteenth century, the prestige of the order was widespread among the highest nobility and royalty in Western Europe. By joining the order, the young Maximilian thus entered into Burgundian noble culture. Nevertheless, Maximilian's policies would quickly lead to unrest. His favoritism toward German nobles displeased the Burgundian and Flemish elite. Various knights of the Order of the Golden Fleece, such as Adolf of Cleves and Louis of Gruuthuse, would join the Flemish cities in the revolt of 1482–92 against the Habsburg ruler. These noblemen were eventually prosecuted by the order in 1491 for their involvement in the revolt.[10]   LD

REFERENCES: Oosterman 2002; Boulton 2006; Haemers 2007; Haemers 2008; Demets 2016; Demets and Dumolyn 2016

1. Demets 2016.
2. Oosterman 2002.
3. Universiteitsbibliotheek, Leuven, MS 1336.
4. Openbare Bibliotheek Brugge, MS 437.
5. Openbare Bibliotheek Brugge, MS 436.
6. Demets and Dumolyn 2016.
7. Koninklijke Bibliotheek van België, Brussels, MS 13073-74, fols. 332v–337v.
8. Koninklijke Bibliotheek van België, Brussels, MS 13073-74, fol. 335r: "Het joncq vanden aren/tsijnen twintich jaren/woude tsoysoens pleghen/mey avend te Brugghe/tsent salvatoors vlugghe/wals rudder ghesleghen" (The young of the eagle/at the age of twenty years/wanted to become a member of the Order of the Golden Fleece/on an evening in May in Bruges/quickly at Saint Salvator's/he was knighted).
9. Boulton 2006.
10. Haemers 2007; Haemers 2008. See also "Justifications de feu monseigneur de Ravestain des cherges a lui bailliés à l'Ordre de la Thoison d'Or," Français 18997, fol. 62v, Département des Manuscrits, Bibliothèque Nationale de France, Paris.

RECTO

VERSO

Cat. 95

Coat of Arms of Maximilian I as King of the Romans (recto)
and *Coat of Arms of Florian Waldauf von Waldenstein*
(verso), from the *Revelations of Saint Bridget of
Sweden* (*Revelationes caelestes mit Vita abbreviata
sanctae Birgittae*)

Circle of Albrecht Dürer

Published by Anton Koberger (ca. 1445–1513)

South German (Nuremberg), 1502

Woodcut

9¹⁵⁄₁₆ x 6¼ in. (25.2 x 15.8 cm)

The Metropolitan Museum of Art, New York, George Khuner
Collection, Bequest of Marianne Khuner, 1984 (1984.1201.36)

As thanks for his miraculous delivery while accompanying
Maximilian I in a terrifying snowstorm on the Zuiderzee,
a shallow bay in the North Sea, in 1498, the Austrian knight
Florian Waldauf, the emperor's favorite adviser and protono-

tary, vowed to erect a chapel in the church of Saint Nicholas
in Hall, Tyrol. The chapel was also to serve as a setting for
Waldauf's extensive collection of relics. Maximilian himself
contributed to this important collection, which was commemorated in a series of more than one hundred woodcuts by Hans
Burgkmair.[1] Larry Silver notes that Maximilian "had a genuine
desire, akin to the religious education projects of learned
humanists in Germany, to make religious ideas available in
print to a large, vernacular audience in the empire."[2] In 1500,
spurred by this desire, Maximilian instructed the renowned
Nuremberg publisher Anton Koberger to print an edition first
in Latin and then in German of the medieval best seller the
Revelations of Saint Bridget of Sweden.[3] Using Waldauf as his
messenger, Maximilian sent Koberger a 1492 illustrated edition of the text from Lübeck to use as his model.[4]

This double-sided woodcut, with Maximilian's and
Waldauf's insignia on opposite sides, comes from the German
edition of 1502. Waldauf's own enthusiasm for Saint Bridget

was considerable: his relics collection included an important wood remnant of her desk, and he was a member of her monastic order, the Order of the Holy Savior. His devotion to the saint also led him to commission Augsburg's Lukas Zeissenmair to print a small German edition of the *Revelations* in the same year as this Nuremberg edition, but with different, less sophisticated woodcuts.

As noted by Susanne Schröer-Trambowsky, the authorship of these woodcuts is much debated.[5] Scholars agree that two different artists were involved and that Waldauf's coat of arms is less refined than Maximilian's. Both artists do, however, adhere to the style of woodcuts being produced in the circle of Albrecht Dürer in Nuremberg during this period. The letterpress inscription above Maximilian's coat of arms identifies the insignia as that of his "Royal Majesty," a title he used prior to his official coronation as Holy Roman Emperor in 1508. Contained within the collar of the Order of the Golden Fleece are five shields: the topmost displays the Imperial Eagle; the three at center represent the duchy of Austria, the kingdom of Hungary, and the duchy of Burgundy, respectively; and the lowermost is for the county of Tyrol. Two griffins, one with the cross of Saint Andrew, the other with a flint and steel, flank the shield at the top. Together they represent the coat of arms of Burgundy and symbolize Maximilian's military might.

On the recto, Waldauf's arms appear with intertwined dragon heads, the shield is surmounted by two helmets with elaborate crests, and all are surrounded by the collar of the Order of the Swan, devoted to the Virgin Mary. The collar on the left is that of the Aragonese Order of the Stole, to which Maximilian belonged, while that on the right, known as the collar of Esses, features the badges of the royal House of Lancaster.   FS

REFERENCES: Anna Scherbaum in Schoch, Mende, and Scherbaum 2001–4, vol. 3 (2004), pp. 487–88, 490, no. A 34; Susanne Schröer-Trambowsky in Schoch, Mende, and Scherbaum 2001–4, vol. 3, pp. 488–90, nos. A 34.1–A 34.3

1. For more on Burgkmair's woodcuts for the *Hallesches Heiltumsbuch*, see Garber 1915; West 2006.
2. Silver 2008, p. 134.
3. During the early sixteenth century, Saint Bridget was extremely popular in Germany and Italy because of her writings on the cult of the Virgin and the Passion of Christ. In 1513 Hans Schäufelein, who apprenticed in Dürer's workshop, designed a woodcut that showed her giving the rule to her order; see Smith 1983, p. 144, no. 46, ill.
4. Silver 2008, p. 134.
5. Susanne Schröer-Trambowsky in Schoch, Mende, and Scherbaum 2001–4, vol. 3 (2004), pp. 489–90.

Cat. 96

Bard Presented by Maximilian I to Henry VIII

Wrought by Guillem Margot (first recorded 1505, died before 1533)
Punched and engraved by Paul van Vrelant (active 1504–1520)
South Netherlandish (Brussels), ca. 1505
Steel, silver, gold, copper alloy, and leather
As mounted: H. 76⅜ in. (194 cm), W. 39¾ in. (101 cm),
D. 94½ in. (240 cm), Wt. 71 lb. 8 oz. (32,460 g)
Royal Armouries, Leeds (VI.6–12)

Presented under unknown circumstances by Maximilian I to Henry VIII of England, this horse bard is likely to have originally been made for Maximilian or his son, Philip I. Unique for the themes and combined techniques of its decoration, the bard consists of a shaffron for the horse's head, a crinet for its neck, and a peytral, flanchards, and a crupper for its body, as well as rein guards of steel, and pommel and cantle plates for a war saddle. The bard was originally silvered overall and either wholly or partly gilded. The principal elements of the bard are embossed and engraved with foliate scrollwork and pomegranates, and, most prominently, with raguly crosses and fire steels, the well-known badges of the Order of the Golden Fleece. The rein guards are fretted with similar designs, whereas the crinet is engraved with a pattern of overlapping feathers.

Although the pomegranates would have been a suitable reference to Catherine of Aragon, Henry's first wife, from 1509 to 1533, the absence of roses, portcullises, and other Tudor emblems make it doubtful that the bard was specially made for Henry, as was long believed. Instead, the prominence of the badges of the Golden Fleece, which are repeated on all elements, and which form a nearly uninterrupted sequence along the bard's lower border, strongly suggests that the bard was originally made for a member of the House of Habsburg. The pomegranates could equally refer to Philip's status as king consort of Castile during the final part of his life and to the prestigious possession of Granada that the position entailed (see cat. 78). Alternatively, they could represent the fruit Maximilian chose as his personal emblem (see cat. 166).

A gift of one's personal armor was just as desirable, if not more so, as a specimen specially made for the recipient precisely because it was a personal possession and its very bestowal implied that the donor was willing to part with something dear. The bard was presumably presented on one of the many occasions when Maximilian needed to strengthen his ties with the younger king in order to secure an advantage against his enemies, the Venetians and the French.

The mark of the letter M surmounted by a crescent, which is struck on the crupper, securely identifies the bard as a work of the Brussels armorer Guillem Margot. The occurrence of the same mark on the remnants of three bards believed to originate from the Habsburgs' armory in Brussels, the evidence provided by the detailed accounts of their treasurers in the Low Countries that record he was the only armorer who delivered bards of steel to the Brussels armory from 1494 to 1530, and the fact that the letter in the mark matches the initial of his family name establish beyond reasonable doubt that the mark belonged to Margot, and that the works bearing it were made by him. An armorer of note who also wrought body armor for the personal use of Philip and his sons, Charles V and Ferdinand I, as well as suits that were presented as gifts, Margot perhaps achieved greatest recognition as a maker of luxury bards (see cat. 123).[1] It is not known when he created the spectacular example that Maximilian eventually gave to Henry VIII. It might have occurred during the time his son personally ruled over the Low Countries, from 1494 to 1506, when Maximilian could no longer instruct the treasurers there to pay for his acquisitions and had to rely on other means, for which there is no comparable documentation.

The style and execution of the bard's punched and engraved decoration exhibit the unmistakable hand of Paul van Vrelant, a Netherlandish goldsmith known to have decorated armor for the Habsburgs in Brussels from 1505 until about 1514, when he entered Henry VIII's service in England, an arrangement that does not seem to have prevented him from subsequently fulfilling commissions for Charles V in the Low Countries.[2] The original effect of the punched and engraved ornament, however, is now difficult to fully appreciate as a result of the near-complete loss of the silver and gold that once covered the bard's entire surface. First mentioned in 1519, when it already was in England in the care of the king's clerk of the stables, the bard remained in the royal palace at Greenwich until 1644, when it was transferred to the Tower of London.[3] PT

REFERENCES: Blair 1965, pp. 37–38, pls. XIII, d (detail), XVI, a; Thom Richardson in *Henry VIII* 2009, pp. 164–65, no. 18, ill.; Terjanian 2009, pp. 156–59

1. Terjanian 2006, pp. 150, 154; Terjanian 2009, pp. 157–59.
2. On Van Vrelant, see Blair 1965, pp. 26–31, 36–41.
3. See Thom Richardson in *Henry VIII* 2009, p. 164.

pear-shaped pommel, a collar, and a straight cross guard, all of gilded-copper alloy; a wood grip that is covered in leather molded and cut with longitudinal bands of foliate scrollwork; and a long, double-edged, straight-steel blade that gradually tapers to a point and has a shallow fuller at each side. Every other facet of the pommel and one side of the cross guard are engraved with fire steels, flaming flints, and the raguly crosses of Saint Andrew, all of which are badges of the Burgundian Order of the Golden Fleece. Similar ornamentation appears on the opposite side of the cross guard, along with the letters HMIADM interspersed with rosettes. These letters are short-hand for Maximilian's motto and name, "Moderation in All Things, Maximilian" (*Halt Mass in allen Dingen, Maximilian*), and identify him as the original owner of the sword. The engravings on the blade's fuller further confirm Maximilian's ownership.[1] On one side are the words *Halt Mass* flanked by the same badges of the order, a running cloud band pattern, and stout late Gothic gables. On the other side is the abraded and partly obliterated pious invocation "God . . . George" (*Gott . . . iorg*), which is framed by the badges of the order, foliate scrollwork, and tall late Gothic gables.

Deep cuts and nicks on the edges of the guard that face the point of the blade prove that the weapon saw active service in combat, despite the profusion of emblems and words engraved on its parts that could have otherwise suggested it was intended for ceremonial use. Although the majority of his surviving armors were designed for tournaments, this sword is among the few extant battle swords known to have belonged to him.

The representation of the badges of the Order of the Golden Fleece on the hilt and blade establishes that the sword was made no earlier than 1478, when Maximilian was admitted into the prestigious Burgundian order and became its sovereign. It is traditionally believed to be the weapon he carried on his triumphal entry into the town of Luxembourg on September 29, 1480, and was long associated with the armor thought to have been worn on the same occasion (cats. 16, 17).[2] Both were in the imperial armory of Vienna until 1889, when they became part of the Kunsthistorisches Museum's Arms Collection (Waffensammlung).[3]   PT

REFERENCES: Gamber 1961, pp. 28–29, and p. 27, figs. 24, 25; Thomas and Gamber 1976, pp. 107–8, no. A 139, fig. 36b

1. The blade is engraved and not etched, contrary to the description provided in Gamber 1961, p. 28; Thomas and Gamber 1976, p. 107, no. A 139.
2. On this tradition, see Gamber 1961, p. 29.
3. The Imperial Armoury department was known as the Waffensammlung until 1989.

Cat. 97

Sword of Maximilian I

Possibly Netherlandish, ca. 1480
Steel, copper alloy, gold, wood, and leather
L. 55¹⁵⁄₁₆ in. (142 cm), W. 11³⁄₁₆ in. (28.5 cm)
Kunsthistorisches Museum, Vienna, Imperial Armoury (A 139)

Maximilian I repeatedly risked life and limb in battle, often sustaining injuries and running the risk of being captured. Intended for use in the field, this slender sword has a faceted,

Cat. 98

Saint George and the Dragon
South German, possibly Swabian, ca. 1460–70
Limewood with paint and gilding
H. 32⁷⁄₁₆ in. (82.4 cm, with lance), W. 13⅜ in. (34 cm),
D. 8¹¹⁄₁₆ in. (22 cm)
The Metropolitan Museum of Art, New York, Gift of George
Blumenthal, 1941 (41.100.213)

Saint George, a soldier of Emperor Diocletian (r. 284–305)—
who oversaw the largest and bloodiest persecution of
Christianity in the Roman Empire—became a significant
martyr when he chose torture and death over renouncing
his Christian faith. Widely venerated in the Middle Ages, he
was especially admired for his bravery. According to a story
compiled in the thirteenth century, he rescued the entire pop-
ulation of a Libyan town from a dragon by singlehandedly
defeating the beast in combat and ultimately killing it, saving
in the process a princess that had been offered to it for
appeasement, and sparing her father the disgrace of having
failed to protect her. A valiant and gallant man of faith, George
became a patron saint for crusaders and numerous chivalric
orders, among them the Order of the Garter, which was established by King Edward III of England in 1348.

Carved in wood, polychromed and partly gilded, this
sculpture presents the saint in armor, with his right foot dug
into the neck of the vanquished dragon. As is typical of the
artistic conventions of the time, the armor is in the contemporary, late Gothic style. It exhibits distinctive features—such as
the form and decoration of the plackart, couters, and tassets—
that were especially popular in the Swabian parts of the
German-speaking lands. The same features are found on the
funeral effigy of Ulrich von Rechberg (d. 1458) in Donzdorf.[1]
The saint's pronounced contrapposto; the drapery of the textile suspended from the back of the helmet over the right forearm; the scrupulous representation of every technical detail of
the armor, such as rivets, hinges, buckles, and straps (only the
lance rest seems to have been accidentally omitted); and the
style of the armor suggest that the work might have been
carved by a Swabian artist. These same features, for example,
appear on three knights on a public stone fountain in Ulm,
which were carved about 1482 by Michel Erhart after designs
by Jörg Sürlin the Younger, two of Ulm's foremost sculptors.[2]
The Saint George figure is likely to predate the Ulm works as
the style of the saint's armor is comparatively earlier and rooted
in the 1460s. A detailed fifteenth-century German metalpoint
study of the figure, now in the Worcester Art Museum,

Massachusetts, suggests that the sculpture caught the attention of other artists shortly after it was made, and that it may
have perhaps influenced their works.[3] PT

REFERENCES: *Collection Spitzer* 1893, vol. 1, p. 127, no. 747, pl. XXIV;
Exposition d'art ancien 1906, p. 43, no. 168, ill.

1. See Baum, Klaiber, and Pfeiffer 1914, p. 749, ill.
2. On the fountain and the knight figures, see Broschek 1973, pp. 158–65,
pls. XXVII–XXIX; Rommé 2002.
3. Worcester Art Museum, Massachusetts (1994.249).

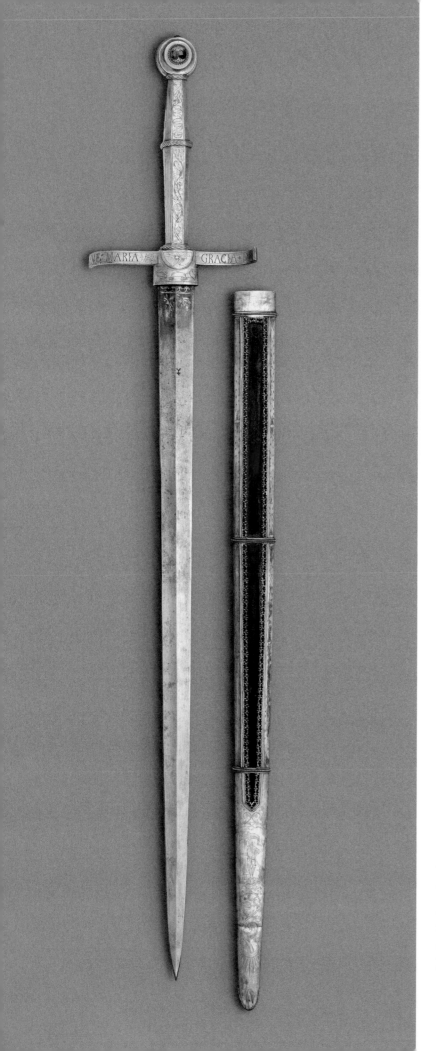

Cats. 99, 100

Sword and Scabbard of Johann Siebenhirter

South German, dated 1499
Steel, silver, gold, enamel, wood, leather, textile, and copper alloy
Sword: L. 46⅛ in. (117.3 cm), W. 8⅛ in. (20.5 cm); scabbard:
L. 34³⁄₁₆ in. (86.9 cm), W. 2¼ in. (5.7 cm)
Landesmuseum für Kärnten, Klagenfurt, Austria (LG 4300)

Made for Johann Siebenhirter (ca. 1420–1508), the first grand master of the chivalric Order of Saint George, this sword bears his enameled paternal and maternal heraldic arms inlaid into one side of the pommel (obverse), and a banderole with the date 1499 engraved on the other (reverse).[1] The hilt and hand-and-a-half grip are made of gilded silver, en suite with the massive overlay of the scabbard that complements the sword. The straight, double-edged steel blade is of flattened-diamond shape in cross section, and it begins to taper to a point approximately four-fifths down. The grip is octagonally shaped and divided into upper and lower sections by a roped collar that matches a collar at the base of the pommel and another one at the base of the cross guard. The grip's facets are adorned with panels that are alternatively void or engraved. The upper and lower central panels on the obverse feature banderoles and scrolling thistles, respectively. The upper and lower side panels feature the same designs, but in reverse, with the upper panels enclosing thistles and the lower ones banderoles. Finally, the central panels on the reverse are each engraved with a radiating crescent moon near the collar and a pattern of flame-like designs that perhaps represent light. The cross guard has two arms that curve outward and inward at their extremities and an overlaid gilded-silver scabbard throat cover. The arms of the cross guard are engraved with scrolling foliage and the invocation AVE MARIA GRACIA PLENA (Hail Mary, full of grace) on the obverse (see detail), and with radiating beams and flame-like designs on the reverse. The throat cover is engraved with the head of a flower and a banderole on the obverse, and with radiating beams and flame-like designs on the reverse, thus en suite with the remainder of the hilt.

The blade is struck at each side with the mark of a cross rising from a crescent, which is similar to the mark on the blade of Maximilian I's battle sword (cat. 97). The bladesmith who used it to sign his works has not been identified. The section of the blade closest to the throat cover retains traces of gilded ornamentation on a blued ground on each side. On the reverse, the lower halves of two figures are still visible; the staff found to the side of one of them suggests that he may have been Saint Christopher. On the obverse, only the feet

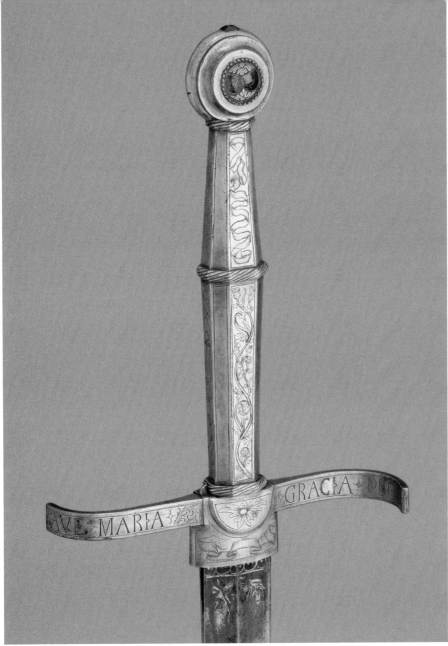

and folds of two figures in either robes or mantles remain. In technique and character, this residual decor is analogous to that of the blades of swords and hunting knives made by the swordsmith Hans Sumersperger in Hall in Tyrol for Maximilian and his great-uncle Archduke Sigismund.[2] However, the mark on the blade is different from the one occurring on Sumersperger's works, and too much of the ornament is lost for a close comparison to be made. The blade may thus have been made by another craftsman.

The leather- and fabric-covered wood scabbard has a chape and a deep locket of gilded silver. Four gilded-silver strips extend down its sides and are joined together by two collars that are similar to the one that borders the lower edge of the locket. The tip of the chape is reinforced with a soldered gilded-silver piece shaped like the folded petals of a four-leaved flower. As it would normally be covered by the hilt's

scabbard throat cover, the locket is left undecorated. By contrast, the side strips are each bordered by a raised molding and a row of stylized foliage on the obverse. Additionally, they are engraved with radiating beams and flame-like designs. The chape is decorated in the same manner as the side strips and engraved on its face with scrolling foliage rising from a radiating crescent moon, with flame-like designs strewn beneath it. Above the moon is a representation of Saint George standing on a dragon and holding his banner in his right hand, and over him is a gable formed by the entwined branches of two rose trees (see detail). On the obverse, the side strips are plain and the chape is only adorned with a radiating moon.

This luxurious sword is similar in form, construction, and proportions to that held by Siebenhirter on his funeral effigy in Millstatt, though on the latter the scabbard is plain.[3] Although its blade would have been serviceable in combat, the use of

The Patron Saints of Austria. Below the figures, Latin inscriptions read:

S. Quirinus Archiepiscopus Lauriacensis deinde patriarcha Aquilegiensis martyr. — S. Maximilianus Archiepiscopus Lauriacensis martyr. — S. Florianus Tribunus militum martyr Lauriaci passus. — S. Severinus post Attilam regem hunorum defunctum secundarius Austrie apostolus. — S. Colomanus martyr apud Stokharau passus. — S. Leopoldus Princeps pius Marchio austrie. — S. Poppo Marchio orientalis Archiepiscopus Treuerensis. — S. Otto Marchio orientalis Episcopus Frisingensis.

silver, a soft metal, for the hilt and grip, and of enamel, another delicate material, for representing the grand master's family heraldic arms on the pommel strongly suggests that the weapon was intended for ceremonial use. The completion of the grand master's castle that Siebenhirter had built in Millstatt, where the order had its seat, in 1499, may have been solemnly celebrated and warranted the commission of this sword and the prominent display of the same date on the pommel. The sword appears to have been kept in the parish church of Millstatt from prior to or shortly after the dissolution of the Order of Saint George until 1849, when it was purchased by the Geschichtsverein für Kärnten (Historical Society for Carinthia). PT

REFERENCES: Bergmann 1868, p. 172; Lind 1873a, p. 315, and p. 310, fig. 11; Lind 1873b, p. 171; *Maximilian I.* 1969, "Katalog," p. 62, no. 244, fig. 40; Thomas and Fritz 1978, p. 15, and p. 11, fig. 14, p. 12, fig. 16, p. 13, fig. 17 (detail); Meinrad Pizzinini in *Circa 1500* 2000, p. 127, no. 1-6-13, ill.; Wlattnig 2015

1. The richer decoration on one side is taken to distinguish the obverse of the object, as this is the side that would have been visible when the sword was sheathed and carried at the hip. Similarly, the more elaborate edge decoration on the silver-gilded overlay is taken to distinguish the obverse of the scabbard. On the Order of Saint George and Siebenhirter, see cats. 99, 105, 106, 110, 112.
2. On Hans Sumersperger's career and accomplishments, see Thomas 1950–51/1977; Thomas 1955/1977.
3. Helfert 1889, pp. 229–30, and p. 234, fig. 259.

Cat. 101

The Patron Saints of Austria
Albrecht Dürer (1471–1528) and possibly Hans Springinklee (ca. 1495–after 1522)
South German (Nuremberg), 1515/17
Woodcut
7 1/16 x 14 5/16 in. (18 x 36.4 cm)
The Metropolitan Museum of Art, New York, Rogers Fund, 1919 (19.70.5)

Even though the Habsburg line of descent could be traced back no farther than the tenth century, Maximilian I, like other rulers before him, had no reservations about crafting a genealogy that linked his family to mythological heroes, to biblical and historical figures, and above all to Christian saints. In this way, the emperor could ensure both his secular and his sacred *memoria*.

In this woodcut, originally conceived by Albrecht Dürer as six saints and likely supplemented by his apprentice Hans Springinklee, eight male saints associated with the House of Habsburg are shown standing along a darkened ground and holding their attributes. Beyond their regalia, the figures are clearly identified by the Latin inscriptions below their feet. Notably, those represented—Quirinus, Maximilian, Florian, Severinus, Koloman, Leopold, Poppo, and Otto—are not found in the *Golden Legend*, the popular medieval collection of the lives of saints. They do appear, however, in the manuscript version of Maximilian's *Book of Habsburg Family Saints* (*Sipp-, Mag- und Schwägerschaft*, 1516–18).[1] By focusing on these more obscure saints who lack long traditions of representation in either texts or images, Maximilian, with the aid of genealogists and historians such as Jacob Mennel and Johannes Stabius, could create a vast family tree for the Habsburgs that seemed authentic.

This sheet is from the second edition of the woodcut, which has the two saints in a separate block at the right likely added by Springinklee in 1517. It is also missing a long inscription by Stabius that would have appeared below the saints and their descriptions. A panegyric to the emperor, Stabius's verses include a dedication to the prominent Viennese humanist, astronomer, and mathematician Andreas Stöberl, alias Stiborius, who was also the parish priest of Stockerau. There, the martyr Kolomon was linked not only to Maximilian but also to the multitalented Stabius, who had had Dürer depict himself in the guise of the saint in 1513.[2]

The saints most directly connected with Maximilian—his namesake and Leopold, the canonized margrave of Austria—also reappear together on Springinklee's *Maximilian Presented by His Patron Saints to the Almighty* (cat. 102), while Leopold also figures prominently on the *Arch of Honor* (cat. 165). FS

REFERENCES: Thomas Schauerte in Schoch, Mende, and Scherbaum 2001–4, vol. 2 (2002), pp. 383–88, no. 237; Schauerte in *Emperor Maximilian I* 2012, p. 175, no. 25

1. The manuscript has been attributed to Jörg Kölderer. It is housed in the Österreichische Nationalbibliothek, Vienna, Cod. Ser. n. 4711. For more on the miniatures, see Laschitzer 1886–87. Only Koloman, Leopold, Poppo, and Otto are found in Leonhard Beck's woodcuts for the printed edition. For Beck's woodcuts, see Messling 2007, vol. 1, pp. 3–153, nos. 1–123.
2. Thomas Schauerte in Schoch, Mende, and Scherbaum 2001–4, vol. 2 (2002), pp. 374–77, no. 234, ill.

Cat. 102

Maximilian Presented by His Patron Saints to the Almighty

Hans Springinklee (ca. 1495–after 1522)

South German (Nuremberg), 1519

Woodcut

21⅜ x 15¼ in. (54.3 x 38.7 cm)

The Metropolitan Museum of Art, New York, Purchase, Jacob H. Schiff Bequest, 1922 (22.78.1)

Primarily a designer of woodcuts, Hans Springinklee was an apprentice in Albrecht Dürer's workshop by 1507. During the second decade of the sixteenth century, he worked closely with Dürer on various single-leaf prints and became involved

in the master's larger commissions for Maximilian I, such as the *Arch of Honor* (cat. 165), the *Triumphal Procession* (cat. 162), and the *Weisskunig* (cats. 114–17).

Maximilian's court historian and astronomer Johannes Stabius devised the iconographic program for *Maximilian Presented by His Patron Saints to the Almighty*. Springinklee acknowledges Stabius's contribution directly by including his coat of arms in the lower left corner of the print. There is some disagreement in the literature as to when this woodcut was made. Thomas Schauerte recently argued that the woodcut was executed several years before Maximilian's death, between 1515 and 1517, though he offers no evidence for this new dating.[1] It seems more likely that it was produced sometime in 1519, just after the death of the emperor, which is also the case with Springinklee's the *Imperial Family Mourning the Death of Maximilian I*.[2]

In this monumental woodcut, Springinklee presents an apotheosis of Maximilian. The emperor, whose titles and princely virtues Stabius extols in the Latin text below, kneels at the Gates of Heaven before Christ, who raises his hand in blessing. In the banderole issuing from Maximilian's mouth, he addresses Christ directly: "Moreover, you O Lord are my supporter / You are my glory and you glorify my reign." Wearing rich robes and carrying a cross-bearing orb, identical to the one lying beside a scepter before Maximilian, Christ blesses the emperor: "I came before him with sweet blessings / On his head I placed a crown of precious stones & I caused / Him to rejoice at the sight of my countenance."[3] Between Christ and the emperor stand the Virgin and Christ, this time a child in her arms, who act as the primary intercessors between them. Behind Maximilian are six of his patron saints. In the most prominent position, closest to the Virgin, is Saint George, the patron of the chivalric order founded by his father in 1469. Andrew stands behind Maximilian as patron of the Order of the Golden Fleece, headed by the emperor. Saint Maximilian, his namesake, is before Barbara and above Sebastian. Those two are the patrons of artillery soldiers and archers, respectively, and they indicate Maximilian's military prowess. Along the left edge in the corner is Leopold, the canonized margrave of Austria, who also is depicted with Saint Maximilian on Dürer and Springinklee's 1517 the *Patron Saints of Austria* (cat. 101) and on the *Arch of Honor*. As Campbell Dodgson noted, these same seven saints were also to appear on the *Arch of Devotion*, a religious counterpart to the *Arch of Honor* that was never designed.[4] Though Maximilian's devotional arch never came to fruition, his leading genealogist, the Freiburg lawyer Jacob Mennel, repeatedly emphasizes the focus on Maximilian's saintly patrons and ancestors, among whom he claims Saint Leopold. As a supplement to his earlier volume on saints connected to the House of Habsburg of about 1516–18, Mennel's fifth volume of the 1518 *Mirror of Birth* (*Geburtsspigel*), also catalogues the saints and blessed figures among the ancestors and relatives of the Habsburgs.[5]   FS

REFERENCES: Dodgson 1903–11, vol. 1, pp. 407–9, no. 78; Francis 1953; Hollstein 1954–2014, vol. 75 (2010), p. 26, no. 18

1. Thomas Schauerte in *Emperor Maximilian I* 2012, p. 385, no. 129.
2. Hollstein 1954–2014, vol. 76 (2010), p. 46, no. 272.
3. The inscriptions are transcribed and translated in Smith 1983, p. 157, no. 57.
4. Dodgson 1903–11, vol. 1, p. 408.
5. The fifth volume is in two parts (Österreichische Nationalbibliothek, Vienna, Cod. 3076 and Cod. 3077). For more on these volumes, see Silver 2008, pp. 44–49.

Cat. 103

Saint George and Emperor Maximilian, from *Images of Saints and of Saints Descended from the Family of Emperor Maximilian I* (*Images de Saints et de Saints Issus de la Famille de l'Empereur Maximilian I*)
Hans Springinklee (ca. 1495–after 1522)
South German (Nuremberg), ca. 1516–18
Published by Adam von Bartsch, Vienna, 1799
Woodcut
9⅜ x 8¼ in. (23.8 x 21 cm)
The Metropolitan Museum of Art, New York, The Elisha Whittelsey Collection, The Elisha Whittelsey Fund, 2017 (2017.431)

As part of Maximilian's larger memorial project, a series of 123 woodcuts by the printmaker Leonhard Beck was planned for a volume of saints connected to the House of Habsburg by the court historian Jacob Mennel. The work was supervised by the Augsburg city secretary Conrad Peutinger, who from 1491 advised Maximilian I on legal as well as artistic matters. Beck, who also contributed to *Theuerdank* (cats. 108, 109) and the *Weisskunig* (cats. 114–17), never completed the series, as it was abandoned after the emperor's death in 1519. Beck did produce eighty-nine woodcuts for the project between 1516 and 1518. This same selection of woodcuts appears in the earliest book edition of Mennel's Habsburg saints, published sometime between 1522 and 1551 on the command of Maximilian's grandson Ferdinand I.[1] These woodcuts follow earlier miniatures, arrayed in sketchbooks produced for Maximilian by the anonymous Master of the Miracles of Mariazell and by the court artist Jörg Kölderer.[2] The miniatures and Beck woodcuts show individual standing saints with their coats of arms.

Hans Springinklee's woodcut of Maximilian wearing full armor beneath a luxurious mantle and kneeling before his patron saint was perhaps not originally conceived as part of the series. Although the saint's coat of arms is not depicted, George does hold a banner bearing the emblem of the Order of Saint George—the cross inside a circle. The Cappadocian dragon slayer held a special place in Maximilian's conception of self throughout his life and often appears in his propagandistic imagery. Maximilian was obsessed with triumphing over the Ottoman Turks, and like George, he wanted to vanquish the "Turkish Dragon." In 1469, as a military response to this threat, Frederick III had founded the Order of Saint George, which Maximilian joined in 1511. As early as 1493, Maximilian also initiated the Fraternity of Saint George, and in 1503 the Society of Saint George (see cat. 105).

Springinklee likely produced this woodcut while working as an apprentice in the workshop of Albrecht Dürer, who was laboring hard on other large imperial projects, such as the *Arch of Honor* (cat. 165) and *Triumphal Procession* (see cat. 162). Although no sixteenth-century impressions exist of this composition, it was published as a part of a volume containing 118 woodcuts of the Habsburg saints by the renowned Viennese art historian and printmaker Adam von Bartsch in 1799.   FS

REFERENCE: Hollstein 1954–2014, vol. 76 (2010), p. 91, no. 308

1. For more on Beck's woodcuts and the editions of the Habsburg saints, see Messling 2006, pp. 41–51; Messling 2007, vol. 1, pp. 3–4.
2. Österreichische Nationalbibliothek, Vienna, Cod. 2857, and Cod. Ser. n. 4711.

Cat. 104

Saint George Standing with Two Angels
Lucas Cranach the Elder (1472–1553)
German, 1506
Woodcut
15⅛ x 11 in. (38.4 x 27.9 cm)
The Metropolitan Museum of Art, New York, Gift of Felix M. Warburg, 1920 (20.64.5)

In 1504 Lucas Cranach the Elder was called from Vienna to Wittenberg by Frederick the Wise, prince elector of Saxony. During his tenure as court artist to this extremely ambitious duke, Cranach created prints, drawings, and paintings that rivaled those made for Maximilian I. This large-scale woodcut of Saint George reflects how much Cranach relied on Albrecht Dürer's depictions of the saint as well as how diligently he worked to further Frederick's ambitions.

Dürer paid copious tribute to Saint George, the exemplary Christian knight whose cult was born out of Maximilian's Crusade obsession—in a painting (ca. 1500), two engravings (ca. 1502; 1505/8), a woodcut (ca. 1504), and his *Prayer Book* (1513–ca. 1515), dedicated for use by the Order of Saint George, to which Cranach contributed eight drawings.[1] The proportions of Dürer's earliest printed depiction of a standing Saint George anticipate those of Cranach's woodcut, though on a much smaller scale. Cranach shows George in full armor before a vast landscape; his emphatic halo marking him out as saintly, he stands upon the slain dragon of his most celebrated triumph. While Dürer's Saint George is wearing field armor with only his discarded helm and the prone dragon at his feet, Cranach's figure is wearing armor for both the field and free tourney (*Freiturnier*), and is surrounded by additional pieces of armor: a buffe for the chin at the lower left, below the angel

holding the helmet; a proper left pauldron reinforce held by the angel at the right; and a proper left tasset reinforce at the feet of the angel on the right. The sequence of the free tourney may explain the choice of George's armor: it begins with knights charging at each other with their lances; then, after they have broken a number of lances (by hitting their target), they would discard the reinforcing pieces and continue with the sword. Similarly, George first disabled the dragon with his lance, then "leashed" the beast, and finally dispatched it with his sword. These anterior narrative scenes can be found in miniature in the Cranach landscape, along with the maiden and lamb George saved from the dragon.

Aside from inspiring images and texts in honor of Maximilian, the cult of Saint George also caused ambitious rivals to compete on their own terms with the emperor. Frederick the Wise avidly acquired saintly relics, building on a collection that he had inherited after a pilgrimage to the

Holy Land in 1492.[2] By 1509 he had already assembled in his castle church more than five thousand relics, which were displayed annually to the public. In the same year, Frederick commissioned Cranach to create woodcuts for a collection catalogue, known as the *Wittenberger Heiltumsbuch*.[3] Predating Cranach's catalogue, the present woodcut and the artist's two prints of the saint on horseback were created between 1506 and 1510, along with other single-leaf prints of saints, such as Anthony and Christopher, all of which bear the Saxon coat of arms and broadly advertise the contents of the prince elector's growing collection and devotion to the cult of saints.[4]   FS

REFERENCES: Hollstein 1954–2014, vol. 6 (1959), p. 60, no. 83; Koepplin and Falk 1974–76, vol. 1, pp. 60–62, no. 11

1. *The Paumgartner Altarpiece*, Alte Pinakothek, Munich (706); Schoch, Mende, and Scherbaum 2001–4, vol. 1 (2000), pp. 100–101, no. 34, ill. (entry by Rainer Schoch), pp. 116–17, no. 41, ill. (entry by Anna Scherbaum), vol. 2 (2002), pp. 135–37, no. 138 (entry by Bernd Mayer); the illustrated *Prayer Book* sections are in the Bayerische Staatsbibliothek, Munich (VD16 M 1657), and the Bibliothèque Municipale, Besançon.
2. For more on Frederick and his collections of relics, see Ainsworth, Hindriks, and Terjanian 2015.
3. For a detailed discussion of the *Wittenberger Heiltumsbuch*, see Cárdenas 2002.
4. Hollstein 1954–2014, vol. 6 (1959), *Saint Anthony*, p. 52, no. 76, *Saint Christopher*, p. 56, no. 79, *Saint George*, p. 58, no. 81, p. 59, no. 82.

Cat. 105

Emperor Maximilian I in the Guise of Saint George

Daniel Hopfer (1471–1536)

South German (Augsburg), ca. 1509/10

Etching

Sheet (trimmed to plate mark): 8¹⁵⁄₁₆ x 6³⁄₁₆ in. (22.8 x 15.7 cm)

National Gallery of Art, Washington, D.C., Andrew W. Mellon Fund (1968.18.14)

This allegorical portrait of Maximilian I provides a supplement or alternative to Leonhard Beck's woodcuts for the *Book of Habsburg Family Saints (Sipp-, Mag- und Schwägerschaft)*. Rather than Beck's simple though imaginative genealogy, Hopfer endows Maximilian with sainthood by transforming him into the Cappodocian Saint George, whose noble ancestry and military prowess led to his designation as the patron of knights. As Larry Silver points out, the famous legend of George and the Dragon—the epic battle between good and evil— seems to have been a product of the crusaders, for it cannot be traced to an earlier period.[1]

In 1469 Maximilian's father, Emperor Frederick III, founded the knightly Order of Saint George, which was confirmed by Pope Paul II that winter. Frederick intended the

order to act as a check against the advance of the Ottomans into Habsburg lands. This crusading spirit was vigorously adopted by Maximilian, who sought to strengthen the order by establishing a Fraternity of Saint George in 1493 and a Society of Saint George in 1503. During periods of relative calm within the empire (1490, 1493–94, 1502–3, 1508, and 1517–18), he also made calls for a Crusade against the infidel Turks.[2] Such a Crusade became a recurring theme in both the literature and the art produced by artists working for the court.

In this print, Maximilian is attended by angels, who hold George's sword, banner, and shield while he gestures emphatically above the vanquished beast. Even though Maximilian's accoutrements communicate the military power and strength of the saint, as does the prominent halo that circles his profile,

his features and dress represent him as a private man, without his crown and the other attributes of an emperor. This iconography may be indebted to multiple versions of a portrait of Maximilian, made by the imperial painter Bernhard Strigel and his workshop, that portray the ruler in profile wearing a fur-lined cloak, a beret, and the collar of the Order of the Golden Fleece.[3]

Most of Hopfer's etched portraits, however, rely on contemporary medallic sources, including those of Charles V and Kunz von der Rosen, Maximilian's adviser and bodyguard.[4] The image of Maximilian as a private man, with cropped hair, beret, and fur-lined cloak, appears in three near-contemporary medals of the emperor. One of these was made by the Italian medalist Giovanni Maria Pomedelli, whose work Hopfer also copied in his portrait of Charles V.[5] The other two are attributed to the Augsburg sculptor Hans Daucher, who notably also executed the limestone relief *Maximilian on Horseback in the Guise of Saint George* (cat. 112).[6]   FS

REFERENCES: Metzger 2009, pp. 377–79, no. 55; Christof Metzger in *Emperor Maximilian I* 2012, p. 354, no. 115

1. For a full discussion of Saint George and Maximilian, see Silver 2008, chap. 4, "*Caesar Divus*: Leader of Christendom," pp. 109–45, 261–70.
2. In 1508 Maximilian concluded the League of Cambrai with Pope Julius II and the kings of France and Aragon by calling for a Crusade. In 1518 there was another such call by the general assembly of the estates of Austria that was answered by Pope Leo X.
3. There are several extant versions. For more information on Strigel and illustrations of these paintings, see Otto 1964, pp. 101–2, nos. 57–60, frontispiece, and ill. nos. 126–28. Not included in Otto is the version in the Kunsthistorisches Museum, Vienna, Gemäldegalerie (922).
4. Metzger 2009, pp. 419–20, no. 94, ill. p. 205; Tobias Güthner and Christof Metzger in Metzger 2009, pp. 429–30, no. 103, ill. pp. 212, 213.
5. Hill 1930/1984, vol. 1, pp. 152–53, no. 601, vol. 2, pl. 108. The obverse of this medal shows Maximilian, while its reverse shows Charles V as "REX CATOLICVS." Hopfer's elaborately ornamented *Portrait of Charles V* copies the reverse of this same Pomedelli medal; see Metzger 2009, pp. 419–20, no. 94, ill. p. 205.
6. For attributions, see Habich 1929–34, vol. 1, pt. 1 (1929), p. 11, no. 38, pl. V, 1, p. 17, no. 71, pl. X, 1, p. 17, no. 78, pl. XI, 1, p. 19, no. 89, pl. XXXVII, 2; Eser 1996, pp. 192–99, nos. 23–25, figs. 42–44. A related low-relief sculpture, formerly attributed by Georg Habich to Daucher (see Habich 1929–34, vol. 1, pt. 1, p. 13, fig. 21), shows a similar portrayal of Maximilian. Now in the Germanisches Nationalmuseum, Nuremberg (Pl.O.713), it is currently considered "South German," from about 1600. For more information on this relief, see Herbert Beck and Bernhard Decker in *Dürers Verwandlung in der Skulptur* 1981, p. 92, no. 43, ill. Thomas Eser also mentions another plaster relief, after a lost casting model, related to Daucher's portrayal of Maximilian (Eser 1996, p. 195). This relief differs from the previous examples in showing Maximilian wearing armor while seated behind a stone parapet.

Cat. 106

Saint George on Horseback

Hans Burgkmair (1473–1531)
Printed by Jost de Negker (1485–1544)
South German (Augsburg), dated 1508, printed 1518
Chiaroscuro woodcut from two blocks
$12^{13}/_{16}$ x $9^{1}/_{16}$ in. (32.5 x 23.1 cm)
The Metropolitan Museum of Art, New York, Harris Brisbane Dick Fund, 1931 (31.81.4)

Cat. 107

Emperor Maximilian I on Horseback

Hans Burgkmair (1473–1531)
Printed by Jost de Negker (1485–1544)
South German (Augsburg), dated 1508, printed 1518
Chiaroscuro woodcut from two blocks
$12^{13}/_{16}$ x $8^{15}/_{16}$ in. (32.5 x 22.7 cm)
National Gallery of Art, Washington, D.C., Rosenwald Collection (1948.11.14)

The year 1508 was a milestone in the life of Maximilian I. In February of that year he journeyed to his southernmost territory, the city of Trento, to proclaim himself "elected Holy Roman Emperor," because Venetian opposition prevented him from making the traditional trip to Rome for formal coronation as emperor by the pope. To commemorate this event, he commissioned several multiple works bearing his image as ruler.

The first appeared in 1508 on a large presentation coin designed by Ulrich Ursentaler (cat. 87).[1] Its obverse shows the emperor in profile on horseback, facing right, wearing the imperial crown and carrying the flag of the imperial double-headed eagle. Both Maximilian and his horse are armored, and the X-shaped cross of Saint Andrew, patron saint of Burgundy, which his army carried into battle on banners, appears on the crupper of the steed.[2] On the reverse, twelve coats of arms of Maximilian's territories surround the heraldic insignia of the emperor and the seven prince electors of the Holy Roman Empire.

The other commemorative multiples were on paper, a pair of pendant woodcuts designed by Hans Burgkmair of Augsburg. The first image, like that on Ursentaler's coin, shows both the emperor and his horse, armored, in profile, and facing left (cat. 107). That Maximilian's patronage of armor was a lifelong passion is revealed both in this volume and in the later Burgkmair woodcut image of his fictional avatar, the White King, visiting the armorers' forge (cats. 114, 115). Behind the emperor, the double-headed eagle hangs on a tapestry with its

DIVVS·GEORGIVS
CHRISTIANORVM·
MILITVM·PRO·
PVGNATOR

·H·BVRGKMAIR·

Jost de Negker.

inescutcheon, Austria on the dexter side and Burgundy on the sinister. Eagles adorn the peytral, while the shield of Austria appears on the crupper. Holding a baton of military command, Maximilian wears at his side an elaborate battle sword, similar to one in this volume (cat. 97). His helmet is topped by a prominent peacock's tail, claimed as a heraldic symbol by the Habsburgs, in part because medieval animal lore viewed the bird, whose flesh supposedly did not decay, as a symbol of the resurrected Christ.[3] Both Maximilian and his mount appear beneath a convincingly classical triumphal arch, executed in accordance with ancient Roman imperial models. This authenticity adds support to the hypothesis that Burgkmair might have visited Italy about 1507.

To this woodcut, Burgkmair added a pendant print of one of Maximilian's favorite holy figures, Saint George (cat. 106). His father, Emperor Frederick III, founded the knightly Order of Saint George, which the son reaffirmed and committed to a Crusade mission, which Maximilian illustrated in an Albrecht Altdorfer woodcut on the side tower of the *Arch of Honor* (cat. 165).[4] Facing the emperor from the left, George is similarly armored and mounted on horseback. The saint and his steed are shown astride his most famous conquest, the dragon that he slew to save a princess, who kneels before him under an arch similar to Maximilian's. Both George's helmet ornament and the decorations on the horse bard show the cross, for the saint was prized as the patron saint of Christian warriors, particularly crusaders.[5] Indeed, Maximilian's own partisan calls for Crusades spanned his entire reign, and his illustrated chivalric quest, *Theuerdank* (cats. 108, 109), ends with a woodcut of the hero setting out on one. That image closely resembles those on the Ursentaler coin and the Burgkmair woodcut of 1508, but also includes the red cross banner of Saint George himself. Here, the Latin inscription in the clouds above calls the saint the "vanguard of the army of Christians." Of course, in reality, Maximilian was blocked by his regional rivals, Venice and France, from even reaching Rome for his coronation.

The *Saint George* also adds further evidence of Burgkmair's supposed trip to Italy, especially Venice, since the aggressive turn of the saint's body and the lowered placement of his baton (translated into a broken lance) echo features of Andrea del Verrocchio's bronze equestrian portrait of Bartolomeo Colleoni in Venice (1488). In addition, the angled, arched structure of *Saint George* actually adapts the nave arches and triforium of San Marco.

By the time he devised these woodcuts, Burgkmair had already begun to design prints for the emperor in Augsburg

under the supervision of the city secretary Conrad Peutinger (see cat. 150). A serious antiquarian and collector of ancient Roman coins, Peutinger had by 1505 commissioned the artist to prepare illustrations for his proposed history of the emperors (the *Kaiserbuch*; never published). He would therefore have appreciated the authenticity of the depicted triumphal arch in the 1508 print.

In addition, the printing history of the Maximilian woodcut holds special significance, because it was a pioneering experiment in color printing. These chiaroscuro woodcuts were created by superimposing separate color blocks onto the basic black-and-white main block. Although several rare impressions of the Maximilian print bear the date 1508, it was reprinted more extensively in 1518, with Burgkmair's signature at the lower right removed; in its place appears the name of Jost de Negker, a skilled Netherlandish woodblock carver, who would later boldly take credit for the invention of color prints.[6]

The history of this crucial experimental period is complicated, and in addition to Negker the Saxon court artist Lucas Cranach the Elder weighed in with his own claims, laid out clearly by Peter Parshall.[7] The key document is a September 1508 letter from Peutinger to Cranach's patron, Frederick the Wise, prince elector of Saxony, referring to a Cranach woodcut "in gold and silver," presumably the 1507 profile *Saint George in a Landscape* on blue tinted paper, now in the British Museum, London.[8] That work fueled Burgkmair's own ambition and led Peutinger to send back to Saxony similar samples on parchment of "knights in silver and gold," namely, these pendant portraits of Saint George and Maximilian from that year.[9]

Not many of the 1508 prints survive. The finest of them, in the collection of the Art Institute of Chicago, has the basic black-and-white outlines of the main block supplemented with gold highlights printed from a second line block.[10] Burgkmair also experimented with the use of tinted papers, and the Ashmolean Museum has two colored 1508 impressions of these pendants, *Saint George* on blue paper and *Maximilian* on red.[11]

But the story does not stop there. In 1509 Cranach, not content with his claim to have invented the technique used for the *Saint George* colored print, produced several more nicely coordinated color woodcuts, including *Saint Christopher* and *Venus and Cupid* (a few dated impressions of these survive), but backdated them to 1506 to secure his place in printmaking history.[12] Moreover, Negker would later claim, in a 1512 solicitation letter to Maximilian, that he himself had invented color woodcut printing. He would reprint the *Maximilian* woodcut with the altered year of 1518 and even substituted his own name in place of Burgkmair's signature at the lower right in

IMP·CAES·MAXIMIL·AVG

Jost de Negker.

H · BVRGKMAIR

some impressions.[13] The chiaroscuro impression in this volume exemplifies that latter phase in production of *Maximilian on Horseback.*   LS

REFERENCES: Chmelarz 1894; Falk 1968, pp. 69–71; Falk 1973, n.p., nos. 21, 22; Silver 1985; Peter Parshall in Landau and Parshall 1994, pp. 187–91

1. Jungwith 1969.
2. On horse and rider armor, see Pyhrr, La Rocca, and Breiding 2005; Terjanian 2011.
3. Thomas Schauerte in *Emperor Maximilian I* 2012, pp. 165–67, no. 19, ill.
4. Winkelbauer 1954; Silver 2008, pp. 112–27.
5. Volbach 1917; Braunfels-Esche 1976.
6. For successive states of the woodcut and the changes among them, see Dodgson 1903–11, vol. 2, pp. 74–77, nos. 14, 15. See also Peter Parshall in Landau and Parshall 1994, pp. 190–91.
7. Parshall in Landau and Parshall 1994, pp. 184–87.
8. British Museum, London (1895-1-22-264); discussed in Bartrum 1995, pp. 171–72, no. 173, pl. 7. For the letter, see König 1923, pp. 97–98, no. 55; English translation, Joachim 1961, p. 8.
9. König 1923, pp. 97–98, no. 55; English translation, Joachim 1961, p. 8.
10. Art Institute of Chicago (1961.3); see Silver 1985.
11. Ibid., pp. 12, 13, figs. 6, 8. A third print of *Maximilian*, on blue paper but with white rather than gold or silver highlights, is at the Cleveland Museum of Art (50.72); ibid., p. 12, and p. 13, fig. 7. For the later history of the technique, see Bialler 1992, especially p. 17, no. B 1, ill.
12. The prints must date after 1508, when Cranach received from Frederick the Wise his own personal coat of arms, a winged serpent, which appears on both images.
13. On Negker, including his 1512 letter to Maximilian, see Parshall in Landau and Parshall 1994, pp. 200–202.

Cats. 108, 109

Theuerdank Leads a Crusade and *Theuerdank Accompanied by Ehrenhold*, from *Theuerdank*

Leonhard Beck (1480–1542), Hans Burgkmair (1473–1531), and Hans Schäufelein (ca. 1480–ca. 1540)
Printed by Hans Schönsperger the Elder (ca. 1455–1521)
South German (Augsburg), 1519
Illustrated verse epic with woodcuts
H. 14¾ in. (37.5 cm), W. 9¹³⁄₁₆ in. (25 cm), D. 2⁹⁄₁₆ in. (6.5 cm)
The Metropolitan Museum of Art, New York, Gift of Mortimer L. Schiff, 1918 (18.57.7)

Only two of Maximilian I's ambitious illustrated projects were published during his lifetime: the *Arch of Honor* (cat. 165) and this lavish book, *Theuerdank*, named for its allegorical hero. Based on late medieval courtly romances, the volume presents half-page woodcut images to accompany each of its 118 chapters.[1] Its lavish font, Fraktur, complete with movable printed flourishes, was specially designed for Maximilian in Augsburg by Vinzenz Rockner to simulate the ornate script of court scribes. The images were delegated to a team of Augsburg artists, led by Leonhard Beck, who produced many of the woodcuts for the emperor's other illustrated projects: the *Weisskunig* (cats. 114–17) and the *Book of Habsburg Family Saints* (*Sipp-, Mag- und Schwägerschaft*). Beck was responsible for most of the images; the others were assigned to Hans Burgkmair and Hans Schäufelein, who had earlier been active in Albrecht Dürer's workshop, while the designers of eight remain anonymous.

A number of volumes of *Theuerdank* survive with carefully colored woodcuts, the paid labor of *Briefmaler* (literally, letter-painters). The printer, Hans Schönsperger the Elder, had also recently provided Maximilian with samples of his projected prayer book, dedicated to the knights of the emperor's Order of Saint George and their crusader mission. Final editing of the text was completed in Nuremberg by Melchior Pfinzing, the provost of the church of Saint Sebald, who appended a "key" (*Clavis*) to identify the main characters and suggest the ties to actual biographical events in Maximilian's life. A planned Latin translation under the title *Magnanimus* was never completed for publication.

Theuerdank's ongoing, almost picaresque plot is loosely based on the exploits of the youthful Maximilian. Featuring dangerous hunts of wild animals in alpine mountains, it also includes tests of knightly prowess in jousts and tournaments and occasional warfare. The goal of Theuerdank's quest is to claim his princess bride, Ehrenreich (Rich in Honor), an allegorized representation of his first wife, Mary of Burgundy. Throughout his progress, the hero is accompanied by two companions, one of whom is his faithful, ever-present herald, Ehrenhold. The other is one of three implacable foes—allegorical antagonists, all vices of youth, who attempt to subvert or even sabotage his success through arranged dangers: first, Fürwittig (Impetuousness); then Unfalo (Accident), and finally, Neidelhart (Envy). A good example of the dangerous situations that these enemies arranged for Theuerdank, related to the military novelties Maximilian himself employed in warfare (and seen elsewhere in this volume), is depicted in a Schäufelein woodcut (no. 39), in which Unfalo shows him a cannon that is overcharged with powder and invites him to inspect it with a lighted torch. Theuerdank's nimble maneuvering, however, enables him to escape unscathed.

An early image by Schäufelein (no. 10) even presents the young hero tempted by an "evil spirit," dressed as a scholar but revealed by his clawed feet to be the devil. Near the end of his quest, Theuerdank is visited by an angel (no. 115), who bolsters his courage and urges him to undertake a Crusade. The chapter of the book containing Beck's image of the hero's subsequent departure as a crusader (no. 117; cat. 108),

CAT. 108

CAT. 109

launched under the red cross banner of Saint George, is the only one that does not have text added, in anticipation of a future real-life Crusade by Maximilian, to be fictionalized in later editions of the volume. In the final image, by Burgkmair (no. 118; cat. 109), Theuerdank appears in full armor within a magic circle of swords; still accompanied by Ehrenhold, he faces a future confident of the Lord's protection.

In the latter portion of the text, the hero proves his valor to his princess bride through successful combat at her court (nos. 98–112), during which he overcomes six knights

(nos. 101–6). In the accompanying illustrations, he wears armor and wields lances or swords based on the innovations in tournaments initiated by Maximilian himself, discussed in this volume and commemorated in his unpublished fictional roster, *Freydal* (cats. 39–55).   LS

REFERENCES: Engels, Geck, and Musper 1968; Appuhn 1979; Müller 1982, pp. 108–30, 159–72; Tennant 1989; Füssel 2003; Silver 2008, pp. 7, 21–22, 35, 138–40, 176–80; Ziegeler 2015

1. Silver 1986; Kohnen 2015.

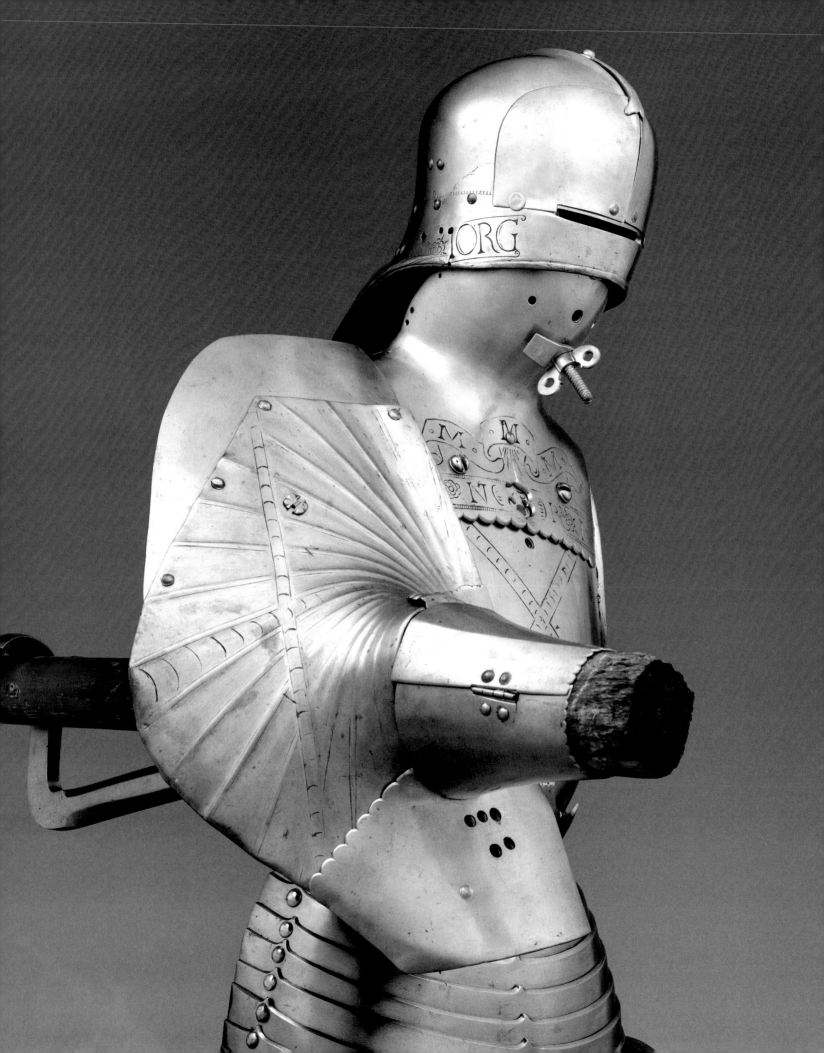

Cat. 110

Armor for the Joust of War

Austrian (Innsbruck), ca. 1500 and later

Steel and leather

As mounted: H. 75 in. (190.5 cm, including mount), W. 33⅞ in. (86 cm), D. 37⅝ in. (95.5 cm)

Kunsthistorisches Museum, Vienna, Imperial Armoury (R. VII)

Among the many armors owned by Maximilian I, this example for the joust of war is unique for the invocation of Saint George on its sallet and the representation of the cross of Saint Andrew on its breastplate. A patron saint of the dukes of Burgundy and their prestigious Order of the Golden Fleece, Andrew became one of Maximilian's special protectors from the time he succeeded Charles the Bold. In fact, the X-shaped cross on which Andrew was thought to have been crucified, originally a Burgundian badge, evolved into a Habsburg one, adorning the military dress, standards, armor, and even artillery of the family and anyone in its service (see cats. 77, 96).[1] The engraved cross on this jousting armor would have been concealed by a large, overlapping targe, but it would have been exposed when the targe, struck properly by the opponent's lance, separated from the armor and was lifted up into the air. In contrast, the invocation of Saint George—HILF HEILIGER RITTER IORG (Help, Holy Knight George), engraved in large letters around the crown of the sallet—would have remained visible at all times. Although many other European sovereigns favored this patron saint, Maximilian had a special attachment to him: beyond George's exemplary prowess as a knight, he embodied the defense of the Christian faith and, by implication, the ideal of the Crusades, in which Maximilian showed a continued interest (see cats. 106, 107). Not unsurprisingly, the saint is invoked on other martial objects owned by Maximilian, among them a lavish ceremonial sword made by Hans Sumersperger in Hall in Tyrol, now in the Kunsthistorisches Museum's collection.[2]

Composed of elements selected in 1952 on the grounds of their stylistic coherence and close fit, the armor as presently assembled comprises a sallet, a buffe, a breastplate with a queue, and a fauld with tassets. It is complemented by a vamplate with lance socket, a lance head, a targe, and tilting sockets; in order to be complete, it would need a backplate. Engraved like the sallet and the breastplate, the buffe features the letters MMM inside a banderole and the letters INRI interspersed with roses along the lower edge. Whereas the meaning of the former is uncertain, that of the latter is a reference to, and invocation of, Jesus Christ.

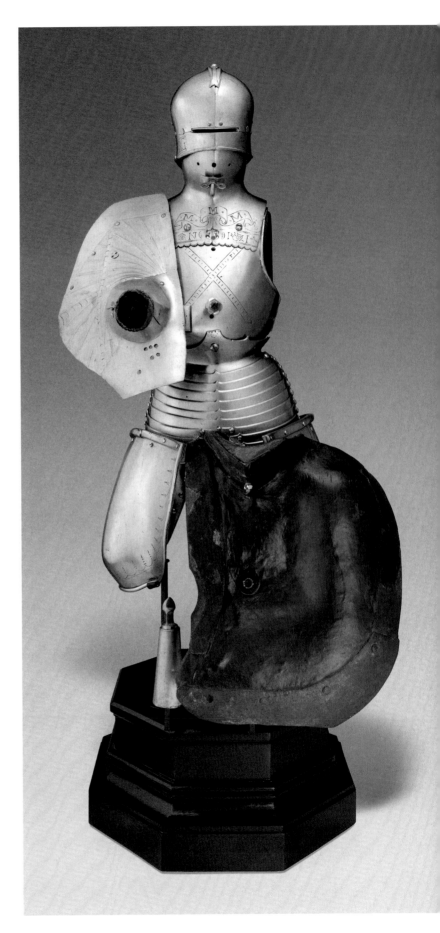

The elements of this armor are notable for the fact that they saw active use and were subjected to certain alterations. For example, the tail of the sallet was trimmed and made more fashionable, according to the standards of the 1520s, with the application of a roped band along its rim. The buffe and breastplate are designed for two forms of the joust war: one that employed mechanical devices capable of ejecting a targe, and the other in which the targe would have been firmly bolted to the breastplate, the chief purpose being to unhorse one's opponent.   PT

REFERENCES: Thomas and Gamber 1954, pp. 69–70, no. 75; Thomas and Gamber 1976, pp. 162–63 (erroneously as no. S. VII)

1. Pyhrr 1989, pp. 99–102, figs. 26–31.
2. Thomas 1955/1977, p. 1439, ill.

Cat. 111

Design for the Crypt of Maximilian I

South German, ca. 1512
Pen and ink and tempera on parchment
Sheet: 16⅛ x 11¹³⁄₁₆ in. (41 x 30 cm)
Tiroler Landesmuseum Ferdinandeum, Innsbruck,
Austria, Grafische Sammlungen (AD 40)

As Maximilian I prepared for his death, he commissioned this design for his own crypt, which he envisioned as the centerpiece of a grand mausoleum that would record and commemorate his earthly accomplishments. Although the intended site of his burial had long remained uncertain, the emperor was insistent that the church to be given the honor of receiving his remains, whether it be renovated or newly constructed, had to be the property of the Order of Saint George.[1]

Maximilian may have failed to endow the chivalric order founded by his father with substantial resources, to increase its ranks and turn it into a mighty organization capable of repelling Ottoman incursions, yet every indication suggests that his attachment to it was sincere. Despite ultimately abandoning the idea of becoming the order's grand master, he spared no effort to enhance its prestige, not least by securing papal support and by openly associating himself with the order and the saint for whom it was named.[2]

In addition to desiring a grand crypt worthy of his legacy, Maximilian envisioned the posthumous foundation of imperial charitable institutions across the German-speaking lands and beyond, as well as the creation of new branches of the Order of Saint George. The program articulated in this drawing, known from Maximilian's last will and testament, comprises seven scenes on each side of the central wall. The left wall celebrates the anticipated foundation of hospices for elderly men in various locations: from top to bottom, Rottenburg on the Neckar (Swabia), Millstatt (Carinthia), Graz (Styria), Rain (Styria), Vienna (Lower Austria), Mechelen (Flanders), and Innsbruck (Tyrol). Occupying the center of each scene is the particular patron saint whom Maximilian designated for the particular foundation, flanked by grateful beneficiaries, clerics, and even pilgrims. These saints, as well as the Virgin, were Maximilian's seven patrons, and six of them are depicted presenting him to the Almighty in a woodcut by the Nuremberg artist Hans Springinklee (cat. 102).[3]

If this wall was devoted to Maximilian's charitable works, the one opposite focuses entirely on his planned expansion of the Order of Saint George. The top scene honors the saint, with groups of men and women praying before what seems to be the cauldron of his martyrdom, with his shield hanging above. Farther down, from top to bottom, five scenes celebrate Maximilian's prescribed establishment of branches of the order in the county of Artois, Freiburg im Breisgau (Swabia), Wiener Neustadt (Lower Austria), Rain (Carniola), and Ebersdorf (Lower Austria). At the bottom, the final scene depicts two shields of Saint George resting on pillows at each end of Maximilian's sarcophagus.

On the central wall, Maximilian appears in the next-to-last panel. Identified by a heraldic shield impaled with the arms of the empire and Austria, he holds an orb and wears a mantle with the cross of Saint Andrew. He is in the company of similarly attired knights, the members of the order honored with the task of caring for his sepulcher. The mantle and its emblem were described in Maximilian's testament as the old vestment of the order, which the sixteen members in charge of his sepulcher were to wear. The three scenes immediately above refer to the rules of the order, while the one at the very bottom introduces a pilgrim entering the sanctuary.

As Maximilian's grand plans proved difficult to implement, the Order of Saint George did not receive the expected support and failed to expand after the emperor's death. Instead, it stagnated as Maximilian's successors lost interest in associating themselves with it. The order was finally dissolved in 1598.   PT

REFERENCES: *Maximilian I*. 1969, "Katalog," p. 64, no. 251; Brauneis 1976; Schmid 1984, pp. 760–61

1. On the order, see Bergmann 1868; Brauneis 1976, pp. 173–74; H. Koller 1980.
2. See Winkelbauer 1954, pp. 529–47; Schmid 1984, p. 759.
3. On Maximilian's testamentary prescriptions for the Order of Saint George, see Schmid 1984, pp. 772–76. For the identification of the figures in this design and the significance of the iconographic program, see Brauneis 1976, pp. 169–72; Schmid 1984, pp. 760–61.

Cat. 112

Maximilian I on Horseback in the Guise of Saint George
Hans Daucher (1486–1538)
South German (Augsburg), ca. 1522
Solnhofener stone
H. 9¹⁄₁₆ in. (23 cm), W. 6¹⁄₁₆ in. (15.5 cm), D. 1¹⁄₁₆ in. (2.8 cm)
Kunsthistorisches Museum, Vienna, Kunstkammer (7236)

This work is one of several carved reliefs by the Augsburg
artist Hans Daucher that feature a posthumous portrait of
Maximilian I as either the central figure or a participant in
the overall composition (see cat. 156). Here, the abbreviated
Latin inscription on the edge of the arch over the emperor's
head identifies him as the main subject: "Emperor Caesar the
August Maximilian" (IMP. CAES. MAXIMILIANVS. AVGVSTV).
The inscription was one Maximilian seems to have personally
favored, as suggested by its inclusion in a woodcut that he
commissioned from Hans Burgkmair (cat. 107) which, in
reverse, has such a similar composition that it might have been
the inspiration for this work. It is also found on the design for
an equestrian statue of the emperor, which Burgkmair had
prepared for the sculptor Gregor Erhart (cat. 161).

As is typical of Daucher's works, the armor and horse bard
are represented in great detail and demonstrate an unusual
understanding of their form and construction, leading the
viewer to experience the image as if it were a historical document. The authority of the representation is enhanced by the
careful rendering of Maximilian's physiognomy as it is recorded
in portraits dating from the end of his life (see cat. 154).

The presence of a dead dragon trampled by his horse
leaves no doubt that Maximilian is here depicted in the guise
of Saint George. The horse bard celebrates his association
with the saint and the order, fraternity, and society of Saint
George that Maximilian supported to bolster the defense of
his lands, particularly against the threat of Ottoman expansion
(see cat. 105). Prominently featured on the boss of the peytral
(as it also appears in a woodcut in *Theuerdank*, see cat. 108),
the cross of Saint George is explicitly associated with the arms
of Austria, which adorn the escutcheon on the horse's shaffron
as well as the breast of the imperial double-headed eagle on
its crupper.   PT

REFERENCES: *Maximilian I*. 1959, pp. 185–86, no. 536, pl. 92; Eser 1996,
pp. 159–65, no. 15, fig. 28; Veronika Sandbichler in *Werke für die Ewigkeit*
2002, pp. 67–68, no. 24, ill.

FIG. 38 *Investiture of the First Grand Master of the Order of Saint George,
Johann Siebenhirter, by Pope Paul II and Emperor Frederick III on January 1,
1469, in the Lateran Basilica in Rome*, detail. Austrian, ca. 1490. Tempera on
panel. Landesmuseum für Kärten, Klagenfurt, Austria (K 86)

The Armorers

Maximilian commissioned armor from the foremost masters across Europe. The armorers whom he patronized in the Franche-Comté, the German-speaking lands, Italy, and the Low Countries possessed their own trade secrets and worked in different styles. A steel skirt speaks to the technical mastery and creativity of Hans Seusenhofer, an armorer whom Maximilian hired to establish and direct a court workshop in Innsbruck. A saddle with a so-called iron hand, a contraption designed to hold the shaft of a military standard, is a reminder of the contributions from locksmiths and even clockmakers to the armorer's art during this period. As someone who wore armor regularly and had put it to the test in battles and tournaments, Maximilian was a great connoisseur. He was deeply interested in the details of the armors that he ordered, and often meddled with the work of the armorers entrusted with the commissions. He regarded his expertise in armor design and his patronage as manifestations of his greatness, as is shown in the text and illustrations of the *Weisskunig*, one of his many pseudo-autobiographical works.

Maximilian did not rely solely on the services of independent armorers. In return for wages or subsidies, masters contractually committed to give him preferential or exclusive treatment, work in specific places, or make set types and quantities of armors every year. Maximilian established privileged relationships with armorers in Arbois, Augsburg, Innsbruck, Graz, Ljubljana, Vienna, and Wiener Neustadt. These and other armorers supplied his arsenals, outfitted his troops, and provided the armors he needed for his personal use and for presentation as gifts to his courtiers, family, officials, and peers. Many masters had successful careers in his service and attained the highest honors by securing the ennoblement of their families. Yet, not all armorers fared so well, and many remained unpaid by the time of their deaths. Maximilian's ongoing need for luxury armor and the kernel importance of these works for the success of his grand designs belong to the chief reasons the armorer's art blossomed under his patronage.

Cat. 113

Maximilian I in Imperial Regalia
Bernhard Strigel (1460–1528)
South German (Memmingen), after 1508
Oil on wood panel
33¹/₁₆ x 20⅜ in. (84 x 51.8 cm)
Tiroler Landesmuseum Ferdinandeum, Innsbruck, Austria,
Ältere Kunstgeschichtliche Sammlungen, on long-term loan
from a private collection (Gem 136)

Among the many portraits of Maximilian I to have been
painted in Bernhard Strigel's workshop—and their copies—
the Innsbruck panel stands out. Not only is it one of the

largest of these paintings, but it also combines familiar
visual elements, yielding a sort of summary of the portraits
preceding it. Recent research has shown, however, that a
host of analogies exists between this panel and a portrait of
Maximilian's father, Frederick III, housed in Vienna.[1]

Maximilian is shown in three-quarter profile before a deep
red background, wearing blackened armor with gold trim,
which may be one produced by the Augsburg armorer Lorenz
Helmschmid before 1508. He dons the collar of the Order of
the Golden Fleece (of which he was once the sovereign and
remained a prominent member) and the insignia of his imperial might, gained in 1508—scepter, sword, mitered crown,
and mantle.

The mantle's splendid beadwork, gold-trimmed borders and bands, and precious stones appear in a similar fashion on the mitered crown. The crown differs from those seen in earlier depictions, but many of its numerous details correspond to descriptions of one in inventories from after 1550. It may be the work mentioned in an order that was placed with Leonhard Strassburger during the Imperial Diet of Constance in 1507, for the production of a miter for the crown to be used in the planned imperial coronation the following year.[2] The Republic of Venice hindered Maximilian's passage to Rome, however, resulting in his proclamation as Holy Roman Emperor elect in Trento Cathedral on February 4, 1508. The scepter—held in his right hand, resting on an opulent brocade cushion—cuts diagonally across the foreground of the painting. Its upper section comprises a chalice opening over a ring of pomegranates, from which a finial bursts forth. This scepter is very similar to the one depicted on the imperial florin.

The sword is noteworthy because it is unlike any of those depicted or surviving that belonged to the emperor. Importantly, Maximilian's hand does not cover the lower section of the hilt, which is unusual in painted depictions. This choice directs the viewers' attention toward the image on the hilt of a crown placed upon a shield with a double-headed imperial eagle. An allegorical female figure, outfitted with crown and halo, appears below; she carries a sword in her left hand, but the object in her right is no longer identifiable. She may be the allegorical figure of Justice or Magnanimity—two sovereign virtues. The presence of the halo, however, strongly suggests the figure is a personification of the church (*Ecclesia*), a symbol that underscores Maximilian's special claim as defender of the Christian faith and savior of the empire, and foregrounds the religious and secular legitimacy of his emperorship.

The Innsbruck panel is the visual manifestation of Maximilian's concepts of sovereignty and self-representation. In an added expression of gravitas, the emperor is depicted in front of a red background reminiscent of the rulers' color in Roman antiquity. In contrast to the cloths of honor or landscape views commonly found in the backgrounds of other portraits, the red focuses attention on the splendid, detailed rendering of the imperial insignia and blackened armor trimmed in gold. The battle-ready armor—which supplants the decorative golden armor used in other paintings—proclaims the emperor's chivalry and defensive power.

The propaganda embedded in this portrait was likely aimed at a courtly audience. Unlike depictions of Maximilian in print and on coins, which had much wider circulation,

the Innsbruck panel is a more exclusive, individually composed image of the emperor.[3] Although it was not drawn from life, the picture nonetheless implies authenticity by means of the shadow on the red background, which announces the emperor's physical presence. This staging was ultimately meant to bind the courtly elite to his power and inspire them to emulate his virtuousness.　PS

REFERENCES: Honold 1967; Gert Ammann in *Hispania—Austria* 1992, pp. 261–62, no. 77, ill.; Eisenbeiss 2005, pp. 156–58, 162, 173, 279–80, figs. 126 (detail), 127

1. Kunsthistorisches Museum, Vienna, Gemäldegalerie (4397); see Eisenbeiss 2005, p. 156.
2. Gert Ammann in *Hispania—Austria* 1992, p. 261.
3. Madersbacher 2000, p. 369; see also Lukas Madersbacher in *Circa 1500* 2000, pp. 370–71, nos. 2-15-1-2-15-6.

Cat. 114

The Skillfulness and Wit of Armor Making, from *Der Weisskunig*

Hans Burgkmair (1473–1531), Leonhard Beck (1480–1542), Hans Springinklee (ca. 1495–after 1522), and Hans Schäufelein (ca. 1480–ca. 1540)
Compiled by Marx Treitzsaurwein (ca. 1450–1527)
South German, ca. 1510–16
Bound album with 119 woodcuts, 52 drawings, and manuscript text
H. 17 1/16 in. (43.4 cm), W. 12 in. (30.5 cm), D. 2 3/4 in. (7 cm)
Museum of Fine Arts, Boston, Katherine E. Bullard Fund (57.40)

Cat. 115

The Skillfulness and Wit of Armor Making, from *Der Weisskunig*

Hans Burgkmair (1473–1531)
South German, 1514–16
Woodblock
H. 8 11/16 in. (22.1 cm), W. 7 5/8 in. (4 cm), D. 15/16 in. (2.3 cm)
Albertina Museum, Vienna (HO2006/347)

Cat. 116

The White King as a Child Playing with Other Children, from *Der Weisskunig*

Hans Burgkmair (1473–1531)
South German, 1514–16, printed 1775
Woodcut
8 3/4 x 7 13/16 in. (22.3 x 19.8 cm)
The Metropolitan Museum of Art, New York, Gift of Harry G. Friedman, 1962 (62.635.124)

CAT. 114

Cat. 117

The White King Learning to Enclose a Camp with Wagons, from *Der Weisskunig*

Hans Burgkmair (1473–1531)

South German, 1514–16, printed 1775

Woodcut proof

8¾ x 7¹⁵⁄₁₆ in. (22.2 x 20.2 cm)

The Metropolitan Museum of Art, New York, Rogers Fund, 1917 (17.72.40)

Although Maximilian I's most ambitious book project, the *Weisskunig*, was never published, the numerous surviving woodcut blocks prepared for it during the middle teens of the sixteenth century were eventually printed by Habsburg descendants in the late eighteenth century (1775).[1] Like other projects of the emperor, such as the *Triumphal Procession* (cat. 162) and *Arch of Honor* (cat. 165), the text was personally

CAT. 115

CAT. 116

CAT. 117

conceived by the emperor and dictated to his private secretary, Marx Treitzsaurwein, who followed up with a correction book (*Fragbuch*, 1515) that refined details of both the texts and the images. Like *Theuerdank* (cats. 108, 109), the *Weisskunig* was intended for publication in Augsburg by the imperial printer Hans Schönsperger the Elder under the local direction of the city secretary Conrad Peutinger.

The 251 full-page images, three of which are presented here alongside one of the surviving woodblocks, were assigned to a team of Augsburg designers. Chief among these were Hans Burgkmair, responsible for 118, most monogrammed with his initials HB, and Leonhard Beck, who provided designs for 127, while Hans Schäufelein contributed two or three; all three artists also supplied the illustrations to *Theuerdank*. Most of the blocks were cut during the period between 1514 and 1516, presumably by the Augsburg carver Jost de Negker. They survive in eleven proof impressions (including those in Treitzsaurwein's own layout book), which give a strong indication of the final layout and its close coordination between texts and images.[2] One of the most precious of those ensembles of the book-in-progress (Manuscript G), once in the collection of the princes of Liechtenstein and

now in Boston (cat. 114), contains both proofs of woodcuts (119) and drawings (52) for revisions and additions. It also includes Maximilian's own handwritten notes, which indicate his close concern with how his reign was represented, especially in the accuracy of battle scenes.[3]

Like *Theuerdank*, the *Weisskunig* draws on late medieval German court literature for its text, especially the *Heldenbücher* (hero books), and although it is intended to be an autobiography, it fictionalizes the characters and takes on the nature of an allegory. The various kings, for example, are designated by colors, based on their heraldry. The White, or "Wise," King (the pun is close in German) represents Maximilian in a color that denotes purity; his father, Frederick III, is called the Old White King. His nemesis, the French monarch, is the Blue King; Hungary, the Green King; and Venice (in reality, a kingless republic), the Fish King.

Comprising three sections, the book begins with the chronicle of the Old White King, who, as Maximilian's predecessor, pursues his own bride and then goes to Rome for his imperial coronation. Next, a middle section considers the White King's youth and his training in multifarious fields, showing his interests and abilities but also his principles.

The monogrammed Burgkmair image here appears in this part, in which Maximilian's childhood familiarity with weapons and armored jousting provides the foundation for his adult achievements as a ruler (cat. 116). The woodcut shows children playing while teams of adults sitting around a table are busy manipulating toy jousters with lances, the same kind of toys (akin to modern sports video games) discussed elsewhere in this catalogue (cats. 71–73). Appearing, with his laurel crown, in several places in the image, the White King not only frolics in wrestling games with adults but also engages in serious play with various contemporary weapons—cannon, crossbow, and longbow—as toys.

Another Burgkmair woodcut from the same middle section shows an older Maximilian still in military training but learning the latest tactics in field warfare (cat. 117). In this case, he literally "circles the wagons," as he employs armaments to construct a mobile army siege fortification (*Wagenburg*, or "wagon castle"). At the back of the encampment, large-scale cannons defend the site. The same formation, with imperial banners from the age of Frederick III, had previously been depicted in the military drawings of the *Housebook*, a court volume compiled in the Middle Rhine region about 1475–80.[4] The text accompanying the present woodcut characteristically declares—after an inventory of the White King's various interests, both practical (cooking, hunting, warfare, armor) and cultural (art, music, languages)—that he soon came to surpass his teachers. These princely preoccupations reappear in both the *Arch of Honor* towers and the *Triumphal Procession*. Thus, Maximilian proclaims himself to be a Renaissance ruler, jack-of-all-trades but master of all.

Another surviving woodcut reiterates this lesson, as it shows the White King visiting with his armorers and offering them advice in their own workshop (cats. 114, 115). This image, designed by Burgkmair, is framed within an open doorway, and all the tools appear on a foreground ledge with armor parts; complete armor hangs in segments on the wall behind. Although its corresponding text appears in the 1775 printing, the woodcut itself does not.

The third and largest section of the *Weisskunig* recounts Maximilian's reign from his 1477 marriage to Mary of Burgundy through his wars and diplomacy (and shifting alliances) up to the year 1513. This part is given over to numerous battle scenes, whose documentary value remained very important to the emperor, as his corrections reveal.[5] The armies are distinguished by their battle ensigns, Maximilian's featuring the X-shaped cross of Saint Andrew, patron saint of Burgundy. Most of the forces display the three major divisions of contemporary warfare: cavalry, infantry (with teams of pikes), and artillery, with the novel weaponry of cannons. — LS

REFERENCES: Musper 1956; *Maximilian I.* 1959, pp. 25–30, nos. 76–89, p. 119, nos. 387–90; Falk 1973, n.p., nos. 178–203; Müller 1982, pp. 130–48; Silver 2008, pp. 1–7, 30–36, 136–39, 156–66, 170–76, 182, 193–94, 206–10; Bossmeyer 2015; Werner 2015

1. For the posthumous publication history, see Bossmeyer 2015, pp. 21–36.
2. Österreichische Nationalbibliothek, Vienna, Cod. 3032, is Treitzsaurwein's layout book.
3. Petermann 1956, pp. 72–89 ("Die Zeichnungen"), and for the Museum of Fine Arts, Boston, printing (Manuscript G) and its drawings, see pp. 67–68 ("Zustand III").
4. Schloss Wolfegg, Fürstlich Waldburg-Wolfeggische Sammlungen, "Mittelalterliche Hausbuch," fols. 53r–v; see Waldburg Wolfegg 1998, pp. 92–100.
5. See especially Bossmeyer 2015, passim; see also Cuneo 2002.

Cat. 118

Giuliano de' Medici (1479–1516), Duke of Nemours
Workshop(?) of Raphael
Italian, 1515
Oil on canvas
32¾ x 26 in. (83.2 x 66 cm)
The Metropolitan Museum of Art, New York,
The Jules Bache Collection, 1949 (49.7.12)

Giuliano de' Medici, the youngest son of Lorenzo de' Medici, Il Magnifico, and a brother of Giovanni, who became Pope Leo X in 1513, spent much of his early life in exile from Florence. He was well known at various courts, above all at Urbino, where he would have met Raphael. Florence was restored to the Medici in 1512, and Giuliano briefly acted as its administrator, but Leo X soon relocated him to Rome and assigned him various strategic tasks. To buttress a family connection with France, and to help strengthen the papacy against the Holy Roman Empire, in 1515, Giuliano married Philiberte of Savoy, and Francis I made him duke of Nemours. That same year Leo appointed him as captain-general of the Church, although Giuliano's illness and then early death meant that he did not play a role in the complex and dangerous maneuvers between the pope and the great powers of Europe, including the emperor—now against the French.[1] Writing of Giuliano's death in April 1516, the author Pietro Bembo mentioned that Raphael—or probably one of his pupils—had recently painted his portrait.[2] It is possible that the occasion of the portrait was, as is so often the case, the sitter's engagement; alternatively, it may have been done when he became *capitano generale*. This could explain the prominence given to the view of the Castel Sant'Angelo in the background. Long-running debate has not resolved whether

CAT. 118

this is a damaged painting by Raphael, perhaps with assistance; a work painted on his design by another artist in his
workshop; or a fine contemporary copy.[3] In any case, its design
became the basis for other official portraits, including that by
Giorgio Vasari in a fresco in the Sala di Leone Decimo in the
Palazzo Vecchio, Florence.   AB

REFERENCES: Meyer zur Capellen 2008, pp. 183–88, no. A22, ill., and
colorpl. p. 81; Tom Henry in *Late Raphael* 2012, pp. 262–65, no. 72, ill.
For full cataloguing, see www.metmuseum.org/collections

1. For Giuliano's biography, see Tabacchi 2009.
2. Pietro Bembo to Cardinal Bernardo Bibbiena, April 19, 1516, in Shearman
2003, vol. 1, pp. 240–41.
3. For a range of proposals, see Fahy 2008, p. 22; Meyer zur Capellen
2008, pp. 183–88, no. A22; Tom Henry in *Late Raphael* 2012,
pp. 262–65, no. 72.

Cat. 119

Foot Combat Armor of Giuliano de' Medici

Attributed to Conrad Seusenhofer (first recorded 1500, died 1517)
Austrian (Innsbruck), dated 1515
Steel, leather, and copper alloy
H. 68⅞ in. (175 cm), W. 27⁹⁄₁₆ in. (70 cm), D. 11¹³⁄₁₆ in. (30 cm)
Musée de l'Armée, Paris (G 179)

Made in 1515 for a member of the Medici family, this work
may be a rare surviving example of an armor that Maximilian I
presented as a diplomatic gift. Designed for the perilous foot
combat—a duel-like contest fought with pollaxes, swords,
or daggers inside an enclosure—it includes a close helmet, a
gorget, a cuirass, pauldrons made in one with the vambraces
and the gauntlets, trunks, a rump defense, a codpiece, full leg

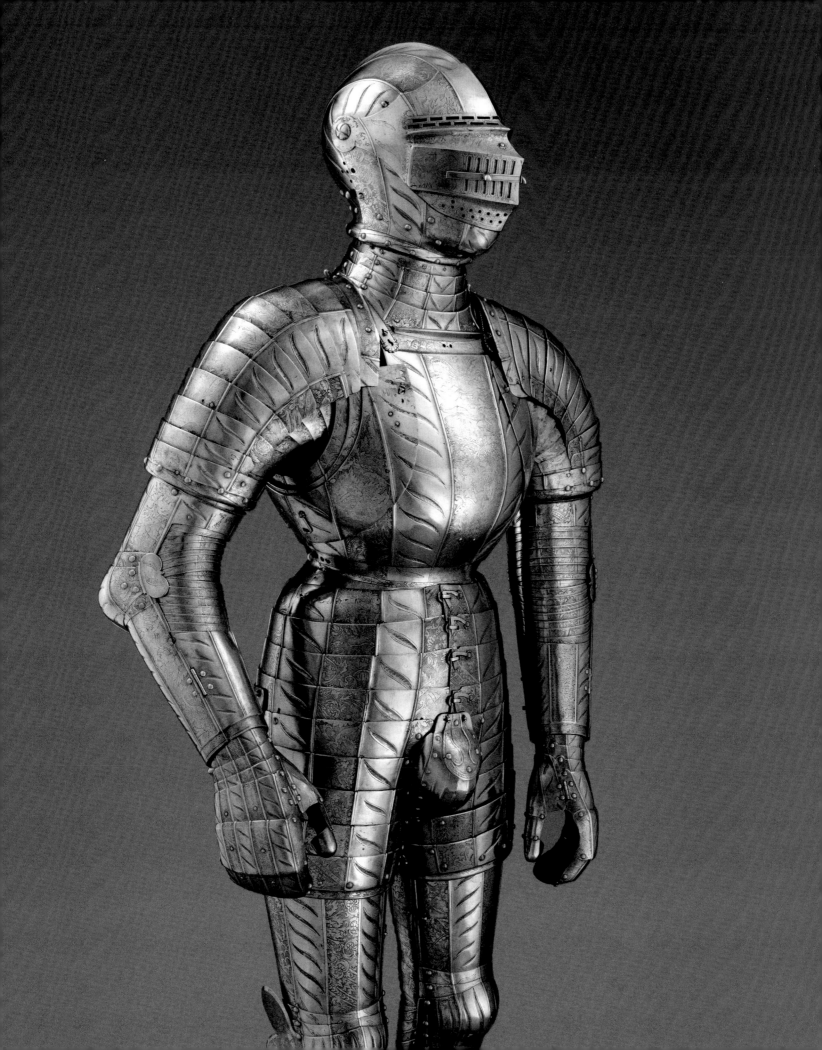

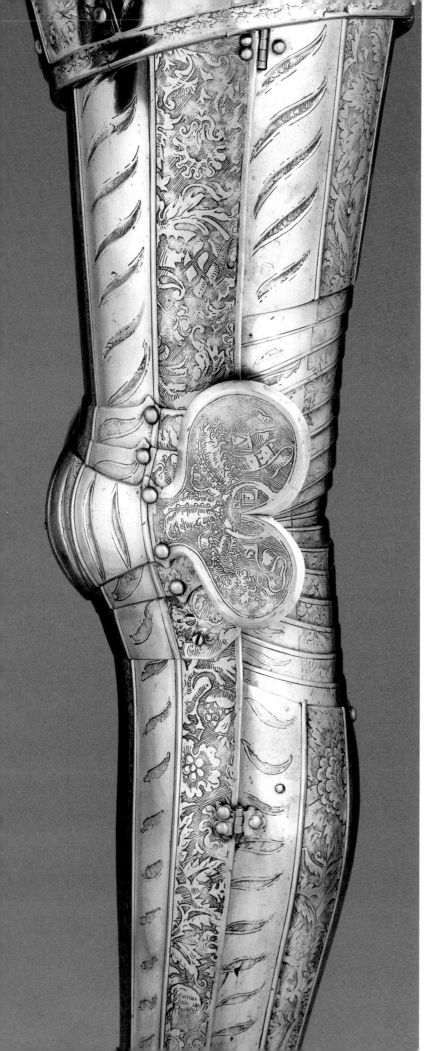

defenses, and sabatons, leaving nothing exposed other than the palms of the hands.

The armor is etched overall with a pattern of longitudinal bands that are alternatively filled with rich brocade and slanted designs simulating the slashes of fashionable clothing from the period. The helmet, cuirass, pauldrons, vambraces, and leg defenses are further decorated with Piero de' Medici's (1416–1468) emblem of a diamond ring with three ostrich feathers, and his Latin motto SEMPER (forever), as well as Pope Leo X's (r. 1513–1521, born Giovanni de' Medici) emblem of a yoke surmounted by the letter N, and his Latin motto SUAVE (sweet).[1] Although various members of the Medici family often used the same emblems,[2] the date 1515 etched on the inner wrist plate of each gauntlet provides helpful limitations. The only male members of the family who could have had use for an armor at that time were Leo X's younger brother Giuliano (1479–1516), his nephew Lorenzo II (1492–1519), and a more distant relative, Lodovico (later known as Giovanni dalle Bande Nere, 1498–1526), who was from a different branch of the Medici but in Giuliano's service in the papal army.

Constructional details and the nature of its ornamentation strongly suggest that the armor was made and decorated in Innsbruck. The swivel hooks closing the trunks at the front, for example, are very similar in construction to those on an armored skirt, or base, that has been attributed to the Innsbruck armorer Conrad Seusenhofer (cat. 140).[3] The comparable etching style on both pieces and on several other works attributed to Conrad further confirms an Innsbruck origin. The treatment of the foliage making up the brocade pattern and of the hatched ground against which it is set is analogous to the handling of etched ornamentation on an armet and a matching pair of complete leg defenses in the Wallace Collection, London, and to that on the gauntlets belonging to the same armor, which are in the Kunsthistorisches Museum, Vienna.[4] The decoration on the foot combat armor compares even more closely to that on a pair of complete leg defenses, also attributed to Conrad, which are part of a composite armor of Maximilian, also in the Kunsthistorisches Museum.[5] In each case, the foliate designs gracefully unwind over a swiftly executed hatched ground and dashes give a texture to the foliage.

In view of its Innsbruck characteristics, Medici emblems, and etched date of 1515, there can be little doubt that the armor is one of the two that Maximilian commissioned from Conrad Seusenhofer on July 25, 1514. Both were to be presented as gifts to Giuliano de' Medici, but just one appears to have ultimately been made. As Conrad had estimated that with the help of four assistants he would need four months to forge it, and as work had not yet begun by November 14, the armor intended for Giuliano was only completed in 1515, which is when Conrad and his staff, as well as the widow of a master who had made its various metal fittings, were paid.[6]

It has often been suggested that the armor was probably commissioned in anticipation of Giuliano's wedding with Philiberte of Savoy, on February 22, 1515. This suggestion, however, is doubtful since this union meant that Giuliano was associating himself with the king of France (his wife's nephew), this after Maximilian had offered Giuliano the hand of his daughter to win him over to his side. It is more likely that Maximilian commissioned the armor right after Leo X bought the fief of Modena from him in 1514 with the intent of giving it, along with Parma and Piacenza, to Giuliano, as the pope's purchase demonstrated his intention to turn his younger brother into a powerful secular ruler.[7] Maximilian might have given this armor to honor this rising figure during a period when he was hoping to improve his relations with the papacy.

The armor was in the armory of the princes of Condé at Chantilly by 1783. Confiscated in 1793, it was deposited in the Dépôt d'Artillerie, Paris, in 1798. Mistakenly thought to be the armor of the French knight Bayard by 1825, it was eventually recognized as belonging to the Medici by 1859.[8] PT

REFERENCES: Carré 1795, pl. XXII, fig. E; Musée de l'Artillerie 1825, p. 10, no. 49; Harzen 1859, p. 121; Penguilly L'Haridon 1862, pp. 218–19, no. G. 117, ill.; Robert 1889–93, vol. 2 (1890), pp. 86–87, no. G. 179; Maindron 1894, pp. 263–64; Thomas 1949/1977, p. 572, and p. 567, fig. 25; Thomas and Gamber 1954, p. 69, no. 73; Reverseau 1982, p. 72, and p. 73, ill. no. 12

1. For the representation of the same emblem and motto on the back of a tondo in the Metropolitan Museum's collection, see Pope-Hennessy and Christiansen 1980, pp. 10–11, no. 6, ill.
2. See Cummings 1991, pp. 84–85.
3. Note by Donald La Rocca, May 1989, on object card, curatorial files, Department of Arms and Armor, The Metropolitan Museum of Art, New York.
4. See Thomas 1949/1977, pp. 575–76, and p. 571, fig. 30, p. 576, fig. 33; Thomas and Gamber 1954, p. 68, nos. 68–70; Mann 1962, vol. 1, pp. 130–31, no. A154, pl. 69, pp. 186–87, nos. A285, A286, pl. 84; Norman 1986, pp. 57–58, nos. A154, A285, A286.
5. See Thomas 1949/1977, p. 575, and p. 573, fig. 31.
6. See Schönherr 1884, p. LXVII, nos. 1173, 1179, p. LXXV, nos. 1221, 1222.
7. See Tewes 2011, p. 1096; Metzig 2016, p. 239.
8. The author is grateful to Stuart W. Pyhrr for the corrected provenance information.

Cat. 120

Letter from Maximilian I to Philip I Regarding the Brussels Armorer Pieter Wambaix

Dated Augsburg, April 1496
Haus-, Hof- und Staatsarchiv, Vienna (Reichskanzlei, Maximiliana 5 [alt 3b], Konv. 2, fol. 136)

In this document, Maximilian I informs his son, Philip I, of a debt of 777 livres 12 sols, currency of Flanders, to the Brussels armorer Pieter Wambaix for several armors and related works that had already been delivered. After several unsuccessful attempts to collect payment, Wambaix ran into financial difficulties and reportedly was about to lose all of his property to satisfy his creditors. Maximilian urges his son to pay Wambaix at least a portion of the sum in cash and to assign the balance on future revenues to be collected by the treasurer of Brabant. Maximilian explains that these expenses were incurred in relation to his "voyage to Utrecht," by which he probably means the siege he laid to the city in the summer of 1483.

Maximilian experienced chronic shortages of funds throughout his life, and thirteen years after delivering armor, the unfortunate master had still not been fully compensated for his work. Many of the armorers Maximilian patronized in the Burgundian Low Countries had to be paid out of subsidies awarded (mostly to fight wars) by the representative assemblies, or estates, of his various dominions, which in practice his treasurers often failed to collect in time and in full. It is not known whether the debt to Wambaix was ever settled.   PT

REFERENCE: Zimerman 1883, p. XXXIV, no. 200

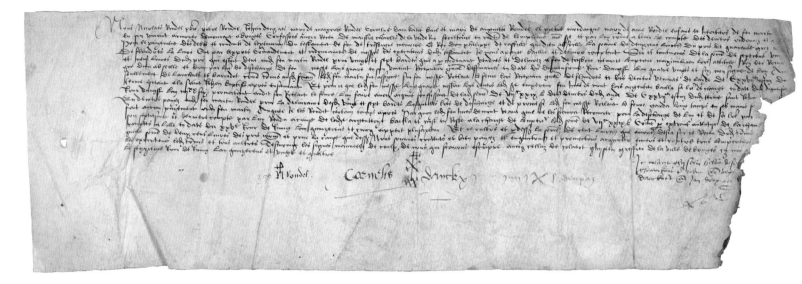

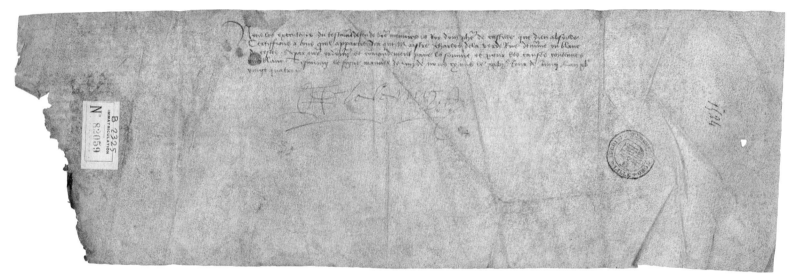

Cat. 121

Receipt from the Heirs of the Bruges Armorer Martin Rondeel

Dated June 16, 1524

Archives Départementales du Nord, Lille, France (B 2325, no. 82059)

Although frequently unable to fund his projects, Maximilian I was generally successful in finding ways to secure the services or goods that he needed. An expedient to which he commonly resorted was to borrow against revenues to which he was entitled but that had not yet materialized. In this document, the children and heirs of the Bruges armorer Martin Rondeel acknowledge having received the sum of 220 livres, currency of Flanders, in addition to 100 livres recently paid to them, in lieu of the sum of 729 livres owed to Rondeel for twenty-seven horse bards he had delivered to Maximilian in 1486. Assigned on August 19, 1486, to the receiver of the subsidies granted by the Netherlandish Estates to Maximilian, the 729 livres still had not been paid by 1505. By the time this receipt was written in 1524, Maximilian and Rondeel had both died. At the end of the document the heirs declare their satisfaction with the payment of what amounted to less than half of the original sum, this some thirty-eight years after the valuable horse bards had been delivered.

Born in Milan, Rondeel became a burgher of Bruges in 1464, and he seems to have achieved some prominence by the mid-1470s.[1] He had clients in England and referred to himself as the "armorer of my lord the Bastard of Burgundy," thus of Anthony of Burgundy (1421–1504), an illegitimate son of Duke Philip the Good. Rondeel was one of many European armorers who struggled to be paid in a timely fashion for works supplied to Maximilian (see cat. 120).   PT

1. On Rondeel, see Gaier 1973, pp. 122–23.

Cat. 122

Cuirass from a Field Armor

Master of the Crowned W Mark (active ca. 1500–1510)

South Netherlandish, ca. 1500–1510

Steel and leather

H. 18⅞ in. (48 cm), W. 14¼ in. (36.2 cm), Wt. 11 lb. 14 oz. (5,410 g)

Royal Armouries, Leeds (III.71–72)

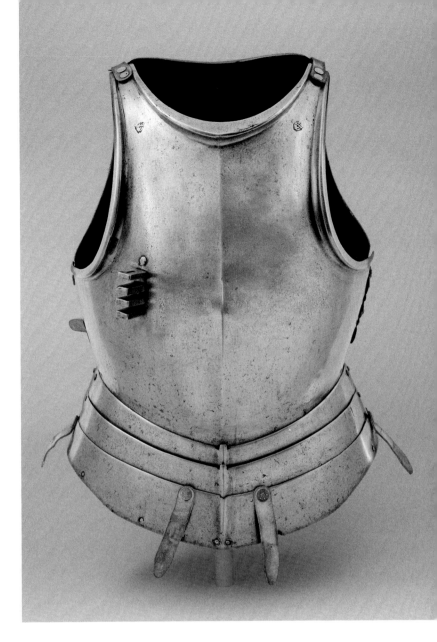

The breastplate of this cuirass has on its right side four of the original five studs, through which a pin could be inserted from above to attach a lance rest—a feature that indicates that the piece was designed for cavalry use. Of a type intended for the field, the cuirass comprises a breastplate with three fauld lames and a backplate with two (originally more) culet lames. The breastplate and backplate were originally secured together by a hinge on the left side, as they are currently by a modern replacement, and by a strap and buckle at the right. They are not articulated with separate plates at the gussets, in keeping with the standard design of most Netherlandish, Italian, and Spanish examples from the period. Instead the edges forming the arm openings are turned inward; in the case of the breastplate, they are markedly boxed, for increased strength. The leather straps riveted to the bottom fauld lame are replacements for the decayed originals, to which a pair of tassets, now lost, would have been attached by buckles.

This cuirass is typologically important as a rare homogeneous and complete example from the turn of the sixteenth century, made in the style favored in Italy and areas of Europe under strong Italian influence (as the Low Countries were). It is also noteworthy for the mark of the letter w surmounted by an open coronet, which is struck at the shoulders of the breastplate and again in the middle of the backplate, immediately below the turned upper edge.

Since the letter w saw little use in the Italian language and would have not aptly referred to an Italian, Spanish, or French name, its presence here precludes the possibility that the mark could have belonged to an armorer living in or originating from those Romance-language lands. Conversely, the stylistic analogies of the cuirass to Italian prototypes make it highly unlikely that it could have been made in Germany,[1] from which it follows that the mark too must have belonged to a master active in another cultural area. Such considerations, along with evidence that the cuirass was already in the royal palace at Greenwich by the seventeenth century, are the probable reasons why the mark has recently been attributed to Jacob de Watte, a Netherlandish armorer who worked in

England for King Henry VIII from no later than 1511 until his death, sometime between 1533 and 1538.[2]

It is questionable whether an armorer in the permanent employ of the king would have had the need for a maker's mark (those working under analogous conditions for Henry VIII in Greenwich and for Maximilian I in Innsbruck did not use any). In addition, the presence of a pair of gauntlets bearing the same mark in the collection of the Real Armería, Madrid—which includes a notable contingent of weapons and armors originally made for Philip I and Charles V in the Low Countries (see cat. 96)—casts serious doubt on the idea that the mark may have belonged to Jacob de Watte, especially since these sovereigns never received armor made in England and neither De Watte nor his Netherlandish colleague Peter Fevers appears to have ever worked for them before moving to England.[3]

Instead, and especially since the Habsburgs owned armor struck with the mark, it seems likely that the armorer to whom it belonged was among the masters known to have supplied the armory of Philip and Charles in Brussels. Among these, two individuals seem strong candidates—provided, of course, that the w in the mark follows the custom of referring to their surnames. The first is the Brussels armorer Pieter Wambaix, about whom very little is known other than that he was patronized by Maximilian in 1483 and was still owed a considerable sum thirteen years later for armor he had supplied to him (see cat. 120). Jehan Wat, the second candidate, was active in Brussels and a much more prominent figure at court. He was one of Philip I's preferred armorers and, as *valet de chambre*, also a member of his household. The record of his deliveries during Philip's reign includes no fewer than seventy-six distinct works, including armors for the field, the joust, and the foot combat, many of which were for the sovereign's personal use. Unlike Wambaix, whose name vanishes from the records in the late 1490s, Wat was very much active during the first decade of the sixteenth century, and for that additional reason is the likelier of the two to have made this cuirass.[4] The cuirass was in the royal palace at Greenwich by 1644, when it was transferred to the Tower of London.[5]   PT

REFERENCE: Thom Richardson in *Henry VIII* 2009, pp. 176–77, no. 22, ill.

1. Compare, for example, the cuirass of Giano II Fregoso's armor in the Kunsthistorisches Museum, Vienna; Thomas and Gamber 1976, pp. 193–94, no. A 11, fig. 90.
2. On Jacob de Watte, see Blair 1965, p. 34. For the attribution of the mark, see Thom Richardson in *Henry VIII* 2009, p. 176.
3. See Valencia de Don Juan 1898, pp. 90–91, no. A. 277, fig. 57.
4. Terjanian 2006, pp. 153–56.
5. See Richardson in *Henry VIII* 2009, p. 176.

Cat. 123

Armet

Guillem Margot (first recorded 1505, died before 1533)
South Netherlandish (Brussels), ca. 1505
Steel
H. 12 in. (30.5 cm), W. 8⁷⁄₁₆ in. (21.4 cm), D. 13 in. (33 cm),
Wt. 9 lb. 4 oz. (4,195 g)
The Metropolitan Museum of Art, New York, Bashford Dean Memorial Collection, Funds from various donors, 1929 (29.158.52)

In addition to being perhaps the only surviving example of its kind that was demonstrably made in the Burgundian Low Countries, this helmet is remarkable for the fact that its maker may be identified and that he was a foremost armorer in Brussels. Constructed with hinged cheekpieces and thus of a type known as an armet, the helmet is reinforced at the front by a large brow plate, but it no longer retains the original visor

that would have been secured by hinge and pin to the sides of its bowl. Unlike Italian examples from the period to which it is closely related in style and by which it was presumably inspired, it has no holes along the lower edge of its cheekpieces for attaching leather or metal straps from which mail defenses for the neck would have been suspended.[1] The rear edges of the cheekpieces have notches to accommodate a post fitted with a rondel (now lost) that would have guarded this vulnerable area of the nape of the neck.

The mark of the letter m surmounted by a crescent, which is struck on the rear right side of the bowl, occurs on many pieces known to have belonged to the Habsburgs, including the richly decorated horse bard that Maximilian I presented as a gift to King Henry VIII of England (cat. 96), the remnants of three bards once in the armory of Charles V and now in the Real Armería, Madrid, and the elements of a man's armor formerly in the imperial armory of Vienna and now in the Magyar Nemzeti Múzeum, Budapest. The provenance of Charles's bards establishes beyond reasonable doubt that their maker and the owner of the mark was Guillem Margot.[2] The archival record of Margot's activity shows that he fulfilled important commissions for Philip I, Charles V, and even Ferdinand I,

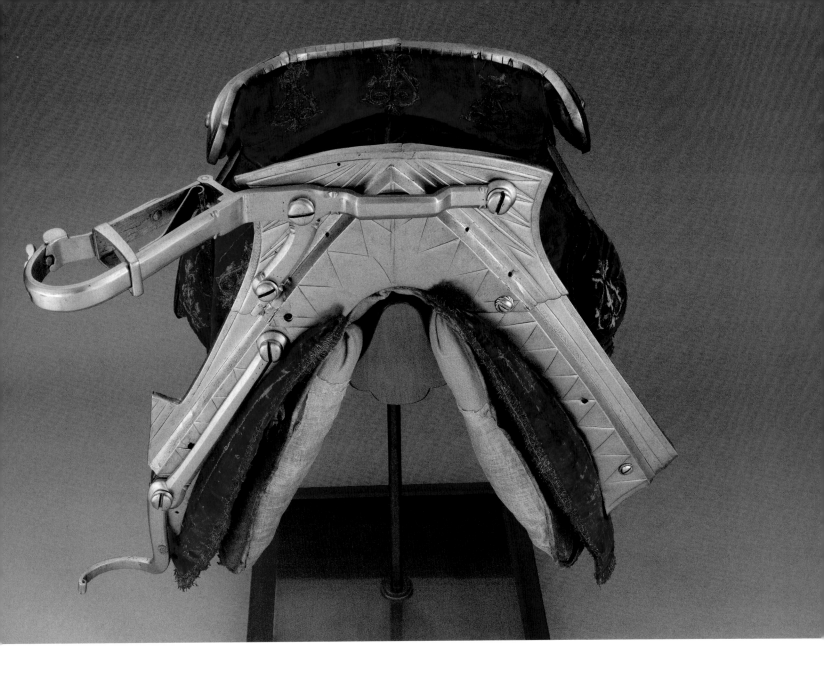

while the bard given to Henry VIII suggests that he also was patronized by Maximilian. Three other pieces by this master are in the Metropolitan Museum.[3] This helmet was in the collection of Bashford Dean of Riverdale, New York, and purchased by the Metropolitan Museum from his estate in 1929.   PT

REFERENCES: Stephen V. Grancsay in Kienbusch and Grancsay 1933, p. 129, no. 44, pl. IV; Blair 1965, p. 37, pl. XIV, a, b; Terjanian 2009, pp. 156, 159

1. For similarly formed Italian examples preserved in Udine and Mantua, see Boccia 1982, figs. 164, 376–82.
2. On Margot and his works, see Terjanian 2006, p. 154; Terjanian 2009, pp. 156–59.
3. Pyhrr 2000, pp. 15–16, nos. 18, 19, ill.

Cat. 124

Armored Saddle with Iron Hand

South Netherlandish, ca. 1500–1510
Steel, wood, leather, and textile
H. 22¹⁄₁₆ in. (56 cm), W. 27⁹⁄₁₆ in. (70 cm), D. 25⁹⁄₁₆ in. (65 cm)
Patrimonio Nacional, Madrid, Real Armería (F. 6)

This war saddle is unusual for the two large brackets secured by broad screws to its central and right pommel plates. Forged in steel, these elements are designed to allow the rider to free up his right hand by stowing his lance in front of him. The upper bracket, spring-loaded to open and close around the shaft of the lance, can be locked by a winged screw. The lower bracket follows the lower edge of the right pommel plate and is angled to line up with the upper one; farther down, it

projects outward, curving to follow the contour of the lance and keep it in a vertical position.

Used for carrying standards on horseback, the uncommon, ingenious contraption known as the iron or steel hand was a Habsburg favorite. The concept behind it certainly appealed to Maximilian I, who commissioned three war saddles with steel hands to carry his standards from the Brussels saddler Guillaume Lempereur. These were delivered to his armory in Brussels and paid for in 1479.[1] As no earlier references to such saddles are known, it is possible that they were specially devised for, or perhaps even by, Maximilian, who had an active interest in mechanical innovation in armor and, significantly perhaps, employed a locksmith to maintain his personal armor.

Maximilian's successors certainly appreciated the benefits of these devices: two saddles "armed to carry the standard" and a loose "iron hand" were in Philip I's armory when it was incorporated into that of his son Charles V in 1510.[2] The objects cited are likely to have been the saddle for a standard that the Brussels clockmaker Hans van Trostemberch serviced in Philip's armory in 1501, and the two mechanical devices "for carrying the standard of my lord" that the same individual made and delivered in 1504, of which only one might have

been mounted on a saddle. Although Charles inherited these saddles, it is clear that he added to them. In 1520 a Brussels clockmaker named Nicolas van Trostemberch, who in view of his last name probably was a relative and pupil of Hans, was paid for having made "an iron hand to a saddle to carry the great standard for the entry into Aachen," the solemn procession marking Charles's coronation as King of the Romans that year.[3] Not unsurprisingly perhaps, Philip II of Spain came to own six such saddles after his acquisition of Charles's armory in 1564.[4] The present saddle is one of only four surviving examples. Its style suggests a tentative dating to the first decade of the sixteenth century, and thus it may have originally belonged to Philip.   PT

REFERENCES: Valencia de Don Juan 1898, pp. 173–74, no. F. 6; Quintana Lacaci 1987, ill. p. 37; José A. Godoy in *Tapices y armaduras del Renacimiento* 1992, p. 132; Terjanian 2006, pp. 150–51, ill.

1. Archives Départementales du Nord, Lille, B 2118, fol. 356v.
2. Terjanian 2006, p. 159, no. 68, p. 158, no. 34, respectively.
3. For these deliveries, see Archives Départementales du Nord, Lille, B 2173, fol. 217v, B 2185, fol. 203v, B 2294, fol. 326v.
4. For these saddles, their designation, and their representation in documents from the period, see Valencia de Don Juan 1898, pp. 3–5, nos. A. 3, A. 4, p. 46, no. A. 128, pp. 173–74, no. F. 6; José A. Godoy in *Tapices y armaduras del Renacimiento* 1992, p. 132; Terjanian 2006, pp. 150–51. See also Patrimonio Nacional, Madrid, Real Armería, N18A, fol. 35r, N18B, fol. 30r.

Agreement between Maximilian I and Gabriele da Merate for the Establishment of an Armorer's Workshop at Arbois

Dated Worms, April 17, 1495

Haus-, Hof- und Staatsarchiv, Vienna (Reichskanzlei, Maximiliana 4 [alt 2b, 3a], fols. 160–61)

Written in French, this legal agreement was concluded in the German city of Worms on April 17, 1495, between Maximilian I, acting in his own name and on behalf of his son, Philip I, and the Milanese armorer Gabriele da Merate, acting in his own name and on behalf of his brother Francesco. Valid for a period of three years and renewable, the agreement obliges Gabriele or his brother to take up residence and practice their trade at Arbois in the county of Burgundy. They are to establish an armorer's workshop to make and deliver specific pieces of armor every year, which they cannot sell to anyone other than Maximilian without his express permission. In return, Maximilian grants them a thousand francs, currency of Burgundy, to cover expenses including setting up a forge and acquiring tools. In addition, he grants the Merate brothers a loan of a thousand florins, currency of the Rhine, of which they must pay back a third every year. Maximilian places at their disposal a house with a water-powered mill on the Cuisance River, which they can alter at will so that it may be used for forging and polishing armor on the proviso that they return it in good condition at the expiration of the agreement. The brothers are to receive together a yearly pension, or subsidy, of 100 francs for the duration of the agreement. They are exempted of all taxes and dues as long as they make and deliver the required pieces of armor every year. These consist of fifty well-made field armors in the Burgundian fashion, forged from good metal, each of which is to be struck with the workshop's distinctive mark. Each of these armors must be composed of an armet, a cuirass, pauldron reinforces, arm defenses, gauntlets, and leg defenses; the workshop will be paid 40 francs for each one. In addition, the workshop must produce a hundred armets with buffes, for which they will receive 10 francs apiece; a hundred pauldron reinforces, for 5 francs apiece; and a hundred pairs of arm defenses, for 40 francs altogether. Maximilian commits to acquiring the listed pieces and agrees to pay in two equal installments every year.

Signed by Gabriele da Merate in the presence of Erasmo Brasca, the duke of Milan's ambassador; Jehan Bontemps, treasurer general of Burgundy; Antoine de Waudripont, Maximilian's secretary; and additional unnamed individuals,

this document resulted in the establishment of an armorer's workshop at Arbois of which Francesco da Merate, Gabriele's brother, assumed the direction.[1] A foot combat armor made for Maximilian (cat. 20) and the remnants of a field armor in Zurich, both bearing the workshop's mark of the letters ARBOIS, show that it was capable of outfitting Maximilian himself and of making classic field armors for men-at-arms, which, although made in the Burgundian fashion, now seem virtually indistinguishable from the style of Italian examples from the period.[2] The workshop perhaps fulfilled another prestigious commission, for between 1498 and 1499 two armors described as the property of Philip, who had taken possession of the county of Burgundy in 1499, were sent under escort from Besançon, about twenty-five miles northeast of Arbois, to him in Brussels.[3] It is not known when exactly the workshop ceased its activity. PT

REFERENCES: Zimerman 1883, p. XXXIII, no. 197; Genevoy 1955

1. Motta 1914, p. 223.
2. Boccia 1982, p. 288, no. 96, and figs. 168, 169, 205a, b.
3. Gauthier 1883–95, vol. 2 (1887), p. 272, no. B. 1124.

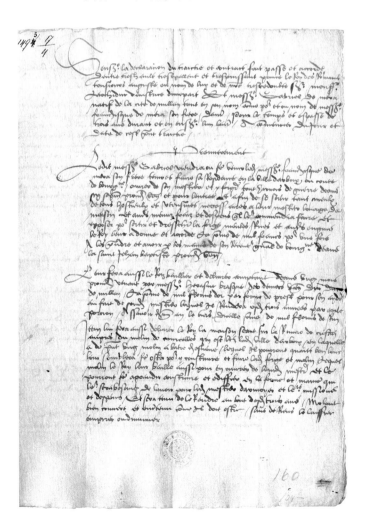

Cat. 126

Sallet of Maximilian I

Attributed to Hans Grünewald (first recorded 1457, died 1503)
South German (Nuremberg), ca. 1490
Steel and copper alloy
H. 8¹¹⁄₁₆ in. (22 cm), W. 9¹⁄₁₆ in. (23 cm), D. 16⁵⁄₁₆ in. (41.5 cm)
Kunsthistorisches Museum, Vienna, Imperial Armoury (A 60 b 2)

Internationally renowned for the sturdy construction and reliability of their works, the armorers of Nuremberg were numerous and capable of fulfilling large commissions of munition-quality armor, enough to outfit entire regiments or stock arsenals. Because the local regulations of their trade required them to specialize in the manufacture of given types of armor elements—either helmets, cuirasses, arm defenses, leg defenses, or gauntlets—the completion of an armor in Nuremberg necessitated contributions from multiple armorers. Their economic interdependence and frequent collaboration promoted the adoption of standardized designs, so that their respective works could be harmoniously combined, and each master could focus on high-volume production.

Even though these regulations were designed to prevent one master from rising above another, a handful of Nuremberg armorers succeeded in securing one by one the rights to make all armor elements. This, in turn, allowed them to attract the patronage of powerful nobles, for whom they wrought complete made-to-measure armors. One of these select armorers made this sallet.

Forged in one piece and fitted with a visor that pivots on the sides of the bowl, the sallet is outstanding for the precise treatment of its outline, the bold profile of its visor, and the

tight fit of its parts. The applied copper-alloy band currently adorning its lower edge is a nineteenth-century replacement for the lost original, which was specially made when the helmet was used to complement one of Maximilian I's field armors by Lorenz Helmschmid, whose original headpiece was already missing (see cats. 16, 17).[1]

The place of manufacture is established by the presence of an inspection mark representing Nuremberg's heraldic arms of a half eagle, which is struck on the left side of the sallet's tail, and by another mark, the letter N in a rectangular cartouche, which may be an additional control mark, struck on the same side. The master who made the helmet is in turn identified by the maker's mark of a shield enclosing indistinct designs, perhaps a crescent moon within a horseshoe, which is struck on each side of the tail.[2]

This mark may be tentatively attributed to Hans Grünewald, one of the foremost and wealthiest armorers of Nuremberg, on the grounds that the sallet originates from Vienna's imperial armory and can only have been made for Maximilian. Grünewald and Cuntz Poler are the only two Nuremberg masters he is known to have patronized. As Poler appears to have exclusively supplied jousting armors, and as the Nuremberg jousting armors owned by Maximilian bear a different maker's mark, the sallet is likely to have been made by Grünewald, from whom Maximilian commissioned armors for his personal use in 1489. Since Maximilian had access to many capable armorers in Augsburg, Innsbruck, and the Low Countries, his choice of Grünewald is likely to have been motivated by the latter's ability to create something that could not be had elsewhere. It is also possible that Sigmund Prüschenk, Frederick III's chief chamberlain, with whom Maximilian had close ties, and for whom Grünewald had recently made an armor, recommended Grünewald to Maximilian.[3] The sallet originates from the imperial armory of Vienna and entered the Kunsthistorisches Museum's Arms Collection (Waffensammlung) in 1889.[4]   PT

REFERENCES: Thomas 1963/1977, pp. 1310–11, 1314, fig. 1; Thomas and Gamber 1976, p. 97, no. A 60; Stefan Krause in *Kaiser Maximilian I.* 2014, p. 35, no. I.6, ill.

1. See Thomas 1963/1977, p. 1314.
2. Two of these marks are illustrated in a section of marks at the end of Thomas and Gamber 1976, "Plattnermarken: Nürnberg," no. A 60.
3. On Cuntz Poler, see Thomas 1956/1977, pp. 1142–45; Thomas 1963/1977, pp. 1311, 1314, fig. 2; Reitzenstein 1967, p. 722, n. 146a; on Hans Grünewald and the armor he made for Maximilian, see Reitzenstein 1967, pp. 712–15; on Maximilian's relations to Prüschenk, see Kraus 1875, pp. 19–23.
4. The Imperial Armoury department was known as the Waffensammlung until 1989.

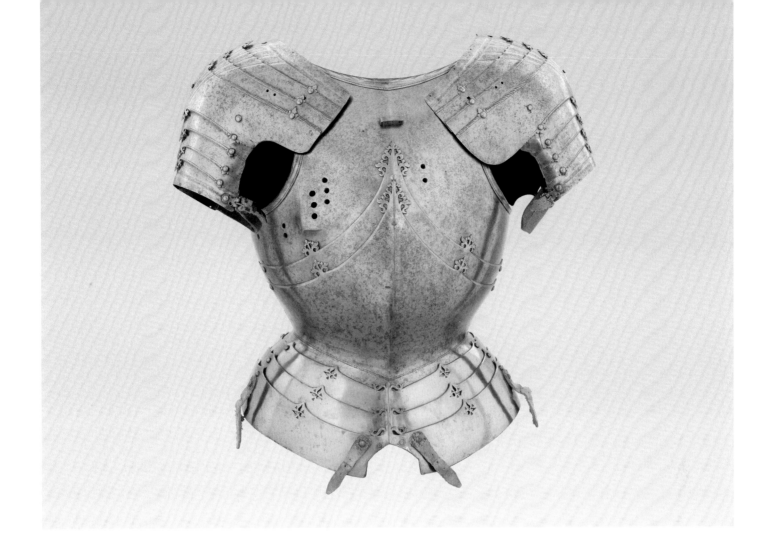

Cat. 127

Cuirass and Pauldrons

Lorenz Helmschmid (first recorded 1467, died 1516)
South German (Augsburg), ca. 1480–90 and later
Steel and leather
Breastplate: H. 21¼ in. (53.7 cm), W. 14¾ in. (37.5 cm), D. 7⅜ in. (18.7 cm), Wt. 8 lb. 8 oz. (3,855.5 g); backplate: H. 20¾ in. (52.7 cm), W. 14½ in. (36.8 cm), D. 7⅝ in. (19.4 cm), Wt. 5 lb. 8 oz. (2,494.7 g); left pauldron: H. 8½ in. (21.6 cm), W. 12 in. (30.5 cm), D. 11¼ in. (28.6 cm), Wt. 1 lb. 10.4 oz. (748.4 g); right pauldron: H. 9½ in. (24.1 cm), W. 11¾ in. (29.8 cm), D. 11½ in. (29.2 cm), Wt. 2 lb. 3.2 oz. (997.9 g)
Detroit Institute of Arts, Gift of William Randolph Hearst Foundation (53.193.4, .5, .6A, .6B)

Although this cuirass and the pair of pauldrons now complementing it did not originally belong to the same armor, they were all made during the same period and in the workshop of Lorenz Helmschmid, Maximilian I's court armorer in Augsburg. The only example of its kind known to survive, the cuirass was probably intended for a variant of the joust of war known in German as the *Geschiftsrennen*, in which each contestant wore a large steel targe overlaid with plates that would disperse in the air when the targe was properly struck and propelled above the head.[1] The pauldrons, by contrast, are more likely to have belonged to a field armor. Although also shaped and decorated in the late Gothic style, they differ from the cuirass in the detail of their pierced ornamentation and the embellishment of the edges of their individual plates with a file-roped pattern.

Bearing the maker's mark of Lorenz and the inspection mark of Augsburg at the right shoulder, the breastplate and backplate making up the cuirass are both constructed of multiple plates over the trunk and extended below the waist by modern replacements for the missing fauld and culet lames, respectively. The three original plates of the breastplate underlap each other downward and are secured together by rivets down the middle and the sides. The upper one has outwardly turned edges decorated with a roped pattern executed with a punch at the neck and gussets. In the manner of breastplates for the joust, it is embossed at the right side in order to provide a flattened surface for attaching a lance rest

workmanship of the present example is in keeping with the high quality of Maximilian's armor.

The cuirass and pauldrons are parts of a composite, partly restored, late Gothic armor that the princes of Hohenzollern-Sigmaringen owned and sold in 1929 to Arnold Seligmann, Rey & Co., New York. Purchased by William Randolph Hearst in 1930, the armor was donated by the William Randolph Hearst Foundation to the Detroit Institute of Arts in 1953.[2]   PT

REFERENCES: Detroit Institute of Arts 1954, p. 6, ill. p. 7; Thomas 1956/1977, pp. 1131–32; Gamber 1957, pp. 43, 48, and p. 46, figs. 51, 52; Stuart W. Pyhrr in Levkoff 2008, pp. 159–60, no. 20, ill.; Pyhrr 2014, pp. 87–88, fig. 17

1. On this contest, see Appelbaum 1964, p. 8, pl. 51; Pfaffenbichler 2017, pp. 102–4.
2. See Pyhrr 2014, pp. 87–88, fig. 17.

Cat. 128

Combination Sallet and Bevor

Lorenz Helmschmid (first recorded 1467, died 1516)
South German (Augsburg), ca. 1495
Steel, leather, copper alloy, and gold
H. 15 in. (38 cm), W. 13⅝ in. (34.5 cm), D. 8¹⁵⁄₁₆ in. (22.7 cm)
Kunsthistorisches Museum, Vienna, Imperial Armoury (A 110 1)

Celebrated today for his technical virtuosity and innovative designs, the Augsburg armorer Lorenz Helmschmid was highly regarded for the very same reasons during his own lifetime. His extant works and the available record of the commissions he fulfilled suggest that in Maximilian I he found a patron who not only valued his drive to push the conventional boundaries of his craft, but one who also would encourage him to create armors unlike anything seen before.

Alongside his unique horse bards made with fully articulated defenses for the belly and legs (see cats. 87, 88, and fig. 5), which in conception are comparable to contemporary armor for men, this sallet ranks among Lorenz's most remarkable and ingenious designs. Constructed with a bevor that pivots on the same points as the visor, this helmet succeeds in protecting the wearer's skull, nape, face, and throat all at once. Although Lorenz did make sallets with separate bevors (see cats. 16, 17), as was the norm, it is clear that he was not content with the customary arrangement and looked for novel solutions to a familiar problem. The present helmet is one of three such examples made by or attributed to him, and it is by far the most opulent.[1]

The sallet has several notable mechanical features that make it possible for its brow plate, visor, and bevor to pivot; for the nape lames to flex; for the upper two bevor plates to be

and perhaps also a queue to hold the rear extremity of the lance's shaft. The two plates supplementing it peak toward the neck and develop into symmetrical bundles of stylized foliage in the late Gothic tradition at the top and on each side. Both have a medial ridge, and the lowermost one is decorated with a punched line across the waist. The staple on the upper plate is a modern addition.

The backplate is more richly decorated than the breastplate, as its surface is enlivened by bundles of flutes sprouting from the loins and bordering edges of the gussets. It is constructed of four original plates, the three lowermost of which overlap downward and are riveted together at the sides; the uppermost one underlaps the next and is rigidly secured to it by six rivets. The extension plates added at the sides are modern additions. Decorated en suite with the breastplate with punched-roped ornament at the gussets and with a continuous punched line across the waist, the backplate has a row of small holes along the upper edge of the second plate from the top to accommodate rivets that would have held in place an applied border of the kind Lorenz often used to adorn his works (see cats. 16, 17, 128).

In the arrangement of the flutes and the outline and piercing of the stylized foliage, the cuirass compares closely to an armor Lorenz made for Maximilian, which he delivered to him in the Low Countries in 1480 along with other armors, including examples for the joust of war (see cats. 16, 17). The

released or propped up; and for the bevor and skull, as well as the visor and top bevor plate, to be locked together. Its form and surface treatment are sophisticated, displaying a combination of techniques, including hammering, filing, piercing, etching, heat-bluing, gilding, and overlay, which together bestow flair and majesty to this extraordinary helmet.

Of all the armorers known to have experimented with helmet design, Lorenz was one of the most imaginative. In addition to the surviving helmets, an album of drawings in the Uměleckoprůmyslové Museum, Prague, documents series of equally unconventional models, made or perhaps merely imagined, which may be confidently attributed to Lorenz (see cat. 129).

This sallet was in Ambras Castle by 1596, and it was by then already part of a composite armor of Maximilian. Removed to Vienna in 1806, it entered the Kunsthistorisches Museum's Arms Collection (Waffensammlung) in 1898.[2] PT

REFERENCES: Norman 1959, pp. 16–19, figs. 1, 2; Thomas and Gamber 1976, pp. 115–16, no. A 110, fig. 43; Stefan Krause in *Kaiser Maximilian I.* 2014, p. 33, no. I.4, ill.

1. On these helmets, see Norman 1959, pp. 17–18, and pp. 20, 21, figs. 5, 6. One is in the Kunsthistorisches Museum, Vienna (A 205), and the other is in The Metropolitan Museum of Art (29.156.45).
2. See Luchner 1958, p. 56. The Imperial Armoury department was known as the Waffensammlung until 1989.

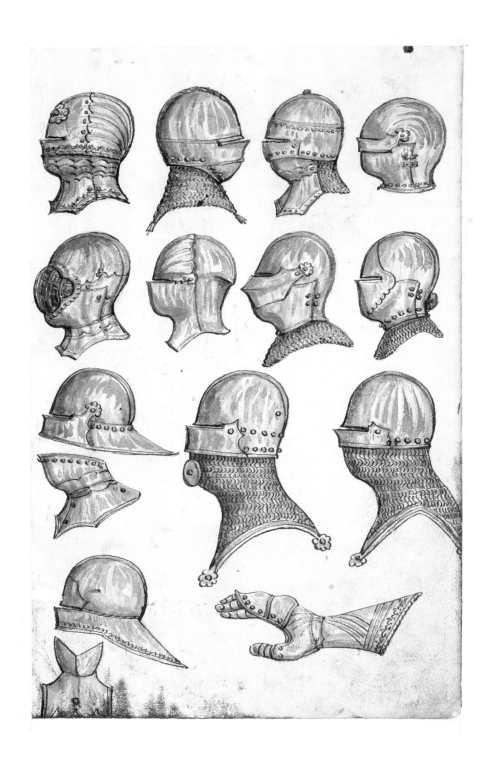

Cat. 129

Album of Armor Drawings

South German, ca. 1460–1600

Lead point, ink, watercolor, and metallic pigments on paper;
bound in vellum

12⅜ x 9½ in. (31.4 x 24 cm)

Uměleckoprůmyslové Museum, Prague (GK II.572–B, fol. n70v)

This album consists of drawings from several different
sources that were bound together in the seventeenth century.

The majority of the images represent armors by leading
Augsburg armorers of the fifteenth and sixteenth centuries.
The largest group among them sheds invaluable light on the
accomplishments of Lorenz Helmschmid and his son Kolman.
As his court armorers in Augsburg, both men fulfilled many
commissions for Maximilian I. The drawings document
works that they completed, or at times perhaps merely
imagined, in his service.

One of these drawings features a most unusual horse bard
of steel constructed with fully articulated leg defenses, which

Lorenz is known to have made for Maximilian and delivered to him in the Low Countries in 1480 (cats. 87, 88, and fig. 5). Invented by the master—perhaps with encouragements from his patron—the bard is shown on a horse ridden by Maximilian, who wears full body armor and is identifiable by his nose and the eagle-shaped mount for the plume on his hat.[1] Other drawings call attention to the range of equally unusual helmets devised by Lorenz, including what may be the model for a combination sallet and bevor (cat. 128), and several foot combat helms of which an example in the Philadelphia Museum of Art's collection may be a remnant.[2]   PT

REFERENCES: Gamber 1957; Gamber 1959a; Terjanian 2011–12

1. See Terjanian 2011–12, pp. 307–8, fig. 5, pp. 342–43, image 30.
2. For examples of these helmets, see ibid., pp. 340–41, 346–47, 376–77, 378–79, 382–83, images 27, 28, 38, 94, 99, 108. On the helm in Philadelphia, see *Kretzschmar von Kienbusch Collection* 1963, pp. 57–58, no. 56, pl. XLIII.

Cat. 130

Sallet for the Joust of War

Jörg Helmschmid the Younger (first recorded 1488, died 1502)
Austrian (Vienna), ca. 1497–1502
Steel and copper alloy
H. 12³⁄₁₆ in. (31 cm), W. 10¼ in. (26 cm), D. 13⅜ in. (34 cm)
Kunsthistorisches Museum, Vienna, Imperial Armoury (B 182)

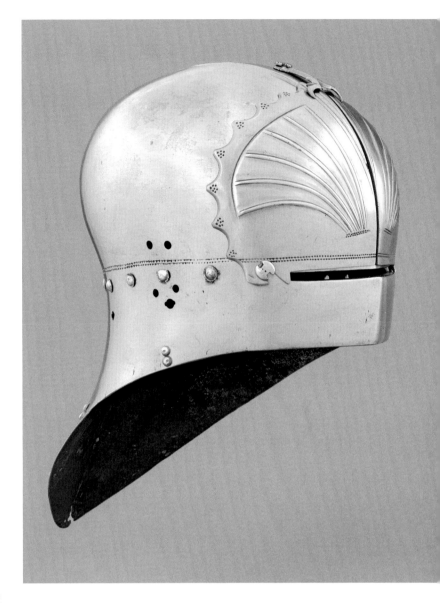

This sallet was designed for use in one of the many variants of the joust of war. Forged from a single piece, it is fitted with two detachable brow plates that rest on rivets with protruding heads at each side of the sight and are further secured by a forked pin at the top. When struck by the opponent's lance, the plates would slip upward and separate in the air. This sallet is unique for the pronounced downward slope of its integral nape defense, or tail, and for the two marks that are struck at each side of its tip; one of which, a jousting helm facing sinister, is the mark of Jörg Helmschmid the Younger and the other, a shield filled with a cross, that of the city of Vienna.

Jörg was born in Augsburg and worked there until 1497, when he relocated to become Maximilian I's court armorer in Vienna. Although today not as famous as his brother Lorenz, he was an exceptional armorer in his own right, as his surviving oeuvre demonstrates. This sallet is one of only two works known to remain from the years he resided in Vienna.[1] The mark representing the heraldic arms of the city was presumably struck on the sallet by the wardens of Vienna's armorers to indicate that they had inspected the piece and determined that it met the metallurgical standards prescribed by the regulations of their trade.[2] The sallet was in the imperial armory of Vienna until 1889, when it became part of the Kunsthistorisches Museum's Arms Collection (Waffensammlung).[3]   PT

REFERENCES: Thomas 1956/1977, pp. 1137, 1138, figs. 37, 38, and p. 1144, fig. 43b; Hummelberger 1961, p. 92, and p. 93, figs. 1, 2; Thomas and Gamber 1976, pp. 169–70, no. B 182, fig. 80; Stefan Krause in *Kaiser Maximilian I.* 2014, p. 162, no. II.41, ill.

1. Boccia 1975, pt. 1, p. 82, no. 140, pt. 2, pl. 134.
2. Hummelberger 1961, pp. 92, 94, 95.
3. The Imperial Armoury department was known as the Waffensammlung until 1989.

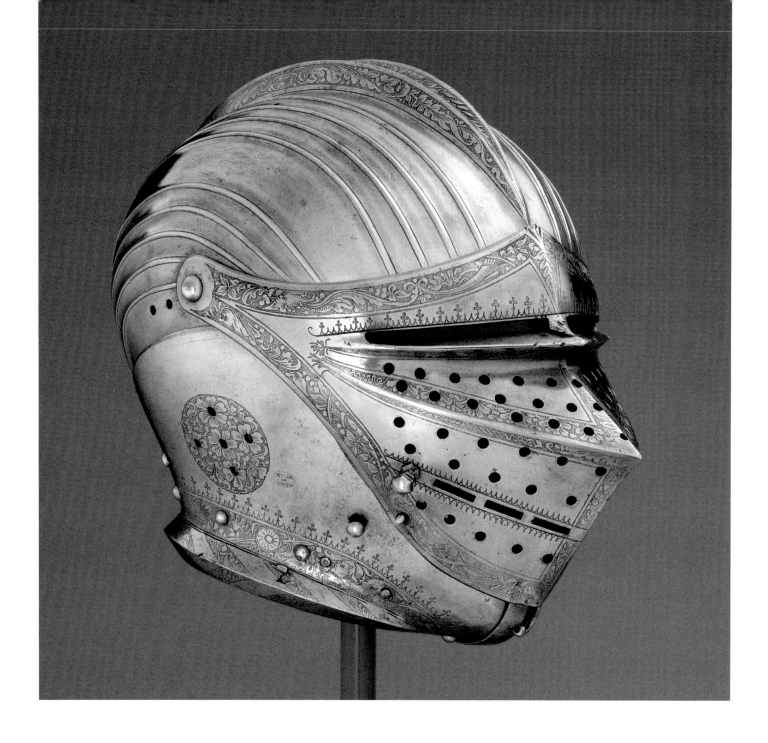

Cat. 131

Armet

Attributed to Lorenz Helmschmid (first recorded 1467, died 1516)
or Kolman Helmschmid (1471–1532)

South German (Augsburg), ca. 1515–20

Steel and copper alloy

H. 10¼ in. (26 cm), W. 9½ in. (24 cm), D. 13⅝ in. (34.5 cm)

Musée de l'Armée, Paris (H 63)

This fine helmet has a bowl, a pair of cheekpieces secured
to it by hinges along their rear edges, and a visor that pivots on
its sides and that can be locked once lowered by a spring catch

with a push-button release on the right cheekpiece. The helmet is flanged along the lower edge to fit over and rotate
around the upper rim of a gorget. The bowl is decorated with
two sprays of flutes at each side of the medial comb and with
etched ornament, also seen on the remainder of the helmet.
The etched ornament consists of bands of foliage, cornucopia,
trophies of arms, masks, and harpies, all set against a dotted
ground; medallions enclosing foliage and rosettes; chevrons
filled with foliage; and cusped lines rhythmically surmounted
by stylized trefoils.

Although the helmet is unmarked, it compares closely
in construction, form, and decoration to one belonging to a

field armor, now preserved in the Historisches Museum, Bern, which bears the inspection mark of Augsburg and the maker's mark of Lorenz Helmschmid on its breastplate.[1] The similarities include the shape of the bowl, the outline of the cheekpieces, and the flanged lower edge, as well as the distribution of the ornament, from the flutes that continue down the bowl to the very front of the brow, to the etched design on the lower edge of the sight. At the same time, the helmet is very similar to one from an armor of Count Ottheinrich of the Palatinate, now in the Kunsthistorisches Museum, Vienna, which is also unmarked but has been attributed to Lorenz or his son Kolman.[2] While the helmet in Vienna is not fluted in the same manner and its sight is wider, it is otherwise most closely related to the present helmet, down to the type and placement of the hearing and ventilation holes, and to the etched patterns.

In the absence of decisive evidence, the present helmet cannot be specifically attributed to Lorenz or Kolman, though there is no doubt that it was made by one of them. Although they may have run separate businesses, father and son were simultaneously active and shared the same house and workshop over a twenty-three-year period. Family ties and shared work space created an environment in which each must have been able to learn from the other and continually exchange ideas and designs.[3] In this light, it is not surprising that Maximilian I was quick to patronize Kolman and entrust him with the making of his silver armor shortly after Lorenz's death (see cat. 160). This helmet was in the collections of the Musée de l'Artillerie, Paris, by 1890.[4]   PT

REFERENCE: Robert 1889–93, vol. 2 (1890), p. 179, no. H. 63

1. On this armor, see Wegeli 1920–48, vol. 1 (1920), pp. 55–60, no. 81, figs. 32, 33, pls. X, XII.
2. On this armor, see Thomas 1938/1977; Thomas and Gamber 1976, pp. 223–24, no. A 239, fig. 105.
3. Kolman began to pay taxes in 1492 and had thus probably graduated to master status that year. For biographical information on the two masters, see Reitzenstein 1951, pp. 180–89.
4. The Musée de l'Artillerie, Paris, merged with the Musée Historique de l'Armée in 1905 to form the Musée de l'Armée.

Medal of Kolman Helmschmid

After a model by Hans Kels the Younger (1508/10–1565)
South German (Augsburg), dated 1532
Lead
Diam. 1¹⁵⁄₁₆ in. (5 cm)
The Metropolitan Museum of Art, New York, Purchase, Kenneth and Vivian Lam Gift, 2015 (2015.597)

Generally commissioned by the social elite—sovereigns, nobility, and successful merchants—Renaissance medals rarely feature craftsmen. The first of only three European armorers known to have been celebrated in this fashion, Kolman Helmschmid has the additional distinction of having inspired two distinct medals, one while he was alive and the other probably after his death. This medal is one of only four known lead casts of the latter.[1]

The obverse has a bust portrait of the master in profile encircled by an inscription stating his name, age (sixty-two), and the year of his death (1532). Kolman is shown wearing a fashionable hat and a pleated shirt under a brocade doublet, the trappings of a prosperous man. The reverse of the medal features his coat of arms—a rooster wearing a sallet, holding a mace in its right claw, and facing dexter—within an escutcheon encircled by a wreath of laurels.

Designed by the Kaufbeuren medalist Hans Kels the Younger, the medal is among his earliest works. Perhaps commissioned by Kolman's relatives and friends, it provides a compelling testimony of his superior standing among the armorers of his day and records his contemporaries' wish to preserve his memory.   PT

REFERENCE: La Rocca 2017, p. 67, fig. 73

1. On the medals of Kolman, see Habich 1929–34, vol. 1, pt. 1 (1929), p. 26, no. 125, pl. XIX, 3, p. 112, no. 767, pl. XCIV, 4. On the earlier medal, see also Kastenholz 2006, p. 157, no. 26, fig. 47.

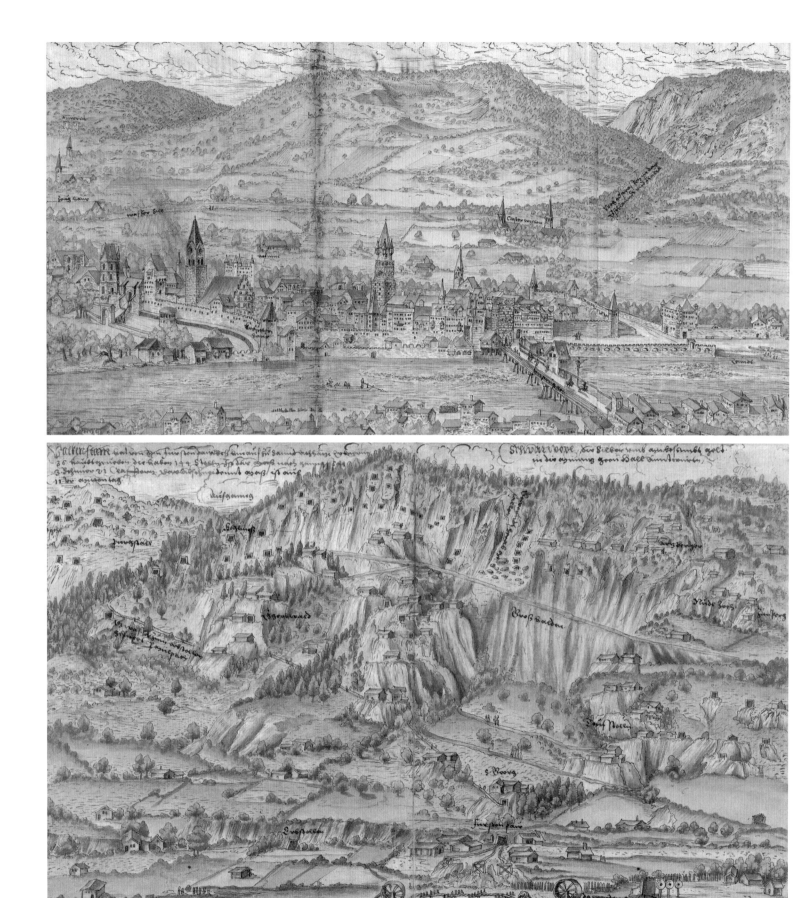

Cats. 133, 134

Innsbruck and *Valkenstein*, from the *Schwaz Mining Book* (*Schwazer Bergbuch*)

Jörg Kölber (active 1545–1568)
Austrian (Schwaz), 1556
Calligraphy pen in ink and watercolor
12¹⁄₁₆ x 8¹⁄₁₆ in. (30.6 x 20.4 cm)
Tiroler Landesmuseum Ferdinandeum, Innsbruck,
Austria, Bibliothek (FB 4312, pls. 15, 16)

Silver mining had begun in the town of Schwaz in Tyrol before the mid-fifteenth century, reaching its heyday around 1520. From 1446 onward, Falkenstein (Valkenstein) was the primary mining region for the rapidly expanding industry, engaging approximately four thousand laborers at the height of production. By 1447 Archduke Sigismund had issued mining regulations for Schwaz, which introduced workers' rights and established the payments owed to the local ruler. Prominent mercantile families of Augsburg who made their money from the silver trade, such as the Fugger family, immediately benefited from what soon became the largest silver and copper mining area in Europe.

Mercantile families were not alone in profiting from the mineral ores; the territorial princes of Tyrol also earned handsomely from taxes levied on the mines, but this income was insufficient to cover their exorbitant, largely military, expenditures. After Maximilian I took control of Tyrol in 1490, the Schwaz mines came to play an important role in his military campaigns, providing not only raw material but also desperately needed revenue to settle, for example, the enormous debts incurred for his war against Venice (1508–16). Over the course of the sixteenth century, however, output from the mines decreased.

The 1556 *Schwaz Mining Book* (*Schwazer Bergbuch*), in which these views originally appeared, belongs to the late medieval tradition of illuminated manuscripts. The choice of this form, which was already outmoded, reveals the commissioner's attitudes toward preserving tradition and classic art forms. Innsbruck experienced great economic prosperity under Maximilian, which led to major building projects. The view of Innsbruck faces south, with the distinctive city tower at center. In the image of Falkenstein, the tunnels and service roads are clearly marked on the page, pointing to the vital role these arteries played in the removal and transportation of the valuable raw material from the mines.   RS

REFERENCES: Bartels and Bingener 2006; Brandstätter 2013; Bartels and Bingener 2015; Bingener and Bartels 2015; Thomas Kuster in *Ferdinand II* 2017, p. 113, no. 1.6, ill.

DETAIL OF CAT. 133

an outwardly turned lower edge that gradually rises to a point at the front and rear of the helmet. The crown is encircled by a row of plain iron rivets with slightly domed heads that secure a leather strap on the interior, to which a textile lining is stitched in place. As is typical of many works made in Innsbruck and Mühlau during the same period, the helmet is free of ornament and exudes simplicity of form.

This sallet was in the ancestral armory of the Counts Trapp at Churburg Castle, South Tyrol, until 1923, when it was sold to Clarence H. Mackay of Roslyn, Long Island, New York. It was acquired from Mackay's estate by Stephen V. Grancsay, who donated it to the Metropolitan Museum in 1942.   PT

REFERENCE: Scalini 1996, p. 98, and p. 24, ill. no. I.5, p. 104, ill. no. III.12

1. On this armor, see Zimerman 1885, p. LXXXIII, no. 2955; Thomas and Gamber 1954, p. 53.

Cat. 135

Sallet

Caspar Rieder (recorded 1452–1499)
Austrian (Mühlau), ca. 1480
Steel, leather, and textile
H. 9½ in. (24.1 cm), W. 9 in. (22.9 cm), D. 14⅞ in. (37.8 cm),
Wt. 6 lb. 8 oz. (2,948 g)
The Metropolitan Museum of Art, New York,
Gift of Stephen V. Grancsay, 1942 (42.50.32)

When Maximilian I succeeded his great-uncle as archduke of Tyrol in 1490 he immediately gained convenient access to a new pool of highly skilled armorers who had distinguished themselves in the service of his predecessor. One of the most prominent among them was master Caspar Rieder. Active in Mühlau, just across from Innsbruck, Rieder was a seasoned professional. With nearly forty years of experience and a distinguished record—for example, in 1472 he made, in collaboration with others, several armors for King Ferdinand I of Naples—Rieder caught the attention of Maximilian and made for him an armor that its owner would describe in 1496 as being his favorite.[1] Now seemingly lost, the armor was so dear to Maximilian that it was singled out in an inventory of his possessions after his death and sent to his grandson Charles V, who, in 1521, had requested it especially.

One of Rieder's few extant works, this sallet is forged from a single piece and struck on the left side of the tail with the master's personal mark, a rectangle enclosing the letters KASP. It has a medial ridge that develops into a low, slightly flattened keel-shaped comb over the rounded bowl, a stepped sight, and

Cats. 136, 137

Breastplate and Backplate

Hans Prunner (first recorded 1482, died before 1503)
Austrian (Innsbruck), ca. 1485–95
Steel and leather
Breastplate: H. 19⅝ in. (49.8 cm), W. 14 in. (35.6 cm), Wt. 6 lb. 8 oz. (2,948 g); backplate: H. 19¾ in. (50.2 cm), W. 15 in. (38.1 cm), Wt. 4 lb. 15 oz. (2,240 g)
The Metropolitan Museum of Art, New York, Bashford Dean Memorial Collection, Bequest of Bashford Dean, 1928 (29.150.80, .70)

Although these two elements did not originally belong to the same armor, they are from the same period and by the same master. The breastplate is constructed with movable gussets (both later replacements) and three fauld lames (the lowermost also a replacement), and pierced at the right side to attach a lance rest. It is a remarkable piece that uses a single main plate to protect the full length of the torso, contrary to the late Gothic tradition of joining two or more plates together for the same purpose. The backplate is also formed from a single main plate, with integral gussets and five culet lames, and it would have been considered modern in its day for the very same reasons. Unlike the ornamentation on the breastplate, the decoration on the backplate follows late Gothic conventions: sunken lines descend from the shoulders and converge to a point between the shoulder blades, and the waistline rises to a point over the base of the spine, from which two flutes sprout to adorn the shoulders, and from which a bundle of ridges alternating with sunken channels spreads toward the buttocks

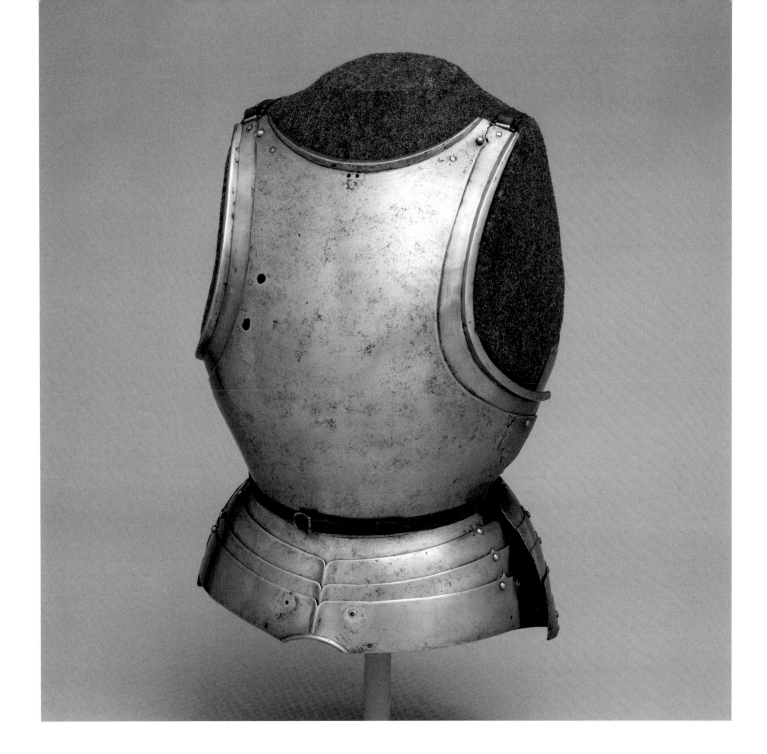

in the manner of pleats in a garment. The sunken bands bordering the gussets and the bottom edge of the lowermost culet lame successfully tie the upper and lower parts of the backplate together.

The mark of a tournament helm facing sinister, which is struck beneath the upper edge of each element, identifies them both as works by the Innsbruck armorer Hans Prunner. Prunner fulfilled a number of prestigious commissions for Maximilian I, including an armor for King John I Albert of Poland in 1493 and another for Maximilian himself in 1497.[1] A near-complete field armor that he made for Philip I is preserved in the Kunsthistorisches Museum, Vienna.[2] These two elements were in the collection of Bashford Dean of Riverdale, New York, and were bequeathed by him to the Metropolitan Museum in 1928.   PT

REFERENCES: cat. 136: Stephen V. Grancsay in Kienbusch and Grancsay 1933, p. 140, no. 56, pl. XXXIV; Thomas and Gamber 1954, p. 59, no. 35, pl. 20; cat. 137: Grancsay in Kienbusch and Grancsay 1933, pp. 142–43, no. 62, pl. XXXV; Thomas and Gamber 1954, p. 59, no. 35, pl. 21

1. On Prunner, see Thomas and Gamber 1954, pp. 32, 59; Trapp 1954.
2. On Philip I's armor, see Thomas and Gamber 1976, pp. 125–26, no. A 9, figs. 50, 51.

Cat. 138

Armet

Hans Rabeiler (first recorded 1501, died 1519)
Austrian (Innsbruck), ca. 1500
Steel and leather
H. 11⁷⁄₁₆ in. (29 cm), W. 7⁷⁄₁₆ in. (19 cm), D. 13 in. (33 cm),
Wt. 7 lb. 8.3 oz. (3,410 g)
Royal Armouries, Leeds (IV.468)

One of only two works by his hand known to survive (the second is cat. 81), this armet by Hans Rabeiler uniquely bears his maker's mark, a band containing the letters and numeral H9R above a shield-shaped cartouche showing a sallet facing sinister. Imaginatively designed and impeccably executed, it has an ovoid form, with deep cheekpieces that taper at the neck in the manner of an hourglass, and a peaked visor reminiscent of the short conical beak of a sparrow. In addition to its distinctive silhouette, the helmet is remarkable for the attachment of the cheekpieces to the bowl by hinges at the top rather than the rear; for the placement of those hinges off center,

immediately behind the bolts around which the visor is pivoted; and for the presence of a spring catch on the right cheekpiece to hold the visor in place once it is fully lowered. The visor's unusually long, narrow shanks, the decorative cusps on its upper edge, and the two rows of horizontal breathing slits on each side give this helmet an incomparable flair.

The post supporting the replaced rondel at the back strongly suggests that the helmet was meant to be worn along with a buffe, a reinforcing element that would have overlapped the lower half of the visor and continued down over the wearer's throat. The buffe would have been secured by strap and buckle round the nape of the neck. Reportedly acquired before 1880 in Padua by Baron Charles Alexander de Cosson, the helmet was purchased by the Royal Armouries at the posthumous sale of his collection at Sotheby's, London, in 1946.[1]   PT

REFERENCES: Cosson and Burges 1881, p. 56, no. 39, fig. 35; Laking 1920–22, vol. 2 (1920), p. 85, fig. 438, c; Thomas and Gamber 1954, p. 63, no. 52; Scalini 1996, p. 120, and p. 131, ill. no. IV.20

1. Sotheby's 1946, p. 16, no. 180, ill. facing p. 13.

Cat. 139

Close Helmet

Hans Maystetter (recorded 1510–1533)
Austrian (Innsbruck), ca. 1505–10
Steel and leather
H. 11 in. (27.9 cm), W. 9 in. (22.9 cm), D. 10⅜ in. (26.4 cm),
Wt. 5 lb. 8 oz. (2,495 g)
The Metropolitan Museum of Art, New York, Bashford Dean
Memorial Collection, Funds from various donors, 1929 (29.158.35)

Recorded in 1511 as one of the skillful armorers in charge of making fine armor in Maximilian I's court workshop in Innsbruck, Hans Maystetter abruptly left the establishment in 1517, the year the armorer Conrad Seusenhofer, its leader and artistic director, died and was succeeded by his brother Hans. A quarrel with Hans over Conrad's succession strongly suggests that the two men did not get along particularly well, and that Maystetter's departure was probably motivated by the prospect of having to work for someone who only a few years before had been the workshop's foreman. An independent armorer again,

Maystetter remained in Innsbruck, where he apparently continued to enjoy free lodging on the grounds of the court armory. The available record suggests that from then onward his chief activity was the manufacture of munition-quality armor, which he regularly delivered to the Innsbruck Arsenal until 1530.[1]

Constructed with an ovoid bowl fitted with three nape lames, and a visor and lower bevor pivoted on its sides, this helmet is struck with Maystetter's mark in the middle of the lowermost nape lame. This mark consists of a shield enclosing a cross between two stars; there is a circle at the base of the cross, and two branches extend downward from the cross's middle and rise again at their extremities. The helmet is striking for the severe appearance of its face defense and the near-complete absence of ornament. Aside from the flattened comb and the sprays of three flutes bordering it on the rear side of the bowl, the helmet is an uncompromisingly plain piece reserved for military use. The survival of a similar example by Maystetter, along with the existence of several comparable helmets, many of which are unmarked, suggests that the type enjoyed some popularity.[2] This helmet was previously in the

collection of Bashford Dean of Riverdale, New York, and was purchased by the Metropolitan Museum from his estate in 1929.   PT

REFERENCES: Grancsay 1933, p. 9, no. 32, ill.; Stephen V. Grancsay in Kienbusch and Grancsay 1933, p. 132, no. 47, pl. IV; Thomas and Gamber 1954, p. 73, no. 89

1. On Maystetter's career, see Boeheim 1899, pp. 291, 305, 307, 309; Thomas and Gamber 1954, pp. 31, 72–73.
2. On the related helmet by Maystetter, see Thomas 1974, p. 188, and p. 190, fig. 128. On analogous helmets, see Stephen V. Grancsay in Kienbusch and Grancsay 1933, p. 133, no. 49, pl. IV (MMA 29.158.34); *Kretzschmar von Kienbusch Collection* 1963, p. 59, no. 59, pl. XLIV.

Cat. 140

Steel Skirt (Base)

Attributed to Conrad Seusenhofer (first recorded 1500, died 1517)
Austrian (Innsbruck), ca. 1510–15
Steel and gold
H. 22 in. (55.9 cm), W. 26¼ in. (66.7 cm), D. 23½ in. (59.7 cm),
Wt. 12 lb. 14 oz. (5,840 g)
The Metropolitan Museum of Art, New York, Gift of William H. Riggs, 1913 (14.25.790a, b)

Constructed in two halves secured by hinge and pin at the rear and by hook and eye at the front, this steel skirt, or base, is composed of six plates that are gadrooned longitudinally to simulate the folds of a skirt. It has a wide opening at the front and back to enable the wearer to sit on a saddle. The removable panels used to close these openings when wearing the base on foot are lost. The folds are alternatively plain with broad ribs extending down the middle, or etched overall with elaborate foliage set against a hatched ground in imitation of a brocade pattern and decorated with series of oblique sunken designs simulating the slashes in contemporary dress.

Quite rare and seemingly reserved for luxury armors, bases of this sort epitomize the close relationship between the armorer's art and male fashion during the first four decades of the sixteenth century, when a handful of accomplished armorers sought to emulate in steel the characteristics of puffed and slashed clothing (see cat. 81). This example is attributed to Conrad Seusenhofer, Maximilian I's court armorer in Innsbruck, in view of its close constructional similarities to the base of an armor that he made for Charles V between 1512 and 1514 (cat. 82). Maximilian is known to have asked Conrad to make a number of armors with this feature, which the emperor wished to present as gifts to his courtiers as well as to German and foreign rulers such as Frederick the Wise, prince elector of Saxony, and Henry VIII, king of England. This base was acquired from the collection of Prince

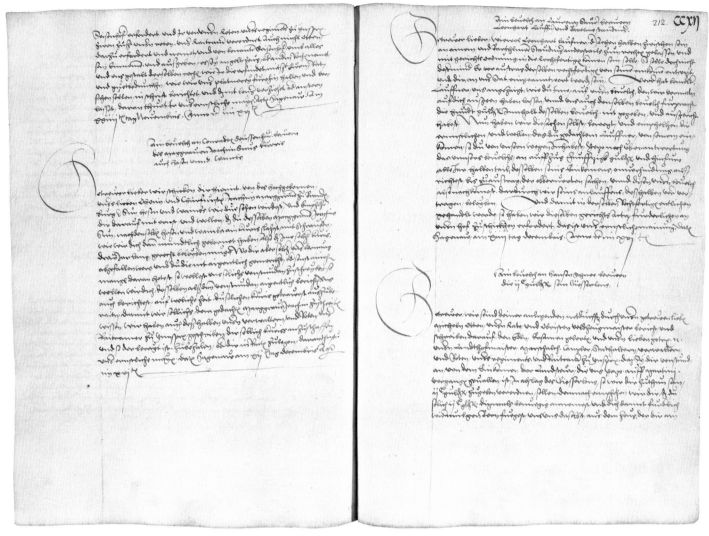

CAT. 141

Peter Soltykoff, Paris, by William Henry Riggs, Paris, in about 1860, and donated by him to the Metropolitan Museum in 1913.   PT

REFERENCES: Grancsay 1931, pp. 202–3, and p. 200, fig. 13, p. 201, fig. 15; Thomas and Gamber 1954, p. 67, no. 65, pl. 39; Blair 1965, p. 20, n. 3, pp. 32–33, pl. v, c

Cat. 141

Maximilian I to the Innsbruck Armorer Conrad Seusenhofer

Dated Hagenau, December 12, 1516

Haus-, Hof- und Staatsarchiv, Vienna (Reichsregister Z, fol. 211v)

This copy of a letter from Maximilian I provides a glimpse of his keen interest in armor design and the authoritative way he conveyed his knowledge of technical matters to one of the foremost armorers in the German-speaking lands. In the letter, Maximilian informs Conrad Seusenhofer, his court armorer in Innsbruck, that he is sending the doublet and hoses of Joachim II Hector of Brandenburg, the son of Joachim I Nestor, prince elector of Brandenburg, so that Conrad can use them as a reference to forge an armor that will fit the eleven-year-old Joachim II. Maximilian reminds the master to construct the armor with bolts, as he has already personally shown him, so that the armor will continue to fit the growing boy for at least three years. As if this recommendation were not enough, Maximilian reminds Conrad that he must write back if he is unsure and needs the method explained to him again. The letter ends with an exhortation to waste no time and to notify the emperor when the armor is finished so that he can, in turn, inform the boy's father.

While this letter seems to verify the section of the *Weisskunig* in which Maximilian claims to provide his armorers with technical advice, the recommendation of using bolts to make an armor adjustable to different sizes was hardly a novel idea (see cat. 26). Although the emperor had a sincere interest in armor design, not to mention a tendency to micromanage, his concern might simply have been a corrective action. The foot combat armor of Louis II of Hungary, which is attributed to Conrad, and which would have been made about a year earlier, was apparently never delivered, possibly because it could no longer fit the boy by the time it was ready (cat. 86). Still unfinished six months after it had been ordered, the armor commissioned in this letter was perhaps never delivered.[1] PT

REFERENCE: Zimerman 1883, p. LXVIII, no. 417

1. Schönherr 1884, p. LXXXII, nos. 1272, 1276.

Cat. 142

Shaffron of Maximilian I

Conrad Seusenhofer (first recorded 1500, died 1517)
Austrian (Innsbruck), 1513
Steel and copper alloy
H. 26⅜ in. (67 cm), W. 15 in. (38 cm), D. 26⅜ in. (67 cm)
Patrimonio Nacional, Madrid, Real Armería (A. 38)

In 1508 Maximilian became Holy Roman Emperor without having been crowned by the pope in Rome, as was normally required. The pope had consented to this historic exception as a diplomatic solution to the prospect of an armed conflict (which occurred anyway) between Maximilian and the Venetians, who denied him free passage through the territories that they controlled for him to be able to reach Rome. Prepared to force his way through, Maximilian was in Trento at the head of a large army when he was granted papal permission to be proclaimed emperor there. On February 4, he took on the title of "emperor elect," the wording of which called attention to the fact that he had been rightfully elected to the imperial throne by a college of ecclesiastical and secular princes, in accordance with a prescription from 1356. It was presumably intended to mitigate the consequences of not having been crowned by the pope himself.

Maximilian had coveted the title of emperor for many years, and although he did not obtain it as formally as he would have liked, at last he had secured it. *Kaiser*, German for emperor, is a corruption of the Latin word *caesar*, and Maximilian, like his predecessors, viewed himself as the legitimate heir and worthy continuator of the greatness of ancient Rome. Because of its implied connection with a noble past and people, and the legitimacy and authority that it conferred, which could be claimed to surpass that of kings, the imperial dignity that had finally been awarded to him, fourteen years

after his father had died, meant a great deal to Maximilian. Not unsurprisingly, he took immediate steps to ensure that his new station in life would be known by all and, whenever possible, celebrated. He even had one of his representatives in Italy present coins that had been specially minted in honor of his recent coronation to the senate of Venice to show that they had failed to prevent his rise (cat. 87).[1]

Maximilian's desire to proclaim his status as head of the empire was not confined to portable, though impactful, objects; in fact, it permeated everything the emperor conceived from his autobiographical and genealogical works to his plans for a grand mausoleum. It was only natural that the same preoccupation would also inform the design of his armors.

Exceptional for its ample proportions, elegant form, and striking decoration, this massive shaffron was made for Maximilian's horses along with another shaffron and three crinets in 1513.[2] The two shaffrons and one of the crinets are among the very few works that can be securely identified as having been made by Conrad Seusenhofer, Maximilian's court armorer in Innsbruck.[3]

Excluding the plume holder on the brow plate, which may not be original, the present shaffron is constructed of twelve plates skillfully forged and riveted together to encase the horse's brow, nose, and jaws and to protect its ears, eyes, and poll. A double-headed eagle with open wings, which is embossed in relief, finely etched, and set against an etched ground of leafy tendrils, dominates the surface. The etcher made resourceful use of the shaffron's form to allow the bicephalic eagle—the heraldic attribute of the emperor and by extension of the empire—to wrap itself around and effectively conquer the horse's entire head. When the shaffron was worn the eyes of the horse would have appeared to be peeking through the eagle's wings. The brow plate proved to be too narrow to include the large imperial crown that normally surmounted the eagle's two heads, and in a departure from convention, the ear plates were cleverly adorned with a smaller version of the crown above each head instead. As a whole, the shaffron was a formidable three-dimensional representation of the emperor's heraldry, especially when it was complemented by a small steel escutcheon, now lost, that could be secured to it between the horse's eyes. Especially when viewed from a distance, the escutcheon, which would have represented the heraldic arms of Austria and Burgundy (as does that of the related shaffron in Vienna), would have looked like the superimposed shield (called an inescutcheon) that graced Maximilian's imperial arms.

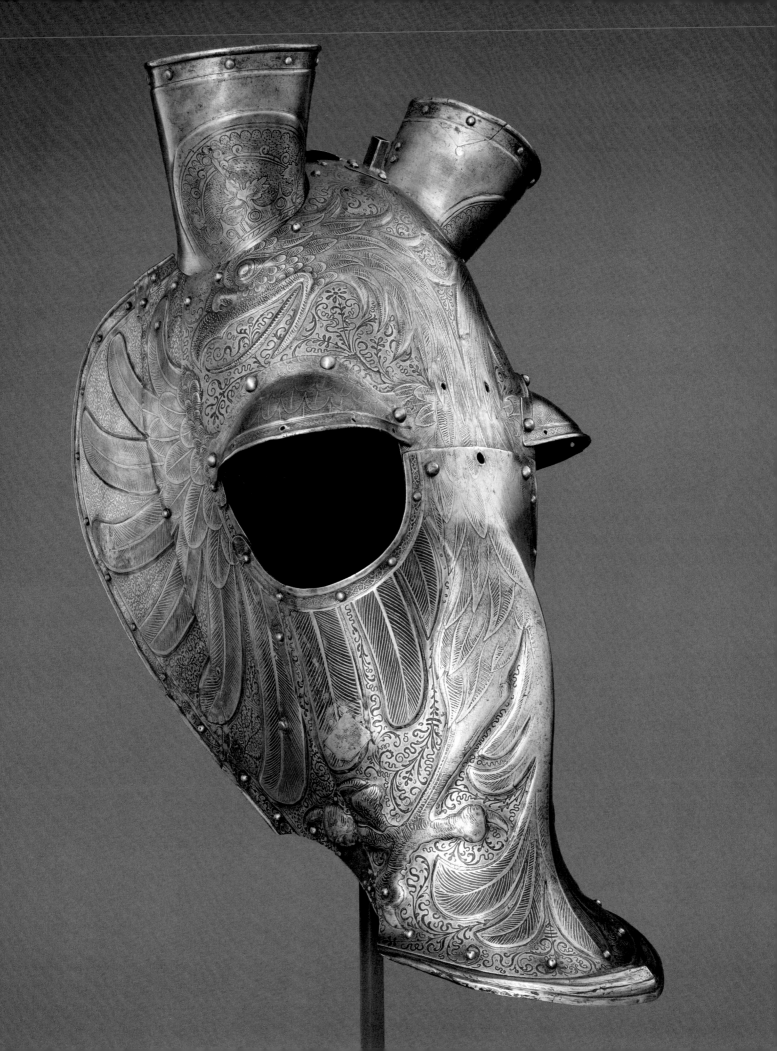

Although it is not illustrated in the pictorial inventory of his armory, which in its current state may not provide a complete record of its contents, there can be little doubt that Charles V inherited the shaffron and that it was subsequently acquired, along with other parts of his armory, by his son Philip II, who incorporated it into his own armory in Madrid.　PT

REFERENCES: Schönherr 1884, p. LXV, no. 1140; Valencia de Don Juan 1898, pp. 23–24, no. A. 38; Álvaro Soler del Campo in *Paz y la guerra* 1994, p. 297, no. 229, ill.; *Arte y caballería en España* 2007, pp. 206–7, 501, no. 52, ill.

1. On the circumstances for the presentation of this coin, see Luschin von Ebengreuth 1903.
2. The second shaffron and one of the crinets are preserved in the Kunsthistorisches Museum, Vienna (A 69; Thomas and Gamber 1976, p. 216, no. A 69, fig. 112). The other two crinets do not appear to survive.
3. On the pieces in Vienna and the group to which they belong, see Schönherr 1884, p. LXV, no. 1140; Thomas 1949/1977, p. 570, and p. 563, fig. 21, p. 564, fig. 22; Thomas and Gamber 1954, p. 67, nos. 63, 64, pl. 47.

Cat. 143

Invoice from Conrad Seusenhofer for Armor Made at the Orders of Maximilian I

Dated Innsbruck, after April 6, 1504

Haus-, Hof- und Staatsarchiv, Vienna (Reichskanzlei, Maximilian 14, fols. 142–43)

In addition to the pieces that he acquired for his personal use, Maximilian I continuously commissioned armors to be presented as gifts to courtiers and various men in his service, to his children and grandchildren, and to princes of the empire, foreign rulers, and their ambassadors. In this document, Conrad Seusenhofer, Maximilian's court armorer in Innsbruck, invoices his master for recently completed armors, for his wages and those of his assistants, and for work carried out by a goldsmith and a shoemaker.

In this instance, Maximilian appears to have given Conrad his orders verbally, as no written instructions for the commission are known. The varying social standing of the beneficiaries of these armors is readily apparent in the enumeration of the items that Conrad has made. These include a complete armor in the Italian style for the papal legate Cardinal Raimond Pérault, then a sixty-nine-year-old man; a cuirass with long tassets "and fluted like the Netherlanders' pleats" for a certain Dyllemee; two cuirasses with arm defenses and light helmets for two noblemen, who are referred to as Herr Eberhardt and Herr Alexander; a cuirass, a "corset" (probably a brigandine), a vambrace (probably a pair), and a pair of gauntlets, all gilded, plus a helmet, for Philip I, Maximilian's son; a cuirass with gilded edges for one of Philip's counselors; and six cuirasses with tassets for Maximilian's bodyguards. Finally, the invoice lists cuisses and a waist plate with a fauld for one of Maximilian's personal armors for the joust of war.

The invoice, which was not intended for Maximilian but for his financial officers in Innsbruck, captures the activity of the court workshop only three months after Maximilian had appointed Conrad as court armorer for a period of six years and committed to an annual payment of 150 florins for his wages, with one additional florin per week for each of his assistants.[1] At the time, Conrad employed only two hammermen and two armor polishers. Four years later, in 1508, this workforce would prove insufficient, and Maximilian personally went to the Low Countries to recruit four additional journeymen.[2] By the following year, Conrad's staff had risen to a total of six hammermen, four polishers, and two apprentice armorers, in an attempt to keep up with Maximilian's continuous flow of new orders.[3]　PT

REFERENCE: Zimerman 1883, p. XLIII, no. 234

1. Schönherr 1884, p. XX, no. 731.
2. Ibid., p. XXXIX, no. 917.
3. Ibid., p. XLII, no. 930.

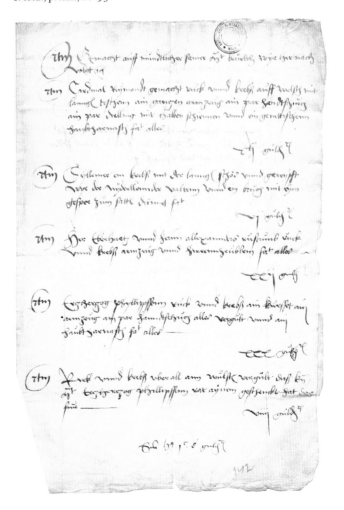

Cat. 144

Breastplate

South German (Augsburg), ca. 1510

Steel

H. 17 in. (43.2 cm), W. 13¾ in. (34.9 cm), Wt. 5 lb. 4.5 oz. (2,395.5 g)

The Metropolitan Museum of Art, New York, Bashford Dean
Memorial Collection, Funds from various donors, 1929 (29.158.154)

This work may be one of the thousands of munition-quality
breastplates that Maximilian I commissioned in anticipation
of his coronation as Holy Roman Emperor. As tradition
required that the coronation take place in the presence of the
pope in Rome, Maximilian would have to cross territories in
the hands of hostile powers, especially the Republic of Venice,
in order to reach the Eternal City. Once it became clear that he
was unlikely to be granted free passage, Maximilian prepared
for war and formally requested his subjects' assistance in the
form of money and contingents of men. As there was no
standing army, the majority of his troops had to be raised for

the occasion. It was thus imperative that he provide the equipment they needed to fight. What followed was one of the largest commissions of munition armor ever recorded, with
Maximilian ordering infantry breastplates by the thousands
from across the German-speaking lands, in places such as
Augsburg, Cologne, Innsbruck, and Nuremberg, which were
all notable centers of armor manufacture during the period.[1]

Forged from a single plate and fitted with two fauld lames,
the breastplate is of a type that was sometimes worn without a
backplate and secured by strap and buckle across the wearer's
back. Basic and inexpensive in comparison to examples worn
by knights, the breastplate was nevertheless carefully made.
The mark of a fir cone, which is struck at the left shoulder,
indicates that it was wrought and inspected in Augsburg. The
breastplate was previously in the collection of Bashford Dean
of Riverdale, New York, and acquired from his estate by the
Metropolitan Museum in 1929.   PT

1. On examples of breastplates made for Maximilian's journey to Rome, see
Düriegl 1977, p. 12; *Wiener Bürgerliche Zeughaus* 1977, pp. 76–77, nos. 52–54.

Cat. 145

Armet

Attributed to Hans Seusenhofer (1470/71–1555)
Austrian (Innsbruck), ca. 1515–20
Steel and copper alloy
H. 9¼ in. (23.5 cm), W. 10 in. (25.4 cm), D. 12½ in. (31.8 cm)
Private collection, New York

Constructed of a bowl reinforced with a deep plate over the brow, a pair of cheekpieces hinged to the bowl at the rear, and a visor that pivots on its sides, this armet is an outstanding example of a helmet with a mask-like face defense. This style was popular in the German-speaking lands between about 1500 and 1540, and seemingly often worn in tournaments.[1] The bold embossing of the nose, the delicate modeling of the lips, the application of separate plates to delineate the eyes, and above all the imaginative quality and flowing execution of the etched ornamentation set it apart from the majority of known specimens.[2]

Although the armet is unsigned, distinctive features of construction and decoration suggest that it was probably made in Innsbruck. Whereas the cheekpieces' low profile, rounded rear edges, and attachment to the bowl by hinges riveted immediately above the neckline are features common to armets made in both Augsburg and Innsbruck,[3] the stout, slightly flattened shape of the bowl, its adornment with multiple keel-shaped ridges, and the decorative cut of the visor's upper edge with a central brace-like design point more decidedly to Innsbruck as the likely place of manufacture.[4]

The conception and execution of the etched ornamentation, from the wrinkles around the bridge of the nose through the eyelashes around the eyes, large rosettes over the hearing holes, to the small rosettes round the holes for lining rivets, further support an Innsbruck origin. In particular, such features occur on armets and detached visors created by Conrad and Hans Seusenhofer. The handling of the wiry, curled mustache on the present armet, for example, closely resembles the treatment of the wrinkles on the face defense of a helmet

produced by Conrad, probably in collaboration with Hans, that Maximilian presented as part of a complete armor as a gift to King Henry VIII of England. In addition, these details are even more closely related to the hair on a mutilated visor that has been convincingly attributed to Hans, which is also constructed with applied plates for the eyes.[5] Thus, in light of the available evidence it seems likely that the present armet was made in Maximilian's court workshop in Innsbruck either during the final years of Conrad's tenure, which ended on his death in 1517, or under the direction of his brother and successor, Hans, in the years that followed.

Said to have been acquired by the earl of Meath on June 21, 1827, at the sale of a collection advertised as having come from the castles of Starhemberg and Ambras, this armet was purchased by the current owner at Christie's, South Kensington, London, in 1987.[6]   PT

REFERENCES: Christie's 1987, pp. 78–79, no. 222, ill.; Pyhrr 2011, pp. 78–79, fig. 17; *Ronald S. Lauder Collection* 2011, p. 524, no. 65, and p. 197, pl. 65; Terjanian 2018, ill. p. 28

1. For a representation of such helmets in a tournament, see Christof Metzger in *Ritter!* 2013, pp. 160–61, no. 3.15, ill.
2. For examples of armets and close helmets with mask-like face defenses, see Blair 1965, pp. 17–19, pl. X, a, c; Dufty and Reid 1968, pl. XC; Thomas and Gamber 1976, p. 231, no. A 342, fig. 109, pp. 232–33, no. A 237, fig. 120; Reverseau 1990, p. 29, no. 15, ill.; Pyhrr 2000, p. 19, no. 25, ill.; Fliegel 2007, pp. 64, 185, no. 65, ill.; Capwell 2011, p. 69, no. A85, ill.; Terjanian 2011, p. 17, fig. 15; Matthias Pfaffenbichler in *Feste feiern* 2016, p. 214, no. 77.1, ill. For detached visors, see Gamber 1988, p. 107, figs. 4–6.

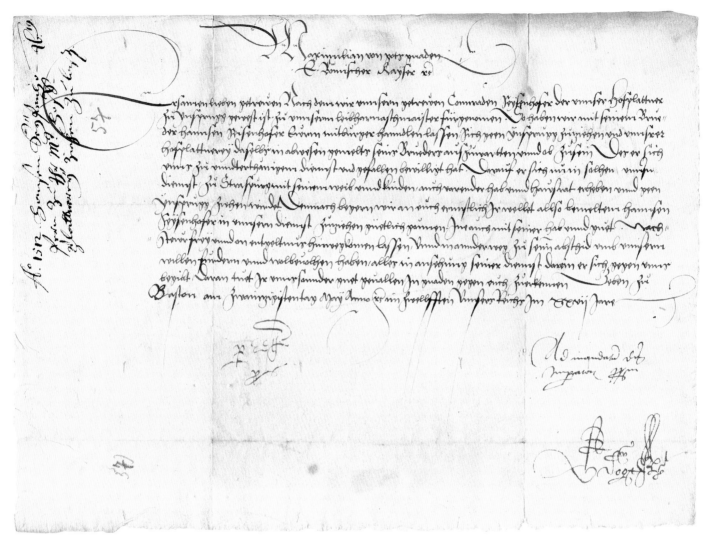

CAT. 146

3. For Augsburg examples, see Wegeli 1920–48, vol. 1 (1920), pp. 55–60, no. 81, pl. X; Thomas 1938/1977, pp. 1151–52, figs. 3, 4; for Innsbruck examples, see Thomas 1949/1977, p. 545, and p. 547, fig. 3, p. 548, fig. 4; Mann 1962, vol. 1, pp. 130–31, no. A154, pl. 69; Blair 1965, pl. X, a.

4. For an armet with a similarly proportioned bowl and cheekpieces, and with a visor with comparable decorative cut, see Wegeli 1920–48, vol. 1 (1920), pp. 60–63, no. 82, pls. XI, XII; Thomas and Gamber 1954, p. 64, no. 54; for an armet with a bowl divided longitudinally by multiple roped ridges, see Thomas and Gamber 1976, p. 234, no. A 461, fig. 113.

5. On the helmet presented to Henry VIII, see Blair 1965, pp. 17–19, pl. X, a, c; Blair 1974, especially pp. 146, 171, 176, pls. LI, LV, a, b, LXIII, a, LXVII, b; Thom Richardson in *Henry VIII* 2009, pp. 166–67, no. 19, ill.; on Hans Seusenhofer's anthropomorphic mask visors, see Gamber 1988, pp. 106–7, figs. 4–6.

6. Christie's 1987, pp. 78–79, no. 222, ill.; see also Pyhrr 2011, pp. 78–79, 87, n. 38.

Letter from Maximilian I to the Magistrate of Strasbourg

Dated Bastogne, May 20, 1512
Archives de la Ville et de l'Eurométropole, Strasbourg, France (AA 333)

Diploma Ennobling Hans Seusenhofer

Dated Vienna, October 26, 1537
Tiroler Landesarchiv, Innsbruck, Austria (Adelsachen Nr. 1626)

Epitaph of Hans Seusenhofer and Apollonia Forchheimer

Designed by Veit Arnberger (died 1551)
Cast by Gregor Löffler (ca. 1490–1565)
Austrian (Innsbruck), 1555
Bronze
23³⁄₁₆ x 19⁷⁄₈ in. (59 x 50.5 cm)
Tiroler Landesmuseum Ferdinandeum, Innsbruck,
Austria, Ältere Kunstgeschichtliche Sammlungen (B 206)

These objects capture pivotal moments in the life of Hans Seusenhofer, an armorer who owed his rise to prominence and ultimate ennoblement to Maximilian I and his grandson Ferdinand I. A master originally active in the free imperial city

CAT. 147

of Strasbourg, Hans was called by Maximilian to relocate and take a senior position in the court workshop at Innsbruck, which was headed by Hans's brother Conrad. In his letter to the municipal authorities of Strasbourg, dated May 20, 1512, Maximilian explains that as a result of Conrad's recent promotion to master keeper of his body armors (*Leibharnischmeister*), Hans had been invited to enter his service and take care of the court workshop in his brother's absence. Since Hans had accepted the offer, the municipality was to allow him to freely leave the city with his wife, children, and property, waive the taxes normally required in such instances, and accept his resignation as a burgher of Strasbourg. It was customary for Maximilian to use his authority to hire valuable servitors and ease their relocation. He had done the same, albeit more politely perhaps, when he wrote Ludovico Sforza to secure the services of Milanese armorers who had agreed to establish a workshop in his realms, in the town of Arbois (see cat. 125).

Hans left Strasbourg for Innsbruck, and in 1514, he personally delivered the armors made in the Innsbruck court workshop, probably with his help, to King Henry VIII of England and to Charles V (see cat. 82). The following year

Maximilian appointed Hans foreman (*Meisterknecht*), second in command but yielding the same power as Conrad in his absence at the Innsbruck workshop. Two months after Conrad died in 1517, Hans was promoted to keeper (*Wappenmeister*) of Maximilian's personal armory.

The diploma ennobling Hans and his descendants was granted by Ferdinand, Maximilian's successor in Tyrol, on October 26, 1537. Having petitioned for the honor two years earlier, Hans succeeded in securing a privilege seldom awarded to craftsmen, with the reservation that any of his descendants who earned a living from an artisanal profession would be prohibited from enjoying the privileges conferred by the letter. By that time, Hans had already retired from active duty and his son Jörg had taken over many of his responsibilities; yet, Hans was still eligible to receive yearly emoluments for his distinguished accomplishments. The diploma indicates that the privileges of nobility were conferred in recognition of Hans's deeds in the service of Emperors Frederick III and Maximilian I, especially for those in relation to Maximilian's "military expeditions, wars, and battles," as well as for those he had provided to Ferdinand as master keeper of his armors

CAT. 148

and personal armory. In reality, Hans had also been Ferdinand's court armorer, producing two richly decorated armors for him, another two for his master of the horse in 1528, and an etched and gilded horse bard for Ferdinand the following year.[1] The occupation is not referenced in the diploma because it was socially inferior to the other positions Hans had held.

After his ennoblement, Hans's family coat of arms was augmented: the helm for the tourney, which only noblemen could use, replaced the jousting helm, which signaled a commoner's status, above the shield. These arms appear on the bronze epitaph for the master and his wife, along with those of her family. As she was a spouse and not a descendant, her family arms are surmounted by a commoner's helm. The epithet *Edelvest*, a title reserved exclusively for noblemen, appears before Hans's name in the text in the cartouche and signals his high standing. While Hans's son Jörg, as an armorer, had to forfeit the privileges granted by Ferdinand, Jörg's daughter Marie Salome married into the nobility. The bronze epitaph for her and her husband, the imperial chief postmaster Josef, baron von Taxis, is also preserved in the collection of the Tiroler Landesmuseum Ferdinandeum.[2] PT

REFERENCES: cat. 146: Terjanian 2018, p. 30; cat. 147: Boeheim 1899, pp. 310–11; Thomas and Gamber 1954, p. 101, no. 192; Terjanian 2018, p. 31; cat. 148: Boeheim 1899, p. 311, fig. 11; Thomas and Gamber 1954, p. 103, no. 202; Hans Joachim Spiegelhalter in *Kaiser Maximilian I.* 2002, p. 313, no. 811, ill.; Terjanian 2018, p. 26, n. 1, ill. p. 29

1. On these commissions, see Boeheim 1899, pp. 307–19, and on Hans's life and career, pp. 293, 301–4, 306–12; Thomas and Gamber 1954, pp. 23–25, 34, 64; Blair 1965, pp. 12–13; Terjanian 2018.
2. See Boeheim 1899, pp. 318–19, fig. 14; Thomas and Gamber 1954, p. 103, no. 203.

Legacy

Maximilian left an extraordinary legacy. Through advantageous marriages and alliances, he successfully expanded Habsburg power in Europe and beyond. In his quest to shape opinion on his qualities and achievements he commissioned outstanding triumphs on paper, which include some of the most ambitious prints ever conceived, plans for a grand mausoleum, and stunning armors. Maximilian's accomplishments as patron of armorers eclipses, inasmuch as they are known, those of all other European rulers from his era and their successors. Yet, the epithet of the "Last Knight," which his pursuits and deeds fully warrant, is too reductive. His actions were by no means conservative: he relied on performance, communication, and commemoration to influence opinion, and he promoted the use of infantry and artillery in warfare. His embrace of the printing press, then still a relatively new media, shows that he saw and actively pursued new possibilities while defending and cultivating an image of himself that conformed to traditional models of leadership.

Maximilian's descendants and successors honored him and his remarkable accomplishments, completing, albeit with some notable adjustments, projects that had been close to his heart, such as the grand mausoleum that was eventually installed in the court church of Innsbruck. To preserve the memory of his outstanding spirit, Charles V took a pair of his grandfather's gauntlets with him to Spain, while Ferdinand II of Tyrol exhibited an armored figure of his great-grandfather in a gallery of heroes installed in his castle at Ambras. Ultimately, Maximilian's lifelong campaign to shape his self-image as that of an unforgettable knight is one of his most enduring successes.

Und ist gestorbn, mit Ieder mans betrübnüs · als ergelebt 68. Iar 9.
Monat. und 19 tag. bis aufu 12 Fener Ao 15·19

Cat. 149

Death Portrait of Maximilian I

South German or Austrian, after 1519

Oil on wood panel

17¹⁵⁄₁₆ x 13 in. (45.5 x 33 cm)

Tiroler Landesmuseum Ferdinandeum, Innsbruck, Austria, Ältere Kunstgeschichtliche Sammlungen (Gem 3152)

Rulers are born and die in the public eye. By today's standards, however, there is no precedent for the idea that Maximilian I would commission a death portrait of himself. Although no documentation exists for this commission, Maximilian personally and meticulously oversaw the preparations for his memorial projects, and it is difficult to believe that he would have allowed anyone else to commission such a work. Remarkably, the sovereign is not shown here in the customary attire of precious fabrics with imperial insignia that would reflect his preeminence. His head, clothed in a red earflap cap, rests diagonally on a black and dark green pillow decorated with white checkers. A black brocade funeral pall covers his torso. His face—with light stubble, open mouth, furrowed brow, and drooping left eye—is gaunt and marked by the struggles of his final days. Robbed of every last hint of majesty, Maximilian is barely recognizable; the characteristic shape of his nose alone recalls the face so well known from his many portraits.

This realistic portrayal is reminiscent of death masks, which were cast from the faces of the deceased to serve as effigies. Yet, in its radical and expressive manner of representation, the image transcends mimesis. It also reflects the tendency in early sixteenth-century depictions of the Passion to exaggerate and humanize Christ's suffering, a practice that reached its peak around the time of Maximilian's death portrait.[1]

Research indicates that Maximilian intended for his piety and humility, as portrayed here, to convey a religious message to his subjects.[2] This principle is further reflected in the plans for his passing. Casting himself as a contrite penitent, Maximilian ordered that his body be whipped, his head shaved, and his teeth knocked out following his death. Such efforts also served his aim of posthumously functioning as the model secular head of Christendom.

The image also operates on a political level, as it bears authentic testimony that Maximilian, the man, is truly dead. By doing so, it relates to a central premodern notion of sovereignty. Medieval juristic and theological thought assigned monarchs two bodies: a natural, and therefore mortal, one, and a supernatural, immortal one that was bound to the ruler's position and majesty. When the mortal body expired, the supernatural one endured, and this continuity, which was based in divine right, justified the monarch's continued dominion. This notion of distinguishing between office and person would provide a key basis for the development of a modern theory of the state.[3]

The concept of the two bodies also informs Maximilian's death portrait in Zittau.[4] This diptych shows the living emperor, clothed according to his rank with the collar of the Order of the Golden Fleece, on the left panel; on the right the deceased Maximilian appears dressed simply, his face haggard, as in the present portrait. The immortal, divinely appointed ruler and the mortal man are not merely juxtaposed—the diptych format binds them together, as they were thought to be in the figure of Maximilian.

As the final image of the monarch, Maximilian's death portrait assumed the authentic and replicable quality of an icon. This explains the many extant versions and copies, which were presumably sent to allied houses and distant family members, just as portraits of him were shared during his lifetime.[5] The desire to view the dead emperor may not in fact be as foreign to contemporary culture as thought, if we consider our relationship with visual media and the deluge of photographic documentation that surrounds the death of many public figures.   PS

REFERENCES: Helga Hensle-Wlasak in *Welt, Macht, Geist* 2002, pp. 244–46, under no. A 3; Eisenbeiss 2005, pp. 292–93; Gernot Mayer in *Emperor*

Maximilian I 2012, pp. 380–83, under no. 127, fig. 2; Christof Metzger in *Face to Face* 2014, pp. 190–91, no. 6.6, ill.

1. In paintings by Matthias Grünewald, for instance, the Crucifixions in the Kunstmuseum Basel (269) and the National Gallery of Art, Washington, D.C. (1961.9.19).
2. Gernot Mayer in *Emperor Maximilian I* 2012, p. 381.
3. Kantorowicz 1957.
4. Städtische Museen, Zittau (2.690/60); *Emperor Maximilian I* 2012, p. 380, fig. 1.
5. Magyar Nemzeti Múzeum, Budapest (179), and Universalmuseum Joanneum, Schloss Eggenberg, Graz (392).

Cat. 150

Imperial Eagle

Hans Burgkmair (1473–1531)
South German (Augsburg), 1507
Woodcut
12⅞ x 8⁵⁄₁₆ in. (32.7 x 21.1 cm)
The Metropolitan Museum of Art, New York, Harris Brisbane Dick Fund, 1926 (26.72.87)

Monogrammed by the Augsburg painter and printmaker Hans Burgkmair on either side of the spouting fountain, this complex allegorical image of a crowned, double-headed eagle represents the Holy Roman Empire and its creative potential under Maximilian I. As elucidated by Peter Luh, its elaborate program probably derives from Maximilian's poet laureate, the learned German humanist Conrad Celtis.[1]

In the center of the print, above the fountain containing the nine classical Muses, sits the enthroned, crowned emperor bearing his regalia of office and flanked by two heralds. In place of the god Apollo, who normally presides over the Muses, this image substitutes Maximilian himself as the promoter of the arts, especially poetry and music, the importance of the latter indicated by the instruments played by the nude Muses. Laurel wreaths symbolizing Apollo's recognition (and that of poets like Celtis) hang from the eagle's two beaks. Two sequences of roundels unfold on the bird's wings. Its right wing enumerates the seven days of Creation, as given in Genesis; its left presents the Seven Mechanical Arts, a medieval cycle summarizing the practical crafts and labors that balance the learning and intellect of the Seven Liberal Arts.[2] Those latter branches of medieval learning appear with their attributes at the base of the fountain, with four figures of the *quadrivium* (Geometry, Arithmetic, Music, and Astronomy), above the traditional *trivium* (Grammar, Rhetoric, and Logic) at the foundation, all presided over from above by an enthroned and crowned Philosophia with her foot on a globe.

Before the base of the structure a negative example unfolds: the image of the Judgment of Paris. There, guided by Mercury, the Trojan prince selects the fairest among the three principal classical goddesses (his ill-advised awarding of the prize to Venus, under the influence of Discord, brought him Helen of Troy, but also initiated the disastrous Trojan War).[3] Thus the entire sequence of decoration on the fountain suggests that earthly, God-given resources will be used wisely by the emperor's subjects and that German intellectuals and artists in the empire will thrive under his benevolent rule.

The entire woodcut displays Latin captions in the uncial capitals of ancient Roman inscriptions, which are appropriate to its learned classical references and to the program by Celtis, who had recently, in 1501, established a College of Poets and Mathematicians in Vienna. This print means to suggest that Maximilian's reign will follow that program and promote a true Northern Renaissance.

Like his Nuremberg contemporary Albrecht Dürer, Burgkmair strove to create Northern Renaissance images that engaged visually with both classical ornament and Italianate forms. He connected to Maximilian and to Celtis through the Augsburg city secretary, Conrad Peutinger, who would supervise both the production and printing of many of the emperor's illustrated projects.   LS

REFERENCES: Falk 1968, pp. 49–51; Falk 1973, n.p., no. 17; Larry Silver in *Emperor Maximilian I* 2012, pp. 192–93, no. 36

1. Luh 2001, pp. 220–38, discusses the Apollo theme in the works of Conrad Celtis for Maximilian; on Augsburg publications for the emperor, see pp. 247–312.
2. The Mechanical Arts consisted of weaving, agriculture, architecture, hunting and warfare, navigation, cooking and medicine, and metallurgy; Summers 1987, pp. 235–65.
3. Maximilian, like many other dynastic rulers in early modern Europe, claimed descent from the ancient Trojans, specifically from their arch hero Hector, whose image is the first in the emperor's *Genealogy*, also designed by Burgkmair (cat. 166).

SACELLVM D. VIRGINIS, ET PRAECIPVI ORNATVS.

Cornelius Galle sculpsit.

1. *Statua sacra.* 2. *Duodecim Apostoli argentei, donum Philippi Boni.* 3. *Statua Diuæ argentea, eiusdem munus.*
4. *Maximilianus Imp. Albertus Dux Saxoniæ, & quidam procerum.* 5. *Arbor aurea Maximiliani, inscripta*
ANNO VIIII. 6. *Lampas argentea Iulij* II. P.M. *inscripta,* ANNO VIIII. IVLIVS PONT. MAX.
7. *Paludamentum Caroli V. Imp.* 8. *Statua argentea viri geniculantis, donum Fuggerorum.*

Cat. 151

Diva Virgo Hallensis: Beneficia Eius & Miracula Fide Atque Ordine Decsripta

Cornelis Galle the Elder (1576–1650)
Written by Justus Lipsius (1547–1606)
South Netherlandish (Antwerp), 1604
Bound volume with engraved illustrations
University of Pennsylvania Libraries, Philadelphia, Kislak Center
for Special Collections, Rare Books and Manuscripts
(BT660.H35 L57 1604)

Cat. 152

The High Altar of the Church of Our Lady at Halle

Lucas Vorsterman the Younger (1624–after 1666)
South Netherlandish (Antwerp), dated 1658
Etching
21¹¹⁄₁₆ x 17¹¹⁄₁₆ in. (55 x 45 cm)
Koninklijke Bibliotheek van België, Brussels
(EST P° - Vorsterman (L.) Junior - R/2009/14832)

In August 1512 the chief treasurer of Maximilian I and Charles V in the Low Countries paid the sum of ten livres to an armorer of Brussels for the costs of having cleaned and repaired a full field armor that sometime ago had been placed in the Church of "Notre Dame de Haulx" at Maximilian's orders. The circumstances surrounding this affair are known through an entry recording this payment in the treasurer's account book: The emperor had asked for the armor to be removed from the sanctuary and replaced with "his statue, armed with another armor, brand new." Once refurbished, the older armor was to be shipped to him in Germany.[1]

Located in Halle, about nine miles (fifteen kilometers) southwest of Brussels, the place in which Maximilian had a statue of himself in full armor was no ordinary church. Famous for a miracle-working statue of the Virgin Mary donated in the thirteenth century, the church (now basilica) of Notre Dame was a major center of Marian devotion and one of the most popular pilgrimage sites in the Low Countries. Like Philip the Good, Charles the Bold, and many other rulers before them, Maximilian joined the church's Confraternity of Our Lady and periodically visited the building, paying homage to the Virgin and seeking her help with prayers. In addition to pious donations, he displayed trophies of war in the church, such as a banner he had captured from the Venetians.[2]

Although nothing of his armored statue is known to remain, it was probably among the church's treasures lost or destroyed following the French invasion of the Low Countries

CAT. 152

DETAIL OF CAT. 152

in 1794.[3] Fortunately, its general appearance and placement within the church are preserved in two prints. The earliest one is an illustration by Cornelis Galle the Elder in a book by the Netherlandish humanist Justus Lipsius that was first published in 1604 and that recounts the miraculous history of the Virgin's statue in the church. The other is a print by the Antwerp artist Lucas Vorsterman the Younger, which is dated 1658. In both works one can see the votive figures of men in armor to the altar's left. However, while there were three figures in 1604, by 1658 there were only two, positioned higher up on the same wall. Lipsius's text, the coats of arms placed near the figures, and the captions for the illustrations that were later installed in the church conclusively identify the two armored figures that were still in situ in 1658 as representing Maximilian I and Duke Albrecht of Saxony, who served Maximilian and his son, Philip I, as governor-general of the Burgundian Low Countries from 1488 until 1494, when Philip came of age.[4]

The treasurer's accounts, Lipsius's book, and Vorsterman's print indicate that Maximilian had introduced a lifesize image of himself in a prominent place of worship sometime before 1512, probably in emulation of several medieval traditions. Many others before him had donated wax effigies to the same church as the result of vows they had made. Medieval men-at-arms and rulers across Europe also occasionally gave their personal armor to a church after having promised to do so if God provided the assistance needed to secure a victory or survive a battle.[5]

The fact that in 1512 Maximilian chose to have the original armor replaced with another suggests that the first was a memento of a special event in his life and that it was perhaps too dear to be allowed to remain in anyone else's custody. As the armor was kept in the Burgundian Low Countries until Maximilian requested it, it is conceivable that it had been wrought in those lands either during the time he resided there or on the occasion of his later stays. If so, the possibility that a cuirass made for him by the Brussels armorer Anthonis van Ghindertaelen, which is now in the Kunsthistorisches Museum, Vienna, and which by the late sixteenth century had been incorporated into a composite armor kept at Ambras Castle, might be the remnant of the armor once in Halle, ought to be considered (see cat. 159).[6]   PT

REFERENCES: cat. 151: Van der Velden 2000, pp. 170, 176–77, and p. 171, fig. 87, p. 176, fig. 90 (detail); cat. 152: Hollstein 1949–2010, vol. 42 (1993), p. 111, no. 44, ill. p. 110; Van der Velden 2000, p. 172, and p. 174, fig. 89

1. Archives Départementales du Nord, Lille, B 2224, fol. 397v.
2. Van der Velden 2000, p. 177.
3. Kieckens 1894.
4. The third figure is thought to have been Hugues de Melun, viscount of Ghent, one of Maximilian's trusted servitors; see Van der Velden 2000, p. 177.
5. On gifts of figural representations of the donors to the church, see ibid., pp. 171–77. On votive gifts of armor, see Merlet 1885, pp. 134–38; Baron 1968; Boccia 1982; Dirk H. Breiding in *Ritterwelten im Spätmittelalter* 2009, pp. 140–45, no. 1.
6. On this cuirass, see Thomas 1949/1977, pp. 574–75; Thomas and Gamber 1976, pp. 179–80, no. A 110.

Cat. 153

Inventory of Maximilian I's Armaments in Tyrol

Jörg Kölderer (ca. 1456/70–1540)
Written by Ludwig Stecher (active 1507–1533) and Hans Kugler (first recorded 1507, died 1524)
Austrian (Innsbruck), ca. 1504–8
Pen in ink and watercolor on paper with calf binding
Sheet: 16^{15}⁄$_{16}$ x 11^{7}⁄$_{16}$ in. (43 x 29 cm)
Yale Center for British Art, New Haven, Connecticut (Folio A 2011 36)

No matter how much he prized hand-to-hand combat in battle and the tournament, Maximilian I was perfectly aware of the latest developments in warfare and quite interested in technological advances that might give his troops an advantage. As a result, he embraced the invention and use of artillery, then still a relatively novel branch of warfare, and promoted the casting of bronze cannons and handguns.

Featuring sixty-three drawings in pen and ink and watercolor, this manuscript is one of several inventories Maximilian commissioned shortly before 1507 to confirm the available stock of weapons and related equipment kept in his arsenals as well as in all cities and castles across his hereditary lands, thus not only in several Austrian duchies but also in territories under his rule in Alsace, Vorarlberg, and Swabia. Compiled under the direction of Bartholome Freyssleben, his chief master of armaments (*Oberst Hauszeugmeister*), the resulting inventories record what was found in situ as well as call attention to the items that had been specially made or purchased at Maximilian's request, including artillery and handguns. Illustrated by Jörg Kölderer, Maximilian's court artist in Innsbruck, the inventories provide an impressive overview of the raw materials, weapons, and munitions kept at Maximilian's disposal, and even document the carefully managed, orderly stores, which must have given Freyssleben and his powerful master much satisfaction.

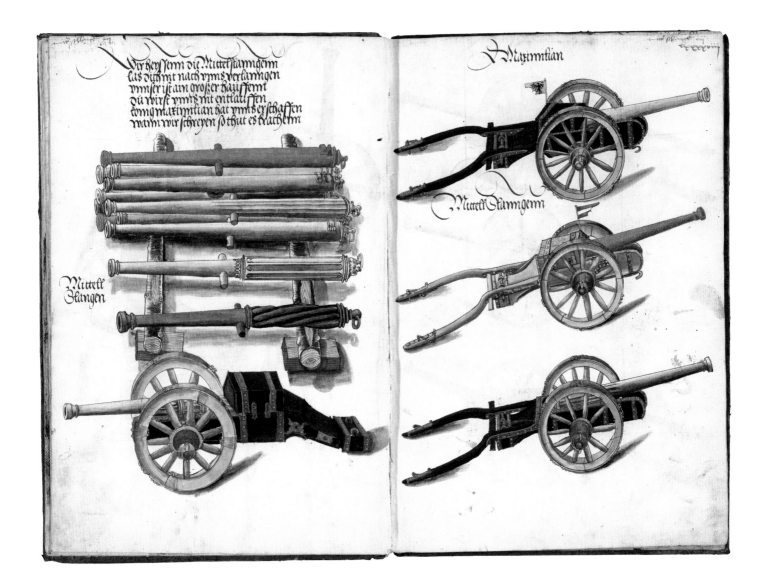

The manuscript now at Yale is devoted to the weapons located in Tyrol, and suitably features interior and exterior views of the new arsenal of Innsbruck, which had just been built at Maximilian's orders. It includes depictions of numerous cannons and handguns that Maximilian had commissioned and even named, a number of which were undoubtedly cast in nearby Mühlau, where he had established three foundries.[1]

The Yale manuscript is related to a pictorial inventory now in the Bayerische Staatsbibliothek, Munich, which includes some of the same illustrations, and to another one in the Österreichische Nationalbibliothek, Vienna, which, with a few exceptions, has the same images in the same order. [2] The chief difference between the copies in Munich and Vienna lies in the execution of the drawings, which in the latter are not outlined in black ink and in the former are perhaps more ambitiously painted. The existence of multiple copies of varying quality may be explained by the process of their creation, which began with simpler versions and ended with presentation-quality copies on vellum for Maximilian and possibly others.[3] Furthermore, Freyssleben and other officials likely wished to have their own copies of the work.   PT

REFERENCE: Nachod 1952

1. On cannons cast for Maximilian in Tyrol, see Egg 1961, pp. 49–55, 69–91.
2. Bayerische Staatsbibliothek, Munich, Cod.icon. 222; Österreichische Nationalbibliothek, Vienna, Cod. 10816.
3. On such copies, see Boeheim 1892, especially pp. 94–99; Egg 1961, pp. 50–52; Maximilian I. 1969, "Katalog," pp. 121–22, nos. 475, 476; Thomas and Gamber 1976, p. 213, nos. P 5074, P 5075, P 5076, fig. 103.

IMPERATOR
DIVVS MAXI
PIVS FELIX

CAESAR
MILIANVS
AVGVSTVS·

Cat. 154

Maximilian I

Hans Weiditz the Younger (before 1500–ca. 1536)
After Albrecht Dürer (1471–1528)
South German (Augsburg), 1519
Woodcut
21¹³⁄₁₆ x 14¹⁵⁄₁₆ in. (55.4 x 38 cm)
The Metropolitan Museum of Art, New York, The George Khuner Collection, Gift of Mrs. George Khuner, 1975 (1975.653.108)

Hans Weiditz the Younger was first trained in Strasbourg, where he contributed one woodcut for Maximilian's *Theuerdank*. He is most associated with the production of woodcuts for illustrated books, but he also created some remarkable single-leaf woodcuts, such as this large-scale and highly ornamented portrait of Maximilian.

By 1518 Weiditz was working as a journeyman in Hans Burgkmair's Augsburg workshop. In that year, the city hosted Maximilian's final Imperial Diet, at which Albrecht Dürer sat with the emperor "high up in the palace in his [Maximilian's] little chamber," and drew him from life.[1] This finely executed chalk drawing, now in Vienna, has become the canonical portrait of Maximilian.[2] It shows the emperor at bust-length, wearing a fur-trimmed hat, a brocade cloak, and the collar of the Order of the Golden Fleece. He turns away from the viewer, demonstrating what Erwin Panofsky calls "noble aloofness and innate benevolence, but also his fatigue and deep disillusionment."[3]

Dürer himself created two paintings and a large woodcut based on the drawing, all likely made just after the emperor's death to satisfy the public's voracious appetite for Maximilian's image.[4] The popularity of Dürer's likeness and of the living memory of Maximilian was assured by three other woodcuts produced just after the emperor's death, which replicate his exact conception.[5] In his version of the portrait, instead of showing the emperor against a blank abstracted space, Weiditz places Maximilian below an elaborately ornamented archway. The flanking columns are adorned with foliage, grotesques, hybrids, and harpies—a style of ornament closely associated with the Italian Renaissance and widely exploited in works across media by Augsburg artists and craftsmen during this period. The columns are topped by griffins that hold symbols of Maximilian's authority, such as the imperial crown and coat of arms, as well as the same Burgundian flints that bind the chain for the collar of the Order of the Golden Fleece. Conceived in the wake of the emperor's death, Weiditz's portrait celebrates Maximilian's power as the direct descendant of Imperial Rome and emphasizes his embrace of Italian Renaissance sensibilities.

Unlike Dürer's own woodcut, which astonishingly lacks his monogram, Weiditz's version includes Dürer's celebrated initials, not only to appeal to a larger market but also to honor the original designer of the image. Weiditz's print also has the same Latin text found on Dürer's woodcut, which declares, "Emperor, Caesar, Divine Maximilian Pious Propitious August" (IMPERATOR / CAESAR / DIVUS MAX I / MILIANUS / PIUS FELIX / AUGUSTUS), emphasizing Maximilian's identification with the ancient Roman Caesars. In addition, this inscription further elevates the emperor after death with the title of Divine, following ancient Roman custom.   FS

REFERENCES: Hollstein 1954–2014, vol. 7 (1960), p. 206, no. 255; Dagmar Eichberger in Schoch, Mende, and Scherbaum 2001–4, vol. 2 (2002), pp. 456–59, under no. 252 (Weiditz, woodblock 4)

1. The drawing bears this inscription by Dürer. See Ashcroft 2017, vol. 1, p. 490, no. 126.1.
2. Albertina Museum, Vienna (4852); Karl Schütz in *Emperor Maximilian I* 2012, pp. 292–95, no. 75, ill.
3. Panofsky 1955, p. 193.
4. For these works, see Luber 1991. The painting in Vienna at the Kunsthistorisches Museum, Gemäldegalerie (825), is on panel, while the one in Nuremberg at the Germanisches Nationalmuseum (169) is on canvas.
5. There are three other woodcut versions of Dürer's portrait of Maximilian including Weiditz's. For a discussion of the different woodcuts, see Dagmar Eichberger in Schoch, Mende, and Scherbaum 2001–4, vol. 2 (2002), pp. 456–59, no. 252.

Cat. 155

Maximilian I

Workshop or follower of Albrecht Dürer
German, ca. 1525–30(?)
Oil on linden panel
15¹¹⁄₁₆ x 12¼ in. (39.8 x 31.1 cm)
Kunsthistorisches Museum, Vienna, Gemäldegalerie (880)

Maximilian I employed clever marital politics to lay the groundwork for the Habsburgs' becoming one of Europe's longest-standing, most powerful dynasties. Also an active collector and writer, the emperor patronized many of the preeminent artists of the day, including Albrecht Dürer, although the theme common to most of his commissions was self-commemoration.

With regard to type, this portrait is tied closely to an undated woodcut and to two paintings, one in Nuremberg, the other in Vienna, which, according to the artist's detailed inscriptions, Dürer completed in 1519, shortly after the emperor's death.[1] All can be traced back to a drawing of Maximilian that Dürer made during his time at the Imperial

Diet in Augsburg in June 1518.[2] Notably, the emperor's features in the drawing correspond in size not only to those in the woodcut and the two paintings from 1519, as Katherine Crawford Luber has established, but also to those of the present panel and another, nearly identical version in Hannover.[3]

It may have been for the sake of economy that Dürer pounced the original study, as evidenced by trace marks on the drawing.[4] He may also have employed this mechanical method of reproduction in an effort to endow the painted and woodcut portraits of Maximilian with the utmost authenticity. That the 1519 paintings in Nuremberg and Vienna (ceremonious half-length portraits of the monarch) and the woodcut (a portrayal reduced to the bust) could have been ordered by Maximilian himself is suggested by the portrait session he had granted Dürer, according to Dürer's inscription on the drawing.

Even after Maximilian's death, however, the monarch's memory called out for depiction: in fact, the woodcut portrait was reproduced with four different printing blocks until about

1600 (see cat. 154). About 1530, it served as inspiration for the present painting and the closely corresponding one in Hannover, further versions of which may well have existed. As comparatively modest works, the two occupy a place somewhere between the printed portraits and the two more ambitious paintings from 1519. Both of the former portraits may have originated from Dürer's workshop or from one of the artists trained there, as evidenced not only by the head of the subject, which was again the same size and thus also traced, but also by the manner of painting flesh tones and hair as well as by the fact that both combine elements from the earlier Nuremberg and Vienna half-length portraits.   GM

REFERENCES: *Maximilian I.* 1969, "Katalog," pp. 150–51, no. 561, fig. 110; Karl Schütz in Schütz 1994, p. 142, no. 47, ill.; Guido Messling in *Lucas Cranach the Elder* 2016, pp. 36–38, no. 1, ill.

1. Germanisches Nationalmuseum, Nuremberg (169); Kunsthistorisches Museum, Vienna, Gemäldegalerie (825). On the various versions of Dürer's portraits of Maximilian I, see Luber 1991. On the woodcut, see especially Dagmar Eichberger in Schoch, Mende, and Scherbaum 2001–4, vol. 2 (2002), pp. 456–59, no. 252, ill.
2. Albertina Museum, Vienna (4852); Winkler 1936–39, vol. 3 (1938), pp. 68–69, no. 635, ill.
3. Luber 1991, pp. 31–46. Niedersächsisches Landesmuseum Hannover (KM 43); Wolfson 1992, pp. 71–72, no. 18, ill.
4. See Luber 1991, p. 31, and p. 32, fig. 1.

Cat. 156

Allegory of the Vices and Virtues

Hans Daucher (1486–1538)
South German (Augsburg), dated 1522
Honestone (Jurassic limestone) with traces of gilding
H. 11⅛ in. (28.3 cm), W. 18⁷⁄₁₆ in. (46.8 cm), D. 1¾ in. (4.4 cm)
The Metropolitan Museum of Art, New York, Gift of J. Pierpont Morgan, 1917 (17.190.745)

The subject of this elaborate relief was taken from *Jüngere Titurel* (*Younger Titurel*), a romance begun by Wolfram von Eschenbach and thought to have been continued by the thirteenth-century poet Albrecht von Scharfenberg. The scene features King Arthur and his retinue crossing a magical bridge to meet the heathen King Clarisidun. Crossing the parapetless bridge is an allegorical test of the travelers' virtuousness, and seven of Arthur's knights, each guilty of various sins, fall into the river and are condemned to drown.[1]

At the head of the cortege, in the foreground, is the figure of either Charles V or his younger brother Ferdinand I. The presence of the double-headed imperial eagle on the bridge's tower and the physical similarities of the figure to a depiction of Charles in another relief by Hans Daucher lend support

to the argument that this horseman is the elder brother (see cat. 91). However, the bard of his horse is not adorned with the imperial eagle, but rather with the arms of Austria and, most significantly, the cross of Saint George, a likely reference to the chivalric order of the same name of which Ferdinand was apparently already considered the protector by 1521.[2] Whether the horseman is Charles or Ferdinand, the person riding by his side, placed in the background but clearly visible, has the unmistakable profile of their grandfather Maximilian I. Although already deceased by 1522, the emperor is included in the composition and awarded the distinction of being crowned with a wreath of laurels, either as an attribute of his imperial majesty or as a marker of his heroic virtue. Given the close observance of details from the story that inspired this allegorical representation, it is conceivable that Maximilian is equated here with the legendary King Arthur.[3]   PT

REFERENCES: Ettlinger 1956; Eser 1996, pp. 106–14, no. 5, fig. 9; Thomas Eser in *Emperor Maximilian I* 2012, pp. 274–75, no. 69, ill.

1. Thomas Eser in *Emperor Maximilian I* 2012, p. 274.
2. See Bergmann 1868, p. 173.
3. On the correlated number of figures in the cortege and in the water, see Eser in *Emperor Maximilian I* 2012, p. 274.

Cat. 157

Charles V on Horseback

Hans Daucher (1486–1538)
South German (Augsburg), 1522
Sandstone (presumably Solnhofener stone) with traces of pigment and gilding
H. 7¹³⁄₁₆ in. (19.9 cm), W. 5⁵⁄₁₆ in. (13.5 cm), D. 1¹⁄₁₆ in. (2.7 cm)
Tiroler Landesmuseum Ferdinandeum, Innsbruck, Austria, Ältere Kunstgeschichtliche Sammlungen (P 168)

This relief depicts Charles V on horseback, flanked by two truncated trees. The sloping background leads the eye to a fortress on the upper edge of the picture; the landscape in the middle ground is largely undefined. In the foreground, the horse rears toward the left, a movement emphasized by the emperor's posture, the billowing feathers on his helmet, and the horse's tail. Charles's left hand grips a scepter, and his right hand, clutching the reins out in front, underscores the twist of his torso turned toward the viewer. The composition gives the impression of speed as if the image were a snapshot of a hunting scene.

The horse's peytral is adorned with the coat of arms of Austria and Saint George's cross, the symbol of the Order of Saint George, whose patron saint was the paragon of chivalric virtue and believed to provide succor to crusaders.[1] Hans Daucher also represented this connection in his posthumous relief of Maximilian I, in which the emperor is portrayed in profile as an armor-clad Saint George on horseback (cat. 112).[2]

Daucher also created other reliefs of Charles V. One of these belongs to a private collection in France, and while it resembles the Innsbruck piece, it is more decorative.[3] The rider's facial expression and clothing as well as the horse's pose and bard are the same in both pieces, but the main figures do not occupy as much space in the French relief. Thomas Eser has suggested that the Innsbruck relief is a second version of the French piece, which Daucher manufactured in order to cast replicas of Charles's portrait.[4] Two of these bronze plaques are known: one is in the Germanisches Nationalmuseum in Nuremberg and the other in the Maximilianmuseum in Augsburg.[5]   CZ

REFERENCES: Gert Ammann in *Hispania—Austria* 1992, p. 399, no. 217, ill.; Eser 1996, pp. 119–23, no. 7, fig. 12

1. The Order of Saint George was founded in 1469 by Frederick III, in response to the 1453 fall of Constantinople and ensuing Ottoman threat. Maximilian expanded the order to include a fraternity, with which he attempted (unsuccessfully) to realize his father's vision of a Crusade to recapture Constantinople. For further discussion on Saint George, see Margot Rauch in *Ritter!* 2013, pp. 124–25, no. 2.13; Krause 2014b.
2. *Kaiser Maximilian I. zu Pferd als Ritter Georg*, 1520/30, Kunsthistorisches Museum, Vienna, Kunstkammer (7236); Eser 1996, pp. 159–65, no. 15, fig. 28. Regarding the portrayal of Saint George, see Poeschel 2014, pp. 238–40.
3. *Kaiser Karl V. zu Pferd*, private collection, France; Eser 1996, pp. 115–18, no. 6, fig. 11.
4. Ibid., p. 122.
5. *Karl V.* (plaque), 1522, Germanisches Nationalmuseum, Nuremberg (Pl.O.880); ibid., p. 123, under no. 7. *Kaiser Karl V. zu Pferd*, Maximilianmuseum, Augsburg (9211); ibid., p. 123, under no. 7, and p. 122, fig. 13.

Pair of Gauntlets of Maximilian I

Attributed to Lorenz Helmschmid (first recorded 1467, died 1516)

South German (Augsburg), ca. 1490

Steel

Right gauntlet: L. 16 in. (40.5 cm), W. 4⅛ in. (10.5 cm), D. 4⅜ in. (11 cm); left gauntlet: L. 15¾ in. (40 cm), W. 4⅛ in. (10.5 cm), D. 4⅜ in. (11 cm)

Patrimonio Nacional, Madrid, Real Armería (E. 88, E. 89)

This very fine pair of gauntlets in the late Gothic German fashion belongs to the group of objects Charles V appears to have brought from the Low Countries to Spain following his abdication as duke of Burgundy in 1555 and Holy Roman Emperor in 1556.[1] Their scale, style, and probable date of manufacture about 1490 preclude the possibility that they were made for Charles or even his father, Philip I, who at the time still would have been an adolescent. They can thus be identified as originally having belonged to Charles's paternal grandfather, Maximilian I. Charles was keenly interested in preserving his grandfather's memory by reclaiming the emperor's favorite armor shortly after his death (see cat. 135). It seems probable that Charles saw in these gauntlets a memento of a formidable figure in his life, to whom the House of Habsburg owed much of its recently expanded prestige and dominions.

The gauntlets are symmetrical and each one is constructed out of twenty-seven plates that are secured together by rivets. In addition to the elaborate articulation and great refinement of form, the gauntlets are outstanding for their sophisticated ornamentation. The cuffs and the plates protecting the thumb and the back of the hand are decorated with sprays of flutes and with sunken bands. The edges of most plates are shaped and pierced with stylized floral designs in the late Gothic tradition. The upper edges of the cuffs are further adorned with overlaid plates fretted with comparable ornament, and various sections of the gauntlets, including the metacarpal lames, are embellished with etched foliate patterns.

Unusual on late Gothic armor, the combination of elaborate piercing and etching is a hallmark of armor made by the Augsburg armorers and brothers Lorenz and Jörg Helmschmid. Examples of the application of both techniques include a combination sallet by Lorenz (cat. 128) and an armor for the joust of peace by Jörg in the Kunsthistorisches Museum, Vienna.[2] The gauntlets of a field armor made by Lorenz, which exhibit comparable construction and workmanship, arrangement of the flutes, and use of pierced overlays along the edges of the cuffs, leave little doubt that the present pair was also made in his workshop, though probably a decade later because it also includes etched ornament, which is a later decorative technique.[3] PT

REFERENCES: Valencia de Don Juan 1898, pp. 168–69, nos. E. 88, E. 89, fig. 97; Álvaro Soler del Campo in *Paz y la guerra* 1994, pp. 300–301, no. 234, ill.

1. Álvaro Soler del Campo in *Paz y la guerra* 1994, pp. 300–301, no. 234, ill.
2. Thomas 1956/1977, p. 1135, fig. 36.
3. On this armor, see Thomas and Gamber 1976, pp. 108–10, no. A 62, figs. 34, 35; for a good illustration of the gauntlets, see Krause 2014a, p. 114, fig. 2.

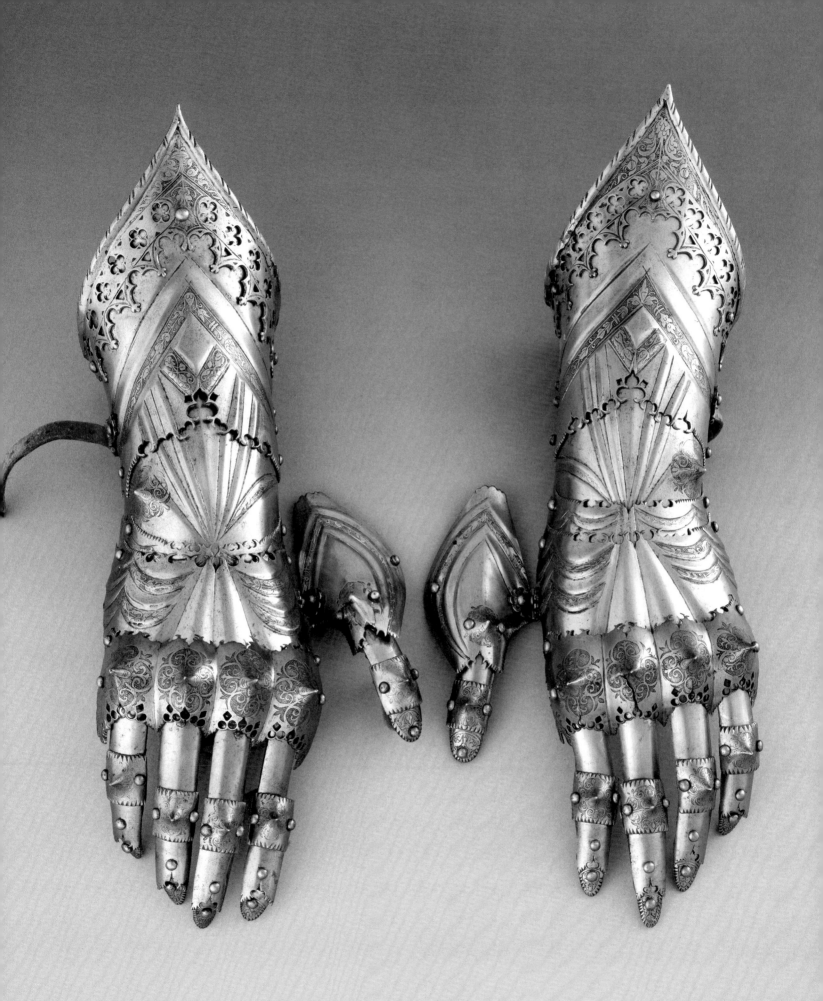

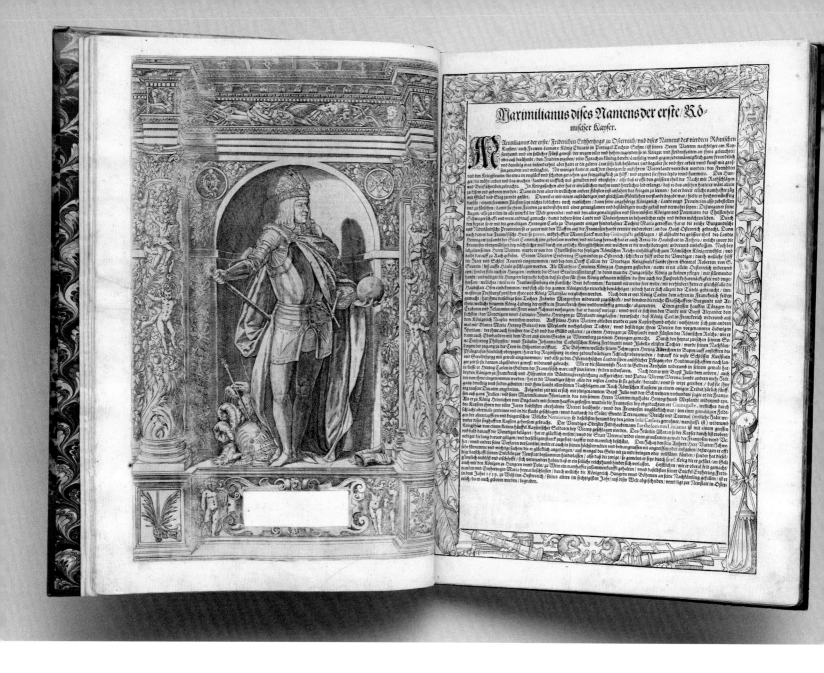

Cat. 159

Catalogue of the Armory of Heroes

Dominicus Custos (after 1550–1612)

After Giovanni Battista Fontana (1524–1587)

Written by Jakob Schrenck von Notzing (1539–1612)

Austrian (Innsbruck), 1603

Printed book with engraved illustrations

The Metropolitan Museum of Art, New York, Library of the
Department of Arms and Armor (147.1Am1C244 Q)

Among the first printed collection catalogues to appear in
Europe, this substantial volume records objects from the
prestigious collection of armors assembled by Archduke
Ferdinand II of Tyrol (1529–1595) and exhibited at Ambras
Castle, his palace near Innsbruck. Ferdinand, a great-
grandson of Maximilian I, amassed armors and weapons of
his illustrious predecessors, as well as those of their allies, and
even their foes, which he presented as relics that invoked their
identities and exploits.[1] Ferdinand described his collection—
widely known as the Armory of Heroes—as an "honorable
society," and included himself among its ranks by installing
his own armor alongside those of his forebearers. The collection and its catalogue gave tangible form to the archduke's
Habsburg-Burgundian lineage and celebrated Maximilian as a
heroic forefather and knightly exemplar. In doing so, it echoed
Maximilian's own genealogical and commemorative projects
(see cats. 64, 166, 167).

   Although not completed until after Ferdinand's death in
1595, the printed catalogue was conceived before 1582 by the
archduke in collaboration with his secretary, Jakob Schrenck

von Notzing, and its preparation spanned two decades. The first edition—in Latin—was published in Innsbruck in 1601. The German edition, exemplified by the present copy, followed in 1603 and was given the title *Of the Most Serene and Powerful Emperors, Kings and Archdukes, Princes, as Well as Counts, Lords of the Nobility and Other Appropriately Famous War Heroes, Whose Weapons and Armor, Some Whole, Some in Pieces, from Nearly Every Country in the World, Some with Great Cost and Effort, Have Been Brought Together*.[2] For the printed volumes, the Augsburg-based printmaker Dominicus Custos engraved the frontispiece and the 125 armored portraits based on designs by Ferdinand's court artist, the Italian Giovanni Battista Fontana. Featuring an armor in Ferdinand's collection, each portrait is complemented by a biographical note on the sitter's life and key military deeds.

Maximilian's portrait occupies an eminent position near the beginning of the volume, among other emperors of the House of Habsburg. He holds the imperial orb and a commander's baton, while at his feet an eagle grasps his scepter in its beak. He is depicted wearing an armor from Ferdinand's collection that is now in the Kunsthistorisches Museum, Vienna.[3] The armor is heterogeneous and combines elements made for him by various armorers in the Low Countries and the German-speaking lands. These include an unusual combination sallet and bevor forged by Lorenz Helmschmid (cat. 128). During the early sixteenth century, probably about 1510, the form and decoration of the pauldrons were altered by armorers in Innsbruck in order to more closely match the breastplate, tassets, vambraces, and gauntlets that are pictured here.[4] Thus, this engraving may illustrate a composite armor that was assembled during Maximilian's lifetime.

Although Ferdinand was a connoisseur and avid patron of luxury armors, he valued the objects in his Armory of Heroes more as historical mementos than as works of art. In his collection at Ambras, many historical figures were represented by composite armors or fragments, often exhibited alongside painted bust-length portraits of the men with whom the objects were associated. This pairing amplified the commemorative and didactic tone of the displays.[5] The printed catalogue enlivened the objects further by depicting them as parts of complete ensembles of armor or military costume worn by the full-length figures portrayed in the engraved illustrations. Like the other engravings that populate this volume and the collection that they record, this print of Maximilian presents armors as objects of memory and persistent embodiments of their wearers' identities.   CK

REFERENCES: Schrenck von Notzing 1601 and 1603/1981; Luchner 1958

1. Luchner 1958, pp. 114–17; Scheicher 1990, p. 71; Beaufort-Spontin 2010, pp. 126–27.
2. The original German title is *Der aller durchleuchtigsten und grossmächtigen Kayser . . . Königen und Ertzhertzogen . . . Fürsten, wie auch Grafen, Herren vom Adel, und anderer treflicher berühmbter Kriegsshelden . . . deren Waffen und Rüstungen zum theil gantz, zum theil stuckweiss . . . fast auss allen Landen der Welt, theils mit grosser mühe und kosten zusamen gebracht . . . in dem Fürstlichen Schloss Ombrass.*
3. Thomas and Gamber 1976, pp. 179–81, no. A 110.
4. Ibid.; see also the commentary by Bruno Thomas for pl. 4 in Schrenck von Notzing 1601 and 1603/1981.
5. Kuster 2018, p. 51.

Cat. 160

Saint Maurice

Lucas Cranach the Elder (1472–1553) and workshop
German, ca. 1520–25
Oil on linden
54 x 15½ in. (137.2 x 39.4 cm)
The Metropolitan Museum of Art, New York, Bequest of Eva F. Kollsman, 2005 (2006.469)

Cardinal Albrecht of Brandenburg's impressive collection of saints' relics, one of the largest of its kind in Germany, was catalogued twice, first in published form in 1520 and again in manuscript form in 1526 or 1527. A comparison of the two documents, the richly illustrated *Hallesches Heiltumsbuch* and the later, equally informative *Liber ostensionis*, shows that the cardinal traded in or sold some of the 235 reliquaries he owned in 1520 and simultaneously acquired many new ones, as by 1527 his collection totaled 353 reliquaries.[1]

Among these later acquisitions was a remarkable reliquary statue of Saint Maurice, the Roman legionnaire and Christian martyr, that was deeply venerated in the archdiocese of Magdeburg, of which Albrecht was the archbishop and as such the territorial ruler from 1513 to 1545. The statue was prominently exhibited in Halle, the town in which he had his palace, in a church that Albrecht had succeeded in elevating to the status of a collegiate church, had completely renovated, and had richly furnished so that his subjects and guests would experience the full measure of his piety and magnificence.

Fully illuminated by thirteen main lamps and seven subsidiary ones, prominently exhibited near the high altar, and installed on a pillow of brocade silk, the reliquary statue made a strong impression on visitors, not least because of its scale and the lifesize silver armor that formed most of it. The armor, of a type intended for field use, was designed in a style popular in the German-speaking lands during the first three decades of

FIG. 39 Workshop of Lucas Cranach the Elder (Simon Franck?). *Reliquary Statue of Saint Maurice*, from the *Liber ostensionis*. German, 1526/27. Pen and wash on parchment. Sheet: 13¾ x 10 in. (35 x 25.5 cm). Hofbibliothek, Aschaffenburg, Germany (Sign. Ms. 14, fol. 227v)

the sixteenth century. Reports from people who saw it and the terms chosen to designate it in documents from the period make it clear enough that the armor was a real one, not a sculpted imitation in polychrome wood or metal.[2] Certain telling constructional features also support this idea, including the correct articulation of its various elements with multiple lames and the presence of fastening devices such as a hook and eye on the greaves to secure their hinged halves together on the inner side and attach the sabatons at the bottom. In fact, a definitive confirmation that the armor consisted of genuine, separable elements is provided by evidence that the right vambrace, the couter of which would have extended into a wing on

the outer side to guard the inside of the elbow, had visibly been taken off and inadvertently remounted on the wrong side of the body by the time it was depicted in the *Liber ostensionis*, with the result that the wing then incorrectly faced the torso.

The panel of Saint Maurice is a fragment of one of no fewer than sixteen altarpieces that the artist Lucas Cranach the Elder and his workshop painted from 1519 to 1525 for Halle's collegiate church, almost all of which are now lost. It represents the same armor recorded in the *Liber ostensionis* (fig. 39), and in some ways supplies even more information about its features, for example by carefully reproducing the cusped line with stylized trefoils that commonly adorned the edges of luxury examples from the period, especially those made or decorated in Augsburg (see cats. 82, 131).[3] It thus appears to have been based on a study of the reliquary's armor rather than having been copied from the comparatively more precise, though perhaps more selective, illustration in the *Liber ostensionis*.

The painting and drawing provide precious information about the origin of the armor, for they show that its pauldrons were adorned with the gilded cross of Saint Andrew, flints, and fire steels, and the upper part of its breastplate was similarly decorated with a gilded sheepskin. The presence of these badges and the pendant of the Burgundian Order of the Golden Fleece are hallmarks of armor made for the Habsburgs, who as sovereigns of the order had adopted them as part of their insignia (see cats. 75–77, 82, 96, 110).

Of the four Habsburgs who could have conceivably owned this armor—Maximilian I, Philip I, Charles V, and Ferdinand I— the first is the only one known to have desired and actually commissioned a full armor of silver. Mentioned in his notebooks as likely to cost the fabulous sum of a thousand florins, the armor was ordered in 1516 from Kolman Helmschmid, his court armorer in Augsburg, and an unnamed goldsmith through the services of the humanist Conrad Peutinger. Since Maximilian failed to fully pay for it, the armor was found in Kolman's possession in April 1519, almost four months after the emperor's death, and although it was finished the armorer would not surrender it until he was paid what he was still owed for its manufacture.[4] Charles V, who had initiated the search for the armor, must have been able to give Kolman satisfaction, for on the day preceding his coronation as King of the Romans in Aachen on October 23, 1520, he solemnly entered the city in a long procession, accompanied by Albrecht of Brandenburg, and wearing a gold-and-silver armor that was described as dazzling.[5] In the absence of documentary evidence that Charles ever commissioned an armor of silver for

himself, and considering that the preparation for his coronation is recorded in great detail in the book of accounts of his chief treasurer in the Low Countries (where he sojourned several months before going to Aachen), there can be little doubt that the armor he wore on the glorious circumstance was the one that had originally been ordered by his grandfather.

Further support for the view that the reliquary's armor is likely to have been that commissioned by Maximilian for himself is provided by a fragmentary drawing, which is annotated on the verso with the words "design for his majesty's silver armor."[6] Believed to be a preliminary design by Gilg Sesselschreiber, Maximilian's court painter in Innsbruck, for a statue of the emperor that would become part of his elaborate mausoleum, the drawing shows a fluted armor constructed with the same distinctive type of one-piece rectangular tassets and, more important, decorated with comparable and very unconventional rows of gems set within bands along the edges of its elements. The slight discrepancies between the drawing and the reliquary's armor—observable in the form of the elbow defenses, the fluting of the surface, and the treatment of the turned edges—suggest that Sesselschreiber did not sketch Maximilian's armor from life, as it was still being made in Augsburg. Rather, he may have relied on one of the multiple and seemingly divergent designs that had been supplied to Kolman in 1516 and about which Peutinger had requested clearer instructions.[7] Since there still was uncertainty about the armor's final design, and since it never left Kolman's workshop during Maximilian's lifetime, it is hardly surprising that the completed armor would have had the same character as—and yet a slightly different form and surface decoration than—that which Sesselschreiber had represented in his drawing.

If, as seems likely, Maximilian's silver armor is the one that Albrecht of Brandenburg came to own and repurposed into a spectacular reliquary, Charles's coronation provides the likeliest explanation for its change of ownership and for the fact that the printed catalogue of the cardinal's collection makes no mention of it.[8] In addition to being archbishop of Magdeburg, Albrecht was prince elector of Mainz (r. 1514–1545), and as such one of the seven princes who had elected Charles as Maximilian's successor on June 28, 1519. Thought to have initially been in favor of another candidate, King Francis I of France, and capable of winning over the other electors, Albrecht was a highly influential man. Charles was indebted to him for his ultimate support of his candidacy, and following the coronation ceremony he publicly gave him marks of esteem.[9] As Maximilian had presented Albrecht with a highly symbolic object, the papal presentation sword that he had received from Leo X,[10] Charles may have given the powerful cardinal the costly silver armor as a token of gratitude—too late, however, for it to be readily transformed into a reliquary and included in the *Hallesches Heiltumsbuch*, which was published two months later. The gift may have included the standard held by Maurice's reliquary statue, since it suitably features the single-headed eagle bearing the King of the Romans' crown on its head as well as the badges of the Order of the Golden Fleece.

An extravagant object decorated with pearls and other gemstones, the armor proved too valuable to remain intact long, despite its distinguished provenance and the central place it held in Albrecht's collegiate church and the veneration of the saint. Pressed by creditors, the cardinal sold it along with many other objects in 1540. A year later, when it had again already changed hands, it was melted down and the gems, which had evidently been carefully removed, were repurposed, completing the destruction of one of Maximilian's most ambitious projects.[11]   PT

REFERENCES: Redlich 1900, pp. 165–66; Steinmann 1968; Ainsworth, Hindriks, and Terjanian 2015

1. On these two catalogues, see Redlich 1900, pp. 238–57; Eichberger 1996; Ainsworth, Hindriks, and Terjanian 2015, pp. 18–22.
2. On visitors' impressions, see Redlich 1900, p. 165, suppl., p. 112*; Smith 2006, p. 37. On the documents, see Bösch 1887–89, p. 127; Redlich 1900, pp. 336–37, suppl., pp. 140*–43*, nos. 31a, 31b.
3. For these details, see Ainsworth, Hindriks, and Terjanian 2015, p. 14, figs. 13, 14.
4. On this commission, see Zimerman 1885, p. LXXXIV, no. 2956; Boeheim 1891, pp. 177–78.
5. On the gift of the armor, see Steinmann 1968, pp. 98–100; Ziermann 2001, pp. 174–76; Smith 2006, p. 30; for an account stating that Charles's armor was made of gold and silver, see Maurus 1523; Meyer 1781, vol. 1, p. 435.
6. The drawing is in a private collection; see Ainsworth, Hindriks, and Terjanian 2015, p. 27, and p. 28, fig. 34.
7. Boeheim 1891, p. 177.
8. *Hallesche Heiltumbuch* 1520/2001.
9. On the cardinal's relationship with Charles, see Hennes 1858, pp. 89–99, 130; Térey 1892, pp. 65–66; Redlich 1900, pp. 42–43, 163–64; Weicker 1901.
10. On the sword, see Hennes 1858, pp. 69–70; Bösch 1887–89, p. 126; Térey 1892, p. 12; Redlich 1900, p. 280; Ainsworth, Hindriks, and Terjanian 2015, p. 29, and p. 30, fig. 36.
11. On the sale and destruction of the armor, see Bösch 1887–89, p. 127; Redlich 1900, pp. 336–37, suppl., pp. 140*–43*, nos. 31a, 31b.

Design for an Equestrian Monument of Emperor Maximilian I

Hans Burgkmair (1473–1531)
South German (Augsburg), ca. 1508–9
Pen in brown-black and gray wash on paper
16 15/16 x 11 3/16 in. (43.1 x 28.4 cm)
Albertina Museum, Vienna (22447)

Hans Burgkmair, who in 1508 had completed the design for the profile equestrian woodcut portrait of Maximilian I as newly crowned emperor (cat. 107), was soon called upon to design an imposing, three-dimensional representation. Assigned to "Maister Gregori," the leading Augsburg sculptor Gregor Erhart, the statue was planned as the first full-scale equestrian portrait in northern Europe.[1] The proposed site, in Augsburg, lay near the church of Saints Ulrich and Afra, where Maximilian had in 1500 laid the foundation stone of the choir. The stone to be carved for the monument is documented in 1509, and Erhart would have prepared a wood model, now lost. Unfortunately, the untimely death in 1510 of the sponsoring abbot and the reallocation of the designated funds brought the project to a halt.

In Burgkmair's design, the sturdiness of the stone statue was assured by the four-square stance of the armored horse.[2] The emperor appears upright, in contemporary armor, one of his major interests (see cats. 114, 115), and he bears a magnificent broadsword, similar to his actual ceremonial sword, which was made in 1496 by Hans Sumersperger and decorated with the heraldry of his territories.[3] In full regalia, he wears the imperial crown; at his feet sit the imperial orb and a scepter. The office of Holy Roman Emperor is reaffirmed by the meticulous italic lettering by the noted Augsburg calligrapher Leonhard Wagner. Added to the drawing as a planned Latin inscription for the sculpture, it proclaims Maximilian by his rank: "Imp[erator] Cae[sar] Maximilianus Aug[ustus]."

This beautiful drawing, which was anticipated by several smaller sketches, is a highly finished presentation piece executed in both pen and brush. Scholars speculate about whether Burgkmair managed to travel, most likely about 1507, to Italy. There he might have seen the large bronze equestrian portrait of the military commander Gattamelata by Donatello in Padua (1453), although it seems more likely that the artist used Andrea del Verrocchio's bronze of Bartolomeo Colleoni in Venice (1488) as the model for his woodcut *Saint George* (cat. 106), the pendant to his 1508 equestrian profile of Maximilian.[4] The ultimate surviving ancient equestrian monument is the bronze

Imp·Cæ·Maximilianus Aug·Chori huius primum
a fundamentis lapidem posuit exædificationē
quæ eius solita liberalitate innit.
Ann·M·D·III·kls Julia.

Marcus Aurelius on the Capitoline Hill in Rome, but Germany also had medieval precedents for mounted imperial portraits, principally the *Magdeburg Rider*, a crowned public statue of Emperor Otto the Great.   LS

REFERENCES: Habich 1913; Halm 1962, pp. 127–30, 162; Falk 1968, pp. 71–73, ill. no. 44; Smith 1994, pp. 318–19, fig. 278; Christof Metzger in *Emperor Maximilian I* 2012, pp. 348–53, no. 111, ill.

1. Leonardo da Vinci's equestrian monument project in Milan for Ludovico Sforza, never completed, would have been familiar to Maximilian, who married the duke's niece, Bianca Maria Sforza of Milan, in 1493; see *Leonardo da Vinci* 2003, especially pp. 426–35, nos. 63, 64 (entries by Carmen C. Bambach).
2. For the armored horse and rider in the era of Maximilian, see Pyhrr, La Rocca, and Breiding 2005; Terjanian 2011 (for this drawing, see p. 15, fig. 12).
3. Thomas 1950–51/1977.
4. Janson 1967/1973.

Cat. 162

Triumphal Procession of Maximilian I
Albrecht Altdorfer (ca. 1480–1538) and his workshop
South German (Regensburg), ca. 1512–15
Watercolor and gouache on parchment
Each panel: 17¹¹/₁₆ x 37⁷/₁₆ in. (45 x 95 cm)
Albertina Museum, Vienna (25220–25222, 25247–25249)

The *Triumphal Procession of Maximilian I* is a magnificent painted cycle originally composed of 109 parchment panels.[1] The extant sixty panels, housed together in Vienna, measure a remarkable 176.5 feet (53.8 meters); complete the *Triumphal Procession* was more than 328 feet (over 100 meters) long. The *Triumphal Procession* is one of the most ambitious commissions by Maximilian I to preserve his fame as part of his *Gedächtnis*, or memorial, and it

follows the process by which many of the other imperial projects were executed. The first mention of a triumphal chariot is found in the memorial book that Maximilian kept between 1505 and 1508,[2] but the complex written program conceived by Johannes Stabius for the *Triumphal Procession* was dictated by Maximilian himself to his private secretary Marx Treitzsaurwein in 1512. A preliminary sketch is believed to have been made by Jörg Kölderer, and the project was then contracted out to a roster of artists who had worked on other imperial commissions, such as Albrecht Altdorfer, Hans Burgkmair, Albrecht Dürer, and Hans Springinklee. Unlike the woodcut version of the *Triumphal Procession*, this monumental painted miniature, akin to Maximilian's *Prayer Book* (1513–ca. 1515) and illuminated copies of *Freydal* (cats. 39–43), was likely meant as a display copy for the emperor's personal use.[3]

The panels range in style and quality, and different materials were used to create the scenes—some are made from carbon-based inks, others from iron-gall inks—and so the attribution of the ensemble has been a source of debate. In 1966 Franz Winzinger settled the argument by assigning them to the Regensburg artist Albrecht Altdorfer, a prolific printmaker and draftsman as well as a talented painter, who produced extremely fine and delicately wrought works.[4] Altdorfer was favored by Maximilian and had participated in other imperial projects, such as the *History of Frederick and Maximilian* (*Historia Frederici et Maximiliani*; ca. 1508–10), *Prayer Book*, and *Arch of Honor* (cat. 165). In concert with what must have been a large and efficient workshop, Altdorfer is believed to have completed the *Triumphal Procession* sometime between 1512 and 1515, a period during which Stabius took up residence in Regensburg, perhaps to oversee the project.

Stabius's program stresses Maximilian's legitimacy and the historical continuity of his reign over the Holy Roman Empire, ideas that reappear in other visual propaganda. The doctrine of imperial migration known as the *translatio imperii* did not begin with Maximilian; it had a long history. However, Maximilian's large-scale projects, including the *Arch of Honor* and the *Triumphal Procession*, rely on the premise that the modern Holy Roman Empire of the German Nation is an uninterrupted continuation of the ancient Roman one that became Christian through the fourth-century conversion of Emperor Constantine.[5] This doctrine not only dictated the forms that Maximilian's monuments took—the triumphal arch and procession in homage to symbols that were central to ancient Roman pageantry—but also the content of those monuments with the emphases placed on military might and on conveying an elaborate and very public display of power. The

Triumphal Procession includes a dazzling portrayal of the spectacle of courtly life: drummers, pipers, hunters of different kinds of game, a court cook, a barber, a tailor, a shoemaker, minstrels, jesters, fencers, jousters, and an array of artillery soldiers with state-of-the-art weaponry populate the scene. There are also standard-bearers of the Habsburg and Burgundian lands, depictions of key marriages and battle scenes, and a lavish chariot filled with Maximilian and his immediate family, underscoring the importance he placed on family and the supremacy of the Habsburg dynasty. FS

REFERENCES: Winzinger 1966; Winzinger 1972–73; Lukas Madersbacher in *Hispania—Austria* 1992, pp. 330–31, under no. 144; Eva Michel in *Emperor Maximilian I* 2012, pp. 224–37, no. 53, ill.; Michel 2012

1. The existence of two complete copies in the Österreichische National-bibliothek, Vienna, establishes the entirety of the procession and proves that it was together and extant at least until the early seventeenth century. For more on the copies, see *Emperor Maximilian I* 2012, pp. 244–47, no. 54 (entry by Eva Michel), pp. 248–49, no. 54a (entry by Susanna Zapke).
2. Hofkammerarchiv, Vienna, "Gedenkbuch" (1505–8), fol. 92r.
3. The woodcut edition was executed by Altdorfer, Burgkmair, Dürer, Springinklee, and other unknown artists likely in Dürer's workshop. For a description of the project, see Mielke 1997, pp. 153–80; Eva Michel in *Emperor Maximilian I* 2012, pp. 268–71, no. 68, ill. Dürer's *Triumphal Chariot* stems from this commission but was removed and done independent of it. See cat. 164 in this volume.
4. Winzinger 1966.
5. For more on the concept of *translatio imperii*, see Silver 2008, especially pp. 80–81.

Cat. 163

The Trophy Wagon, from The Triumphal Procession of Maximilian I

Hans Springinklee (ca. 1495–after 1522)
Block cut by Jan de Bonn (active 16th century)
South German (Nuremberg), 1516–18
Woodblock
H. 15¹⁄₁₆ in. (38.3 cm), W. 14¹⁵⁄₁₆ in. (38 cm), D. 1¹⁄₁₆ in. (2.8 cm)
Albertina Museum, Vienna (HO2006/271)

In order to secure the legacy of his fame and accomplishments for posterity, Maximilian I recognized that he needed to disseminate his memorial projects to a broad audience; thus, he commissioned a print version of the *Triumphal Procession* alongside the deluxe painted panels that Albrecht Altdorfer and his workshop produced for his private use (see cat. 162). As the task of designing and cutting the necessary woodblocks was enormous, multiple artists were hired to undertake the work. This woodblock is one of twenty-two that the Nuremberg artist Hans Springinklee contributed to the project.[1]

Cut by Jan de Bonn, the block features a luxurious wagon loaded with glorious spoils of war, including armor elements for man and horse, swords, and an array of lances and military standards. The splendor of these objects is purposeful, as it lends greater weight to the significance of their capture. Although they look randomly piled up at the bottom of the wagon, the trophies are otherwise neatly arranged around a central mast to form a pleasing, symmetrical composition. The palms and wreaths of laurels visible above them suitably celebrate the deeds and merits of the victor.

The idea for the processional display of splendid trophies of war originates from the rediscovery of a similar Roman tradition, and it is characteristic of the Renaissance fascination with ancient Rome. However, the image is not purely allegorical; it is also likely a reference to Maximilian's documented practice of collecting trophies of war, examples of which include an infantry shield taken from the Bohemians at the battle of Wenzenbach near Regensburg in 1504, which was supplemented with an inscription recording the circumstance of its capture (see fig. 4).[2] PT

REFERENCE: Schestag 1883, p. 179

1. On this project, see Schestag 1883; Eva Michel in *Emperor Maximilian I* 2012, pp. 268–71, no. 68.
2. Musée de l'Armée, Paris (I.12); Reverseau 1982, p. 42, and p. 43, ill. no. 72.

The Triumphal Chariot of Maximilian I

Albrecht Dürer (1471–1528)
South German (Nuremberg), probably finished ca. 1518, published 1522
Woodcut from eight blocks
Each sheet: 19½ x 13¼ in. (49.5 x 33.7 cm)
The Metropolitan Museum of Art, New York, Gift of Junius Spencer Morgan, 1919 (19.73.226–.233)

In the same way that Maximilian I firmly controlled the creation of the visual elements of the *Arch of Honor* (cat. 165), he closely supervised the production of its complement, the *Triumphal Procession of Maximilian I*. The *Triumphal Procession* was to encompass the entertainments of court life, territories, marriages, wars, ancestors, imperial majesty, and princes, as well as soldiers, trophies, and captives, following the ancient Roman imperial model. Initial ideas for the *Triumphal Procession* were dictated by the emperor to his private secretary Marx Treitzsaurwein in 1512. A manuscript version, likely made for Maximilian, with two full-page illuminations and the dictated text of the imaginary procession is housed in the Österreichische Nationalbibliothek in Vienna.[1] The project was then delegated to court artist Jörg Kölderer, who made preliminary line drawings and employed a team of artists to flesh out the ideas, seeking the help of Albrecht Altdorfer in Regensburg, Hans Burgkmair in Augsburg, and Albrecht Dürer in Nuremberg. At this moment Dürer and his workshop were busy with the *Arch of Honor*, so the artistic coordinator in Augsburg, city secretary Conrad Peutinger, assigned the bulk of the work for the *Triumphal Procession* to Burgkmair, entrusting him with the written copy of the program.

The idea for a triumphal procession emerged at the same moment as that for the *Arch of Honor*. Both speak to Maximilian's obsession with the notion of *translatio imperii*, the doctrine of imperial migration whereby power is transferred from one great empire to the next, and both revive ancient Roman imperial celebrations in the form of triumphal arches that were erected and paraded through after significant military victories. For Maximilian, the ancient Roman claims to world domination were sanctified through the fourth-century conversion of Emperor Constantine, when they were fused with the religious truth and universal supremacy of Christianity. Bolstered by his court genealogists, historians, and humanists, Maximilian traced an unbroken line from Julius Caesar through Charlemagne, situating himself as the inheritor of an august lineage.

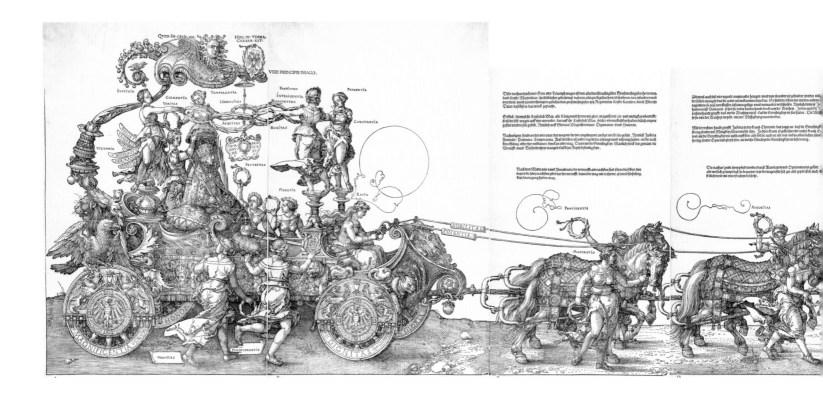

Like most of Maximilian's other printed monuments, the *Triumphal Procession* was left unfinished at his death in 1519. Between 1512 and 1515, Altdorfer and his workshop completed a painted version of the *Triumphal Procession*, likely meant as a display copy for the emperor (cat. 162), as well as thirty-two woodcuts for the printed version that would broadcast Maximilian's *Gedächtnis*, or memorial. This version was to have two hundred prints, but only 137 were executed. Along with those made by Altdorfer, Burgkmair produced sixty-seven, including the first fifty-seven in the sequence. Additionally, Hans Springinklee created twenty-two; Leonhard Beck seven; Wolf Huber five; Hans Schäufelein two; and Dürer two. The blocks were cut between 1516 and 1518, but the first edition of the fragmentary procession was printed in 1526 by Ferdinand I, Maximilian's grandson and heir in the Habsburg regions, who also supplemented and printed the *Arch of Honor* in the same year.

Dürer's *Triumphal Chariot* was to be the centerpiece of the *Triumphal Procession*. The iconographic program of Dürer's woodcut, however, deviates from Maximilian's original conception, which Treitzsaurwein noted was to show the emperor with his closest family members, including his two wives as well as his children and their spouses. This program is followed by Altdorfer in his miniature and by Dürer in his

initial drawing for the chariot, executed in about 1512.[2] Dürer's eventual woodcut presents a different concept developed by the artist with his friend and mentor, the Nuremberg humanist Willibald Pirckheimer. Maximilian only learned of the new concept through the Nuremberg provost Melchior Pfinzing, and he wrote to Pirckheimer in February 1518 to ask for a drawing to be sent to him immediately;[3] this pen-and-ink drawing with watercolor retains the larger chariot holding Maximilian's family, but it also includes many of the allegorical aspects of Pirckheimer's newer plan.[4] In Pirckheimer's letter to Maximilian, he appealed to the emperor as follows:

Most Gracious Lord, this chariot, which I invented, need not necessarily remain as it is. Your Majesty being most knowledgeable in such matters, if it should prove unsuitable it can easily be altered, corrected, or even redone. I am, however, humbly confident that my invention, which is no ordinary triumph, but one of philosophy and morality, will not displease Your Majesty, and that my diligent research and sincere loyalty will continue undiminished no matter what faults might be found in this, my invention. . . . Most gracious Lord, the reason for the delay in the dispatch of this chariot is the following: it has taken a long time to arrange the virtues in proper order. Were it not for the

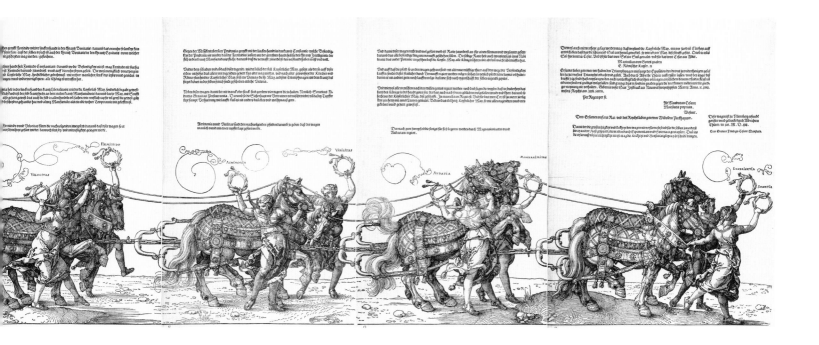

exemplary diligence of Your Majesty's servant Albrecht Dürer, and for the fact that he took this matter into his own hands, the project would have taken yet longer and would have been even more difficult.[5]

Maximilian replied to Pirckheimer that he was satisfied with the imagery and its explanation, and that he was looking forward to seeing it accompanying "our 'Triumph.'"[6] Ultimately, because of mounting frustrations with the pace of publishing the rest of the *Triumphal Procession*, Dürer, at his own expense, published the *Triumphal Chariot* as a stand-alone monument to the late emperor in 1522, annotated with German inscriptions by Pirckheimer. In 1523 a Latin edition was printed, followed by six more before 1600, attesting to the popularity of both Maximilian and Dürer. The *Triumphal Chariot* was also used by Georg Pencz and other artists connected to Dürer's workshop in about 1520 for a mural on the north wall of the great hall of Nuremberg's city hall.[7]

In Dürer's woodcut version, Maximilian is shown seated without his family, wearing the imperial robes and crown of the Holy Roman Emperor. He is accompanied by numerous allegorical figures. Reason guides his magnificent carriage, while Fame, Magnificence, Dignity, and Honor make up the four wheels that ensure his successful journey. Justice,

Courage, Wisdom, and Temperance—the four Cardinal (or "angelic," as Pirckheimer wrote) Virtues—are arranged on pedestals that ring the emperor; they hold an intertwined laurel wreath of honor above Maximilian's head, who is doubly crowned by Victory. Above the chariot is a baldachin, a pennant with the imperial arms, and an inscription reading, "What the sun is in the heavens, the emperor is on earth." Dürer and Pirckheimer thus deemphasize the importance of genealogy and focus instead on the timeless glorification of this truly Renaissance emperor.   FS

REFERENCES: Smith 1983, pp. 120–21, no. 26; Thomas Schauerte in Schoch, Mende, and Scherbaum 2001–4, vol. 2 (2002), pp. 470–83, no. 257; Silver 2008, pp. 26–27, and pp. 28–29, fig. 11; Eva Michel in *Emperor Maximilian I* 2012, pp. 258–61, no. 60

1. Österreichische Nationalbibliothek, Vienna, Cod. 2835.
2. Altdorfer, Albertina Museum, Vienna (25246); Dürer, Albertina Museum (3140).
3. Maximilian I to Willibald Pirckheimer, Augsburg, February 5, 1518, quoted in Strauss 1974, vol. 3, p. 1700; cited by Eva Michel in *Emperor Maximilian I* 2012, p. 258.
4. Dürer, Albertina Museum (685).
5. Pirckheimer to Maximilian I, Nuremberg, [early 1518]; Rupprich 1956, p. 261, no. 40; English translation, Strauss 1974, vol. 3, pp. 1700–1701 (quotation on p. 1700).
6. Maximilian I to Pirckheimer, Innsbruck, March 29, 1518; Rupprich 1956, p. 261, no. 41; English translation, Strauss 1974, vol. 3, p. 1701.
7. For more on the mural, see Mende 1979, pp. 224–45.

QVOD·IN·CELIS·SOL·   HOC·IN·TERRA·
CAESAR·EST·

VERI PRINCIPIS IMAGO.

IVSTICIA   CLEMENTIA   TEMPERANTIA   FORTITVDO
VERITAS   LIBERALITAS   INTELICENTIA
MANSVETVDO

AEQVITAS

GALLIS
VNGARIS
ELVETIS
BOHEMIS
GERMANIS
VENETIS

VICTORIA   BONITAS

IN·M   REG
ANV   IS·E·
DE   ST
I

SECVRITAS

FIDENTIA

HONOR

MAGNIFICENTIA   DIG

GRAVITAS   PERSEVERANTIA

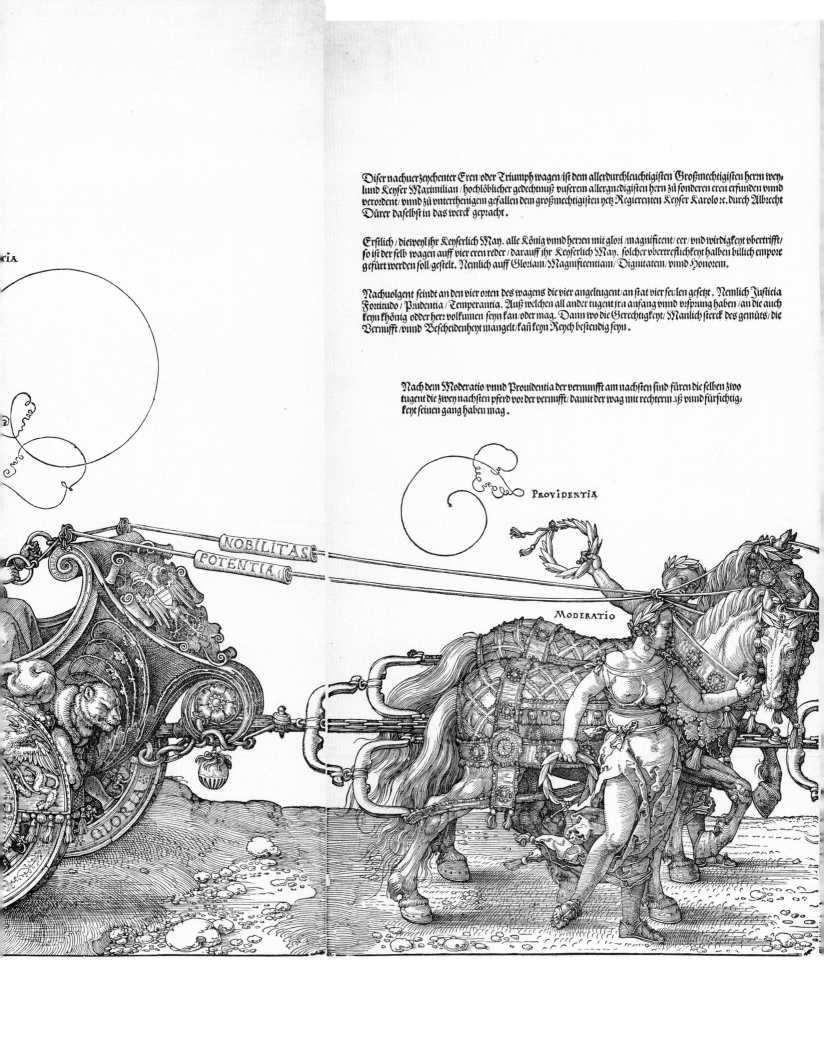

Difer nacher zeychenter Eren/oder Triumph wagen/ift dem allerdurchleuchtigiften Großmechtigiften herrn wey,
lund Keyfer Maximilian/hochlöblicher gedechtnuß vuferem allergnedigiften herrn zů fonderen eren erfunden vnnd
verordent/vnnd zů vnterthenigem gefallen dem großmechtigiften yetz Regierenten Keyfer Karolo ec. durch Albrecht
Dürer dafelbft in das werck geracht.

Erftlich/dieweyl ihr Keyferlich May. alle König vnnd herren mit glori/magnificent/eer/vnd wirdigkeyt vbertrifft/
fo ift der felb wagen auff vier eren reder/darauff ihr Keyferlich May. folcher vbertreflichkeyt halben billich empore
gefürt werden foll/geftelt. Nemlich auff Gloriam/Magnificentiam/Dignitatem/vnnd Honorem.

Nachuolgent feindt an den vier orten des wagens die vier angeltugent/an ftat vier feulen gefetzt. Nemlich Jufticia
Fortitudo/Prudentia/Temperantia. Auß welchen all ander tugent jra anfang vnnd vrfprung haben/an die auch
keyn khönig odder herr volkumen feyn kan/oder mag. Dann wo die Gerechtigkeyt/Manlich fterck des gemüts/die
Vernufft/vnnd Befcheidenheyt mangelt/kañ keyn Reych beftendig feyn.

Nach dem Moderatio/vnnd Prouidentia der vernufft am nachften find/füren die felben zwo
tugent die zwey nachften pferd vor der vernufft/damit der wag mit rechterm .aß vnnd fürfichtig,
keyt feinen gang haben mag.

PROVIDENTIA

NOBILITAS

POTENTIA

MODERATIO

Cat. 165

Arch of Honor

Albrecht Dürer (1471–1528), Albrecht Altdorfer (ca. 1480–1538),
Hans Springinklee (ca. 1495–after 1522), and Wolf Traut
(1486–1520)
Blocks cut by Hieronymus Andreae (ca. 1485–1556)
Written by Johannes Stabius (1450–1522)
Calligraphy by Johann Neudörffer (1497–1563)
South German, dated 1515, 1799 edition
42 woodcuts; 2 etchings
Overall size: 11 ft. 7⅜ in. x 9 ft. 9½ in. (354 x 298.5 cm)
National Gallery of Art, Washington, D.C., Gift of David P. Tunick
and Elizabeth S. Tunick, in honor of the appointment of Andrew
Robison as Andrew W. Mellon Senior Curator (1991.200.1)

Selected Sheets from the *Arch of Honor*

Albrecht Altdorfer (ca. 1480–1538), Albrecht Dürer (1471–1528),
and Hans Springinklee (ca. 1495–after 1522)
South German, dated 1515, 1517–18 edition
9 woodcuts with letterpress
Dimensions in order: 18¼ x 24¼ in. (46.4 x 61.6 cm); 18³⁄₁₆ x
24¹³⁄₁₆ in. (46.2 x 63 cm); 18⅜ x 24⁹⁄₁₆ in. (46.7 x 62.4 cm);
18¼ x 24¹⁵⁄₁₆ in. (46.3 x 63.3 cm); 18³⁄₁₆ x 24⁷⁄₁₆ in. (46.2 x 62 cm);
18¼ x 24¹⁵⁄₁₆ in. (46.4 x 63.4 cm); 18¹⁄₁₆ x 24¹⁵⁄₁₆ in. (45.9 x
63.4 cm); 17¹⁵⁄₁₆ x 24 in. (45.6 x 60.9 cm); 18⁵⁄₁₆ x 24⅝ in.
(46.5 x 62.6 cm)
The Metropolitan Museum of Art, New York, Harry Brisbane Dick
Fund, 1928 (28.82.22, .25, .27, .28, .31, .37, .38, .40, .42)

The *Arch of Honor* is the *summa* of Maximilian I's ambitions.
The visual and textual program of this monument is composed of thirty-six sheets of large folio paper that have been
printed with roughly 195 woodblocks. It shows Maximilian I's
ancestry, his territories, his extended kinship, his predecessors
as emperor, his deeds and accomplishments, his personal tal-
ents and interests, and thus his glory. It combines elements
from many of his other imperial commissions, including the
Genealogy (cat. 166), the *Patron Saints of Austria* (cat. 101),
Freydal (cats. 39–55), the *Weisskunig* (cats. 114–17) and the
Triumphal Procession (cat. 162). Yet, unlike any of Maximilian's
other large printed testaments of his personality and reign, the
Arch of Honor is the only one that was completed and pub-
lished during his lifetime. In the autobiographically inspired
Weisskunig, the emperor notably wrote:

> He who during his life provides no remembrance for him-
> self has no remembrance after his death and the same

person is forgotten with the tolling of the bell, and therefore
the money that I spend on remembrance is not lost; but the
money that is spared on my remembrance, that is a suppres-
sion of my future remembrance, and what I do not accom-
plish during my life for my memory will not be made up for
after my death, neither by thee nor others.[1]

Maximilian strongly believed in the need for monuments and
memorials (*Gedächtnis*), even those made of the ephemeral
substance of paper, to convey his lasting fame. He engaged
with historians, genealogists, astronomers, and humanists,
as well as many other kinds of scholars, to create a visual and
literary record of his accomplishments. Many of the artists in
his employ, such as Albrecht Altdorfer, Hans Burgkmair, and
Albrecht Dürer, worked on various imperial projects throughout their careers.

The woodblocks for the *Arch of Honor* were designed
mainly in Nuremberg by Dürer with his apprentices Wolf
Traut and Hans Springinklee, though the two flanking towers
are by Altdorfer. The extended descriptive texts by Johannes
Stabius were fabricated by the calligrapher Johann Neudörffer,
who also worked closely with Dürer. All of the woodblocks
were professionally cut by Hieronymus Andreae. According
to a letter that Stabius wrote to Charles V in 1519–20, a first
edition or a large group of proofs was printed in Nuremberg
about 1517–18. Thomas Schauerte recently contended that
Stabius's mention in the letter of "around 700 copies" referred
to sheets and not complete sets, so the emperor likely had
twenty complete sets after the first printing.[2] These were supplemented and distributed by Ferdinand I, Maximilian's
grandson, in 1526. Only a handful of complete first editions
survive, some with hand-coloring and additions of gold, such
as those in Braunschweig and Vienna.[3] A second edition
was printed in Vienna in 1559, by Ferdinand's son Charles II,
archduke of Austria.[4] Most of the blocks are housed in the
Albertina Museum, Vienna; the one remaining block is in the
Österreichisches Museum für angewandte Kunst, Vienna.[5]

The overall program for the *Arch of Honor* was devised by
Maximilian with his private secretary Marx Treitzsaurwein in
1512. The literary program was then further developed by
Stabius and given to Jörg Kölderer, who prepared the initial
design of the overall architecture. The visual program was delegated to Dürer. Stabius, Kölderer, and Dürer are celebrated
as the makers of the *Arch of Honor* by the inclusion of their
coats of arms on the step of the platform in the lower right corner. The date 1515 appears twice on the work, but these are
likely references to when the initial designs were completed

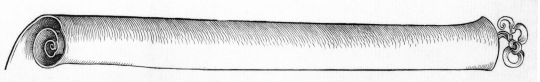

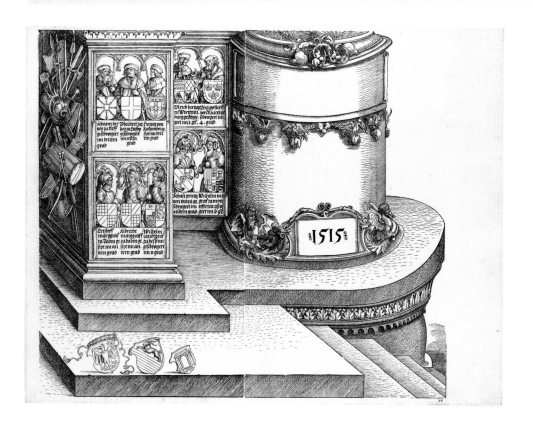

and not when the blocks were cut. Documentary evidence suggests that revisions and work continued on the project into 1517, particularly on the central family tree, and always with the intervention of Maximilian himself.[6]

This *Ehrenpforte*, or *Arch of Honor*, as Stabius describes it in the inscription below the edifice, was conceived and constructed after the triumphal arches of the Roman emperors, such as the Arch of Constantine in the Forum in Rome. Although Maximilian's arch contains three doorways, like its ancient marble predecessors, its structure and program deviate from these models. The central Portal of Honor and Power represents Maximilian's ancestors as well as his children and grandchildren, all surrounded by the coats of arms of the territories claimed by the Habsburg dynasty. The doorway to the right, called the Portal of Nobility, shows Maximilian's royal cousins and the central importance of diplomacy and alliance through marriage. On the left is the Portal of Praise, in which depictions of Roman emperors denote the origins of Maximilian's imperial majesty. Given pride of place in the vast and imaginative family tree—which includes ancient and legendary figures—are the previous Habsburg emperors. Beyond family ties, twenty-four large scenes represent Maximilian's worthy deeds, many of which are military events that focus on his strength and valor. These battles for legitimacy and land, as well as the hard-won alliances that followed, confirm the emperor's strength and illustrious accomplishments in office. Altdorfer's twin towers, as Stabius emphasizes, show Maximilian's own personal interests and qualities, such as his piety and desire to launch a Crusade, his fascination with heraldry and knightly orders, and his love of tournaments and masquerades.

The *Arch of Honor* culminates in a so-called *mysterium* at its pinnacle. In this portrait of the emperor, he is seated on a throne surrounded by animals and symbolic images. The animals are derived from the *Hieroglyphica,* a second- or third-century Greek text by Horus Apollo. About 1513, when Dürer was enlisted to work on the *Arch of Honor*, he was also making drawings for an edition of the *Hieroglyphica* that was being translated into Latin by his friend and mentor Willibald Pirckheimer and was to be dedicated to Maximilian. The *mysterium* mirrors the frontispiece to Dürer and Pirckheimer's manuscript that was presented to Maximilian in Linz in 1514. The hieroglyphic animals that surround Maximilian form a rebus that express the ideas communicated throughout the work regarding the emperor's ancient lineage, courage, power, and desire for lasting fame.   FS

REFERENCES: Schauerte 2001; Thomas Schauerte in Schoch, Mende, and Scherbaum 2001–4, vol. 2 (2002), pp. 393–412, no. 238; Schauerte in *Emperor Maximilian I* 2012, pp. 373–76, no. 124

1. Cited and translated by Larry Silver in Silver 1994, p. 45.
2. Thomas Schauerte in *Emperor Maximilian I* 2012, p. 374. In this entry Schauerte refers to his original conception of the first edition as seven hundred complete sets. For this earlier idea, see Schauerte 2001, p. 421.
3. Herzog Anton Ulrich-Museum, Braunschweig (ADürer WB 2.279); Albertina Museum, Vienna (DG1935/973). There is a list of first editions in Schoch, Mende, and Scherbaum 2001–4, vol. 2 (2002), p. 394. It does not include the full set in The Metropolitan Museum of Art, New York (28.82.7-42). This first edition is also missing from Schauerte 2001, pp. 451–55.
4. A third edition was printed in 1799 by Adam von Bartsch, the artist and art historian who advised Duke Albert of Saxe-Teschen, the founder of the Albertina Museum, on his collection.
5. Albertina Museum, Vienna (HO2006/1-169); Österreichisches Museum für angewandte Kunst, Vienna (F. 447).
6. Letters between Maximilian and Stabius trace the debates over all kinds of details, including genealogy. For more on the correspondence about the *Arch of Honor*, see Silver 2008, pp. 77–85.

Cat. 166

Maximilian (recto) and *Philip the Good* (verso), from *The Genealogy of Emperor Maximilian I*

Hans Burgkmair (1473–1531)
South German (Augsburg), 1509–12
Woodcut, first state of two
8¹⁄₁₆ x 7¹⁄₁₆ in. (20.5 x 18 cm)
The Metropolitan Museum of Art, New York,
Harris Brisbane Dick Fund, 1939 (39.92.1a, b)

When Maximilian I set out on his larger project of *Gedächtnis*, or memorial, he sought first to establish his own family history, so his initial printed project was the *Genealogy*, begun about 1509. To supervise this endeavor, the emperor chose the

learned and reliable city secretary of Augsburg, Conrad Peutinger. As the designer for the woodcut illustrations, which would display all his ancestors, he selected Hans Burgkmair, also of Augsburg. Already an accomplished graphic artist, Burgkmair had previously worked with Peutinger, about 1505, on another project of illustrated biographical history, the uncompleted *Kaiserbuch*, which aimed to present the sequence of Roman emperors as bust profiles. For the *Genealogy*, Burgkmair eventually produced ninety-two individual images, most of them inscribed with his monogram.

The family historical research, both prolonged and serious, was conducted by a team of scholars that included Vienna University professor Ladislaus Sunthaim and the historian Johannes Stabius. Most noteworthy among these was Jacob Mennel, who later presented many of the findings concerning Maximilian's ancestors in a six-volume illuminated manuscript, the *Princely Chronicle* (*Fürstliche Chronik*; 1517–18).[1] Also known as the *Mirror of Birth* (*Geburtsspigel*), this work was summarized in an illustrated digest, the *Handbook* (*Zaiger*),[2] which contained thirty-seven pages of family trees and twenty-one full-page illustrations of Habsburg family history. The digest traced the ancient family back not only to the Frankish kings of central Europe but also, ultimately, to the Trojan prince and hero Hector.

Beginning with Hector, who opens the *Genealogy* with scepter in hand and wearing a fantastic lion armor, the series of woodcuts ends with quite recognizable enthroned portraits of Emperor Frederick III, Maximilian's father, and finally Maximilian himself. All the figures in the series wear armor, real or imagined, and stand or sit in lively poses. A 1512 letter by the emperor, indicating that Maximilian had seen and proofed his full family tree, reveals just how meticulously he supervised all the woodcuts in his memorial initiatives.[3]

Because the precise ancestry of the Habsburgs remained in dispute, the *Genealogy* went unpublished, with the woodcuts stalled in the state achieved by Burgkmair in late 1510. Later, the family tree at the center of Maximilian's *Arch of Honor*, produced by Albrecht Dürer's workshop, relied for its murky origins on allegorical figures of Troia (Troy), Sicambria (Hungary), and Francia (France) before continuing on with individual rulers through Clovis, the first Christian king of the Merovingian Franks (cat. 165).

The series culminates in this handsome profile of Maximilian himself, seated on his lion throne, wearing the imperial crown and elaborate mantle, and carrying the scepter of office as well as a ceremonial sword. His contemporary armor was familiar to Burgkmair, who had used it for the

VERSO

RECTO

emperor's 1508 equestrian portrait, produced on the occasion of his coronation that year in Trento (cat. 107). Like all of his ancestors, Maximilian proudly displays his coat of arms, the haloed eagle of the Holy Roman Empire; his principal territorial arms appear against the wings of the bird. Maximilian's name is proclaimed at the top in proper majuscule Latin letters, derived from ancient Roman imperial inscriptions.

An unusual feature of this final portrait print is the presence of more personal attributes in the upper left of the image: an orb of imperial world dominion, surmounting a wheel of fortune (akin to the heraldry of Prince Theuerdank's herald, Ehrenhold), and a pomegranate at bottom. That fruit, which became a personal emblem for Maximilian, requires some interpretation. As Stabius explains on the *Arch of Honor* colophon: "although a pomegranate's exterior is neither very beautiful nor endowed with a pleasant scent, it is sweet on the inside and is filled with a great many well-shaped seeds. Likewise the Emperor is endowed with many hidden qualities

which become more and more apparent each day and continue to bear fruit."[4] Albrecht Dürer also painted Maximilian holding a pomegranate in his two portraits of the emperor from 1519.[5]

A hand-colored and annotated ensemble of seventy-seven figures of the *Genealogy* from the Habsburg collections survives at the Österreichische Nationalbibliothek, Vienna.[6]   LS

REFERENCES: Laschitzer 1888; *Maximilian I.* 1959, pp. 51–61, nos. 167–98; Geissler 1965; Falk 1973, n.p., nos. 150–66; Larry Silver and Christof Metzger in *Emperor Maximilian I* 2012, pp. 168–69, no. 20

1. Österreichische Nationalbibliothek, Vienna, Cod. 3077*, Cod. 3077**, Cod. 3074–3077.
2. Österreichische Nationalbibliothek, Vienna, Cod. 7892.
3. Maximilian I to Sigmund von Dietrichstein, October 14, 1512, in Schauerte 2001, pp. 411–12, no. Q 20. A few individual sheets bear additional printed frames and rhymed verses that were once planned for the *Genealogy*.
4. Translation in Strauss 1980, p. 731. See also Silver 2008, pp. 211–12.
5. Kunsthistorisches Museum, Vienna (825); Germanisches Nationalmuseum, Nuremberg (169).
6. Österreichische Nationalbibliothek, Vienna, Cod. 8048; Larry Silver and Christof Metzger in *Emperor Maximilian I* 2012, pp. 168–69, no. 20.

Cat. 167

Thirty-Nine Ancestors of Maximilian I
Attributed to Jörg Kölderer (ca. 1456/70–1540)
Austrian (Innsbruck), ca. 1512/14 or 1528
Watercolor and pen and ink on parchment
14⅝ in. x 11 ft. 1⅞ in. (37 x 340 cm)
Kunsthistorisches Museum, Vienna, Schloss Ambras (KK 5333)

This parchment scroll is attributed to Maximilian I's court painter Jörg Kölderer, who held this role from 1498 until 1518, when he was named architect to the imperial court.[1] It depicts thirty-nine figures, including Habsburg rulers and their wives as well as historical and fictitional potentates, each identifiable from their heraldic arms, name, and title below. Clovis I, king of the Franks, is at the head of the line, and Philip the Good, duke of Burgundy, at the end; however, the figures are not arranged in any discernible genealogical or chronological order. Although Clovis is placed upon a column capital, all others stand on a patch of grass. In addition to individuals from the House of Austria, such as Philip I, son of Maximilian and Mary of Burgundy, and members of the Tyrolian line of the Habsburgs, such as Frederick IV, duke of Austria, and his son Sigismund, archduke of Tyrol, there are a number of figures depicted who represent moral qualities. Among them is Charlemagne, the first Christian Holy Roman Emperor, as well as King Arthur and Godfrey of Bouillon, who as soldiers of Christ (*miles Christi*) and two of the Nine Worthies embody the ideals of chivalry. Every aspect of the scroll—from the lettering and stylistic execution of the drawing to the choice of figures and the depiction of their regalia, armor, and ceremonial garb—is connected to Maximilian's genealogical projects. Central to these projects was the celebration of the universal might of the Habsburgs and the promotion of their claim—originating in antiquity—to power and hereditary titles.

The realization of these genealogical projects can be found in the plans for the emperor's tomb and in Albrecht Altdorfer's *Triumphal Procession* (cat. 162), in which the figures largely correspond to the ones featured on the present scroll.[2] In the *Triumphal Procession*, Maximilian's ancestors are depicted as statues, much as they would later appear—cast in bronze, but not gilded, and in smaller number—surrounding the emperor's tomb in the Court Church (Hofkirche) in Innsbruck, although there is no further direct connection between the two works. While a similar program appears on Kölderer's parchment scroll and the tomb, this relationship does not extend to the depiction of the figures themselves. In 1528, after Maximilian's death and at the behest of Ferdinand I, Kölderer made sketches for the arrangement of the forty bronze statues for the planned tomb. The specific group of figures, however, is different on the two works: Julius Caesar, Theudebert I, Elisabeth of Carinthia, queen of Germany, and Ferdinand I of Portugal appear only on the plans for the tomb, while Princess Ita of Habsburg, Count Ottoprecht of Habsburg, and John I of Portugal are depicted only on the parchment scroll. Since none of these figures—with the exception of John I of Portugal—correspond to the later bronze statues, the scroll cannot be considered documentation of their planning. Indeed, the scroll may have served merely to communicate the names and crests to Altdorfer—who was uninvolved in the tomb project—to craft the triumphal procession.

It is not known whether the scroll was created by 1512 or was commissioned later by Ferdinand I. Later mid-sixteenth-century copies of the scroll are housed, in the form of paper codices, in the Bayerische Staatsbibliothek in Munich and the Österreichische Nationalbibliothek in Vienna.[3] With regard to the connections discussed here, this would suggest that the parchment scroll was later received within the context of Maximilian's tomb design.   VS

Ernst Erthergog zu
Osterreich

Leonora Romistde
kayserin

Blanca maria e
Romistge kaysserin

Johanna künigin zu Castilia
Erthergogin zu Osterreich

Maria Erthergogin zu
Osterreich vnd Hertzogin zu
Burgundi

Ma
vnd

REFERENCES: Oberhammer 1935, pp. 42–56, figs. 11–23; Katharina Seidl in *Kaiser Ferdinand I.* 2003, pp. 551–52, no. XI.5; Veronika Sandbichler in *Emperor Maximilian I* 2012, pp. 170–71, no. 21, ill.

1. Oberhammer 1935, p. 42.
2. Katharina Seidl in *Kaiser Ferdinand I.* 2003, pp. 551–52, no. XI.5.
3. Bayerische Staatsbibliothek, Munich, "Wappenbuch des Hauses Habsburg," Cgm. 908; Österreichische Nationalbibliothek, Vienna, Cod. 7867. See Veronika Sandbichler in *Emperor Maximilian I* 2012, pp. 170–71, no. 21.

Cat. 168

Design for a Statue of Godfrey of Bouillon for the Tomb of Maximilian I

Hans Polhaimer the Elder (ca. 1490/1500–1566)

Austrian (Innsbruck), ca. 1530–32

Pen in ink and watercolor on paper

11¹¹⁄₁₆ x 8¼ in. (29.7 x 21 cm)

Tiroler Landesmuseum Ferdinandeum, Innsbruck,

Austria, Grafische Sammlungen (AD 32)

Maximilian I was profoundly concerned with his eternal memorialization and spent much of his life preparing for death, which included designing a monumental imperial tomb. He initially

planned the tomb for the town of Sankt Wolfgang in Upper Austria; shortly before his death, however, he moved its intended location to Saint George's Cathedral in Wiener Neustadt. Unfortunately, the tomb was never finished. The cathedral proved to be unsuitable because it could not structurally support the forty larger-than-life bronze figures—Maximilian's ancestral line—that were to flank the tomb, several of which had already been cast. His grandson Ferdinand I therefore relocated the tomb to Innsbruck, where it was installed in the Court Church (Hofkirche) constructed for the purpose. Maximilian's body, meanwhile, remained in Wiener Neustadt.

The Munich-born Hans Polhaimer the Elder, court painter in Innsbruck from 1528 to 1566, designed the statue of Godfrey (1060–1100), lord of Bouillon and duke of Lower Lorraine. Godfrey was also the leader of the First Crusade in 1099, and later reconquered Jerusalem. In this sketch, he appears on an imagined pedestal, in a static, heavily frontal pose (a conscious nod to the style of medieval sculpture), with legs spread, grasping a short sword in his right hand and a shield bearing the lion of Habsburg and the Jerusalem cross in his left. He wears an elaborate armor of metal scales and greaves that are at once historicizing and fanciful. His collar and waist strap feature medallions that alternate between the lion of Habsburg and the fleur-de-lis of France. The couter, embellished with a grotesque mask of perhaps a Turk's face, might allude to Godfrey's role as liberator of sacred Christian sites. This role is also echoed in the Weapons of Christ (*Arma Christi*)—cross, crown of thorns, whip, and rod—that decorate his helmet. In an otherwise largely fictitious ancestral line, Godfrey serves as a role model for the emperor's self-conception as Christianity's defender and points to Maximilian's desire to become a crusader himself.

Polhaimer's design for the statue of Godfrey largely follows Hans Springinklee's depiction of the figure created between 1512 and 1519 as part of the *Triumphal Procession* print series Maximilian had commissioned. A comparison to the bronze statue of Godfrey that Stefan Godl ultimately cast in 1533, using a model by Leonhard Magt, reveals major alterations that simplified the figure's appearance. The instructions Ferdinand I scrawled next to the sketch, indicating that the sword should be longer and positioned more to the side, suggest that the illustration played a role in creating the final statue, which incorporated these very changes.   PS

REFERENCES: Franz Reitinger and Astrit Schmidt-Burkhardt in *Europa und der Orient* 1989, p. 689, no. 7/13, and p. 691, fig. 772; Lukas Madersbacher in *Ruhm und Sinnlichkeit* 1996, pp. 178–79, no. 45, ill.; Günther Dankl in *Sammellust* 1998, pp. 288–89, ill.

Cat. 169

King Arthur
Heinrich Fuss (1845–1913)
Austrian, ca. 1900
Bronze
H. 23³⁄₁₆ in. (59 cm)
Tiroler Landesmuseum Ferdinandeum, Innsbruck, Austria,
Ältere Kunstgeschichtliche Sammlungen (B 359)

This small-scale replica, approximately one-fifth the size of
the original, was fashioned about 1900 by Austrian sculptor
Heinrich Fuss for the Innsbruck art dealer C. A. Czichna, presumably as a type of souvenir for wealthy buyers. The original
statue belongs to a series of twenty-eight larger-than-life
bronze figures flanking Maximilian I's cenotaph in the Court
Church (Hofkirche), Innsbruck, that were conceived as a sort
of funeral procession in the Burgundian tradition of *pleurants*
(mourners).[1] It was created in 1513, along with one of King
Theoderic, by the Nuremberg workshop of Peter Vischer the
Elder. The designs for both statues are attributed to Albrecht
Dürer, who also provided sketches for three other figures:
Albrecht IV, duke of Austria; Charlemagne; and Ottoprecht,
first count of Habsburg (according to the imperial chronicle of
the court historian Jacob Mennel).[2]

   The congregated "mourners" in the Court Church, composed of actual relations and imaginary ancestors alike, not
only honored the emperor's eternal memory, but were also
a component of Maximilian's political-dynastic propaganda,
intended to illustrate the legitimacy of the Habsburg claim
to power. The legendary King Arthur, model sovereign,
embodies the ideals of chivalric virtues here.

   Work on Maximilian's tomb began in 1502, but casting the
large bronze statues proved problematic from the first, and by
the time the emperor died in 1519, only some of the statues
had been completed. Ferdinand I initially carried on work
according to his grandfather's plans, but it was Maximilian's
great-grandson Ferdinand II who concluded the project, albeit
without fully realizing its intended scope.[3]   BW

1. On this series, see Oberhammer 1935; Madersbacher 1996; Cornelia
Plieger in Naredi-Rainer and Madersbacher 2007, pp. 598–601.
2. See Koreny 1989.
3. In addition to forty larger-than-life ancestral statues, the original plan
included a hundred statues of saints and thirty-four busts of Roman emperors. Ultimately, twenty-eight ancestral figures and twenty-three statues of
saints were finished (housed today in the Court Church, Innsbruck). The
busts of Roman emperors were the only element completed in full: twenty
are in Ambras Castle in Innsbruck, with a further bust at the Bayerisches
Nationalmuseum, Munich. See Cornelia Plieger in Naredi-Rainer and
Madersbacher 2007, p. 598. The location of the remaining busts of Roman
emperors is unknown, and they may not have survived.

CHRONOLOGY

	MAXIMILIAN'S LIFE	HABSBURG FAMILY EVENTS	WIDER POLITICAL EVENTS
1453			Ottoman Turks capture Constantinople
1459	Born in Wiener Neustadt		
1461			Louis XI is crowned king of France
1469		Frederick III establishes the Order of Saint George	
1477	Marries Mary of Burgundy	Charles the Bold dies	
1478	Becomes a member and the sovereign of the Order of the Golden Fleece	Philip I is born	
1479	Wins the battle of Guinegate against the French		
1480		Margaret is born	
1481		Philip I becomes a member of the Order of the Golden Fleece	
1482		Mary of Burgundy dies	
		Philip I becomes the sovereign of the Order of the Golden Fleece following his mother's death	
1483		Margaret is engaged to the dauphin Charles VIII of France	Charles VIII is crowned king of France
1486	Elected King of the Romans		
1488	Imprisoned in Bruges		
1490	Becomes ruler of Tyrol and Further Austria following Sigismund's abdication in his favor		Matthias Corvinus, king of Hungary, dies
	Marries Anne of Brittany by proxy		
1491		Charles VIII of France breaks his engagement to Margaret	Charles VIII of France marries Anne of Brittany
1492			Ferdinand II of Aragon and Isabella I of Castile capture Granada, ending the reconquest of Spain from Islamic rulers
			Alexander VI is elected pope
1493	Establishes the Fraternity of Saint George	Frederick III dies	Peace treaty is agreed between Maximilian and the Netherlandish Estates
	Inherits the remaining Habsburg hereditary lands from his father		
	Marries Bianca Maria Sforza by proxy		

	MAXIMILIAN'S LIFE	HABSBURG FAMILY EVENTS	WIDER POLITICAL EVENTS
1494			Charles VIII of France invades Italy
			Maximilian makes Ludovico Sforza duke of Milan
1495	Joins the Holy League with Venice, Milan, Spain, and the Holy See		
1496		Philip I marries Joanna of Castile	
1498			Louis XII is crowned king of France
1499			After defeating Maximilian's forces at the battle of Dornach, the Old Swiss Confederacy successfully secedes from the Holy Roman Empire
1500		Charles V is born	
1501		Charles V becomes a member of the Order of the Golden Fleece	
1503	Establishes the Society of Saint George	Ferdinand I is born	Beginning of the War of the Succession of Bavaria-Landshut
			Julius II is elected pope
1504			Isabella I of Castile dies
1506		Philip I is crowned king of Castile	
		Philip I dies	
		Charles V becomes the sovereign of the Order of the Golden Fleece following his father's death	
1507		Margaret is appointed regent of the Burgundian Low Countries	
1508	Takes the title of Holy Roman Emperor elect in Trento		Beginning of the long war with Venice
1509			Henry VIII is crowned king of England
1513	With Henry VIII of England, wins the Battle of the Spurs against the French		Leo X is elected pope
1515	Defeated at the battle of Marignano	Charles V becomes duke of Burgundy	Francis I is crowned king of France
		The "double wedding" between the Habsburg and Jagiellion royal families is arranged at the First Congress of Vienna	
1516		Charles V becomes king of Spain, uniting the crowns of Castile and Aragon	Ferdinand II of Aragon dies
1519	Dies in Wels, Upper Austria	Charles V is elected King of the Romans	
1520		Charles V is crowned King of the Romans in Aachen	

FAMILY TREE

Ferdinand II of Aragon
(March 10, 1452–January 23, 1516)
King of Aragon (1479–1516)
King of Castile and León (1475–1504)

Isabella I of Castile
(April 22, 1451–November 26, 1504)
Queen of Castile and León (1474–1504)
Queen consort of Aragon
(1479–1504)

Charles the Bold
(November 10, 1433–January 5, 1477)
Duke of Burgundy (1467–1477)

1. Catherine of France
(1428–July 13, 1446)

2. Isabella of Bourbon
(ca. 1434–September 25, 1465)

3. Margaret of York
(May 3, 1446–November 23, 1503)
Duchess of Burgundy (1468–1477)

1. Mary of Burgundy
(February 13, 1457–March 27, 1482)
Duchess of Burgundy (1477–1482)
Archduchess consort of Austria (1477–1482)

Joanna of Castile
(November 6, 1479–April 12, 1555)
Queen of Castile and León (1504–1555)
Queen of Aragon (1516–1555)

Philip I
(July 22, 1478–September 25, 1506)
Archduke of Austria (1478–1506)
Duke of Burgundy (1494–1506)
King of Castile (1506)

Margaret
(January 10, 1480–December 1, 1530)
Archduchess of Austria (1480–1530)
Fille de France (1483–1491)
Princess consort of Asturias (1497)
Duchess consort of Savoy (1501–1504)
**Regent of the Burgundian Low
Countries** (1507–1515 and 1519–1530)

Eleanor
(November 15, 1498–February 25, 1558)
Archduchess of Austria (1498–1558)
Queen consort of Portugal (1518–1521)
Queen consort of France (1530–1547)

Charles V
(February 24, 1500–September 21, 1558)
Archduke of Austria (1500–1558)
Duke of Burgundy (1515–1555)
King of Spain (1516–1556)
King of the Romans (1519–1530)
Holy Roman Emperor (1530–1556)

Isabella
(July 18, 1501–January 19, 1526)
Archduchess of Austria (1501–1526)
Queen consort of Denmark and Norway (1515–1523)
Queen consort of Sweden (1520–1521)

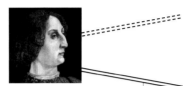

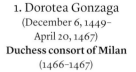

1. Dorotea Gonzaga
(December 6, 1449–
April 20, 1467)
Duchess consort of Milan
(1466–1467)

Frederick III
(September 21, 1415–August 19, 1493)
Archduke of Austria (1453–1493)
King of the Romans (1440–1486)
Holy Roman Emperor (1452–1493)

Eleanor of Portugal
(September 18, 1434–September 3, 1467)
Queen of the Romans (1452–1467)
Holy Roman Empress (1452–1467)

Galeazzo Maria Sforza
(January 24, 1444–December 26, 1476)
Duke of Milan (1466–1476)

2. Bona of Savoy
(August 10, 1449–
November 23, 1503)
Duchess consort of Milan
(1468–1476)

2. Bianca Maria Sforza
(February 4, 1472–December 31, 1510)
Archduchess consort of Austria (1494–1510)
Queen of the Romans (1494–1510)
Holy Roman Empress (1508–1510)

Maximilian I

(March 22, 1459–January 12, 1519)
Archduke of Austria (1459–1519)
Duke consort of Burgundy (1477–1482)
King of the Romans (1486–1519)
Holy Roman Emperor (1508–1519)

Ferdinand I
(March 10, 1503–July 25, 1564)
Archduke of Austria (1503–1564)
King of Bohemia and Hungary (1526–1564)
King of Croatia (1527–1564)
King of the Romans (1531–1556)
Holy Roman Emperor (1556–1564)

Mary
(September 15, 1505–October 18, 1558)
Archduchess of Austria (1505–1558)
Queen consort of Bohemia and Hungary (1515–1526)
Regent of the Burgundian Low Countries (1531–1555)

Catherine
(January 14, 1507–February 12, 1578)
Archduchess of Austria (1507–1578)
Queen consort of Portugal (1525–1557)

MAXIMILIAN I'S ARMORERS

The information on many of these armorers is based primarily on account books, letters, reports, and other original manuscript materials. The principal repositories for these documents are the Staatsarchiv Augsburg; Algemeen Rijksarchief, Brussels; Tiroler Landesarchiv, Innsbruck; Archives Départementales du Nord, Lille; Staatsarchiv, Nuremberg; Archives de la Ville et de l'Eurométropole, Strasbourg; and Haus-, Hof- und Staatsarchiv, Vienna.

Selected References: Van den Leene 1705; Gilliodts-van Severen 1876; Schönherr 1883; Zimerman 1883; Zimerman 1885; Zimerman and Kreyczi 1885; Boeheim 1891; Motta 1914; Buttin 1929; Reitzenstein 1951; Thomas and Gamber 1954; Thomas 1956/1977; Thomas 1958/1977; Hummelberger 1961; Blair 1965; Reitzenstein 1967; Reitzenstein 1969; Gaier 1973; Thomas 1974; Greve and Lebailly 2001–2

Aigner, Sigmund
Armorer in Linz (recorded 1501). Paid for unspecified work (1501).

Barnareggio, Giovan Pietro da
Armorer in Milan (recorded 1495). Made brigandines at the orders of Maximilian (1495).

Brussels, Peter from
Armorer in Innsbruck (recorded 1511). Employed in the Innsbruck court workshop to make high-quality armor (from 1511).

Cantoni, Bernardino
Armorer in Milan (active after 1508). Signed a brigandine of Maximilian in Real Armería, Madrid (C. 11).

Castner, Hans
Armorer in Innsbruck (recorded 1511). Employed in the Innsbruck court workshop to make high-quality armor (from 1511).

Costantino, Zoanne
Armorer in Milan (recorded 1495). Made horse bards at the orders of Maximilian (1495).

Diem, Gordian
Armorer in Ljubljana (recorded 1518). Appointed by Maximilian as his armorer in Ljubljana (1518).

Du Pre, Ancelmy
Armorer in Bruges (recorded 1475–1480). Delivered armors and horse bards to Charles the Bold (before 1477) and Maximilian (1479, 1480, 1481), which they presented as gifts to gentlemen of their households.

Ferat, Amory
Armorer in Brussels (recorded 1483). Made an armor that Maximilian presented as a gift to the squire Jean de Mailly (1483).

Ferrando
Armorer in Milan (recorded 1495). Made unspecified armors at the orders of Maximilian (1495).

Galdere, Jan van
Saddler in Bruges (recorded 1479–1490). Made two horse bards and two war saddles (for which he received payment in 1479) and another three horse bards (payment 1482), all for Maximilian.

Ghindertaelen, Anthonis van
Armorer in Brussels (first recorded 1491, died 1520). Son of Lancelot van Ghindertaelen and Elysabeth van Meeren, alias Bucxken. Made field and tournament armors for the personal use of Philip I (for which he received payments in 1499, 1501, 1505), and Charles V (payments 1511, 1513, 1514, 1516, 1519, 1520). Made armors that Philip and Charles presented as gifts to others, including Ferdinand II of Aragon (payment 1505); Alfonso de Aragon, archbishop of Saragossa and Ferdinand II's natural son (payment 1505); Ferdinand II's great equerry (payment 1505); Count Francis I of Saint Pol (payment 1505); two for Duke John II of Cleves (payments 1505, 1511); either Antoine or Pierre of Werchin (payment 1511); two for Charles of Lannoy (payment 1519, 1520). Likely patronized by Maximilian, as the remnants of an armor made for Maximilian and now in the Kunsthistorisches Museum, Vienna (A 110), bear his armorer's mark of a crowned orb.

Ghindertaelen, Lancelot van
Armorer in Brussels (first recorded 1447, died before 1512). Burgher of Brussels (from 1447). Municipal treasurer (1466, 1469, 1475), councilor (1460, 1467, 1469, 1470, 1474, 1475, 1491), and alderman of Brussels (from 1477). Appointed by Charles the Bold as his court armorer and *valet de chambre* (1463). Made four corsets for Guillaume Fillastre, bishop of Toul and chancellor of the Order of the Golden Fleece (1455), as well as field armors, jousting armors, and brigandines that Charles the Bold presented as gifts to gentlemen of his household, other noblemen, men-at-arms, and members of his guard (for which he received payments in 1468, 1469). Made unspecified armors at the orders of Maximilian (payments of 1,095 livres in 1479, 592 livres 16 sols in 1483).

Grünewald, Hans
Armorer in Nuremberg (first recorded 1457, died 1503). Master armorer (from 1457). Made armors for the personal use of the knight Friedrich von Müllenheim (1478); Margrave Friedrich of Brandenburg (1482); Sigmund Prüschenk, Frederick III's chief chamberlain (1487); and Maximilian (1489). Requested permission from the municipal council of Nuremberg to temporarily employ more journeymen than the regulations permitted, on the grounds that he had to fulfill commissions from many kings and princes (1489). Maximilian wrote the council to the same end, so that the master would be able to complete the armor he was making for him.

Gwerlich, Utz
Armorer in Innsbruck (recorded 1511). Employed in the Innsbruck court workshop to make munition-quality armor (from 1511).

Hamer, Lienhard
Armorer in Wiener Neustadt (first recorded 1512, died before 1549). Appointed by Maximilian as his armorer in Wiener Neustadt (1512) in return for his commitment to make three hundred infantry breastplates per year.

Haym, Jörg
Armorer in Innsbruck (recorded 1511). Employed in the Innsbruck court workshop to make munition-quality armor (from 1511).

Helmschmid, Jörg, the Younger
Armorer in Augsburg and Vienna (first recorded 1488, died 1502). Brother of Lorenz Helmschmid. Active in Augsburg (1488–1497) and Vienna (from 1497). Burgher of Vienna (from 1498). Appointed by Maximilian as his court armorer (1496). Made a helmet and shaffron for Maximilian's personal use (for which he received payment of 100 florins in 1496). Received commissions from Maximilian to make armors to be gifted to Weickhart von Polheim, caretaker of Hainburg Castle and town (1498); Achaz von Mecknitz, caretaker of Weitersfeld Castle (1501); Seyfried von Polheim, a courtier of Frederick III (1501); and Wilhelm von Graben, caretaker of Neuberg Castle (1501).

Helmschmid, Kolman
Armorer in Augsburg (1471–1532). Son of Lorenz Helmschmid and his wife Anna. Master armorer (by 1492). Made several armors for the personal use of Maximilian (1515–19), Charles V (ca. 1515–31), Francesco and Federico Gonzaga, marquises of Mantua (1506–21), and the grand master of the Teutonic Order Albrecht of Brandenburg (1515, 1518, 1525, 1527, 1531, 1532). Made toy jousters that Maximilian presented as gifts to Louis II of Hungary (1516). Made armor that Maximilian presented as gifts to Onoferus Ellenbogen, his usher; Stefan Westner, his secretary; and the knight Friedrich von Ems (all 1517).

Helmschmid, Lorenz
Armorer in Augsburg (first recorded 1467, died 1516). Brother of Jörg Helmschmid the Younger. Master armorer (from 1467). Appointed by Maximilian as his court armorer (1491). Made armors for the personal use of Frederick III (1477, 1490), Maximilian (for which he received payments in 1477, 1480, 1490, 1491, 1492, 1493, 1494, 1496, 1497, 1500, 1503, 1504), and Duke Christoph of Bavaria (before 1483). Made armors for Sigmund Prüschenk, Frederick's chief chamberlain (1477, 1485, 1489) and armors that Maximilian presented as gifts to Blasius Wolf, his treasury secretary (1506); Jörg Golldacker, his marshal (1507); and Ludovico Pico de la Mirandola, count of Concordia (1509).

Heyns, Gregoris
Armorer in Bruges (recorded 1470–1490). Municipal councilor of Bruges (1478–81, 1490–91). Made armors that Maximilian presented as gifts to gentlemen of his household, and to members of his guard (for which he received payments of 650 livres in 1479, 234 livres 10 sols in 1480, 1,104 livres in 1486).

Hirschler, Jörg
Armorer in Nuremberg (recorded 1504). Made armor for Hans Wolf von Landsberg at the orders of Maximilian (for which he received payment in 1504).

Kessler, Hans
Armor polisher in Innsbruck (recorded 1511). Employed in the Innsbruck court workshop to polish munition-quality armor (from 1511).

Koch, Erhard
Armorer in Innsbruck (recorded 1511). Employed in the Innsbruck court workshop to make munition-quality armor (from 1511).

Laubermann, Hans, alias Kölner
Armorer in Innsbruck (recorded 1490–1521). Possibly came from Ulm. Burgher of Innsbruck (from 1498). Municipal councilor (from 1503), judge (1505, 1511, 1513, 1515–17, 1519), and burgomaster of Innsbruck (1507, 1515). Patronized by Sigismund of Tyrol, then by Maximilian. Court armorer of Maximilian (by 1501). Made armors that Maximilian presented as gifts to an Ottoman ambassador (1497) and Italian and German noblemen, including Count Galeotto I Pico della Mirandola (1497); Hans Imer von Gilgenberg, Maximilian's counsel and bailiff in Ensisheim (1500); Hans Walter von Laubenberg, Maximilian's counsel and bailiff in Geislingen (1501); and Jörg von Liechtenstein, Maximilian's counsel and military commander (1513).

Lautterwein, Hans
Armorer in Innsbruck (recorded 1511). Employed in the Innsbruck court workshop to make high-quality armor (from 1511).

Lehenher, Michel
Armorer in Innsbruck (recorded 1501–1511). Employed in the Innsbruck court workshop to make munition-quality armor (1511).

Lempereur, Guillaume
Saddler in Brussels (recorded 1468–1479). Patronized by Charles the Bold (before 1468). Made three war saddles with steel brackets to hold the shafts of standards for Maximilian (for which he received payment in 1479).

Leonardo
Armorer in Milan (recorded 1495). Made horse bards at the orders of Maximilian (1495).

Lusch, Caspar
Armor polisher in Innsbruck (recorded 1511–1530). Employed in the Innsbruck court workshop to polish high-quality armor (1511).

Margot, Guillem
Armorer in Brussels (first recorded 1505, died before 1533). Made field and tournament armors and horse bards for the personal use of Philip I (for which he received payment in 1505), Charles V (payments 1508, 1509, 1511, 1512, 1515), and Ferdinand I (1518, 1520). Made armors that they presented as gifts to others, including Massimiliano Sforza (1511) and Margrave Christoph of Baden (1520). A horse bard in the Royal Armouries, Leeds (VI.6–12), which is struck with his armorer's mark, was presented at an unknown time by Maximilian as a gift to Henry VIII of England.

Maystetter, Hans
Armorer in Innsbruck (recorded 1510–1533).
Appointed by Maximilian as his armorer in
Graz (1510), but perhaps did not relocate there.
Employed in the Innsbruck court workshop to
make high-quality armor (from 1511) and was its
most senior armorer after Conrad Seusenhofer
until Conrad's brother Hans was appointed
as its foreman (1515). Left the court workshop
following Conrad's death (1517) and made
munition-quality armor for Innsbruck's arsenal
(until 1530).

Merate, Francesco da
Armorer in Milan, Ferrara, and Arbois (recorded
1480–1496). Brother of Gabriele da Merate.
Active in Milan (1480, 1492–1495), Ferrara
(1480–1485), and Arbois (from 1495). Court
armorer of the duke of Ferrara (1485). Made
armors for the personal use of Gianfrancesco II
Gonzaga, marquis of Mantua (1485), and
Alfonso I d'Este, duke of Ferrara (1488). Made
unspecified armor at the orders of Maximilian
in Milan (1495). With his brother entered into
an agreement with Maximilian and Philip I to
establish an armorer's workshop at Arbois in the
Franche-Comté (1495).

Merate, Gabriele da
Armorer in Milan (recorded 1495–1529). Brother
of Francesco da Merate. With his brother
entered into an agreement with Maximilian and
Philip I to establish an armorer's workshop at
Arbois in the Franche-Comté (1495). Supplied
armors at Maximilian's orders (1496). Maximilian
commissioned fifty field armors and one hundred leather horse bards from him (1504), the
delivery of which was later intercepted by
the Venetians.

Müllner, Hans
Armor polisher in Innsbruck (recorded 1511).
Employed in the Innsbruck court workshop to
polish munition-quality armor (from 1511).

Pichler, Bartleme
Armor polisher in Innsbruck (recorded 1511–
1514). Employed in the Innsbruck court workshop to polish armor (from 1511).

Poler, Cuntz
Armorer in Nuremberg (recorded 1474–1500).
Burgher of Nuremberg (from 1474). Master
armorer (from 1475). Was owed large sums of
money by Maximilian for armor he had delivered in 1492 and 1498 (for which he received a
partial payment of 1,700 florins in 1500).

Prenner, Wolfgang
Armorer in Innsbruck (recorded 1498–1524).
Made a field armor, shaffron, and crinet that
Maximilian presented as gifts to a member of
the Schurf family, probably Wilhelm Schurf,
caretaker of Ambras Castle (1519). Made armors
for Innsbruck's arsenal (1517, 1522) and armors
that Ferdinand I presented as gifts to his courtiers (1522).

Prunner, Hans
Armorer in Innsbruck and Mühlau (first
recorded 1482, died before 1503). Came from
Augsburg. Recorded in Innsbruck (1482–1501)
and Mühlau (1490–1499). Burgher of Innsbruck
(from 1487). Made armor for Sigismund of
Tyrol's personal use (1493) and to be gifted by
him to others, including Florian Waldauf (1491),
Friedrich and Wilhelm Kappeler (1493), and one
of the sons of Casimir IV of Poland (1493). Made
several armors at the orders of Maximilian,
including one for King John I Albert of Poland
(1493) and one for Maximilian's personal
use (1497).

Rabeiler, Hans, alias Pair (the Bavarian)
Armorer in Innsbruck (first recorded 1501, died
1519). With Michel Witz the Elder made an
armor that Maximilian presented as a gift to
Francesco II Gonzaga, marquis of Mantua (1509).
Made an armor that Maximilian presented to
Girolamo della Torre, a nobleman of Verona
(1511) and another that was intended for
Charles V but never finished (1511).

Reiffart, Ulrich
Armorer in Innsbruck (recorded 1511). Employed
in the Innsbruck court workshop to make high-
quality armor (from 1511).

Rieder(er), Caspar
Armorer in Mühlau (recorded 1452–1499).
Patronized by Sigismund of Tyrol and Maximilian.
In collaboration with others or alone made
armors that Sigismund presented as gifts to King
Ferrante I of Naples (1472); Rudolf von Horb
(1473); the knight Burkhart von Knörigen (1473);
and Sigmund von Welsperg, caretaker of Thaur
Castle (1478). Made an armor for Maximilian's
personal use (1496), which was shipped to him
while he was campaigning in Italy.

Rondeel, Martin
Armorer in Bruges (first recorded 1464, died
before 1524). Born in Milan. Burgher of Bruges
(from 1464). Armorer of Anthony, bastard of
Burgundy (by 1473). Made twenty-seven horse
bards for Maximilian (1486), for which his heirs
eventually obtained a partial payment (1524).

Rosenpusch, Hans
Armorer in Graz (recorded 1484–1522).
Appointed by Maximilian as his armorer in
Graz (1510).

Salzburger, Lienhard
Armorer in Innsbruck (recorded 1511). Employed
in the Innsbruck court workshop to make
munition-quality armor (from 1511).

Schuster, Caspar
Armorer in Innsbruck (recorded 1511). Employed
in the Innsbruck court workshop to make
munition-quality armor (from 1511).

Scroo, Franck
Armorer in Brussels (recorded 1479–1496).
Court armorer of Maximilian (by 1480). Made
armors for the personal use of Maximilian (1479,
1488) and to be gifted by Maximilian to gentlemen of his household, other noblemen, men-at-
arms, and members of his guard (for which he
received payments of 2,107 livres 3 sols in 1480,
60 livres 14 sols in 1483, 564 livres 7 sols in 1487,
884 livres 13 sols in 1488, 97 livres in 1490, 731
livres 6 sols 6 deniers in 1494). The armors for
which he was paid in 1488 were presented to
Philip I; Margrave Bernard III of Baden, Philip's
fourteen year-old companion; either Sigismund
or Friedrich, margrave of Brandenburg;
Wolfgang von Polheim, Maximilian's chamberlain; Vincent von Schwanenburch, marshal of
the archbishop of Cologne; Hugues of Salins,
viscount of Ghent, and one of Maximilian's
stewards; Willem van Reymerswaele, bailiff of
Rotterdam and Schieland; Jan van Houthem,
chancellor of Brabant; Anthon Schenk von
Missbach, an Alsatian nobleman; Jehan Binnot,
alias Wafflart, a mounted crossbowman; and the
squire Philippe van der Ee.

Seusenhofer, Conrad
Armorer in Innsbruck (first recorded 1500, died 1517). Brother of Hans Seusenhofer. Appointed by Maximilian as his court armorer for six years (1504), and indefinitely (1509), and as keeper of his personal armory (1515). Made armors for Maximilian's personal use and to be gifted by him to others, including Cardinal Raimondo della Torre (1504); Philip I and one of his counsels (1504); Christoph Mindorffer (1504); Mattheus Staudigl, knight commander for the Order of Saint George of Rechberg (1505); Georg Ilsung (1510); Frederick, prince elector of Saxony (1511); Henry VIII of England (1511–14); Richard Jernigham, Henry VIII's ambassador (1511–14); Charles V (1512–14); Don Pedro de Urrea, ambassador of Ferdinand II of Aragon (1513); Count Francesco of San Bonifacio (1514); Wolf von Dietrichstein, one of Maximilian's stewards (1514); Captain Albrecht von Stamp (1514); Jörg von Emershoffen, Maximilian's counsel and equerry (1514, 1515); Hermann Aichhorn, a notable of Meran (1515); Eitelhans von Emershofen and his servitor (1515); Ferdinand I (1515); Louis II of Hungary (1515); Giuliano de' Medici (1515); Wilhelm von Reichenpach, counsel and bailiff of Horb (1516); Marcantonio Colonna, a commander of papal forces (1516); Margrave Joachim II Hector of Brandenburg (1516); Nicolaus Rauber, captain of Trieste (1517); Bernhard Boner, customs officer of Leoben (1517); and Count Gianfrancesco Gambara (1518).

Seusenhofer, Hans
Armorer in Strasbourg and Innsbruck (1470/71–1555). Brother of Conrad Seusenhofer. Active in Strasbourg (1501–1512) and Innsbruck (1514–1555). Invited by Maximilian to enter his service and relocate from Strasbourg to Innsbruck (1512). Appointed by Maximilian as foreman of the Innsbruck court workshop (1515), and as keeper of his armory (1516). Appointed by Ferdinand I as his court armorer and keeper of his personal armory (1519). Ennobled (1537).

Teininger, Conz
Armor polisher in Innsbruck (recorded 1511). Employed in the Innsbruck court workshop to polish munition-quality armor (from 1511).

Verurban, Martin
Armorer in Innsbruck (recorded 1511). Employed in the Innsbruck court workshop to make high-quality armor (from 1511).

Vischer, Baltis
Armorer in Innsbruck (recorded 1511). Employed in the Innsbruck court workshop to make munition-quality armor (from 1511).

Wagner, Hans
Armorer in Innsbruck (first recorded 1511, died before 1549). Employed in the Innsbruck court workshop to make munition-quality armor (from 1511).

Wambaix, Pieter
Armorer in Brussels (recorded 1490–1497). Made unspecified armor at the orders of Maximilian (for which he received partial payments in 1483, 1490). Was owed in 1496 a balance of 777 livres 12 sols for armor that he had delivered in 1483.

Weiss, Conrad
Armorer in Landshut (recorded 1459–1493). Made an armor for the joust of peace for Maximilian (1476).

Weymersch, Jacques de
Mail armorer (recorded 1480). Repaired mail armor for Maximilian's personal use (1480).

Widman, Hans
Armorer in Innsbruck (recorded 1511). Employed in the Innsbruck court workshop to make munition-quality armor (from 1511).

Witz, Michel, the Elder
Armorer in Innsbruck (recorded 1509–1549). Municipal councilor of Innsbruck (1533, 1540). With Hans Rabeiler made an armor that Maximilian presented as a gift to Francesco II Gonzaga, marquis of Mantua (1509). Made armors that Maximilian presented as gifts to Niclaus Trautmansdorffer (1510) and Thillman von Brempt, sheriff of Nuremberg (1511), and another armor that Ferdinand I presented as a gift to his military commander Egloff Scheller (1526).

Wolfgang
Armorer in Graz (recorded 1518–1523). Appointed by Maximilian as his armorer in Graz (1518).

GLOSSARY

armet: A helmet that completely encloses the head, with hinged cheekpieces that overlap at the chin and a **visor** that rotates on pivots at the sides of the **bowl**.

armorial (n.): An album of coats of arms.

associated: A piece for an armor that was not originally made as part of the ensemble but integrated at a later date. A **composite** armor is made up of such elements.

backplate: A defense for the back, often extended with a **culet** over the upper buttocks.

bard: A defense for the body of a horse, including its neck and head.

bendy: A heraldic term for a **field** bearing a series of diagonal stripes of alternate colors.

besagew: A small plate that covers the armpit, often worn in pairs. Although usually disk-shaped, its form varies.

bevor: A defense for the chin and throat. It can be an independent element worn with an open-face helmet, such as a **sallet**, or the component of a **close helmet** that covers the lower face and pivots with the **visor** at the sides of the **bowl**.

boss: A convex, often hemispherical area **embossed** onto both sides of the **peytral** to make room for the horse's pectoral muscle and elbow joint. It allows the horse to move more freely and provides additional protection and comfort.

bowl: A component of a helmet that protects the skull.

breastplate: A defense for the front half of the torso, often extended with a **fauld** over the abdomen.

brigandine: A defense for the torso that consists of overlapping plates of iron or steel riveted inside a garment made of cloth or leather.

buffe: A detachable defense for the face and throat worn in combination with an open-face helmet. When it is articulated with **lames** that can be raised and lowered to expose the face, it is called a falling buffe.

Bundrennen: A variant of the **joust of war** in which each contestant bears a large shield that is attached to their **breastplate** using a spring-loaded mechanism. When struck by a **lance**, the mechanism releases, flinging the shields into the air. **Sallets** used in this **joust** are often fitted with rollers to prevent the flying shields from being caught on their lower edges.

cannon: A cylindrical defense that encloses the upper arm (upper cannon) and lower arm (lower cannon).

cantle plate: A plate or plates that enclose the cantle, or rear bow, of a saddle for the field or the **tournament**, protecting not only the saddle's structure but also the rider's buttocks.

close helmet: A helmet that completely encloses the head. It is made up of a **bowl**, **visor**, and **bevor**, all of which pivot from common points on the sides of the head.

coat of arms: A written or pictorial representation of one's identity achieved by the use of colors, partitions, and charges (symbols) within a shield-shaped frame according to heraldic usage. The term can additionally refer to the helm with crest and mantling that often complements and surmounts the shield.

codpiece: A defense for the genitals.

collar: A fitting that encircles the grip of a sword.

composite: An armor composed of elements that were not originally intended to be worn together.

coronel: A blunted lance head with three or more prongs, used in the **joust of peace**.

costume armor: Armor that mimics the appearance of civilian dress, generally designed for visual impact rather than protection in combat.

couch (v.): To lower a weapon, such as a **lance**, to the position of attack with the point directed forward.

couter: A defense for the elbow.

crinet: A defense for the horse's neck, usually made of articulated plates or a combination of plate and mail. It connects to the **poll plate** of the **shaffron** and extends downward to the base of the neck. A closed crinet encloses the entire circumference of the horse's neck.

cross guard: In a sword, a guard that consists of a transverse bar set between the grip and the blade, intended to protect the hand; the two arms that form the cross guard are called quillons.

crupper: A rear element of a **bard**, which covers the horse's rump, hindquarters, and upper hind legs.

cuirass: A defense for the torso, generally made up of a **breastplate** and **backplate**.

cuisse: A defense for the thigh.

culet: A defense for the upper buttocks, either made in one with the **backplate** or a detachable component of it.

dexter: A heraldic term for the right side of a shield or **coat of arms**. Because heraldry is described from the bearer's viewpoint, the dexter appears to the viewer's left.

embossing: A process of selectively raising the surface of metal by hammering it up from the back to sculpt a design in low or high relief.

escutcheon: Either a shield-shaped plate attached to the brow of a **shaffron** or a shield-like frame of a **coat of arms**.

etching: A process of inscribing a design or image into armor plates using acid or other corrosives. After applying a resist, such as wax, to mask the surface, the etcher selectively scratches away the resist to expose the areas to be etched, then immerses the plate in a corrosive to bite the design into the metal.

fauld: A defense for the lower abdomen and hips, generally made in one with the **breastplate**.

field: In heraldry, the ground or surface of a **coat of arms**.

field armor: Armor intended for use in battle.

flutes: Alternating ridges and folds hammered into the surface of an armor plate to provide both ornamentation and strength.

foot combat: In the **tournament**, a **mock combat** in which two contestants fight on foot with **pollaxes**, swords, daggers, and other handheld weapons.

free tourney: A **mock combat** in which two groups of mounted contestants first charge at each other with **lances** with sharpened heads and then continue the fight with blunted swords.

fuller: A vertical groove that reduces the weight of the blade of a sword or dagger without weakening it.

garniture: A matching set of elements (called exchange pieces) that can be assembled to create armor for a variety of uses, including the **field** and the **tournament**, and service on horseback and foot.

gauntlet: A defense for the hand, which can take the form of a mitten or have individually articulated fingers.

Geschiftsrennen: A variant of the **joust of war** in which each contestant has a specialized shield made of several tightly fitted pieces affixed to the **breastplate** using a spring-loaded mechanism. When struck with a **lance**, the mechanism releases, and the shield appears to explode, its pieces flying into the air.

gorget: A defense for the neck worn separately from the helmet.

greave: A defense for the lower leg that either fully encloses the calf or covers only the shin.

gusset: A small piece, sometimes a movable **lame**, attached to the **breastplate** along the line of the armpit to provide additional protection to the joint. Its edges are often roped or rolled to help deflect blows away from the vulnerable armpit.

hasps: Hinged metal plates that form part of the fasteners used to secure elements of armor together. They are frequently pierced with a hole to fit over a projecting staple or peg.

haute-piece: A vertical guard on the right and/or left **pauldron** that is designed to prevent an opponent's weapon from sliding onto the face or neck.

helm: A large, heavy helmet that completely encloses the head and neck, in which the head is generally immobilized. By the end of the fourteenth century, it was used almost exclusively in **tournaments**.

inescutcheon: A heraldic term for a smaller shield that appears within or superimposed on top of the main heraldic shield.

joust: A **mock combat** in which two or more mounted contestants charge at one another with **couched lances**. The object of the **joust** can be to unhorse an opponent, to break one's own lance, or to strike specific areas in order to score points.

joust of peace: A **joust** in which the **lances** are mounted with **coronels**. The contestants wear specialized armor that differs significantly in design from that worn in battle.

joust of war: A **joust** in which the **lances** are mounted with sharpened heads. The contestants wear either **field armor** or specialized armor that evokes the design of **field armor**. From the late fifteenth century onward, the specialized armor for this contest mimicked the appearance of antiquated **field armor**. Many variants of the **joust of war** existed in the German-speaking lands, where it was known as the *Rennen*.

jousting at large: A **joust** in which contestants are not separated by a **tilt**.

jousting sockets: Stationary, shell-shaped plates suspended from the saddle to protect a rider's legs in many variants of the **joust of war**. They replaced heavier full-leg armor used in battle and **tournaments** on foot.

lames: Oblong plates that overlap to articulate an element of armor, increasing its range of movement.

lance: A long, shafted weapon used by a horseman to strike an opponent.

lance rest: A component of the **breastplate** that provides support for the **lance** when charging at an opponent and striking the desired target. It can be immobile or hinged so that it can be folded away when the rider decides to use his sword.

mock combat: A fight in which the intent is not to inflict harm.

pauldron: A defense for the shoulder that often extends down the upper arm.

peytral: A front element of a bard, which covers the horse's chest and upper forelegs.

poleyn: A defense for the knee.

poll plate: A plate attached to the top rear of the **shaffron**, which protects the back of the horse's head (the poll). It is frequently hinged to the **shaffron** and used to connect it to the **crinet**.

pollaxe: A fighting ax mounted on a long shaft, used in both battle and **mock combat**.

pommel: A component of swords and daggers that is fastened to the tang of the blade at one extremity of the grip. It counterbalances the blade, makes the weapon easier to grip, and secures all the elements of the hilt.

pommel plate: A plate or several plates attached to the front bow of a saddle for the field or the **tournament** to protect the front of the saddle and thus the rider's inner thighs and groin.

queue: A horizontal bar attached to the right side of the **breastplate** for the **joust**, which extends backward under the arm to terminate in a hook into which the butt end of a **lance** can be fitted. It eases the **couching** of the **lance**, steadies the **lance** during the contest, and provides a counterbalance to the **lance rest**.

raguly: A heraldic term for an object that has pieces projecting at the sides in a slanting direction like the cut boughs of a tree.

rondel: A circular plate often used to protect a gap at the armpit, elbow, or knee, or to provide additional protection to an armored area, such as the forehead of a **shaffron**.

rump defense: A defense for the buttocks made of articulated **lames**. This element, also known as a hoguine, was used in some variants of the **foot combat**.

sabaton: A defense for the foot.

sallet: A helmet whose **bowl** curves outward at the rear to guard the nape of the neck. It can be open-faced or equipped with **visors**.

shaffron: A defense for the front and often the sides of a horse's head.

sight: A slit in a headpiece or face defense through which the wearer is able to see.

sinister: A heraldic term for the left side of a shield or **coat of arms**. Because heraldry is described from the bearer's viewpoint, the sinister appears to the viewer's right.

targe: In the **joust**, a shield borne over the left side of the **breastplate** and left shoulder. It often serves as a target for an opponent's **lance**.

tassets: Defenses suspended from the **breastplate** to guard the upper thighs.

tilt: A barrier of cloth or planks that separates the horses of jousters as they charge toward each other.

tonlet: A deep skirt of plates primarily worn in variants of the **foot combat**.

tournament: An event that features one or many forms of **mock combat**. Also, a term used as a generic reference to all **mock combats**.

vambrace: A defense for the entire arm, comprising lower and upper **cannons** and a **couter**.

vamplate: A funnel-shaped plate that encircles the shaft of a wood **lance** and guards the hand that holds it.

visor: A component of a helmet that protects the entire face or its upper part and is pivoted to the sides of the **bowl**.

waist plate: A **lame** of a **breastplate** or **backplate** that guards the waist and is extended downward by the **fauld** or **culet**.

war hat: An open-face helmet with a circular brim that evokes the shape of a brimmed hat.

war saddle: A saddle reinforced by a **pommel plate** and a **cantle plate**, and used in battle.

Welschrennen: A variant of the **joust of war** in which combatants are separated by a **tilt** during the charge. Contestants wear either full **field armor** or specialized full armor that evokes the appearance of Italian **field armor**.

Wulstrennen: A dangerous form of the **joust of war** in which contestants wear no helmets or armor on their limbs but are protected instead by a large shield that is bolted to the **breastplate**. These shields are molded to the body from the saddle to the brow and pierced with an eye slit for vision. This event, in which jousters' flamboyant clothing is on full view, is named for the padded textile bolster (or *Wulst*) that is tied around the combatant's brow to absorb shock.

NOTES

THE CURRENCY OF POWER

1. "Dann was ist ainem kunig grössers dann ein harnasch, darynnen sein leib in den streiten versorgt ist?" Treitzsaurwein and Schultz 1888, p. 108. Translation by the present author. For an overview of Maximilian's armors and weapons, see Gamber 1959b; Pfaffenbichler 2014c.

2. On Maximilian's image making and the place of the visual arts in his communication in particular, see Silver 2008.

3. In the *Weisskunig*, chapter 55, Maximilian claims to have taught German to Mary while she taught him French. See Treitzsaurwein and Schultz 1888, p. 137.

4. On Guinegate, see Fugger 1668, p. 891. On a shot fired at him outside Utrecht, see Fugger 1668, p. 921. On the battle of Wenzenbach (September 12, 1504), during which he was pulled down from his horse and rescued at the eleventh hour, see Palacký 1844–67, vol. 5, pt. 2 (1867), p. 91; Teuffenbach 1877, p. 167.

5. Fugger 1668, p. 1377.

6. On the tournament in the age of Maximilian I and on these mock combats in particular, see Appelbaum 1964, pp. 7–8, pls. 41–56; Anglo 2000, pp. 227–70; Breiding 2012; Sandbichler 2013; Niederhäuser 2014; Pfaffenbichler 2014b; Bloh 2017; Jezler 2017; Pfaffenbichler 2017.

7. Fugger 1668, p. 888.

8. Examples from the beginning of his rule include his recorded participation in jousts in Bruges (in 1479; Brown 2000, pp. 324–25); Ghent (in 1479; Archives Départementales du Nord, Lille, B 2118, fols. 351v–352v); 's-Hertogenbosch (in 1479; Archives Départementales du Nord, Lille, B 2118, fols. 351v–352v, B 2124, fol. 259r); Ghent (in 1480; Archives Départementales du Nord, Lille, B 2121, fol. 526r–v); Gornichem (mentioned in 1480; Archives Départementales du Nord, Lille, B 2121, fols. 505r–v); Bruges (in 1481; Archives Départementales du Nord, Lille, B 2124, fol. 259r; Brown 2000, p. 325); Nijmegen (in 1481; Archives Départementales du Nord, Lille, B 2124, fol. 263v); and Ghent (mentioned in 1481; Archives Départementales du Nord, Lille, B 2124, fol. 283v).

9. Maximilian was injured in a joust held in Arnhem in 1481 and again at one in Innsbruck in 1498. See Breiding 2012, p. 71; *Regesta Imperii* 1993, pp. 298–99, no. 5930 (document dated March 2, 1498, Innsbruck), pp. 299–300, no. 5934 (document dated March 3, 1498, Hall near Innsbruck), p. 304, no. 5966 (document dated March 11, 1498, Innsbruck).

10. La Marche 1562/1883–88, vol. 3 (1885), p. 309.

11. Maximilian I to Sigmund Prüschenk, June 24, 1478, in Kraus 1875, p. 35.

12. Fugger 1668, p. 1376.

13. For the crimson satin robe, see Archives Départementales du Nord, Lille, B 2118, fols. 341v–352r; for other robes of taffeta and velvet also acquired to be worn over his armor, see B 2118, fols. 327v–328r, 330v. For Maximilian's use of a leather bard, see Archives Départementales du Nord, Lille, B 2121, fol. 493r.

14. Archives Départementales du Nord, Lille, B 2118, fols. 355r–356r.

15. For the textiles worn over his armor, see Archives Départementales du Nord, Lille, B 2118, fol. 339v, B 2124, fol. 259r; for the plumes worn over his helmets, see B 2118, fols. 361v–362r, B 2127, fols. 285v–286r.

16. Archives Départementales du Nord, Lille, B 2118, fol. 356r–v; for the goldsmiths' work for his plumes, see B 2118, fol. 346r–v; for the acquisition of additional plume holders, see B 2118, fols. 351v–352v, 355r–356r, B 2127, fol. 266r.

17. See, for example, Archives Départementales du Nord, Lille, B 2121, fols. 503r–v, 505r–v, 526r–v, 530r–531v.

18. Archives Départementales du Nord, Lille, B 2118, fols. 351v–352v, B 2124, fol. 259r, B 2121, fols. 530r–531v.

19. Archives Départementales du Nord, Lille, B 2118, fols. 346r–v, 348v–351v.

20. *Regesta Imperii* 1993, pp. 299–300, no. 5934 (document dated March 3, 1498, Hall near Innsbruck); Sanuto 1496–1533/1879–1903, vol. 4 (1880), col. 215 (document dated January 1501, Innsbruck).

21. Maximilian also was an avid hunter, and his skills and tribulations in the hunt were integral parts of the exaltation of his own self; see Silver 2008, especially pp. 147–60; Pfaffenbichler 2014a.

22. La Marche 1562/1883–88, vol. 3, p. 306, n. 1.

23. See, for example, Fugger 1668, pp. 891–92 (entry in Ghent in 1479); Anzelewsky 1963, pp. 81–82, 84 (Luxembourg in 1480 and Strasbourg in 1492); Ranke 1839–47, vol. 1 (1839), pp. 183–84 (Worms in 1509).

24. For the rental of four jousting armors, shields, and saddles, along with vamplates and other lance fittings in 1481, see Archives Départementales du Nord, Lille, B 2124, fols. 263v, 272r–v.

25. Zimerman 1883, p. XLVII, no. 265, pp. LXI–LXII, no. 361; Schönherr 1884, p. LXXXVIII, no. 1352; Zimerman 1885, pp. LXXXII–LXXXIV, no. 2955.

26. Archives Départementales du Nord, Lille, B 2118, fols. 352v–353v.

27. Archives Départementales du Nord, Lille, B 2118, fols. 348v–351v.

28. Archives Départementales du Nord, Lille, B 2121, fols. 495r–496r.

29. Archives Départementales du Nord, Lille, B 2118, fol. 329v; for a caparison, see B 2121, fol. 408r.

30. Maximilian I to Sigmund Prüschenk, June 24, 1478, in Kraus 1875, p. 35.

31. Algemeen Rijksarchief, Brussels, CC 1924, fol. 130r. Other yearly accounts of the *argentier*, the treasurer responsible for Maximilian's household expenses, are destroyed, making it impossible to provide a comprehensive account of Maximilian's patronage of Netherlandish armorers during the period.

32. Maximilian entered into an agreement with Milanese armorers in 1495, with the request that they make at Arbois in the Franche-Comté fifty harnesses "in the fashion of Burgundy" every year. See cat. 125 in this volume.

33. For an example of the interest that the ownership of high-quality foreign armor could generate, see Blair 1965, pp. 9–10, especially p. 10, n. 1.

34. On Charles the Bold, see Gaier 1973, pp. 123–24; on Louis XI, see Picot 1904, pp. 294–95. For an overview of the armor industry of Milan, see Thomas 1958/1977.

35. On Maximilian's commissions of armor in Augsburg during the period, see Buttin 1929, pp. 41–45. On an armor made for him, which transited through Frankfurt in 1478, see Lersner 1734, p. 43. On an armor made for him by Hans Grünewald in Nuremberg in 1489, see Reitzenstein 1967, p. 714. However, it is unclear in this instance whether the armor had been commissioned before or after Maximilian's departure from the Low Countries at the beginning of the year. On an armor made for him in Mühlau and presented to him by his uncle in 1480, see Boeheim 1899, p. 287.

36. Anzelewsky 1963, p. 84.

37. *Meisterwerke der Weltlichen Schatzkammer* 2009, pp. 90–91, no. 28, ill. On the pawning of the sword, see Archives Départementales du Nord, Lille, B 2115, fols. 17v–18r.

38. On the pawning of these armor elements, see Archives Départementales du Nord, Lille, B 2122, no. 68529; B 2129, nos. 69084, 69085; B 2139, no. 69696; B 2141, no. 69856; B 2163, no. 71319; B 3512, no. 123943.

39. Gaier 1973, p. 81.

40. On Maximilian's admission into the order, see Dünnebeil 2016, pp. 49–104.

41. On his knighting, see ibid., p. 96.

42. On the many men knighted by Maximilian in anticipation of the battle of Guinegate, see Molinet 1827–28, vol. 2 (1828), p. 209. On men that he knighted during his Hungarian campaign, see La Marche 1562/1883–88, vol. 3, pp. 307–8.

43. For an armor commissioned in 1517 for presentation to Nicolas Rauber, captain in Trieste, who had recently been knighted by Maximilian, see Zimerman 1883, p. LXVIII, no. 421.

44. Anzelewsky 1963, pp. 81–82.

45. Gachard 1851–52, vol. 2, p. 87, no. CXVI.

46. On Charles the Bold's ambition to lead a Crusade, see Winkelbauer 1954, p. 527; Walsh 1977. On Maximilian's piety and the construction of his self-image as a leader of Christendom, see Silver 2008, pp. 109–45; Krause 2014b.

47. On these institutions under Frederick III and Maximilian I, see Bergmann 1868; Winkelbauer 1954; H. Koller 1980, pp. 423–28; Schmid 1984, pp. 759–60.

48. Winkelbauer 1954, pp. 533, 540; Schnurbein 2008, p. 38.

49. Greve and Lebailly 2001–2, vol. 1, pp. 97–98, nos. 464, 465, pp. 253–54, nos. 1060–62, pp. 349–56, nos. 1502–3, 1505–10, p. 492, no. 2063.

50. These gifts are too numerous to be cited here and are recorded in the registers of accounts of Maximilian's chief treasurer in the Burgundian Low Countries, which are preserved in the Archives Départementales du Nord in Lille.

51. For examples of funds given in anticipation of a military campaign, see Archives Départementales du Nord, Lille, B 2121, fols. 407r–408v, 409v; for examples of funds given to replace lost or damaged armor, see B 2121, fol. 408v.

52. See Archives Départementales du Nord, Lille, B 2121, fol. 408v.

53. As the earlier accounts of his *argentier* are lost, it is not possible to tell whether Maximilian began to give armors in this fashion before 1488.

54. Algemeen Rijksarchief, Brussels, CC 1924, fol. 130r.

55. Schönherr 1884, p. I, no. 505, p. II, no. 506.

56. Ibid., p. VII, no. 579.

57. Laubermann is first mentioned in 1496; see ibid., p. IV, no. 535. He was expressly referred to as Maximilian's court armorer in 1500; ibid., p. XII, no. 620.

58. On Archduke Sigismund's patronage of the armorers of Mühlau, see Schönherr 1883, pp. 196–99.

59. Schönherr 1884, p. XX, no. 731, p. XLII, nos. 929, 930.

60. For orders of armors for Maximilian's guard, see ibid., p. LII, no. 1019, p. LIII, no. 1028, p. LV, no. 1036.

61. For orders given in person, see Zimerman 1883, p. XLIII, no. 234, p. LXVIII, no. 417; for comments on type, design, and fixtures, see p. LXVIII, no. 421.

62. Ibid., p. LIX, no. 347.

63. Ibid., p. XLIII, no. 234.

64. Ibid., p. LXVIII, no. 419.

65. Ibid., p. LIII, no. 308.

66. Schönherr 1884, pp. XXV–XXVI, no. 792.

67. Ibid., p. XIII, no. 636; p. XIV, no. 644; p. XVI, no. 672; p. XIX, no. 718; p. XLV, no. 952; p. XLIX, no. 993; p. LII, no. 1024; p. LIV, nos. 1029, 1032, 1034; p. LXII, no. 1114; p. LXVIII, no. 1180; Zimerman and Kreyczi 1885, p. XXXVII, nos. 2671, 2672.

68. For gifts of armor commissioned from Kolman Helmschmid, see Zimerman 1883, p. LXXI, no. 436. For armor commissioned from Jörg Helmschmid the Younger, see Zimerman and Kreyczi 1885, p. III, no. 2243; p. XVIII, no. 2451; p. XX, no. 2485; pp. XX–XXI, no. 2490; p. XXIII, no. 2518; p. XXVI, no. 2549; p. XXVIII, no. 2560.

69. Tiroler Landesarchiv, Innsbruck, Geschäft von Hof, 1497, fol. 366r (Ottoman ambassador); Zimerman 1883, p. LIII, no. 308 (ambassador of Aragon); Schönherr 1884, p. LIII, no. 1028 (ambassador of England), p. VIII, no. 596 (ambassador of Naples); Zimerman 1883, p. XLIII, no. 234 (Cardinal Raimond Pérault); Schönherr 1884, p. LIX, no. 1088 (cardinal of Ferrara), p. XLV, no. 952 (Gonzaga), p. LIII, no. 1028 (Gonzaga), p. LXVII, no. 1173 (Giuliano de' Medici).

70. Schönherr 1884, p. VIII, no. 596.

71. Ibid., p. LIII, no. 1028.

72. Ibid., p. LXVII, no. 1173.

73. Zimerman and Kreyczi 1885, p. XXXVIII, no. 2681.

74. "Und der gedacht weiss kunig hat in der bemelten seiner platnerey mit diser kunstlichen hert, die allen andern verporgen was, vil kunigen, fursten und mechtigen herrn kirris machn lassen und verert, damit der weiss kunig, aller ander kunig schankung ubertroffen hat." Treitzsaurwein and Schultz 1888, p. 108. Translation by the present author.

75. Algemeen Rijksarchief, Brussels, CC 1924, fol. 130r.

76. Schönherr 1883, p. 197; Boeheim 1899, p. 288.

77. On this armor, see Thomas and Gamber 1954, p. 59, no. 34, pl. 18.

78. "Et treuve que l'acier est plus noble chose que l'or, l'argent, le plomb ne le fer, pour ce que l'acier, comme du plus noble metal, l'on fait les armures et les harnois, dont les plus grans du monde se parent et asseurent leurs corps contre la guerre et autrement." La Marche 1562/1883–88, vol. 3, p. 313. Translation by the present author.

POLITICAL STRUGGLE AND DYNASTIC TRIUMPH

1. The major work on Maximilian I is the five-volume biography written by Hermann Wiesflecker; see Wiesflecker 1971–86. Additional studies include Wiesflecker 1991; *Maximilian I.* 2000; Hollegger 2005; Hollegger 2012.

2. See Pfaffenbichler 2000, p. 50.

3. Ibid., p. 55.

4. Wiesflecker 1971–86, vol. 1 (1971), p. 165.

5. Seton-Watson 1902, p. 17.

6. See Wiesflecker 1971–86, vol. 2 (1977), pp. 288–96.

7. Ibid., p. 287.

8. Wiesflecker 2000, p. 112.

9. Hollegger 2005, p. 68.

10. Lange 2002, p. 153.

11. See Wiesflecker 1971–86, vol. 3 (1977), pp. 186–92.

12. Niederstätter 1996, p. 339.

13. Just 2011, p. 71.

14. Niederstätter 1996, p. 372.

15. Hollegger 2012, p. 25.

THE MAKING OF THE "LAST KNIGHT"

1. Amory Sibley Carhart to John O. Sargent, April 11 (1890?), microfilm, reel 3, John O. Sargent Papers, Massachusetts Historical Society, Boston.

2. Anastasius Grün is a pseudonym for the Austrian politician and poet Count Anton Alexander von Auersperg. For more on Grün's *Last Knight,* see Scharmitzer 2010, pp. 93–103, 452–53, 466–67, 504–5.

3. See Boner 1846; see also Scharmitzer 2009, pp. 149–51, nos. 118, 119, p. 156, no. 122.

4. See Sargent 1871.

5. See Silver 2008.

6. Faber 1519, n.p. [fol. 15v], cited in Zinnhobler 1968–69, p. 58.

7. See Collin 1810b, p. 19, n. (unsigned note written by Joseph von Hormayr); Collin 1810a, p. 238. See also Hormayr 1814, pp. 60–62, n. 53; Franckh 1830, p. 57, 2nd col. Hormayr had not yet begun using the "Last Knight" appellation in 1807; see Hormayr 1807–14, vol. 5 (1807), pp. 86–186.

8. See Jahn 1810, p. 241; Schlechte 1835; Duller 1836, p. 247.

9. For more on the concept of the Last Knight, see Paravicini 2011, pp. 108–12.

10. *Star Wars: Episode VIII—The Last Jedi*, directed by Rian Johnson (Walt Disney Pictures and Lucasfilm, 2017); *Transformers: The Last Knight*, directed by Michael Bay (Paramount Pictures and Hasbro, 2017).

11. For more on the *Weisskunig,* see Larry Silver in *Emperor Maximilian I* 2012, pp. 288–89, no. 74, and on *Theuerdank,* see Silver in *Emperor Maximilian I* 2012, p. 285, no. 73. For *Freydal,* see cats. 39–55 in this volume.

12. For the *Genealogy,* see Silver and Christof Metzger in *Emperor Maximilian I* 2012, pp. 168–69, no. 20; for the *Book of Habsburg Family Saints,* see Thomas Schauerte in *Emperor Maximilian I* 2012, pp. 172–73, nos. 22, 23.

13. For the *Triumphal Procession,* see Eva Michel in ibid., pp. 268–71, no. 68, ill.; for the *Arch of Honor,* see Schauerte in ibid., pp. 373–74, no. 124, ill.; Schauerte 2015.

14. For the tomb, see Lukas Madersbacher in *Spätmittelalter und Renaissance* 2003, pp. 369–72, no. 6, and ill. pp. 94, 100, 101; Schauerte in *Emperor Maximilian I* 2012, pp. 358–61, nos. 118, 119, ill., p. 368, no. 122, ill.; Katharina Seidl in *Emperor Maximilian I* 2012, pp. 362–63, no. 120, ill.; Thomas Kuster in *Emperor Maximilian I* 2012, pp. 366–67, no. 121, ill.; Krause 2014c, pp. 191–92.

15. Draft of a letter from Conrad Peutinger to Emperor Maximilian I, June 9, 1516, Stadtarchiv, Augsburg, Literaliensammlung Personenselekte Peutinger; see König 1923, pp. 268–71, no. 168. Liefrinck's printing blocks for the *Triumphal Procession* are in the Albertina Museum, Vienna (HO2006/197, HO2006/202, HO2006/207, HO2006/215, HO2006/227, HO2006/263, HO2006/269, HO2006/289, HO2006/298).

16. See Michel in *Emperor Maximilian I* 2012, pp. 268–71, no. 68, ill., especially p. 269.

17. For more on the artists involved in the *Freydal* project, see Pokorny 2019.

18. See Rudolf 1980, fig. 7 (following p. 176); Michel in *Emperor Maximilian I* 2012, pp. 155–56, no. 15, ill.; see also cats. 39–43 on the tournament book *Freydal* in this volume.

19. "ain peligan koph; ain gantzen peligcan"; National Gallery of Art, Washington, D.C., Rosenwald Collection (1943.3.4427); on the *Freydal* sketches in Washington, see cats. 44–52 in this volume.

20. For more on the notion of commemoration, see Müller 1987, cols. 208–9; Müller 1998.

21. See Andrea Scheichl in *Emperor Maximilian I* 2012, pp. 314–15, no. 90, p. 317, no. 92, p. 344, no. 107, pp. 346–47, nos. 109, 110.

22. See Österreichische Nationalbibliothek, Vienna, Cod. 2900, fol. 2r. See also "puech der lust gärten und der siben ruem gärten"; Österreichische Nationalbibliothek, Vienna, Cod. Ser. n. 2626, fol. 126r.

23. "nach den Arttickhln, in scatl zu legen"; Österreichische Nationalbibliothek, Vienna, Cod. Ser. n. 2645, fol. 10r.

24. "puecher, cronickhen vnnd dergleichen treulichen zuuerwaren vnnd zufursehen [seien], bis auf vnnser lieben sün/willen, vnnd weyter fursehung"; Steiermärkisches Landesarchiv, Graz, Landschaftliche Urkunden, A 26a, fols. 5v–6r.

25. See Wood 2015, pp. 137, 142, 143–45, 145–50.

26. "die menschen der gedächtnuss so wenig acht nämen"; *Der Weisskunig,* chap. 24, quoted in Musper 1956, vol. 1, p. 225.

27. "und hat befohlen vleissig alle Historicos zusamen zubringen und aus allen ein leideliche Chronica zu machen"; Carion 1533, fol. 173v (chapter titled "Wie und wenn die Churfürsten erstlich eingesatzt sind").

28. "mit allem fleiss solchs auffgezeichnet vnd notiert damit ja hindenach Gelerte Leute so etwa diese hendel beschreiben wolten"; Melanchthon 1569, p. CXLVII, verso. Melanchthon's assertion is based on a personal note from Willibald Pirckheimer.

29. For more on contemporaneous accounts of Maximilian's death, see Wiesflecker 1971–86, vol. 4 (1981), pp. 420–32, 627–28, n. 1. Albrecht Dürer recorded the emperor's age, down to the day, in the inscription on his portrait of Maximilian (fig. 22); see Anzelewsky 1991, pp. 257–59, no. 146, figs. 171–73.

30. See Krause 2014c, pp. 191–93.

31. For more on the inscription, see note 29 above.

32. *Death Portrait of Emperor Maximilian I,* 1519, Universalmuseum Joanneum, Schloss Eggenberg, Graz (392).

33. See Christof Metzger in *Dürer, Cranach, Holbein* 2011, pp. 29–30, no. 3; Gernot Mayer in *Emperor Maximilian I* 2012, pp. 380–83, no. 127, ill.; Sahm 2015.

34. See Krause 2014c, pp. 186–87; see also Rudolf Distelberger in *Kaiser Karl V.* 2000, p. 319, no. 354, ill. p. 321; Sabine Haag in *Kaiser Ferdinand I.* 2003, p. 438, no. VI.9, ill. p. 439.

35. See Alexis Merle du Bourg in *Jordaens* 2013, pp. 198–99, no. III-06, ill.; see also Martin 1972, pp. 66–86.

36. See Busson 1888; Gottlieb 1900, pp. 128–30; Ammann 1996; Krause 2014c, pp. 190–91.

37. See Pighius 1587, pp. 243–46.

38. See Krause 2014c, p. 190, fig. 5.

39. See, for instance, Tobias Verhaecht and (attributed to) Sebastien Vrancx, *Landscape with the Rescue of Emperor Maximilian I from the Martinswand,* 1615, Koninklijke Musea voor Schone Kunsten van België, Brussels (2794); Koninklijke Musea voor Schone Kunsten van België 1984, p. 310, ill. See also the smaller version of the painting in the Musée du Louvre, Paris (M.N.R. 401); Brejon de Lavergnée, Foucart, and Reynaud 1979, p. 145, ill.

40. See Telesko 2006, p. 461, n. 197; Krause 2014c, p. 191; see also Krezdorn 1969.

41. For more on *El segundo blasón,* see Johnson 1980; Arellano and Pinillos 1997; Pinillos 1998. For more on Castilla's release from prison, see Pinillos 1998, pp. 266–67.

42. See Krause 2014c, pp. 190–91.

43. See Telesko 2012; Krause 2014c, pp. 193–94.

44. "die Basis aller neuern Europäischen Verfassung"; Herder 1769, p. 170. "die Stuffe des österreichischen Thrones höher zu bauen"; Treitzsaurwein 1775, n.p. [introduction, p. 2].

45. "mit einem weiss damastenen Kleid, und einem Mantel von roth geblumten Samet angethan"; *Wienerisches Diarium,* April 11, 1770, no. 29, Mittwochsanhang, n.p. [p. 1]. See also Krause 2014c, p. 194.

46. "unter Läutung aller Glocken in der Burg, und in der Stadt"; *Wienerisches Diarium,* April 11, 1770, no. 29, Mittwochsanhang, n.p. [p. 2].

47. See Krause 2014c, p. 185.

48. See Telesko 2012; Krause 2014c, pp. 194–96.

49. See Hormayr 1807–14, vol. 5 (1807), p. 171; Telesko 2006, p. 350 (with bibliography).

50. See Natter 2012, p. 590, no. 155, ill. p. 589, and pp. 580–82, no. 141, ill. For more on the armor (Kunsthistorisches Museum, Vienna, A 60, A 62), see Thomas and Gamber 1976, pp. 106–7, no. A 60, fig. 40, pp. 108–10, no. A 62, figs. 34, 35.

51. See Telesko 2012, pp. 118–21, and figs. 1, 2.

52. Ibid., p. 122; Krause 2014c, p. 194. The title of the work comes from a Latin phrase in a medieval poem, "Bella gerant alii, tu felix Austria nube!" (Let others wage war, you—happy Austria—marry!).

53. Albrecht Dürer Haus, Museen der Stadt Nürnberg (GM 86); see Marianne Frodl in *Traum vom Glück* 1996, vol. 2, pp. 639–40, no. 23.11, ill.; Telesko 2012, p. 118, and p. 126, fig. 8.

54. See Angelina Pötschner in *Traum vom Glück* 1996, vol. 2, p. 639, no. 23.10, ill.; for Van Mander's account of the anecdote (*Het Schilder-boeck*; Van Mander 1616–18, fol. 208v, and Appendix [1617], fol. 208v), see Van Mander 1604/1994–99, vol. 1 (1994), p. 93, lines 14–24, p. 462, lines 15–21, vol. 2 (1995), p. 303; see also Mende 1993; Pötschner in *Traum vom Glück* 1996, vol. 2, p. 639, no. 23.10.

55. "das gelt, so ich auf die gedechtnus ausgib, nit verloren"; *Der Weisskunig,* chap. 24, quoted in Musper 1956, vol. 1, p. 226. See also Silver 1994, p. 45.

A bon droyt 2007
A bon droyt: Spade di uomini liberi, cavalieri e santi/Epées d'hommes libres, chevaliers et saints. Exh. cat., Museo Archeologico Regionale, Aosta. Edited by Mario Scalini. Cinisello Balsamo: Silvana, 2007.

Abadia 1793
Ignacio Abadia. *Resumen sacado del inventario general histórico que se hizo en el año de 1793 de los arneses antiguos, armas blancas y de fuego, con otros efectos de la Real Armería del Rey nuestro señor.* Madrid: Imprenta Real, 1793.

Ainsworth, Hindriks, and Terjanian 2015
Maryan W. Ainsworth, Sandra Hindriks, and Pierre Terjanian. *Lucas Cranach's "Saint Maurice." The Metropolitan Museum of Art Bulletin*, n.s., 72, no. 4 (Spring 2015). [Published in conjunction with the exhibition "Cranach's *Saint Maurice*," held at The Metropolitan Museum of Art, New York, 2015.]

Albertario 2015
Marco Albertario. "Per un 'profilo' dei duchi di Milano." In *Arte lombarda* 2015, pp. 35–37.

Albrecht Dürer 2003
Albrecht Dürer. Exh. cat., Albertina Museum, Vienna. Edited by Klaus Albrecht Schröder and Maria Luise Sternath. Ostfildern: Hatje Cantz, 2003.

Alexander 2016
Jonathan J. G. Alexander. "I libri di scuola di Massimiliano Sforza e il loro contesto." In Jonathan J. G. Alexander, Pier Luigi Mulas, and Marzia Pontone, *Grammatica del Donato e Liber Iesus: Due libri per l'educazione di Massimiliano Sforza*, pp. 9–41. Modena: Franco Cosimo Panini, 2016.

Ammann 1996
Gert Ammann. "Kaiser Maximilians I. Rettung aus der Martinswand." In *Heldenromantik: Tiroler Geschichtsbilder im 19. Jahrhundert von Koch bis Defregger*, edited by Ellen Hastaba, Carl Kraus, and Claudia Sporer-Heis, pp. 30–34. Exh. cat., Tiroler Landeskundliches Museum im Zeughaus Kaiser Maximilians I., Innsbruck, and Südtiroler Landesmuseum, Schloss Tirol. Innsbruck: Tiroler Landesmuseum Ferdinandeum; Tirol: Südtiroler Landesmuseum, 1996.

Angermeier 1981
Heinz Angermeier, ed. *Deutsche Reichstagsakten unter Maximilian I.* Vol. 5, *Reichstag von Worms,*

1495. 2 vols. in 3 pts. Edited by the Bayerische Akademie der Wissenschaften, Historische Kommission. Göttingen: Vandenhoeck & Ruprecht, 1981.

Angermeier 1982
Heinz Angermeier. "Die Sforza und das Reich." In *Gli Sforza a Milano e in Lombardia e i loro rapporti con gli stati italiani ed europei (1450–1535): Convegno internazionale, Milano, 18–21 maggio 1981*, pp. 165–91. Milan: Cisalpino-Goliardica, 1982.

Anglo 2000
Sidney Anglo. *The Martial Arts of Renaissance Europe.* New Haven, Conn.: Yale University Press, 2000.

Anzelewsky 1963
Fedja Anzelewsky. "Erzherzog Maximilians schwerer Rossharnisch von 1480." *Waffen- und Kostümkunde*, 3rd ser., 5, no. 2 (1963), pp. 77–88.

Anzelewsky 1991
Fedja Anzelewsky. *Albrecht Dürer: Das malerische Werk.* 2 vols. 2nd edition. Berlin: Deutscher Verlag für Kunstwissenschaft, 1991.

Anzelewsky and Mielke 1984
Fedja Anzelewsky and Hans Mielke. *Albrecht Dürer: Kritischer Katalog der Zeichnungen.* Berlin: Staatliche Museen Preussischer Kulturbesitz, Kupferstichkabinett, 1984.

Appelbaum 1964
The Triumph of Maximilian I: 137 Woodcuts by Hans Burgkmair and Others. Introduction, translation, and notes by Stanley Appelbaum. New York: Dover Publications, 1964.

Appuhn 1979
Maximilian I, Holy Roman Emperor. *Theuerdank, 1517.* Commentary by Horst Appuhn. Die Bibliophilen Taschenbücher 121. Dortmund: Harenberg Kommunikation, 1979.

Arellano and Pinillos 1997
Pedro Calderón de la Barca. *El segundo blasón del Austria.* Edited by Ignacio Arellano and Carmen Pinillos. Autos sacramentales completos de Calderón 14. Teatro del Siglo de Oro, Ediciones críticas, 81. Pamplona: Universidad de Navarra; Kassel: Edition Reichenberger, 1997.

Art of the Armourer 1963
The Art of the Armourer: An Exhibition of Armour, Swords and Firearms. Exh. cat., Victoria and Albert Museum, London. London: Arms and Armour Society, 1963.

Arte lombarda 2015
Arte lombarda dai Visconti agli Sforza. Exh. cat., Palazzo Reale, Milan. Edited by Mauro Natale and Serena Romano. Milan: Skira, 2015.

Arte y caballería en España 2007
Arte y caballería en España: La Real Armería de Madrid. [In Chinese and Spanish.] Exh. cat., Palace Museum, Forbidden City, Beijing. Edited by Álvaro Soler del Campo. Beijing: Zi Jin Cheng Chubanshe, 2007.

Ashcroft 2017
Jeffrey Ashcroft. *Albrecht Dürer: Documentary Biography.* 2 vols. New Haven, Conn.: Yale University Press, 2017.

Auer 1984
Alfred Auer. *Das Inventarium der Ambraser Sammlungen aus dem Jahr 1621.* Pt. 1, *Die Rüstkammern.* Vienna: A. Schroll, 1984.

Auer et al. 2008
Alfred Auer, Margot Rauch, Veronika Sandbichler, and Katharina Seidl. *Meisterwerke der Sammlungen Schloss Ambras.* Kürzführer durch das Kunsthistorische Museum 9. Vienna: Kunsthistorisches Museum; Milan: Skira, 2008.

Baron 1968
Françoise Baron. "Le cavalier royal de Notre-Dame de Paris et le problème de la statue équestre au Moyen Age." *Bulletin monumental* 126, no. 2 (1968), pp. 141–54.

Bartels and Bingener 2006
Christoph Bartels and Andreas Bingener. *Der Bergbau bei Schwaz in Tirol im mittleren 16. Jahrhundert.* Vol. 3 of *Das Schwazer Bergbuch: "1556 Perckwerch etc.,"* edited by Christoph Bartels, Andreas Bingener, and Rainer Slotta. Veröffentlichungen aus dem Deutschen Bergbau-Museum Bochum 142. Bochum: Deutsches Bergbau-Museum, 2006.

Bartels and Bingener 2015
Christoph Bartels and Andreas Bingener. "Das Schwazer Bergbuch in seinem historischen und technologischen Kontext." In *Bergauf Bergab: 10.000 Jahre Bergbau in den Ostalpen*, edited by Thomas Stöllner and Klaus Oeggl, pp. 519–26. Veröffentlichungen aus dem Deutschen Bergbau-Museum Bochum 207. Bochum: Deutsches Bergbau-Museum; Rahden: In Kommission bei VML Verlag Marie Leidorf, 2015.

Bartolini 1515
Riccardo Bartolini. *Odeporicon, idest, Itinerariu[m] Reuerendissimi in Christo Patris & D[omi]ni. D. Mathei Sancti Angeli, Cardinalis Gurcensis Coadiutoris Saltzburgen[sis]. . . . Quaeq[ue] in Conuentu Maximiliani Caes. Aug. . . . Memoratu Digna Gesta Sunt.* [Vienna]: Hieronymus Vietor impensis Ioannis Vuideman, 1515.

Bartrum 1995
Giulia Bartrum. *German Renaissance Prints, 1490-1550.* Exh. cat., British Museum, London. London: British Museum Press for the Trustees of the British Museum, 1995.

Baum, Klaiber, and Pfeiffer 1914
Julius Baum, Hans Klaiber, and Bertold Pfeiffer. *Die Kunst- und Altertums-Denkmale im Königreich Württemberg.* [Vol. 4], *Inventar: Donaukreis,* pt. 1, *Oberämter Biberach, Blaubeuren, Ehingen, Geislingen.* Stuttgart: Paul Neff, 1914.

Beard 1939a
Charles R. Beard. "Armours from St. Donat's Castle in the Collection of William Randolph Hearst, Esq." *Connoisseur* 103, no. 449 (January 1939), pp. 3-9.

Beard 1939b
Charles R. Beard. "Helmets at St. Donat's Castle in the Collection of William Randolph Hearst, Esq." *Connoisseur* 103, no. 451 (March 1939), pp. 129-35, 177.

Beaufort-Spontin 2010
Christian Beaufort-Spontin. "Die 'Ehrliche Gesellschaft' Erzherzog Ferdinands von Österreich: Die originellste Sammlung des 16. Jahrhunderts?" In *Das Exponat als historisches Zeugnis: Präsentationsformen politischer Ikonographie,* edited by Hans Ottomeyer, pp. 125-30. Dresden: Sandstein; Berlin: Deutsches Historisches Museum, 2010.

Beaufort-Spontin and Pfaffenbichler 2005
Christian Beaufort-Spontin and Matthias Pfaffenbichler. *Meisterwerke der Hofjagd- und Rüstkammer.* Kurzführer durch das Kunsthistorische Museum 3. Vienna: Kunsthistorisches Museum; Milan: Skira, 2005.

Bergmann 1868
Joseph von Bergmann. "Der St. Georgs-Ritterorden vom Jahre 1469-1579." *Mittheilungen der K. K. Central-Commission zur Erforschung und Erhaltung der Baudenkmale* 13 (1868), pp. 169-74.

Bertolotti 1889
Antonino Bertolotti. *Le arti minori alla corte di Mantova nei secoli XV, XVI e XVII: Ricerche storiche negli Archivi Mantovani.* Milan: Tipografia Bortolotti di Giuseppe Prato, 1889.

Bialler 1992
Nancy Bialler. *Chiaroscuro Woodcuts: Hendrick Goltzius (1558-1617) and His Time.* Exh. cat., Rijksmuseum, Amsterdam, and Cleveland Museum of Art. Amsterdam: Rijksmuseum; Ghent: Snoeck-Ducaju & Zoon, 1992.

Bingener and Bartels 2015
Andreas Bingener and Christoph Bartels. "Bergbau in Schwaz im 15. bis 18. Jahrhundert." In *Bergauf Bergab: 10.000 Jahre Bergbau in den Ostalpen,* edited by Thomas Stöllner and Klaus Oeggl, pp. 527-32. Veröffentlichungen aus dem Deutschen Bergbau-Museum Bochum 207. Bochum: Deutsches Bergbau-Museum; Rahden: In Kommission bei VML Verlag Marie Leidorf, 2015.

Bischoff 2003
Georges Bischoff. "'Vive Osteriche et Bourgogne!' Un preux Franc-Comtois au service de Maximilien Iᵉʳ, Louis de Vaudrey." In *La Franche-Comté à la charnière du Moyen Age et de la Renaissance, 1450-1550: Actes du colloque de Besançon, 10-11 octobre 2002,* edited by Paul Delsalle and Laurence Delobette, pp. 161-86. Besançon: Presses Universitaires Franc-Comtoises, 2003.

Blair 1965
Claude Blair. *The Emperor Maximilian's Gift of Armour to King Henry VIII and the Silvered and Engraved Armour at the Tower of London.* Oxford: Printed by Vivian Ridler for the Society of Antiquaries of London, 1965.

Blair 1966
Claude Blair. "Two Toy Jousters." *Waffen- und Kostümkunde,* 3rd ser., 8, no. 1 (1966), pp. 43-47.

Blair 1974
Claude Blair. "Comments on Dr. Borg's 'Horned Helmet.'" *Journal of the Arms and Armour Society* 8, no. 2 (December 1974), pp. 138-85.

Blair 1998
Claude Blair. "The Lullingstone Helm." *Antiquaries Journal* 78 (1998), pp. 289-305.

Bloh 2017
Jutta Charlotte von Bloh. "Rennen, Stechen, Turniere und Mummereien: Die sächsischen Kurfürsten Friedrich III. (1463-1525) und Johann (1468-1532) in Interaktion mit Kaiser Maximilian I." In *Turnier: 1000 Jahre Ritterspiele,* edited by Stefan Krause and Matthias Pfaffenbichler, pp. 253-83. Vienna: KHM-Museumsverband; Munich: Hirmer, 2017.

Boccia 1975
Lionello Giorgio Boccia, ed. *Il Museo Stibbert a Firenze.* Vol. 3, *L'armeria europea.* 2 pts. Milan: Electa, 1975.

Boccia 1982
Lionello Giorgio Boccia, ed. *Le armature di S. Maria delle Grazie di Curtatone di Mantova e l'armatura lombarda del '400.* Busto Arsizio: Bramante, 1982.

Boccia and Coelho 1967
Lionello Giorgio Boccia and E. T. Coelho. *L'arte dell'armatura in Italia.* Milan: Bramante, 1967.

Boccia, Rossi, and Morin 1980
Lionello Giorgio Boccia, Francesco Rossi, and Marco Morin. *Armi et armature lombarde.* Milan: Electa, 1980.

Boeheim 1889
Wendelin Boeheim. *Führer durch die Waffen-Sammlung.* Vienna: Kunsthistorische Sammlungen des Allerhöchsten Kaiserhauses, 1889.

Boeheim 1890
Wendelin Boeheim. *Handbuch der Waffen-kunde: Das Waffenwesen in seiner historischen Entwickelung vom Beginn des Mittelalters bis zum Ende des 18. Jahrhunderts.* Leipzig: E. A. Seemann, 1890.

Boeheim 1891
Wendelin Boeheim. "Augsburger Waffenschmiede: Ihre Werke und ihre Beziehungen zum kaiserlichen und anderen zu Höfen." *Jahrbuch der Kunsthistorischen Sammlungen des Allerhöchsten Kaiserhauses* 12 (1891), pp. 165-227.

Boeheim 1892
Wendelin Boeheim. "Die Zeugbücher des Kaisers Maximilian I." *Jahrbuch der Kunsthistorischen Sammlungen des Allerhöchsten Kaiserhauses* 13 (1892), pp. 94-201.

Boeheim 1898
Wendelin Boeheim. *Album hervorragender Gegenstände aus der Waffensammlung des Allerhöchsten Kaiserhauses.* Vol. 2. Vienna: J. Löwy, 1898.

Boeheim 1899
Wendelin Boeheim. "Die Waffenschmiede Seusenhofer: Ihre Werke und ihre Beziehungen zu habsburgischen und anderen Regenten." *Jahrbuch der Kunsthistorischen Sammlungen des Allerhöchsten Kaiserhauses* 20 (1899), pp. 283-320.

C. G. Boerner 1929
Kupferstiche des XV. bis XVIII. Jahrhunderts: Dabei die Sammlung von Passavant-Gontard, Frankfurt a. M. . . . Originalzeichnungen zum Freydal des Kaisers Maximilian. . . . Sale cat., C. G. Boerner, Leipzig, May 10-15, 1929.

W. Boerner 1927
Wolfgang Boerner. "Der Meister WA." PhD diss., Rheinische Friedrich-Wilhelms-Universität, Bonn, 1927.

Boner 1846
[Charles Boner.] "Anastasius Grün, Count Auersperg." *Literary Gazette* (London), no. 1521 (March 14, 1846), pp. 247–49; no. 1522 (March 21, 1846), pp. 272–74.

Bonnefons de Lavialle 1838
Catalogue descriptif des armures, armes défensives et offensives, meubles et curiosités diverses du Moyen-Age . . . composant la collection de M. le docteur A. Hebray. Sale cat., Bonnefons de Lavialle, Paris, January 29, 1838, and following days.

Borchert 2002
Till-Holger Borchert. *The Age of Van Eyck: The Mediterranean World and Early Netherlandish Painting, 1430–1530.* With contributions by Andreas Beyer et al. Exh. cat., Groeningemuseum, Bruges. New York: Thames & Hudson, 2002.

Bösch 1887–89
Hans Bösch. "Die kirchlichen Kleinodien des Kardinals Albrecht, Erzbischofs und Kurfürsten von Mainz, Markgrafen von Brandenburg." *Mitteilungen aus dem Germanischen Nationalmuseum* 2 (1887–89), pp. 123–52.

Boskovits and Brown 2003
Miklós Boskovits and David Alan Brown, with Robert Echols et al. *Italian Paintings of the Fifteenth Century.* Collections of the National Gallery of Art, Systematic Catalogue. Washington, D.C.: National Gallery of Art, 2003.

Bossmeyer 2015
Christine Bossmeyer. *Visuelle Geschichte in den Zeichnungen und Holzschnitten zum "Weisskunig" Kaiser Maximilians I.* 2 vols. Ostfildern: Jan Thorbecke, 2015.

Boulton 2006
D'Arcy Jonathan Dacre Boulton. "The Order of the Golden Fleece and the Creation of Burgundian National Identity." In *The Ideology of Burgundy: The Promotion of National Consciousness, 1364–1565,* edited by D'Arcy Jonathan Dacre Boulton and Jan R. Veenstra, pp. 21–97. Brill's Studies in Intellectual History 145. Leiden: Brill, 2006.

Brandstätter 2013
Klaus Brandstätter. "Der Bergbau in Schwaz und die Brixlegger Hütte." In *Cuprum Tyrolense: 5550 Jahre Bergbau und Kupferverhüttung in Tirol,* edited by Montanwerke Brixlegg, Klaus Oeggl, and Veronika Schaffer, pp. 233–40. Brixlegg: Edition Tirol, 2013.

Brauneis 1976
Walther Brauneis. "Das Kaisergrab auf dem Bürglstein im Wolfgangland: Ein Grabmalprojekt Maximilians I." *Jahrbuch des Oberösterreichischen Musealvereines* 121, no. 1 (1976), pp. 169–77.

Braunfels-Esche 1976
Sigrid Braunfels-Esche. *Sankt Georg: Legende, Verehrung, Symbol.* Munich: Callwey, 1976.

Breiding 2012
Dirk H. Breiding. "Rennen, Stechen und Turnier zur Zeit Maximilians I." In *"Vor Halbtausend Jahren . . .": Festschrift zur Erinnerung an den Besuch des Kaisers Maximilian I. in St. Wendel,* pp. 51–82. St. Wendel: Stadtmuseum St. Wendel, 2012.

Breiding 2017
Dirk H. Breiding. "Turniere und Turnierausrüstung in Mitteleuropa: Von den Anfängen bis zum ausgehenden 15. Jahrhundert." In *Turnier: 1000 Jahre Ritterspiele,* edited by Stefan Krause and Matthias Pfaffenbichler, pp. 23–39. Vienna: KHM-Museumsverband; Munich: Hirmer, 2017.

Brejon de Lavergnée, Foucart, and Reynaud 1979
Arnauld Brejon de Lavergnée, Jacques Foucart, and Nicole Reynaud. *Catalogue sommaire illustré des peintures du Musée du Louvre.* Vol. 1, *Ecoles flamande et hollandaise.* Paris: Réunion des Musées Nationaux, 1979.

Broschek 1973
Anja Broschek. *Michel Erhart: Ein Beitrag zur schwäbischen Plastik der Spätgotik.* Beiträge zur Kunstgeschichte 8. Berlin: Walter de Gruyter, 1973.

Brown 1999
Andrew Brown. "Bruges and the Burgundian 'Theatre-State': Charles the Bold and Our Lady of the Snow." *History* (Historical Association, Great Britain) 84, no. 276 (1999), pp. 573–89.

Brown 2000
Andrew Brown. "Urban Jousts in the Later Middle Ages: The White Bear of Bruges." *Revue belge de philologie et d'histoire* 78, no. 2 (2000), pp. 315–30.

Buchon 1838
J. A. C. Buchon, ed. *Choix de chroniques et mémoires sur l'histoire de France.* Paris: Auguste Desrez, 1838.

Bücken 2013
Véronique Bücken. "Maître des Portraits princiers." In *Héritage de Rogier van der Weyden* 2013, pp. 225–27.

Busson 1888
Arnold Busson. "Die Sage von Max auf der Martinswand und ihre Entstehung." *Sitzungsberichte der Philosophisch-Historischen Classe der Kaiserlichen Akademie der Wissenschaften* 116 (1888), pp. 455–500.

Buttin 1929
Charles Buttin. *Les bardes articulées au temps de Maximilien Ier: Etude sur l'armement chevaleresque au quinzième et au seizième siècles.* Strasbourg: Librairie Istra, 1929.

Byck 2015
John Byck. "Master W with the Key: New Perspectives on the Engraver and His Art." PhD diss., Institute of Fine Arts, New York University, 2015.

Campbell 2007
Thomas P. Campbell. *Henry VIII and the Art of Majesty: Tapestries at the Tudor Court.* New Haven, Conn.: Yale University Press for the Paul Mellon Centre for Studies in British Art, 2007.

Capwell 2011
Tobias Capwell, with David Edge and Jeremy Warren. *Masterpieces of European Arms and Armour in the Wallace Collection.* London: Wallace Collection and Paul Holberton, 2011.

Capwell 2019
Tobias Capwell. "'By the Action of His Majesty': Jousting in *Freydal.*" In Krause 2019a.

Cárdenas 2002
Livia Cárdenas. *Friedrich der Weise und das Wittenberger Heiltumsbuch: Mediale Repräsentation zwischen Mittelalter und Neuzeit.* Berlin: Lukas, 2002.

Cardinale 1985
Hyginus Eugene Cardinale. *Orders of Knighthood, Awards and the Holy See.* 3rd edition. Edited and revised by Peter Bander van Duren. Gerrards Cross, Buckinghamshire: Van Duren, 1985.

Carion 1533
Johannes Carion. *Chronica durch M. Johan. Carion, vleissig zusamen gezogen. . . .* Wittenberg: Georg Rhau, 1533.

Carré 1795
J. B. L. Carré. *Panoplie, ou Réunion de tout ce qui a trait à la guerre, depuis l'origine de la nation française jusqu'à nos jours.* Châlons-sur-Marne: Pinteville-Bouchard; Paris: Fuchs, 1795.

Catalogue de la collection formée par M. Didier Petit 1843
Catalogue de la collection formée par M. Didier Petit, à Lyon, consistant en émaux, faïences, verres de Venise. . . . Paris: Dentu, 1843.

Caviness et al. 1985
Madeline H. Caviness et al. *Stained Glass before 1700 in American Collections: New England and New York (Corpus Vitrearum Checklist. I).* Studies in the History of Art 15. Monograph Series 1. Washington, D.C.: National Gallery of Art, 1985.

Cermann 2013
Regina Cermann. *Der "Bellifortis" des Konrad Kyeser.* Codices Manuscripti & Impressi, Supplementum 8. Purkersdorf: Brüder Hollinek, 2013.

Certosa di Pavia 2006
Certosa di Pavia. Edited by Franco Maria Ricci. Parma: Cariparma; Piacenza: Grafiche Step, 2006.

Cetto 1977
Anna Maria Cetto. "Cranachs Turnier-holzschnitte von 1509 und der Turnierteppich Friedrichs des Weisen in Valenciennes." In *Akten des Kolloquiums zur Basler Cranach-Ausstellung 1974: Anhang; Das Turnier-Gedicht des Georg Sibutus*, edited by Luzi Schucan, pp. 19–21. Basel: Kunstmuseum, 1977.

Charles-Quint et son temps 1955
Charles-Quint et son temps. Exh. cat., Museum voor Schone Kunsten, Ghent. Ghent: Editions de la Connaissance, 1955.

Charles the Bold 2009
Charles the Bold (1433–1477): Splendour of Burgundy. Exh. cat., Historisches Museum, Bern; Bruggemuseum and Groeningemuseum, Bruges; and Kunsthistorisches Museum, Vienna. Edited by Susan Marti, Till-Holger Borchert, and Gabriele Keck. Brussels: Mercatorfonds, 2009.

Châtelet and Goetghebeur 2006
Albert Châtelet and Nicole Goetghebeur. *Le Musée des Beaux-Arts de Lille.* Brussels: Centre d'Etude de la Peinture du Quinzième Siècle dans les Pays-Bas Méridionaux et la Principauté de Liège, 2006.

Chefs-d'oeuvre de la tapisserie 1973
Chefs-d'oeuvre de la tapisserie du XIVe au XVIe siècle. Exh. cat., Galeries Nationales du Grand Palais, Paris. Edited by Geneviève Souchal. Paris: Editions des Musées Nationaux, 1973.

Chmelarz 1894
Eduard Chmelarz. "Jost de Negker's Helldunkelblätter Kaiser Max und St. Georg." *Jahrbuch der Kunsthistorischen Sammlungen des Allerhöchsten Kaiserhauses* 15 (1894), pp. 392–97.

Christie's 1987
Antique Arms and Armour. Sale cat., Christie's South Kensington, London, October 21, 1987.

Christie's 2001
Fine Antique Arms and Armour and Books from the R. T. Gwynn Collection. Sale cat., Christie's, London, April 24, 2001.

Cinquecento lombardo 2000
Il Cinquecento lombardo: Da Leonardo a Caravaggio. Exh. cat., Palazzo Reale, Milan. Edited by Flavio Caroli. Milan: Skira; Florence: Artificio, 2000.

Circa 1500 2000
Circa 1500: Leonardo e Paola, una coppia diseguale; De ludo globi, il gioco del mondo, alle soglie dell'Impero. Exh. cat., Castel Beseno, Besenello; Palazzo Vescovile, Bressanone; and Schloss Bruck, Lienz. Milan: Skira, 2000.

[German edition, *Circa 1500: Leonhard und Paola, ein ungleiches Paar; De ludo Globi, vom Spiel der Welt, an der Grenze des Reiches.* Geneva: Skira, 2000.]

Codice di Leonardo da Vinci 2006
Il codice di Leonardo da Vinci nel Castello Sforzesco. Exh. cat., Castello Sforzesco, Milan. Edited by Pietro C. Marani and Giovanni M. Piazza. Milan: Electa, 2006.

Collection Spitzer 1893
Catalogue des objets d'art et de haute curiosité: Antiques, du Moyen-Age & de la Renaissance; composant l'importante et précieuse Collection Spitzer. 2 vols. Sale cat., Paris, April 17–June 16, 1893.

Collin 1810a
Heinrich von Collin. "Collin's Rudolphiade." *Archiv für Geographie, Historie, Staats- und Kriegskunst*, [edited by Joseph von Hormayr], 1, nos. 53–54 (May 2–4, 1810), pp. 237–40.

Collin 1810b
Heinrich von Collin. "Kaiser Max auf der Martinswand in Tirol." *Archiv für Geographie, Historie, Staats- und Kriegskunst*, [edited by Joseph von Hormayr], 1, nos. 4–5 (January 8–10, 1810), pp. 19–21.

Cornides 1967
Elisabeth Cornides. *Rose und Schwert im päpstlichen Zeremoniell, von den Anfängen bis zum Pontifikat Gregors XIII.* Wiener Dissertationen aus dem Gebiete der Geschichte 9. Vienna: Wissenschaftliches Antiquariat H. Geyer, 1967.

Cosson and Burges 1881
Charles Alexander, Baron de Cosson, and William Burges. *Ancient Helmets and Examples of Mail.* Exh. cat. London: Royal Archaeological Institute of Great Britain and Ireland, 1881.

Cummings 1991
Anthony M. Cummings. "Giulio de' Medici's Music Books." *Early Music History* 10 (1991), pp. 65–122.

Cuneo 2002
Pia F. Cuneo. "Images of Warfare as Political Legitimization: Jörg Breu the Elder's Rondels for Maximilian I's Hunting Lodge at Lermos (ca. 1516)." In *Artful Armies, Beautiful Battles: Art and Warfare in Early Modern Europe*, edited by Pia F. Cuneo, pp. 87–105. History of Warfare 9. Leiden: Brill, 2002.

Curley 1927
M. Mildred Curley. "An Episode in the Conflict between Boniface VIII and Philip the Fair." *Catholic Historical Review* 13, no. 2 (July 1927), pp. 194–226.

Currency of Fame 1994
The Currency of Fame: Portrait Medals of the Renaissance. Exh. cat., National Gallery of Art, Washington, D.C.; Frick Collection, New York; and National Gallery of Scotland, Edinburgh. Edited by Stephen K. Scher. New York: Harry N. Abrams, in association with the Frick Collection, 1994.

Cuspinian 1515
Johannes Cuspinian. *Der namhaftigen kay: Ma. vnd dreyer kuningen zu Hungern Beham vnd Poln zamenkumung vnd versamlu[n]g so zu wienn in dem Heymonat; Nach Christi gepurd M.D.xv. iar geschehe[n] ain kurtze und warhafte erzelung vnd erklarung.* [Vienna]: [Johann Singriener], 1515.

De Schryver 2008
Antoine de Schryver. *The Prayer Book of Charles the Bold: A Study of a Flemish Masterpiece from the Burgundian Court.* Preface by Thomas Kren. Getty Museum Monographs on Illuminated Manuscripts. Los Angeles: J. Paul Getty Museum, 2008. [German edition, *Das Gebetbuch Karls des Kühnen: Ms. 37, The J. Paul Getty Museum, Los Angeles; Ein flämisches Meisterwerk für den Hof von Burgund.* Regensburg: Schnell & Steiner, 2007.]

Decker 2018
John R. Decker. "Aid, Protection, and Social Alliance: The Role of Jewelry in the Margins of the *Hours of Catherine of Cleves.*" *Renaissance Quarterly* 71, no. 1 (Spring 2018), pp. 33–76.

Delmarcel 1999
Guy Delmarcel. *Flemish Tapestry.* London: Thames & Hudson, 1999.

Demets 2016
Lisa Demets. "The Late Medieval Manuscript Transmission of the *Excellente Cronike van Vlaenderen* in Urban Flanders." *Medieval Low Countries* 3 (2016), pp. 123–73.

Demets and Dumolyn 2016
Lisa Demets and Jan Dumolyn. "Urban Chronicle Writing in Late Medieval Flanders: The Case of Bruges during the Flemish Revolt of 1482–1490." *Urban History* 43, no. 1 (February 2016), pp. 28–45.

Detroit Institute of Arts 1954
Detroit Institute of Arts. *A Selection from the William Randolph Hearst Collection of Arms and Armor in the Detroit Institute of Arts.* Commentary by Francis W. Robinson. Detroit: Detroit Institute of Arts, 1954.

Dillon 1902
Harold A. Dillon. *Horse Armour.* London: Harrison and Sons, 1902.

Dodgson 1903–11
Campbell Dodgson. *Catalogue of Early German and Flemish Woodcuts Preserved in the Department of Prints and Drawings in the British Museum.* 2 vols. London: Printed by order of the Trustees, 1903–11. [Reprint, Vaduz, Liechtenstein: Quarto Press, in association with British Museum Publications, 1980.]

Dodgson 1926
Campbell Dodgson. "An Unknown MS. of Freydal." *Burlington Magazine* 48, no. 278 (May 1926), pp. 235–42.

Dodgson 1928
Campbell Dodgson. "More Freydal Drawings." *Burlington Magazine* 53, no. 307 (October 1928), pp. 170–73.

Domínguez Casas 2006
Rafael Domínguez Casas. "Estilo y rituales de corte." In *Felipe I el Hermoso: La belleza y la locura*, edited by Miguel Ángel Zalama and Paul Vandenbroeck, pp. 89–103. Madrid: Centro de Estudios Europa Hispánica; Burgos: Fundación Caja de Burgos; Madrid: Fundación Carlos de Amberes, 2006.

Dubois et al. 2009
Anne Dubois, Roel Slachmuylders, Géraldine Patigny, and Famke Peters. *The Flemish Primitives: Catalogue of Early Netherlandish Painting in the Royal Museums of Fine Arts of Belgium.* Vol. 5, *Anonymous Masters.* Brussels: Brepols, 2009.

Dufty and Reid 1968
Arthur Richard Dufty and William Reid. *European Armour in the Tower of London.* London: Her Majesty's Stationery Office, 1968.

Duller 1836
Eduard Duller. "Der letzte Ritter nimmt Abschied." *Taschenbuch für die vaterländische Geschichte* 15 (1836), pp. 247–49.

Dünnebeil 2016
Sonja Dünnebeil, ed. *Die Protokollbücher des Ordens vom Goldenen Vlies. Teil 4: Der Übergang an das Haus Habsburg (1477 bis 1480).* Frankfurt am Main: Peter Lang, 2016.

Dupont 1936
Jacques Dupont. "Remarques sur l'iconographie de Charles VIII." *Bulletin de la Société de l'Histoire de l'Art Français*, 1936, pp. 186–89.

Dürer, Cranach, Holbein 2011
Dürer, Cranach, Holbein: Die Entdeckung des Menschen; Das deutsche Porträt um 1500. Exh. cat., Kunsthistorisches Museum, Vienna, and Kunsthalle der Hypo-Kulturstiftung, Munich. Edited by Sabine Haag, Christiane Lange, Christof Metzger, and Karl Schütz. Munich: Hirmer, 2011.

Dürers Verwandlung in der Skulptur 1981
Dürers Verwandlung in der Skulptur zwischen Renaissance und Barock. Exh. cat. Frankfurt am Main: Liebieghaus Museum alter Plastik, 1981.

Düriegl 1977
Günter Düriegl. "Das Wiener Bürgerliche Zeughaus: Die Geschichte einer Waffensammlung." In *Wiener Bürgerliche Zeughaus* 1977, pp. 9–19.

Egg 1961
Erich Egg. *Der Tiroler Geschützguss, 1400–1600.* Innsbruck: Universitätsverlag Wagner, 1961.

Eichberger 1996
Dagmar Eichberger. "A Renaissance Reliquary Collection in Halle, and Its Illustrated Inventories." *Art Bulletin of Victoria* 37 (1996), pp. 19–36.

Eichberger 2002
Dagmar Eichberger. *Leben mit Kunst, Wirken durch Kunst: Sammelwesen und Hofkunst unter Margarete von Österreich, Regentin der Niederlande.* Turnhout: Brepols, 2002.

Eisenbeiss 2005
Anja Eisenbeiss. "Einprägsamkeit en gros: Die Porträts Kaiser Maximilians I.; Ein Herrscherbild gewinnt Gestalt." PhD diss., Universität Heidelberg, 2005.

Emperor Maximilian I 2012
Emperor Maximilian I and the Age of Dürer. Exh. cat., Albertina Museum, Vienna. Edited by Eva Michel and Maria Luise Sternath. Munich: Prestel, 2012. [German edition, *Kaiser Maximilian I. und die Kunst der Dürerzeit.* Munich: Prestel, 2012.]

Engels, Geck, and Musper 1968
Maximilian I, Holy Roman Emperor. *Kaiser Maximilians Theuerdank.* 2 vols. [Vol. 1], Commentary by Heinz Engels, Elisabeth Geck, and Heinrich Theodor Musper. [Vol. 2], Facsimile edition of the 1517 edition. Plochingen: Müller und Schindler, 1968.

Epée 2011
L'épée: Usages, mythes et symboles. Exh. cat., Musée de Cluny—Musée National du Moyen Age. Paris: Réunion des Musées Nationaux, 2011.

Ephrussi 1882
Charles Ephrussi. *Albert Dürer et ses dessins.* Paris: A. Quantin, 1882.

Eser 1996
Thomas Eser. *Hans Daucher: Augsburger Kleinplastik der Renaissance.* Kunstwissenschaftliche Studien 65. Munich: Deutscher Kunstverlag, 1996.

Ettlinger 1956
L. D. Ettlinger. "Virtutum et Viciorum Adumbracio." *Journal of the Warburg and Courtauld Institutes* 19, nos. 1–2 (January–June 1956), pp. 155–56.

Europa und der Orient 1989
Europa und der Orient, 800–1900. Exh. cat., Martin-Gropius-Bau, Berlin. Edited by Gereon Sievernich and Hendrik Budde. Gütersloh: Bertelsmann Lexikon, 1989.

Exposition d'art ancien 1906
Exposition d'art ancien. Exh. cat., Palais des Beaux-Arts, Tourcoing. Edited by Jean Masson, with Ch.-Léon Cardon, Maurice Wintrebert, and Pierre Turpin. Lille: L. Danel, 1906.

Faber 1519
Johannes Faber. *Oratio Fvnebris in Depositione Gloriosis. Imp. Caes. Maximiliani Aug.* Augsburg: Sigmund Grimm and Marx Wirsung, 1519.

Face to Face 2014
Face to Face: Die Kunst des Porträts. Exh. cat., Schloss Ambras, Innsbruck. Edited by Sabine Haag. Vienna: Kunsthistorisches Museum, 2014.

Fahy 2008
Everett Fahy. "The Marriage Portrait in the Renaissance, or Some Women Named Ginevra." In *Art and Love in Renaissance Italy*, edited by Andrea Bayer, pp. 17–27. Exh. cat., The Metropolitan Museum of Art, New York, and Kimbell Art Museum, Fort Worth. New York: The Metropolitan Museum of Art, 2008.

Falk 1968
Tilman Falk. *Hans Burgkmair: Studien zu Leben und Werk des Augsburger Malers.* Munich: Bruckmann, 1968.

Falk 1973
Tilman Falk, ed. *Hans Burgkmair, 1473–1973: Das graphische Werk.* With contributions by Tilman Falk, Rolf Biedermann, and Heinrich Geissler. Exh. cat. Augsburg: Städtische Kunstsammlungen Augsburg, 1973.

Fallows 2010
Noel Fallows. *Jousting in Medieval and Renaissance Iberia.* Woodbridge, Suffolk: Boydell Press, 2010.

Ferdinand II 2017
Ferdinand II: 450 Years Sovereign Ruler of Tyrol; Jubilee Exhibition. Exh. cat., Schloss Ambras, Innsbruck. Edited by Sabine Haag and Veronika Sandbichler. Innsbruck: Haymon, 2017. [German edition, *Ferdinand II.: 450 Jahre Tiroler Landesfürst; Jubiläumsausstellung.* Innsbruck: Haymon, 2017.]

Feste feiern 2016
Feste feiern: 125 Jahre Jubiläumsausstellung. Exh. cat., Kunsthistorisches Museum, Vienna. Edited by Sabine Haag and Gudrun Swoboda. Vienna: KHM-Museumsverband, 2016. [English edition, *Celebration! 125 Years—Anniversary Exhibition.* Vienna: KHM-Museumsverband, 2016.]

Flanders in the Fifteenth Century 1960
Flanders in the Fifteenth Century: Art and Civilization. Exh. cat., Detroit Institute of Arts. Detroit: Detroit Institute of Arts; Brussels: Centre National de Recherches Primitifs Flamands, 1960. [Published in conjunction with

the exhibition "Masterpieces of Flemish Art: Van Eyck to Bosch," held at the Detroit Institute of Arts, 1960.]

Fliegel 2007
Stephen N. Fliegel. *Arms & Armor: The Cleveland Museum of Art*. Rev. edition. Cleveland: Cleveland Museum of Art, 2007.

Foster 2014
Marc R. Foster. "The Edict of Restitution (1629) and the Failure of Catholic Restoration." In *The Ashgate Research Companion to the Thirty Years' War*, edited by Olaf Asbach and Peter Schröder, pp. 205–15. Farnham, Surrey: Ashgate, 2014.

Francis 1953
Henry S. Francis. "A Woodcut by Hans Springinklee." *Bulletin of the Cleveland Museum of Art* 40, no. 1 (January 1953), pp. 17–18, 23.

Franckh 1830
F. G. Franckh. Review of *Der letzte Ritter: Romanzen-Kranz*, by Anastasius Grün. *Kritische Blätter der Börsen-Halle* 1, no. 8 (August 23, 1830), pp. 57–59.

Franke and Welzel 2013
Birgit Franke and Barbara Welzel. "Morisken für den Kaiser: Kulturtransfer?" In *Kulturtransfer am Fürstenhof: Höfische Austauschprozesse und ihre Medien im Zeitalter Kaiser Maximilians I.*, edited by Matthias Müller, Karl-Heinz Spiess, and Udo Friedrich, pp. 15–51. Schriften zur Residenzkultur 9. Berlin: Lukas, 2013.

Friedländer 1975
Max J. Friedländer. *Early Netherlandish Painting*. Vol. 12, *Jan van Scorel and Pieter Coeck van Aelst*. Comments and notes by H. Pauwels and G. Lemmens. New York: Praeger, 1975.

Frieling 2013
Kirsten O. Frieling. *Sehen und gesehen werden: Kleidung an Fürstenhöfen an der Schwelle vom Mittelalter zur Neuzeit (ca. 1450–1530)*. Mittelalter-Forschungen 41. Ostfildern: Jan Thorbecke, 2013.

From Van Eyck to Bruegel 1998
From Van Eyck to Bruegel: Early Netherlandish Paintings in The Metropolitan Museum of Art. Exh. cat. Edited by Maryan W. Ainsworth and Keith Christiansen. New York: The Metropolitan Museum of Art, 1998.

Fugger 1668
Johann Jacob Fugger. *Spiegel der Ehren des höchst-löblichsten Kayser- und Königichlen Erzhauses Oesterreich*. Edited by Sigmund von Birken. Nuremberg: Michael und Johann Friderich Endtern, 1668.

Füssel 2003
Maximilian I, Holy Roman Emperor. *Theuerdank: Die Abenteuer des Ritters; Kolorierter Nachdruck der Gesamtausgabe von 1517/The Adventures of the Knight; Complete Coloured Facsimile of the 1517 Edition*. 2 vols. [Vol. 1], Facsimile edition of MS Sign. Rar. 325a in the Bayerische Staatsbibliothek, Munich. [Vol. 2], Commentary by Stephan Füssel. Cologne: Taschen, 2003.

Gachard 1851–52
Louis-Prosper Gachard. *Lettres inédites de Maximilien, duc d'Autriche, roi des Romains et empereur, sur les affaires des Pays-Bas*. 2 vols. Brussels: C. Muquardt, 1851–52.

Gaier 1973
Claude Gaier. *L'industrie et le commerce des armes dans les anciennes principautés belges du XIIIme à la fin du XVme siècle*. Bibliothèque de la Faculté de Philosophie et Lettres de l'Université de Liège 202. Paris: Les Belles Lettres, 1973.

Gailliard 1846
Jean Jacques Gailliard. *Recherches historiques sur la Chapelle du Saint-Sang, à Bruges*. Bruges: Jean Jacques Gailliard, 1846.

Galerie Fischer 1934
Waffensaal des Schlosses Grafenegg, Herzog Viktor von Ratibor. Sale cat., Galerie Fischer, Lucerne, May 2, 1934. Sale held at Zunfthaus zur Meise, Zurich.

Galerie Fischer 1935
Schutz- und Trutzwaffen aus allerhöchstem Besitz: Jagdsammlung de Westerweller. Sale cat., Galerie Fischer, Lucerne, May 7–8, 1935. Sale held at Zunfthaus zur Meise, Zurich.

Galerie Fischer 1953
Mobiliar, Kollektions-Silber, Muselmanische Kunst aus dem 9. bis 13. Jahrhundert, China-Sammlung. Sale cat., Galerie Fischer, Lucerne, June 16–20, 1953.

Galerie Fischer 1961
Waffenauktion: Stangenwaffen, Schwerter, Degen und Fernwaffen; Prunkwaffen, Rüstungen und Rüstungsteile aus deutschem und österreichischem Adelbesitz sowie verschiedener Herkunft. Sale cat., Galerie Fischer, Lucerne, November 27, 1961.

Galerie Sismann 2012
Galerie Sismann. *Galerie Sismann: Sculptures européennes et objets d'art*. Paris: Galerie Sismann, 2012.

Gamber 1957
Ortwin Gamber. "Der Turnierharnisch zur Zeit König Maximilians I. und das Thunsche Skizzenbuch." *Jahrbuch der Kunsthistorischen Sammlungen in Wien* 53 (1957), pp. 33–70.

Gamber 1958
Ortwin Gamber. "Der italienische Harnisch im 16. Jahrhundert." *Jahrbuch der Kunsthistorischen Sammlungen in Wien* 54 (1958), pp. 73–120.

Gamber 1959a
Ortwin Gamber. "Eine Harnischgarnitur Maximilians I. von Lorenz Helmschmied." *Waffen- und Kostümkunde*, 3rd ser., 1, nos. 1–2 (1959), pp. 3–15.

Gamber 1959b
Ortwin Gamber. "Die Waffen Kaiser Maximilians I." *Alte und moderne Kunst* 4, no. 5 (1959), pp. 7–11.

Gamber 1961
Ortwin Gamber. "Die mittelalterlichen Blankwaffen der Wiener Waffensammlung." *Jahrbuch der Kunsthistorischen Sammlungen in Wien* 57 (1961), pp. 7–38.

Gamber 1981
Ortwin Gamber. "Führer durch die Rüstkammern Erzhergoz Ferdinands." In Gamber and Auer 1981, pp. 33–59.

Gamber 1988
Ortwin Gamber. "A Funerary Effigy, Grotesque Helmets and the Seusenhofer Workshop." *Apollo* 127, n.s., no. 312 (February 1988), pp. 105–7.

Gamber and Auer 1981
Ortwin Gamber and Alfred Auer. *Die Rüstkammern*. Kunsthistorisches Museum, Sammlungen Schloss Ambras. Führer durch das Kunsthistorische Museum 30. Vienna: Kunsthistorisches Museum, 1981.

Gamber and Beaufort-Spontin 1978
Ortwin Gamber and Christian Beaufort-Spontin. *Curiositäten und Inventionen aus Kunst- und Rüstkammer*. Vienna: Kunsthistorisches Museum, 1978.

Garber 1915
Josef Garber. "Das Haller Heiltumbuch mit den Unika-Holzschnitten Hans Burgkmairs des Älteren." *Jahrbuch der Kunsthistorischen Sammlungen des Allerhöchsten Kaiserhauses* 32 (1915), pp. I–CLXXVII.

Gauthier 1883–95
Jules Gauthier. *Inventaire sommaire des archives départementales antérieures à 1790. Archives civiles, série B: Chambre des comptes de Franche-Comté*. 3 vols. Département du Doubs. Besançon: Paul Jacquin, 1883–95.

Gebetbuch Karls des Kühnen 2007
Das Gebetbuch Karls des Kühnen/The Prayer Book of Charles the Bold/Le livre de prières de Charles Téméraire. Lucerne: Faksimile Verlag, 2007. [Facsimile edition of MS 37 in the J. Paul Getty Museum, Los Angeles.]

Geissler 1965
Paul Geissler. "Hans Burgkmairs Genealogie Kaisers Maximilians I." *Gutenberg-Jahrbuch*, 1965, pp. 249–61.

Genevoy 1955
Robert Genevoy. "Notes sur l'Armurerie Impériale d'Arbois (1495–1509?) et sur les armures de Claude de Vaudrey et de Maximilien 1er au Kunsthistorisches Museum de Vienne." *La nouvelle revue franc-comtoise*, no. 8 (October 1955), pp. 208–22.

Gilliodts-van Severen 1876
Louis Gilliodts-van Severen. *Inventaire des archives de la ville de Bruges.* Sect. 1, *Inventaire des chartes*, ser. 1, *Treizième au seizième siècle.* Vol. 6. Bruges: Edw. Gailliard & Cie., 1876.

Gottlieb 1900
Theodor Gottlieb. *Büchersammlung Kaiser Maximilians I. mit einer Einleitung über älteren Bücherbesitz im Haus Habsburg.* Die Ambraser Handschriften. Beitrag zur Geschichte der Wiener Hofbibliothek 1. Leipzig: M. Spirgatis, 1900. [Reprint, Amsterdam: Gérard Th. van Heusden, 1968.]

Grancsay 1931
Stephen V. Grancsay. "The Mutual Influence of Costume and Armor: A Study of Specimens in The Metropolitan Museum of Art." *Metropolitan Museum Studies* 3, no. 2 (June 1931), pp. 194–208.

Grancsay 1933
Stephen V. Grancsay. *Loan Exhibition of European Arms and Armor.* Brooklyn, N.Y.: Brooklyn Museum, 1933.

Grancsay 1955
Stephen V. Grancsay. *A Loan Exhibition of Equestrian Equipment from The Metropolitan Museum of Art.* Exh. cat. Louisville, Ky.: J. B. Speed Art Museum, 1955.

Grancsay 1956
Stephen V. Grancsay. "A Jousting Harness." *Philadelphia Museum of Art Bulletin* 52 (Autumn 1956), pp. 3–7.

Greve and Lebailly 2001–2
Anke Greve and Emilie Lebailly, eds. *Comptes de l'argentier de Charles le Téméraire, duc de Bourgogne.* Vols. 1 and 2. Recueil des historiens de la France. Documents financiers et administratifs 10, nos. 1, 2. Paris: Boccard, 2001–2.

Gröber 1928
Karl Gröber. *Kinderspielzeug aus alter Zeit: Eine Geschichte des Spielzeugs.* Berlin: Deutscher Kunstverlag, 1928.

Grosvenor Thomas Collection 1913
The Grosvenor Thomas Collection of Ancient Stained Glass. 2 vols. New York, 1913.

Gruben 1997
Françoise de Gruben. *Les chapitres de la Toison d'Or à l'époque bourguignonne (1430–1477).* Mediaevalia Lovaniensia, ser. 1, Studia 23. Leuven: Leuven University Press, 1997.

Gwynn 2016
Reginald T. Gwynn. *The Gwynn Collection: A Lifetime Passion for Antique Arms and Armour.* Edited by Carlo Paggiarino. Milan: Hans Prunner, 2016.

Habich 1913
Georg Habich. "Das Reiterdenkmal Kaiser Maximilians I. in Augsburg." *Münchner Jahrbuch der bildenden Kunst* 8 (1913), pp. 255–62.

Habich 1929–34
Georg Habich. *Die deutschen Schaumünzen des XVI. Jahrhunderts. 1. Teil, Die deutschen Schaumünzen des XVI. Jahrhunderts, geordnet nach Meistern und Schulen.* 3 vols. in 5. Munich: F. Bruckmann, 1929–34.

Haemers 2007
Jelle Haemers. "Adellijke onvrede: Adolf van Kleef en Lodewijk van Gruuthuse als beschermheren en uitdagers van het Bourgondisch-Habsburgse hof (1477–1482)." *Jaarboek voor middeleeuwse geschiedenis* 10 (2007), pp. 178–215.

Haemers 2008
Jelle Haemers. "Opstand adelt? De rechtvaardiging van het politieke verzet van de adel in de Vlaamse Opstand (1482–1492)." *Bijdragen en mededelingen betreffende de geschiedenis der Nederlanden* 123, no. 4 (2008), pp. 586–608.

Haemers 2014
Jelle Haemers. *De strijd om het regentschap over Filips de Schone: Opstand, facties en geweld in Brugge, Gent en Ieper (1482–1488).* Historische monografieën Vlaanderen 2. Ghent: Academia Press, 2014.

Hallesche Heiltumbuch 1520/2001
Das Hallesche Heiltumbuch von 1520: Nachdruck zum 450. Gründungsjubiläum der Marienbibliothek zu Halle. Edited by Heinrich L. Nickel. Halle an der Saale: Janos Stekovics, 2001.

Halm 1962
Peter Halm. "Hans Burgkmair als Zeichner." *Münchner Jahrbuch der bildenden Kunst*, 3rd ser., 13 (1962), pp. 75–162.

Harzen 1859
E. Harzen. "Ueber die Erfindung der Aetzkunst." *Archiv für die zeichnenden Künste mit besonderer Beziehung auf Kupferstecher- und Holzschneidekunst und ihre Geschichte* 5 (1859), pp. 119–36.

Heilingsetzer 2003
Georg Heilingsetzer. "Ein Baustein zur Entstehung der Habsburgermonarchie: Die Hochzeit Erzherzog Ferdinands in Linz (1521)." In *Kaiser Ferdinand I.* 2003, pp. 67–75.

Heinz and Schütz 1976
Günther Heinz and Karl Schütz. *Porträtgalerie zur Geschichte Österreichs von 1400 bis 1800.* Führer durch das Kunsthistorische Museum 22. Vienna: Kunsthistorisches Museum, 1976.

Helbig 1939
J. Helbig. "A Flemish Armorial Window." *Burlington Magazine* 75, no. 436 (July 1939), p. 42.

Helfert 1889
Josef Alexander von Helfert, ed. *Kunst-Topographie des Herzogthums Kärnten.* Österreichische Kunst-Topographie 1. Vienna: Kubasta & Voigt, 1889.

Hénault 1910
Maurice Hénault. "La tapisserie du 'Tournoi' au Musée de Valenciennes." *Revue de l'art ancien et moderne* 28, no. 161 (August 1910), pp. 145–56.

Hennes 1858
J. H. Hennes. *Albrecht von Brandenburg: Erzbischof von Mainz und von Magdeburg.* Mainz: Franz Kirchheim, 1858.

Henry VIII 2009
Henry VIII: Arms and the Man, 1509–2009. Exh. cat., White Tower, Tower of London. Edited by Graeme Rimer, Thom Richardson, and J. P. D. Cooper. Leeds: Royal Armouries, 2009. [Published in conjunction with the exhibition "Henry VIII: Dressed to Kill," held at the White Tower, Tower of London, 2009–10.]

Herder 1769
Johann Gottfried Herder. "Ueber die Reichsgeschichte: Ein historischer Spaziergang." In *Kritische Wälder, oder Einige Betrachtungen die Wissenschaft und Kunst des Schönen betreffend, nach Maasgabe neuerer Schriften; Drittes Wäldchen*, pp. 156–71. Riga, 1769.

Héritage de Rogier van der Weyden 2013
L'héritage de Rogier van der Weyden: La peinture à Bruxelles, 1450–1520. With contributions by Véronique Bücken et al. Exh. cat., Koninklijke Musea voor Schone Kunsten van België. Tielt: Lannoo, 2013.

Herrlich Wild 2004
Herrlich Wild: Höfische Jagd in Tirol. Exh. cat., Schloss Ambras, Innsbruck. Edited by Wilfried Seipel. Vienna: Kunsthistorisches Museum, 2004.

Hill 1930/1984
George Francis Hill. *A Corpus of Italian Medals of the Renaissance before Cellini.* 2 vols. Reprint, Florence: Studio per Edizioni Scelte, 1984. [1st edition, London: British Museum, 1930.]

Hispania—Austria 1992
Hispania—Austria: Die Katholischen Könige, Maximilian I. und die Anfänge der Casa de Austria in Spanien; Kunst um 1492. Exh. cat., Schloss Ambras, Innsbruck. Edited by Lukas Madersbacher. Milan: Electa, 1992.

Holladay and Ward 2016
Joan A. Holladay and Susan L. Ward. *Gothic Sculpture in America.* Vol. 3, *The Museums of New*

York and Pennsylvania. Publications of the International Center of Medieval Art 6. New York: International Center of Medieval Art, 2016.

Hollegger 2005
Manfred Hollegger. *Maximilian I. (1459–1519): Herrscher und Mensch einer Zeitenwende.* Kohlhammer Urban-Taschenbücher 442. Stuttgart: W. Kohlhammer, 2005.

Hollegger 2012
Manfred Hollegger. "Personality and Reign: The Biography of Emperor Maximilian I." In *Emperor Maximilian I* 2012, pp. 23–35. [German edition, "Persönlichkeit und Herrschaft: Zur Biografie Kaiser Maximilians I." In *Kaiser Maximilian I. und die Kunst der Dürerzeit*, edited by Eva Michel and Maria Luise Sternath, pp. 23–35. Exh. cat., Albertina Museum, Vienna. Munich: Prestel, 2012.]

Hollstein 1949–2010
F. W. H. Hollstein. *Dutch and Flemish Etchings, Engravings, and Woodcuts, ca. 1450–1700.* 72 vols. Amsterdam: Menno Hertzberger; Ouderkerk van den Ijssel: Sound & Vision, 1949–2010.

Hollstein 1954–2014
F. W. H. Hollstein. *German Engravings, Etchings and Woodcuts, ca. 1400–1700.* 82 vols. Amsterdam: Menno Hertzberger; Ouderkerk van den Ijssel: Sound & Vision, 1954–2014.

Honold 1967
Konrad Honold. "Ein unbekanntes Bildnis Kaiser Maximilians I. von Bernhard Strigel." *Tiroler Heimatblätter* 42 (1967), pp. 33–39.

Hormayr 1807–14
Joseph von Hormayr. *Oesterreichischer Plutarch, oder Leben und Bildnisse aller Regenten und der berühmtesten Feldherren, Staatsmänner, Gelehrten und Künstler des österreichischen Kaiserstaates.* 20 vols. Vienna: Anton Doll, 1807–14.

Hormayr 1814
[Joseph von Hormayr]. *Österreich und Deutschland.* Gotha: Becker, 1814.

Hummelberger 1961
Walter Hummelberger. "Die Ordnungen der Wiener Plattner und Sarwürcher." *Waffen- und Kostumkunde*, n.s., 3, no. 2 (1961), pp. 91–107.

Huynh 2011
Michel Huynh. "Usages symboliques." In *Epée* 2011, pp. 53–83.

Hye 1969
Franz-Heinz Hye. "Die heraldischen Denkmale Maximilians I. in Tirol." *Der Schlern: Illustrierte Monatshefte für Heimat- und Volkskunde* 43 (1969), pp. 56–77.

Hye 1997
Franz-Heinz Hye. *Das Goldene Dachl Kaiser Maximilians I. und die Anfänge der Innsbrucker Residenz.* Veröffentlichungen des Innsbrucker Stadtarchivs, n.s., 24. Innsbruck: Stadtmagistrat Innsbruck, 1997.

Hye 2004
Franz-Heinz Hye. *Wappen in Tirol: Zeugen der Geschichte; Handbuch der Tiroler Heraldik.* Schlern-Schriften 321. Innsbruck: Universitätsverlag Wagner, 2004.

Jacobowitz and Stepanek 1983
Ellen S. Jacobowitz and Stephanie Loeb Stepanek. *The Prints of Lucas van Leyden & His Contemporaries.* Exh. cat., National Gallery of Art, Washington, D.C., and Museum of Fine Arts, Boston. Washington, D.C.: National Gallery of Art, 1983.

Jahn 1810
Friedrich Ludwig Jahn. *Deutsches Volksthum.* Lübeck: Niemann und Comp., 1810.

Janson 1967/1973
H. W. Janson. "The Equestrian Monument from Cangrande della Scala to Peter the Great." In *Sixteen Studies*, pp. 157–88. New York: Harry N. Abrams, 1973. [Originally published in *Aspects of the Renaissance: A Symposium*, edited by Archibald R. Lewis, pp. 73–85. Austin: University of Texas Press, 1967.]

Jezler 2017
Peter Jezler. "Turnierhöfe der oberdeutschen Adelsgesellschaften: Gestech und Rennen, Kolbenturnier, Schwertkampf um die Helmzier, Friedensrat, Standesgericht und Heiratsmarkt." In *Turnier: 1000 Jahre Ritterspiele*, edited by Stefan Krause and Matthias Pfaffenbichler, pp. 41–59. Vienna: KHM-Museumsverband; Munich: Hirmer, 2017.

Joachim 1961
Harold Joachim. "Maximilian I by Burgkmair." *Art Institute of Chicago Quarterly* 55, no. 1 (March 1961), pp. 5–9.

Johnson 1980
Harvey L. Johnson. "Sources of Calderón's *El segundo blasón del Austria.*" *Journal of Hispanic Philology* 5, no. 1 (Autumn 1980), pp. 51–58.

Jordaens 2013
Jordaens, 1593–1678. Exh. cat., Petit Palais, Musée des Beaux-Arts de la Ville de Paris. Edited by Alexis Merle du Bourg. Paris: Paris-Musées, 2013.

Jungwith 1969
Helmut Jungwith. "Münzen und Medaillen Maximilians I." In *Maximilian I.* 1969, "Beiträge," pp. 65–72.

Just 2011
Thomas Just. "Die Beziehungen zwischen Habsburg und Venedig im 15. und frühen 16. Jahrhundert." In *Venedig: Seemacht,*

Kunst und Karneval, edited by Matthias Pfaffenbichler, pp. 68–72. Exh. cat., Schloss Schallaburg. Schallaburg: Schallaburg Kulturbetriebsgesellschaft; Vienna: Kunsthistorisches Museum, 2011.

***Kaiser Ferdinand I.* 2003**
Kaiser Ferdinand I., 1503–1564: Das Werden der Habsburgermonarchie. Exh. cat. Edited by Wilfried Seipel. Vienna: Kunsthistorisches Museum, 2003.

***Kaiser Karl V.* 2000**
Kaiser Karl V. (1500–1558): Macht und Ohnmacht Europas. Exh. cat. Bonn: Kunst- und Ausstellungshalle der Bundesrepublik Deutschland; Vienna: Kunsthistorisches Museum, 2000.

***Kaiser Maximilian I.* 2002**
Kaiser Maximilian I.: Bewahrer und Reformer. Exh. cat., Reichskammergerichtsmuseum Wetzlar. Edited by Georg Schmidt-von Rhein. Ramstein: Paqué, 2002.

***Kaiser Maximilian I.* 2014**
Kaiser Maximilian I.: Der letzte Ritter und das höfische Turnier. Exh. cat., Reiss-Engelhorn-Museen, Mannheim. Edited by Sabine Haag, Alfried Wieczorek, Matthias Pfaffenbichler, and Hans-Jürgen Buderer. Regensburg: Schnell & Steiner, 2014.

***Kaiser, Reich, Reformen* 1995**
1495—Kaiser, Reich, Reformen: Der Reichstag zu Worms. Exh. cat., Museum der Stadt Worms. Koblenz: Landesarchivverwaltung Rheinland-Pfalz, 1995.

Kantorowicz 1957
Ernst H. Kantorowicz. *The King's Two Bodies: A Study in Mediaeval Political Theology.* Princeton, N.J.: Princeton University Press, 1957.

Kastenholz 2006
Richard Kastenholz. *Hans Schwarz: Ein Augsburger Bildhauer und Medailleur der Renaissance.* Kunstwissenschaftliche Studien 126. Munich: Deutscher Kunstverlag, 2006.

Kieckens 1894
J.-F. Kieckens. "Le trésor de Notre-Dame de Hal à la fin du XVIIIe siècle: D'après des documents inédits." *Précis historiques: Bulletin mensuel des missions belges de la Compagnie de Jésus*, ser. 3, 3 (1894), pp. 278–87.

Kienbusch and Grancsay 1933
Carl Otto Kretzschmar von Kienbusch and Stephen V. Grancsay. *The Bashford Dean Collection of Arms and Armor in The Metropolitan Museum of Art.* Portland, Me.: Southworth Press for the Armor and Arms Club of New York City, 1933.

Kings, Queens, and Courtiers 2011
Kings, Queens, and Courtiers: Art in Early Renaissance France. Exh. cat., Galeries Nationales du Grand Palais, Paris, and Art Institute of Chicago. Edited by Martha Wolff. Chicago: Art Institute of Chicago; New Haven, Conn.: Yale University Press, 2011. [French edition, *France 1500: Entre Moyen Age et Renaissance.* Edited by Elisabeth Taburet-Delahaye, Geneviève Bresc-Bautier, and Thierry Crépin-Leblond. Paris: Réunion des Musées Nationaux, 2010.]

Kittel 1970
Erich Kittel. *Siegel.* Bibliothek für Kunst- und Antiquitätenfreunde 11. Braunschweig: Klinkhardt & Biermann, 1970.

Koepplin and Falk 1974–76
Dieter Koepplin and Tilman Falk. *Lukas Cranach: Gemälde, Zeichnungen, Druckgraphik.* 2 vols. Exh. cat., Kunstmuseum Basel. Basel: Birkhäuser, 1974–76.

Kohnen 2015
Rabea Kohnen. "*Das mer gehoert zuo eim Ritter auserkorn*: Überlegungen zum *Theuerdank.*" In *Maximilians Ruhmeswerk: Künste und Wissenschaften im Umkreis Kaiser Maximilians I.*, edited by Jan-Dirk Müller and Hans-Joachim Ziegeler, pp. 269–94. Frühe Neuzeit 190. Berlin: Walter de Gruyter, 2015.

H. Koller 1980
Heinrich Koller. "Der St. Georgs-Ritterorden Kaiser Friedrichs III." In *Die geistlichen Ritterorden Europas*, edited by Josef Fleckenstein and Manfred Hellmann, pp. 417–29. Vorträge und Forschungen 26. Sigmaringen: Jan Thorbecke, 1980.

M. Koller 2001
Manfred Koller. "Das 'Goldene Dachl' in Innsbruck: Weiss-goldene Figurenreliefs um 1500." *Restauro: Zeitschrift für Kunsttechniken, Restaurierung und Museumsfragen*, April–May 2001, p. 173.

König 1923
Konrad Peutinger. *Konrad Peutingers Briefwechsel.* Edited by Erich König. Veröffentlichungen der Kommission für Erforschung der Geschichte der Reformation und Gegenreformation, Humanisten-briefe 1. Munich: Oskar Beck, 1923.

Koninklijke Musea voor Schone Kunsten van België 1984
Koninklijke Musea voor Schone Kunsten van België. *Catalogue inventaire de la peinture ancienne.* Brussels: Musées Royaux des Beaux-Arts de Belgique, 1984.

Koreny 1989
Fritz Koreny. "'Ottoprecht Fürscht': Eine unbekannte Zeichnung von Albrecht Dürer; Kaiser Maximilian I. und sein Grabmal in der Hofkirche zu Innsbruck." *Jahrbuch der Berliner Museen* 31 (1989), pp. 127–48.

Kraus 1875
Victor von Kraus, ed. *Maximilians I. vertraulicher Briefwechsel mit Sigmund Prüschenk Freiherrn zu Stettenberg, nebst einer Anzahl zeitgenössischer das Leben am Hofe beleuchtender Briefe.* Innsbruck: Wagner'sche Universitaets-Buchhandlung, 1875.

Krause 2008
Stefan Krause. "Die Porträts von Hans Maler: Studien zum frühneuzeitlichen Standesporträt." PhD diss., Universität Wien, 2008.

Krause 2011–12
Stefan Krause. "Der Augsburger Druckgraphiker Daniel Hopfer (1471–1536) als Waffendekorateur." *Jahrbuch des Kunsthistorischen Museums Wien*, n.s., 13–14 (2011–12), pp. 53–75.

Krause 2012
Stefan Krause. "Die Porträts von Hans Maler: Der Schwazer Silberrausch der frühen Neuzeit und seine Akteure." *Münchner Jahrbuch der bildenden Kunst*, 3rd ser., 63 (2012), pp. 69–102.

Krause 2014a
Stefan Krause. "'die leuchtende Fackel, [. . .] die uns den ehrenhaften Weg zeigt': Deutsche Rüstungen der Zeit Maximilians I. und ihr Dekor." In *Kaiser Maximilian I.* 2014, pp. 114–27.

Krause 2014b
Stefan Krause. "'vnnser leib soll bestett werden in sannd Jörgen kirchen zu der newstat in Österreich': Kaiser Maximilian I. und der hl. Georg." In *Kaiser Maximilian I.* 2014, pp. 99–102.

Krause 2014c
Stefan Krause. "'zum staeten Andenken diesen dem Herze Oesterreichs unvergesslichen Kaisers': Zur Rezeption Kaiser Maximilians I." In *Kaiser Maximilian I.* 2014, pp. 185–201.

Krause 2016
Stefan Krause. *Mode in Stahl: Der Kostümharnisch des Wilhelm von Rogendorf.* Vienna: Album Verlag, 2016.

Krause 2019a
Stefan Krause, ed. "*Freydal:* Forschungen zu einem unvollendeten Gedächtniswerk Kaiser Maximilians I." Special issue, *Jahrbuch des Kunsthistorischen Museums Wien*, n.s., 21 (2019). Forthcoming.

Krause 2019b
Stefan Krause, ed. *Freydal: Medieval Games; The Book of Tournaments of Emperor Maximilian I.* [In English, German, and French.] Cologne: Taschen, 2019.

Krause 2019c
Stefan Krause. "*Freydal:* Werkbeschreibungen." In Krause 2019a.

Kren 2003
Thomas Kren. "Revolution and Transformation: Painting in Devotional Manuscripts, circa 1467–1485." In Kren and McKendrick 2003, pp. 121–25.

Kren and McKendrick 2003
Thomas Kren and Scot McKendrick. *Illuminating the Renaissance: The Triumph of Flemish Manuscript Painting in Europe.* With contributions by Maryan W. Ainsworth et al. Exh. cat., J. Paul Getty Museum, Los Angeles, and Royal Academy of Arts, London. Los Angeles: J. Paul Getty Museum, 2003.

Kretschmar 1909–11
Colonel von Kretschmar. "Der Turnierteppich im Museum zu Valenciennes." *Zeitschrift für historische Waffenkunde* 5 (1909–11), pp. 166–71.

Kretzschmar von Kienbusch Collection 1963
The Kretzschmar von Kienbusch Collection of Armor and Arms. Princeton, N.J.: Princeton University Library, 1963.

Krezdorn 1969
Siegfried Krezdorn. "Kaiser Maximilian in der Martinswand." *Tiroler Heimatblätter* 44 (1969), pp. 42–43.

Kuster 2018
Thomas Kuster. "Eine Ruhmeshalle aus Eisen: Bemerkungen zur Heldenrüstkammer von Schloss Ambras." *Waffen- und Kostümkunde*, 3rd ser., 60, no. 1 (2018), pp. 39–64.

La Marche 1562/1883–88
Olivier de La Marche. *Mémoires d'Olivier de La Marche, maître d'hôtel et capitaine des gardes de Charles le Téméraire.* Edited by Henri Beaune and J. d'Arbaumont. 4 vols. Paris: Librairie Renouard, 1883–88. [Originally published as *Les memoires de messire Olivier de La Marche, premier maistred'hostel de l'Archeduc Philippe d'Austriche, comte de Flandres.* Lyon: Guillaume Rouille, 1562.]

La Rocca 2017
Donald J. La Rocca. *How to Read European Armor.* New York: The Metropolitan Museum of Art, 2017.

Laking 1920–22
Guy Francis Laking. *A Record of European Armour and Arms through Seven Centuries.* 5 vols. Introduction by Charles Alexander, Baron de Cosson. Vols. 2–5 edited by Francis Henry Cripps-Day. London: G. Bell and Sons, 1920–22.

Landau and Parshall 1994
David Landau and Peter Parshall. *The Renaissance Print, 1470–1550.* New Haven, Conn.: Yale University Press, 1994.

Landshuter Plattnerkunst 1975
Landshuter Plattnerkunst: Ein Überblick. Exh. cat., Stadtresidenz, Landshut. Landshut: K. Möginger, 1975.

Lange 2002
Ulrich Lange. "Deutschland im Zeitalter der Reichsreform: Der kirchlichen Erneuerung und der Glaubenskämpfe (1495–1648)." In *Deutsche Geschichte: Von den Anfängen bis zur Gegenwart*, edited by Martin Vogt, pp. 144–217. New edition. Frankfurt am Main: Fischer, 2002.

Laschitzer 1886–87
Simon Laschitzer. "Die Heiligen aus der 'Sipp-, Mag- und Schwägerschaft' des Kaisers Maximilian I." *Jahrbuch der Kunsthistorischen Sammlungen des Allerhöchsten Kaiserhauses* 4 (1886), pp. 70–288; 5 (1887), pp. 117–261.

Laschitzer 1888
Simon Laschitzer. "Die Genealogie des Kaisers Maximilian I." *Jahrbuch der Kunsthistorischen Sammlungen des Allerhöchsten Kaiserhauses* 7 (1888), pp. 1–200.

Late Raphael 2012
Late Raphael. Exh. cat., Museo Nacional del Prado, Madrid, and Musée du Louvre, Paris. Edited by Tom Henry and Paul Joannides. Madrid: Museo Nacional del Prado, 2012.

Van den Leene 1705
Joseph van den Leene. *Le theatre de la noblesse de Brabant representant . . . les creations des chevaleries, & octroys des marques d'honneur & de noblesse accordez par les princes souverains ducs de Brabant, jusques au Roy Philippe V. . . .* Liège: Jean Francois Broncaert, 1705.

Leitner 1866–70
Quirin von Leitner, ed. *Die Waffensammlung des österreichischen Kaiserhauses im K. K. Artillerie-Arsenal-Museum in Wien*. Vienna: H. Martin, 1866–70.

Leitner 1880–82
Quirin von Leitner. *Freydal: Des Kaisers Maximilian I. Turniere und Mummereien*. 2 vols. Vienna: Adolf Holzhausen, 1880–82.

Leman 1927
Henri Leman. *La collection Foulc: Objets d'art du Moyen Age et de la Renaissance*. 2 vols. Paris: Les Beaux-Arts, Edition d'Etudes et de Documents, 1927.

Leng 2002
Rainer Leng. *Ars belli: Deutsche taktische und kriegstechnische Bilderhandschriften und Traktate im 15. und 16. Jahrhundert*. Vol. 1, *Entstehung und Entwicklung*. Imagines Medii Aevi 12, no. 1. Wiesbaden: Reichert, 2002.

Leng 2009
Rainer Leng. "Feuerwerks- und Kriegsbücher." In *Katalog der deutschsprachigen illustrierten Handschriften des Mittelalters*, vol. 4, no. 2, pts. 3–4, pp. 145–512. Munich: C. H. Beck, 2009.

Leo X 1521
Pope Leo X. *Bulla Erectionis Officii Dominorum Militum S. Petri: De Numero Participantium Nuncupatorum Quamplurimis Privilegiis Decorati*. Rome, 1521.

Leonardo da Vinci 2003
Leonardo da Vinci: Master Draftsman. Exh. cat. Edited by Carmen C. Bambach. New York: The Metropolitan Museum of Art, 2003.

Lersner 1734
Achill August von Lersner. *Chronica der weitberühmten freyen Reichs- Wahl- und Handels-Stadt Franckfurth am Mayn, oder zweyter Theil der ordentlichen Beschreibung der Stadt Franckfurth Ursprung, und wie selbige nach und nach zugenommen, wie auch allerley denckwürdiger Begebenheiten und geschichten. . . .* Edited by Georg August von Lersner. Frankfurt am Main: Georg August von Lersner, 1734.

Levkoff 2008
Mary L. Levkoff. *Hearst the Collector*. With contributions by Christine E. Brennan et al. Exh. cat. New York: Harry N. Abrams; Los Angeles: Los Angeles County Museum of Art, 2008.

Lightbown 1992
Ronald W. Lightbown. *Mediaeval European Jewellery, with a Catalogue of the Collection in the Victoria & Albert Museum*. London: Victoria & Albert Museum, 1992.

Limouze 1989
Dorothy Limouze. "Aegidius Sadeler: Imperial Printmaker." *Philadelphia Museum of Art Bulletin* 85, no. 362 (Spring 1989), pp. 1, 3–24. [Published in conjunction with the exhibition "The Sadelers: Engravers from the Golden Age of Antwerp and Prague," held at the Philadelphia Museum of Art, 1989.]

Lind 1873a
Karl Lind. "Die Gruppe XXIV. der Wiener Weltausstellung." *Mittheilungen der K. K. Central-Commission zur Erforschung und Erhaltung der Baudenkmale* 18 (1873), pp. 300–315.

Lind 1873b
Karl Lind. "Die österreichische kunsthistorische Abtheilung der Wiener-Weltausstellung." *Mittheilungen der K. K. Central-Commission zur Erforschung und Erhaltung der Baudenkmale* 18 (1873), pp. 149–220.

Liske 1866
Xaver Liske. "Der Kongress zu Wien im Jahre 1515: Eine kritische-historische Studie." *Forschungen zur deutschen Geschichte* 7 (1866), pp. 463–558.

Lorentz and Comblen-Sonkes 2001
Philippe Lorentz and Micheline Comblen-Sonkes. *Musée du Louvre, Paris*. Vol. 3. 2 pts. Corpus de la peinture des anciens Pays-Bas méridionaux et de la principauté de Liège au quinzième siècle 19. Brussels: Centre International d'Etude de la Peinture Médiévale des Bassins de l'Escaut et de la Meuse; Paris: Réunion des Musées Nationaux, 2001.

Lorey 1941
Hermann Lorey. *Liste der 1940 aus Frankreich zurückgeführten militärischen Gegenstände*. Berlin: Thormann & Goetsch, 1941.

Luber 1991
Katherine Crawford Luber. "Albrecht Dürer's Maximilian Portraits: An Investigation of Versions." *Master Drawings* 29, no. 1 (Spring 1991), pp. 30–47.

Lucas Cranach the Elder 2016
Lucas Cranach the Elder: 500 Years of the Power of Temptation. [In English and Japanese.] Exh. cat., National Museum of Western Art, Tokyo, and National Museum of Art, Osaka. Edited by Guido Messling and Atsushi Shinfuji. Tokyo: TBS Television, 2016.

Luchner 1958
Laurin Luchner. *Denkmal eines Renaissancefürsten: Versuch einer Rekonstruktion des Ambraser Museums von 1583*. Edited by the Kunsthistorisches Museum, Vienna. Vienna: Anton Schroll & Co., 1958.

Luh 2001
Peter Luh. *Kaiser Maximilian gewidmet: Die unvollendete Werkausgabe des Conrad Celtis und ihre Holzschnitte*. Frankfurt am Main: Peter Lang, 2001.

Luschin von Ebengreuth 1903
Arnold Luschin von Ebengreuth. "Denkmünzen Kaiser Maximilians I. auf die Annahme des Kaisertitels (4. Februar 1508)." *Numismatische Zeitschrift* 35 (1903; pub. 1904), pp. 221–24.

Mackowitz 1955
Heinz Mackowitz. "Ein Verlobungsbild der Königin Anna von Ungarn." *Tiroler Heimatblätter*, 1955, nos. 7–9, pp. 77–79.

Madersbacher 1996
Lukas Madersbacher. "Das Maximiliansgrabmal." In *Ruhm und Sinnlichkeit* 1996, pp. 124–39.

Madersbacher 2000
Lukas Madersbacher. "Massimiliano: Una nuova immagine di sovrano?" In *Circa 1500* 2000, pp. 368–69. [German edition, "Maximilian: Ein neues Bild des Herrschers?" In *Circa 1500: Leonhard und Paola, ein ungleiches Paar; De ludo globi, vom Spiel der Welt, an der Grenze des Reiches*, pp. 368–69. Exh. cat., Castel Beseno, Besenello; Palazzo Vescovile, Bressanone; and Schloss Bruck, Lienz. Geneva: Skira, 2000.]

Magie du verre 1986
Magie du verre. Exh. cat., Galerie CGER, Brussels. Brussels: R. Reyns, 1986.

Maindron 1894
Maurice Maindron. "Les collections d'armes du Musée d'Artillerie." *Gazette des beaux-arts* 35, no. 3 (March 1894), pp. 253–64.

Van Mander 1604/1994–99
Karel van Mander. *The Lives of the Illustrious Netherlandish and German Painters, from the First Edition of the "Schilder-boeck" (1603–1604): Preceded by the Lineage, Circumstances and Place of Birth, Life and Works of Karel van Mander . . . from the Second Edition of the "Schilder-boeck" (1616–1618).* Edited and translated by Hessel Miedema. 6 vols. Doornspijk: Davaco, 1994–99.

Van Mander 1616–18
Karel van Mander. *Het Schilder-boeck.* 2nd edition. 7 pts. Amsterdam, 1616–18.

Mann 1962
James Gow Mann. *European Arms and Armour.* 2 vols. Wallace Collection Catalogues. London: Printed for the Trustees by William Clowes and Sons, 1962.

Marsh 2009
Ann Marsh. "Stained and Painted Glass from the Chapel of the Holy Blood, Bruges." *V&A Conservation Journal*, no. 58 (Autumn 2009), pp. 41–42.

Marti 2009a
Susan Marti. "The Burgundian Army." In *Charles the Bold* 2009, pp. 322–23. [German edition, "Das burgundische Heer." In *Karl der Kühne (1433–1477): Kunst, Krieg und Hofkultur*, edited by Susan Marti, Till-Holger Borchert, and Gabriele Keck, pp. 322–23. Stuttgart: Belser Verlag, 2008.]

Marti 2009b
Susan Marti. "The Meeting in Trier, 1473: Circumstances and Sequence of Events." In *Charles the Bold* 2009, pp. 264–65. [German edition, "Treffen in Trier 1473: Anlass und Verlauf." In *Karl der Kühne (1433–1477): Kunst, Krieg und Hofkultur*, edited by Susan Marti, Till-Holger Borchert, and Gabriele Keck, pp. 264–65. Stuttgart: Belser Verlag, 2008.]

Martin 1972
John Rupert Martin. *The Decorations for the Pompa Introitus Ferdinandi.* Corpus Rubenianum Ludwig Burchard 16. London: Phaidon, 1972.

Master of Flémalle 2009
The Master of Flémalle and Rogier van der Weyden. Exh. cat., Städel Museum, Frankfurt am Main, and Staatliche Museen zu Berlin, Gemäldegalerie. Edited by Stephan Kemperdick and Jochen Sander. Ostfildern: Hatje Cantz, 2009.

Maurus 1523
Hartmann Maurus. *Coronatio Invictissimi Caroli Hispaniarum Regis Catholici in Romanorum Regem.* Nuremberg: Peypus, 1523.

Maximilian I. 1959
Maximilian I., 1459–1519. Exh. cat., Österreichische Nationalbibliothek, Vienna; Graphische Sammlung Albertina, Vienna; and Kunsthistorisches Museum, Vienna, Waffensammlung. Biblos-Schriften 23. Vienna: Österreichische Nationalbibliothek, 1959.

Maximilian I. 1969
Ausstellung Maximilian I.: Innsbruck; Katalog. Exh. cat., Museum in Zeughaus, Tiroler Landesmuseen, Innsbruck. Edited by Erich Egg. Innsbruck: Verlagsanstalt Tyrolia, 1969.

Maximilian I. 2000
Maximilian I.: Der Aufstieg eines Kaisers, von seiner Geburt bis zur Alleinherrschaft, 1459–1493. Exh. cat., Stadtmuseum Wiener Neustadt. Wiener Neustadt: MWN, Stadtmuseum Statutarstadt Wiener Neustadt, 2000.

Maximilian I. 2005
Maximilian I.: Triumph eines Kaisers; Herrscher mit europäischen Visionen. Exh. cat., Kaiserliche Hofburg, Innsbruck. Kulturgüter in Tirol 6. Innsbruck: Amt der Tiroler Landesregierung, 2005.

M. P. McDonald 2005
Mark P. McDonald. *Ferdinand Columbus: Renaissance Collector (1488–1539).* Exh. cat., British Museum, London. London: British Museum Press, 2005.

W. C. McDonald 1976
William C. McDonald. "Maximilian I of Habsburg and the Veneration of Hercules: On the Revival of Myth and the German Renaissance." *Journal of Medieval and Renaissance Studies* 6, no. 1 (Spring 1976), pp. 139–54.

Meder 1932
Joseph Meder. *Dürer-Katalog: Ein Handbuch über Albrecht Dürers Stiche, Radierungen, Holzschnitte, deren Zustände, Ausgaben und Wasserzeichen.* Vienna: Gilhofer & Ranschburg, 1932.

Meisterwerke der Weltlichen Schatzkammer 2009
Meisterwerke der Weltlichen Schatzkammer. Edited by Sabine Haag. Kurzführer durch das Kunsthistorische Museum 2. Vienna: Kunsthistorisches Museum, 2009.

Melanchthon 1569
Philipp Melanchthon. *Newe volkommene Chronica Philippi Melanthonis: Zeytbuch vnd warhafftige Beschreibung, Was von anfang der Welt biss auff diss gegenwertige Jar . . . sich zugetragen, furgenommen, verhandelt, vnnd aussgefürt ist worden. . . .* Frankfurt am Main: Sigmund Feyerabend, 1569.

Mende 1979
Matthias Mende. *Das alte Nürnberger Rathaus: Baugeschichte und Ausstattung des grossen Saales und der Ratsstube.* Vol. 1. Exh. cat., Nürnberger Rathaus. Nuremberg: Stadtgeschichtliche Museen Nürnberg, 1979.

Mende 1993
Matthias Mende. "Kaiser Maximilian I. hält Albrecht Dürer die Leiter: Ein neuerworbenes Gemälde von August Siegert, 1849." *Monats Anzeiger* (Germanisches Nationalmuseum Nuremberg), no. 146 (May 1993), pp. 1170–71.

Mende 2004
Matthias Mende. "Freydal." In Schoch, Mende, and Scherbaum 2001–4, vol. 3 (2004), pp. 152–53, 164.

Menéndez Pidal de Navascués 1982
Faustino Menéndez Pidal de Navascués. *Heráldica medieval española.* Vol. 1, *La Casa Real de León y Castilla.* Madrid: Hidalguía, 1982.

Merlet 1885
Lucien Merlet. *Catalogue des reliques & joyaux de Notre-Dame de Chartres.* Chartres: Garnier, 1885.

Messling 2006
Guido Messling. *Leonhard Beck: Der Augsburger Maler und Zeichner und sein Umkreis; Studien zur Augsburger Tafelmalerei und Zeichnung des frühen 16. Jahrhunderts.* Dresden: Thelem, 2006.

Messling 2007
Guido Messling, comp. *Leonhard Beck.* Edited by Hans-Martin Kaulbach. 2 vols. New Hollstein German Engravings, Etchings and Woodcuts, 1400–1700. Ouderkerk aan den IJssel: Sound & Vision, 2007.

Metzger 2009
Christof Metzger. *Daniel Hopfer: Ein Augsburger Meister der Renaissance; Eisenradierungen, Holzschnitte, Zeichnungen, Waffenätzungen.* With contributions by Tobias Güthner et al. Exh. cat., Pinakothek der Moderne, Munich. Munich: Staatliche Graphische Sammlung and Deutscher Kunstverlag, 2009.

Metzig 2016
Gregor M. Metzig. *Kommunikation und Konfrontation: Diplomatie und Gesandtschaftswesen Kaiser Maximilians I. (1486–1519).* Bibliothek des Deutschen Historischen Instituts in Rom 130. Berlin: Walter de Gruyter, 2016.

Meyer 1781
Karl Franz Meyer. *Aachensche Geschichten überhaupt als Beyträge zur Reichs-allgemeinen, insbesondere aber zur Anlage einer vollständigen Historie über den Königlichen Stuhl und des Heiligen Römischen Reichs freye Haupt-Kron- und Cur-Stadt Aachen. . . .* 3 vols. Aachen: Karl Franz Meyer, 1781.

Meyer zur Capellen 2008
Jürg Meyer zur Capellen. *Raphael: A Critical Catalogue of His Paintings.* Vol. 3, *The Roman Portraits, ca. 1508–1520.* Landshut: Arcos, 2008.

Michael 1983
Nicholas Michael. *Armies of Medieval Burgundy, 1364–1477.* London: Osprey, 1983.

Michel 2012
Eva Michel. "'For Praise and Eternal Memory': Albrecht Altdorfer's *Triumphal Procession* for Emperor Maximilian I." In *Emperor Maximilian I* 2012, pp. 49–65. [German edition, "'Zu lob und ewiger Gedechtnus': Albrecht Altdorfers *Triumphzug* für Kaiser Maximilian I." In *Kaiser Maximilian I. und die Kunst der Dürerzeit,* edited by Eva Michel and Maria Luise Sternath, pp. 49–65. Exh. cat., Albertina Museum, Vienna. Munich: Prestel, 2012.]

Mielke 1997
Ursula Mielke, comp. *Albrecht and Erhard Altdorfer.* Edited by Holm Bevers and Ger Luijten. New Hollstein German Engravings, Etchings and Woodcuts, 1400–1700. Rotterdam: Sound & Vision, 1997.

Modern 1901
Heinrich Modern. "Geweihte Schwerter und Hüte in den Kunsthistorischen Sammlungen des Allerhöchsten Kaiserhauses." *Jahrbuch der Kunsthistorischen Sammlungen des Allerhöchsten Kaiserhauses* 22 (1901), pp. 127–68.

Molinet 1827–28
Jean Molinet. *Chroniques de Jean Molinet.* Edited by J. A. C. Buchon. 5 vols. Paris: Verdière, 1827–28.

Montagnini 1769
Carlo Ignazio Montagnini. *Memorie risguardanti la superiorità imperiale sopra le città di Genova e di S. Remo come pure sopra tutta la Liguria.* 3 vols. Regensburg: Giuseppe Allegrini, 1769.

Moraht-Fromm 2016
Anna Moraht-Fromm. *Von einem, der auszog . . . : Das Werk Hans Malers von Ulm, Maler zu Schwaz.* Ostfildern: Jan Thorbecke, 2016.

Morrison 2015
Elizabeth Morrison. "The Genius of Visual Narrative." In Elizabeth Morrison and Zrinka Stahuljak, *The Adventures of Gillion de Trazegnies: Chivalry and Romance in the Medieval East,* pp. 103–39. Los Angeles: J. Paul Getty Museum, 2015.

Morscher and Grossmann 2004
Lukas Morscher and G. Ulrich Grossmann. *Das Goldene Dachl in Innsbruck.* With a contribution by Anja Grebe. Burgen, Schlösser und Wehrbauten in Mitteleuropa 18. Regensburg: Schnell & Steiner, 2004.

Motta 1914
Emilio Motta. "Armaiuoli milanesi nel periodo Visconteo-Sforzesco." *Archivio storico Lombardo,* ser. 5, 1 (1914), pp. 187–232.

Mulas 2016
Pier Luigi Mulas. "L'iconografia ducale nei libri miniati al tempo di Ludovico Sforza." In Jonathan J. G. Alexander, Pier Luigi Mulas, and Marzia Pontone, *Grammatica del Donato e Liber Iesus: Due libri per l'educazione di Massimiliano Sforza,* pp. 43–92. Modena: Franco Cosimo Panini, 2016.

Müller 1982
Jan-Dirk Müller. *Gedechtnus: Literatur und Hofgesellschaft um Maximilian I.* Forschungen zur Geschichte der älteren deutschen Literatur 2. Munich: Wilhelm Fink, 1982.

Müller 1987
Jan-Dirk Müller. "Maximilian I." In *Die deutsche Literatur des Mittelalters: Verfasserlexikon,* vol. 6, cols. 204–36. 2nd edition. Berlin: Walter de Gruyter, 1987.

Müller 1998
Jan-Dirk Müller. "Archiv und Inszenierung: Der 'letzte Ritter' und das Register der Ehre." In *Kultureller Austausch und Literaturgeschichte im Mittelalter: Kolloquium im Deutschen Historischen Institut, Paris, 16.–18.3.1995,* edited by Ingrid Kasten, Werner Paravicini, and René Pérennec, pp. 115–26. Sigmaringen: Jan Thorbecke, 1998.

Musée de l'Artillerie 1825
Musée de l'Artillerie. *Notice abrégée des collections dont se compose le Musée de l'Artillerie.* Paris: Imprimerie de Fain, 1825.

Musper 1956
Maximilian I, Holy Roman Emperor. *Kaiser Maximilians I. Weisskunig.* Compiled by Marx Treitzsaurwein. 2 vols. [Vol. 1], Text and commentary by Heinrich Theodor Musper, with Rudolf Buchner, Heinz-Otto Burger, and Erwin Petermann. Stuttgart: W. Kohlhammer, 1956.

Mythos Burg **2010**
Mythos Burg. Exh. cat., Germanisches Nationalmuseum, Nuremberg. Edited by G. Ulrich Grossmann. Nürnberg. Dresden: Sandstein, 2010.

Nachod 1952
Hans Nachod. *The Emperor Maximilian's Armories: A Recently Discovered Early XVIth-Century Codex with Joerg Koelderer's Watercolors.* New York: H. P. Kraus, 1952.

Naredi-Rainer and Madersbacher 2007
Paul Naredi-Rainer and Lukas Madersbacher, eds. *Kunst in Tirol.* Vol. 1, *Von den Anfängen bis zur Renaissance.* Kunstgeschichtliche Studien, Innsbruck, n.s., 3. Innsbruck: Tyrolia; Bozen: Verlagsanstalt Athesia, 2007.

Natter 2012
Tobias G. Natter, ed. *Gustav Klimt: The Complete Paintings.* Cologne: Taschen, 2012. [German edition, *Gustav Klimt: Sämtliche Gemälde.* Cologne: Taschen, 2012.]

Newe Zeitung **1515**
Newe Zeitung wie vnd welcher gestalt Kaiserlich Maiestat mit sambt den Künigen von Ungern vnd Polen. Am sechzehenden tag Julii. Tausend Fünffhundert Fünzehen. Zu Wienn eingeriten ist. vnnd was sich aldo verlauffen hat. [Nuremberg, 1515.]

Niederhäuser 2014
Peter Niederhäuser. "'In allen Ritterspielen unübertrefflich': Kaiser Maximilian als Turnierkämpfer." In *Ritterturnier* 2014, pp. 93–101.

Niederstätter 1996
Alois Niederstätter. *Das Jahrhundert der Mitte: An der Wende vom Mittelalter zur Neuzeit.* Österreichische Geschichte, 1400–1522. Vienna: Ueberreuter, 1996.

Nogueira 2015
Alison Manges Nogueira. "An Illuminated Schoolbook for Ludovico Sforza: Portraiture in Educational Manuscripts at the Court of Milan." *Manuscripta* 59, no. 2 (2015), pp. 187–222.

Norman 1959
A. V. B. Norman. "A Comparison of Three Helmets." *Waffen- und Kostümkunde,* 3rd ser., 1, nos. 1–2 (1959), pp. 16–21.

Norman 1986
A. V. B. Norman. *European Arms and Armour Supplement.* Wallace Collection Catalogues. London: Printed for the Trustees by Balding & Mansell, 1986.

Norman and Eaves 2016
A. V. B. Norman and Ian Eaves. *Arms & Armour in the Collection of Her Majesty the Queen: European Armour.* London: Royal Collection Trust, 2016.

Norman and Wilson 1982
A. V. B. Norman and G. M. Wilson. *Treasures from the Tower of London: An Exhibition of Arms and Armour.* Exh. cat., Sainsbury Centre for Visual Arts, University of East Anglia, Norwich; Cincinnati Art Museum, Cincinnati, Ohio; and Royal Ontario Museum, Toronto. Norwich: Sainsbury Centre for Visual Arts, University of East Anglia, 1982.

Oberhammer 1935
Vinzenz Oberhammer. *Die Bronzestandbilder des Maximiliangrabmales in der Hofkirche zu Innsbruck.* Innsbruck: Tyrolia, 1935.

Oosterman 2002
Johan Oosterman. "De *Excellente cronike van Vlaenderen* en Anthonis de Roovere." *Tijdschrift voor Nederlandse taal- en letterkunde* 118 (2002), pp. 22–37.

Orell Füssli-Hof 1928
Auktion: Waffensammlung aus herzoglich Anhalt-Dessauischem, deutschem und schweizerischem Privatbesitz/Auction: Collection of Weapons from the Anhalt-Dessau Ducal Collection and from Swiss and German Private Collections. Sale cat., Orell Füssli-Hof, Zurich, October 19–20, 1928.

Otto 1964
Gertrud Otto. *Bernhard Strigel.* Kunstwissenschaftliche Studien 33. Munich: Deutsche Kunstverlag, 1964.

Palacký 1844–67
Franz Palacký. *Geschichte von Böhmen.* 5 vols. in 10. Prague: Friedrich Tempsky, 1844–67.

Palme 2000
Rudolf Palme. *Das Messingwerk Mühlau bei Innsbruck: Ein Innovationsversuch Kaiser Maximilians I.; Aus den Quellen dargestellt.* Hall in Tirol: Berenkamp, 2000.

Panofsky 1955
Erwin Panofsky. *The Life and Art of Albrecht Dürer.* 4th edition. Princeton, N.J.: Princeton University Press, 1955.

Paravicini 2011
Werner Paravicini. *Die ritterlich-höfische Kultur des Mittelalters.* 3rd edition. Enzyklopädie deutscher Geschichte 32. Munich: Oldenbourg, 2011.

Paz y la guerra 1994
La paz y la guerra en la época del Tratado de Tordesillas. Exh. cat., Monasterio de San Juan and Convento de las Bernardas, Burgos. Madrid: Electa, 1994.

Penguilly L'Haridon 1862
Octave Penguilly L'Haridon. *Catalogue des collections composant le Musée d'Artillerie.* Paris: Charles de Mourgues Frères, 1862.

Périer-D'Ieteren 1990
Catheline Périer-D'Ieteren. "Contributions to the Study of the *Triptych with the Miracles of Christ*: The Marriage of Cana." *Art Bulletin of Victoria*, no. 31 (1990), pp. 2–19.

Périer-D'Ieteren 2013
Catheline Périer-D'Ieteren. "Le portrait à Bruxelles au tournant du XVᵉ siècle." In *Héritage de Rogier van der Weyden* 2013, pp. 67–79.

Petermann 1956
Erwin Petermann. "Die Formschnitte des Weisskunig." In Musper 1956, [vol. 1], pp. 57–147.

Pfaffenbichler 2000
Matthias Pfaffenbichler. "Maximilian und Burgund." In *Maximilian I.* 2000, pp. 49–63.

Pfaffenbichler 2014a
Matthias Pfaffenbichler. "'wie der jung [...] kunig [...] het hirschen, gembsen, stainpöck, wiltswein und peren zu jagen': Maximilian und die höfische Jagd." In *Kaiser Maximilian I.* 2014, pp. 63–65.

Pfaffenbichler 2014b
Matthias Pfaffenbichler. "'wie der jung [...] kunig in allen ritterspilen, auch in teutschen und welschen stechen ubertreffenlichen was': Maximilian I. und das höfische Turnier." In *Kaiser Maximilian I.* 2014, pp. 129–39.

Pfaffenbichler 2014c
Matthias Pfaffenbichler. "'wie der [...] kunig gar künstlichen was in der platnerey und harnaschmaisterey': Maximilian als Förderer des Plattnerwesens." In *Kaiser Maximilian I.* 2014, pp. 109–12.

Pfaffenbichler 2017
Matthias Pfaffenbichler. "Kaiser Maximilian I.: Der letzte Ritter und das höfische Turnier." In *Turnier: 1000 Jahre Ritterspiele*, edited by Stefan Krause and Matthias Pfaffenbichler, pp. 93–109. Vienna: KHM-Museumsverband; Munich: Hirmer, 2017.

Piccard 1970
Gerhard Piccard. *Die Wasserzeichenkartei Piccard im Hauptstaatsarchiv Stuttgart: Findbuch.* Vol. 3, *Die Turm-Wasserzeichen.* Stuttgart: W. Kohlhammer, 1970.

Picot 1904
Emile Picot. "Les Italiens en France au XVIᵉ siècle: Les artistes italiens en France." *Bulletin italien* 4 (1904), pp. 294–315.

Pierpont Morgan Library 1993
Pierpont Morgan Library. *In August Company: The Collections of the Pierpont Morgan Library.* New York: Pierpont Morgan Library, in association with Harry N. Abrams, 1993.

Pighius 1587
Stephanus Vinandus Pighius. *Hercules Prodicius, seu Principis Juventutis Vita et Peregrinatio.* Antwerp, 1587.

Pinacoteca di Brera 1988
Pinacoteca di Brera: Scuole lombarda e piemontese, 1300–1535. Edited by Federico Zeri. Musei e gallerie di Milano. Milan: Electa, 1988.

Pinillos 1998
Carmen Pinillos. "Prácticas escénicas del auto: *El segundo blasón del Austria* de Calderón de la Barca." In *Teatro español del Siglo de Oro: Teoría y práctica*, edited by Christoph Strosetzki, pp. 263–82. Studia hispanica 7. Frankfurt am Main: Vervuert; Madrid: Iberoamericana, 1998.

Poeschel 2014
Sabine Poeschel. *Handbuch der Ikonographie: Sakrale und profane Themen der bildenden Kunst.* 5th edition. Darmstadt: Philipp von Zabern, 2014.

Pokorny 2019
Erwin Pokorny. "Die Maler der Wiener *Freydal*-Miniaturen." In Krause 2019a.

Polleross 2012
Friedrich Polleross. "Tradition and Innovation: Emperor Maximilian I and His Portraits." In *Emperor Maximilian I* 2012, pp. 101–15. [German edition, "Tradition und Innovation: Kaiser Maximilian I. im Porträt." In *Kaiser Maximilian I. und die Kunst der Dürerzeit*, edited by Eva Michel and Maria Luise Sternath, pp. 101–15. Exh. cat., Albertina Museum, Vienna. Munich: Prestel, 2012.]

Pontone 2016
Marzia Pontone. "*La Grammatica del Donato* e il *Liber Iesus* tra storia e scrittura nella Milano di Ludovico il Moro." In Jonathan J. G. Alexander, Pier Luigi Mulas, and Marzia Pontone, *Grammatica del Donato e Liber Iesus: Due libri per l'educazione di Massimiliano Sforza*, pp. 93–117. Modena: Franco Cosimo Panini, 2016.

Pope-Hennessy and Christiansen 1980
John Pope-Hennessy and Keith Christiansen. "Secular Painting in 15th-Century Tuscany: Birth Trays, Cassone Panels, and Portraits." *The Metropolitan Museum of Art Bulletin*, n.s., 38, no. 1 (Summer 1980).

Post 1939
Paul Post. "Zum 'Silbernen Harnisch' Kaiser Maximilians I von Coloman Kolman mit Ätzentwürfen Albrecht Dürers." *Zeitschrift für historische Waffen- und Kostümkunde*, n.s., 6, no. 12 (1939), pp. 253–58.

Primisser 1819
Alois Primisser. *Die Kaiserlich-Königliche Ambraser-Sammlung.* Vienna, 1819.

Pyhrr 1989
Stuart W. Pyhrr. "European Armor from the Imperial Ottoman Arsenal." *Metropolitan Museum Journal* 24 (1989), pp. 85–116.

Pyhrr 2000
Stuart W. Pyhrr. *European Helmets, 1450–1650: Treasures from the Reserve Collection.* Exh. cat. New York: The Metropolitan Museum of Art, 2000.

Pyhrr 2011
Stuart W. Pyhrr. "Arms and Armor." In *Ronald S. Lauder Collection* 2011, pp. 59–87.

Pyhrr 2014
Stuart W. Pyhrr. "'I would prefer Gothic': William Randolph Hearst as an Armor Collector." In *The Spring 2014 London Park Lane Arms Fair*, pp. 76–105. N.p.: David A. Oliver, 2014.

Pyhrr and Godoy 1998
Stuart W. Pyhrr and José A. Godoy. *Heroic Armor of the Italian Renaissance: Filippo Negroli and His Contemporaries.* Exh. cat. New York: The Metropolitan Museum of Art, 1998.

Pyhrr, La Rocca, and Breiding 2005
Stuart W. Pyhrr, Donald J. La Rocca, and Dirk H. Breiding. *The Armored Horse in Europe, 1480–1620.* Exh. cat. New York: The Metropolitan Museum of Art, 2005.

Quintana Lacaci 1987
Guillermo Quintana Lacaci. *Armería del Palacio Real de Madrid.* Madrid: Editorial Patrimonio Nacional, 1987.

Rackham 1940
Bernard Rackham. "The Stained Glass in the Chapel of the Holy Blood at Bruges." *Journal of the British Society of Master Glass-Painters* 8, no. 2 (April 1940), pp. 45–50.

Ramade 1995
Patrick Ramade. "Les tournois." In *Châteaux chevaliers en Hainaut au Moyen Age*, pp. 241–44. Exh. cat., Musée des Beaux-Arts, Valenciennes. Brussels: Crédit Communal, 1995.

Ranke 1839–47
Leopold Ranke. *Deutsche Geschichte im Zeitalter der Reformation.* 6 vols. Berlin: Duncker und Humblot, 1839–47.

Raurell 2003
Ana Mur Raurell. "'Ex Hispaniis Sequuti': Der Hof Ferdinands I. und die spanischen Ritterorden." In *Kaiser Ferdinand I.* 2003, pp. 53–61.

Redlich 1900
Paul Clemens Redlich. *Cardinal Albrecht von Brandenburg und das Neue Stift zu Halle, 1520–1541: Eine kirchen- und kunstgeschichtliche Studie.* Mainz: Franz Kirchheim, 1900.

Regesta Imperii 1993
J. F. Böhmer. *Regesta Imperii.* Vol. 14, *Ausgewählte Regesten des Kaiserreiches unter Maximilian I., 1493–1519.* Vol. 2, pt. 1, *Maximilian I., 1496–1498.* Edited by Hermann Wiesflecker, with Manfred Hollegger, Kurt Riedl, and Ingeborg Wiesflecker-Friedhuber. Cologne: Böhlau, 1993.

Regesta Imperii 2002
J. F. Böhmer. *Regesta Imperii.* Vol. 14, *Ausgewählte Regesten des Kaiserreiches unter Maximilian I., 1493–1519.* Vol. 4, pt. 1, *Maximilian I., 1502–1504.* Edited by Hermann Wiesflecker, Ingeborg Wiesflecker-Friedhuber, and Manfred Hollegger, with Christa Beer. Cologne: Böhlau, 2002.

Reitzenstein 1951
Alexander von Reitzenstein. "Die Augsburger Plattnersippe der Helmschmied." *Münchner Jahrbuch der bildenden Kunst*, 3rd ser., 2 (1951), pp. 179–94.

Reitzenstein 1963
Alexander von Reitzenstein. "Der Landshuter Plattner Matthes Deutsch." *Waffen- und Kostümkunde*, 3rd ser., 5, no. 2 (1963), pp. 89–98.

Reitzenstein 1967
Alexander von Reitzenstein. "Die Nürnberger Plattner." In *Beiträge zur Wirtschaftsgeschichte Nürnbergs*, vol. 2, pp. 700–725. Nuremberg: Stadtrat, 1967.

Reitzenstein 1969
Alexander von Reitzenstein. "Die Landshuter Plattner: Ihre Ordnungen und ihre Meister." *Waffen- und Kostümkunde*, 3rd ser., 11, no. 1 (1969), pp. 20–32.

Renaissance Portrait 2011
The Renaissance Portrait from Donatello to Bellini. Exh. cat., Bode-Museum, Berlin, and The Metropolitan Museum of Art, New York. Edited by Keith Christiansen and Stefan Weppelmann. New York: The Metropolitan Museum of Art, 2011.

Resplendence of the Spanish Monarchy 1991
Resplendence of the Spanish Monarchy: Renaissance Tapestries and Armor from the Patrimonio Nacional. Exh. cat. New York: The Metropolitan Museum of Art, 1991.

Reverseau 1982
Jean-Pierre Reverseau. *Musée de l'Armée, Paris: Les armes et la vie.* Paris: Dargaud, 1982.

Reverseau 1990
Jean-Pierre Reverseau. *Armes insolites du XVIᵉ au XVIIIᵉ siècle.* Exh. cat. Paris: Réunion des Musées Nationaux and Musée de l'Armée, 1990.

Ritter! 2013
Ritter! Traum & Wirklichkeit. Exh. cat., Schloss Ambras, Innsbruck. Edited by Sabine Haag. Vienna: Kunsthistorisches Museum, 2013.

Ritterturnier 2014
Ritterturnier: Geschichte einer Festkultur. Exh. cat., Museum zu Allerheiligen Schaffhausen. Edited by Peter Jezler, Peter Niederhäuser, and Elke Jezler. Lucerne: Quaternio, 2014.

Ritterwelten im Spätmittelalter 2009
Ritterwelten im Spätmittelalter: Höfisch-ritterliche Kultur der Reichen Herzöge von Bayern-Landshut. Exh. cat., Spitalkirche Heiliggeist of the Museen der Stadt Landshut. Schriften aus den Museen der Stadt Landshut 29. Landshut: Museen der Stadt Landshut, 2009.

Robert 1889–93
Léon Robert. *Catalogue des collections composant le Musée d'Artillerie en 1889.* 5 vols. Paris: Imprimerie Nationale, 1889–93.

Roberts 2004
Ann M. Roberts. "The Horse and the Hawk: Representations of Mary of Burgundy as Sovereign." In *Excavating the Medieval Image: Manuscripts, Artists, Audiences; Essays in Honor of Sandra Hindman*, edited by Davis S. Areford and Nina A. Rowe, pp. 135–50. Aldershot: Ashgate, 2004.

Roberts 2008
Ann M. Roberts. "The Posthumous Image of Mary of Burgundy." In *Women and Portraits in Early Modern Europe: Gender, Agency, Identity*, edited by Andrea Pearson, pp. 55–70. Aldershot: Ashgate, 2008.

Rommé 2002
Barbara Rommé. "Der Ulmer Fischkasten: Eine weitere Kooperation der beiden Syrlins mit Michel Erhart." In *Michel Erhart & Jörg Syrlin d. Ä.: Spätgotik in Ulm*, edited by Stefan Roller and Michael Roth, pp. 180–93. Stuttgart: Konrad Theiss, 2002.

Ronald S. Lauder Collection 2011
The Ronald S. Lauder Collection: Selections from the 3rd Century BC to the 20th Century; Germany, Austria, and France. Exh. cat., Neue Galerie, New York. Munich: Prestel, 2011.

Rorimer 1938
James J. Rorimer. "New Acquisitions for the Cloisters." *Bulletin of The Metropolitan Museum of Art* 33, no. 5, pt. 2 (May 1938).

Rudolf 1980
Karl Friedrich Rudolf. "'Das gemäl ist also recht': Die Zeichnungen zum 'Weisskunig' Maximilians I. des Vaticanus Latinus 8570." *Römische historische Mitteilungen* 22 (1980), pp. 167–207.

Rudolf 2003
Karl Friedrich Rudolf. "'Yo el infante—ich, der Infant': Ferdinand, 'Prinz in Hispanien.'" In *Kaiser Ferdinand I.* 2003, pp. 31–51.

Ruhm und Sinnlichkeit 1996
Ruhm und Sinnlichkeit: Innsbrucker Bronzeguss, 1500–1650; Von Kaiser Maximilian I. bis Erzherzog Ferdinand Karl. Exh. cat. Innsbruck: Tiroler Landesmuseum Ferdinandeum, 1996.

Rupprich 1956
Hans Rupprich, ed. *Dürer: Schriftlicher Nachlass.* Vol. 1. Berlin: Deutscher Verein für Kunstwissenschaft, 1956.

Sacken 1855
Eduard von Sacken. *Die K. K. Ambraser-Sammlung.* 2 vols. Vienna: Wilhelm Braumüller, 1855.

Sacken 1859
Eduard von Sacken. *Die vorzüglichsten Rüstungen und Waffen der K. K. Ambraser-Sammlung, in Original-Photographien.* Vol. 1, *Deutsche Fürsten und Herren.* Vienna: Wilhelm Braumüller, 1859.

Sahm 2015
Heike Sahm. "Der Körper des Kaisers und der Tod: Zur Frage der Kontinuität von Maximilians Selbstentwürfen." In *Maximilians Ruhmeswerk: Künste und Wissenschaften im Umkreis Kaiser Maximilians I.,* edited by Jan-Dirk Müller and Hans-Joachim Ziegeler, pp. 395–411. Frühe Neuzeit 190. Berlin: Walter de Gruyter, 2015.

Sammellust 1998
Sammellust: 175 Jahre Tiroler Landesmuseum Ferdinandeum. Innsbruck: Tyrolia, 1998.

Sammlung von Passavant-Gontard 1929
Ausstellung der Hauptblätter der Sammlung Julius Model, Berlin, und der Sammlung von Passavant-Gontard, Frankfurt am Main. Exh. cat., C. G. Boerner, Leipzig. Leipzig, 1929.

Sandbichler 2004
Veronika Sandbichler. "Vogeljagd und Vogelfang." In *Herrlich Wild* 2004, pp. 135–36.

Sandbichler 2013
Veronika Sandbichler. "'turnieren daz ist ritter-lîch.'" In *Ritter!* 2013, pp. 39–47.

Sandrart 1675
Joachim von Sandrart. *L'academia todesca della architectura, scultura & pittura, oder Teutsche Academie der edlen Bau-, Bild- und Mahlerey-Künste.* 2 pts. Nuremberg: Jacob von Sandrart and Matthaeus Merian, 1675.

Sanuto 1496–1533/1879–1903
Marino Sanuto. *I diarii di Marino Sanuto (MCCCCXCVI–MDXXXIII) dall'autografo Marciano ital. cl. VII codd. CDXIX–CDLXXVII.* Edited by Federico Stefani et al. 58 vols. Venice: Fratelli Visentini, 1879–1903.

Sargent 1871
Anastasius Grün. *The Last Knight: A Romance-Garland.* Translated by John O. Sargent. New York: Hurd and Houghton, 1871.

Scalini 1996
Mario Scalini, with Rudolf H. Wackernagel and Ian Evans. *L'armeria Trapp di Castel Coira/Die Churburger Rüstkammer/The Armoury of the Castle of Churburg.* 2 vols. Udine: Magnus, 1996.

Scalini 2007
Mario Scalini. "La cristianizzazione e la santifi-cazione della spada, simbolo dell'*imperium* e della giustizia: Iconografia medievale del potere civile e religioso"/"La christianisation et la sanct-ification de l'épée, symbole de l'*imperium* et de la justice: Iconographie médiévale du pouvoir civil et religieux." In *A bon droyt* 2007, pp. 39–57.

Scharmitzer 2009
Dietmar Scharmitzer, ed. *So eine Art lyrisches Kaffeehaus: Briefwechsel Anastasius Grün mit dem Weidmann-Verlag, 1832–1876.* Manu Scripta 1. Vienna: Böhlau, 2009.

Scharmitzer 2010
Dietmar Scharmitzer. *Anastasius Grün (1806–1876): Leben und Werk.* Literatur und Leben, n.s., 79. Vienna: Böhlau, 2010.

Schauerte 2001
Thomas Schauerte. *Die Ehrenpforte für Kaiser Maximilian I.: Dürer und Altdorfer im Dienst des Herrschers.* Kunstwissenschaftliche Studien 95. Munich: Deutscher Kunstverlag, 2001.

Schauerte 2015
Thomas Schauerte. "*Pour éternelle mémoire . . .*: Burgundische Wurzeln der *Ehrenpforte.*" In *Maximilians Ruhmeswerk: Künste und Wissenschaften im Umkreis Kaiser Maximilians I.,* edited by Jan-Dirk Müller and Hans-Joachim Ziegeler, pp. 107–30. Frühe Neuzeit 190. Berlin: Walter de Gruyter, 2015.

Scheicher 1990
Elisabeth Scheicher. "Historiography and Display: The 'Heldenrüstkammer' of Archduke Ferdinand II in Schloss Ambras." *Journal of the History of Collections* 2, no. 1 (1990), pp. 69–79.

Schenck 2019
Kimberly Schenck. "Jousting and Jubilation: A Technical Investigation of the Washington *Freydal.*" In Krause 2019a.

Schestag 1883
Franz Schestag. "Kaiser Maximilian I. Triumph." *Jahrbuch der Kunsthistorischen Sammlungen des Allerhöchsten Kaiserhauses* 1 (1883), pp. 154–81.

Schlechte 1835
Leopold Schlechte. "Der letzte Ritter Engelhaus." *Der Wanderer auf das Jahr 1835* (Vienna), no. 96 (April 6, 1835), n.p. [pp. 1–2].

Schmid 1984
Karl Schmid. "'Andacht und Stift': Zur Grabmalplanung Kaiser Maximilians I." In *Memoria: Der geschichtliche Zeugniswert des litur-gischen Gedenkens im Mittelalter,* edited by Karl Schmid and Joachim Wollasch, pp. 750–86. Münsterische Mittelalter-Schriften 48. Munich: Wilhelm Fink, 1984.

Schmutz 2009
Daniel Schmutz. "Giovanni Candida: An Italian Medallist at the Court of Charles the Bold." In *Charles the Bold* 2009, pp. 224–25. [German edi-tion, "Giovanni Candida: Ein italienischer Medailleur am Hof Karls des Kühnen." In *Karl der Kühne (1433–1477): Kunst, Krieg und Hofkultur,* edited by Susan Marti, Till-Holger Borchert, and Gabriele Keck, pp. 224–25. Stuttgart: Belser Verlag, 2008.]

Schnurbein 2008
Vladimir von Schnurbein. "Die Bemühungen des Hauses Habsburg zur Ansiedlung von Ritterorden beim Aufbau der Militärgrenze." *Militär und Gesellschaft in der frühen Neuzeit* 12, no. 1 (2008), pp. 36–52.

Schoch, Mende, and Scherbaum 2001–4
Rainer Schoch, Matthias Mende, and Anna Scherbaum. *Albrecht Dürer: Das druckgraphische Werk.* 3 vols. Munich: Prestel, 2001–4.

Schönherr 1883
David Schönherr. "Die Kunstbestrebungen Erzherzogs Sigmund von Tyrol: Nach Urkunden und Acten des K. K. Statthalterei-Archivs in Innsbruck." *Jahrbuch der Kunsthistorischen Sammlungen des Allerhöchsten Kaiserhauses* 1 (1883), pp. 182–212.

Schönherr 1884
David Schönherr, ed. "Urkunden und Regesten aus dem K. K. Statthalterei-Archiv in Innsbruck." *Jahrbuch der Kunsthistorischen Sammlungen des Allerhöchsten Kaiserhauses* 2 (1884), pp. I–CLXXII.

Schönherr 1890
David Schönherr, ed. "Urkunden und Regesten aus dem K. K. Statthalterei-Archiv in Innsbruck." *Jahrbuch der Kunsthistorischen Sammlungen des Allerhöchsten Kaiserhauses* 11 (1890), pp. LXXXIV–CCXLI.

Schrenck von Notzing 1601 and 1603/1981
Jakob Schrenck von Notzing. *Die Helden-rüstkammer (Armamentarium Heroicum) Erzherzog Ferdinands II. auf Schloss Ambras bei Innsbruck: Faksimiledruck der lateinischen und der deutschen Ausgabe des Kupferstich-Bildinventars von 1601 bzw. 1603.* Introduction and commen-tary on the plates by Bruno Thomas. Osnabrück: Biblio Verlag, 1981.

Schütz 1994
Karl Schütz. *Albrecht Dürer im Kunsthistorischen Museum.* With contributions by Rotraud Bauer et al. Exh. cat., Kunsthistorisches Museum, Vienna. Milan: Electa, 1994.

Seton-Watson 1902
R. W. Seton-Watson. *Maximilian I: Holy Roman Emperor (Stanhope Historical Essay, 1901).* Westminster: Archibald Constable & Co., 1902.

Shearman 2003
John Shearman. *Raphael in Early Modern Sources (1483–1602).* 2 vols. Römische Forschungen der Bibliotheca Hertziana 30, 31. New Haven, Conn.: Yale University Press, 2003.

Shell 1998
Janice Shell. "Ambrogio de Predis." In *I Leonardeschi: L'eredità di Leonardo in Lombardia,* pp. 123–30. Milan: Skira, 1998. [English edition, "Ambrogio de Predis." In *The Legacy of Leonardo: Painters in Lombardy, 1490–1530,* pp. 123–30. Milan: Skira, 1998.]

Silver 1985
Larry Silver. "Shining Armor: Maximilian I as Holy Roman Emperor." *Art Institute of Chicago Museum Studies* 12, no. 1 (Fall 1985), pp. 9–29.

Silver 1986
Larry Silver. "'Die guten alten istory': Emperor Maximilian I, 'Teuerdank', and the 'Heldenbuch' Tradition." *Jahrbuch des Zentralinstituts für Kunstgeschichte* 2 (1986), pp. 71–106.

Silver 1994
Larry Silver. "Power of the Press: Dürer's *Arch of Honor.*" In *Albrecht Dürer in the Collection of the National Gallery of Victoria,* edited by Irena Zdanowicz, pp. 45–62. Melbourne: National Gallery of Victoria, 1994.

Silver 2005
Larry Silver. "*Blijde Uitgave*: Early Dutch Large Woodcut Ensembles and Politics." In *Florissant: Bijdragen tot de kunstgeschiedenis der Nederlanden (15de–17de eeuw); Liber Amicorum Carl van de Velde,* edited by Arnout Balis et al., pp. 65–77. Brussels: VUB Press, 2005.

Silver 2008
Larry Silver. *Marketing Maximilian: The Visual Ideology of a Holy Roman Emperor.* Princeton, N.J.: Princeton University Press, 2008.

Sismann 2006
Gabriela Sismann. "Un portrait inédit de la Renaissance italienne." *L'estampille/L'objet d'art,* no. 419 (December 2006), pp. 19–20.

Smith 1983
Jeffrey Chipps Smith. *Nuremberg: A Renaissance City, 1500–1618.* Exh. cat. Austin: University of Texas Press for the Archer M. Huntington Art Gallery, University of Texas at Austin, 1983.

Smith 1994
Jeffrey Chipps Smith. *German Sculpture of the Later Renaissance, c. 1520–1580: Art in an Age of Uncertainty.* Princeton, N.J.: Princeton University Press, 1994.

Smith 2006
Jeffrey Chipps Smith. "Die Kunst des Scheiterns: Albrecht von Brandenburg und das Neue Stift in Halle." In *Der Kardinal Albrecht von Brandenburg: Renaissancefürst und Mäzen,* vol. 1, *Katalog,* edited by Thomas Schauerte, pp. 17–51. Katalog der Stiftung Moritzburg, Kunstmuseum des Landes Sachsen-Anhalt, Halle. Regensburg: Schnell & Steiner, 2006.

Soler del Campo 1998
Álvaro Soler del Campo. "La armería de Felipe II." *Reales sitios* 35, no. 135 (1998), pp. 24–37.

Soler del Campo 2009
Álvaro Soler del Campo. *The Art of Power: Royal Armor and Portraits from Imperial Spain/El arte del poder: Armaduras y retratos de la España imperial.* Exh. cat., National Gallery of Art, Washington, D.C. Madrid: Sociedad Estatal para la Acción Cultural Exterior; Patrimonio Nacional; and Tf Editores, 2009.

Sotheby's 1923
Catalogue of an Important Collection of Drawings by Old Masters. Sale cat., Sotheby, Wilkinson & Hodge, London, July 4, 1923.

Sotheby's 1936
Catalogue of Valuable Armour and Weapons. Sale cat., Sotheby & Co., London, July 2, 1936.

Sotheby's 1946
Catalogue of Armour and Weapons from the Collection of the Late Baron C. A. de Cosson. . . . Sale cat., Sotheby & Co., London, May 23, 1946.

Sotheby's 1952
Catalogue of Fine Armour and Weapons. . . . Sale cat., Sotheby & Co., London, December 12, 1952.

Spätmittelalter und Renaissance 2003
Spätmittelalter und Renaissance. Edited by Artur Rosenauer. Vol. 3 of *Geschichte der bildenden Kunst in Österreich.* Österreichische Akademie der Wissenschaften, Vienna. Munich: Prestel, 2003.

"Stained-Glass Windows" 1971–72
"Stained-Glass Windows: An Exhibition of Glass in the Metropolian Museum's Collection." *The Metropolitan Museum of Art Bulletin,* n.s., 30, no. 3 (December 1971–January 1972).

Steinberg 1939
S. H. Steinberg. "A Flemish Armorial Window." *Burlington Magazine* 74, no. 434 (May 1939), pp. 218–22.

Steinherz 1906
S. Steinherz. "Ein Bericht über die Werke Maximilians I." *Mitteilungen des Instituts für Österreichische Geschichtsforschung* 27 (1906), pp. 152–55.

Steinmann 1968
Ulrich Steinmann. "Der Bilderschmuck der Stiftskirche zu Halle: Cranachs Passionszyklus und Grünewalds Erasmus-Mauritius-Tafel." *Forschungen und Berichte* (Staatliche Museen, Berlin, Preussischer Kulturbesitz) 11 (1968), pp. 69–104.

Sterling et al. 1998
Charles Sterling et al. *Fifteenth- to Eighteenth-Century European Paintings: France, Central Europe, the Netherlands, Spain, and Great Britain.* Robert Lehman Collection 2. New York: The Metropolitan Museum of Art, in association with Princeton University Press, 1998.

Strauss 1974
Walter L. Strauss. *The Complete Drawings of Albrecht Dürer.* 6 vols. New York: Abaris Books, 1974.

Strauss 1980
Walter L. Strauss, ed. *Albrecht Dürer: Woodcuts and Wood Blocks.* New York: Abaris Books, 1980.

Summers 1987
David Summers. *The Judgment of Sense: Renaissance Naturalism and the Rise of Aesthetics.* Ideas in Context. Cambridge: Cambridge University Press, 1987.

Tabacchi 2009
Stefano Tabacchi. "Medici, Giuliano de'." In *Dizionario biografico degli italiani,* vol. 73, pp. 84–88. Rome: Istituto della Enciclopedia Italiana, 2009.

Tapices y armaduras del Renacimiento 1992
Tapices y armaduras del Renacimiento: Joyas de la colecciones reales. Exh. cat., Reales Atarazanas, Barcelona, and Palacio de Velázquez, Madrid. Barcelona: Lunwerg; Madrid: Patrimonio Nacional, 1992.

Taylor 1931
[Francis Henry Taylor.] "Handbook of the Display Collection of the Art of the Middle Ages." *Pennsylvania Museum Bulletin* 26, no. 140 (March 1931), pp. 2–47.

Telesko 2006
Werner Telesko. *Geschichtsraum Österreich: Die Habsburger und ihre Geschichte in der bildenden Kunst des 19. Jahrhunderts.* Vienna: Böhlau, 2006.

Telesko 2012
Werner Telesko. "*Imperator Perpetuus?* The Reception of Emperor Maximilian I from the Eighteenth to the Early Twentieth Centuries." In *Emperor Maximilian I* 2012, pp. 117–27. [German edition, "Imperator Perpetuus? Zur Rezeption Kaiser Maximilians I. vom 18. bis zum frühen 20. Jahrhundert." In *Kaiser Maximilian I. und die Kunst der Dürerzeit,* edited by Eva Michel and Maria Luise Sternath, pp. 117–27. Exh. cat., Albertina Museum, Vienna. Munich: Prestel, 2012.]

Tennant 1989
Elaine C. Tennant. "'Understanding with the Eyes': The Visual Gloss to Maximilian's *Theuerdank.*" In *Entzauberung der Welt: Deutsche Literatur, 1200–1500,* edited by James F. Poag and Thomas C. Fox, pp. 211–75. Tübingen: Francke, 1989.

Térey 1892
Gábor von Térey. *Cardinal Albrecht von Brandenburg und das Halle'sche Heiligthumsbuch von 1520: Eine kunsthistorische Studie.* Strasbourg: Heitz & Mündel, 1892.

Terjanian 2006
Pierre Terjanian. "La armería de Felipe el Hermoso." In *Felipe I el Hermoso: La belleza y la locura,* edited by Miguel Ángel Zalama and Paul Vandenbroeck, pp. 143–62. Madrid: Centro de Estudios Europa Hispánica; Burgos: Fundación Caja de Burgos; Madrid: Fundación Carlos de Amberes, 2006.

Terjanian 2009
Pierre Terjanian. "The King and the Armourers of Flanders." In *Henry VIII 2009*, pp. 155–59, 336.

Terjanian 2011
Pierre Terjanian. "Princely Armor in the Age of Dürer: A Renaissance Masterpiece in the Philadelphia Museum of Art." *Philadelphia Museum of Art Bulletin*, n.s., [no. 5] (2011).

Terjanian 2011–12
Pierre Terjanian. "The Art of the Armorer in Late Medieval and Renaissance Augsburg: The Rediscovery of the *Thun Sketchbooks*." *Jahrbuch des Kunsthistorischen Museums Wien*, n.s., 13–14 (2011–12), pp. 299–395.

Terjanian 2018
Pierre Terjanian. "Notes on the Early Life and Career of Hans Seusenhofer, Court Armorer of Emperors Maximilian I and Ferdinand I in Innsbruck." In *The Antique Arms Fair at Olympia, London: 21 April 2018*, pp. 26–32. N.p., [2018].

Teuffenbach 1877
Albin Reichsfreiherr von Teuffenbach, ed. *Vaterländisches Ehrenbuch: Geschichtliche Denkwürdigkeiten aus allen Ländern der österreichisch-ungarischen Monarchie*. Vienna: Karl Prochaska, 1877.

Tewes 2011
Götz-Rüdiger Tewes. *Kampf um Florenz: Die Medici im Exil (1494–1512)*. Cologne: Böhlau, 2011.

Thomas 1938/1977
Bruno Thomas. "Der Wiener Ottheinrich-Harnisch von Koloman Colman (recte Helmschmid): Stilkritik und Waffenkunde." In Bruno Thomas, *Gesammelte Schriften zur historischen Waffenkunde*, vol. 2, pp. 1147–55. Graz: Akademische Druck- u. Verlagsanstalt, 1977. [Originally published in *Zeitschrift für historische Waffen- und Kostümkunde*, n.s., 6, no. 6 (1938), pp. 116–23.]

Thomas 1949/1977
Bruno Thomas. "Konrad Seusenhofer: Studien zu seinen Spätwerken zwischen 1511 und 1517." In Bruno Thomas, *Gesammelte Schriften zur historischen Waffenkunde*, vol. 1, pp. 541–76. With a contribution by Ortwin Gamber, pp. 562–70. Graz: Akademische Druck- u. Verlagsanstalt, 1977. [Originally published in *Konsthistorisk tidskrift* 18, nos. 2–3 (October 1949), pp. 37–70.]

Thomas 1950–51/1977
Bruno Thomas. "Kejsar Maximilian I's tre Pragtsvaerd i Wien og København/Die Prunkschwerter Maximilians I. in Wien und Kopenhagen." In Bruno Thomas, *Gesammelte Schriften zur historischen Waffenkunde*, vol. 2, pp. 1347–1435. With contributions by Alphons Lhotsky, pp. 1370–82, 1408–16, and H. D. Schepelern, pp. 1429–35. Graz: Akademische Druck- u. Verlagsanstalt, 1977. [Originally published in *Vaabenhistoriske aarbøger* 6, nos. b–c (1950–51), pp. 105–91.]

Thomas 1955/1977
Bruno Thomas. "The Hunting Knives of Emperor Maximilian I." In Bruno Thomas, *Gesammelte Schriften zur historischen Waffenkunde*, vol. 2, pp. 1437–46. Graz: Akademische Druck- u. Verlagsanstalt, 1977. [Originally published in *The Metropolitan Museum of Art Bulletin*, n.s., 13, no. 6 (February 1955), pp. 201–8.]

Thomas 1956/1977
Bruno Thomas. "Jörg Helmschmied d. J.: Plattner Maximilians I. in Augsburg und Wien." In Bruno Thomas, *Gesammelte Schriften zur historischen Waffenkunde*, vol. 2, pp. 1127–46. Graz: Akademische Druck- u. Verlagsanstalt, 1977. [Originally published in *Jahrbuch der Kunsthistorischen Sammlungen in Wien* 52 (1956), pp. 33–50.]

Thomas 1958/1977
Bruno Thomas. "Die Mailänder Plattnerkunst." In Bruno Thomas, *Gesammelte Schriften zur historischen Waffenkunde*, vol. 2, pp. 971–1098. With a contribution by Ortwin Gamber, pp. 980–1028. Graz: Akademische Druck- u. Verlagsanstalt, 1977. [Originally published as "L'arte milanese dell'armatura." In *Storia di Milano*, vol. 11, pp. 697–841. Milan: Fondazione Trecanni degli Alfieri per la Storia di Milano, 1958.]

Thomas 1963/1977
Bruno Thomas. "Nürnberger Plattnerkunst in Wien." In Bruno Thomas, *Gesammelte Schriften zur historischen Waffenkunde*, vol. 2, pp. 1307–19. Graz: Akademische Druck- u. Verlagsanstalt, 1977. [Originally published in *Anzeiger des Germanischen Nationalmuseums*, 1963, pp. 89–99.]

Thomas 1971
Bruno Thomas. "Die Polonica der Wiener Waffensammlung." *Jahrbuch der Kunsthistorischen Sammlungen in Wien* 67 (1971), pp. 47–104.

Thomas 1974
Bruno Thomas. "Die Innsbrucker Plattnerkunst: Ein Nachtrag." *Jahrbuch der Kunsthistorischen Sammlungen in Wien* 70 (1974), pp. 179–220.

Thomas and Fritz 1978
Bruno Thomas and Johann Michael Fritz. "Unbekannte Werke spätmittelalterlicher Waffenschmiedekunst in Karlsruhe." *Waffen- und Kostümkunde*, 3rd ser., 20, no. 1 (1978), pp. 1–18.

Thomas and Gamber 1954
Bruno Thomas and Ortwin Gamber. *Die Innsbrucker Plattnerkunst: Katalog*. Exh. cat. Innsbruck: Tiroler Landesmuseum Ferdinandeum, 1954.

Thomas and Gamber 1976
Bruno Thomas and Ortwin Gamber. *Katalog der Leibrüstkammer*. Pt. 1, *Der Zeitraum von 500 bis 1530*. Kunsthistorisches Museum, Vienna, Waffensammlung. Führer durch das Kunsthistorische Museum 13. Vienna: Kunsthistorisches Museum, 1976.

Tietze and Tietze-Conrat 1928–38
Hans Tietze and Erika Tietze-Conrat. *Kritisches Verzeichnis der Werke Albrecht Dürers*. 2 vols. in 3. Augsburg: B. Filser; Basel: Holbein-Verlag, 1928–38.

Tilmans 1988
Karin Tilmans. *Aurelius en de Divisiekroniek van 1517: Historiografie en humanisme in Holland in de tijd van Erasmus*. Hollandse studiën 21. Hilversum: Historische Vereniging Holland, 1988.

Tiroler Landesmuseum Ferdinandeum 1979
Tiroler Landesmuseum Ferdinandeum, ed. *Tiroler Landesmuseum Ferdinandeum, Innsbruck: Führer durch die Schausammlungen*. Innsbruck: Tiroler Landesmuseum Ferdinandeum, 1979.

***Toison d'Or* 1962**
La Toison d'Or: Cinq siècles d'art et d'histoire. Exh. cat., Groeningemuseum, Bruges. Bruges: Administration Communale de Bruges, 1962.

Trapp 1954
Oswald Trapp. "Hans Prunner: Plattner in Innsbruck." *Tiroler Heimatblätter* 29, (1954), pp. 34–36.

***Traum vom Glück* 1996**
Der Traum vom Glück: Die Kunst des Historismus in Europa. 2 vols. Exh. cat., Künstlerhaus and Akademie der Bildenden Künste, Vienna. Edited by Hermann Fillitz and Werner Telesko. Vienna: Künstlerhaus, 1996.

Treitzsaurwein 1775
Maximilian I, Holy Roman Emperor. *Der Weiss Kunig: Eine Erzehlung von den Thaten Kaiser Maximilian des Ersten*. Compiled by Marx Treitzsaurwein. Vienna: Auf Kosten J. Kurzböckens, 1775.

Treitzsaurwein and Schultz 1888
Maximilian I, Holy Roman Emperor. "Der Weisskunig." Compiled by Marx Treitzsaurwein. Edited by Alwin Schultz. *Jahrbuch der Kunsthistorischen Sammlungen des Allerhöchsten Kaiserhauses* 6 (1888).

Unterkircher 1983
Franz Unterkircher. "Bücher aus dem Besitz der Kaiserin Bianca Maria in der Österreichischen Nationalbibliothek." In *Domus Austriae: Eine Festgabe Hermann Wiesflecker zum 70. Geburtstag*, edited by Walter Höflechner, Helmut J. Mezler-Andelberg, and Othmar Pickl, pp. 407–11. Graz: Akademische Druck- u. Verlagsanstalt, 1983.

Valencia de Don Juan 1898
Juan Bautista Crooke y Navarrot, conde de Valencia de Don Juan. *Catálogo histórico-descriptivo de la Real Armería de Madrid*. Madrid, 1898.

Vallance 1911
Aymer Vallance. "Some Flemish Painted Glass Panels." *Burlington Magazine* 19, no. 100 (July 1911), pp. 189–92.

Vanden Bemden 2000
Yvette Vanden Bemden. *Les vitraux de la première moitié du XVIᵉ siècle conservés en Belgique: Province du Hainaut*. Vol. 1, *La collégiale Sainte-Waudru Mons*. Corpus Vitrearum, Belgique, 5, no. 1. Collection "Histoire, art & archéologie" 3. Namur, Belgium: Presses Universitaires de Namur, 2000.

Vaughan 2002
Richard Vaughan. *Charles the Bold: The Last Valois Duke of Burgundy*. New edition. Woodbridge, Suffolk: Boydell Press, 2002.

Van der Velden 2000
Hugo van der Velden. *The Donor's Image: Gerard Loyet and the Votive Portraits of Charles the Bold*. Burgundica 2. Turnhout: Brepols, 2000.

Venturelli 1996
Paola Venturelli. "Un gioiello per Bianca Maria Sforza e il ritratto di Washington." *Arte lombarda*, n.s., no. 116 (1996), no. 1, pp. 50–53.

Villinger 1515
Jacob Villinger. *Congressus ac Celeberrimi Conventus Caesaris Max. et Trium Regum Hungariae, Boemiae, et Poloniae. In Vienna Panoniae, Mense Iulio. Anno M.D.X.V. . . .* [Vienna]: [Johann Singriener], 1515.

Vogelaar et al. 2011
Christiaan Vogelaar et al. *Lucas van Leyden en de Renaissance*. Exh. cat., Museum De Lakenhal, Leuven. Antwerp: Ludion, 2011.

Volbach 1917
Wolfgang Fritz Volbach. *Der Hlg. Georg: Bildliche Darstellung in Süddeutschland mit Berücksichtigung der norddeutschen Typen bis zur Renaissance*. Studien zur deutschen Kunstgeschichte 199. Strasbourg: Heitz, 1917.

Waldburg Wolfegg 1998
Christoph, Graf zu Waldburg Wolfegg. *Venus and Mars: The World of the Medieval Housebook*. Exh. cat., National Gallery of Art, Washington, D.C., and Frick Collection, New York. Munich: Prestel, 1998.

Waldman 1994
Louis Waldman. "Giovanni Filangieri Candida (born c. 1445–50, died c. 1498–99?)." In *Currency of Fame* 1994, pp. 121–22.

Walsh 1977
Richard J. Walsh. "Charles the Bold and the Crusade: Politics and Propaganda." *Journal of Medieval History* 3, no. 1 (1977), pp. 53–86.

Wegeli 1920–48
Rudolf Wegeli, with W. Blum and Rudolf Münger. *Inventar der Waffensammlung des Bernischen historischen Museums in Bern*. 4 vols. Bern: K. J. Wyss Erben, 1920–48.

Weicker 1901
Bernhard Weicker. *Die Stellung der Kurfürsten zur Wahl Karls V. im Jahr 1519*. Historische Studien 22. Berlin: E. Ebering, 1901.

Weihrauch 1963
Hans R. Weihrauch. "Ein verkanntes Spielzeug der Dürerzeit." *Waffen- und Kostümkunde*, 3rd ser., 5, no. 1 (1963), pp. 17–20.

Weiss 2010
Sabine Weiss. *Die vergessene Kaiserin: Bianca Maria Sforza, Kaiser Maximilians zweite Gemahlin*. Innsbruck: Tyrolia, 2010.

Welch 1995
Evelyn S. Welch. *Art and Authority in Renaissance Milan*. New Haven, Conn.: Yale University Press, 1995.

Welt, Macht, Geist 2002
Welt, Macht, Geist: Das Haus Habsburg und die Oberlausitz, 1526–1635. Exh. cat., Städtische Museen Zittau. Edited by Joachim Bahlcke and Volker Dudeck. Görlitz: Gunter Oettel, 2002.

Werke für die Ewigkeit 2002
Werke für die Ewigkeit: Kaiser Maximilian I. und Erzherzog Ferdinand II. Exh. cat., Schloss Ambras, Innsbruck. Edited by Wilfried Seipel. Vienna: Kunsthistorisches Museum, 2002.

Werner 2015
Elke Anna Werner. "Kaiser Maximilians *Weisskunig*: Einige Beobachtungen zur Werkgenese der Illustrationen." In *Maximilians Ruhmeswerk: Künste und Wissenschaften im Umkreis Kaiser Maximilians I.*, edited by Jan-Dirk Müller and Hans-Joachim Ziegeler, pp. 349–80. Frühe Neuzeit 190. Berlin: Walter de Gruyter, 2015.

West 2006
Ashley West. "Hans Burgkmair the Elder (1473–1531) and the Visualization of Knowledge." PhD diss., University of Pennsylvania, Philadelphia, 2006.

Wiener Bürgerliche Zeughaus 1977
Das Wiener Bürgerliche Zeughaus: Rüstungen und Waffen aus fünf Jahrhunderten. Exh. cat., Schloss Schallaburg. Sonderausstellung des Historischen Museums der Stadt Wien 49. Vienna: Eigenverlag der Museen der Stadt Wien, 1977.

Wiesflecker 1971–86
Hermann Wiesflecker. *Kaiser Maximilian I.: Das Reich, Österreich und Europa an der Wende zur Neuzeit*. 5 vols. Munich: R. Oldenbourg, 1971–86.

Wiesflecker 1991
Hermann Wiesflecker. *Maximilian I.: Die Fundamente des habsburgischen Weltreiches*. Vienna: Verlag für Geschichte und Politik; Munich: R. Oldenbourg, 1991.

Wiesflecker 2000
Hermann Wiesflecker. "Die Wiederherstellung der habsburgischen Macht im Osten." In *Maximilian I.* 2000, pp. 111–14.

Williams 1941
Hermann Warner Williams Jr. "Dürer's Designs for Maximilian's Silvered Armor." *Art in America* 29, no. 2 (April 1941), pp. 73–82.

Williamson 2003
Paul Williamson. *Medieval and Renaissance Stained Glass in the Victoria and Albert Museum*. London: V&A Publications, 2003.

Winkelbauer 1954
Walter Winkelbauer. "Kaiser Maximilian I. und St. Georg." *Mitteilungen des österreichischen Staatsarchives* 7 (1954), pp. 523–50.

Winkler 1936–39
Friedrich Winkler. *Die Zeichnungen Albrecht Dürers*. 4 vols. Berlin: Deutscher Verein für Kunstwissenschaft, 1936–39.

Winter 2014
Heinz Winter. "'und in sonderhait hat er grosse munz schlagen lassen': Die Schaumünzen Maximilians I. aus der Prägestätte Hall in Tirol." In *Kaiser Maximilian I.* 2014, pp. 203–9.

Winzinger 1966
Franz Winzinger. "Albrecht Altdorfer und die Miniaturen des Triumphzuges Kaiser Maximilians I." *Jahrbuch der Kunsthistorischen Sammlungen in Wien* 62 (1966), pp. 157–72.

Winzinger 1972–73
Die Miniaturen zum Triumphzug Kaiser Maximilians I. 2 vols. [Vol. 2], Commentary by Franz Winzinger. Veröffentlichungen der Albertina 5. Graz: Akademische Druck- u. Verlagsanstalt, 1972–73.

Wlattnig 2015
Robert Wlattnig. "Das Siebenhirter-Schwert aus Millstatt: Ein vom Geschichtsverein für Kärnten gerettetes Kunstwerk der Spätgotik von europäischer Bedeutung." *Bulletin* (Geschichtsverein für Kärnten) ([July–December] 2015), pp. 94–97.

Wolfson 1992
Michael Wolfson. *Die deutschen und niederländischen Gemälde bis 1550: Kritischer Katalog mit Abbildungen aller Werke.* Niedersächsisches Landesmuseum Hannover, Landesgalerie. Hannover: Niedersächsisches Landesmuseum Hannover, 1992.

Wood 2005
Christopher S. Wood. "Maximilian I as Archeologist." *Renaissance Quarterly* 58, no. 4 (Winter 2005), pp. 1128–74.

Wood 2015
Christopher S. Wood. "Maximilian als Archäologe." In *Maximilians Ruhmeswerk: Künste und Wissenschaften im Umkreis Kaiser Maximilians I.,* edited by Jan-Dirk Müller and Hans-Joachim Ziegeler, pp. 131–84. Frühe Neuzeit 190. Berlin: Walter de Gruyter, 2015.

Woods-Marsden 2013
Joanna Woods-Marsden. "The Sword in Titian's Portraits of Emperor Charles V." *Artibus et Historiae* 34, no. 67 (2013), pp. 201–18.

Woollett and Van Suchtelen 2006
Anne T. Woollett and Ariane van Suchtelen. *Rubens & Brueghel: A Working Friendship.* Exh. cat., J. Paul Getty Museum, Los Angeles, and Royal Picture Gallery Mauritshuis, The Hague. Los Angeles: J. Paul Getty Museum, 2006.

Wree 1639
Olivier de Wree. *Sigilla Comitum Flandriae et Inscriptiones Diplomatum ab Iis Editorum cum Expositione Historica.* Bruges, 1639.

Zaffignani 1991
Gianni Zaffignani. "Fasti, allegorie e misteri dei medaglioni." In *Il cortile d'onore,* pp. 86–93. Società Storica Vigevanese. Vigevano: Diakronia, 1991.

Zalama 2006
Miguel Ángel Zalama. "Felipe I el Hermoso y las artes." In *Felipe I el Hermoso: La belleza y la locura,* edited by Miguel Ángel Zalama and Paul Vandenbroeck, pp. 17–48. Madrid: Centro de Estudios Europa Hispánica; Burgos: Fundación Caja de Burgos; Madrid: Fundación Carlos de Amberes, 2006.

Zastrow 1993
Oleg Zastrow. *Museo d'arti applicate: Oreficerie.* Musei e gallerie di Milano. Milan: Electa, 1993.

Ziegeler 2015
Hans-Joachim Ziegeler. "Beobachtungen zur Entstehungsgeschichte von Kaiser Maximilians *Theuerdank.*" In *Maximilians Ruhmeswerk: Künste und Wissenschaften im Umkreis Kaiser Maximilians I.,* edited by Jan-Dirk Müller and Hans-Joachim Ziegeler, pp. 211–54. Frühe Neuzeit 190. Berlin: Walter de Gruyter, 2015.

Ziermann 2001
Horst Ziermann, with Erika Beissel. *Matthias Grünewald.* Munich: Prestel, 2001.

Zimerman 1883
Heinrich Zimerman, ed. "Urkunden und Regesten aus dem K. u. K. Haus-, Hof- und Staats-Archiv in Wien." *Jahrbuch der Kunsthistorischen Sammlungen des Allerhöchsten Kaiserhauses* 1 (1883), pp. I–LXXVIII.

Zimerman 1885
Heinrich Zimerman, ed. "Urkunden und Regesten aus dem K. u. K. Haus-, Hof- und Staats-Archiv in Wien." *Jahrbuch der Kunsthistorischen Sammlungen des Allerhöchsten Kaiserhauses* 3 (1885), pp. LXXXII–CLII.

Zimerman and Kreyczi 1885
Heinrich Zimerman and Franz Kreyczi, eds. "Urkunden un d Regesten aus dem K. u. K. Reichs-Finanz-Archiv." *Jahrbuch der Kunsthistorischen Sammlungen des Allerhöchsten Kaiserhauses* 3 (1885), pp. I–LXXXI.

Zinnhobler 1968–69
Rudolf Zinnhobler. "Johannes Fabers Leichenrede auf Maximilian I. (Gehalten in Wels am 16. Jänner 1519)." *Jahrbuch des Musealvereins Wels* 15 (1968–69), pp. 35–87.

INDEX

PHOTOGRAPHY CREDITS